JAVA FOUNDATION CLASSES

McGRAW-HILL
JAVA MASTERS TITLES

Java Foundation Classes

Matthew T. Nelson

McGraw-Hill
New York • San Francisco • Washington, D.C. • Auckland
Bogotá • Caracas • Lisbon • London • Madrid • Mexico City
Milan • Montreal • New Delhi • San Juan • Singapore
Sydney • Tokyo • Toronto

Library of Congress Cataloging-in-Publication Data

Nelson, Matthew T.
  Java foundation classes / Matthew T. Nelson.
      p.   cm.
  Includes index.
  ISBN 0-07-913758-X
  1. Java (Computer program language)   2. Java foundation classes.
I. Title.
QA76.73.J38N45   1998
005.13'3—dc21   98-6455
                                                                   CIP

McGraw-Hill

A Division of The **McGraw-Hill** Companies

1 2 3 4 5 6 7 8 9 0   DOC/DOC   9 0 3 2 1 0 9 8

P/N 047165-7
PART OF ISBN 0-07-913758-X

*The sponsoring editor for this book was Judy Brief and the production
supervisor was Sherri Souffrance. It was set in Century Schoolbook by Douglas
& Gayle Limited.*

Printed and bound by R. R. Donnelley & Sons Company.

McGraw-Hill books are available at special quantity discounts to use as
premiums and sales promotions, or for use in corporate training programs.
For more information, please write to Director of Special Sales, McGraw-Hill,
11 West 19th Street, New York, NY 10011. Or contact your local bookstore.

This book is printed on recycled, acid-free paper containing a minimum of 50%
recycled de-inked fiber.

To my parents, Virginia and Thomas

CONTENTS

Contents

Contents

Contents

Contents

Contents

Contents

INTRODUCTION

What Are the Java Foundation Classes?

If you go down to your local software store and look around, don't be surprised if you can't find a single application written in Java. With the exception of a few tools to help you write your own Java, there aren't any. Why?

■ **Performance:** We have to face the fact that Java, as an interpreted language, is slow. It might be acceptable for some user interface implementations and for network functions like mobile agents and other applications where Java's capabilities are more important than performance, but for just about everything else, it's too slow.

■ **Functionality and Appearance:** In the Windows world, users have come to expect a lot from applications. Interfaces are slick and generally intuitive; programs can work together; online help can be built in; and user interface components pretty much work the way you would expect. Java, in its current state, doesn't match up.

The *Java Foundation Classes* (JFC) will help programmers make their *graphical user interfaces* (GUIs) slightly faster than before, but the main hope for better performance is the future HotSpot high-speed virtual machine. On the other hand, the JFC can definitely help with functionality and appearance.

The JFC gives programmers the components we need to write great interfaces (see Figure I-1). All the trees, tables, toolbars, tooltips, and so forth are now available, usable, and stable.

The Java Foundation Classes are made up of the following parts:

■ **The Swing classes:** They include replacement classes for the *Abstract Windowing Toolkit* (AWT) components and many more useful GUI components.

■ **The Accessibility *Application Programming Interface* (API):** This is used to give components a standard interface so they can be displayed to the disabled user in an easily understood way.

■ **The Java 2D classes:** They are used to give Java better fonts and drawing capabilities.

■ **Drag-and-drop:** This feature lets you program in the ability to drag items around your application and drop them on different destinations.

Figure I-1

A simple example of
what you can do
using the JFC.

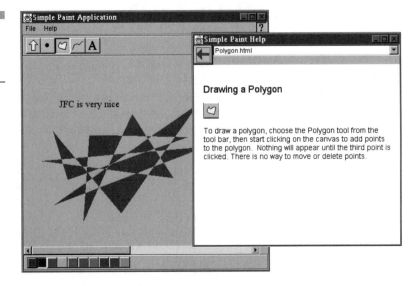

Why Do We Need the JFC When We Have the AWT?

Java is a *great* language. It's amazingly easy to learn and use, it encourages good programming practices, and it makes writing reusable code seem natural. Unfortunately, the AWT that Java supplies for creating user interfaces isn't at all satisfactory for creating commercial software.

The AWT was designed to use each platform's native components (buttons, scrollbars, file dialogs, and so forth). This is not a bad thing. After all, giving the user an interface he or she is comfortable with cuts down on frustration and increases productivity. However, there was a severe downside to this approach.

The problem was that a button on one platform wasn't the same as a button on another platform. If a button under X/Motif had a makeMeRound() method, and a button on Windows NT did not, the AWT button couldn't support that method. What would happen when you tried to make a round button on NT? There were other problems with the timing and sequence of things happening on one platform versus another platform, too. Fundamentally, because they use these native components, the AWT components are less useful than the equivalent native ones on any single platform.

Interestingly, the JFC fixes the AWT's component problems by using the AWT's own drawing methods. The JFC completely controls drawing all its components. If you want a button, the JFC uses lines to draw the borders and shading and a rectangle to draw the interior. No native components are used except for the most basic ones, such as frames and windows.

One problem with not using native components is that you lose the platform-specific look-and-feel that the user expects. The JFC deals with this problem by allowing pluggable look-and-feel. Using this feature, you can create an application that retains the platform's expected look-and-feel without recoding, as long as a look-and-feel library exists for each platform. Initially, the JFC comes with a Windows 95 library, a Motif library, and a new Java library. Although a platform-consistent look-and-feel is generally preferred, pluggable look-and-feel can be useful for maintaining a consistent look across different platforms, so a user who moves around can always get the look he or she is comfortable with.

Why You Will Love the JFC

If you have been trying to write attractive user interfaces that are at all complex, you will love the JFC simply because it works the way you think it should. If you realized early on that the AWT scrollbars not only had bugs, but had different bugs on different platforms, you will love the JFC because your life won't be one workaround after another. Mostly, you will love the JFC because it's as easy to use as the rest of Java (excluding the AWT, of course).

Here are some other reasons you will love the JFC:

- You can make your GUIs run faster because when you paint, you know which parts actually need to be repainted and which don't.

- The swing part of JFC is written totally in Java, so it's instantly portable. You might have to wait six months between a JavaSoft JDK release and the equivalent Linux JDK release, but when a new JFC comes out, you just copy and go.

- The AWT was the main reason Java went from "write once, run anywhere" to "write once, debug everywhere." The JFC puts this right.

- The JFC has lots of great components that weren't in the AWT, and they actually work!

- The JFC was written by the combined efforts of JavaSoft, Netscape, and IBM, so it doesn't serve the interests of any one company (naming no names).

- The JFC components are all JavaBeans, so they can be used in existing development tools.

How Does the JFC Compare to the IFC?

For a long time, Netscape's *Internet Foundation Classes* (IFC) were the best (only) way to create good user interfaces in Java. They were easy to use, they looked attractive, and they truly worked. JavaSoft showed solid common sense by including Netscape in the design of the JFC, and Netscape did the same by joining up. Netscape further showed its support for the JFC by announcing it would be including the JFC in future releases of Navigator and would be freezing the IFC.

Many of the best things in the IFC have been included in the JFC:

- Internal frames
- Event targets
- Accelerator keys
- Icons
- Auto-scrolling
- Timers
- Drag-and-drop

If you're learning the JFC so you can port your IFC applications, you will find that although the details are different, most of the concepts are still there, along with much more.

What You Will Find in This Book

This book is written from one Java programmer to another. You won't find a lot of pretty language here. What you *will* find is a load of information to help you on your way. The heart of the book is Chapter 7, "JFC by Concept," and Chapter 8, "JFC by Class." Each important component is covered in those chapters with step-by-step instructions on how to quickly get started using each new component, followed by more advanced examples to help you understand what the component really *is*. It's impossible to imagine all the ways a component can be used, so this book tries to help you find the *essence* of the component so you can more easily make it do what you need it to do.

A Quick Summary of the Chapters

Chapter 1, "Getting Started with the JFC" This chapter steps you through creating a simple JFC application on top of which you can build your own applications. It also points you to where you can find out about the concepts it introduces.

Chapter 2, "Moving from AWT to JFC"   This chapter gives you some advice about what to do when you port your AWT applications to JFC. It goes through the AWT components and briefly discusses how they map to JFC components.

Chapter 3, "The JComponent Class"   This chapter explores the JFC's most important class—JComponent. It discussed the capabilities JComponent adds and also covers JComponent's most important methods, including inherited ones.

Chapter 4, "Pluggable Look-and-Feel"   This chapter discusses the concepts behind the JFC's pluggable look-and-feel and goes through the different levels of working with it.

Chapter 5, "JFC Documents"   This chapter discusses the Document concept that JFC text components use.

Chapter 6, "Accessibility"   This chapter talks about JFC's built-in support for access technology and the methods you can use to extend that support.

Chapter 7, "JFC by Concept"   This chapter approaches the JFC from a functional standpoint. Go here when you have a problem but don't know which JFC classes can be used to fix the problem.

Chapter 8, "JFC by Class"   This chapter is the reference section of the book. It has a section for each important class. Each section includes step-by-step instructions on how to use the class, a basic example illustrating the more commonly used methods of the class, and often one or more advanced examples as well.

Chapter 9, "Future JFC Technologies"   This chapter discusses the parts of the JFC that haven't been released yet, including Java 2D.

Chapter 10, "Integrating JFC Example 1: A File Browser"   This chapter implements a file browser that has been verified to work on Windows and UNIX. It discusses each of the example's classes in detail, including which JFC classes were used and why, as well as how the different classes in the example work together.

Chapter 11, "Integrating JFC Example 2: Adding Items to and Removing Items from JTrees"   This chapter illustrates the ideas behind changing the JFC tree component. It discusses each of the example's classes in detail, including which JFC classes were used and why, as well as how the different classes in the example work together.

Chapter 12, "Integrating JFC Example 3: A Simple Paint Program" This chapter creates a simple paint application that shows how to use toggle buttons and color choosers and much more. It discusses each of the example's classes in detail, including which JFC classes were used and why, as well as how the different classes in the example work together.

Chapter 13, "Integrating JFC Example 4: A Simple Word Processor" This chapter implements a basic word processing program that illustrates many of the features of the JFC text components. It discusses each of the example's classes in detail, including which JFC classes were used and why, as well as how the different classes in the example work together.

SUMMARY

In this chapter, we've tried to begin convincing you that the Java Foundation Classes fill a void that has been gaping in Java for two years. If you have worked much with Java, you already know that since Java was initially released, the AWT has sat on top of it like a pimple on the face of the Mona Lisa. As you continue reading this book, we hope you come to believe that the sore has been healed and that GUI programming in Java has become as simple and flexible as the rest of Java.

Getting Started with the JFC

This chapter is intended to give you a simple application that's easy for you to add to. I have found that the best way to learn something is to play around with it one piece at a time; to do that, you need a simple, solid foundation from which to start. The nature of learning is that every answer brings more questions. This chapter will raise many questions, but it will also, I hope, point you toward the answers.

A Simple Example

The JFC is a set of classes that help you produce visually appealing things with Java, so it only seems natural that a simple example would result in putting something on your screen. This example does just that, and at every step points you toward the tools you will need to make your own user interfaces look great.

Step 1: Create Your Main Class

Every application must have a class with a main() method in it. Usually, all the main() method does is create an instance of the class that really cranks up your application. That's what we will do here. The SimpleApp class contains a main() method (static, of course), and all the main() method does is create an instance of SimpleApp. For this step, SimpleApp doesn't actually do anything.

Here's the code for creating your main class:

```
public class SimpleApp
    {
    public SimpleApp()
    {
    }

    public static void main( String args[] )
    {
        new SimpleApp();
    }
}
```

When you run SimpleApp, it does nothing—just returns.

Step 2: Make SimpleApp Display a Frame

Most applications use a frame as their main window. It's where the main menu resides, and it typically controls all other windows. In this step, we make SimpleApp display a JFC frame.

The steps for creating and displaying a JFC frame (JFrame) are as follows:

Create the JFrame. You can do this in a couple of ways (see Chapter 8, "JFC by Class"), but we'll just create it with a string that shows up in its title bar:

```
JFrame myFrame = new JFrame( "Frame Title" );
```

Now that the JFrame is created, we have to specify where it should go, and how big it should be. For this, we use the setBounds() method from java.awt.Component. We want the JFrame's upper-left corner to be 100 pixels from the left edge of the screen and 50 pixels from the top of the screen. We also want it to be 300 pixels wide and 200 pixels tall, as shown here:

```
myFrame.setBounds( 100, 50, 300, 200 );
```

We have created the JFrame and specified its location and size, so now we must tell it to display itself. To do so, we use the setVisible() method that JFrame inherited from java.awt.Frame:

```
myFrame.setVisible(true);
```

JFrame is one of the few JFC components that descends from an AWT component that uses a *peer* (a native component). That's because JFrame interacts directly with the operating system and so must assume a form that is acceptable to it.

Here is the revised source for SimpleApp with the changes in italic. Notice that we also added an import statement so JFrame can be found.

```
import com.sun.java.swing.*;

public class SimpleApp
{
    public SimpleApp()
    {
        JFrame myFrame = new JFrame( "Frame Title" );
        myFrame.setBounds( 100, 50, 300, 200 );
        myFrame.show();
    }

    public static void main( String args[] )
    {
        new SimpleApp();
    }
}
```

Figure 1-1 shows what the JFrame should look like so far.

Figure 1-1
An empty JFrame.

SimpleApp is so simple that it can't even close itself. You have to press Ctrl+C in the window where you started it to make it go away. See "A Quick Review of the JDK 1.1 Event Model" in Chapter 7, "JFC by Concept," for a discussion of events in general. The JFrame section in Chapter 8, "JFC by Class" includes an example of how to properly close a JFrame.

NOTE: *For lots more information on frames and other windows, see the "Windows" section in Chapter 7. Also see the following sections in Chapter 8: "JDialog," "JFrame," "JInternalPane," "JRootPane," and "JWindow."*

Step 3: Create Your Own JFrame

The previous step displayed a JFrame very nicely, but because this JFrame will act as our application's main window, it makes things much easier if we subclass JFrame. This method gives us more control and also encapsulates our main window's behavior.

For this step, the subclass, called MyFrame, is very simple and acts just like the JFrame in Step 2. It's made up of an import of the main JFC package and a simple class that extends JFrame. MyFrame just has the one constructor, and all it does is call JFrame's matching constructor.

Here's the revised source code for the SimpleApp class with changes in italic. Notice that the import of the main JFC package was removed (SimpleApp needed it because it used JFrame, but doesn't need it now), and all references to JFrame were changed to MyFrame:

```
public class SimpleApp
{
    public SimpleApp()
    {
        MyFrame myFrame = new MyFrame( "Frame Title" );
        myFrame.setBounds( 100, 50, 300, 200 );
        myFrame.show();
    }

    public static void main( String args[] )
    {
        new SimpleApp();
    }
}
```

Here's the source for the new MyFrame class:

```
import com.sun.java.swing.*;

public class MyFrame extends JFrame
{
    public MyFrame( String titleString )
```

```
    {
        super( titleString );
    }
}
```

If you run SimpleApp, it should look just like it did after Step 2. All we did was move the JFrame stuff into a separate class.

Step 4: Understanding Root Panes

It's important to understand root panes because you can't really use a JFrame without them. You should never try to add items (menus, buttons, and so forth) directly to a JFrame. The JFrame has what you might call an "agent" that handles that kind of task. That agent is a *root pane*, which is an instance of the JRootPane class. It has four parts, any of which can be accessed directly or replaced with your own versions:

- The menu bar. There's no menu bar that automatically comes with a JRootPane. To use a menu bar with a JFrame, you must make your own JMenuBar.
- The content pane. This is a container where you add items like buttons and other panels. You can use the default content pane, which is a JPanel, or you can replace it with your own.
- The layered pane. This part actually contains the menu bar and content pane on one layer, and supports adding things like popup menus at higher layers.
- The glass pane. This is an invisible component that overlays everything else. It's not often used, but can be handy for temporarily blocking events or for drawing over the top of everything else in the JFrame.

 NOTE: *For more information about root panes, see the "JFC Containers" and "Menus" sections in Chapter 7. Also see the "JRootPane," "JMenuBar," "JLayered-Pane," "JFrame," "JWindow," "JDialog," and "JInternalFrame" sections in Chapter 8.*

Step 5: Add a Menu Bar

Basically, any application that uses a main window has a menu bar in it. The menu bar is where the application gives the user access to all its options and child windows. Creating a menu bar, with all its menus and items, can be done by following the steps outlined in this section.

First, create the menu bar. This means creating an instance of JMenuBar, which we do in MyFrame's constructor:

```
JMenuBar menuBar = new JMenuBar();
```

The next step is to make MyFrame use the menu bar as its main menu bar, which is done through the root pane:

```
getRootPane().setMenuBar( menuBar );
```

A menu bar doesn't show inside the JFrame until it contains a menu. Each menu is represented by an instance of JMenu. Here, we're going to create a File menu. The word *File* will show up in the menu bar after we add the menu to the menu bar, as shown here:

```
JMenu fileMenu = new JMenu( "File" );
```

Now add the menu to the menu bar:

```
menuBar.add( fileMenu );
```

Now that the menu bar has been created and attached to the JFrame and a menu has been attached to the menu bar, the menu bar is visible. However, if you try to access the File menu, nothing happens because there are no menu items in the File menu. Menu items can be almost any type of component, but they are normally JMenuItem, JRadioButtonMenuItem, or JCheckBoxMenuItem. For this example, we'll just use a single JMenuItem labeled "Exit":

```
JMenuItem exitItem = new JMenuItem( "Exit" );
```

The menu item is created, so now it must be added to the menu. Now there will be a menu bar with a single menu attached to it, and the menu will have a single item in it:

```
fileMenu.add( exitItem );
```

Here is the revised code for MyFrame with changes in italic near the end of the listing. SimpleApp's code is not listed because it hasn't changed.

```
import com.sun.java.swing.*;

public class MyFrame extends JFrame
{
    public MyFrame( String titleString )
    {
        super( titleString );
```

```
JMenuBar menuBar = new JMenuBar();
getRootPane().setMenuBar( menuBar );
JMenu fileMenu = new JMenu( "File" );
menuBar.add( fileMenu );
JMenuItem exitItem = new JMenuItem( "Exit" );
fileMenu.add( exitItem );
    }
}
```

Figure 1-2 shows what our frame looks like now. The menu bar is visible, and you can open the File menu and see an item labeled "Exit." When you choose Exit, however, not much happens. Refer to "A Quick Review of the JDK 1.1 Event Model" in Chapter 7 and the "JMenuItem" section in Chapter 8 for information about capturing menu item events.

NOTE: *For more information about menus, see the "Menus" section in Chapter 7, and the "JCheckBoxMenuItem," "JMenu," "JMenuBar," "JMenuItem," "JPopupMenu," and "JRadioButtonMenuItem" sections in Chapter 8.*

Step 6: Add Components to the JFrame

You won't always want to add components like buttons into your JFrame. Many times, the JFrame's main area is reserved as a workspace where windows float around. For this example, we'll add a single button at the bottom of the JFrame and save the rest of the workspace for floating windows (added in the next step).

When adding components to a JFrame, you have to go through the root pane. The root pane controls a panel called the *content pane*, which is where components such as buttons get put. The content pane fills the entire inside area of the JFrame except where the menu bar is. Although you can replace the default content pane, it's generally not necessary to do so. Follow the steps outlined here to create a component and add it to the JFrame.

First, you have to create the component. We'll just create a JFC button (JButton):

```
JButton okButton = new JButton( "Ok" );
```

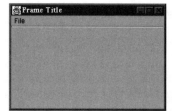

Figure 1-2
JFrame with a menu bar.

To know where the button goes when we add it, we need to know what the layout manager is for the container where the button is being added. The container is the JFrame's content pane, accessible by using getRoot-Pane().getContentPane(). Its default layout manager is BorderLayout, which serves our purpose just fine. The button will be laid out along the bottom edge of the JFrame:

```
getRootPane().getContentPane().add( "South", okButton );
```

Here's the revised source code for MyFrame with changes in italic near the end of the listing:

```
import com.sun.java.swing.*;

public class MyFrame extends JFrame
{
    public MyFrame( String titleString )
    {
        super( titleString );

        JMenuBar menuBar = new JMenuBar();
        getRootPane().setMenuBar( menuBar );
        JMenu fileMenu = new JMenu( "File" );
        menuBar.add( fileMenu );
        JMenuItem exitItem = new JMenuItem( "Exit" );
        fileMenu.add( exitItem );

        JButton okButton = new JButton( "Ok" );
        getRootPane().getContentPane().add( "South", okButton );
    }
}
```

NOTE: *We use getRootPane().getContentPane() to get the JFrame's content pane. JFrame has a convenience method—getContentPane()—that does the same thing and is a little less ponderous.*

Figure 1-3 shows our frame after adding the button. The button is laid out just where it's supposed to be, but if you click it, it doesn't do anything beyond looking pressed down. "A Quick Review of the JDK 1.1 Event Model" in Chapter 8 has some information on capturing button events.

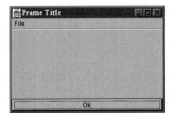

Figure 1-3
JFrame with a menu bar and a button.

NOTE: *For more information on JFC components, see the "Double Buffering," "Allowing the User to Trigger Actions," "Selecting Items from Lists," "Component Borders," "Text," "Keyboard Navigation," and "JFC Layout Managers" sections in Chapter 7. Also see Chapter 8.*

Step 7: Adding Internal Frames

Many applications have a single main window with a variety of child windows inside. A child window can hold a document (as in a word processor), a tool palette (as in a paint program), or a chart (as in a spreadsheet program). The JFC includes a component called an *internal frame* that can be used as a child window; it's implemented in the JInternalFrame class.

JInternalFrames are typically added to a specialized pane called a *desktop pane*, called that because it acts as your own private desktop that manages windows and icons much as your operating system's desktop does. In this step, we first create a desktop pane (class JDesktopPane) and then add a JInternalFrame to it.

First, we create the JDesktopPane:

```
JDesktopPane desktop = new JDesktopPane();
```

Then we add it to the content pane:

```
getRootPane().getContentPane().add( "Center", desktop );
```

Remember that the content pane is using a BorderLayout, so if we add our desktop pane to its center position, the desktop pane will fill the content pane's remaining area.

The desktop pane is created and ready, so we create the JInternalFrame, giving it a title string to put in its title bar (we could set some other properties, but you can find out more about them in Chapter 8):

```
JInternalFrame inFrame = new JInternalFrame( "Internal Frame" );
```

The internal frame doesn't know how big it should be or where it should go within the desktop pane. We set this information with the setBounds() method, just as we did with the JFrame:

```
inFrame.setBounds( 10, 20, 150, 80 );
```

The values 10 and 20 are the location of the internal frame's upper-left corner in relation to the desktop pane's upper-left corner; 150 and 80 are the internal frame's width and height in pixels.

Now that the internal frame is ready, we just add it to the desktop pane. A desktop pane can hold more than one internal frame, but we'll add just one to keep it simple:

```
desktop.add( inFrame );
```

You can drag the internal frame around inside the desktop pane, but it can't pass outside of the pane. You can also make the internal frame useful by putting items inside it, like buttons or text.

Here's the revised source code to MyFrame with changes in italic near the end of the listing:

```
import com.sun.java.swing.*;

public class MyFrame extends JFrame
{
    public MyFrame( String titleString )
    {
        super( titleString );

        JMenuBar menuBar = new JMenuBar();
        getRootPane().setMenuBar( menuBar );
        JMenu fileMenu = new JMenu( "File" );
        menuBar.add( fileMenu );
        JMenuItem exitItem = new JMenuItem( "Exit" );
        fileMenu.add( exitItem );

        JButton okButton = new JButton( "Ok" );
        getRootPane().getContentPane().add( "South", okButton );

        JDesktopPane desktop = new JDesktopPane();
        getRootPane().getContentPane().add( "Center", desktop );
        JInternalFrame inFrame = new JInternalFrame( "Internal
                                                      Frame" );
        inFrame.setBounds( 10, 20, 150, 80 );
        desktop.add( inFrame );
    }
}
```

Figure 1-4 shows our frame after adding the JDesktopPane and JInternalFrame.

Figure 1-4

JFrame with an internal frame.

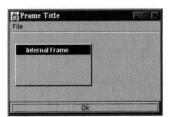

NOTE: *For more information on internal frames, see the "JFC Containers" and "Windows" sections in Chapter 7. Also see the "JDesktopPane" and "JInternal-Frame" sections in Chapter 8.*

SUMMARY

When you're just starting to learn a new programming language or set of classes, it's nice to have a simple test application that you can play with. This chapter has given you that example to use as a place to try out JFC's other features.

2

Moving from AWT to JFC

Whenever a company decides to replace an old library with a new one, people who have applications that use the old library get a little uneasy. They know they will have to port their code to the new library sooner or later, and there's no guarantee that the port will be easy. How difficult the port is depends greatly on how much consideration the library designers gave to porting problems. Fortunately for us, the JFC team seems to have given ease of porting a fairly high priority.

If you have Java code that uses the AWT components and are thinking about porting it to use JFC components, you have some options:

■ Option 1: Leave your existing code alone.

Nothing about the JFC or JDK 1.2 will make your existing code work any worse than it does already. All the AWT components will work the same as they did before JFC. If you choose this route, you will probably want to make any later additions using the AWT as well because JFC components will probably clash visually with your AWT components.

- Option 2: Rewrite your code from scratch using the JFC.

  Typically, this option isn't necessary, but if you hate the existing code, you might find switching to the JFC a convenient excuse for a full rewrite. Also, if your existing code uses the JDK 1.0.2 event model and the code will be in use for a while, at least a partial rewrite might be good idea.

- Option 3: Convert your AWT components into JFC components.

  If your code has a future and already uses the JDK 1.1 event model, this is probably your best bet.

Porting Information

If you take your AWT-JFC port slowly, you shouldn't have too many problems. The JFC designers tried to make new components that include the same functionality as the equivalent AWT components. For example, the AWT Button component has a JFC counterpart called "JButton." JButton is what JavaSoft calls "source compatible" with Button, which means that JButton has pretty much all of Button's methods with the same parameters. So, in this case, all you have to do is change the word *Button* to *JButton* when you declare and construct the component and you should be set to go.

You might previously have overridden addNotify() in your AWT code to find out when a component's peer was created. Of course, the JFC doesn't use peers, so this technique won't work the same. It might be a good idea, then, to use a ComponentListener or WindowListener instead. Any other code that deals with peer creation could also cause problems.

The best way to approach AWT-JFC porting is to convert one component at a time, if possible. That way you can change the component, then see if it behaves the way it should, and then move on to the next one. Do this at least until you get a feel for the kinds of problems you're running into. Otherwise, if you make changes wholesale, it will be more difficult to pinpoint exactly which component conversion causes whatever problems (if any) you encounter.

The first step is to add the JFC import statement:

```
import com.sun.java.swing.*;
```

Then you can start converting your components.

AWT-JFC Component Comparison

Here is a list of AWT components and porting details about each:

■ **Applet:** The JFC has a component called "JApplet," which is a descendant of Applet. However, JApplet gives access to its space via a JRootPane, so if you want to convert your Applet to a JApplet, it requires a little work.

■ **Button:** The JFC has an equivalent component called "JButton." JButton has more features, including the ability to display an icon on the button, but it has all of Button's methods.

■ **Canvas:** It's still the same component it was. It can be used as it has always been used, although you might prefer to use one of the JFC panes, such as JPanel, or you can subclass JComponent.

■ **Checkbox:** The JFC has an equivalent component called "JCheckBox." JCheckBox has more features than Checkbox, but includes its methods. If you're using Checkbox to display radio buttons, you should change them to JRadioButtons. You will also have to change your CheckboxGroup to a ButtonGroup.

■ **CheckboxGroup:** The JFC doesn't have an exact equivalent for this component. The AWT uses multiple Checkboxes in a CheckboxGroup to display radio buttons. The JFC has an actual radio button component called "JRadioButton," but it's not grouped by using a CheckboxGroup. It uses a ButtonGroup, so you need to replace CheckboxGroup with ButtonGroup. The two don't have exactly the same methods, so you might need to change method calls, too.

■ **CheckboxMenuItem:** The JFC has an equivalent component called "JCheckBoxMenuItem." JCheckBoxMenuItem has more features than CheckboxMenuItem, but includes its methods. If you are using it with a CheckboxGroup to imitate radio buttons, you need to change your JCheckBoxMenuItems to JRadioButtonMenuItems and your CheckboxGroup to a ButtonGroup.

■ **Choice:** There's no exact equivalent for this component in the JFC. Instead, the JFC uses a JComboBox to fill the same need. Unfortunately, JComboBox is not source compatible with Choice, so you have to rewrite the code that deals with Choice.

■ **Component:** Component is still the same old Component and is fine to use. In fact, most of the JFC components have Component in their ancestry somewhere. You might want to change over to a subclass of JComponent (JComponent is abstract) if you want the extra features that adds, but it's not necessary.

■ **Container:** Much like Component, Container is still the same as it was, and most JFC components also have Container as an ancestor. You can subclass JComponent for use as a container if you want the added features, but it's not necessary.

- **Dialog:** The JFC has a JDialog class that's actually a descendent of Dialog. However, JDialog gives access to its space via its JRootPane, which, of course, Dialog doesn't have. You can continue to use Dialog, but you might want to change to JDialog because it seems to have avoided the bugs that have plagued Dialog.

- **FileDialog:** You can continue to use FileDialog if you like, or you can use the JFC's JFileChooser class if you want it to be visually consistent with the rest of your JFC components. JFileChooser also gives you more control over what's going on than FileDialog does. JFileChooser doesn't use the same methods as FileDialog. For Swing 1.0, the JFileChooser API is not complete.

- **Frame:** The JFC has a JFrame class that's a descendent of Frame. Like JDialog, JFrame gives access to its area via a JRootPane, so you have to make some changes to your code to convert from Frame to JFrame.

- **Label:** The JFC has an equivalent component called "JLabel." JLabel has extra features that Label doesn't have, but it includes Label's methods.

- **List:** The JFC has no exact equivalent for this component. Instead, it has a new component called "JList" that fills the same need. Unfortunately, JList is significantly different from List, so you will have to redo your List code.

- **Menu:** The JFC has an equivalent component called "JMenu." JMenu has extra features, but includes Menu's methods.

- **MenuBar:** The JFC has an equivalent component called "JMenuBar." JMenuBar has extra features, but includes MenuBar's methods.

- **MenuComponent:** The JFC has no exact equivalent for this component. Depending on what you used it for, you might want to try a JMenuItem or subclass JComponent.

- **MenuItem:** The JFC has an equivalent component called "JMenuItem." JMenuItem has more features, but includes MenuItem's methods.

- **Panel:** The JFC has an equivalent component called "JPanel." JPanel has many more features than Panel, including support for double-buffering and borders.

- **PopupMenu:** The JFC has an equivalent component called "JPopupMenu." JPopupMenu has more features, but also includes all of PopupMenu's methods.

- **ScrollPane:** The JFC has a JScrollPane component that does the same types of things, but it isn't source compatible with ScrollPane. In fact, the two are quite different, so you will have some rewriting to do.

■ **Scrollbar:** The JFC has an equivalent component called "JScrollBar." JScrollBar is source compatible with Scrollbar, but they didn't include Scrollbar's bugs in JScrollBar.

■ **TextArea:** The JFC has an equivalent component called "JTextArea." JTextArea has much more functionality than TextArea, but includes TextArea's methods.

■ **TextComponent:** The JFC has an equivalent component called "JTextComponent." JTextComponent has extra features but includes TextComponent's methods.

■ **TextField:** The JFC has an equivalent component called "JTextField" that has much more functionality but also includes TextField's methods.

■ **Window:** The JFC has a component called "JWindow" that's a descendent of Window. However, JWindow gives access to its space via a JRootPane, so if you want to convert your Window to a JWindow, it requires a little work.

Combining AWT and JFC Components

If you want to, you can combine AWT and JFC components without too many problems. Because most JFC components descend from java.awt.Component, AWT and JFC components generally act the same as far as basic operation and component layout go. Therefore, you can put JFC components into AWT containers, and you can put AWT components into JFC containers. There are only a couple of things to worry about.

The most obvious problem with combining AWT and JFC components is that AWT components use the native look-and-feel, but JFC components use whatever look-and-feel is in effect. Not only do the two types of component look different, the differences change from platform to platform.

Another problem is the interaction between components with peers and lightweight (peer-less) components. The problem is that if an AWT and a JFC component overlap, the AWT component always displays on top. This is true even if the JFC component is a JInternalFrame in a JDesktopPane and it uses a layer of 1,000,000. This isn't a problem in most cases because components don't generally overlap. It should be noted that AWT components go on top of JFC components only within the same container. Also, layering doesn't work with AWT components—not even among themselves.

If you use a JFC component in an AWT container, you will need to implement double-buffering so the component doesn't flash. In the JFC, you can just use a JPanel with double-buffering turned on.

SUMMARY

If you have read this chapter, you have no doubt been working with the AWT and are more than ready to move over to the JFC. There's no magical way to port from the AWT to the JFC, but the information covered in this chapter should help as you begin.

The JComponent Class

Perhaps the most important class in the JFC is the JComponent class. Most of the new components defined in the JFC are subclasses of this abstract class.

What Makes a JFC Component?

Before JDK 1.1, all Java components used the components that occur natively on each platform. That is, an AWT button was just a wrapper around a Windows button or an X/Motif button or a Macintosh button. The Java component relied on the local operating system to define its appearance and its behavior.

With JDK 1.1 came the concept of lightweight components. A *lightweight component* is responsible for everything about itself, from drawing the component in all its possible states (enabled, selected, disabled, and so forth) to reacting to user input. This feature gives the developer much more control over exactly how the component acts. All JFC components are lightweight components, with the exception of the ones directly managed by the operating system: JWindow, JFrame, and JDialog.

Like AWT components, all JFC components (including JComponent) have java.awt.Component as an ancestor. Most JFC components derive from the JComponent class, which automatically gives them some useful capabilities.

JComponent

JComponent's ancestry looks like this:

```
java.lang.Object
  |
  +—java.awt.Component
      |
      +—java.awt.Container
          |
          +—com.sun.java.swing.JComponent
```

As you can see, JComponent descends from java.awt.Container—a fact that some of the more complex JFC components use extensively. For example, a JMenuBar acts as a container for JMenus (it uses a BoxLayout). Although the JFC components are quite different from the AWT components we're used to, much of the core functionality still comes from java.awt.Component and java.awt.Container.

What JComponent Provides

JComponent supplies a useful set of features you would have had to otherwise create yourself. They are listed briefly here, and then JComponent's capabilities are explained in the following sections. JComponent's new features include the following:

- Ability to change a component's borders
- Pluggable look-and-feel
- More advanced painting
- Built-in scrolling features
- Ability to set preferred, minimum, and maximum size
- Improved focus handling
- Better keyboard navigation
- Tool tips
- Double-buffering
- Notification of changes in the window hierarchy
- Accessibility information

ABILITY TO CHANGE A COMPONENT'S BORDERS The JFC introduces the concept of borders to the Java world. A *border* simply describes how the edge of a component should be drawn.

PLUGGABLE LOOK-AND-FEEL The JFC separates each component into parts: the Model (its internal state/data), the Look-and-Feel (how it draws and responds to events), and the component itself (its external state). This separation makes it possible to keep the parts of a component that deal with storing internal and external properties while changing the way the component looks and behaves.

MORE ADVANCED PAINTING JComponent provides the ability to specify transparency of components, paint parts of components, and paint with a pluggable look-and-feel.

BUILT-IN SCROLLING FEATURES Although JComponent itself doesn't do scrolling, it does offer some helper methods that let components control their behavior somewhat while scrolling.

ABILITY TO SET PREFERRED, MINIMUM, AND MAXIMUM SIZE Layout managers (particularly new JFC ones) often look at a component's minimum, preferred, and maximum size to decide how to lay out the component. JComponent includes methods that let you change these sizes without having to subclass the component.

IMPROVED FOCUS HANDLING The AWT supplied some focus management, and the JFC has made it better.

BETTER KEYBOARD NAVIGATION The JFC has much improved the ability to create a user interface that doesn't require a mouse.

TOOL TIPS A *tool tip* is a small text window associated with a component; it's displayed when the user places the mouse over the component and lets it rest there momentarily. Tool tips are very useful, particularly with components like tool bar buttons that don't have text or a label with the component.

DOUBLE-BUFFERING Because almost all JFC components are lightweight, display flashing is a major concern, making double-buffering a necessity. So even though you could implement double-buffering yourself, JComponent does so for you in a memory-efficient way.

NOTIFICATION OF CHANGES IN THE WINDOW HIERARCHY
Now a component can ask to be informed when a component above it in the display hierarchy changes in some way (made visible or invisible or removed from its container).

ACCESSIBILITY INFORMATION Most JFC components automatically provide a basic amount of information for use by screen readers, and so forth. JComponent includes a single method that helps you add even more information.

JComponent's Capabilities Including What It Inherits

It's important to understand all of JComponent's methods so we know what built-in abilities its subclasses have. This includes understanding the methods it inherits from java.awt.Container and java.awt.Component. The following sections break most of these methods down into groups and explain each of them.

PLACEMENT IN A CONTAINER All subclasses of JComponent are added into other containers, so there are several methods that try to control where they are placed and at what size:

- **public boolean contains(int x, int y)** From JComponent; given a point x,y in relation to the component, this method asks the component if the point is in it.

- **public boolean contains(Point p)** From Component; it's the same as the previous method, except that the point is passed in as a Point, instead of as integers x and y.

- **public float getAlignmentX()** From JComponent. Some layout managers want direction on how to place components. A vertical BoxLayout, for example, might have some components that don't fill the area horizontally. It uses the components' X alignment to decide whether to center them, align them left or right, and so on. The alignment value is from 0.0 to 1.0. This method lets you find out a component's X alignment value.

▪ **public float getAlignmentY()**   From JComponent; it's the same as the previous method, except that it tells you the component's vertical alignment value.

▪ **public Rectangle getBounds()**   From Component; gets the component's location within its container and its size in pixels as a Rectangle variable.

▪ **public Rectangle getBounds(Rectangle rect)**   From JComponent; just like the previous method, except it passes in a Rectangle variable so the method won't have to make a new one.

▪ **public int getHeight()**   From JComponent; returns the pixel height of the component.

▪ **public Point getLocation()**   From Component; it returns the location of the component's upper-left corner in pixels in relation to its container.

▪ **public Point getLocation(Point loc)**   From JComponent; it's the same as the previous method, except you pass in a Point variable. The same Point variable is returned from the method, so an extra Point variable doesn't have to be allocated in the method.

▪ **public Point getLocationOnScreen()**   From Component; it returns the component's upper-left corner in pixels in relation to the screen origin instead of to the container origin. Useful for placing or moving windows and dialogs in relation to a component.

▪ **public Dimension getMaximumSize()**   From JComponent. Each component has a size beyond which it would rather not be drawn. This method tells the component to figure out that size and return it in a Dimension. The maximum size depends mostly on the type of component and less on its properties. A button looks silly when it's too big, but a panel has essentially an unlimited maximum size.

▪ **public Dimension getMinimumSize()**   From JComponent. Each component has a size it thinks is the smallest at which it can be drawn and still be effective. This method tells the component to figure that size out and return it in a Dimension variable. The minimum size varies depending on the component's type and current properties. For example, a button's minimum size is partly determined by the length of its text string.

▪ **public Dimension getPreferredSize()**   From JComponent. Each component has a size it thinks makes it work most effectively—and it prefers to be drawn at this size. This method tells the component to figure out what that size is and return it in a Dimension variable. The preferred size depends on the type of component and its properties.

- **public Dimension getSize()** From Component; returns the pixel size of the component as a Dimension class.

- **public Dimension getSize(Dimension size)** From JComponent; just like the previous method, except you pass in a Dimension. The size is put into the Dimension variable and also returned from the method, so the method doesn't have to allocate a new Dimension variable.

- **public int getWidth()** From JComponent; returns the pixel width of the component.

- **public int getX()** From JComponent; it returns the location of the component's left side in pixels in relation to its container.

- **public int getY()** From JComponent; it returns the location of the component's top side in pixels in relation to its container.

- **public void setAlignmentX(float align)** From JComponent. Some layout managers want direction on how to place components. A vertical BoxLayout, for example, might have some components that don't fill the area horizontally. It uses the components' X alignment to decide whether to center them, align them left or right, and so on. The alignment value is from 0.0 to 1.0. This method lets you set how a component should behave in these situations. Not all layout managers use the alignment; java.awt.Component has a series of constants that can be passed to this method for certain alignments.

- **public void setAlignmentY(float align)** From JComponent; it's the same as the previous method, except it's used to set the component's Y alignment.

- **public void setBounds(int x, int y, int width, int height)** From JComponent; sets the component's location within its container and its size in pixels.

- **public void setBounds(Rectangle rect)** From JComponent; same as the previous method, except the location and size are passed in as a Rectangle.

- **public void setLocation(int x, int y)** From Component; it moves the component so that its upper-left corner is at position x,y in pixels in relation to its container. Some layout managers don't allow this, and others might allow it and then move the component somewhere else when the container gets laid out again.

- **public void setLocation(Point loc)** From Component; just like the previous method, except x and y are passed in as a Point.

- **public void setMaximumSize(Dimension size)** From JComponent; tells the component that it shouldn't be drawn larger than the given size. Layout managers frequently use a component's maximum size when the container has extra space to fill, and the layout manager must decide which components can grow to fill the space.

- **public void setMinimumSize(Dimension size)**   From JComponent; tells the component that it shouldn't be drawn smaller than the given size. This method is useful in affecting how layout managers treat the component because they sometimes use a component's minimum size in determining how it should be laid out.

- **public void setPreferredSize(Dimension size)**   From JComponent; tells the component what its ideal size is. Layout managers often use a component's preferred size in initially laying out its container.

- **public void setSize(Dimension size)**   From Component; sets the component's size in pixels. The upper-left corner of the component stays at its same location. The container's layout manager might not allow the component to grow in response to this method, and it could cause the component to change its location as a result of the change in size.

COMPONENT BORDERS   The JFC adds the ability to change a component's border—how its edge looks. Whether changing the component's border is a good idea depends on the component, and whether a component honors the change is up to its look-and-feel. For example, a button uses its border to show whether it's pressed or not, so changing borders affects that. Also, some components, like radio buttons, typically don't draw a border. Here are the methods that deal with borders:

- **public Border getBorder()**   From JComponent; it returns the border currently being used by the component. Border is the interface that all border classes must implement.

- **public Insets getInsets()**   From JComponent. If a border is being used, it returns the border's width on each side of the component. Otherwise, it calls Container's getInsets() method.

- **public void setBorder(Border border)**   From JComponent; it makes the component use the specified border.

TOOL TIPS   Tool tips are new with the JFC. Normally, you just use the setToolTipText() method. Using the getToolTipText() method is less common.

- **public Point getToolTipLocation(MouseEvent event)**   From JComponent; returns the point at which the toll tip should appear relative to the component's origin. Override this method to provide special behavior. The "event" argument is either a mouse entered event or a mouse moved event.

- **public String getToolTipText()**   From JComponent; returns the string that's currently displayed over the component. Can be null.

- **public String getToolTipText(MouseEvent event)**   From JComponent; returns the tool tip text associated with the properties

of the "event" argument. By default, this calls getToolTipText() with
no arguments. Override it to display different tool tip text for
different locations in the component. The "event" argument is either
a mouse entered event or a mouse moved event.

■ **public void setToolTipText(String text)**   From JComponent;
specifies the text that should be displayed in the component's tool tip.

DOUBLE-BUFFERING   Double-buffering is absolutely required for JFC
applications because JFC components cause screen flashing otherwise.
JComponent takes care of double-buffering for you with these methods:

■ **public boolean isDoubleBuffered()**   From JComponent; says
whether the component is double-buffered. Even though a component
might say it's not double-buffered, its double-buffering needs are taken
care of if one of its ancestors in the display hierarchy is double-buffered.

■ **public void setDoubleBuffered(boolean buffer)**   From JComponent;
turns double-buffering on or off for a component. You almost never need to
turn double-buffering on because it's normally taken care of by the content
pane of the frame, dialog, or window the component is in.

ADDING COMPONENTS TO A JCOMPONENT   Because JCompo-
nent is a subclass of java.awt.Container, you can add other components into
subclasses of JComponent. Here are several methods from java.awt.Con-
tainer and its superclass java.awt.Component that deal with adding components and managing them once they have been added:

■ **public Component add(Component comp)**   From Container; it
adds the specified component to your component. The return value
is the added component. What happens when you call this method
depends on your component's layout manager.

■ **public Component add(Component comp, int index)**   From
Container; it adds the specified component to your component. The
index is used by some layout managers to position the components
relatively. Using an index with some layout managers can cause an
error. The return value is the added component.

■ **public Component add(Component comp, Object constraints)**
From Container; it's used to add the specified component to your
component when your component is using a layout manager (like
GridBagLayout) that requires a separate object to tell it how to lay
the component out. The return value is the added component.

■ **public Component add(Component comp, Object constraints,
int index)**   From Container; it's used for adding a component to
your component when your component is using a layout manager
that requires a constraints object and can use an index. The return
value is the added component.

- **public Component add(String position, Component comp)** From Container; it adds the specified component to your component. It's used when your component uses a layout manager that accepts a string and is most commonly used with a BorderLayout. The return value is the added component.

- **public void doLayout()** From Container; causes your component to lay itself out. It's best to call the validate() method instead of calling doLayout() directly because validate() makes sure both the component and its children get laid out properly.

- **public Component getComponent(int n)** From Container; returns the *n*th component in your component. It doesn't require that the components be added to your component with indices.

- **public Component getComponentAt(int x, int y)** From Container. Given a point at x,y in relation to your component, it returns the component at that point. If there are multiple components at that point, the topmost is returned.

- **public Component getComponentAt(Point p)** From Container; it's the same as the previous method, except the point is passed in as a Point instead of as integers x and y.

- **public int getComponentCount()** From Container; it returns the number of components in your component.

- **public Component[] getComponents()** From Container; it returns an array holding all the components in your component. This method is often used by layout managers when they are laying things out.

- **public LayoutManager getLayout()** From Container; returns the layout manager that your component is currently using.

- **public Container getParent()** From Component; returns the container to which this component was added.

- **public JRootPane getRootPane()** From JComponent; returns the component's root pane if it has one. Otherwise, it looks up the display hierarchy to get the first one it comes across.

- **public void invalidate()** From Container; it tells your component that it and its parents need to be laid out again.

- **public boolean isValidateRoot()** From JComponent; if it returns true, then if one of the component's descendents calls revalidate(), it works its way up to the component. When it gets there, the component causes all of its descendents to be validated. The only component that returns true by default is JScrollPane. This helps a JScrollPane to change when the component it's scrolling changes size.

- **public void remove(Component comp)** From Container; it removes the specified component from your component. The component would have previously been added to your component by using one of the preceding add() methods. If the component is not in your component, no error is generated.

- **public void remove(int index)**   From Container; it removes the component at the specified index from your component. The component would have been added to your component by using add(Component, int) or add(Component, Object, int) defined previously.

- **public void removeAll()**   From Container; it removes all components from your component.

- **public void revalidate()**   From JComponent; it invalidates the current component and causes its nearest ancestor whose isValidateRoot() method returns true to validate all its descendants. Normally called by a component being scrolled by a JScrollPane. JScrollPane's isValidateRoot() method returns true, so when this component calls revalidate(), its JScrollPane validates itself and its descendants.

- **public void setLayout(LayoutManager layout)**   From Container; it tells your component which layout manager to use.

- **public void validate()**   From Container; causes your component and all its children to be laid out. It's useful when you or the user have done something that changes the size of a child component.

EVENT AND EVENT HANDLERS   Many things can happen to components and containers, so there's a need for many types of events and ways for those events to be captured. Here are the methods from Component, Container, and JComponent that deal with events:

- **public synchronized void addAncestorListener(Ancestor-Listener l)**   From JComponent. It tells the component which class should be notified when one of the following happens to the component or one of its ancestors in the display hierarchy: It's made visible or is added to the hierarchy, it's moved, or it's made invisible or is removed from the hierarchy. More than one class can be registered in this way, and all registered classes are notified when any of these events takes place.

- **public synchronized void addComponentListener (ComponentListener l)**   From Component. It tells the component which class should be notified when one of the following happens to the component: It's hidden, shown, resized, or moved. More than one class can be registered in this way, and all registered classes are notified when any of these events takes place.

- **public void addContainerListener(ContainerListener l)**   From Container. It tells the component which class should be notified when one of the following happens to it: A component is added to the component, or a component is removed from the component. More than one class can be registered in this way, and all registered classes are notified when either of these events takes place.

- **public synchronized void addFocusListener(FocusListener l)**
  From Component. It tells the component which class should be notified when one of the following happens to the component: It gains focus, or it loses focus. More than one class can be registered in this way, and all registered classes are notified when either of these events takes place.

- **public synchronized void addKeyListener(KeyListener l)**
  From Component. It tells the component which class should be notified when one of the following happens to the component: A key is pressed when it has the focus, a key is released when it has the focus, or a key is typed (pressed and released) when it has the focus. More than one class can be registered in this way, and all registered classes are notified when any of these events takes place.

- **public synchronized void addMouseListener(MouseListener l)**
  From Component. It tells the component which class should be notified when one of the following happens to the component: The mouse is clicked (pressed and released) in its area, the mouse is pressed in its area, the mouse is released in its area, the mouse enters its area, or the mouse exits its area. More than one class can be registered in this way, and all registered classes are notified when any of these events takes place.

- **public synchronized void addMouseMotionListener (MouseMotionListener l)** From Component. It tells the component which class should be notified when one of the following happens to the component: The mouse moves within its area, or the mouse is dragged within its area. More than one class can be registered in this way, and all registered classes are notified when either of these events takes place.

- **public synchronized void addPropertyChangeListener (PropertyChangeListener l)** From JComponent; it tells the component which class should be notified when a bound property is set. More than one class can be registered in this way, and all registered classes are notified when either of these events takes place.

- **public synchronized void addVetoableChangeListener (VetoableChangeListener l)** From JComponent; it tells the component which class should be notified when a vetoable change happens. More than one class can be registered in this way, and all registered classes are notified when either of these events takes place.

- **protected final void disableEvents(long eventsMask)** From Component; it's set by a component to specify what types of events it shouldn't receive. The valid flags that can be part of this mask are defined in AWTEvent.

■ **public final void dispatchEvent(AWTEvent event)** From Component; it sends an event to the component.

■ **protected final void enableEvents(long eventsMask)** From Component; it's set by a component to specify what types of events it should receive. The valid flags that can be part of this mask are defined in AWTEvent.

■ **protected void processComponentEvent(ComponentEvent e)** From Component. This method is usually called by the processEvent() method that has recognized the event as a component event and passed it to this method for proper processing. This method figures out what type of component event it is (hidden, moved, resized, shown). Then it sends the event to the appropriate ComponentListener method of each registered ComponentListener.

■ **protected void processContainerEvent(ContainerEvent e)** From Container. This method is usually called by the processEvent() method that has recognized the event as a container event and passed it to this method for proper processing. This method figures out what type of container event it is (added or removed). Then it sends the event to the appropriate ContainerListener method of each registered ContainerListener.

■ **protected void processEvent(AWTEvent event)** From Component. This is where an event enters a component. For example, if the mouse is clicked on the component, a MouseEvent is generated and sent to the component's processEvent() method. The event is sent to the component only if the component either has listeners registered for that type of event or has used the enableEvents() method to enable that type of event. The processEvent() method typically checks the type of the event and sends it off to the processMouseEvent() method, the processKeyEvent() method, and so forth.

■ **protected void processFocusEvent(FocusEvent e)** From Component. This method is usually called by the processEvent() method that has recognized the event as a focus event and passed it to this method for proper processing. This method figures out what type of focus event it is (got focus or lost focus). Then it sends the event to the appropriate FocusListener method of each registered FocusListener.

■ **protected void processKeyEvent(KeyEvent e)** From JComponent. This method is usually called by the processEvent() method that has recognized the event as a key event and passed it to this method for proper processing. This method figures out what type of key event it is (pressed, released, typed). Then it sends the event to the appropriate KeyListener method of each registered KeyListener.

■ **protected void processMouseEvent(MouseEvent e)** From Component. This method is usually called by the processEvent() method that has recognized the event as a mouse event and passed it to this method for proper processing. This method figures out what type of mouse event it is (pressed, released, clicked, entered, exited). Then it sends the event to the appropriate MouseListener method of each registered MouseListener.

- **protected void processMouseMotionEvent(MouseEvent e)**
From JComponent. This method is usually called by the processEvent() method that has recognized the event as a mouse motion event and passed it to this method for proper processing. This method figures out what type of mouse motion event it is (moved or dragged). Then it sends the event to the appropriate MouseMotionListener method of each registered MouseMotionListener.

- **public synchronized void removeAncestorListener (AncestorListener l)**   From JComponent; it tells the component to stop notifying the specified class when ancestor events occur on it. The AncestorListener should have first been added by using the addAncestorListener() method.

- **public synchronized void removeComponentListener (ComponentListener l)**   From Component; it tells the component to stop notifying the specified class when component events occur on it. The ComponentListener should have first been added by using the addComponentListener() method.

- **public void removeContainerListener(ContainerListener l)**
From Container; it tells the component to stop notifying the specified class when container events happen. The ContainerListener should have first been added by using the addContainerListener() method.

- **public synchronized void removeFocusListener (FocusListener l)**
From Component; it tells the component to stop notifying the specified class when focus events occur on it. The FocusListener should have first been added by using the addFocusListener() method.

- **public synchronized void removeKeyListener(KeyListener l)**
From Component; it tells the component to stop notifying the specified class when key events occur on it. The KeyListener should have first been added by using the addKeyListener() method.

- **public synchronized void removeMouseListener (MouseListener l)**   From Component; it tells the component to stop notifying the specified class when mouse events occur on it. The MouseListener should have first been added by using the addMouseListener() method.

- **public synchronized void removeMouseMotionListener (MouseMotionListener l)**   From Component; it tells the component to stop notifying the specified class when mouse motion events occur on it. The MouseMotionListener should have first been added by using the addMouseMotionListener() method.

■ **public synchronized void removePropertyChangeListener (PropertyChangeListener l)**   From JComponent; it tells the component to stop notifying the specified class when bound properties change. The PropertyChangeListener should have first been added by using the addPropertyChangeListener() method.

■ **public synchronized void removeVetoableChangeListener (VetoableChangeListener l)**   From JComponent; it tells the component to stop notifying the specified class when vetoable changes happen. The VetoableChangeListener should have first been added by using the addVetoableChangeListener() method.

LOOK-AND-FEEL   JComponent defines the basic methods that allow a component to have a different look-and-feel:

■ **public String getUIClassID()**   From JComponent; returns the component's look-up name for looking up its user interface (UI) component in the active look-and-feel. It's overridden when you create your own JComponent subclass that has pluggable look-and-feel.

■ **protected void setUI(ComponentUI uicomp)**   From JComponent; assigns a UI class to the component.

■ **public void updateUI()**   From JComponent; it's called to tell the component that its look-and-feel has changed. The component then usually asks the UIManager for the new UI class.

GETTING AND SETTING COMPONENT STATE   There are basic states every component recognizes that can be toggled on and off. Here are some methods that handle these states:

■ **public boolean isEnabled()**   From Component; says whether the component can accept input at this time.

■ **public boolean isShowing()**   From Component; says if the component is visible and is in a container that's visible and showing.

■ **public boolean isValid()**   From Component; says whether the component is valid or if it needs to be laid out again.

■ **public boolean isVisible()**   From Component; says whether the component is visible.

■ **public void setEnabled(boolean newState)**   From Component; tells the component whether it can receive input.

■ **public void setVisible(boolean newState)**   From JComponent; tells the component whether it's visible.

GRAPHICS   Painting, printing, and graphical properties are crucial to components. Here are the related Component, Container, and JComponent methods:

■ **public Color getBackground()**   From Component; returns the color the component is using for its background.

■ **public Cursor getCursor()**   From Component; returns the component's current cursor. It's useful for getting its normal cursor so it can be saved while a temporary cursor is being used.

■ **public Font getFont()**   From Component; returns the font the component is using. It can be null.

■ **public FontMetrics getFontMetrics(Font font)**   From Component; returns the font description of the specified font. The specified font isn't necessarily the component's current font. You can also get the component's current font metrics in the paint() method by using the Graphics class's getFontMetrics() method.

■ **public Color getForeground()**   From Component; gets the color the component is using for its foreground operations.

■ **public Graphics getGraphics()**   From JComponent; it returns a graphics context for the component. You can draw into this Graphics object just as you can within the paint() method. You should use this only in unusual circumstances, such as when you need to draw on a component that you can't override. Normally, you should do your drawing in one of the paint methods or in a look-and-feel UI class.

■ **public Toolkit getToolkit()**   From Component; it returns the component's toolkit, which can be used to get all kinds of interesting information.

■ **public boolean isOpaque()**   From JComponent; it returns false by default but should be overridden to return true if the component is guaranteed to draw its entire area.

■ **public void paint(Graphics g)**   From JComponent. For JComponent subclasses, this method calls the paintComponent(), paintBorder(), and paintChildren() methods in that order. Those methods are responsible for calling the UI methods to paint these component parts. The paint() method should not be called directly. Instead, you should call one of the repaint() methods or paintImmediately(). As with earlier JDK releases, you can override the paint() method if you want to completely control the component's appearance, but then the component won't take advantage of the JFC's pluggable look-and-feel capabilities.

■ **public void paintAll(Graphics g)**   From Component; it calls the paint() method for the component if it's lightweight (which subclasses of JComponent are) or the peer.paint() method for peered components (old AWT components).

- **protected void paintBorder(Graphics g)**   From JComponent. This method, called by the paint() method, is used to control the painting of the component's border. If you don't override it, this method calls the component's UI class to do the actual painting. If you just want to change the way a component's border looks without changing the rest of the component's appearance, you can override this. You might be better off in that case if you just use the component's setBorder() method.

- **protected void paintChildren(Graphics g)**   From JComponent. This method, called by the paint() method, is used to control the painting of the component's child components, if any.

- **protected void paintComponent(Graphics g)**   From JComponent. This method, called by the paint() method, is used to control the painting of the component's main area (everything except the border and the children). For JComponent subclasses, this method calls the component's UI class to do the actual painting. If you want to let the UI class handle painting the border and the children, you can override this method to do your own drawing. This is useful for components like buttons that rely on the UI class's treatment of the border for proper display of whether the button is pressed.

- **public void paintComponents(Graphics g)**   From Container; it causes all of a component's child components to be painted without repainting the component itself. Ultimately, it calls each of the component's paint methods. Notice that this method is public, but paintChildren() is protected.

- **public void paintImmediately(int x, int y, int width, int height)**   From JComponent; it causes the paint() method to be called to paint the specified rectangle. Calling this method could actually slow down drawing compared to calling the repaint() method if calls are frequent. That's because the repaint() method can combine duplicate paint calls into a single one.

- **public void paintImmediately(Rectangle rect)**   From JComponent; it's the same as the previous method, except the region to be painted is passed in as a Rectangle.

- **public void print(Graphics g)**   From Container; causes the component and its children to be printed. See the PrintJob class (in the JDK documentation) for information on getting the Graphics instance this call needs.

- **public void printAll(Graphics g)**   From Component; it causes the component to be printed. See the PrintJob class (in the JDK documentation) for information on getting the Graphics instance this call needs.

...mponents(**Graphics g**) From Container; ...child components (if any) to be printed. See ... JDK documentation) for information on ...nce this call needs.

...om Component; it tells the component to ...ing might have changed. It ultimately ...ich in turn calls the paint() method.

...**y, int width, int height**) From ... to redraw the specified area. This ...g part of a component is likely to be ...ole thing.

...(**Rectangle r**) From JComponent; this is the ...ious method except that the redraw area is given as

...c void repaint(long time) From Component; it tells the ...component to redraw itself within the specified time in milliseconds. The repaint() calls that don't specify a time will redraw as soon as possible, so this method isn't faster than the other repaint() calls; it could be slower.

- **public void repaint(long time, int x, int y, int width, int height)** From JComponent; it's just like the previous method, except it specifies a particular area that needs redrawing.

- **public void setBackground(Color color)** From Component; it specifies the color the component uses for its background, typically the color that fills the component's rectangle wherever other drawing hasn't been done. However, its use depends on the component type as well as on the current look-and-feel. For example, the JFC JButton class, using the "windows" look-and-feel, applies the background color not only to its main area, but also uses variations on the color in its border.

- **public synchronized void setCursor(Cursor newCursor)** From Component; it changes the component's cursor. It can be set to a predefined cursor or to a custom cursor (new with the JFC). If the new cursor is just for temporary use, you might want to save the existing cursor before calling this method.

- **public void setFont(Font font)** From Component; it specifies the font the component should use for its text (if any). The component isn't guaranteed to use the font—it depends on the type of component and its current look-and-feel.

- **public void setForeground(Color color)** From Component; specifies the color the component uses for its foreground operations. What this means varies from component to component, as well as between a component's different look-and-feels. It often affects items like text color, checkmarks, and so forth.

Chapter Three

From JComponent; ...aint its background ...ponent; just calls ...thod which ...esn't handle ...ontend with

- **public void setOpaque(boolean opaq)** tells the component whether or not it should ~~p~~ rectangle.
- **public void update(Graphics g)** From JCom~~p~~ paint(g). This overrides Component's update(g) m~~e~~ painted the background rectangle.

SCROLLING-RELATED METHODS JComponent d~~~~ scrolling, but has several methods that help your component~~~~ scrolling-related difficulties:

- **public void computeVisibleRect(Rectangle rect)** From~~~~ JComponent; calculates the area of the component that's visible~~~~ taking the intersection of its area with its ancestors'. The solution~~~~ placed in the passed-in rectangle.
- **public boolean getAutoscrolls()** From JComponent; returns true~~~~ the component supports automatically scrolling its contents when drags occur.
- **public Rectangle getVisibleRect()** From JComponent; it's the same as computeVisibleRect(Rectangle), except you get the solution as a return value.
- **public void scrollRectToVisible(Rectangle rect)** From JComponent. The component can call this method with its bounding rectangle and, if one of its ancestors is a JViewport, the component becomes visible. This is useful in tables when you're moving around using tabs or arrows.
- **public void setAutoscrolls(boolean autoscrolls)** From JComponent; set to true if the component should support automatic scrolling when drags occur.

KEYBOARD FOCUS JComponent includes a set of methods that help make keyboard focus control more flexible:

- **public Component getNextFocusableComponent()** From JComponent; it returns the component that should get the keyboard focus after the component if the component knows. Usually it returns null, which means the focus manager will decide.
- **public boolean hasFocus()** From JComponent; it returns true if the component currently has the keyboard focus or false, otherwise.
- **public boolean isFocusTraversable()** From JComponent; it tells whether the component can have the keyboard focus. There's no setFocusTraversable() method—you have to override this method to change the behavior.

- **public boolean isManagingFocus()**   From JComponent; it returns true if the component is managing the focus. This is useful if you want to use tabs as tabs instead of as triggers for focus changes.

- **public boolean isRequestFocusEnabled()**   From JComponent; it returns true if the component can request focus by using the requestFocus() method.

- **public boolean requestDefaultFocus()**   From JComponent; attempts to give the focus to the component that gets the focus by default. This is usually the first focus-traversable component.

- **public void requestFocus()**   From JComponent. This method is how the component asks to be given the keyboard focus. If the isRequestFocusEnabled() method returns false, this method can be called, but doesn't do anything.

- **public void setNextFocusableComponent(Component comp)** From JComponent. If you set this method, it's returned when the getNextFocusableComponent() method is called and overrides the default focus order.

- **public void setRequestFocusEnabled(boolean enabled)** From JComponent; it tells the component whether it can request the keyboard focus by using the requestFocus() method.

KEYSTROKES AND ACTIONS   These methods address managing Key-Stroke/Action pairs registered with the component:

- **public Action getActionForKeyStroke(KeyStroke aKeyStroke)**   From JComponent; returns the Action that's triggered when the given KeyStroke happens.

- **public int getConditionForKeyStroke(KeyStroke aKeyStroke)**   From JComponent; returns the condition (see the registerKeyboardAction() method) under which the given KeyStroke triggers its Action.

- **public KeyStroke[] getRegisteredKeyStrokes()**   From JComponent; returns an array of the KeyStrokes registered with the component.

- **public void registerKeyboardAction(Action anAction, KeyStroke keystroke, int condition)**   From JComponent. Registers an Action/KeyStroke pair with the component so that when the KeyStroke occurs, the Action is triggered. The "condition" argument specifies under what condition the KeyStroke should trigger the Action and is one of the following: WHEN_FOCUSED, WHEN_IN_FOCUSED_WINDOW, or WHEN_ANCESTOR_OF_FOCUSED_COMPONENT.

■ **public void registerKeyboardAction(ActionListener anAction,String aCommand,KeyStroke aKeyStroke,int aCondition)** From Jcomponent. This is just like the previous method except that the "aCommand" argument is set as the action command in generated ActionEvents.

■ **public void resetKeyboardActions()** From JComponent; unregisters all KeyStrokes registered with the component.

■ **public void unregisterKeyboardAction(KeyStroke keystroke)** From JComponent; unregisters the Action associated with the given KeyStroke, so that when the KeyStroke happens, the Action is no longer triggered.

DISPLAY HIERARCHY These methods deal with the component's display hierarchy, including changes to it:

■ **public void addNotify()** From JComponent; it's called as soon as the component is added to a Container.

■ **public Container getTopLevelAncestor()** From JComponent; returns the top-level ancestor of the component. It can be an application's main window or an applet's applet window.

■ **public void removeNotify()** From JComponent; it's called when the component is removed from its Container.

ACCESSIBILITY

■ **public AccessibleContext getAccessibleContext()** From JComponent; it's a component's entry point to its accessibility information. An AccessibleContext has a set of methods you can call to get different kinds of information, depending on the type of component.

SUMMARY

The JComponent class is an ancestor of most of the classes described in this book, so it contains much of the functionality of those classes. You can't completely understand what a class can do until you understand its ancestors. This chapter has accumulated the methods in JComponent and its ancestors Container and Component to help give you that understanding.

CHAPTER 4

Pluggable Look
and Feel

The term *look-and-feel* describes what the standard graphical parts of an application or operating system look like and how they work. Look-and-feel consists mainly of what basic components like buttons and text fields look like and how they behave during user interaction on different operating systems. If you use Windows, a button is essentially the same, no matter what application you're running. The text color is the same; the background color is the same; and when you click it, it looks the same whether you're configuring your display or working in your favorite word processor. If you use a Macintosh, a button looks different from a Windows button but looks basically the same for all applications you run on the Macintosh. You can say that a button maintains a consistent "Windows look-and-feel" on one machine and a consistent "Macintosh look-and-feel" on the other.

Look-and-feel doesn't just have to do with appearance—that's only the "look" part. The "feel" part comes from how components interact with the user—how they respond to events. If you have a list box onscreen and you want to select more than one item from the list, how you do that varies from operating system to operating system. It might require a Ctrl+click on one computer but a Shift+click on another.

The Advantages of Being Consistent on a Single Computer

It's very important that all applications on a particular computer maintain a consistent look-and-feel. If your applications had different ways of accessing menu items (or even differently placed menus), you would have to figure it out over and over for each application. If each application's help system was accessed differently, the same would be true, and on and on for every conceivable aspect of your applications. Operating system vendors publish style guides that describe how to design interfaces that correspond with their specific look-and-feel, and application developers are happy to comply because being consistent with the operating system is a good way to make products easier to learn and use.

The Advantages of Being Consistent on Multiple Computers

Just as it's important for a user to have a familiar user interface between applications on a single computer, it's important for a user who uses more than one type of computer to be able to have a familiar interface, no matter which type he or she is working on. This is becoming more important as network computers are released from a variety of vendors. Imagine that you use a PC when you're in the office but use a special purpose network computer when you're on the road. If you use the same mail application on both, and each has its own look-and-feel, it will be more difficult to initially learn the application and more awkward when you have to switch between the two computers. If both computers have the same look-and-feel, you learn the application on one and are instantly comfortable on the other.

Java and Look-and-Feel

The AWT

The AWT attempted to make it possible for Java applications to maintain the native look-and-feel of the operating system they were running on. It did this by having Java component classes that acted as wrappers around actual native components called "peers;" the components acted just like native components because they *were* native components. Unfortunately, there were some drawbacks. First, the AWT wrapper class for a component could only implement functionality that was natively supported for the component on *all* potential platforms. That meant the amount you could customize the component was a kind of least common denominator, giving only limited control over the component's appearance and size. Second, because native components were used, the ability you had to change the behavior of components was very limited. Third, each Java Virtual Machine had to implement the component wrapper classes, which required extra native code and prompted delays and inconsistencies across platforms.

Throughout Java's brief history, the AWT has been a serious problem, mainly because of its reliance on these native controls. Making complex user interfaces that were attractive across platforms was painfully difficult, and a lot of time was spent working around AWT bugs and inconsistencies.

The IFC

Netscape's Internet Foundation Classes (IFC) were the first good replacement for AWT's components. IFC components didn't use native components, but drew themselves by using the AWT line, fill, and image capabilities. IFC allowed developers to write truly professional-quality user interfaces that were totally cross-platform. For the IFC, Netscape created a brand-new look-and-feel, so an IFC application looked the same whether it ran under Windows, on a Macintosh, or in a Web browser. This was a case of keeping a consistent look-and-feel across computers at the cost of having a look-and-feel different from all other applications.

For this and other reasons, Netscape has said that the JFC will be replacing the IFC and will ship with future versions of its Navigator Web browser.

The JFC

The JFC has abandoned using native components, except when it was necessary to use native components because the operating system would be handling them directly (as in frames, windows, dialogs). Like the IFC, JFC components are drawn by using the AWT's line, fill, and image methods. For this reason, you can have a consistent look-and-feel across different computers, as with the IFC. However, unlike the IFC, you can also switch look-and-feel at will, so you can use either a look-and-feel that's on other computers or the look-and-feel of the computer you're using. This ability is what pluggable look-and-feel is all about.

How Pluggable Look-and-Feel Works

The general idea behind *pluggable look-and-feel* is that can you have multiple appearances and behaviors for a single component class without having to subclass the component for every look-and-feel. This is done by separating the part of the component that has to do with appearance and behavior from the part that has to do with storing internal states and interfacing with other Java classes. The part that controls appearance and behavior is called the "UI" (for "user interface"). Each JFC component has multiple UIs—one for each different look-and-feel. These UIs take care of drawing the component and responding to events. Each JFC component also has a main component class that keeps track of general attributes, such as text alignment, icon, and border style. This main component class represents the component to the rest of the Java world. In addition, each component has what's called a "model" that stores the component's current internal state, which includes information such as whether the component is enabled or has the focus. When you want to create a JFC component, you don't have to create its UI and model. You just create an instance of its main component (JButton, JTextField, and so forth), and it takes care of creating the correct UI and model.

As an example, we'll look at the JFC button component JButton. JButton is a subclass of AbstractButton, which contains most of the interesting stuff, so most of what we associate with the JButton class actually comes from its parent class.

The Main Component Class JButton/ AbstractButton

If you look at JButton's variables, you can see that, with the exception of "model," all the variables have to do with the component's external state:

```
protected ButtonModel  model                  = null;
private String         text                   = null;
private Insets         pad                    = null;
private Icon           defaultIcon            = null;
private Icon           pressedIcon            = null;
private Icon           selectedIcon           = null;
private Icon           rollOverIcon           = null;
private Icon           disabledIcon           = null;
private boolean        paintBorder            = true;
private boolean        paintFocus             = true;
private int            verticalAlignment      = CENTER;
private int            horizontalAlignment    = CENTER;
private int            verticalTextPosition   = CENTER;
private int            horizontalTextPosition = RIGHT;
protected Border       border                 = null;
```

The graphical parts are stored in these variables, as well as positional information like text alignment, but notice that information about whether the button is enabled or pressed is not stored here.

The Model Class DefaultButtonModel

DefaultButtonModel class implements the ButtonModel interface. You can replace the model by creating your own class that implements ButtonModel, and then pass it to the main component's setModel() method. It's not likely you will ever have reason to do so. This class keeps track of whether the button is pressed, whether the mouse is over the button (triggering the use of the rollover icon, if any), whether the button is enabled, and so on. For JButton, you don't generally have to access the model directly.

Some JFC components require you to work directly with the model. When you deal with a JTree, you're actually adding items to and removing items from a class that implements the TreeModel interface (usually Default-TreeModel). This is typical of components that store complex data.

The UI Class

The class used for the UI implements the ButtonUI interface and depends on which look-and-feel is currently being used. The default look-and-feel is a new one called "Metal." The JFC also includes a look-and-feel for Windows and one for Motif. Future releases are expected to include a Macintosh look-and-feel, too. Each look-and-feel shipped with the JFC is in its own subdirectory under com.sun.java.swing.plaf.

Essentially, the UI class contains no data. It accesses the main component and the model to get what it needs. It asks the main component for the text string, icon, and alignment information, and asks the model whether the component is enabled or disabled, pressed or not, and so on. Then it uses that information to paint the component so it reflects its state.

Using Pluggable Look-and-Feel

You can use pluggable look-and-feel in several different ways. First, you can make it possible for your JFC application to support more than one look-and-feel. Second, you can create your own component, specifying that it change its look-and-feel as the JFC components' look-and-feel changes. Third, you can create a different look-and-feel by replacing one or more component UIs in an existing look-and-feel. Or fourth, you can create a completely new look-and-feel.

Supporting Existing Look-and-Feels

If you want your Java application to support more than just the default look-and-feel, you need to give the user some way to switch to a new one. You can only switch between look-and-feels whose JAR files are available in your application's CLASSPATH. The JAR files for the look-and-feels shipped with the JFC are in the directory where the JFC is installed and are called windows.jar, and motif.jar. The "Metal" look-and-feel is included in the swing.jar file.

Changing look-and-feel is easy. All you have to do is call UIManager's set-LookAndFeel() method with the name of the new look-and-feel's subclass of the LookAndFeel class. That procedure might not *sound* simple, but it actually is. Here's the code needed to change to the Motif look-and-feel:

```
try
{
    UIManager.setLookAndFeel(
        "com.sun.java.swing.plaf.motif.MotifLookAndFeel" );
}
catch ( ClassNotFoundException ex )
{
    System.err.println(
        "Motif:  Could not find the look-and-feel" );
}
catch ( InstantiationException ex )
{
    System.err.println(
        "Motif:  Could not create the look-and-feel" );
}
catch ( IllegalAccessException ex )
{
    System.err.println(
        "Motif:  Could not access the look-and-feel" );
}
catch ( UnsupportedLookAndFeelException ex )
{
    System.err.println(
        "Motif:  Motif look-and-feel not supported" );
}
```

Notice that the work is done in a single line:

```
UIManager.setLookAndFeel( "com.sun.java.swing.motif.
                          MotifLookAndFeel" );
```

The rest of the code is for handling exceptions that are thrown when the JAR file for the look-and-feel is not in the CLASSPATH, or the supplied look-and-feel class name is incorrect, and so forth.

When a component is created, it takes the current look-and-feel. If you change the look-and-feel, components that were created with a previous look-and-feel don't automatically change to the new one. They keep their original look-and-feel until their updateUI() method is called. You can change the look-and-feel for a container *and* its child components by calling the SwingUtilities updateComponentTreeUI() method.

EXAMPLE 4-1   Combining Look-and-Feels

This example contains a frame that has three panels, each with a different look-and-feel. The first has the "Windows" look-and-feel, the second has the "Motif" look-and-feel, and the third has the "Metal" look-and-feel. The first two panels get their look-and-feels from the ones installed when they were created. The third gets its look-and-feel by first creating the panel and its components and then calling the SwingUtilities updateComponentTreeUI() method. Figure 4-1 shows the example as it first comes up.

Important points to notice:

- Each panel contains a single checked JCheckBox so you can see the differences between each look-and-feel.
- Each JFC look-and-feel has its own package under com.sun.java.swing.

Here is the source code:

```
import com.sun.java.swing.*;
import com.sun.java.swing.border.*;
import java.awt.*;
import java.util.*;

public class MyFrame extends JFrame
{
    public MyFrame()
    {
        setTitle( "Plaf1" );

        // Store the content pane in a variable for easier
        // access.

        JPanel contentPane = (JPanel)getContentPane();

        // Set up the content pane to hold three sub-panes.

        contentPane.setLayout( new GridLayout( 3, 1 ) );
```

Figure 4-1
Combining look-and-feels.

```
// Try to make "windows" the current look-and-feel.

try
{
   UIManager.setLookAndFeel( "com.sun.java.swing." +
                  "plaf.windows.WindowsLookAndFeel" );
}
catch ( ClassNotFoundException ex )
{
   System.err.println(
   "Windows:  Could not find the look-and-feel" );
}
catch ( InstantiationException ex )
{
   System.err.println(
   "Windows:  Could not create the look-and-feel" );
}
catch ( IllegalAccessException ex )
{
   System.err.println(
   "Windows:  Could not access the look-and-feel" );
}
catch ( UnsupportedLookAndFeelException ex )
{
   System.err.println(
   "Windows:  Could not access the look-and-feel" );
}

// Create a pane for the "windows" look-and-feel.

JPanel pane1 = new JPanel();
pane1.setBorder( new TitledBorder(
                  "Windows look-and-feel" ) );
pane1.setLayout( new FlowLayout() );

// Add a component.

JCheckBox windowsBtn = new JCheckBox( "Windows" );
windowsBtn.setSelected( true );
pane1.add( windowsBtn );

// Add the "windows" pane to the content pane.

contentPane.add( pane1 );

// Try to make "motif" the current look-and-feel.

try
{
   UIManager.setLookAndFeel( "com.sun.java.swing." +
                  "plaf.motif.MotifLookAndFeel" );
}
catch ( ClassNotFoundException ex )
{
   System.err.println(
```

```
            "Motif:  Could not find the look-and-feel" );
}
catch ( InstantiationException ex )
{
   System.err.println(
   "Motif:  Could not create the look-and-feel" );
}
catch ( IllegalAccessException ex )
{
   System.err.println(
   "Motif:  Could not access the look-and-feel" );
}
catch ( UnsupportedLookAndFeelException ex )
{
   System.err.println(
   "Motif:  Could not access the look-and-feel" );
}

// Create a pane for the "motif" look-and-feel.

JPanel pane2 = new JPanel();
pane2.setBorder(
      new TitledBorder( "Motif look-and-feel" ) );
pane2.setLayout( new FlowLayout() );

// Create a component and add it to the "motif" pane.

JCheckBox motifBtn = new JCheckBox( "Motif" );
motifBtn.setSelected( true );
pane2.add( motifBtn );

// Add the "motif" pane to the content pane.

contentPane.add( pane2 );

// For the "metal" pane, we will create the pane
// first, then tell it to change its (and its
// contents) look-and-feel by calling the
// SwingUtilities.updateComponentTreeUI() method.

// Create a "metal" pane.  It and its contents will
// initially be created with the "motif" look-and-feel
// since that is the current one.

JPanel pane3 = new JPanel();
pane3.setBorder( new TitledBorder(
                  "Java look-and-feel" ) );
pane3.setLayout( new FlowLayout() );

// Add a component to the "metal" pane.

JCheckBox metalBtn = new JCheckBox( "Metal" );
metalBtn.setSelected( true );
pane3.add( metalBtn );
```

```
// try to make "metal" the current look-and-feel.

try
{
   UIManager.setLookAndFeel( "com.sun.java.swing." +
                         "plaf.metal.MetalLookAndFeel" );
}
catch ( ClassNotFoundException ex )
{
   System.err.println(
        "metal:  Could not find the look-and-feel" );
}
catch ( InstantiationException ex )
{
   System.err.println(
      "metal:  Could not create the look-and-feel" );
}
catch ( IllegalAccessException ex )
{
   System.err.println(
      "metal:  Could not access the look-and-feel" );
}
catch ( UnsupportedLookAndFeelException ex )
{
   System.err.println(
      "metal:  Could not access the look-and-feel" );
}

// Add the "metal" pane to the content pane.

contentPane.add( pane3 );

// Tell 'pane3' to change over to the new
// look-and-feel, and to tell all of the components
// under it to do the same.

SwingUtilities.updateComponentTreeUI( pane3 );
   }
}
```

Normally, you want to change the look-and-feel all the way across your application instead of just in certain containers.

Creating and Using Custom Look-and-Feel Classes

At times, you might not like the way a particular component looks or behaves when a specific look-and-feel is installed. With pluggable look-and-feel, you can subclass an existing look-and-feel and modify how a single component looks and behaves without affecting other components. You probably won't do this often, but it's a useful example of how to create a custom look-and-feel. Here are the steps you should follow:

1. Subclass an existing LookAndFeel subclass. BasicLookAndFeel is a good place to start. In fact, WindowsLookAndFeel, MotifLookAndFeel, and MetalLookAndFeel are all subclasses of BasicLookAndFeel. You need to override the LookAndFeel class's getDefaults() method to replace the look-and-feel normally associated with the component. The getDefaults() method is used to return a hashtable associating the ID strings that components' getUIClassID() methods return with the actual UI classes that draw the components. So, by overriding the getDefaults() method, we can replace the UI class used for check boxes with one of our own. You need to make sure the isNativeLookAndFeel() and isSupportedLookAndFeel() methods are implemented. It's also a good idea to override the getName() and getDescription() methods, or they will return misleading information from your superclass. The getName() method returns a string that identifies your look-and-feel, and getDescription() returns a brief description of it.

2. Subclass the class that the component uses for its appearance and behavior in the look-and-feel we're subclassing. This allows us to make the changes we want to make so the component is drawn as we would like it to be drawn. If we subclassed WindowsLookAndFeel in step 1, and the component whose look-and-feel we're changing is JCheckBox, we would subclass WindowsCheckBoxUI. You need to override at least the createUI() method so it creates and returns a copy of our UI class, and the paint() method so we can draw the component differently.

3. Use your new look-and-feel where you would normally have used the one you subclassed.

NOTE: *See the "LookAndFeel," "UIDefaults," and "UIManager" sections in Chapter 8, "JFC by Class," for more information about look-and-feel classes.*

EXAMPLE 4-2 Subclassing MotifLookAndFeel to Replace the CheckBoxUI Class

This example implements the preceding steps. It has four radio buttons so the user can switch between look-and-feels. One of the radio buttons represents a custom look-and-feel that's the same as the Motif look-and-feel, except the UI class used by check boxes has been replaced. It also has a single check box at the bottom so you can see it change. Figure 4-2 shows the example as it initially comes up.

Important points to notice:

Figure 4-2
Subclassing
MotifLookAndFeel
to replace the
CheckBoxUI class.

■ This example includes three important classes: MyFrame.java, MyLookAndFeel.java, and MyCheckBoxUI.java. MyFrame is the application's main frame class that contains all of the components and changes the look-and-feel when a radio button is selected. MyLookAndFeel is a subclass of MotifLookAndFeel, and MyCheckBoxUI is a subclass of MotifCheckBoxUI.

■ MyLookAndFeel.java and MyCheckBoxUI.java are in a separate package called "MyLookAndFeel."

■ Because the size a component is displayed at is determined by its look-and-feel class, you might want to lay out the container again after changing look-and-feel.

■ When the look-and-feel changes, we call SwingUtilities.updateComponentTreeUI() to propagate the look-and-feel change throughout the frame's component hiearchy.

■ In MyLookAndFeel.java, notice the use of the put() method to associate a UI class with a UI class ID. That UI class ID is the same string returned by JCheckBox's getUIClassID() method.

■ Notice that the JComponent passed to MyCheckBoxUI's paint() method is cast to an AbstractButton so we can access the check box's text string and button model.

Here's the source code to MyFrame.java (the source to the look-and-feel classes follows it):

```
import com.sun.java.swing.*;
import com.sun.java.swing.border.*;
import java.awt.*;
import java.awt.event.*;
import com.sun.java.swing.plaf.metal.*;

public class MyFrame extends JFrame implements ItemListener
{
    // The four look-and-feel radio buttons.

    private JRadioButton mMotif;
    private JRadioButton mWindows;
    private JRadioButton mMetal;
    private JRadioButton mCustom;
```

```java
public MyFrame()
{
    setTitle( "Plaf2" );

    // Store the content pane in a variable for easier
    // access.

    JPanel contentPane = (JPanel)getContentPane();

    // Components will all be added to this panel.

    contentPane.setLayout( new BorderLayout() );

    // Create the four look-and-feel radio buttons and
    // make it so this class is notified when they are
    // selected.

    mMotif = new JRadioButton( "Motif" );
    mMotif.addItemListener( this );
    mWindows = new JRadioButton( "Windows" );
    mWindows.addItemListener( this );
    mMetal = new JRadioButton( "Metal" );
    mMetal.addItemListener( this );
    mCustom = new JRadioButton( "Motif-modified" );
    mCustom.addItemListener( this );

    // Create a button group for the radio buttons and
    // add them to it.

    ButtonGroup group = new ButtonGroup();
    group.add( mMotif );
    group.add( mWindows );
    group.add( mMetal );
    group.add( mCustom );

    // Create a panel to hold the radio buttons, and add
    // them to it.

    JPanel l_f_pane = new JPanel();
    l_f_pane.setBorder( new TitledBorder(
                        "Which look-and-feel?" ) );
    l_f_pane.setLayout( new BoxLayout( l_f_pane,
                        BoxLayout.Y_AXIS ) );
    l_f_pane.add( mMotif );
    l_f_pane.add( mWindows );
    l_f_pane.add( mMetal );
    l_f_pane.add( mCustom );

    // Add the radio button panel to the content pane.

    contentPane.add( "Center", l_f_pane );

    // Select the custom look-and-feel initially.
    // Selecting it here causes an item event to be
    // generated so the look-and-feel is
```

```
    // automatically set.

    mCustom.setSelected( true );

    // Create a regular JCheckBox and place it at the
    // bottom of the content pane.

    JCheckBox jcb = new JCheckBox( "Normal Check Box" );
    jcb.setSelected( true );
    contentPane.add( "South", jcb );
}

// This is called when one of the radio buttons changes
// state.

public void itemStateChanged( ItemEvent e )
{
    String l_f_name;

    // We ignore de-select events.

    if ( e.getStateChange() == ItemEvent.SELECTED )
    {
        // Based on the radio button that generated the
        // event, set the look-and-feel class' name.

        if ( e.getSource() == mMotif )
        {
            l_f_name = "com.sun.java.swing." +
                       "plaf.motif.MotifLookAndFeel";
        }
        else if ( e.getSource() == mWindows )
        {
            l_f_name = "com.sun.java.swing." +
                       "plaf.windows.WindowsLookAndFeel";
        }
        else if ( e.getSource() == mMetal )
        {
            l_f_name = "com.sun.java.swing." +
                       "plaf.metal.MetalLookAndFeel";
        }
        else
        {
            l_f_name = "MyLookAndFeel.MyLookAndFeel";
        }

        try
        {
            // Try to set the look-and-feel.

            UIManager.setLookAndFeel( l_f_name );

            // Propagate the new look-and-feel to all
            // components in the frame.
```

```
                    SwingUtilities.updateComponentTreeUI( this );

                    // Make the display reflect the change.

                    repaint();
                }
                catch ( Exception ex )
                {
                    System.out.println( ex );
                }
            }
        }
    }
```

Here is the source code for MyLookAndFeel.java:

```
package MyLookAndFeel;

import com.sun.java.swing.plaf.motif.*;
import com.sun.java.swing.*;
import java.util.*;
import com.sun.java.swing.plaf.*;
import java.awt.*;

public class MyLookAndFeel extends MotifLookAndFeel
{
    // Overridden so we can replace the check box UI class.

    public UIDefaults getDefaults()
    {
        // Get MotifLookAndFeel's list of UI classes.

        UIDefaults defs = super.getDefaults();

        try
        {
            // Replace the UI class associated with
            // "CheckBoxUI".

            defs.put( "CheckBoxUI",
                        "MyLookAndFeel.MyCheckBoxUI" );
        }
        catch ( Exception e )
        {
            System.out.println( e );
        }

        // Return the modified UIDefaults.

        return defs;
    }

    // Return a string name for the look-and-feel.

    public String getName()
```

```
{
    return "MyLookAndFeel";
}

// Return a one-line description of the look-and-feel.

public String getDescription()
{
    String retval = "A subclass of MotifLookAndFeel "+
                    "which replaces the CheckBoxUI";
    return retval;
}

public boolean isNativeLookAndFeel()
{
    return false;
}

public boolean isSupportedLookAndFeel()
{
    return true;
}

}
```

Here is the source code for MyCheckBoxUI.java:

```
package MyLookAndFeel;

import com.sun.java.swing.*;
import com.sun.java.swing.border.*;
import com.sun.java.swing.plaf.motif.*;
import java.awt.*;
import com.sun.java.swing.plaf.*;

public class MyCheckBoxUI extends MotifCheckBoxUI
{
    public static ComponentUI createUI( JComponent c )
    {
        // Create and return an instance of this class.

        return new MyCheckBoxUI();
    }

    // Paint our custom check box.

    public synchronized void paint( Graphics g,
                                    JComponent c )
    {
        // Cast so we can get the model, etc.

        AbstractButton btn = (AbstractButton)c;

        // Get the border insets so we don't overwrite the
        // border.
```

```
Insets insets = getDefaultMargin( btn );

// Use the insets to discover the available drawing
// area.

int width = btn.getWidth() - insets.left -
           insets.right;
int height = btn.getHeight() - insets.top -
            insets.bottom;

// Get the metrics so we can place the string.

FontMetrics metrics = g.getFontMetrics();

// Fill the background rectangle.

g.setColor( btn.getBackground() );
g.fillRect( insets.left, insets.top, width, height );

// Retrieve the check box's model.

ButtonModel model = btn.getModel();

// Draw a red 'x' in the box if the check box is
// selected.

if ( model.isSelected() )
{
   g.setColor( Color.red );
   g.drawLine( insets.left, insets.top, height,
              height );
   g.drawLine( insets.left, height, height,
              insets.top );
}

// Draw the text in black.  Notice that we get the
// text from the component class.

g.setColor( Color.black );
g.drawRect( insets.left, insets.top, height - 1,
           height - 1 );
g.drawString( btn.getText(), insets.left + height + 2,
             insets.top + metrics.getAscent() );
   }
}
```

Making Your Own Components Use Pluggable Look-and-Feel

Before the JFC, you could subclass Component and create your own components in which you could completely control appearance and behavior. You can still do this and it will work fine—you don't *have* to create multiple look-and-feels for your own components. Without multiple look-and-feels, your components will have the same appearance and behavior no matter what platform the application is running on and no matter what look-and-feel the JFC components are using.

There's also a hybrid solution. In the JFC, unless it's overridden, the paint() method still controls the painting process, but it doesn't contain the painting code any more. Instead, it causes different parts of the component to be painted by using different standard methods:

- **paintBorder():** Causes the component's border to paint itself.
- **paintComponent():** Paints the area of the component that lies within the border.
- **paintChildren():** Causes the component's child components (if any) to be painted.

So, if you want a custom button but you don't want to write your own look-and-feel, you can simply override the paintComponent() method. That way, the button's border still acts the same as it normally would, and changing the button's look-and-feel from Windows to Motif makes the button visually match the application's other JFC components.

If you want to support extra look-and-feels for your own components, it's not too difficult. Following are a pair of examples designed to help step you through it.

EXAMPLE 4-3 **Creating a Check Box That Always Uses the Motif Look-and-Feel**

This example creates a subclass of JCheckBox that will use the Motif look-and-feel no matter what look-and-feel is currently installed. The most important part of this example is overriding the updateUI() method, which is called whenever the component is told to update its look-and-feel to match the currently installed one. Figure 4-3 shows the example as it comes up initially. Notice that the two check boxes look different.

Important points to notice:

- There are two classes: MyFrame.java and MyCheckBox.java. MyFrame is the application's main frame, and MyCheckBox is our custom subclass of JCheckBox.
- MyFrame contains an instance of our custom check box and an instance of a normal JCheckBox.
- MyFrame sets the look-and-feel to Metal so we can see the difference between the custom check box and the normal one.
- For simplicity, MyCheckBox has only the one constructor.
- MyCheckBox overrides the updateUI() method, which is normally called to tell a component to check with the UIManager to update its

Figure 4-3
Creating a check box
that always uses the
Motif look-and-feel.

Figure 4-3
Creating a check box
that always uses the
Motif look-and-feel.

look-and-feel. In this method, we save the current look-and-feel so other components aren't affected. Next, we set the look-and-feel to Motif, and then get the Motif look-and-feel version of CheckBoxUI and apply it to our component. Finally, we restore the normal look-and-feel.

Here is the source code for MyFrame.java, followed by the source code for MyCheckBox.java:

```java
import com.sun.java.swing.*;
import java.awt.*;

public class MyFrame extends JFrame
{
    public MyFrame()
    {
        setTitle( "Plaf3" );

        // Store the content pane in a variable for easier
        // access.

        JPanel contentPane = (JPanel)getContentPane();

        // Components will all be added to this panel.

        contentPane.setLayout( new BorderLayout() );

        // Set the look-and-feel to "metal", and apply it
        // to the content pane.

        try
        {
            UIManager.setLookAndFeel( "com.sun.java.swing." +
                            "plaf.metal.MetalLookAndFeel" );
            contentPane.updateUI();
        }
        catch ( Exception e )
        {
            System.out.println( e );
        }

        // Create an instance of our custom check box and make
        // it so it will appear at the top of the content
        // pane.

        MyCheckBox mcb = new MyCheckBox( "My Check Box" );
        mcb.setSelected( true );
```

```
        contentPane.add( "North", mcb );

        // Create an instance of JCheckBox and add it on the
        // bottom edge of the content pane.

        JCheckBox jcb = new JCheckBox( "Metal Check Box" );
        jcb.setSelected( true );

        contentPane.add( "South", jcb );
    }
}
```

Here is the source code for MyCheckBox.java:

```
import com.sun.java.swing.*;
import com.sun.java.swing.plaf.*;

public class MyCheckBox extends JCheckBox
{
    // We only support this constructor to keep it simple.

    public MyCheckBox( String text )
    {
        super( text );
    }

    // Override the updateUI() method so we can always set
    // our look-and-feel to "motif".

    public void updateUI()
    {
        // Save the current look-and-feel so we can restore it
        // so other components are not affected.

        LookAndFeel oldLF = UIManager.getLookAndFeel();

        // Make "motif" the current look-and-feel, get
        // "motif"s CheckButtonUI class, and apply it to this
        // class.

        try
        {
            UIManager.setLookAndFeel( "com.sun.java.swing." +
                            "plaf.motif.MotifLookAndFeel" );
            ButtonUI newUI = (ButtonUI)UIManager.getUI( this );
            setUI( newUI );
        }
        catch ( Exception e )
        {
            System.out.println( e );
        }

        // Restore the normal look-and-feel.

        try
```

```
        {
            UIManager.setLookAndFeel( oldLF );
        }
        catch ( Exception e )
        {
            System.out.println( e );
        }
    }
}
```

EXAMPLE 4-4 **Changing Your Component's Look-and-Feel Based on the Installed Look-and-Feel**

You might create a custom component that you want to use on different platforms, but you don't want it to clash with JFC components when the installed look-and-feel changes. If you create a custom button component that looks like a Windows button, when you take it to a UNIX machine, its appearance will clash with JFC components there because they will be using the Motif look-and-feel. So maybe you want to create two look-and-feels for your component—one that looks like a Windows component, and one that looks like a Motif component. This example shows how to do so.

The example consists of six main classes:

■ **MyFrame.java:** This is the main frame class. It creates an instance of a custom button plus two radio buttons. The radio buttons allow the user to switch between the Windows and Motif look-and-feels.

■ **MyButton.java:** This is the custom button. It extends JButton and overrides the getUIClassID() method because we need the look-and-feel to install the proper UI class. It also overrides the updateUI() method. In that method, it does the following:

Saves the current plugged-in look-and-feel.

Gets the name of the plugged-in look-and-feel.

If the name is "Windows," it installs our custom look-and-feel that extends WindowsLookAndFeel.

If the name is something else, it installs our custom look-and-feel that extends MotifLookAndFeel.

It applies the look-and-feel to the custom button.

It reinstalls the original look-and-feel so other classes are not affected.

■ **MyMotifLookAndFeel.java:** This class extends MotifLookAndFeel. It overrides the getDefaults() method so it can associate the custom button's ID string with its Motif look-alike UI class. It overrides the getName() and getDescription methods to identify the look-and-feel, and also overrides the isNativeLookAndFeel() and isSupportedLookAndFeel() methods.

■ **MyWindowsLookAndFeel.java:** This class extends WindowsLookAndFeel. It overrides the getDefaults() method so it can associate the custom button's ID string with its Windows look-alike UI class. It overrides the getName() and getDescription() methods to identify the look-and-feel, and also overrides isNativeLookAndFeel() and isSupportedLookAndFeel().

- **MyMotifButtonUI.java:** This class extends MotifButtonUI. It overrides the createUI() method to create an instance of itself, and also overrides the paint() method. In that method, it calls the parent's paint() method, and then draws a red × through it.

- **MyWindowsButtonUI.java:** This class extends WindowsButtonUI. It overrides the createUI() method to create an instance of itself and also overrides the paint() method. In that method, it calls the parent's paint() method and then draws a green × through it.

When the user switches look-and-feel, MyButton's updateUI() method gets called. That method checks the name of the look-and-feel and, based on that, temporarily installs a custom look-and-feel that contains a UI class for MyButton that doesn't clash with the look-and-feel the user just switched to.

Figure 4-4 shows the example as it looks initially.

Here is the source code. MyFrame.java is listed first, then MyButton.java, MyMotifLookAndFeel.java, and MyMotifButtonUI.java. The two Windows classes aren't listed here because they are so similar to the Motif ones, but they're on the book's CD-ROM.

Here is MyFrame.java:

```java
import com.sun.java.swing.*;
import com.sun.java.swing.border.*;
import java.awt.*;
import java.awt.event.*;

public class MyFrame extends JFrame implements ItemListener
{
    private JRadioButton mMotif;
    private JRadioButton mWindows;

    public MyFrame()
    {
        setTitle( "Plaf4" );

        // Store the content pane in a variable for easier
```

Figure 4-4

Changing your component's look-and-feel based on the installed look-and-feel.

```
                   // access.

                   JPanel contentPane = (JPanel)getContentPane();

                   // Components will all be added to this panel.

                   contentPane.setLayout( new BorderLayout() );

                   // Create a custom button.

                   MyButton btn = new MyButton( "My Button" );

                   // Add the button at the top of the content pane.

                   contentPane.add( "North", btn );

                   // Create two radio buttons for shifting
                   // look-and-feel.

                   mMotif = new JRadioButton( "Motif" );
                   mMotif.addItemListener( this );
                   mWindows = new JRadioButton( "Windows" );
                   mWindows.addItemListener( this );

                   // Create a button group for the radio buttons and add
                   // them to it.

                   ButtonGroup group = new ButtonGroup();
                   group.add( mMotif );
                   group.add( mWindows );

                   // Create a panel to hold the radio buttons, and add
                   // them to it.

                   JPanel l_f_pane = new JPanel();
                   l_f_pane.setBorder( new TitledBorder(
                                    "Which look-and-feel?" ) );
                   l_f_pane.setLayout( new BoxLayout(
                                    l_f_pane, BoxLayout.Y_AXIS ) );
                   l_f_pane.add( mMotif );
                   l_f_pane.add( mWindows );

                   // Add the radio button panel to the content pane.

                   contentPane.add( "Center", l_f_pane );

                   // Select the custom look-and-feel initially.
                   // Selecting it here causes an item event to be
                   // generated so the look-and-feel is
                   // automatically set.

                   mMotif.setSelected( true );
               }

           // This is called when one of the radio buttons changes
```

```
                         // state.

                      public void itemStateChanged( ItemEvent e )
                      {
                         String l_f_name = "";

                         // We ignore de-select events.

                         if ( e.getStateChange() == ItemEvent.SELECTED )
                         {
                            // Based on the radio button that generated the
                            // event, set the look-and-feel class' name.

                            if ( e.getSource() == mMotif )
                            {
                               l_f_name = "com.sun.java.swing." +
                                           "plaf.motif.MotifLookAndFeel";
                            }
                            else if ( e.getSource() == mWindows )
                            {
                               l_f_name = "com.sun.java.swing." +
                                           "plaf.windows.WindowsLookAndFeel";
                            }

                            try
                            {
                               // Try to set the look-and-feel.

                               UIManager.setLookAndFeel( l_f_name );

                               // Propagate the new look-and-feel to all
                               // components in the frame.

                               SwingUtilities.updateComponentTreeUI( this );

                               // Make the display reflect the change.

                               repaint();
                            }
                            catch ( Exception ex )
                            {
                               System.out.println( ex );
                            }
                         }
                      }
                   }
```

Here is MyButton.java:

```
import com.sun.java.swing.*;
import com.sun.java.swing.plaf.*;

public class MyButton extends JButton
{
```

```java
public MyButton( String text )
{
   super( text );
}

// Return the ID string that the look-and-feel will use
// to assign a UI class.

public String getUIClassID()
{
   return "MyButtonUI";
}

// Someone wants this component to check with the
// currently installed look-and-feel to get a new UI
// class.  Since there is no UI class for the
// "MyButtonUI" ID string, we check which look-and-feel
// is installed, and temporarily install
// our own look-and-feel.

public void updateUI()
{
   // Get the name of the look-and-feel.

   String lfName = UIManager.getLookAndFeel().getName();

   // Save the look-and-feel so we can put it back.

   LookAndFeel oldLF = UIManager.getLookAndFeel();

   // If the look-and-feel is the "windows"
   // look-and-feel, install our subclass of the windows
   // look-and-feel.  Otherwise, install our subclass of
   // the Motif look-and-feel.

   try
   {
   if ( lfName.equals( "Windows" ) )
   {
      // Install our windows look-and-feel.

      UIManager.setLookAndFeel(
        "MyWindowsLookAndFeel.MyWindowsLookAndFeel" );
   }
   else
   {
      // Install our motif look-and-feel.

      UIManager.setLookAndFeel(
         "MyMotifLookAndFeel.MyMotifLookAndFeel" );
   }

      // Get the MyButtonUI class from the look-and-feel.

      ButtonUI newUI = (ButtonUI)UIManager.getUI( this );
```

```
    // Tell the custom button what its new
    // look-and-feel is.

    setUI( newUI );

}
catch ( Exception e )
{
    e.printStackTrace();
}

// Restore the general look-and-feel.

try
{
    UIManager.setLookAndFeel( oldLF );
}
catch ( Exception e )
{
    System.out.println( e );
}
    }
}
```

Here is MyMotifLookAndFeel.java:

```
package MyMotifLookAndFeel;

import com.sun.java.swing.plaf.motif.*;
import com.sun.java.swing.*;
import java.util.*;
import com.sun.java.swing.plaf.*;
import java.awt.*;

public class MyMotifLookAndFeel extends MotifLookAndFeel
{
    // Overridden so we can add the MyButtonUI class.

    public UIDefaults getDefaults()
    {
        // Get MotifLookAndFeel's list of UI classes.

        UIDefaults defs = super.getDefaults();

        try
        {
            // Add the class for the custom button's UI.

            defs.put( "MyButtonUI",
                      "MyMotifLookAndFeel.MyMotifButtonUI" );
        }
        catch ( Exception e )
        {
            System.out.println( e );
        }
```

```
        // Return the modified UIDefaults.

        return defs;
    }

    // Return a string name for the look-and-feel.

    public String getName()
    {
        return "MyMotifLookAndFeel";
    }

    // Return a one-line description of the look-and-feel.

    public String getDescription()
    {
        String retval = "A subclass of MotifLookAndFeel " +
                        "which adds MyButtonUI";
        return retval;
    }

    // This is not the native look-and-feel.

    public boolean isNativeLookAndFeel()
    {
        return false;
    }

    // This look-and-feel is always supported.

    public boolean isSupportedLookAndFeel()
    {
        return true;
    }
}
```

Here is MyMotifButtonUI.java:

```
package MyMotifLookAndFeel;

import com.sun.java.swing.*;
import com.sun.java.swing.border.*;
import com.sun.java.swing.plaf.motif.*;
import java.awt.*;
import com.sun.java.swing.plaf.*;

public class MyMotifButtonUI extends MotifButtonUI
{
    public static ComponentUI createUI( JComponent c )
    {
        // Create and return an instance of this class.

        return new MyMotifButtonUI();
    }
```

```
// Paint our custom button.

public synchronized void paint( Graphics g,
                                 JComponent c )
{
    super.paint( g, c );

    g.setColor( Color.red );

    g.drawLine( 0, 0, c.getWidth() - 1,
                c.getHeight() - 1 );
    g.drawLine( 0, c.getHeight() - 1,
                c.getWidth() - 1, 0 );
}
}
```

Creating a Complete Custom Look-and-Feel

If you need to create a completely new look-and-feel, your best bet is to sub-class one of the existing look-and-feels—Motif or Metal. That way, you can subclass the other look-and-feel's UI classes if you just want to change how they look, not how they respond to events. If you choose not to subclass MetalLookAndFeel or MotifLookAndFeel, you should at least subclass the abstract BasicLookAndFeel class.

Making an entire custom look-and-feel is a huge task—especially when you get to JTree and JTable—so it's beyond the scope of this book. However, the four examples in this chapter should give you a place to start.

SUMMARY

Pluggable look-and-feel is one of the fundamental concepts in the JFC. You can happily use the JFC components without understanding the details of look-and-feel, but as you begin to subclass them and change their behavior, it will gradually become more important for you to learn. This chapter has explained what JavaSoft means by *pluggable look-and-feel* and covered the different levels at which it can affect your applications. It has also explained how to begin implementing your own look-and-feel and making your own components change look-and-feel as the JFC components do.

JFC Documents and Text Components

JFC's text-related classes can be very hard to understand for several reasons. First, there are *so* many classes that interact. It's not immediately clear what they all do and which classes control which other classes. Second, several undocumented inner classes are used. They typically implement known interfaces, but it's unclear what else they do. Third, the problem being addressed is complex, so it takes some time to understand.

In this chapter, we go through the important classes and interfaces, discussing what each part's responsibilities are, what classes it interacts with, and how it interacts.

The Pieces of the Puzzle

When you first look at the JFC text classes, it's a little like looking at a jig-saw puzzle for the first time. You have seen what the final product should look like, but all you can see in the box is a random jumble of confusing shapes. Now it's time to open the box and look at each piece in the following sections. Once we have done that, we can start putting them together.

The Text Component

This is the class that represents a text control to the rest of the world. It does not hold much of the information about the text control, but can get it.

The Document

This is where the characters for the text control actually reside. This class also has a reference to where the text attributes (font, bold, italic, and so on) are stored but doesn't store them itself.

The Element

Elements associate text attributes with ranges of characters.

The Caret

The Caret stores what the user thinks of as the current location in the text control. The Caret position is where a character is inserted when the user types. It's responsible for drawing itself and usually appears as a vertical line between characters.

The Attribute Set

This holds a set of text attributes, including font family, font size, bold, italic, and text alignment.

The Style Context

This holds a set of named Attribute Sets that define commonly used combinations of attributes.

The Position

This is assigned to a particular place in the Document, like the beginning of a specific word and moves around as that place moves around. At any time, you can ask it for its current location.

The Key Map

This associates keystrokes that happen on the text control with actions that should occur in response. Not all keystrokes are mapped—only the ones that require special handling.

The View

This handles the drawing of a single Element.

The UI

This is the text component's look-and-feel class and is what coordinates the drawing of the entire text control. It also handles catching and processing input events.

How the Pieces Fit Together

Now that we have seen the pieces, we can go through each one, show the text-related classes and interfaces that the JFC uses to implement the piece, and describe how it interacts with the other pieces.

The Text Component

The Text Component has the following classes:

- **JTextField:** A simple editor for single line text. It uses only one font.
- **JTextArea:** A simple editor for multi-line text. It also uses only one font.
- **JTextPane:** A sophisticated editor for multi-line text. It supports word wrapping, multiple fonts, bold, italic, underlining, insertion of components and images, and more.
- **JTextComponent:** The abstract class that all of the preceding classes extend.

The Text Component has the following items:

- External state information, such as the border, whether the control is editable, and so on. For JTextField and JTextArea, it also contains the font the control will use.
- A reference to the Document.
- A reference to the Look-and-Feel.
- A reference to the Caret.

INTERACTING WITH DOCUMENTS When the Text Component is created, you can typically pass in a text string and a Document if you want to, or you can create the Text Component with no arguments. In that case, a default Document is created. You can use the getDocument() method to gain access to the Document. With JTextPane, you can also call the get-StyledDocument() method. You can replace the Document by using the set-Document() or setStyledDocument() method.

INTERACTING WITH THE UI When created, a Text Component gets a UI class from UIManager. This class controls drawing the text control, handles its input events, creates the Caret, and has a View factory that generates Views for Elements. To get access to the UI, you can call the getUI() method. You can also call the setUI() method to replace the class, although that's not advisable; setUI() is more for interaction between the component and the installed look-and-feel.

INTERACTING WITH THE CARET You can get access to the Caret by calling the getCaret() method. You can also set the Caret by using the setCaret() method. The Text Component also has methods for moving the caret and changing its color.

INTERACTING WITH THE STYLE CONTEXT JTextPane has convenience methods for interacting with a StyledDocument's Style Context.

INTERACTING WITH THE REST OF THE WORLD The Text Component is created so it can be placed in a container of some kind. It's placed in the container just like other components (it has java.awt.Component as one of its ancestors). The Text Components have many convenience methods for accessing and changing things that are stored in its associated classes.

The Document

The Document component has the following interfaces:

- **Document:** Defines the minimum behavior for accessing and modifying text and attributes, and for tracking text positions and changes. Documents used by JTextField or JTextArea must implement this interface.
- **StyledDocument:** Extends the Document interface to define extra attribute-handling behavior. Documents used by JTextPane must implement this interface.

Document has the following classes:

- **PlainDocument:** This class implements the Document interface and is the default Document created by JTextField and JTextArea.
- **DefaultStyledDocument:** This class implements the StyledDocument interface and is the default Document created by JTextPane.
- **AbstractDocument:** This is the abstract class that's the parent of both PlainDocument and DefaultStyledDocument. It implements the Document interface, so it defines most of the most useful Document functionality for its subclasses.

The Document contains the following items:

- The actual text for the text control.
- One or more root Elements. Each root Element contains a complete Element tree that associates attributes with character positions in the

Document. You can use multiple root Elements to hold different sets of attributes for the entire Document, but there's normally just one root Element.

■ A list of classes that implement the DocumentListener interface and that are to be notified when text is inserted or removed or when attributes change.

■ DefaultStyledDocument contains a reference to a Style Context.

INTERACTING WITH TEXT COMPONENTS A Document class can either be created on its own or be created by default by the Text Component. If no Document is specified in its constructor, the Text Component creates a PlainDocument or DefaultStyledDocument, depending on the type of Text Component. The Document can be accessed by using the getDocument() method or replaced with the setDocument() method. There are corresponding getStyledDocument() and setStyledDocument() methods in JTextPane. The Text Component has a set of convenience methods for accessing and changing information stored in the Document.

INTERACTING WITH ELEMENTS Besides storing one or more root Elements, the Document supplies a set of convenience methods for locating which Elements correspond to which character positions and for getting and setting Element attributes. The Document is responsible for accepting attribute changes and modifying the Element tree to reflect the changes.

INTERACTING WITH ATTRIBUTE SETS The Document receives Attribute Sets when a request is made to change attributes. The Document has to decide how the change affects the Element tree. It also passes out Attribute Sets when requests are made for attributes associated with character positions or paragraphs.

INTERACTING WITH THE STYLE CONTEXT A DefaultStyledDocument can accept a Style Context as an argument to its constructor; otherwise, it creates its own. It has convenience methods for accessing and modifying the named Attribute Sets that the Style Context contains.

INTERACTING WITH POSITIONS You can create a Position by calling the Document's createPosition() method.

INTERACTING WITH THE UI When the UI class is drawing the text control, it has to get text and Elements from the Document. Otherwise, it wouldn't know what text to draw or how to draw it. For JTextField and JTextArea, the Elements aren't as important because attributes aren't used.

The Element

For interfaces, the Element component has the Element interface itself. Any class that wants to be used as an Element must implement this interface.

The only actual Element classes in the JFC are the ones defined as inner classes within the Document classes.

Elements contain the following items:

- They can contain other Elements. An Element might be a root Element, it might represent a paragraph, or it might represent a range of characters (in which case it won't contain other Elements). An Element that doesn't contain other Elements is called a "leaf Element."

- An Attribute Set. An Element always contains the set of Attributes that define how the document, paragraph, or range of text should look. Attributes in Elements that are lower down in the Element tree override attributes in Elements that are higher up. For example, if you have a root Element that contains a paragraph Element containing a leaf Element, when drawing the leaf, all attributes defined in the leaf are applied. Any attributes defined in the paragraph that aren't defined in the leaf are applied, and any attributes defined in the root that aren't defined in the paragraph or the leaf are applied.

- A start position and an end position, if the Element is a leaf Element. They specify what range of characters the Element's attributes are applied to. When you ask a non-leaf Element for its starting position, it returns the starting position of its initial leaf Element.

INTERACTING WITH DOCUMENTS A Document contains one or more root Elements, with each root Element providing a complete mapping of Document characters to attributes. When attributes change for some part of the Document, the Document is responsible for modifying the affected Element tree to reflect the change. The Document might also be asked for the Element that corresponds to a paragraph or a character position and is responsible for finding the proper Element and returning it.

INTERACTING WITH VIEWS Because a View is used to draw an Element, it needs to get the Element from the Document so it can get the range of characters to draw and the attributes.

INTERACTING WITH THE UI The UI class retrieves each Element from the Document and creates a View that knows how to draw each one.

The Caret

Caret is the interface that any Caret class must implement. DefaultCaret is the standard Caret class used if a special one is not assigned.

The Caret contains the following items:

- The current caret position, referred to as the "Dot position." If there's a text selection, it represents the end of the selection.
- The Mark position. This is the same as the Dot position unless there's a current text selection, in which case it marks the beginning of the selection.

INTERACTING WITH THE TEXT COMPONENT The Text Component has a reference to the Caret and supplies methods for moving the Caret and for changing its color.

INTERACTING WITH ATTRIBUTE SETS When text is inserted at the Caret position, it uses the attributes active at that position. The JTextPane setCharacterAttributes() method sets the attributes at the current Caret position or within the text selection defined by the Mark and Dot positions.

INTERACTING WITH THE UI The UI class creates the caret and gives it to the Text Component. The UI class calls the Caret's paint() method so the Caret marker (typically a vertical line) can be drawn.

The Attribute Set

NOTE: *See the "StyleConstants" section in Chapter 8 to see how they can be used to make dealing with Attribute Sets simpler.*

The Attribute Set has the following interfaces:

- **AttributeSet:** Defines the basic behavior for accessing attributes from within a set of attributes.
- **MutableAttributeSet:** Extends the AttributeSet interface to define behavior for adding attributes to and removing attributes from the Attribute Set.
- **Style:** Extends the MutableAttributeSet interface to define behavior for accessing the Style name and for tracking changes to attributes.

The Attribute Set has one class:

■ **SimpleAttributeSet:** Implements the MutableAttributeSet interface. It's useful for creating attribute sets, changing attributes within a set, or copying or inheriting from one set to another.

The Attribute Set contains the following items:

■ A set of attributes stored in name/value pairs.
■ Possibly a "Resolve Parent," which is another Attribute Set that this one contains a reference to. The main set makes itself different from the Resolve Parent by adding extra attributes or overriding one or more of the Resolve Parent's attributes.

INTERACTING WITH THE TEXT COMPONENT The Text Component has a set of convenience methods that apply attributes to characters, paragraphs, and so forth.

INTERACTING WITH THE DOCUMENT A Document might have to change the Element tree when attributes change. A StyledDocument also contains a reference to a Style Context that contains named Attribute Sets. StyledDocument includes convenience methods for accessing and modifying the Style Context.

INTERACTING WITH ELEMENTS An Element stores an Attribute Set that defines attributes for the character range that the Element represents.

INTERACTING WITH VIEWS Because a View is used to draw an Element, it uses the Element's attributes to know how to draw the characters represented by the Element.

The Style Context

NOTE: *See the "StyleConstants" section in Chapter 8 to find out how to make it easier to access a Style's attributes.*

The Style Context component has only one class:

■ **StyleContext:** Stores the Styles (named Attribute Sets), provides access to the Styles, and allows tracking changes.

The Style Context contains the following items:

■ A list of name/style pairs so you can retrieve any Style by its name or get all names.

■ A list of ChangeListeners that are notified when Styles are added and removed.

INTERACTING WITH TEXT COMPONENTS   JTextPane has a set of convenience methods for accessing and modifying its StyledDocument's Style Context.

INTERACTING WITH DOCUMENTS   A StyledDocument contains a Style Context and provides convenience methods for accessing and modifying its contents.

INTERACTING WITH ATTRIBUTE SETS   Each Style in the Style Context is just a named AttributeSet. Style extends the MutableAttributeSet interface, which extends the AttributeSet interface.

The Position

The Position component has a single interface:

■ **Position:** Defines a single method for accessing the Position's current offset.

The only JFC classes that implement the Position interface are undocumented inner classes of the Document classes.
The Position component typically includes the following item:

■ Its current offset within the Document.

INTERACTING WITH DOCUMENTS   Positions are created by using the Document's createPosition() method.

The Key Map

The Key Map component has a single interface:

■ **Keymap:** Defines the behavior required to add keystroke/action pairs to the Key Map, to remove keystroke/action pairs from the Key Map, and to access the Key Map's contents.

The only JFC classes that implement the Keymap interface are ones generated by the Text Component's UI class.
The Key Map contains the following items:

■ A list of keystroke/action pairs.

■ Possibly a Resolve Parent, which is another Key Map that this one can inherit keystroke/action pairs from. A Key Map with a Resolve Parent adds actions for keystrokes the parent didn't define and replaces some of the keystroke actions with others.

INTERACTING WITH TEXT COMPONENTS The Text Component supplies convenience methods for accessing and replacing the Key Map.

INTERACTING WITH THE UI The UI class defines a Key Map that makes the associated component act as expected, which includes providing actions for when arrow keys are pressed, and so forth.

The View

The View component has a single interface:

■ **ViewFactory:** The UI class uses a class that implements this interface to create a View for each Element.

These classes define how to draw different types of Elements. View is the abstract parent of the rest in the list:

■ BoxView
■ ComponentView
■ CompositeView
■ FieldView
■ IconView
■ LabelView
■ ParagraphView
■ PasswordView
■ PlainView
■ View

INTERACTING WITH THE UI When the UI class is drawing the component, it gets the Document and goes through it Element by Element. For each Element to be drawn, it uses its ViewFactory to create a View for that Element.

INTERACTING WITH ELEMENTS A View is used to draw a single Element that it gets from the UI class, which in turn got it from the Document.

INTERACTING WITH ATTRIBUTE SETS   To draw an Element, the View must get and interpret the Element's Attribute Set.

The UI

Each Look-and-Feel has a different UI class for each Text Component. The Look-and-Feel class includes the following:

- A reference to the current Key Map.
- A reference back to the Text Component.
- A reference to the Caret.
- A ViewFactory for creating Views from Elements.
- Code for drawing the component and handling events.

INTERACTING WITH TEXT COMPONENTS   The UI class is responsible for drawing the component. It also handles input events, such as mouse clicks and key presses. It might be replaced at any time by the equivalent UI class from another Look-and-Feel package. The UI class uses the Text Component's access methods to get the Document when it's time to draw. It also accesses the Text Component's information about borders and more.

INTERACTING WITH DOCUMENTS   The UI class doesn't know what the text control contains or what the contents should look like, so it gets the Document by using the Text Component's getDocument() or getStyled-Document() method. It then accesses the correct Element tree from the Document and creates Views for the Elements.

INTERACTING WITH ELEMENTS   The UI class gets the Elements from the Document and creates Views to match. It uses the Elements' references to character ranges to get the text that needs to be drawn, and the Elements' Attribute Sets to get the attributes that should be applied.

INTERACTING WITH CARETS   The UI class creates the Caret and gives a reference to it to the Text Component. It also listens for when the Caret is changed through the Text Component's convenience methods.

INTERACTING WITH ATTRIBUTE SETS   The UI class accesses Elements' Attribute Sets to tell how the text referred to by the Elements should be drawn.

INTERACTING WITH KEY MAPS   The UI class creates the Key Map and gives a reference to it to the Text Component. It also listens for when the Key Map is changed through the Text Component's convenience methods.

INTERACTING WITH VIEWS   When the UI class is drawing the text control, it uses its ViewFactory to create Views from Elements. It uses the Views to draw the Elements.

SUMMARY

JFC Text Components can be complicated to use because there are so many interdependent classes to know about. This chapter has tried to explain what all the classes are and how the complex relationships between them work. Implementation details haven't been included because they tend to obscure the relationships; however, they are covered in detail in Chapter 8.

Accessibility

The goal of the JFC Accessibility *Application Programming Interface* (API) is to make it easy for programmers to make their applications work with access technologies that can sit on top of the *Java Virtual Machine* (JVM). *Access technology*, which includes screen readers and magnifiers, Braille keyboards, and other devices, helps disabled users use the computer (see

`http://java.sun.`
`com/products/jfc/accessibility.html`).

JFC accessibility, when fully implemented, helps the user understand what each component does and what its state is. It also describes relationships between components and containers and between lists and list items. All components that ship with the JFC have access methods built in, to some extent. JComponent includes access to the accessibility methods so that all its children can have them as well, although any subclass of JComponent needs to do some work to make its access information meaningful. JFC components like Box, JFrame, JWindow, and JDialog that aren't subclasses of JComponent also offer the same access.

There are two sides to providing accessible functionality with Java. The first side concerns what the programmer has to do to make an application accessible. JFC includes a package called "com.sun.java.accessibility" that contains the interfaces different types of components should implement to provide support for access technologies. These interfaces are as follows:

- **Accessible:** Contains a single method, getAccessibleContext(), through which all accessible information can be reached. This method returns either null or a subclass of the abstract AccessibleContext class. AccessibleContext contains methods that either give accessible information directly or return classes that give specific types of accessible information.

- **AccessibleAction:** Describes the behavior required to give accessible access to a component's actions (registered or not) so the user can see what they are and can trigger them. To find out about a component's accessible actions, you have to call its AccessibleContext's getAccessibleAction() method. The method returns null if the component doesn't support accessible actions or returns a class that implements the AccessibleAction interface.

- **AccessibleComponent:** Describes the basic required behavior for a component that wants to be accessible, including information about whether the component can get focus, what its colors and fonts are, whether it's visible, and so forth. Most of the methods in AccessibleComponent are already defined in JComponent. So, if you extend JComponent, you have almost completely implemented this interface. To get access to the class that implements the AccessibleComponent interface, you call the component's AccessibleContext's getAccessibleComponent() method. It returns null if the interface is not supported, or it returns the class that implements it. The returned class is frequently the component itself.

- **AccessibleSelection:** Defines accessible behavior for components that contain things that can be selected, such as lists, combo boxes, trees, and more. It lets the user get and modify information about the current selection state. The class that implements the AccessibleSelection interface can be accessed by using the component's AccessibleContext's getAccessibleSelection() method. If the component doesn't support the interface, the method returns null.

- **AccessibleText:** Defines the behavior that Text Components should implement to allow accessible reading of the text contents. This behavior includes finding out the caret position; reading characters, words, and sentences; and getting the selected text (if any). The class that implements the AccessibleText interface can be accessed by using the component's AccessibleContext's getAccessibleText() method. The method returns null if the component doesn't support the interface.

■ **AccessibleValue:** Defines the behavior a component that contains or represents a changing numeric value should implement to be accessible. This behavior includes getting and setting the current value as well as finding out the maximum and minimum values allowed. The class that implements the AccessibleValue interface can be accessed by using the component's AccessibleContext's getAccessibleValue() method. The method returns null if the component doesn't support the interface.

The second side of accessibility concerns how developers of access technologies can interact with the JVM to get applications' accessibility information. JavaSoft supplies a set of classes and utilities called "Java Accessibility" shipped separately from the JFC. Although we will focus on the accessibility classes provided with the JFC, we will also discuss how some of the utilities in the Java Accessibility can be used to test your applications' access functionality.

NOTE: *For information on implementing the Accessible interface in your own components, see the "AccessibleContext" section in Chapter 8, "JFC by Class."*

The com.sun.java.accessibility. Accessible Interface

This interface must be implemented for a component to expose any accessible information. It defines a single method that gives access to all of a component's defined accessibility information:

■ **AccessibleContext getAccessibleContext():** This method returns a class that extends the abstract AccessibleContext class. AccessibleContext contains some methods that return general accessibility information and other methods that give access to more specialized accessibility information.

The com.sun.java.accessibility. AccessibleAction Interface

This interface must be implemented to give accessible access to the things that can be done to a component. For example, a button can be pressed, so something like a "Press" action should be available to be triggered. A common use for the methods in this interface is to list the actions available for a component and let the user choose one to execute. Here are the available methods:

■ **boolean doAccessibleAction(int i):** This method causes the component's action identified by the given index to be executed. For a button, if the index referred to a "Press" action, the method should cause the button to be pressed.

■ **int getAccessibleActionCount():** Returns the number of accessible actions the component supports.

■ **String getAccessibleActionDescription(int i):** Returns a String that describes the *i*-th accessible action the component supports.

The com.sun.java.accessible. AccessibleComponent Interface

This interface gives access to a component's graphical state and allows the user to change it. All the methods in this interface, except the getAccessibleAt() method, are defined in JComponent, or JComponent inherits them. So, if a component extends JComponent, it already almost implements the AccessibleComponent interface. Here are the available methods:

■ **void addFocusListener(FocusListener l):** Tells the component to notify the given class when the focus is gained or lost.

■ **boolean contains(Point p):** Returns true if the given Point is within this component's bounds.

■ **Accessible getAccessibleAt(Point p):** Returns the topmost Accessible component at the given Point, if there is one.

■ **Color getBackground():** Returns this component's current background color.

■ **Rectangle getBounds():** Returns this component's origin and size in relation to its container.

■ **Cursor getCursor():** Returns this component's current cursor.

■ **Font getFont():** Returns this component's current font.

■ **FontMetrics getFontMetrics(Font f):** Returns the FontMetrics for the given font.

■ **Color getForeground():** Returns this component's current foreground color.

■ **Point getLocation():** Returns this component's origin in relation to its container.

- **Point getLocationOnScreen():** Returns this component's origin in relation to the display's origin.
- **Dimension getSize():** Returns the size of this component.
- **boolean isEnabled():** Returns true if this component is enabled.
- **boolean isFocusTraversable():** Returns true if this component can get the focus through Tab or Shift+Tab.
- **boolean isShowing():** Returns true if this component is currently being displayed onscreen.
- **boolean isVisible():** Returns true if this component is currently visible. It might be visible but not showing if one of its display ancestors is not showing.
- **void removeFocusListener(FocusListener l):** Tells the component to stop notifying the given class when this component gains or loses focus.
- **void requestFocus():** Asks to have the focus transferred to this component.
- **void setBackground(Color c):** Specifies the color this component uses to draw its background rectangle.
- **void setBounds(Rectangle r):** Specifies where this component's origin is in relation to its container and sets its size.
- **void setCursor(Cursor cursor):** Specifies what this component's cursor should be.
- **void setEnabled(boolean b):** Specifies whether this component is enabled or disabled.
- **void setFont(Font f):** Specifies this component's current font.
- **void setForeground(Color c):** Specifies the color this component should use for its foreground operations.
- **void setLocation(Point p):** Specifies this component's origin point in relation to its container.
- **void setSize(Dimension d):** Specifies this component's size.
- **void setVisible(boolean b):** Specifies whether this component is visible or invisible.

The com.sun.java.accessible. AccessibleSelection Interface

This interface specifies the methods that an accessible component containing selectable items should implement. It gives accessible access to the current selection state and allows the user to change that state. Here are the available methods:

- **void addAccessibleSelection(int i):** Adds the item at the given index to the list of currently selected accessible items.
- **void clearAccessibleSelection():** Makes it so that no accessible items are selected.
- **Accessible getAccessibleSelection(int i):** Returns the *i*-th selected accessible item.
- **int getAccessibleSelectionCount():** Returns the number of currently selected accessible items.
- **boolean isAccessibleChildSelected(int i):** Returns true if the *i*-th accessible item is currently selected.
- **void removeAccessibleSelection(int i):** Removes the *i*-th accessible item from the current selection.
- **void selectAllAccessibleSelection():** Causes all accessible items to become selected.

The com.sun.java.accessibility. AccessibleText Interface

This interface defines how Text Components can give accessible access to their contents. It includes retrieving characters, words, and sentences; getting the caret position; finding out about text selection; and checking characters' attributes. Here are the available methods:

- **String getAfterIndex(int part,int index):** Given a character index and a constant identifying what to return, this method returns the character after the index, the word after the word in which the index falls, or the sentence after the sentence in which the index falls. The constant is AccessibleText.CHARACTER, AccessibleText.WORD, or AccessibleText.SENTENCE.
- **String getAtIndex(int part,int index):** Given a character index and a constant identifying what to return, this method returns the character at the index, the word in which the index falls, or the sentence in which the index falls. The constant is AccessibleText.CHARACTER, AccessibleText.WORD, or AccessibleText.SENTENCE.
- **String getBeforeIndex(int part,int index):** Given a character index and a constant identifying what to return, this method returns

the character before the index, the word before the word in which the index falls, or the sentence before the sentence in which the index falls. The constant is AccessibleText.CHARACTER, AccessibleText.WORD, or AccessibleText.SENTENCE.

- **int getCaretPosition():** Returns the index at which the caret is currently positioned.
- **AttributeSet getCharacterAttribute(int i):** Returns the attributes in effect for the character at the given index.
- **Rectangle getCharacterBounds(int i):** Returns the bounding box of the character at the given index.
- **int getCharCount():** Returns the number of characters in the component.
- **int getIndexAtPoint(Point p):** Returns the index of the character under the given point.
- **String getSelectedText():** Returns the currently selected text, if any.
- **int getSelectionEnd():** Returns the offset of the end of the current text selection. If there's no selection, it returns the caret position.
- **int getSelectionStart():** Returns the offset of the beginning of the current text selection. If there's no selection, it returns the caret position.

The com.sun.java.accessibility. AccessibleValue Interface

This interface defines how a component that stores or represents a changeable numeric value can give accessible access to that value. Here are the available methods:

- **Number getCurrentAccessibleValue():** Returns the component's current value.
- **Number getMaximumAccessibleValue():** Returns the component's maximum acceptable value.
- **Number getMinimumAccessibleValue():** Returns the component's minimum acceptable value.
- **boolean setCurrentAccessibleValue(Number n):** Sets the component's value. Returns true if the value was acceptable and was set.

Utilities for Testing the Accessibility of Your Applications

The separate Java Accessibility pack discussed in this chapter's overview has several utilities, three of which are useful for our purposes. All three attach to the JVM and allow you to find accessibility information about *graphical user interface* (GUI) applications that the JVM runs. Each utility gives a different view into accessibility information, so you might find that you use one utility for one situation and another utility for another situation.

Each utility starts up its own window when your application starts up, and the information in that window changes as the state of your application changes. To get these utilities, you must download them separately from Java-Soft—they aren't included with the JFC.

NOTE: *The release of the Java Accessibility pack discussed in this section is lagging behind the release of the JFC at publication time, so the utilities explained here might be different from the ones ultimately released.*

JavaMonitor

JavaMonitor is a handy utility that not only offers accessibility information, but also tracks a variety of events.

SETTING UP YOUR ENVIRONMENT   You have to do a little work to prepare your environment to run this utility because the JVM has to know to start it up whenever you run a Java application. Follow these steps to prepare your environment:

1. Change your CLASSPATH.

   You need to add the jaccess.jar file to your CLASSPATH. This file is located in the directory where you installed the Java Accessibility pack.

   You also need to add the JavaMonitor directory to your CLASSPATH. It's a directory called "JavaMonitor" under the examples subdirectory in the directory where you installed the Java Accessibility pack.

2. Change your awt.properties file.

   There's an awt.properties file in the lib subdirectory under the directory where your JDK is installed. You need to add the following two lines to the end of that file:

   ```
   AWT.EventQueueClass=com.sun.java.accessibility.EventQueueMonitor
   AWT.AutoLoadClasses=JavaMonitor
   ```

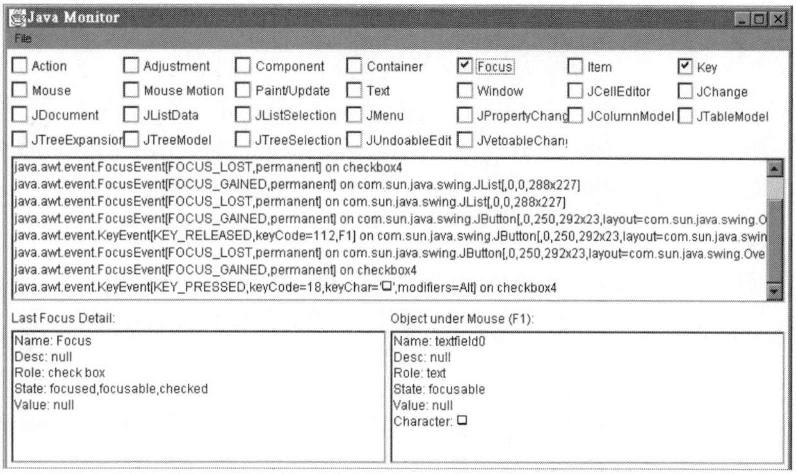

Figure 6-1
The JavaMonitor
window.

Figure 6-1
The JavaMonitor
window.

USING JAVAMONITOR   Once you have changed your environment as described in the preceding steps, the JavaMonitor utility will start up every time you run a Java application, and your application will be running in its own window separate from the JavaMonitor window. Figure 6-1 shows a sample of what JavaMonitor will look like.

At the top of the JavaMonitor screen is a set of check boxes you can click to see different types of information. The available types of information go well beyond just accessible information. You can see all sorts of events simply by selecting different check boxes. Notice that JavaMonitor doesn't restrict itself to tracking events in your application—it catches events that happen to itself as well.

Just below the check boxes is a list box that displays information about events as they happen. If you have checked the "Mouse Motion" check box, this list box is where all the mouse motion events are displayed.

At the bottom of the JavaMonitor window are two more list boxes called "Last Focus Detail:" and "Object Under Mouse (F1):"; they are where accessibility information is displayed.

To get accessibility information, you need to at least check the "Key" check box. Then, when you place the mouse cursor over a component and press the F1 key, the accessibility information about the component under the mouse is displayed in the "Object Under Mouse (F1):" list box. You can also check the "Focus" check box. Once you do that, whenever a component gets the focus, its accessibility information shows up in the "Last Focus Detail:" list box.

Explorer

Explorer shows strictly accessibility information and is the most useful utility for getting that information. When you move the mouse over a component and then pause it, Explorer shows the accessibility information for the component the mouse is placed over.

SETTING UP YOUR ENVIRONMENT You have to do a little work to prepare your environment to run this utility because the JVM has to know to start it up whenever you run a Java application. Follow these steps to prepare your environment:

1. Change your CLASSPATH.

   You need to add the jaccess.jar file to your CLASSPATH. This file is located in the directory where you installed the Java Accessibility pack.

   You also need to add the Explorer directory to your CLASSPATH. It's a directory called "Explorer" under the examples subdirectory in the directory where you installed the Java Accessibility pack.

2. Change your awt.properties file.

   There's an awt.properties file in the lib subdirectory under the directory where your JDK is installed. You need to add the following two lines to the end of that file:

   ```
   AWT.EventQueueClass=com.sun.java.accessibility.EventQueueMonitor
   AWT.AutoLoadClasses=Explorer
   ```

USING EXPLORER Using Explorer is very simple. All you have to do is move the mouse over the component you want accessibility information for and let it rest there for a moment. Once Explorer senses the pause, it gets the component's accessibility information and displays it. Of course, when you move the mouse to other components, the Explorer's information changes. Figure 6-2 shows a sample of what Explorer looks like.

Figure 6-2
The Explorer utility.

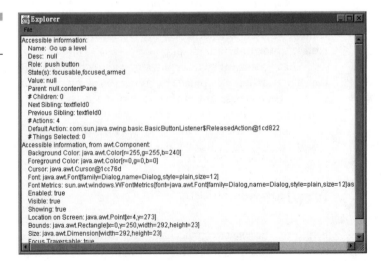

This utility is particularly useful because of the complete information it gives. The JavaMonitor utility gives a much more limited set of accessibility information.

Monkey

The Monkey utility allows you to compare the actual display hierarchy with the hierarchy of Accessible components.

SETTING UP YOUR ENVIRONMENT   You have to do a little work to prepare your environment to run this utility because the JVM has to know to start it up whenever you run a Java application. Follow these steps to prepare your environment:

1. Change your CLASSPATH.

    You need to add the jaccess.jar file to your CLASSPATH. This file is located in the directory where you installed the Java Accessibility pack.

    You also need to add the Monkey directory to your CLASSPATH. It's a directory called "Monkey" under the examples subdirectory in the directory where you installed the Java Accessibility pack.

2. Change your awt.properties file.

    There's an awt.properties file in the lib subdirectory under the directory where your JDK is installed. You need to add the following two lines to the end of that file:

```
AWT.EventQueueClass=com.sun.java.accessibility.EventQueueMonitor
AWT.AutoLoadClasses=Monkey
```

USING MONKEY   Monkey automatically comes up when you run your Java application. It displays a split pane, shown in Figure 6-3; the left side is a component hierarchy of your application, and the right side is the same thing except it's a hierarchy of accessible components. You can use the File menu's Refresh Trees option to update it.

Figure 6-3

The Monkey utility's split pane.

SUMMARY

This chapter has explored the different interfaces in the com.sun.java. accessibility package and has explained how to use different tools to see how accessible your applications look from the outside.

Adding accessibility to an application isn't always at the top of the corporate priority list. However, it's something that makes an application useful to more people. With the Accessibility API, JavaSoft has made it relatively easy to add accessible information to components and, therefore, to applications.

7

JFC by Concept

Chapter 8, "JFC by Class," covers the JFC classes in detail, one by one. In the real world, however, you don't generally look at a JFC class and say "What can I do with this class?" Instead, you look at the problem you're trying to solve and say "Which class or classes can help me solve this problem?" This chapter looks at the JFC as groups of components that solve particular types of problems, as well as the processes that tie them together. It should help you get from the type of problem you need to solve to the specific class you need. Although there's some necessary duplication between this chapter and Chapter 8, always look to that chapter for truly detailed information about specific JFC classes.

A Quick Review of the JDK 1.1 Event Model

The Need for Event Handling

The JFC has some great new components that let you make truly professional-looking user interfaces. No matter how great your interface looks, however, it's useless if it doesn't respond to user input. That's where event handling comes in.

Recognizing and dealing with user-initiated events is really the core of creating useful user interfaces. When the user clicks a button, he or she expects something to happen. What happens is handled by catching and reacting to events.

When input happens to a component—a mouse click on a button or entry into a text field—the default effect is for the component to do something with the input, but not to tell anyone the event happened. For instance, if you click the mouse on a button, the button changes its appearance so it looks pressed, but it doesn't notify any other class that it has been pressed—mainly because it doesn't know what classes to tell. Event handling, therefore, consists mostly of telling a component which classes it should notify when events happen and exactly which types of events these classes want to know about. Then, when a class is told that a particular type of event has happened to the component, the class can take appropriate action.

Event Listeners

Any class that wants to receive events is called a *listener*. To tell a component which listeners to notify about a particular type of event, you pass the listener class to one of the component's add . . . Listener() methods. What goes in the place of " . . . " depends on the type of event being listened for. If you want to listen for ActionEvents, for example, the method is addActionListener(); if you want to listen for MouseEvents, the method is addMouseListener().

The following line tells a JButton called "myButton" that another class called "myListener" wants to know when ActionEvents are generated:

```
myButton.addActionListener( myListener );
```

When myButton is pressed, it checks its list of registered action listeners and calls each of their actionPerformed() methods. That means each of these listener classes must *have* an actionPerformed() method. That's what the ActionListener interface, as shown here, is for:

```
public interface ActionListener extends EventListener
{
    public void actionPerformed( ActionEvent e );
}
```

So, any class passed as the argument to addActionListener() must implement the ActionListener interface.

Here are the steps for handling ActionEvents:

1. One or more classes register themselves as ActionListeners for myButton by using myButton's addActionListener() method. These registered classes have implemented the ActionListener interface.

2. The user clicks the myButton component.

3. myButton sees the click and figures that the click means the user has pressed the button.

4. myButton creates an ActionEvent because pressing a button is considered an action.

5. myButton goes through its list of registered ActionListeners and calls each one's actionPerformed() method, passing the just-created ActionEvent.

6. Each ActionListener's actionPerformed() method does something that's an appropriate response to myButton being pressed.

Different types of events have their own Listener interfaces. Here are the AWT Listener interfaces:

- **ActionListener:** Used for ActionEvents. Generated by buttons of different sorts (JButton, JCheckBox, JRadioButton, JMenuItem, and so on) and by JTextField.

- **AdjustmentListener:** Used for AdjustmentEvents. Generated by scrollbars.

- **ComponentListener:** Used for ComponentEvents. Generated by any component when it changes size, hides, or becomes visible.

- **ContainerListener:** Used for ContainerEvents. Generated by any container when a component is added to or removed from the container.

- **FocusListener:** Used for FocusEvents. Generated by components when they gain or lose focus.

- **ItemListener:** Used for ItemEvents. Generated by components that represent lists of things (JList, JComboBox) or by components that have a selected and a deselected state (JCheckBox, JRadioButton, JToggleButton) when an item changes state.

- **KeyListener:** Used for KeyEvents. Mostly generated by text components.

- **MouseListener:** Used for MouseEvents except for mouse motion events. Generated by any component when the mouse is clicked or released or enters or exits the component.
- **MouseMotionListener:** Used for MouseEvents that say when the mouse is moved or dragged.
- **TextListener:** Used for TextEvents. Generated by text components when the contents change.
- **WindowListener:** Used for WindowEvents. Generated by JWindow, JFrame, and JDialog when they change size, are opened, or are closed.

Here are the JFC Listener classes:

- **AncestorListener:** Used for AncestorEvents. Generated by any subclass of JComponent when it or one of its ancestors in the display hierarchy becomes visible or invisible or is added to or removed from the display hierarchy.
- **ChangeListener:** Used for ChangeEvents. Generated by a variety of components when something about them changes. A ChangeEvent is a kind of general statement of change; you have to ask the event source what the change was.
- **DocumentListener:** Used for events that implement the Document interface. Generated by Text Components when document elements are changed, inserted, or removed.
- **HyperlinkListener:** Used for HyperlinkEvents. Generated by a JEditorPane when the user clicks a hyperlink.
- **ListDataListener:** Used for ListDataEvents. Generated by a ListModel when when items are added or when one or more of its items change or are removed.
- **ListSelectionListener:** Used for ListSelectionEvents. Generated by a ListSelectionModel when its current selection changes.
- **MenuListener:** Used for MenuEvents. Generated by a JMenu when it displays or disappears or is cancelled.
- **PopupMenuListener:** Used for PopupMenuEvents. Generated by a JPopupMenu when it appears and disappears.
- **TableColumnModelListener:** Used for TableColumnModel events. Generated by a JTable's TableColumnModel when a column is added, moved, or removed, or when the column margins change or the column selection changes.
- **TableModelListener:** Used for TableModelEvents. Generated by a JTable's TableModel when its contents change.
- **TreeExpansionListener:** Used for TreeExpansionEvents. Generated by a JTree when a node that can have child nodes is expanded or collapsed.

- **TreeModelListener:** Used for TreeModelEvents. Generated by a JTree's TreeModel when its contents change.
- **TreeSelectionListener:** Used for TreeSelectionEvents. Generated by a JTree's TreeSelectionModel when nodes are selected or deselected.

NOTE: *See the component sections in this chapter for some additional information and also see each JFC component's section in Chapter 8 for examples of how many of these events are handled.*

Event Adapters

Many listener interfaces have more than one method that must be implemented. For example, the MouseListener interface looks like this:

```
public interface MouseListener extends EventListener
{
    public void mouseClicked(MouseEvent e);

    public void mousePressed(MouseEvent e);

    public void mouseReleased(MouseEvent e);

    public void mouseEntered(MouseEvent e);

    public void mouseExited(MouseEvent e);
}
```

If you want your class to be able to receive MouseEvents from another class, your class looks something like this:

```
import java.awt.event.*;

public class MyClass implements MouseListener
{
    public void mouseClicked( MouseEvent e )
    {
        // The event generating component just got
        // mouse-clicked.
    }

    public void mousePressed( MouseEvent e )
    {
        // The event generating component just got
        // mouse-pressed.
    }

    public void mouseReleased( MouseEvent e )
    {
```

```
        // The event generating component just got
        // mouse-released.
    }

    public void mouseEntered( MouseEvent e )
    {
        // The mouse just entered the event generating
        // component.
    }

    public void mouseExited( MouseEvent e )
    {
        // The mouse just left the event generating component.
    }
}
```

If you only care about one or two of these events, it's unfortunate that you have to implement the other three or four methods, even though you don't use them. To clean this up, Java has the concept of Adapter classes. Many event Listener interfaces that have more than one method to implement have an associated Adapter. All the Adapter does is implement a Listener's methods as empty methods. So, the MouseAdapter looks just like "MyClass" defined previously in that it implements the five MouseListener methods, and the methods don't do anything.

NOTE: *EventListeners introduced with the JFC don't have event adapters.*

Here's how to create a class that implements the MouseListener interface, but really just wants to know when the mouse enters or exits the event-generating component:

```
import java.awt.event.*;

public class MyAdapter extends MouseAdapter
{
    public void mouseEntered( MouseEvent e )
    {
        System.out.println
        ( "The mouse has entered the component" );
    }

    public void mouseExited( MouseEvent e )
    {
        System.out.println( "The mouse has left the
        component" );
    }
}
```

EXAMPLE 7-1 **Using an Event Adapter to Change a Component**

This example is built around a frame that contains two components: a Button and a TextField. We want the text field's contents to change whenever the mouse enters or exits the button, so we extend the MouseAdapter class to receive the button's mouse events. Notice that the text field is an instance variable, unlike the button itself, which is defined inside the frame's constructor. This is necessary so the MouseAdapter can modify the text field directly. We could have set it up so that the text field was passed to the MouseAdapter through a constructor, but that would limit the adapter to being able to listen to only a single component's events. Implementing the MouseAdapter as an inner class of a container is a standard practice because it gives the adapter access to the class's variables. Figure 7-1 shows the example after the mouse has been dragged through the button.

Following is the source code for the frame, including the inner class that listens for events. The parts that have to do with event handling are in italic. Everything in this example is straight JDK 1.1—there's nothing new introduced:

```java
import java.awt.*;
import java.awt.event.*;

public class MyFrame extends Frame
{
    // This is a class variable so that instances of
    // MyMouseListener can access it.

    TextField textField;

    public MyFrame()
    {
        // Set the frame's layout manager.

        setLayout( new BorderLayout() );

        // Create the Button.

        Button myButton = new Button( "Roll over me" );
        myButton.setBackground( Color.lightGray );

        // Place the Button in the frame's main display area.

        add( "North", myButton );

        // Create an instance of our mouse adapter.
```

Figure 7-1
The text field's contents change after the mouse exits the button.

```
    MyMouseListener mouser = new MyMouseListener();

    // Tell the Button to notify our mouse adapter when
    // mouse events occur on the Button.

    myButton.addMouseListener( mouser );

    // Create the text field.

    textField = new TextField();

    // Add the text field to the frame's main display
    // area.

    add( "South", textField );
}

// Here is our mouse adapter class.  It only overrides
// 'mouseEntered()' and 'mouseExited()'.  When the mouse
// passes over the class this adapter is listening to
// ('myButton' defined above), the Button calls the
// adapter's methods.  When the mouse enters the Button,
// the text field's string is set to "Entered".  When
// the mouse exits the Button, the text field's contents
// are set to "Exited".

private class MyMouseListener extends MouseAdapter
{
    public void mouseEntered( MouseEvent e )
    {
        textField.setText( "Entered" );
    }

    public void mouseExited( MouseEvent e )
    {
        textField.setText( "Exited" );
    }
}
}
```

Identifying the Source of an Event

Event Listener methods are generally used to cause something to happen to
another class, so the Listener methods need access to information from outside their Listener methods and often from outside their Listener class.
EventListeners are also used to handle events from more than one component, so when a Listener method like mouseExited() is called, you need to
know which component the mouse just exited. All events have a getSource()
method you can call to get the Object that generated the event:

```
public void mouseEntered( MouseEvent e )
{
    if ( e.getSource() == button1 )
        System.out.println( "Entered first button" );
    else if ( e.getSource() == button2 )
        System.out.println( "Entered second button" );
}
```

Of course, for this method to work, "button1" and "button2" must be visible to the mouseEntered() method, just as "textField" had to be visible in the previous example.

Some components like Button can associate a string with an event. This string can be used to identify the source of an event without the Listener method requiring access to the generating component. The string is associated with a Button by using the setActionCommand() method:

```
Button myButton = new Button( "Button 1" );
myButton.addActionListener( someActionListenerClass );
myButton.setActionCommand( "Button 1" );
```

An ActionListener listens for when a Button is pressed. The ActionListener interface has only one method: actionPerformed(). To get the action command string associated with an ActionEvent, we use the getActionCommand() method:

```
public void actionPerformed( ActionEvent e )
{
    if ( e.getActionCommand().equals( "Button 1" ) )
        System.out.println( "Button 1 was pressed" );
}
```

Notice that we had to put the string "Button 1" in two places: in the setActionCommand() method, and as a comparison to the getActionCommand() method. Instead of doing this, you might want to make a string constant and refer to it instead. That way, if you have to change the string, you don't have to change it in two places.

How Events Get from a Component to Its Event Listeners

Although it might seem so, events aren't magically transported from a component to its event listeners. There are certain steps an event passes through to get where it needs to be.

THE PROCESSEVENT(AWTEVENT) METHOD Every component has a processEvent() method, inherited initially from java.awt.Component. In this method, an event first becomes known to a component. For example, if you click the mouse on a component, a MouseEvent is generated through the virtual machine and the windowing system. Then the MouseEvent is sent to the component through its processEvent() method.

Normally, the processEvent() method then looks at the event and figures out its type (mouse event, key event, and so on). Based on the event's type, the processEvent() method then calls the method—usually one like processMouseEvent() or processKeyEvent()—that handles processing that type of event. These methods typically look at the details of the event, such as its ID, and then, for each EventListener registered for notification of that type of event, call the appropriate EventListener method.

For the MouseEvent mentioned previously, the MouseEvent is sent to the component through the component's processEvent() method. The processEvent() method sees that the event is a MouseEvent and sends it to the component's processMouseEvent() method. The processMouseEvent() method looks at the event and sees that it's a mouse click. Therefore, for every registered MouseListener, it calls the listener's mouseClicked() method, passing the MouseEvent.

The processEvent() method never gets events it will do nothing with. If the component doesn't use a particular type of event, and there are no listeners registered for that type of event, the component's processEvent() method isn't called when that type of event happens. If a component has any listeners registered for a type of event, processEvent() is called whenever an event of that type happens to the component.

Also, if the component has explicitly said it wants to get a type of event, regardless of whether there are any registered listeners, it can call the enableEvents() method and pass it the mask that corresponds to the type of event. The enableEvents() method is typically used when a component needs to catch an event that affects its appearance or when one type of event results in generating a different type of event. When the mouse is clicked on a button, the button should respond by altering its appearance so it looks pressed. The button can have registered MouseListeners, but usually other classes want to listen to ActionEvents, not MouseEvents. Therefore, the button will want to call enableEvents() with the mouse event mask set.

If you want to catch a component's event before it gets propagated to registered listeners, you should override the processEvent() method or one of the methods it calls (processMouseEvent(), processKeyEvent(), and so on). If you do this, make sure you call the superclass's version of the method when you're through if you want normal event processing to happen.

Double-Buffering

Before getting to double-buffering, you should understand the distinction between *lightweight* and *peered* components. All JFC components, with the exception of the ones managed by the operating system (JFrame, JWindow, JDialog), are lightweight components. A *lightweight component* is completely responsible for all aspects of its appearance and behavior; it draws every part of itself and defines how it handles all the events that come its way. This behavior is in contrast to AWT components—they are peered components. A *peered component* is a Java wrapper around a native control (called a "peer"). Peered components don't draw themselves; they let the operating system draw them. This distinction is important here because it means that using JFC components requires much more drawing, and more drawing makes double-buffering more important.

When you draw a JFC component, you typically lay down a colored background rectangle, and then draw the main body of the component, its border, and its children (if any). So what happens when you have a JFC button (JButton) on the screen and you press it? First, it draws a background rectangle, obscuring the JButton as it was drawn in its unpressed state, and then it draws itself in its pressed state. When you release the JButton, it overwrites itself again with its background rectangle, and then redraws itself in its unpressed state. Not surprisingly, this process makes the JButton look like it flashes every time it's redrawn, making your interface look amateurish. Flashing wasn't a problem with AWT components because the operating system took care of it automatically. It *was*, however, a problem in the AWT if you were drawing on a Canvas.

Double-buffering's main use is to cure flashing. When you use double-buffering, you draw to an offscreen buffer instead of drawing directly to the screen. Then, when the draw is complete, the offscreen buffer is slapped onto the screen all at once. That means you don't see a background rectangle being laid down, and you don't see individual parts being drawn. There's no flashing, and your user interface looks great.

Double-buffering is also used in animation. If you have an animation sequence made up of four images, you don't want the user to see that Image 1 has to be cleared away before Image 2 can be drawn. You want a smooth transition. So, you draw Image 2 to an offscreen buffer, and then you slap the buffer directly to the screen, completely overwriting Image 1. This method makes your animation much smoother and more professional-looking.

It wasn't too difficult to carry out double-buffering in the AWT, but you were definitely responsible for it yourself. If you had a Canvas you were drawing in and you wanted to double-buffer it, you had to do the following:

1. Allocate the offscreen buffer.
2. Make sure the buffer changes size whenever the Canvas changes size.
3. Paint into the offscreen buffer.
4. Paint the offscreen buffer to the display when drawing is finished.

If you had many double-buffered components, you also had many offscreen buffers, which took up more memory than it should have—especially if the buffered components overlapped on the screen.

Recognizing that the JFC definitely requires double-buffering, the JavaSoft people have made it the default behavior. JComponent, where most JFC components come from, implements double-buffering for you. You can still turn double-buffering off if you need to.

When you create a JFrame, its main display area is a JPanel with double-buffering turned on. If you add other panels to that panel, their double-buffering is taken care of by the main JPanel. If you run into a flashing problem, it's probably because the JFrame's main display JPanel has been replaced with another panel that's not double-buffered.

NOTE: *For related information, see the "JPanel," "JRootPane," "JComponent," and "JFrame" sections in Chapter 8.*

Allowing the User to Trigger Actions with Buttons

Every set of user interface components includes a control the user can press to cause something to happen. This type of control is generally called a *button*. The JFC includes a button component called "JButton." Figure 7-2 shows several examples.

JButton is typically a rectangular component that can include a text string, an icon, or both. When enabled, it has two possible states: normal and pressed. When you click the mouse on a JButton, it appears to be pushed down into its container while the mouse button is held down. Otherwise, the JButton looks like it's slightly raised, ready to be pushed in.

Commonly Set Properties

As mentioned, a JButton can display an icon. In fact, it can display different icons depending on its current state. It can have an icon for when it's pressed, when it's disabled, or when the mouse is passing over the component.

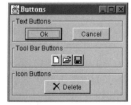

Figure 7-2
Some examples of JButton.

You can also change where the text/icon is displayed in relation to the button itself (upper-left, center, lower-right) as well as where the text is in relation to the icon (left, right, above, and so on).

Triggering the Action

When pressed and released, a JButton creates an ActionEvent and sends it out to each registered ActionListener. This procedure is how the JButton notifies other classes that it has been pressed. The JButton can have a command string, identifying which component generated the event, that it adds to every ActionEvent it generates.

Required Classes

The JButton class is one of three classes required to make a JFC button work. The other two are the ButtonModel and the look-and-feel class that extends the ButtonUI class. You don't have to create the ButtonModel and look-and-feel classes. JButton creates a DefaultButtonModel class and gets the look-and-feel class from the currently plugged-in look-and-feel. Here's how the three classes split up the work:

- **JButton:** This class is the one other classes interact with—it's the outside world's view of a JFC button. JButton stores the visual attributes needed to draw the button, as well as the instances of the ButtonModel and the look-and-feel class. Visual attributes include the border, the icons, the text string, and so on. JButton contains the paint() method, but the paint() method calls other methods that allow the look-and-feel class to do the actual drawing.

- **ButtonModel:** This class stores the button's internal state, indicating whether the button is disabled, whether it's pressed, whether the mouse is rolling over the button, and so on. The look-and-feel class uses this state information when it's drawing the button so it can represent the button's current state properly.

- **The look-and-feel class:** This class defines the button's appearance and behavior and is called something like BasicButtonUI or MotifButtonUI. It responds to events and does the actual painting of the button, using information from both the JButton and ButtonModel classes to draw the button accurately. That's because the look-and-feel class doesn't store any state information. This class is associated with the look-and-feel currently in use. When a new look-and-feel is plugged in, this class is replaced by another class that also implements the ButtonUI interface. Because these look-and-feel classes don't store any state information, you can plug in new look-and-feels on the fly without changing the button's internal state.

NOTE: *For more information, see the "JButton," "AbstractButton," "ImageIcon," and "DefaultButtonModel" sections in Chapter 8. You can also refer back to Chapter 4, "Pluggable Look-and-Feel."*

Components That Can Be Turned On and Off

Most user interfaces have certain components that control whether a property is turned on or off or whether a particular tool or option is selected. These components are either selected or not selected, and their current state is reflected in their appearance. Figure 7-3 shows some JFC components in their selected or deselected states.

JCheckBox is a component that's typically used to allow the user to turn a particular property on and off. It normally has a text string that describes the property being set and a box or an icon used to show the property's current state. If a box is used instead of an icon, it's empty if the property is off or contains a checkmark if the property is on. If an icon is used, one icon should represent the on state and another should represent the off state. When the mouse is clicked on the JCheckBox's text or box/icon, its state changes.

A JCheckBox could be used when, for example, you want to give users the opportunity to turn the status bar off in your application. You could give them a JCheckBox with the text "Status Bar" and an initial state of on. If they click the component, the status bar goes away, but they can always click it again to make the status bar come back.

JRadioButton is a component that normally occurs as one of a set of JRadioButtons. The set represents a group of options, and only one can be selected at a time. When one of the set is clicked, the set's previously selected button becomes deselected, and the clicked one becomes selected. By de-

Figure 7-3

Components' appearances reflect their current state.

fault, JRadioButtons don't enforce the one-at-a-time rule because they don't know which other JRadioButtons make up their set. To associate them in a set, add them to a ButtonGroup to make sure only one of the set is selected at any time.

A JRadioButton is like a JCheckBox in that it has a text string that briefly describes the item being selected or deselected and a box or an icon that indicates its current state. The main difference is that a JRadioButton's box is often a circle rather than a square and contains a dot instead of a checkmark. Like a JCheckBox, if you use an icon, you need to specify two to represent both the selected and deselected states.

JRadioButtons can be used when, for example, your application needs to allow users to choose printing in either portrait or landscape mode. Obviously, you can't print in both, so you must be able to prevent the user from choosing both. You might start with landscape mode turned on, and then when they click on portrait mode, landscape is deselected and portrait is selected.

JToggleButton is another component often used as one of a set, although it doesn't have to be. A JToggleButton looks like a regular button, but when the user presses it, it stays pressed even when the user releases the mouse. It doesn't come back up until it's clicked again. In this way, it's like a JCheckBox or a JRadioButton because it always has a selected or deselected state and visually reflects what its current state is. Although a JToggleButton can have text like a regular button, it's far more common to leave the text off and just give it an icon.

Unlike JCheckBox and JRadioButton, it's not standard to change the icon when the JToggleButton's state changes. Instead, the change of state is reflected by the JToggleButton appearing to be pushed in when it's selected. You *can* change the icon as well, but it's not necessary.

JToggleButtons can be used like JCheckBoxes to represent the state of a single property or like JRadioButtons to show which one of a set of items is selected. They can be added to a ButtonGroup to enforce the rule that only one of the set can be selected at a time.

JToggleButtons are often used in toolbars and tool palettes. For example, a paint program's tool palette might have six tools: a select tool, a line draw tool, a circle tool, a text tool, a fill tool, and a polygon tool. Each tool could be represented as a JToggleButton with an icon. In this case, the six JToggleButtons would be added to a ButtonGroup because you want only one of them selected at a time.

Commonly Set Properties

If you use an icon on these components, you can replace it with other icons to show changes in the components' states. You can change it to reflect whether the component is selected, whether it's disabled, and whether the mouse is currently placed over it.

You can also change where the text/icon/box is located within the component (upper-left, upper-right, and so on), as well as where the text is in relation to the icon (left, right, above, and so on).

State-Change Events

The most important event from JCheckBoxes, JRadioButtons, and JToggle-Buttons is the ItemEvent. When one of these components changes its state, it creates an ItemEvent and sends it to all its registered ItemListeners. As descendants of the AbstractButton class, these classes can also generate ActionEvents when clicked. ActionEvents aren't as useful as ItemEvents because they don't carry the clicked component's new state, and they are generated even if a state change didn't result from the click (if an already selected JRadioButton was clicked).

When a component that's part of a ButtonGroup gets selected, you actually get two events because its selection also causes the previously selected item to be deselected. Therefore, registered ItemListeners get one event when the previously selected item is deselected and another when the new item is selected.

Required Classes

JCheckBox, JRadioButton, and JToggleButton each require two other classes to work: a ButtonModel class and a look-and-feel class that extends the abstract ButtonUI class. You don't have to create these classes yourself. Each of the three components creates its own DefaultButtonModel class, and they get their look-and-feel classes from the currently plugged-in look-and-feel. Here's how the classes divide up the work:

- **JCheckBox, JRadioButton, JToggleButton:** These classes are how the rest of the world sees these components. They contain references to their ButtonModel and look-and-feel classes. They also contain information about their external state, such as the current border, text string, and icons. They don't do any painting—their paint() methods by default call other methods that tell the look-and-feel to do it. Only by overriding the paint() method or one of the methods it calls can you make these classes draw themselves.

- **ButtonModel:** This class contains the component's internal state—whether it's selected, whether it's disabled, and so on. The look-and-feel class accesses this class's information so it can draw the component accurately.

■ **ButtonGroup:** This class is used with JRadioButtons and can be used with JToggleButtons to make sure only one of the set of buttons added to the ButtonGroup can be selected at a time.

■ **The look-and-feel class:** JCheckBox, JRadioButton, and JToggleButton use different look-and-feel classes because they look and behave differently. Their look-and-feel classes have names like WindowsCheckBoxUI, WindowsRadioButtonUI, and MotifToggleButtonUI ("Windows" and "Motif" are from the currently plugged-in look-and-feel). These classes take care of actually drawing the components in their current state. They also handle responding to events that occur on the components. The look-and-feel classes don't store any state information, so they must access the main component and ButtonModel classes to get the information they need to draw the components properly.

NOTE: *For more information, see the "JCheckBox," "JRadioButton," "JToggleButton," "AbstractButton," "ImageIcon," "ButtonGroup," and "DefaultButtonModel" sections in Chapter 8. You can also refer back to Chapter 4.*

Component Borders

A *border* is what a component uses to define how its edges look. Not all components support borders—just descendants of JComponent. When a component that supports borders paints itself, it passes its graphics context to its current border, and the border paints itself. Then the component does its usual drawing within that border. Figure 7-4 shows examples of several JFC borders.

All borders implement the Border interface, which includes three methods:

■ **getBorderInsets(Component c):** This method calculates the width of the border on each side of the component and then returns those widths as an Insets class. This is important because the component needs to know where it can draw without overwriting the border.

■ **isBorderOpaque():** This method returns true if the border draws all of its space and false if it draws only in part.

Figure 7-4
Different types
of borders.

■ **paintBorder(Component c, Graphics g, int x, int y, int width, int height):** This method allows the border to paint itself on the component.

When a descendant of JComponent is painted, its paint() method calls its paintBorder() method, which calls the border's paintBorder() method. Then it uses the border's getBorderInsets() method to find out how much space it has left in which to draw itself. If the component's paint() method is overridden and paintBorder() never gets called, the border isn't drawn.

Borders can be used in different ways. They are often used to group related components in a dialog box. They can also be used to make a component appear set into its container or raised above it, or they can be used to emphasize a particular component to make it look important. You can also combine borders to make them more intricate.

All the JFC borders are subclasses of the AbstractBorder class. Here are the JFC borders:

■ **BevelBorder:** This border creates the effect that the component it surrounds is raised or lowered in relation to the surrounding container. It's used to make text fields appear set into their container or to make internal frames appear raised above their container.

■ **CompoundBorder:** This border combines two borders, one inside the other, to make a single, more complex border.

■ **EmptyBorder:** This border puts empty space around the edge of a component. If you create a panel and want all its components to be at least 10 pixels from the edge, you could use an EmptyBorder.

■ **EtchedBorder:** This border makes it look like a thin groove has been carved into its component all the way around. EtchedBorder is most commonly used as part of a TitledBorder.

■ **LineBorder:** This border draws a line all the way around the edge of a component. You can set the line's color and width.

■ **MatteBorder:** This border covers the edge of a component, either with a solid color or with copies of an image. You set the width of the border on each side of its component and then specify the color or the image used to fill the border.

■ **SoftBevelBorder:** This border is just like a BevelBorder except that the corners are slightly rounded.

■ **TitledBorder:** This border takes another border and places a text string in a break in the border. TitledBorders often use EtchedBorders —in fact, the simplest constructor for TitledBorder uses an EtchedBorder by default. TitledBorders are commonly used to group related components in dialogs because the text string helps tell the user why the components are grouped.

Because descendants of JComponent have the setBorder() method, which can be used to change their borders, some interesting effects can be achieved by doing so. For example, you can change an internal frame's border to a lowered BevelBorder so it looks sunken into its desktop pane, or you can give a text field an EmptyBorder so it blends into its container. However, this technique doesn't work well on some components. A JButton, for instance, relies on its own special border to show whether it's pressed. Other components, such as JCheckBox, show no effect when you change the border.

It's important to note that a component's look-and-feel doesn't have to honor changes to the component's border. The look-and-feel is free to hard-code the border, so calling setBorder() would have no effect.

NOTE: *For more information, see the "AbstractBorder," "BevelBorder," "CompoundBorder," "EmptyBorder," "EtchedBorder," "LineBorder," "MatteBorder," "SoftBevelBorder," and "TitledBorder" sections in Chapter 8. You can also refer back to Chapter 3, "The JComponent Class" for methods used to assign a border to a component.*

Menus

Menus let you give users access to all your application's capabilities without having to clutter the display. Through menus, the user can set properties, display and hide application windows and dialogs, exit the application, access help, and do many other things. Figure 7-5 shows an application frame with a menu attached to a menu bar.

JFC menus are either attached as frame menus to a menu bar or appear as popup menus in response to special user actions. Whether a menu is attached to a menu bar or pops up somewhere else, the menu's capabilities are the same. Menus typically have one or more menu items, which are standard menu items, radio button menu items, check box menu items, or other menus. When the user clicks on one of these items, the result depends on the type of item it is.

Figure 7-5
A menu attached to a menu bar.

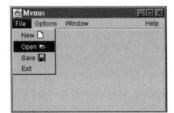

The Menu Components

JMENUBAR   This component typically appears at the top of a JFrame, JWindow, or JInternalFrame. In these cases, it's added through the JFrame, JWindow, or JInternalFrame's root pane. A JMenuBar is just a component, so it can be added to a container just as any other component can, but that's not commonly done. A JMenuBar contains a set of JMenus, with each JMenu represented as a text string within the JMenuBar. When the user clicks one of the text strings, the associated menu pops up under the text string and displays its menu items.

JMenuBar, like all JComponent descendants, is also a descendant of java.awt.Container. It uses a BoxLayout layout manager. Although usually only JMenus are added to a JMenuBar, there's no reason why other components can't be added, as long as they implement the MenuElement interface.

It's not commonly done, but you can change some JMenuBar properties, such as its border.

JMENUBAR'S REQUIRED CLASSES   JMenuBar requires two other classes to do its job: a class that implements the SingleSelectionModel interface, and a look-and-feel class that extends the abstract MenuBarUI class. You don't have to create these classes yourself—JMenuBar creates a DefaultSingleSelectionModel class and gets a class that extends the MenuBar UI class from the currently plugged-in look-and-feel. Here's how the classes divide the work:

- **JMenuBar:** This class represents the menu bar to the rest of the world. It contains references to the SingleSelectionModel class and the look-and-feel class. It also stores information about the component's external appearance, such as what its current border is. As a descendant of Container, JMenuBar also stores child components, such as JMenus, and whatever else you add.

- **SingleSelectionModel:** This class keeps track of what menu is currently selected, if any. When a menu is clicked, the look-and-feel class is notified. It then figures out which menu is selected, gets the SingleSelectionModel from the JMenuBar class, and sets it to reflect the new selection.

- **The look-and-feel class:** This class is responsible for drawing the menu bar and for responding to events that occur in it. It doesn't store any state information, so it has to get information about properties such as its border from the JMenuBar class and information about which menu is selected from the SingleSelectionModel class, so it can properly draw the menu bar in its current state. The actual class is gotten from the currently plugged-in look-and-feel and has a name like WindowsMenuBarUI or MotifMenuBarUI.

NOTE: *For more information, see the "JMenuBar" and "DefaultSingleSelection-Model" sections in Chapter 8. You can also refer back to Chapter 4.*

JMENU This component appears in two ways. When it's added to a JMenuBar, it appears as a text string inside the JMenuBar. When the user clicks on that text string, the JMenu expands the real menu under its menu bar text string, displaying all its menu items. Only one of a menu bar's menus is expanded at a time.

As a descendant of JComponent, JMenu is also a descendant of java.awt.Container, so you can add other components into it. Usually, they include only the standard menu items: JMenuItem, JCheckBoxMenuItem, JRadioButtonMenuItem, JSeparator, and other JMenus, but there's no prohibition against adding other components, as long as they implement the MenuElement interface. If you add other components, you might have to do some special processing. Normally, when you click on a menu item, the menu closes up unless the item is another menu, in which case the original menu remains showing and the submenu is also displayed. When you add a non-menu item component to a JMenu, it works fine, except the JMenu doesn't close up after you press on the component.

JMenu actually uses a JPopupMenu to display itself in its expanded state. This is reasonable because at that point, it's a popup menu placed so that it looks attached to the menu bar.

You can set JMenu properties, such as the font it uses in its menu bar text string. You can also give it an icon to accompany that text.

JMENU REQUIRED CLASSES Besides JMenuBar, JMenu requires two other classes to do its job: the JPopupMenu it uses to display itself expanded and a look-and-feel class that extends the MenuUI abstract class. You don't have to create these classes yourself—JMenu creates a JPopupMenu class and gets its look-and-feel class from the currently plugged-in look-and-feel. Here's how the classes divide the work:

- **JMenu:** This class represents the menu to the rest of the world. It contains references to the JPopupMenu and look-and-feel classes. It also contains information about its external state, such as its text string and font. As far as the menu items added to the JMenu, they are actually stored inside the JPopupMenu class.

- **JPopupMenu:** This class is used to display the JMenu's menu items when the user brings the JMenu up. It includes all the configurability of a regular JPopupMenu. It actually has its own look-and-feel class, but that's discussed in the next section.

- **The look-and-feel class:** This class is responsible for drawing the menu as it appears in the menu bar and for responding to events that occur on it there. It's not responsible for the popup menu's look-and-feel, and it doesn't store any state information. It gets information like the text string, icon, and font from the JMenu class so it can draw the component properly. The actual class is gotten from the currently plugged-in look-and-feel and has a name like WindowsMenuUI or MotifMenuUI.

NOTE: *For more information, see the "JMenu" and "JPopupMenu" sections in Chapter 8. You can also refer back to Chapter 4.*

JPOPUPMENU   This component is used to display an expanded menu. It's either used by itself as a menu that appears anywhere or used as part of a JMenu—apparently attached to a menu bar. It looks like a rectangular window and contains one or more menu items. These items can include almost any component that implements the MenuElement interface but are normally one of the standard menu item components: JMenuItem, JCheckBoxMenuItem, JRadioButtonMenuItem, or JMenu. The same difficulties with nonmenu items in JMenus applies to JPopupMenus.

When you use a JPopupMenu directly (not as part of a JMenu), you usually display it in response to some user event. For example, in Windows 95, when you right-click on an icon, a popup menu comes up that allows you to see information about the icon and the thing it represents. The popup menu is typically displayed at the point where the mouse was right-clicked. This kind of context-sensitive popup menu is common.

JPopupMenu is displayed as either a Frame or a JPanel. If it fits within the area of its parent frame, it's displayed as a JPanel; if it extends outside its parent frame, it's displayed as a Frame.

Within a JDialog, JPopupMenus are always displayed as JPanels, so it is important to make your dialogs large enough to display your menus.

JPOPUPMENU REQUIRED CLASSES   JPopupMenu requires two other classes to get its job done: a class that implements the SingleSelectionModel interface, and a look-and-feel class that extends the abstract PopupMenuUI class. You don't have to create either of these classes. JPopupMenu creates a DefaultSingleSelectionModel and gets its look-and-feel class from the currently plugged-in look-and-feel. Here's how the classes divide up the work:

■ **JPopupMenu:** This class represents the popup menu to the rest of the world. It contains references to the SingleSelectionModel class and the look-and-feel class. As a Container, it stores the menu item components that have been added to it. It also stores information about its external state, like its border.

■ **SingleSelectionModel:** This class stores which menu item is currently selected, if any. When a menu item is clicked, the look-and-feel class is notified. It then gets the SingleSelectionModel class from the JPopupMenu class and modifies it so that it reflects the new selection.

- **The look-and-feel class:** This class is responsible for drawing the JPopupMenu and for responding to events that occur on it. It doesn't store any state information, so it has to get information such as the border from the JPopupMenu class and information about which item is selected from the SingleSelectionModel, so it can properly draw the popup menu in its current state. The actual class is gotten from the currently plugged-in look-and-feel and is called something like WindowsPopupMenuUI or MotifPopupMenuUI.

NOTE: *For more information, see the "JPopupMenu" and "DefaultSingleSelectionModel" sections in Chapter 8. You can also refer back to Chapter 4.*

JMENUITEM This component is like a button in a menu. It typically appears as a text string (possibly with an icon) in a JMenu or JPopupMenu. When you press it, it causes something to happen. Unlike a JButton, pressing a JMenuItem doesn't change its appearance. Instead, when you press and release the mouse on a JMenuItem, the menu that contains it closes up.

You can change a JMenuItem's appearance by changing its font, its border, and its background and text colors. You can cause its icon (if used) to change when the mouse is clicked on the item. You can also change how the item's text/icon is aligned, as well as their positions in relation to each other. Much of this functionality comes from JMenuItem being descended from AbstractButton.

MAKING THINGS HAPPEN When a JMenuItem is clicked and released, it generates an ActionEvent and distributes it to all registered ActionListeners. This is how JMenuItem tells other classes it has been clicked. You can also assign a command string that's delivered with any ActionEvents a JMenuItem generates, which can be used to help identify the component generating the events.

JMENUITEM REQUIRED CLASSES JMenuItem requires two other classes to do its job: a class that implements the ButtonModel interface and a look-and-feel class that extends the abstract MenuItemUI class. You don't have to create either of these classes. JMenuItem creates a DefaultButtonModel class, and gets the look-and-feel class from the currently plugged-in look-and-feel. Here's how the classes divide up the work:

- **JMenuItem:** This class is the one that other classes interact with— it's the outside world's view of a menu item. JMenuItem stores references to the ButtonModel and the look-and-feel class. It also stores the visual attributes needed to draw the menu item, such as the border, the icons, the text string, and so on. It contains the paint() method, but the paint() method calls other methods that allow the look-and-feel class to do the actual drawing.

■ **ButtonModel:** This class stores the menu item's internal state, such as whether the menu item is disabled, pressed, and so on. The look-and-feel class accesses this state information when it's drawing the menu item so that it can represent the menu item's current state properly.

■ **The look-and-feel class:** This class defines the appearance and behavior of the menu item and is called something like WindowsMenuItemUI or MotifMenuItemUI. It responds to events and does the actual painting of the menu item. This class has to access information from both the JMenuItem and ButtonModel classes to draw the menu item accurately because it doesn't store any state information. This class is associated with the look-and-feel currently in use.

NOTE: *For more information, see the "JMenuItem," "AbstractButton," and "DefaultButtonModel" sections in Chapter 8. You can also refer back to Chapter 4.*

JCHECKBOXMENUITEM This is basically a check box in a menu. A JCheckBoxMenuItem is always either selected or deselected, and its appearance reflects its current state. When a JCheckBoxMenuItem is selected, it has a checkmark next to it. If not, there's no checkmark. A JCheckBoxMenuItem has a text string and/or an icon. Unlike JCheckBox, the icon is just for decoration; it doesn't change to reflect the component's current state.

You can set a variety of display properties for a JCheckBoxMenuItem. You can set its font, icon and text string, and background color. You can also specify where in the control the text/icon is displayed (left-aligned, for example). You can specify the text's position in relation to the icon, too (if you're using both text and icon).

REACTING WHEN A JCHECKBOXMENUITEM IS CLICKED When a JCheckBoxMenuItem is clicked, its state changes. When that happens, the JCheckBoxMenuItem creates an ItemEvent and distributes it to all registered ItemListeners. When an ItemListener is notified of the change, it can ask the ItemEvent what the new state is.

JCHECKBOXMENUITEM REQUIRED CLASSES JCheckBoxMenuItem requires two other classes to do its job: a class that implements the ButtonModel interface, and a look-and-feel class that extends the abstract CheckBoxMenuItemUI class. You don't have to create either class. JCheckBoxMenuItem creates a DefaultButtonModel class and gets the look-and-feel class from the currently plugged-in look-and-feel. Here's how the classes divide up the work:

■ **JCheckBoxMenuItem:** This is the class that represents the check box menu item to the rest of the world. It contains references to the ButtonModel and look-and-feel classes. It also stores information about the check box menu item's external state, such as the text

string, the icon, and the background color. It contains the paint()
method, but that method calls other ones that pass off the actual
painting to the look-and-feel class.

■ **ButtonModel:** This class stores the check box menu item's internal
state—whether it's selected, disabled, and so on. The look-and-feel
class accesses this information so it can draw the component in its
current state.

■ **The look-and-feel class:** This class defines the appearance and
behavior of the check box menu item. It responds to events on the
component and also does the actual drawing of the component. It
accesses the text string, icon, and so on from the
JCheckBoxMenuItem class and the state information from the
ButtonModel class. This class doesn't store information itself because
a new look-and-feel class could be plugged in at any time. The actual
look-and-feel class being used is called something like
WindowsCheckBoxMenuItemUI or MotifCheckBoxMenuItemUI.

NOTE: *For more information, see the "JCheckBoxMenuItem," "AbstractButton,"
and "DefaultButtonModel" sections in Chapter 8. You can also refer back to
Chapter 4.*

JRADIOBUTTONMENUITEM   JRadioButtonMenuItem is basically a
radio button in a menu. It typically occurs as one of a set of JRadioButton-
MenuItems, with all of them part of a ButtonGroup so that only one can be
selected at a time. A JRadioButtonMenuItem has a text string and/or an
icon and displays its current state (selected or deselected) by placing a dot
to the left of the text icon. Unlike a JRadioButton, if a JRadioButtonMenu-
Item uses an icon, it's for decoration only—it doesn't reflect the component's
current state.

You can set a variety of JRadioButtonMenuItem properties, such as the
font, the text string and icon, and the background color. You can also specify
where the text/icon appears within the component (upper-left, for example) as
well as the text string's location in relation to the icon (if there is one).

REACTING WHEN A JRADIOBUTTONMENUITEM CHANGES STATE   When a JRadioButtonMenuItem is clicked, one of two things happens. First, if it's already
selected, it remains selected. Second, if it's not already selected, the currently
selected item from its ButtonGroup becomes deselected, and the clicked item
becomes selected. Every time a JRadioButtonMenuItem changes state, it creates an ItemEvent and distributes it to all its registered ItemListeners. When
the user selects a new item, then, two events are generated—one from the
previously selected item as it becomes deselected and one from the newly selected item. When an ItemListener is notified of a state change, it can query
the ItemEvent for the changed item's new state.

JRADIOBUTTONMENUITEM REQUIRED CLASSES JRadioButtonMenuItem requires two other classes to do its job: a class that implements the Button-Model interface and a look-and-feel class that extends the abstract RadioButtonMenuItemUI class. You don't have to create either class. JRadioButtonMenuItem creates a DefaultButtonModel class and gets the look-and-feel class from the currently plugged-in look-and-feel. Here's how the classes divide up the work:

- ■ **JRadioButtonMenuItem:** This is the class that represents the radio button menu item to the rest of the world. It contains references to the ButtonModel and look-and-feel classes. It also stores information about the radio button menu item's external state, such as the text string, the icon, and the background color. In addition, it contains the paint() method, but that method passes off the actual painting to the look-and-feel class.

- ■ **ButtonModel:** This class stores the radio button menu item's internal state—whether it's selected, disabled, and so on. The look-and-feel class accesses this information so that it can draw the component in its current state.

- ■ **ButtonGroup:** Related JRadioButtonMenuItems are added to a ButtonGroup so that only one of the items can be selected at a time.

- ■ **The look-and-feel class:** This class defines the appearance and behavior of the radio button menu item. It responds to events on the component and also does the actual drawing of the component. It accesses the text string, icon, and so on from the JRadioButtonMenuItem class and the state information from the ButtonModel class. This class doesn't store information itself because a new look-and-feel class could be plugged in at any time. The actual look-and-feel class being used is called something like WindowsRadioButtonMenuItemUI or MotifRadioButtonMenuItemUI.

NOTE: *For more information, see the "JRadioButtonMenuItem," "ButtonGroup," "AbstractButton," and "DefaultButtonModel" sections in Chapter 8. You can also refer back to Chapter 4.*

JFC Containers

The JFC has components, called *containers*, whose main function is to hold other components. Some are general and can be heavily configured, and others are very specialized for a particular use. One of the benefits of containers

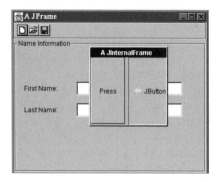

Figure 7-6
Types of JFC
containers.

is that you can add other containers to them, so if a single type of container doesn't meet your needs, perhaps a combination of containers will. Figure 7-6 shows several different types of JFC containers (JPanel, JToolBar, JDesktopPane, JRootPane, and JSplitPane). JFrame and JInternalFrame are actually covered in the "Windows" section of this chapter.

All the JFC containers in this section (except for Box, which is a special case) are descendants of JComponent, so they can have different look-and-feels, tool tips, and borders, among other things.

Because all descendants of JComponent are also descendants of Container, they all have the potential to contain other components. The difference between the classes in this section and the other JFC classes is that these classes contain other components as their main function.

JPanel

JPanel is a very general container. It's the class you will most often use to group components together. You can also use it as a drawing canvas. You can set the border to whatever you want and set the layout manager, too, without disrupting JPanel's designed operation.

Not only will you often add components to a JPanel, you will also add other JPanels frequently. This is usually the way a user interface is built up—you create the different parts with their own layouts and borders, and then you put the parts together.

JPANEL REQUIRED CLASSES JPanel doesn't require any other classes. It's a lightweight container with no look-and-feel class.

NOTE: *For more information, see the "JPanel" section in Chapter 8, the "Component Borders" section in this chapter, and Chapter 3, "The JComponent Class." You can also refer back to Chapter 4.*

Box

Box is different from the other JFC containers, not just because it doesn't descend from JComponent, but also because its greatest value is in the static methods it provides for creating padding components. Box is a direct descendant of java.awt.Container. It uses a BoxLayout, and you can't change the layout manager. A Box is useful for holding a row or a column of components.

Even if you never use a Box, you will probably use the Box class's static methods for creating padding components, especially if you use a BoxLayout. These methods create dummy components that either grow (in one or both directions) as the container grows or take up a preset amount of space (in one or both directions), no matter how the container grows or shrinks. The components created are very useful for controlling the spacing between components as a container changes size.

Because Box isn't a descendant of JComponent, you can't give it a border. If you want to use a Box but need a border, try using a JPanel instead and give it a BoxLayout.

NOTE: *For more information, see the "Box" and "BoxLayout" sections in Chapter 8.*

JLayeredPane

JLayeredPane is a general container for controlling components that overlap. Its main role is as the parent class of JDesktopPane.

When you add components to a JLayeredPane, you should use the component's setBounds() method to place it because JLayeredPane uses a null layout manager. Although you're allowed to change the layout manager, it's not advisable.

Components added to a JLayeredPane can be given relative layer values, which determine what components are on top of other components.

JLAYEREDPANE REQUIRED CLASSES   JLayered doesn't require any other classes. It's a lightweight container with no look-and-feel class.

NOTE: *For more information, see the "JLayeredPane" and "JDesktopPane" sections in Chapter 8. You can also refer back to Chapter 4.*

JDesktopPane

JDesktopPane is a container used for managing JInternalFrames. You can add JInternalFrames to a JDesktopPane, which takes care of how they resize and minimize. Because JDesktopPane is a descendant of JLayered-Pane, you can set the relative layers of the JInternalFrames. Like JLay-eredPane, JDesktopPane uses a null layout manager. Don't change the layout manager, or the JDesktopPane's JInternalFrames will always be layed out again by it when the pane is resized or layed out again for any other reason. By setting the layout manager, you lose much of what you want from JInternalFrames.

JDESKTOPPANE REQUIRED CLASSES JDesktopPane requires two other classes to get its work done: a class that implements the Desktop-Manager interface and a look-and-feel class that extends the abstract Desk-topPaneUI class. You don't have to create these classes yourself. JDesktopPane creates a DefaultDesktopManager class and gets the look-and-feel class from the currently plugged-in look-and-feel. Here's how the classes divide up the work:

- **JDesktopPane:** This class is how the rest of the world interacts with the desktop pane. It contains references to the DesktopManager class and the look-and-feel class. As a descendant of Container, it stores all the JInternalFrames added to it. It also stores all layer information and provides access to its contents either on a component-by-component basis or by layer.
- **DesktopManager:** The JDesktopPane uses a class that implements the DesktopManager interface to take care of look-and-feel–dependent operations with its internal frames.
- **DesktopPaneUI:** This class handles drawing the desktop pane, but not the internal frames—they have their own look-and-feel classes. The actual class, called something like WindowsDesktopPaneUI or MotifDesktopPaneUI, is gotten from the currently plugged-in look-and-feel.

NOTE: *For more information, see the "JDesktopPane," "JLayeredPane," and "JInternalFrame," sections in Chapter 8. You can also refer back to Chapter 4.*

JRootPane

JRootPane is a unique component with a well-defined role. It acts as the only child for JWindows, JDialogs, JFrames, and JInternalFrames, and completely controls access to its parent's display area. In the AWT, you add components directly to the Window, Frame, or Dialog. You should no longer do so, however; you should always add components through the root pane.

A JRootPane has four parts: the Menu Bar, the Content Pane, the Layered Pane, and the Glass Pane.

THE MENU BAR   This represents the window, dialog, frame, or internal frame's main menu bar, which appears just below the title bar (if there is one). There's no default Menu Bar assigned to a root pane, so if you want to use one, you have to add it yourself. You do this by creating a JMenuBar and passing it to the root pane with its setMenuBar() method.

THE CONTENT PANE   This represents the main display area of the window, dialog, frame, or internal frame. If you want to add components, the Content Pane is where you add them. You can use the default Content Pane, which is an instance of JPanel, by using the root pane's getContentPane() method, or you can replace the Content Pane with a container of your own by using the root pane's setContentPane() method.

THE LAYERED PANE   The Layered Pane is an instance of JLayeredPane and acts as the parent to the Menu Bar, the Content Pane, and the Glass Pane. It puts the Menu Bar and Content Pane in the same layer (FRAME_CONTENT_LAYER).

THE GLASS PANE   This pane is transparent and can completely overlay the window, dialog, frame, or internal frame's main area. When set to visible, it's still invisible but can be used to intercept any input to the components in the root pane's Content Pane or Layered Pane.

NOTE: *For more information, see the "JRootPane," "JMenuBar," "JLayered-Pane," "JPanel," "JFrame," "JWindow," "JDialog," and "JInternalFrame" sections in Chapter 8.*

JToolBar

JToolBar is a fairly general container that can be dragged around inside its parent container and "docked" in a new position or left floating in its own window. To support the "docking" behavior, the JToolBar's parent container should use a BorderLayout.

To drag a JToolBar, click in an area that doesn't have components in it and drag. Move it away from its original position and drop it; it becomes a stand-alone window with the JToolBar in it. To dock the JToolBar, drag it from the standalone window to its new position. When the outline changes color, drop it.

Using dockable JToolBars is not advisable since the behavior is confusing and still has some bugs.

By default, JToolBar uses a horizontal BoxLayout. You can change that to another layout, if you like.

JToolBars generally contain icon-only JButtons or icon-only JToggleBut-tons, depending on how you want them to work. The components in a JTool-

Bar can also be spaced with a separator or one of the Box component's padding components.

You can also set the JToolBar's border style to give it a new look.

JTOOLBAR REQUIRED CLASSES JToolBar requires one other class to do its job: a look-and-feel class that extends the abstract ComponentUI class. Here's how the classes divide up the work:

- **JToolBar:** This is the class that represents the toolbar to the rest of the world. It contains a reference to the look-and-feel class. As a descendant of Container, it stores all the components added to it. It also stores information about its external state, such as its current border.
- **The look-and-feel class:** This class does the actual drawing of the toolbar and responds to events that happen in it. It gets information from JToolBar so that it can draw the toolbar accurately. This class doesn't store any state information because it can be replaced on the fly when the look-and-feel is changed. The actual class, called something like WindowsToolBarUI or MotifToolBarUI, is gotten from the current look-and-feel.

NOTE: *For more information, see the "JToolBar," "BoxLayout," "JButton," and "JToggleButton" sections in Chepter 8. You can also refer back to Chapter 4.*

JTabbedPane

JTabbedPane is a useful container for items like properties dialogs, used to configure a single type of object that has many options and several categories of options. A JTabbedPane allows you to show one category's options at a time and switch between categories by clicking a tab that looks like a file folder tab. You can get this effect by using several panels in a CardLayout, but JTabbed-Pane takes care of drawing the tabs and so on for you.

A JTabbedPane has one file folder–like tab for each category of options. Each tab is associated with its own pane that actually displays the options. These panes can be any kind of pane you want.

Each tab has a text string and/or an icon. You can also change the tab's font and specify whether the tabs appear at the top, bottom, right, or left.

JTABBEDPANE REQUIRED CLASSES JTabbedPane requires two other classes to get its job done: a class that implements the SingleSelection-Model interface, and a class that extends the abstract TabbedPaneUI class. You don't have to create these classes. JTabbedPane creates a DefaultSin-gleSelectionModel class and gets the look-and-feel class from the currently plugged-in look-and-feel. Here's how the classes divide up the work:

- **JTabbedPane:** This class represents the tabbed pane to the outside world. It contains references to the SingleSelectionModel class and the look-and-feel class. As a descendant of Container, it stores the tab panels added to it. It also stores information about its external state, such as each tab's text and icon.

- **SingleSelectionModel:** This class keeps track of which tab panel is currently selected. When a different tab is selected, the look-and-feel class is notified and asks the JTabbedPane class for the SingleSelectionModel, which it changes to reflect the new selection.

- **The look-and-feel class:** This class is responsible for drawing the tabs and for responding to events within the component. When it draws the component, it asks JTabbedPane for information about text and icons and asks the SingleSelectionModel for information about the current selection, so that it can accurately draw the component in its current state. This class doesn't store information because it can be replaced at any time if a new look-and-feel gets plugged in. The class, called something like WindowsTabbedPaneUI or MotifTabbedPaneUI, is gotten by JTabbedPane from the current look-and-feel.

NOTE: *For more information, see the "JTabbedPane" and "DefaultSingleSelectionModel" sections in Chapter 8. You can also refer back to Chapter 4.*

JSplitPane

JSplitPane is another somewhat specialized container. It has two main components, usually containers themselves, separated by a divider that can be moved so that one of the components gets more space at the expense of the other. The divider can be horizontal, so that the two components are displayed one above the other, or vertical, so that the two components appear side by side. This concept can be handy for when you want to show different panes at the same time, but you want the user to be able to allocate more screen space to one of them.

JSplitPanes are very similar to the HTML frames you see when browsing the Web. Although a JSplitPane separates only two components, you can embed JSplitPanes within JSplitPanes to divide an area into more panes—all with adjustable sizes.

You can dynamically change the panes being displayed and move the divider around programmatically. You're allowed to change the border, but doing so generally produces bad results.

JSPLITPANE REQUIRED CLASSES   JSplitPane requires one other class to get its job done: a look-and-feel class that extends the abstract Split-PaneUI class. You don't have to create the look-and-feel class—JSplitPane gets it from the currently plugged-in look-and-feel. Here's how the classes divide up the work:

- **JSplitPane:** This class represents the split pane to the rest of the world. It contains a reference to the look-and-feel class and holds information about the split pane's external state, such as the divider location and orientation. As a descendant of Container, it also holds the two components it's splitting.

- **The look-and-feel class:** This class takes care of drawing the component and responding to events that happen on it, such as when the user drags the divider. When drawing the component, this class must ask JSplitPane for information about the component's external state so that it can represent the component accurately onscreen. This class doesn't contain any state information because it can be replaced at any time if a new look-and-feel is plugged in. JSplitPane gets the actual look-and-feel class from the currently plugged-in look-and-feel, and the class's name is something like WindowsSplitPaneUI or MotifSplitPaneUI.

NOTE: *For more information, see the "JSplitPane" section in Chapter 8. You can also refer back to Chapter 4 and the "Windows" section in this chapter.*

Trees: JTree

Certain types of data lend themselves to hierarchical storage, in which a set of data can be broken down into classifications; the classifications can be further broken down into sub-classifications; and so on. With books, for example, you can split them into fiction and nonfiction and then break down the fiction group into literature, mystery, adventure, and so on. The basic structure has a root node that gives access to subnodes that can themselves contain other subnodes, which can contain their own subnodes. Things that naturally fall into this hierarchical model lend themselves to being displayed with a tree. The JFC tree component is called "JTree." Figure 7-7 shows a simple JTree.

Using a JTree can be fairly complicated, especially if the contents of the tree change often. If your tree just gets loaded up and never changes, using JTree is pretty straightforward.

Figure 7-7
A simple JTree.

Monitoring JTree Events

The two most important types of events JTrees can generate are TreeSelectionEvents and TreeExpansionEvents. TreeSelectionEvents are generated when the current selection within the tree changes—usually when the user clicks on a tree node. TreeExpansionEvents are generated when a node within the tree is expanded, displaying its child nodes, or when a node is collapsed.

JTree Required Classes

JTree requires seven other classes to do its job:

- A class that implements the TreeModel interface
- Node classes that implement the TreeNode interface
- A class that implements the TreeSelectionModel interface
- Instances of the TreePath class
- A class that implements the TreeCellRenderer interface
- A class that implements the TreeCellEditor interface
- A look-and-feel class that extends the abstract TreeUI class

You don't have to create all these classes. JTree creates a DefaultTreeModel class, a DefaultTreeSelectionModel class, a class that implements TreeCellRenderer, and a DefaultCellEditor class. JTree gets the look-and-feel class from the currently plugged-in look-and-feel. TreePaths are generated by JTree as required while using the JTree, although you can generate them yourself. You do have to create the nodes—typically by using the DefaultMutableTreeNode class. Here's how the classes divide up the work:

- **JTree:** This class is how the tree is represented to the rest of the world. It stores references to the other required classes. It also stores changeable information about what the tree looks like, including how the root node should be displayed.

- **TreeModel:** This class is where all the tree's data is stored and accessed. When nodes are added to or removed from the tree, it's done through the TreeModel or through individual tree nodes. It's typically better to do these things through the TreeModel, or you will have to go through the extra step of notifying the TreeModel that the changes have been made.

■ **TreeNode:** This contains the data for a single tree node. It doesn't draw itself; instead, when a tree node is being drawn, a TreeNode class is passed to the current TreeCellRenderer, which reads the data in the TreeNode and draws it accordingly.

■ **TreePath:** This is the list of TreeNodes you have to pass to get from one node in a tree to another node. TreePaths are generally created by JTree methods when you ask for things such as the currently selected nodes.

■ **TreeSelectionModel:** This class keeps track of a tree's current selection state (which nodes are selected) and holds information about whether multiple nodes can be selected at a time. When a node in the tree is clicked, the look-and-feel class asks the JTree class for the TreeSelectionModel class, finds out what type of selection is active from the TreeSelectionModel class, and then changes the TreeSelectionModel's contents so that it stores the revised selection state.

■ **TreeCellEditor:** This is a graphical class used when a tree node is to be edited. You must explicitly specify that tree nodes can be edited because they aren't editable by default. The DefaultCellEditor class offers three different constructors that fit most needs.

■ **TreeCellRenderer:** This is a graphical class used to draw tree nodes. By default, a JTree gets a TreeCellRenderer class from its look-and-feel class. You can create your own TreeCellRenderer without too much trouble if you need special functionality.

■ **The look-and-feel class:** This class controls drawing the tree and responding to events that happen to it. Because it doesn't store information about the tree's contents, the changeable visual attributes, or the cell renderer or editor, this class must ask the other classes for this information. JTree gets the actual look-and-feel class from the currently plugged-in look-and-feel; its name is something like WindowsTreeUI or MotifTreeUI.

NOTE: *For more information, see the "JTree," "DefaultMutableTreeNode," "DefaultTreeModel," "TreePath," "DefaultTreeSelectionModel," and "DefaultCellEditor" sections in Chapter 8. Chapters 10, "Integrating JFC Example1: A File Browser," and 11, "Integrating JFC Example2: Adding Items to and Removing Items from JTrees," also illustrate how to do different things with trees, and you can refer back to Chapter 4.*

File Browsing

Before the JFC, it was extremely difficult to use Java to browse file systems without using any native code. This problem has been fixed with the introduction of the DirectoryModel class.

The JFC introduces two graphical classes—JDirectoryPane and JFile-Chooser—that rely on the DirectoryModel class and take care of many of your file-browsing needs, although they don't implement full file browsing. The JFC also introduces two nongraphical classes, FileType and TypedFile, that the other three classes use extensively to identify file types and to determine whether a file is actually a directory. Figure 7-8 shows an example of a JDirectoryPane.

NOTE: *With the release of JFC1.1 (Swing 1.0), all file browsing classes have been moved to the com.sum.java.swing.preview package. This means that their APIs will change in the next release.*

DirectoryModel

This is a nongraphical class that represents the computer's file system. It has the concept of a current directory from which you can go up to the parent directory or down into subdirectories. It can also get the entire contents of a directory by using TypedFiles, which store enough information about each file that a graphical component based on DirectoryModel can visually show that the types of files are different.

NOTE: *For more information, see the "DirectoryModel," "FileType," and "Typed-File" sections in Chapter 8. You can also refer to Chapter 10.*

Figure 7-8
A JDirectoryPane.

TypedFile

This is a subclass of the java.io.File class that adds the ability to store the file type with the other file information. This file type information is in the form of a class that implements the FileType interface.

TypedFiles are what DirectoryModel returns when it gets the contents of a directory. The contents are passed to the JDirectoryPane and JFileChooser classes that use the file type information to customize how files are represented onscreen.

NOTE: *For more information, see the "TypedFile" and "FileType" sections in Chapter 8.*

FileType

This is an interface that, when implemented, stores information about a file type, such as a string that describes the file type, an icon for the file type, whether the type of file can contain other files (is it a directory?), and a method for finding out if a file is of this type.

FileType actually has a set of predefined general types that cover things like generic files, folders, and so on. FileType is mostly used as a member of a TypedFile, describing what type the file is. Its icon is often displayed next to the filename in a JDirectoryPane or JFileChooser.

NOTE: *For more information, see the "FileType" and "TypedFile" sections in Chapter 8.*

JDirectoryPane

A JDirectoryPane displays the contents of a directory in a window, including both files and subdirectories. If you double-click on a subdirectory, the subdirectory's contents are loaded and replace the window's previous contents. That means you can't browse upward through the file system using a JDirectoryPane by itself. A JDirectoryPane is much like the right-hand window of Windows Explorer.

JDirectoryPane relies heavily on the DirectoryModel class for its access to the file system.

LISTENING FOR FILE SELECTION EVENTS   When a file or directory is single- or double-clicked in a JDirectoryPane, the JDirectoryPane gen-

erates an ActionEvent. You can differentiate between single-clicks and double-clicks by using the event's action command because JDirectoryPane lets
you specify an extra action command string for double-clicks.

JDIRECTORYPANE REQUIRED CLASSES   In addition to the other
classes in this section, JDirectoryPane also requires two additional classes to
get its job done: a class that implements the ListSelectionModel, and a look-
and-feel class that extends the abstract DirectoryPaneUI class. You don't have
to create these classes. JDirectoryPane creates a DefaultListSelectionModel
class and gets the look-and-feel class from the currently plugged-in look-and-
feel. Here's how the classes divide up the work:

■ **JDirectoryPane:** This class is how the directory pane is represented
to the rest of the world. It contains references to the DirectoryModel,
the ListSelectionModel, and the look-and-feel class.

■ **ListSelectionModel:** This class stores the directory pane's current
selection state. When an item is clicked in the directory pane, the
look-and-feel class is notified. It asks the JDirectoryPane class for the
reference to the ListSelectionModel, which it modifies to reflect the
new selection state.

■ **The look-and-feel class:** This class is responsible for drawing the
directory pane and responding to events that happen within it. To
draw the directory pane and accurately reflect its current state, the
look-and-feel class asks the JDirectoryPane for information like border
and background color, asks the DirectoryModel for the contents of the
directory being drawn, and asks the ListSelectionModel what items
are currently selected. The look-and-feel class itself doesn't store any
state information because it's likely to be replaced if a new look-and-
feel is plugged in. The actual class, called something like
WindowsDirectoryPaneUI or Motif DirectoryPaneUI, is gotten from
the currently plugged-in look-and-feel.

NOTE: *For more information, see the "DirectoryModel," "TypedFile," "FileType,"*
"JDirectoryPane," "JFileChooser," and "DefaultListSelectionModel" sections in
Chapter 8. You can also refer back to Chapter 4.

JFileChooser

JFileChooser is a 100 percent–Java version of the old FileDialog from the
AWT. It contains an instance of JDirectoryPane with controls added to allow
browsing up *and* down through the file system. It also allows the user to pick
which types of files should be shown.

JFileChooser can be displayed as an added standard component to a panel or within its own dialog. To choose a file, the user can either double-click on it or enter the filename and click the OK button.

JFileChooser, containing an instance of JDirectoryPane, requires basically the same supporting classes, so they aren't repeated here. The only difference is that the look-and-feel class extends the abstract FileChooserUI class and is called something like WindowsFileChooserUI or MotifFileChooserUI. JFileChooser also handles single- and double-click notification the same way JDirectoryPane does.

NOTE: *For JFC 1.1 (Swing 1.0), the JFileChooser API is incomplete. For more information, see the "JFileChooser," "JDirectoryPane," "DirectoryMode," "TypedFile," and "FileType" sections in Chapter 8.*

Managing Event Listeners

When you create a component that generates an event, you have to be able to register listeners for that type of event. This registration can be automatically taken care of if you subclassed a component that already generates the type of event in question. For example, if you create a subclass of JButton and you want it to generate an ActionEvent not just when the button is released, but also when it's pressed, you don't have to worry about managing ActionListeners because JButton handles it for you. If, on the other hand, you want to generate an ActionEvent and your parent class doesn't manage ActionListeners, you need the EventListenerList class.

EventListenerList doesn't take care of your class's interface to its listeners. You still have to write short methods such as addActionListener() and removeActionListener(). EventListenerList makes sure you don't have synchronization problems and makes it easier to add a new listener and iterate through the registered listeners when it's time to distribute an event.

NOTE: *For more information, see "A Quick Review of the JDK 1.1 Event Model" in this chapter, and the "EventListenerList" section in Chapter 8. Also, Chapters 10, 11, and 12, "Integrating JFC Example 3: A Simple Paint Program," use EventListenerLists.*

Selecting Items from Lists

When building a user interface, often you need to display a list of items and allow the user to select from among the items. The JFC fills this need with

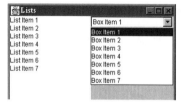

Figure 7-9

A JList and a
JComboCox.

two components: JList and JComboBox. Figure 7-9 shows an example of a JList and a JComboBox side by side. The JComboBox's list is expanded so you can see its items.

JList

JList is a panel in which a list of items is displayed. The user can select one or more items from the list. If there are too many items to display within a JList, you should place the JList in a JScrollPane that lets the user see all the items.

If you need to customize the way items are displayed in the list, you can create your own ListCellRenderer class and tell the JList to use it.

LISTENING FOR JLIST EVENTS JList generates two types of events that are commonly caught: ListSelectionEvents and ListDataEvents. List-SelectionEvents are generated when the selection state of a JList changes (the user clicks a list item); ListDataEvents are generated when the actual items in the list change. To register as a ListSelectionListener, you have to ask the JList for its ListSelectionModel and register with it. To register as a ListDataListener, you have to ask the JList for its ListModel and register with it.

JLIST REQUIRED CLASSES JList requires four other classes to do its job: a class that implements the ListModel interface, a class that implements the ListSelectionModel interface, a class that implements the ListCellRenderer interface, and a look-and-feel class that extends the abstract ListUI class. You don't have to create these classes yourself. JList creates a DefaultListModel class, a DefaultListSelectionModel class, and a class that implements ListCellRenderer and gets the look-and-feel class from the currently plugged-in look-and-feel. Here's how the classes divide the work:

- **JList:** This class represents the list to the rest of the world. It contains references to the ListModel, the ListSelectionModel, the ListCellRenderer, and the look-and-feel class. It also stores changeable information about the list's appearance, such as its border.

- **ListModel:** This class holds all the list items and is used to add items to the list and remove items from the list. It generates ListDataEvents when its contents change.
- **ListSelectionModel:** This class stores the list's current selection state—which items are currently selected. When a list item is clicked, the look-and-feel class is notified. It asks the JList class for the ListSelectionModel class and modifies it to reflect the new selection state. When the state changes, the ListSelectionModel generates ListSelectionEvents.
- **ListCellRenderer:** This class is responsible for drawing each list item. By default, it draws them like labels, but it's not difficult to create your own ListCellRenderer and use it if you need special functionality.
- **The look-and-feel class:** This class controls drawing the component and responding to events within the component. When the component needs to be drawn, the look-and-feel class must access information stored in the other classes so it can reflect the current state in its drawing. It asks the ListModel for the list items, it asks the JList for things like the border, it asks the ListSelectionModel which items are currently selected, and it controls the use of the ListCellRenderer in drawing individual items. This class doesn't store any state information because it can be replaced if a new look-and-feel gets plugged-in. The actual class, called something like WindowsListUI or MotifListUI, is gotten from the current look-and-feel.

NOTE: *For more information, see the "JList," "DefaultListModel," and "Default-ListSelectionModel" sections in Chapter 8. You can also refer back to Chapter 4.*

JComboBox

A JComboBox looks like a text field with an arrow next to it. What's displayed in the text field is the JComboBox's current value. If you click on the arrow next to it, the list of possible values is displayed and the user can select a new value from that list. If the JComboBox is set to be editable, users can type their own values in the text field or select an item from the list. Only one item can be selected at a time.

By default, items in the list are displayed as labels, and the editor works like a text field. You can create a custom cell renderer or editor, however, if you need special functionality. You can also set simpler properties, such as border and text or background colors.

LISTENING FOR NEW SELECTIONS When the user clicks a new item in the list, the item is selected. When that happens, the JComboBox generates an ItemEvent and distributes it to all registered ItemListeners. When the selection changes, you get two ItemEvents—one when the previously selected item becomes deselected and another when the clicked item becomes selected.

You can also listen for when the combo box's list changes by catching List-DataEvents. To register for these events, you have to get the JComboBox's data model and register with it.

JCOMBOBOX REQUIRED CLASSES   JComboBox requires four other classes to do its job: a class that implements the ComboBoxModel interface, a class that implements the ComboBoxEditor interface (if the JComboBox is editable), a class that implements the ListCellRenderer interface, and a look-and-feel class that extends the abstract ComboBoxUI class. You don't have to create these classes yourself. JComboBox creates a class that implements ComboBoxModel, a class that implements ComboBoxEditor, and a class that implements ListCellRenderer, and gets the look-and-feel class from the currently plugged-in look-and-feel. Here's how the classes divide the work:

- **JComboBox:** This class represents the combo box to the rest of the world. It contains references to the ComboBoxModel, the ComboBoxEditor, the ListCellRenderer, and the look-and-feel class. It also stores changeable information about appearance, such as the border and background color.
- **ComboBoxModel:** This class contains the items in the list and gives access to them. It also generates ListDataEvents when items are added or removed and keeps track of which item is currently selected. The model class is defined as an inner class within JComboBox.
- **ComboBoxEditor:** This class is used when JComboBox has been set to be editable. It interacts with the user so he or she can enter a new value for the JComboBox. The editor class is gotten from the currently plugged-in look-and-feel. You can create your own if you need special behavior.
- **ListCellRenderer:** This class is used to draw each individual item in the list. The renderer class is gotten from the currently plugged-in look-and-feel. You can create your own if you need special behavior.
- **The look-and-feel class:** This class controls drawing the component and responding to events. Because this class isn't allowed to store state information about the component, it must access the other classes to draw the component and accurately reflect its current state. It has to ask the ComboBoxModel for the list of items and the currently selected item. It has to ask the JComboBox for information about the border and background colors, and so on. It has to get the cell renderer and use it on each item being drawn. The actual class, called something like WindowsComboBoxUI or MotifComboBoxUI, is gotten from the currently plugged-in look-and-feel.

NOTE: *For more information, see the "JComboBox" section in Chapter 8. You can also refer back to Chapter 4.*

Windows

A window is a container that's visually separate from its surroundings and can be dragged around the screen. The seven components in this section can be divided into two groups: external windows and internal windows. Figure 7-10 shows one external window (a JFrame) that contains an internal window (a JInternalFrame).

The external windows are JWindow, JDialog, and JFrame—all descendants of java.awt.Window. They are managed by the native operating system, so they can float everywhere on the screen. Because they are managed by the operating system, their appearance is consistent with the operating system's look and has only limited configurability. JOptionPane and JColorChooser can create their own JDialogs and place themselves within, so in that sense they can be considered external windows.

The internal windows are JInternalFrame and JApplet. JOptionPane and JColorChooser can create JInternalFrames and be displayed within them, so in that way they can be considered internal windows. JInternalFrames are completely Java—they aren't managed by the operating system, so their appearance and behavior are completely configurable. They are typically managed by a JDesktopPane and can't be dragged beyond their parent component's boundaries. JApplets are internal windows because they are designed to appear within Web pages.

JWindow, JDialog, JFrame, JApplet, and JInternalFrame are similar in giving access to their display areas through a JRootPane. Tasks such as setting the menu bar, adding components, and so on are done that way.

Figure 7-10
A JFrame containing a JInternalFrame.

Window Events

The external window classes can generate WindowEvents when they are opened, closed, and so on. JInternalFrame can't; it relies on ComponentEvents. JApplet has methods called by the browser when important things happen.

JWindow

A JWindow is a featureless window—just a colored rectangle. You can use it if you want an external window you can customize. Other external windows have preset frame borders and title bars with close and minimize buttons. Of course, you also have to implement any dragging or resizing of the JWindow.

JDialog

A JDialog is a framed window with a title bar, normally used as a subwindow in an application. It's used to get a specific set of input from the user or to hold a toolbar or tool palette. While it's up, it can either block input into the application's other windows or allow the user to continue working with the rest of the application.

JFrame

A JFrame is a framed window with a title bar and can be used as an application's main window or as a subwindow. As a subwindow, it doesn't keep the user from working with the application's other windows.

JInternalFrame

A JInternalFrame is an internal window with a title bar. Because it's an internal window, it can't be used as an application's main window. JInternal-Frames are typically added to and managed by a JDesktopPane. When minimized, JInternalFrames become icons within their parent JDesktop-Panes. You have great control over JInternalFrames, including setting borders, making portions transparent, specifying whether they can be minimized, and so forth.

As a completely Java component, JInternalFrame uses a look-and-feel class that extends the abstract InternalFrameUI class. JInternalFrame stores all state information, such as its root pane and border, and the look-and-feel class accesses JInternalFrame's information and uses it to draw the component to reflect that information. The look-and-feel class, called something like WindowsInternalFrameUI or MotifInternalFrameUI, is gotten from the current look-and-feel.

JOptionPane

JOptionPane is a way to create simple dialogs without much trouble. JOption-Pane is, in itself, not a window at all. It's just a normal JFC component that contains the controls needed for a dialog. It's a window in that it has static methods for displaying itself as the main pane in a JDialog or a JInternalFrame.

JOptionPane uses a look-and-feel class that extends the abstract Option-PaneUI class. JOptionPane stores the components added to it, as well as other changeable information, such as its border. The look-and-feel class accesses JOptionPane's information and uses it to draw the component properly. The look-and-feel class, called something like WindowsOptionPaneUI or Motif-OptionPaneUI, is gotten from the current look-and-feel.

JColorChooser

JColorChooser is a way to let the user easily choose a color. It's actually just a JFC panel rather than a window, but it has the ability to display itself inside a JDialog or a JInternalFrame. It's rarely used just as a panel, so it belongs in this section.

JColorChooser doesn't use a look-and-feel class.

JApplet

JApplet is used instead of the old Applet class to place JFC Java into Web pages. It doesn't use a look-and-feel class.

NOTE: *For more information, see the "Component Borders" section in this chapter and the "JWindow," "JDialog," "JFrame," "JOptionPane," "JInternalFrame," "JRootPane," "JApplet," and "JDesktopPane" sections in Chapter 8. You can also refer back to Chapter 4.*

Figure 7-11
The four components
for text entry and
editing.

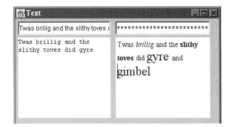

Text Entry and Editing

User interfaces commonly need a place for text entry. Applications require entering and modifying filenames, people's names, e-mail addresses, e-mail messages, and more complicated items, such as documents. The JFC has four components for text entry and editing, shown in Figure 7-11.

NOTE: *The four components are discussed briefly here. An in-depth discussion of Text Components and their many associated classes can be found in Chapter 5, "JFC Documents and Text Components." Each component is discussed individually in detail in Chapter 8.*

JTextField

JTextField is used for single-line text entry and editing. Although you can change the font, the one that's set applies to all characters in the component.

JPasswordField

JPasswordField is just a JTextField that displays a special echo character so other people can't read your password as you type it in.

JTextArea

JTextArea is a multiline component used for text entry and editing. Like JTextField, it uses only one font at a time.

JTextPane

JTextPane is the deluxe text editor. It supports word wrapping, multiple fonts and colors, text alignment, insertion of icons and components, and more.

Scrolling

Often, you have a pane that's just too big to be displayed within your application's frame. Scrolling lets you display part of the pane, while letting the user change which part of the pane is displayed, thus making it possible to see all of the pane part by part.

The JFC has made scrolling much simpler than it used to be. Figure 7-12 shows a JScrollPane being used to scroll around a panel containing a raster image.

JScrollBar

JScrollBar is a long, thin control that lets you move a position indicator from one end to the other. It's a way to represent a range of possible values and either a value within that range or a subrange of values within that range. For scrolling a pane, there are two JScrollBars—one horizontal and one vertical. The length of the JScrollBar represents the length of a side of the pane being scrolled. The location of the position indicator represents the lowest coordinate visible in the JScrollBar's direction (X or Y). The length of the position indicator represents the portion of the pane that's visible in relation to its total size in that direction. The user moves the position indicator to make different parts of the pane visible.

In the JFC, you generally don't have to deal directly with JScrollBars when scrolling a pane. JScrollPane handles that kind of thing automatically. You can still use single JScrollBars for other purposes, such as changing a value within a range.

Figure 7-12
Scrolling through a panel with a JScroll-Pane.

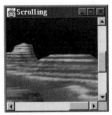

LISTENING FOR CHANGES IN THE JSCROLLBAR   The AWT deals with changes in its Scrollbar component by generating AdjustmentEvents. Although they are still generated by JScrollBar for backward compatibility, JScrollBar also generates ChangeEvents whenever any change takes place. You should catch the ChangeEvents if you want to monitor changes in a JScrollBar.

JSCROLLBAR REQUIRED CLASSES   JScrollBar requires two other classes to get its job done: a class that implements the BoundedRangeModel interface, and a look-and-feel class that extends the abstract ScrollBarUI class. You don't have to create these classes. JScrollBar creates a Default-BoundedRangeModel class and gets the look-and-feel class from the currently plugged-in look-and-feel. Here's how the classes divide up the work:

- **JScrollBar:** This class represents the scrollbar to the rest of the world. It contains references to the BoundedRangeModel class and the look-and-feel class. It stores information about properties such as the border and background color that the look-and-feel class needs so it can draw the scrollbar. JScrollBar also stores the unit increment and block increment used to define how much the position indicator moves in different situations.

- **BoundedRangeModel:** This class stores information about what values the ends of the scrollbar and the position indicator really represent. It contains the scrollbar's minimum and maximum values, the value at the position indicator's low end, and the extent represented by the length of the position indicator. This class's units aren't the same as the scrollbar's. For example, say you have a 2,000 pixel by 2,000 pixel image in a pane, but you have a viewing area that's only 500 × 500 pixels. Ignoring the buttons on the ends of the scrollbar for simplicity, the scrollbar on either side will be 500 pixels long, but represent the full 2,000-pixel size of the pane on that side. The position indicator will represent 500 pixels because that's how much of the pane is visible at one time. The length of the position indicator represents the part of the pane that's currently visible, which is 500 pixels, or 25 percent of the pane size. So, the position indicator's actual length will be 25 percent of 500, which is 125 pixels.

- **The look-and-feel class:** This class is responsible for drawing the scrollbar and responding to events that happen to it. When the user uses the mouse within the JScrollBar, the look-and-feel class is notified. It checks whether the mouse event is a drag of the position indicator, a click on an end button, or a click between the position indicator and an end button. If one of these actions happens, the look-and-feel class asks the JScrollBar class for the BoundedRangeModel and updates it to reflect a changed state. The BoundedRangeModel realizes it has been changed, generates a ChangeEvent, and distributes it to its ChangeListeners. To draw the scrollbar, the look-and-feel class must ask the JScrollBar class for information such as border and background color and the BoundedRangeModel for information about where the position indicator is and how long it is. Then it can draw the scrollbar in a way that reflects its current state. The actual look-and-feel class, called something like WindowsScrollBarUI or MotifScrollBarUI, is gotten from the currently plugged-in look-and-feel.

NOTE: *For more information, see the "JScrollBar" and "DefaultBoundedRange-Model" sections of Chapter 8. You can also refer back to Chapter 4.*

JViewport

A JViewport represents the visible area of a component being scrolled. JScrollPane automatically creates a JViewport when you create it with a component or allows you to create one of your own.

JViewport requires no other classes.

NOTE: *For more information, see the "JViewport" and "JScrollPane" sections in Chapter 8.*

JScrollPane

A JScrollPane is a component that's extremely helpful in scrolling around a panel that's too large for its allotted display area. It consists of two JScroll-Bars, one horizontal and one vertical, and a JViewport. Usually, all you have to do is create your large component and then assign it as a JScrollPane's view component. JScrollPane handles scrolling for you and evens takes care of cases when the view component changes size on the fly. It also includes separate row and column header viewports that you can use for items like spreadsheet row and column headers that scroll in only one direction. If you use row and column headers, it leaves a rectangular gap at the JScrollPane's top left. This gap is referred to as the "corner," and you can assign a component to go there, if you want.

By default, the two JScrollBars are displayed only when needed; they aren't there if the view component can be completely seen. You can, however, change this behavior so that one or both JScrollBars are always or never seen. You also have the freedom to replace one or both JScrollBars if you want special functionality, but you have to extend JScrollPane to do so.

JSCROLLPANE REQUIRED CLASSES In addition to the JViewport and the two JScrollBars, JScrollPane also requires a look-and-feel class that extends the abstract ScrollPaneUI class. You don't have to create this class—JScrollPane gets it from the currently plugged-in look-and-feel. Here's how the classes divide up the work:

- **JScrollPane:** This class represents the scroll pane to the rest of the world. It contains references to the scrollbars and the look-and-feel class.

- **The look-and-feel class:** This class handles coordinating events that happen to the scrollbars with changes in the viewport. It's loaded from the currently plugged-in look-and-feel and has a name like WindowsScrollPaneUI or MotifScrollPaneUI.

NOTE: *For more information, see the "JScrollPane," "JScrollBar," "JViewport," and "DefaultBoundedRangeModel" sections in Chapter 8.*

JFC Layout Managers

The JFC classes include a group of new layout managers, with two particularly useful ones. BoxLayout emphasizes specifying how components can stretch and shrink as their container gets larger or smaller. OverlayLayout is more interested in layering components on top of each other and controlling their relationships when one component overlays another.

BoxLayout

BoxLayout is a pretty simple layout manager that lays out a single row or single column of components. It's used by the JMenuBar class to lay out its menus and by JToolBar to lay out its tool buttons. It can be useful for placing OK and Cancel buttons, for example, so that they're evenly spaced out. The Box component includes some static methods for creating special padding components that are particularly useful for BoxLayouts.

OverlayLayout

OverlayLayout is a good layout manager to use when you want to place components on top of each other. It's particularly handy when one or more of the components is at least partly transparent.

NOTE: *For more information, see the "Box," "BoxLayout," and "OverlayLayout" sections in Chapter 8.*

JFC Tables

Often, you want to display data in a spreadsheet fashion. JTable takes care of many of the difficulties involved in making this kind of control. JTable is oriented toward displaying database records in which each row displays a row in the database (or a row from a query, anyway), and each column displays different records' values for the same field (last name, date of birth, whatever). It makes it easy to add headers to your table's columns, but does not provide the same service for the rows. Cells can be editable or not. You can control how cells are displayed as well as the component used to edit them. Figure 7-13 shows an example of a simple JTable.

JTable can be quite easy to use when you just want to display data. When you start modifying data, adding and removing rows and columns and changing the way different cells are treated, it can get fairly complicated.

When you create a JTable, you can give it a bunch of rows and columns of data for it to display, and then just let it go. It's often too big to display within its allotted area, so you should put it in a scroll pane. You can just add it as the view component to a JScrollPane, but the column headers won't show up. JTable includes a special method that creates a JScrollPane configured to show the column headers in their proper place as the scroll pane's column header view. It can do this because it stores the column headers as a separate pane, which explains why they don't show up when you display a JTable without its custom scroll pane.

JTable includes the ability to rearrange table columns by dragging them because it includes the idea of a TableColumnModel that manages all the table's columns. JTable doesn't include the same capabilities for rows, although you can implement it yourself, just as you can create row headers. Cell renderers and editors are also assigned by column, making it difficult to swap the implied roles of rows and columns.

If you don't like the built-in capabilities of the cell renderer or editor, you can easily make your own custom cell renderer or editor. You can also customize the number of mouse clicks required to activate the editor.

Figure 7-13
A simple JTable.

Name	Birthdate	Salary	Job Title
John Q. Public	11-23-61	$50,000	Java Programmer
James T. Doe	12-25-67	$50,000	Java Programmer
Jane S. Person	3-5-66	$60,000	Project Leader
Harold X. Dunno	5-16-68	$35,000	Junior Programmer
Sarah V. Nerd	7-13-68	$65,000	Java Guru

Listening to Tables

The most interesting events generated by a table happen when the contents of the table change or when the user selects one or more cells. You can listen for these TableModelEvents and ListSelectionEvents if your class implements the TableModelListener interface and the ListSelectionListener interface. To be notified of TableModelEvents, you must register your listener class with the JTable's TableModel. To be notified of ListSelectionEvents, you must register your listener class with the JTable's ListSelectionModel for when row selection changes or with the TableColumnModel's ListSelectionModel for when column selection changes.

JTable's Required Classes

JTable requires eight other classes to do its job:

- A class that implements the TableModel interface
- A class that implements the TableColumnModel interface
- A class that implements the ListSelectionModel interface
- A TableColumn class for each column in the table
- A class that implements the TableCellRenderer interface
- A class that implements the TableCellEditor interface (if any cells will be editable)
- A JTableHeader class
- A look-and-feel class that extends the abstract TableUI class

You don't have to create these classes yourself. JTable creates the following:

- A DefaultTableModel class, although you can create this yourself, add data directly to it, and then pass it to a JTable constructor.
- A DefaultTableColumnModel class, although you can create this yourself and pass it to one of the JTable constructors.
- A DefaultListSelectionModel class. Again, you can create this yourself and pass it to a JTable constructor.
- A TableColumn class for each column.
- A JTableHeader class.
- A DefaultTableCellRenderer class.
- A DefaultCellEditor class.

JTable gets the look-and-feel class from the current look-and-feel. Here's how the classes divide up the work:

- **JTable:** This class represents the table to the rest of the world. It contains references to the TableModel, the TableColumnModel, the ListSelectionModel (for row selection), and the JTableHeader. It also stores changeable information about how the tree should look, such as whether the grid should be drawn and what color it should be.

- **TableModel:** This class holds the table's data. You can use it to load new rows and columns and to get values out of the table. It generates a TableModelEvent when its contents change. If you want to create a TableModel you can load complex data into, you might want to extend the AbstractTableModel class.

- **TableColumnModel:** This class stores information about a table's columns in general, including all the TableColumns and column margins. It also has a ListSelectionListener that keeps track of the currently selected column. You can use this class to access TableColumns by index.

- **ListSelectionModel:** This class keeps track of which rows or columns in the table are currently selected.

- **TableColumn:** This class holds all graphical information about a single column, like its current, maximum, and minimum width, its header value, and its cell renderer and editor. It also stores the index of the column it represents in the table model.

- **JTableHeader:** This is the component used to draw a table's column headers. It interacts with the TableColumnModel to get the header strings. You can place it yourself, or, if you use JTable's createScrollPaneForTable() method, the scroll pane uses it as its column header view.

- **DefaultTableCellRenderer:** This is stored in each TableColumn. By default, cells are rendered as labels, but you can create your own renderer class by implementing the TableCellRenderer interface.

- **TableCellEditor:** This is stored in each TableColumn. By default, cells can't be edited. If you make a column's cells editable, then they are edited by using a text field. You can also use the DefaultCellEditor to create cell editors that use a check box or a combo box, or you can create your own custom cell editor.

- **The look-and-feel class:** This is the class that controls the appearance and behavior of the table. It coordinates drawing the table and responding to events within it. This class doesn't store any state information because it can be replaced if the look-and-feel is changed. To draw the table correctly, then, it has to get information from the other classes. It has to talk to JTable to get information such as whether the grid should be drawn. It asks TableModel to get the contents of the cells, TableColumnModel to get the TableColumns and column margins, and TableColumns to get their cell renderers and editors. It also has to talk to the ListSelectionModels to find out which cells are currently selected and use the CellRenderer to draw the cells properly. The actual look-and-feel class, called something like WindowsTableUI or MotifTableUI, is gotten from the currently plugged-in look-and-feel.

NOTE: *For more information, see the "JScrollPane," "JTable," "AbstractTable-Model," "DefaultTableModel," "DefaultTableColumnModel," "DefaultListSelection-Model," "TableColumn," "DefaultTableCellRenderer," "DefaultCellEditor," and "JTableHeader" sections in Chapter 8.*

Placing Static Text

Sometimes you need to place text on the user interface, without making it possible for the user to edit it. The most common example is including a text string next to an editable text field, explaining what the user is expected to put into the text field. This kind of static text component is typically called a "label." The JFC includes a label component called JLabel. Figure 7-14 shows a label being used to explain what the user is expected to enter in a text field.

Commonly Set Properties

Many components can use an *accelerator key*, one that, when pressed along with a special key (Alt on many systems), switches focus to the component. Although JLabel can't get the focus, it can make one of its characters under-lined to indicate the accelerator key for a component next to it. Notice that the *F* in *File Name* is underlined in Figure 7-14. You could, then, switch focus to the text field by pressing Alt+F.

You can also set the JLabel's font and its alignment within its bounding rectangle. A JLabel can include an icon, and you can change how the text and icon are positioned in relation to each other.

Figure 7-14
A JLabel component.

Required Classes

JLabel requires one other class to get its job done: a look-and-feel class that implements the abstract LabelUI class. You don't have to create the look-and-feel class—JLabel gets it from the currently installed look-and-feel. Here's how the two classes split up the work:

- **JLabel:** This class is the outside world's view of a JFC label. It contains a reference to the look-and-feel class. It also stores state information, such as the font, text string, icon, and so forth.

- **The look-and-feel class:** This class defines the appearance of the label. Because it's responsible for drawing the label, but doesn't store state information about it, it has to access JLabel to get the text string, icon, font, and so on. The actual class, called something like WindowsLabelUI or MotifLabelUI, is gotten from the look-and-feel.

NOTE: *For more information, see the "JLabel" and "ImageIcon" sections in Chapter 8. You can also look back at Chapter 4.*

SUMMARY

It's helpful to have a big reference chapter that covers all kinds of classes in lots of detail, but you also need a smaller chapter that can direct you to the right places in the reference chapter and clarify the relationships between the classes. Chapter 8 is the big reference chapter, and this smaller chapter has tried to tie things together and point you in the direction you need to go.

CHAPTER **8**

JFC by Class

The previous chapter covers what you can do with the JFC in general terms. It frequently refers to sections in this chapter for more detailed discussions of individual classes. This chapter goes through 100+ of the most important JFC classes one at a time, giving step-by-step instructions on how to use them in common ways, then provides more advanced examples describing how they can be used in more unusual ways. The point is to make it easy to start using the classes, then to give insights into how the classes can be used to solve more advanced problems.

Some Notes About Examples

Most of the examples in this chapter do not include discussions or listings of a class with a main() method. This is because most of the examples use a class called Test.java that contains a main() method, then creates a JFrame subclass that actually contains the useful code. So, in the interest of efficiency, the Test.java class has not been listed with each example, although it is included for each example on the CD. The basic Test.java source file looks like this:**import com.sun.java.swing.*;**

```
public class Test
{
    public Test()
    {
        String lf = UIManager.getSystemLookAndFeelClassName();

        if ( lf != null )
        {
            try
            {
                UIManager.setLookAndFeel( lf );
            }
            catch ( Exception ex )
            {
                ex.printStackTrace();
            }
        }

        MyFrame mf = new MyFrame();
        mf.setSize( 250, 200 );
        mf.show();
    }

    public static void main( String args[] )
    {
        new Test();
    }

}
```

It has a main() method that creates an instance of the Test class. The Test() constructor creates an instance MyFrame, a JFrame subclass, and places it on the screen. MyFrame.java is the important method for almost every example in this chapter. There are a few classes that are non-graphical, and thus do not use a MyFrame class. These examples include Test.java in their listings.

Test.java also includes code to make the example take on the system's native look-and-feel.

AbstractAction

AbstractAction is an abstract class that implements the Action interface. In its simplest form, its subclasses can be used as ActionListeners since AbstractAction implements the ActionListener interface (Action extends ActionListener).

Certain JFC containers are Action aware. For example, you can subclass AbstractAction and add an instance of your subclass to a JMenu. JMenu is Action aware, so it sees your class, creates a JMenuItem, and adds the JMenuItem to itself. It is for this type of use that the Action interface defines its icon and text manipulation methods. You can create a single Abstract-Action subclass and add it to multiple Action aware containers. For instance, you might want to have a Cut tool in a tool bar and in a menu. You can create your subclass, giving it a text string and an icon, both of which will be placed in the menu and the toolbar. The subclass' actionPerformed() method will be activated when either the menu item or the tool bar button is pressed. You can also disable both the menu item and the tool bar button by disabling the subclass.

AbstractAction subclasses are useful whenever you have more than one way the user can trigger the same action.

Ancestors

```
java.lang.Object
    |
    +-com.sun.java.swing.AbstractAction
```

 NOTE: *For more information, see the "KeyStroke," "JMenu," and "JToolBar" sections of this chapter. Also see "A Quick Review of JDK 1.1 Events" in Chapter 7, "JFC by Concept." The "JTextArea" section in this chapter shows how to use an AbstractAction subclass with a KeyStroke.*

Steps in Extending and Using AbstractAction

1. Create your own class that extends AbstractAction. At the least, you must override the actionPerformed() method.

```
public class MyAction extends AbstractAction
{
    public void actionPerformed( ActionEvent e )
    {
```

```
                // For this example, we print out the component that
                // generated the ActionEvent.
                System.out.println( "Action source component:  " +
                                    e.getSource() );
        }
    }
```

2. You can use an AbstractAction subclass as an ActionListener. Here we create two buttons and use the same listener for both:

```
MyAction myAction = new MyAction();
JButton b1 = new JButton( "Button 1" );
b1.addActionListener( myAction );
JButton b2 = new JButton( "Button 2" );
b2.addActionListener( myAction );
```

3. Create a JMenuItem in a JMenu using an AbstractAction subclass. Notice that the JMenu's add() method returns the JMenuItem that was created.

   Create an AbstractAction subclass that accepts a text string:

```
private class CopyAction extends AbstractAction
{
    public CopyAction( String text )
    {
        super( text );
    }

    public void actionPerformed( ActionEvent e )
    {
        // Do something now you know the "Copy" menu item was
        // pressed.
    }
}
```

   Create an instance of the action and add it to the JMenu:

```
// Create a JMenu.
JMenu editMenu = new JMenu( "Edit" );

// Create an instance of the action.
CopyAction copyAction = new CopyAction( "Copy" );

// Add the action to the JMenu.  This causes a JMenuItem to be
// created and added to the JMenu.  The created JMenuItem is
// returned from the add() method.
JMenuItem copyMenuItem = editMenu.add( copyAction );
```

4. Create a JButton in a JToolBar using an AbstractAction subclass. Notice that JToolBar's add() method returns the created JButton.

   Create an AbstractAction subclass that accepts an icon:

```
private class CopyAction extends AbstractAction
{
    public CopyAction( Icon icon )
```

```
    {
        super( "", icon );
    }

    public void actionPerformed( ActionEvent e )
    {
        // Do something now you know the "Copy" menu item was
        // pressed.
    }
}
```

Create an instance of the action and add it to the JToolBar:

```
// Create a JToolBar.
JToolBar toolbar = new JToolBar();

// Create an instance of the action.
CopyAction copyAction = new CopyAction( new ImageIcon(
                                        "copy.gif" ) );

// Add the action to the JToolBar.  This causes a JButton to be
// created and added to the JToolBar.  The created JButton is
// returned from the add() method.
JButton copyButton = toolbar.add( copyAction );
```

5. Disable the AbstractAction subclass. This also disables the components that were created using it.

```
copyAction.setEnabled( false );
```

6. Find out if the AbstractAction subclass is enabled:

```
boolean actionState = copyAction.isEnabled();
```

7. Set the AbstractAction subclass' text strings. AbstractAction actually allows you to store multiple text strings and icons with the action. The Action interface defines the following string constants that you can associate strings with, and you can also create your own:

```
Action.DEFAULT
Action.NAME
Action.SHORT_DESCRIPTION
Action.LONG_DESCRIPTION
```

If you specified a text string in AbstractAction's constructor, that string is associated with Action.NAME and JMenu uses it as the text for the JMenuItem it creates when an action is passed to JMenu's add() method. You can use the other strings for other purposes like tool tips or accessible descriptions.

Add a long description string to the action, create a JButton with the action, and set the JButton's tool tip:

```
// Create a tool bar.
JToolBar toolbar = new JToolBar();
```

```
// Create an action.
CopyAction copyAction = new CopyAction( new ImageIcon(
                                        "copy.gif" ) );

// Set the action's long description.
copyAction.putValue( Action.LONG_DESCRIPTION, "Copy highlighted text
                     to the clipboard" );

// Add the action to the tool bar, and get back the created button.
JButton copyBtn = toolbar.add( copyAction );

// Use the action's long description as the button's tool tip.
copyBtn.setToolTipText( copyBtn.getValue
                        ( Action.LONG_DESCRIPTION ) );
```

Basic Code Examples

EXAMPLE 8-1 **Controlling Multiple Components with a Single Action**
This example has a menu with Cut, Copy, and Paste menu items, and a tool bar with buttons that are equivalent to the menu items. All of the menu items and tool bar buttons are created with subclasses of AbstractAction, with one action being used for both the Cut menu item and the cut button, and so on for copy and paste. Figure 8-1 shows the example with the menu expanded.

Important points to notice:

■ Our AbstractAction subclass is called WorkingAction. It is also abstract, and each type of action (cut, copy, paste) subclasses it to provide the appropriate actionPerformed() method.

■ WorkingAction's constructor accepts an name, description, and icon. It also has a configureComponent() method that is used to apply the description string to a passed in component as its tool tip and accessible description. This method also sets the accessible name for the passed in component.

■ The main frame class, MyFrame, contains three inner subclasses of WorkingAction—one for cut, one for copy, and one for paste.

■ The action that controls the Cut menu item and the cut tool bar button is disabled at the end of MyFrame's constructor. This demonstrates how disabling the action also disables the associated menu item and toolbar button.

Figure 8-1

■ The toolbar buttons are shifted right so we can see them when the menu is expanded. This is done by adding a padding component using the Box.createHorizontalGlue() method.

Here is the source code for MyFrame.java (WorkingAction.java follows):

```java
import com.sun.java.swing.*;
import java.awt.*;
import java.awt.event.*;
import java.util.*;

public class MyFrame extends JFrame
{
    // The three actions.
    private CopyAction mCopyAction;
    private CutAction mCutAction;
    private PasteAction mPasteAction;

    public MyFrame()
    {
        setTitle( "AbstractAction1" );

        // Store the content pane in a variable for easier
        // access.
        JPanel contentPane = (JPanel)getContentPane();

        // Components will all be added to this panel.
        contentPane.setLayout( new BorderLayout() );

        // Create the menu bar.
        JMenuBar mbar = new JMenuBar();

        // Create an "Edit" menu and add it to the menu bar.
        JMenu edit = new JMenu( "Edit" );
        mbar.add( edit );

        // Create the action for the copy menu item and
        // button.
        mCopyAction = new CopyAction( "Copy",
            "Copy highlighted information to the clipboard",
            new ImageIcon( "copy.gif" ) );

        // Create a menu item in the menu by adding the action
        // to the menu.
        JMenuItem copy = edit.add( mCopyAction );

        // Apply the action's name and description to the menu
        // item as tool tip and accessible information
        // strings.
        mCopyAction.configureComponent( copy );

        // Create the action for the cut menu item and button.
        mCutAction = new CutAction( "Cut",
            "Move the highlighted information to the clipboard",
            new ImageIcon( "cut.gif" ) );
```

```
// Create a menu item in the menu by adding the action
// to the menu.
JMenuItem cut = edit.add( mCutAction );

// Apply the action's name and description to the menu
// item as tool tip and accessible information
// strings.
mCutAction.configureComponent( cut );

// Create the action for the paste menu item and
// button.
mPasteAction = new PasteAction( "Paste",
        "Insert the information from the clipboard",
        new ImageIcon( "paste.gif" ) );

// Create a menu item in the menu by adding the action
// to the menu.
JMenuItem paste = edit.add( mPasteAction );

// Apply the action's name and description to the menu
// item as tool tip and accessible information
// strings.
mPasteAction.configureComponent( paste );

// Use the menu bar as the frame's main menu.
getRootPane().setMenuBar( mbar );

// Create a tool bar.
JToolBar toolbar = new JToolBar();

// Use a padding component to force the toolbar
// buttons to the right.
toolbar.add( Box.createHorizontalGlue() );

// Create a button in the toolbar by adding the
// action.
JButton copyBtn = toolbar.add( mCopyAction );

// Apply the action's name and description to the menu
// item as tool tip and accessible information
// strings.
mCopyAction.configureComponent( copyBtn );

// Create a button in the toolbar by adding the
// action.
JButton cutBtn = toolbar.add( mCutAction );

// Apply the action's name and description to the menu
// item as tool tip and accessible information
// strings.
mCutAction.configureComponent( cutBtn );

// Create a button in the toolbar by adding the
// action.
```

```
        JButton pasteBtn = toolbar.add( mPasteAction );

        // Apply the action's name and description to the menu
        // item as tool tip and accessible information
        // strings.
        mPasteAction.configureComponent( pasteBtn );

        // Add the toolbar to the top of the content pane.
        contentPane.add( "North", toolbar );

        // Disable the "Cut" action, and thereby the
        // associated menu item and button.
        mCutAction.setEnabled( false );
    }

    // This is the action class used for the "Copy" menu item
    // and button.
    private class CopyAction extends WorkingAction
    {
        public CopyAction( String name, String description,
                            Icon icon )
        {
            super( name, description, icon );
        }

        // Called when either the menu item or the button is
        // pressed.
        public void actionPerformed( ActionEvent e )
        {
            System.out.println( "Copy pressed" );
        }
    }

    // This is the action class used for the "Cut" menu item
    // and button.
    private class CutAction extends WorkingAction
    {
        public CutAction( String name, String description,
                            Icon icon )
        {
            super( name, description, icon );
        }

        // Called when either the menu item or the button is
        // pressed.
        public void actionPerformed( ActionEvent e )
        {
            System.out.println( "Cut pressed" );
        }
    }

    // This is the action class used for the "Paste" menu
    // item and button.
    private class PasteAction extends WorkingAction
    {
```

```
    public PasteAction( String name, String description,
                        Icon icon )
    {
        super( name, description, icon );
    }

    // Called when either the menu item or the button is
    // pressed.
    public void actionPerformed( ActionEvent e )
    {
        System.out.println( "Paste pressed" );
    }
    }
}
```

Here is the source code for WorkingAction.java:

```
import com.sun.java.swing.*;
import com.sun.java.accessibility.*;
import java.util.*;
import java.awt.event.*;

abstract public class WorkingAction extends AbstractAction
{
    public WorkingAction( String name, String description,
                          Icon icon )
    {
        // Store the strings as keyed strings that can be
        // accessed using the getText() method.
        putValue( Action.SMALL_ICON, icon );
        putValue( Action.NAME, name );
        putValue( Action.DEFAULT, name );
        putValue( Action.SHORT_DESCRIPTION, description );
        putValue( Action.LONG_DESCRIPTION, description );
    }

    // Apply the name and description strings passed into the
    // constructor as the JComponent's tooltip, accessible
    // name, and accessible description.
    public void configureComponent( JComponent jcomp )
    {
        jcomp.setToolTipText(
            (String)getValue( Action.LONG_DESCRIPTION ) );

        AccessibleContext ac = jcomp.getAccessibleContext();

        if ( ac != null )
        {
            ac.setAccessibleDescription(
                (String)getValue( Action.LONG_DESCRIPTION ) );
            ac.setAccessibleName(
                (String)getValue( Action.NAME ) );
        }
    }
}
```

Advanced Issues

For information on using actions with keysrokes, see the "KeyStroke" section in this chapter.

AbstractAction's Public Methods

```
void addPropertyChangeListener(PropertyChangeListener listener)
```

Tells the AbstractAction subclass to notify the given class when properties (text, icon, etc.) change.

```
Object getValue(String key)
```

Returns the object (typically a String or Icon) associated with the given key.

```
boolean isEnabled()
```

Returns true if the action is enabled.

```
void putValue (String key, object value)
```

Associates an Object (typically a String or Icon) with the given key. The keyString is usually Action.DEFAULT, Action.Name, Action.SHORT_DESCRIPTION, action.LONG-DESCRIPTION, or Action.SMALL_ICON.

```
void removePropertyChangeListener(PropertyChangeListener listener)
```

Tells the AbstractAction subclass to stop notifying the given class when properties change.

```
void setEnabled(boolean newValue)
```

Specifies whether the action is enabled.

AbstractBorder

All of the JFC border classes are descendants of AbstractBorder which is, not surprisingly, an abstract class. AbstractBorder has a basic implementation of the Border interface, and adds a static method for finding the part of a component that can be drawn on without interfering with the border. If you want to create a custom border of your own, AbstractBorder is a good place to start.

A border is not a component itself. It is a class that a component can use to describe how its edge should appear. A component is not required to use a border, but JComponent includes the ability to set, get, and paint a border. Its default paint() method indirectly calls the border's paintBorder() method. If you override the paint() method in your own JComponent subclass, you need to call the border's paintBorder() method or the border will not paint. It is better in those cases to override the paintComponent() method instead of the paint() method.

A border's area is defined using an inset from each edge of the component onto which the border will paint. Your custom borders should override the getBorderInsets() method so other classes can find out where the border will draw.

Ancestors

```
java.lang.Object
    |
    +-com.sun.java.swing.border.AbstractBorder
```

NOTE: *For more information, see the "BevelBorder," "CompoundBorder," "Empty-Border," "EtchedBorder," "LineBorder," "MatteBorder," "SoftBevelBorder," and "TitledBorder" sections of this chapter; Chapter 3, "The JComponent Class;" and the "Component Borders" section of Chapter 7, "JFC by Concept."*

Steps in Subclassing AbstractBorder

1. Create your class' skeleton:

   ```
   // For AbstractBorder.
   import com.sun.java.swing.border.*;

   // For Insets and various painting classes.
   import java.awt.*;

   public class MyBorder extends AbstractBorder
   {
       public MyBorder()
       {
       }
   }
   ```

2. Override the getBorderInsets() method. This tells inquiring classes how much space the border will take up on each side of the component it is attached to. In this case, we say the border is six pixels on each side. If the border is applied to a resizable JInternalFrame, this is also the

area over which the JInternalFrame's resize cursor will appear. Notice that this method takes an argument which is the component onto which the border will be painted:

```
public Insets getBorderInsets( Component c )
{
    return new Insets( 6, 6, 6, 6 );
}
```

3. Override the paintBorder() method. This should be called indirectly by the component's paint() method. If the component fails to call this method, the border will not be painted. Note that the border should not paint in the main area of the component. This paintBorder() method will draw three stripes around the edge of the component. These will be red, green, and blue, and will be two pixels wide each. Notice that the component being drawn on, its graphics context, the border's origin, and the border's width and height are passed to this method.

```
public void paintBorder( Component c, Graphics g, int x, int y,
                         int width, int height )
{
    // Draw the red stripe.
    g.setColor( Color.red );
    g.drawRect( x, y, width, height );
    g.drawRect( x + 1, y + 1, width - 2, height - 2 );

    // Draw the green stripe.
    g.setColor( Color.green );
    g.drawRect( x + 2, y + 2, width - 4, height - 4 );
    g.drawRect( x + 3, y + 3, width - 6, height - 6 );

    // Draw the blue stripe.
    g.setColor( Color.blue );
    g.drawRect( x + 4, y + 4, width - 8, height - 8 );
    g.drawRect( x + 5, y + 5, width - 10, height - 10 );
}
```

4. If your border paints all of its space, you should override the isBorderOpaque() method to return true:

```
public boolean isBorderOpaque()
{
    return true;
}
```

Basic Code Examples

EXAMPLE 8-2   Creating a Custom Border by Subclassing AbstractBorder

This example puts the steps discussed above together. It consists of two classes: one that is a general JFrame subclass called MyFrame on whose con-

Figure 8-2
A custom border.

tent pane we will put the border, and the other is our AbstractBorder subclass called MyBorder which will draw the border. Figure 8-2 shows the example as it first comes up.

Here is the source for MyFrame.java. It is quite simple:

```java
import com.sun.java.swing.*;
import java.awt.*;

public class MyFrame extends JFrame
{
    public MyFrame()
    {
        setTitle( "AbstractBorder1" );

        // Store the content pane in a variable for easier
        // access.
        JPanel contentPane = (JPanel)getContentPane();

        // Set the content pane's border to our custom border.
        contentPane.setBorder( new MyBorder() );
    }
}
```

Here is the source for MyBorder.java. It is just as discussed above:

```java
import com.sun.java.swing.border.*;

// For Insets and various painting classes.
import java.awt.*;

public class MyBorder extends AbstractBorder
{
    public MyBorder()
    {
    }

    // The border is 6 pixels wide all the way around.
    public Insets getBorderInsets( Component c )
    {
        return new Insets( 6, 6, 6, 6 );
    }

    // Paint the border.  It will have a 2-pixel red stripe
    // around a 2-pixel green stripe around a 2-pixel blue
    // stripe.
    public void paintBorder( Component c, Graphics g, int x,
                             int y, int width, int height )
```

```
{
    // Draw the red stripe.
    g.setColor( Color.red );
    g.drawRect( x, y, width, height );
    g.drawRect( x + 1, y + 1, width - 2, height - 2 );

    // Draw the green stripe.
    g.setColor( Color.green );
    g.drawRect( x + 2, y + 2, width - 4, height - 4 );
    g.drawRect( x + 3, y + 3, width - 6, height - 6 );

    // Draw the blue stripe.
    g.setColor( Color.blue );
    g.drawRect( x + 4, y + 4, width - 8, height - 8 );
    g.drawRect( x + 5, y + 5, width - 10, height - 10 );
}

// We paint the entire border area, so we say it is
// opaque.
public boolean isBorderOpaque()
{
    return true;
}
}
```

AbstractBorder's Public Methods

Insets getBorderInsets(Component c)

Returns the border's width on each side of the component.

Rectangle getInteriorRectangle(Component c,int x,int y,int width,int height)

Given the component onto which the border will be drawn and the component's size, returns the rectangle within the border.

static Rectangle getInteriorRectangle(Component c,Border b,int x,int y,int width,int height)

Given the border and the component onto which the border will be drawn and the component's size, this static method returns the rectangle within the border.

boolean isBorderOpaque()

Should return true if the border completely fills its insets or false if not. It returns false by default.

void paintBorder(Component c,Graphics g,int x,int y,int width,int height)

Given the component onto which the border will be drawn, the component's graphics context, location, and size, paint the border.

AbstractButton

AbstractButton is an abstract class which is the parent class of all of the JFC buttons: JButton, JCheckBox, JRadioButton, JToggleButton, JMenuItem, JCheckBoxMenuItem, and JRadioButtonMenuItem. It includes the lion's share of most of these components' functionality—especially the non-menu ones.

Ancestors

```
java.lang.Object
    |
    +-java.awt.Component
            |
            +-java.awt.Container
                    |
                    +-com.sun.java.swing.JComponent
                            |
                            +-com.sun.java.swing.AbstractButton
```

NOTE: *For more information, see the "JButton," "JCheckBox," "JRadioButton," "JToggleButton," "JMenuItem," "JRadioButtonMenuItem," "JCheckBoxMenuItem," "ImageIcon," and "DefaultButtonModel" sections in this chapter. Also see Chapter 3, "The JComponent Class," and Chapter 4, "Pluggable Look-and-Feel."*

Steps in Creating and Using AbstractButton

Since the AbstractButton methods that affect its subclasses are discussed in each of their sections in this chapter, we will not cover them step-by-step here. Also, there is no AbstractButton example since you will normally subclass one of AbstractButton's subclasses rather that AbstractButton itself.

AbstractButton's Public Methods

```
void addActionListener(ActionListener l)
```

Tells the button to notify the passed-in class when the button is pressed.

```
void addChangeListener(ChangeListener l)
```

Tells the button to notify the passed-in class when the ButtonModel changes, like when the mouse rolls over the button or the button is pressed.

```
void addItemListener(ItemListener l)
```

Typically used for AbstractButton subclasses that change state—not JButton or JMenuItem. Tells the button to notify the passed-in class when the button's state changes.

```
void doClick()
```

Programmatically click the button.

```
void doClick(int pressTime)
```

Just like the previous method except that the button remains pressed for the given number of milliseconds.

```
String getActionCommand()
```

Returns the action command string that the button will deliver with its ActionEvents. May be null.

```
Icon getDisabledIcon()
```

Returns the icon (if any) that is displayed on the button when it is disabled. This will return the icon specified through the setDisabledIcon() method, or a gray version of the button's normal icon if one has been defined, or null if the button doesn't use an icon.

```
Icon getDisabledSelectedIcon()
```

Returns the icon (if any) that is displayed on the button when it is disabled in the selected state. This will return the icon specified through the setDisabledSelectedIcon() method, or a gray version of the icon set through the setSelectedIcon() method if there is one, or null.

```
int getHorizontalAlignment()
```

Returns the text/icon's position within the button (LEFT, CENTER, RIGHT).

```
int getHorizontalTextPosition()
```

Returns the button's text string's position relative to the button's icon (if any). It is one of: LEFT, RIGHT, CENTER.

```
Icon getIcon()
```

Returns the button's normal icon (if any).

`Insets getMargin()`

Returns the space between the button's text/icon and its border on all four sides of the button.

`int getMnemonic()`

Returns the accelerator key that, in combination with a special key (Alt on some systems), causes the button to be selected/pressed.

`ButtonModel getModel()`

Returns the ButtonModel, usually a DefaultButtonModel, where the buttons internal state is stored.

`Icon getPressedIcon()`

Returns the icon (if any) that the button displays when pressed. This icon would have been set using the setPressedIcon() method.

`Icon getRolloverIcon()`

Returns the icon (if any) that the button displays if rollover is enabled (using the setRolloverEnabled(true) method) and the mouse is currently over the button.

`Icon getRolloverSelectedIcon()`

Returns the icon (if any) that the button displays if rollover is enabled (using the setRolloverEnabled(true) method), the mouse is currently over the button, and the button is selected.

`Icon getSelectedIcon()`

Returns the icon (if any) the button displays when it is selected.

`Object[] getSelectedObjects()`

This method is used basically just to fill out the ItemSelectable interface that AbstractButton implements. It returns an array containing the button if the button is selected or null otherwise.

`String getText()`

Returns the button's displayed text string (if any).

`ButtonUI getUI()`

Returns the button's look-and-feel class—a class that extends the ButtonUI class.

```
int getVerticalAlignment()
```

Returns the text/icon's location within the button. This can be: CENTER, TOP, or BOTTOM.

```
int getVerticalTextPosition()
```

Returns the text's vertical position relative to the icon. This can be: CENTER, TOP, or BOTTOM.

```
boolean isBorderPainted()
```

Returns true if the border will be painted or false if not.

```
boolean isFocusPainted()
```

Returns true if the rectangle that indicates that the button has focus will be drawn or false if not.

```
boolean isRolloverEnabled()
```

Return's true if the use of rollover icons is enabled.

```
boolean isSelected()
```

Returns true if the button is in a selected state.

```
void removeActionListener(ActionListener l)
```

Tells the button that the passed-in class should no longer be notified when the button is pressed.

```
void removeChangeListener(ChangeListener l)
```

Tells the button that the passed-in class should no longer be notified when the ButtonModel changes.

```
void removeItemListener(ItemListener l)
```

Tells the button that the passed-in class should no longer be notified when the button changes its state.

```
void setActionCommand(String actionCommand)
```

Specifies the String that the button should deliver with its ActionEvents.

```
void setBorderPainted(boolean b)
```

Specifies whether the button's border should be painted or not.

```
void setDisabledIcon(Icon disabledIcon)
```

Specifies the icon that the button should display when it is disabled.

```
void setDisabledSelectedIcon(Icon disabledSelectedIcon)
```

Specifies the icon that the button should display when it is disabled and in the selected state.

```
void setEnabled(boolean b)
```

Enables or disables the button.

```
void setFocusPainted(boolean b)
```

Specifies whether the button should display its focus rectangle when it has the focus.

```
void setHorizontalAlignment(int alignment)
```

Specifies where within the button the text/icon should be displayed (LEFT, CENTER, or RIGHT).

```
void setHorizontalTextPosition(int textPosition)
```

Specifies whether the text should be LEFT or RIGHT of the icon, or in the CENTER so it can be below or above the icon.

```
void setIcon(Icon defaultIcon)
```

Specifies the button's normal icon.

```
void setMargin(Insets m)
```

Specifies the padding size between the text/icon and the button's border on all four of the button's sides.

```
void setMnemonic(int keyAccelerator)
```

Specifies the key which, when pressed with a special key (Alt on some platforms), will cause the button to be pressed or selected/deselected.

```
void setMnemonic(char mnem)
```

Same as the previous method except that the mnemonic is specified as a char.

```
void setModel(ButtonModel newModel)
```

Used to specify a new class to act as the button's model.

```
void setPressedIcon(Icon pressedIcon)
```

Specify the icon that the button should display while it is pressed.

```
void setRolloverEnabled(boolean b)
```

Enables or disables the use of rollover icons.

```
void setRolloverIcon(Icon rolloverIcon)
```

Specifies the icon that the button should display when the use of rollover icons is enabled and the mouse is over the button.

```
void setRolloverSelectedIcon(Icon rolloverSelectedIcon)
```

Specifies the icon that the button should display when the use of rollover icons is enabled, the button is selected, and the mouse is over the button.

```
void setSelected(boolean b)
```

Tells the button that it is now selected/deselected.

```
void setSelectedIcon(Icon selectedIcon)
```

Specifies the icon that the button should display when it is selected.

```
void setText(String text)
```

Specifies the text string that the button should display.

```
void setUI(ButtonUI ui)
```

Gives the button a new look-and-feel class.

```
void setVerticalAlignment(int alignment)
```

Specifies whether the text/icon should display at the TOP, CENTER, or BOTTOM of the button.

```
void setVerticalTextPosition(int textPosition)
```

Specifies whether the text should appear above or below the icon, or vertically level with it. To display above or below, the horizontal alignment should be CENTER. Possible values are: TOP, CENTER, or BOTTOM.

```
void updateUI()
```

Tells the button that its look-and-feel class has been changed.

AbstractDocument

AbstractDocument is an abstract class that the JFC's working Document classes are derived from. A Document is where the various text components store their contents, attributes, etc. AbstractDocument defines the basic behavior for accessing text components' contents and attributes, and for tracking changes to the contents and the text attributes. A single Document may be used by more than one text component at a time.

Ancestors

```
java.lang.Object
   |
   +-com.sun.java.swing.text.AbstractDocument
```

NOTE: For more information, see the "DefaultStyledDocument," "PlainDocument," "Element," "JTextField," "JTextArea," and "JTextPane" sections in this chapter. Also see Chapter 5, "JFC Documents and Text Components," and Chapter 13, "JFC Integration Example 4—A Simple Word Processor."

Steps in Creating and Using AbstractDocument Subclasses

Since AbstractDocument is abstract, these steps refer to PlainDocument, the simplest subclass of AbstractDocument.

1. Create the AbstractDocument subclass. This may be done explicitly, or the various JFC text components will automatically create one. JTextField and JTextArea use PlainDocuments and JTextPane uses a DefaultStyledDocument.

    Create a PlainDocument and apply it to a JTextField:

    ```
    PlainDocument doc = new PlainDocument();
    JTextField jtf = new JTextField();
    jtf.setDocument( doc );
    ```

2. Get the number of characters in the document.

```
int length = doc.getLength();
```

3. Get a specific part of the document's text. There are two getText() methods for this.

Get a copy of the text in a range starting at character 3 and having a length of 4:

```
String part = doc.getText( 3, 4 );
```

Read the same range, but load it into a Segment that gives direct access to the Document's characters:

```
Segment part = new Segment()
String part = doc.getText( 3, 4, part );
```

If you change the contents of the Segment, the text in the document is changed. You can access the characters directly through the Segment's 'array' variable.

4. Insert text into the Document at a specific index. This method takes an AttributeSet argument, but you can set it to null.

Insert the string "inserted string" into the document at index 3.

```
doc.insertString( 3, "inserted string", null );
```

5. Listen for changes to the Document. You will be notified when text is inserted or deleted, or when attributes change.

Specify a class that will be notified of document changes. In this case it is the current class.

```
doc.addDocumentListener( this );
```

Make the event-receiving class (MyFrame) implement the DocumentListener interface:

```
public class MyFrame extends JFrame implements DocumentListener
{
    public void changedUpdate( DocumentEvent e )
    {
        // Atributes changed.
    }

    public void insertUpdate( DocumentEvent e )
    {
        // Text was inserted.
    }

    public void removeUpdate( DocumentEvent e )
    {
        // Text was deleted.
    }
}
```

6. Remove text from the Document.

This removes 4 characters starting at index 3:

```
doc.remove( 3, 4 );
```

Basic Code Example

EXAMPLE 8-3   **Exercising `AbstractDocument`'s capabilities**

This example contains two JTextFields and a JButton. We create a Plain-Document, since that is the AbstractDocument subclass that JTextFields use, and we tell both JTextFields to use it. This way, when you change one JTextField, the contents of the other one change as well. The JButton exercises AbstractDocument's dump() method and also triggers our own dump method that recursively walks through the document's elements, printing out their contents. We also store a Position which represents the beginning of the word "brillig" in the original text (see the "JTextField" section in this chapter for another example of using a Position). As text is inserted or deleted, we check to see if the seven characters following the Position have been changed. Figure 8-3 shows the example as it looks when it first comes up.

Important points to notice:

■ Since we are using JTextFields, setting attributes doesn't have much effect. So, dumping the document's contents just displays the contents as a single element.

Here is the source code:

```java
import com.sun.java.swing.*;
import com.sun.java.swing.event.*;
import com.sun.java.swing.text.*;
import java.awt.*;
import java.awt.event.*;

public class MyFrame extends JFrame implements
        DocumentListener, ActionListener
{
    // The document.  PlainDocument is a subclass of
    // AbstractDocument.
    private PlainDocument mDoc;

    // A stored position.
    private Position mPos;

    public MyFrame()
```

Figure 8-3

```
{
    setTitle( "AbstractDocument1" );

    // Store the content pane in a variable for easier
    // access.
    JPanel contentPane = (JPanel)getContentPane();

    // Components will all be added to this panel.
    contentPane.setLayout( new BorderLayout() );

    // Create a pane to hole the two text fields.
    JPanel fieldPane = new JPanel();
    fieldPane.setLayout( new BorderLayout() );

    // Create the document that the text fields will use.
    mDoc = new PlainDocument();

    // Make it so this class is notified when text is
    // inserted or deleted, or attributes change.
    mDoc.addDocumentListener( this );

    // Create the two text fields.
    JTextField jtf = new JTextField();
    JTextField jtf2 = new JTextField();

    try
    {
        // Give the document some text.
        mDoc.insertString( 0, "Twas brillig", null );

        // Tell the two text fields to use the document.
        jtf.setDocument( mDoc );
        jtf2.setDocument( mDoc );

        // Set the font for the first text field.
        jtf.setFont( new Font( "TimesRoman", Font.BOLD,
                                18 ) );

        // Store a Position which tracks the start of the
        // word "brillig".
        mPos = mDoc.createPosition( 5 );
    }
    catch ( BadLocationException ex )
    {
        System.out.println( ex );
    }

    // Place the text fields in their pane.
    fieldPane.add( "North", jtf );
    fieldPane.add( "South", jtf2 );

    // Add the text fields' pane to the content pane.
    contentPane.add( "North", fieldPane );

    // Create a button that will trigger a dump of the
```

```
      // document.
      JButton dump = new JButton( "Dump" );
      dump.addActionListener( this );
      contentPane.add( "South", dump );
   }

   public void actionPerformed( ActionEvent e )
   {
      // Use AbstractDocument's built in dump() method.
      mDoc.dump( System.out );

      // Use our own method to list the document's elements.
      Element root = mDoc.getDefaultRootElement();

      listElements( root );
   }

   // This method recursively goes through the document and
   // prints out each element's contents.
   private void listElements( Element root )
   {
      try
      {
         // If the passed-in element is a leaf, print it.
         if ( root.isLeaf() )
         {
            System.out.println( "|" +
                     mDoc.getText( root.getStartOffset(),
                     root.getEndOffset() -
                     root.getStartOffset() ) + "|" );
         }
         else
         {
            // If this element has child elements, call this
            // method on each of them.
            int num = root.getElementCount();

            for ( int i = 0; i < num; i++ )
            {
               listElements( root.getElement( i ) );
            }
         }
      }
      catch ( BadLocationException ex )
      {
         System.out.println( ex );
      }
   }

   // This is called when attributes change.
   public void changedUpdate( DocumentEvent e )
   {
      System.out.println( "Changed" );
   }

   // This is called when text is inserted.
```

```
public void insertUpdate( DocumentEvent e )
{
    System.out.println( "Inserted" );

    // See if "brillig" has been changed.
    checkBrillig();
}

// This is called when text is deleted.
public void removeUpdate( DocumentEvent e )
{
    System.out.println( "Removed" );

    // See if "brillig" has been changed.
    checkBrillig();
}

// This method looks at the position created in the
// constructor and compares the next seven characters
// there to see if they still spell "brillig".
private void checkBrillig()
{
    if ( mPos == null )
        return;

    try
    {
        if ( mDoc.getText( mPos.getOffset(), 7 ).equals(
            "brillig" ) )
        {
            System.out.println(
                            "'brillig' has not changed" );
        }
        else
        {
            System.out.println( "'brillig' HAS changed" );
        }
    }
    catch ( BadLocationException ex )
    {
        System.out.println( ex );
    }
}
}
```

AbstractDocument's Public Methods

void addDocumentListener(DocumentListener listener)

Tells the AbsrtactDocument subclass to notify the given class when: text is inserted, text is deleted, or attributes change.

```
void addUndoableEditListener(UndoableEditListener l)
```

Tells the AbstractDocument subclass to notify the given class when an edit that can be undone occurs.

```
Position createPosition(int offs)
```

Create a Position instance that will move right as text is inserted in front of it, or left as text is removed from before it. Use Position's getOffset() method to find its current value. Positions are used to mark a spot in the text so you can keep track of it as the rest of the document changes.

```
void dump(PrintStream out)
```

Prints the AbstractDocument subclass' structure to standard out, including all text and attributes.

```
Element getDefaultRootElement()
```

Returns the AbstractDocument subclass' root element.

```
Dictionary getDocumentProperties()
```

Returns the current set of document properties.

```
Position getEndPosition()
```

Returns a Position representing the end of the text.

```
int getLength()
```

Returns the number of caharacters in the AbstractDocument subclass.

```
Object getProperty(Object key)
```

Retrieve a property Object that was stored within the AbstractDocument subclass. You can store any key/value pair you want.

```
Element[] getRootElements()
```

Get all root elements. There will normally just be one—the one returned by getDefaultRootElement().

```
Position getStartPosition()
```

Returns a Position that represents the start of the text.

```
String getText(int offset,int length)
```

Returns a range of the text, starting at 'offset' and having a length of 'length'.

```
void getText(int offset,int length,Segment txt)
```

Gets a range of text starting a index 'offset' and having a length of 'length'. The range is put into the 'txt' parameter—a Segment.

```
void insertString(int offs,String str, AttributeSet a)
```

Inserts the given String into the AbstractDocument subclass' text at the given offset. The given AttributeSet is applied to the text, but may be null.

```
void putProperty(Object key,Object value)
```

Store a new key/value pair.

```
void remove(int offs,int len)
```

Removes text starting at the given offset and having the given length.

```
void removeDocumentListener(DocumentListener listener)
```

Tells the AbstractDocument subclass to stop notifying the given class of text insertions, text deletion, and attribute changes.

```
void removeUndoableEditListener(UndoableEditListener l)
```

Tells the AbstractDocument subclass to stop notifying the given class when an undoable edit occurs.

```
void render(Runnable r)
```

Allows the document to be rendered in a thread safe manner.

```
void setDocumentProperties(Dictionary x)
```

Sets the document's properties, replacing any existing set.

AbstractTableModel

AbstractTableModel is an abstract class that implements most of the TableModel interface, thus implementing much of the functionality required for a class to be used as a model for a JTable. The TableModel methods that are not implemented are getRowCount(), getColumnCount(), and getValueAt(row,column). By implementing only part of the TableModel interface, AbstractTableModel implements as much as it can without making assumptions about the structure of the data in the model. This makes it ideal for wrapping around your own data model.

Ancestors

```
java.lang.Object
    |
    +-com.sun.java.swing.table.AbstractTableModel
```

NOTE: *For more information, see the "JTable" and "DefaultTableModel" sections in this chapter. Also see the "JFC Tables" section in Chapter 7, "JFC by Concept."*

Steps in Extending and Using AbstractTableModel

1. Create the AbstractTableModel subclass.

Create the skeleton:

```
public class MyTableModel extends AbstractTableModel
{
    // Implement your data storage mechanism.
}
```

Implement the getRowCount() method:

```
public int getRowCount()
{
    // Return the number of rows.
}
```

Implement the getColumnCount() method:

```
public int getColumnCount()
{
    // Return the number of columns.
}
```

Implement the getValueAt() method:

```
public Object getValueAt( int row, int column )
{
    // Return the value at the given row and column.
}
```

2. Create an instance of the AbstractTableModel subclass:

```
MyTableModel model = new MyTableModel();
```

3. Create a JTable using the AbstractTableModel subclass. You can also replace the JTable's model with the new one using JTable's setModel() method.

```
JTable myTable = new JTable( model );
```

4. Now you have a JTable that holds the data from our custom AbstractTableModel. If you want to be able to edit the data, you have to override the isCellEditable() and setValueAt() methods.

Override isCellEditable():

```
public boolean isCellEditable( int row, int column )
{
    // Return true if all cells are editable.
    return true;
}
```

Override setValueAt():

```
public void setValueAt( Object newValue, int row, int column )
{
    // Make sure the row and column are velid, then place the new
    // value into your data storage mechanism.

    // Notify any TableModelListeners that this cell has changed.
    fireTableCellUpdated( row, column );
}
```

There are a number of protected fire…() methods that you can call to notify TableModelListeners when the structure or contents of the model change.

Basic Code Examples

EXAMPLE 8-4 Creating a Custom TableModel from AbstractTableModel

This example creates a simple subclass of AbstractTableModel and creates a JTree that uses it. The data storage consists of a static 3x4 array of Objects. Figure 8-4 shows the example after the cell at column 2, row 1 has been edited.

Important points to notice:

■ We implemented getRowCount(), getColumnCount(), getValueAt(), and setValueAt() to provide information about and to allow change to our specific implementation of the table model.

■ We overrode the isCellEditable() method to allow all cells to be edited.

Figure 8-4

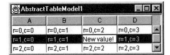

- The main frame class is registered as a TableModelListener on the custom table model, and will print out the string "Changed" when a cell is changed.
- The custom AbstractTableModel is included as an inner class within the main frame class for convenience. It could just as well have been in a class of its own.

Here is the source code:

```java
import com.sun.java.swing.*;
import com.sun.java.swing.event.*;
import com.sun.java.swing.table.*;
import java.awt.*;

public class MyFrame extends JFrame implements
        TableModelListener
{
    public MyFrame()
    {
        setTitle( "AbstractTableModel1" );

        // Store the content pane in a variable for easier
        // access.
        JPanel contentPane = (JPanel)getContentPane();

        // Components will all be added to this panel.
        contentPane.setLayout( new BorderLayout() );

        // Create an instance of our custom table model.
        MyTableModel model = new MyTableModel();

        // Make it so this class is notified when the table
        // model changes.
        model.addTableModelListener( this );

        // Create a JTree using our custom table model.
        JTable myTable = new JTable( model );

        // Create a JScrollPane for the table.
        JScrollPane sp = myTable.createScrollPaneForTable(
                                myTable );

        // Place the scroll pane in content pane's main area.
        contentPane.add( "Center", sp );
    }

    // This is called when the table model changes.
```

```
public void tableChanged( TableModelEvent e )
{
    System.out.println( "Changed" );
}

private class MyTableModel extends AbstractTableModel
{
    // Array holding the table model's data.
    private Object[][] mContents;

    // Rows in the model.
    private int mNumRows = 3;

    // Columns in the model.
    private int mNumColumns = 4;

    public MyTableModel()
    {
        // Allocate the rows.
        mContents = new Object[mNumRows][];

        // Allocate all columns in each row.
        for ( int i = 0; i < mNumRows; i++ )
            mContents[i] = new Object[mNumColumns];

        // Load data into the array.
        mContents[0][0] = "r=0,c=0";
        mContents[1][0] = "r=1,c=0";
        mContents[2][0] = "r=2,c=0";
        mContents[0][1] = "r=0,c=1";
        mContents[1][1] = "r=1,c=1";
        mContents[2][1] = "r=2,c=1";
        mContents[0][2] = "r=0,c=2";
        mContents[1][2] = "r=1,c=2";
        mContents[2][2] = "r=2,c=2";
        mContents[0][3] = "r=0,c=3";
        mContents[1][3] = "r=1,c=3";
        mContents[2][3] = "r=2,c=3";
    }

    // Returns the number of rows in the model.
    public int getRowCount()
    {
        return mNumRows;
    }

    // Returns the number of columns in the model.
    public int getColumnCount()
    {
        return mNumColumns;
    }

    // Returns the value in the cell at the given row and
    // column.
    public Object getValueAt( int row, int column )
```

```
{
    if ( row < mNumRows && row >= 0 &&
         column < mNumColumns && column >= 0 )
       return mContents[row][column];

    return null;
}

// Returns true so all cells are editable.
public boolean isCellEditable( int row, int column )
{
    return true;
}

// Checks that the row and column are valid, and then
// replaces its current item at the given row/coulmn
// with the new one.  Calls the protected
// fireTableCellUpdated() method to notify
// TableModelListeners of the change.
public void setValueAt( Object newValue, int row,
                        int column )
{
    if ( row >= 0 && row < mNumRows &&
         column >= 0 && column < mNumColumns )
    {
        mContents[row][column] = newValue;
        fireTableCellUpdated( row, column );
    }
}
    }
  }
}
```

AbstractTableModel's Public Methods

`void addTableModelListener(TableModelListener l)`

Tells the table model to notify the given classes when the model changes.

`int findColumn(String columnName)`

Returns the index of the table column that has the given name.

`Class getColumnClass(int columnIndex)`

Returns the class associated with the column.

`String getColumnName(int column)`

Returns the name associated with the given column.

`boolean isCellEditable(int rowIndex,int columnIndex)`

Returns true if the cell at the given row/column can be edited.

```
void removeTableModelListener(TableModelListener l)
```

Tells the table model to stop notifying the given class when the model changes.

```
void setValueAt(Object aValue,int rowIndex,intcolumnIndex)
```

Sets the value of the cell at the given row/column to the given value.

AccessibleContext

AccessibleContext as an abstract class located in the com.sun.java. accessibility package. You must extend it in order to support accessibility in your own components. When a screen reader or other access technology asks a component for its accessibility information, it does so by calling the component's getAccessibleContext() method. This method returns a subclass of AccessibleContext which gives the access technology a doorway into the component's accessibility information.

All JFC components include the getAccessibleContext() method, either defined directly, or inherited from JComponent. They also include at least some accessibility information.

Ancestors

```
java.lang.Object
    |
    +-com.sun.java.accessibility.AccessibleContext
```

NOTE: *For more information, see Chapter 6, "Accessibility."*

Steps in Extending and Using AccessibleContext

1. Subclass the abstract AccessibleContext class. This is required if you want to add accessibility information to your own components. JFC components contain their own AccessibleContext subclasses.

   Create your subclass:

```
public class MyAccessibleContext extends AccessibleContext
{
}
```

Implement the abstract getAccessibleRole() method. This method returns a constant from AccessibleRole (or a subclass of it) that defines the kind of component we are talking about. In this case, we will say that the component to which this AccessibleContext will be attached is a button:

```
public AccessibleRole getAccessibleRole()
{
    return AccessibleRole.PUSH_BUTTON;
}
```

Implement the abstract getAccessibleStateSet() method. This method returns a set of AccessibleStates that decribe the current state of the component. In this case, our button's state will be checked to create a AccessibleStateSet:

```
public AccessibleStateSet getAccessibleStateSet()
{
    ButtonModel model = button.getModel();
    AccessibleStateSet set = new AccessibleStateSet();

    if ( model.isEnabled() )
       set.add( AccessibleState.ENABLED );

    if ( model.isPressed() )
       set.add( AccessibleState.PRESSED );

    if ( button.isVisible() )
       set.add( AccessibleState.VISIBLE );

    return set;
}
```

Implement the abstract getAccessibleIndexInParent() method. This returns the accessible index of this component in its parent. SwingUtilities provides a static method that you can use to take care of this:

```
public int getAccessibleIndexInParent()
{
    return SwingUtilities.getAccessibleIndexInParent(
                                               mComponent );
}
```

Implement the abstract getAccessibleChildrenCount(). This returns the number of of accessible children in this component. SwingUtilities provides a static method that you can use to take care of this:

```
public int getAccessibleChildrenCount()
{
```

```
        return SwingUtilities.getAccessibleChildrenCount(
                                                    mComponent );
    }
```

Implement the abstract getAccessibleChild() method. This returns the nth accessible child component within this component. SwingUtilities provides a static method that you can use to take care of this:

```
    public Accessible getAccessibleChild( int n )
    {
        return SwingUtilities.getAccessibleChild( mComponent, n );
    }
```

Implement the abstract getLocale() method. This returns the locale of the component. Component contains a method that can be used to get this:

```
    public Locale getLocale()
    {
        return mComponent.getLocale();
    }
```

Set the accessible name for the component. This is a name that the user can use to identify the component. In this case, it might be "OK button":

```
    setAccessibleName( "OK button" );
```

If you want to set this from outside the AccessibleContext subclass, you can call:

```
    component.getAccessibleContext().setAccessibleName(
                                                    "OK button" );
```

Set the accessible description for the component. This describes the purpose of the component, and should not just be the accessible name:

```
    setAccessibleDescription(
                "Press this to save the dialog's information" );
```

If you want to set the accessible description from outside the AccessibleContext subclass, you can call:

```
    component.getAccessibleContext().setAccessibleDescription(
                "Press this to save the dialog's information" );
```

2. There are five specific types of accessible information that can be added to an AccessibleContext, and they are defined by the interfaces: AccessibleAction, AccessibleComponent, AccessibleSelection, AccessibleText, and AccessibleValue. AccessibleContext has five methods for getting these five types of information: getAccessibleAction(), getAccessibleComponent(), getAccessibleSelection(), getAccessibleText(), and getAccessibleValue(). These methods will return null unless you override them to return actual information. You can create new

classes to implement these interfaces, and/or you can implement them in your component or your AccessibleContext subclass and return those. AccessibleComponent especially lends itself to being returned as the AccessibleComponent because it will already have most of the interface implemented.

Basic Code Examples

EXAMPLE 8-5   **Implementing Accessibility in a Custom Component**

This example shows how to implement accessibility in a subclass of JComponent. It includes a main frame class, a custom component called My-Component, an AccessibleContext subclass that holds the custom component's accessibility information, and a class that implements AccessibleAction and handles accessible access to the AccessibleContext's AccessibleAction information. Figure 8-5 shows the example just after Alt-F has been pressed to transfer focus to the custom component.

Important points to notice:

- There are two actions associated with MyComponent. Alt-F will trigger the MyFocusAction, which requests the focus for the component. Alt-C will trigger the MyColorAction, which causes MyComponent to toggle its background color. These actions are defined so the AccessibleAction implementor will have actions to work with.

- The AccessibleContext subclass, MyAccessibleContext, includes two methods—setAccessibleComponent() and setAccessibleAction()—that are not part of AccessibleContext itself. These allow an outside class to specify classes that implement the AccessibleComponent and AccessibleAction interfaces.

- MyAccessibleAction implements the AccessibleAction interface. It thinks of an accessible action as an action that is registered with a keystroke, and has an action description or name.

- MyAccessibleContext does not override the getAccessibleSelection(), getAccessibleText(), or getAccessibleValue() methods, so they still return null.

Here is the source for the main frame class MyFrame.java (the source for the other classes will follow):

```
import com.sun.java.swing.*;
import com.sun.java.accessibility.*;
import java.awt.*;
import java.awt.event.*;
import java.util.*;
```

Figure 8-5

```
public class MyFrame extends JFrame
{
    public MyFrame()
    {
        setTitle( "Accessibility1" );

        // Store the content pane in a variable for easier
        // access.

        JPanel contentPane = (JPanel)getContentPane();

        // Components will all be added to this panel.

        contentPane.setLayout( new BorderLayout() );

        // Create buttons at the top and bottom of the content
        // pane so we can shift focus away from them.

        JButton b1 = new JButton( "Top Button" );
        contentPane.add( "North", b1 );

        JButton b2 = new JButton( "Bottom Button" );
        contentPane.add( "South", b2 );

        // Create the custom component.

        MyComponent custom = new MyComponent();

        // Make it so the component gets the focus when Alt-F
        // is pressed.

        MyFocusAction focusAction =
                    new MyFocusAction( "Get Focus" );
        custom.registerKeyboardAction( focusAction,
                    KeyStroke.getKeyStroke( KeyEvent.VK_F,
                    ActionEvent.ALT_MASK, true ),
                    JComponent.WHEN_IN_FOCUSED_WINDOW );

        // Make it so the component's background color is
        // toggled when Alt-C is pressed.

        MyColorAction colorAction =
                    new MyColorAction( "Toggle Color" );
        custom.registerKeyboardAction( colorAction,
                    KeyStroke.getKeyStroke( KeyEvent.VK_C,
```

```java
                        ActionEvent.ALT_MASK, true ),
                        JComponent.WHEN_IN_FOCUSED_WINDOW );

        // Add the custom component to the center of the
        // content pane.

        contentPane.add( "Center", custom );

    }

    // When this action is executed, it gives the focus to
    // the source component.

    private class MyFocusAction extends AbstractAction
    {
        // We set the action name and description so the
        // AccessibleContext can use the description as its
        // action description.

        public MyFocusAction( String name )
        {
            super( name );
            putValue( "Request for the focus to be set here",
                    Action.LONG_DESCRIPTION );
        }

        public void actionPerformed( ActionEvent e )
        {
            Component c = (Component)e.getSource();
            c.requestFocus();
        }
    }

    // When this action is executed, the MyComponent source
    // toggles its background color.

    private class MyColorAction extends AbstractAction
    {
        public MyColorAction( String name )
        {
            super( name );
            putValue( "Toggle the background color",
                    Action.LONG_DESCRIPTION );
        }

        public void actionPerformed( ActionEvent e )
        {
            MyComponent c = (MyComponent)e.getSource();
            c.toggleColor();
        }
    }
}
```

Here is the source for the custom component MyComponent.java:

```java
import com.sun.java.accessibility.*;
import com.sun.java.swing.*;
import java.awt.*;
import java.awt.event.*;

public class MyComponent extends JComponent implements
        Accessible, AccessibleComponent, FocusListener
{
    // The AccessibleContext subclass associated with this
    // component.

    private MyAccessibleContext mAccessInfo;

    public MyComponent()
    {
        super();

        // The component is initially yellow.

        setBackground( Color.yellow );

        // Listen for focus changes so we can redraw to show
        // or hide the focus rectangle.

        addFocusListener( this );

        // Create our custom AccessibleContext.

        mAccessInfo = new MyAccessibleContext( this );

        // Set the AccessibleContext's AccessibleAction to our
        // custom one.  Notice that the setAccessibleAction()
        // method is not a normal part of AccessibleContext.

        mAccessInfo.setAccessibleAction(
                            new MyAccessibleAction( this ) );

        // We have made this component implement the
        // AccessibleComponent interface, so we give it to
        // the AccessibleContext for use as its
        // AccessibleComponent.

        mAccessInfo.setAccessibleComponent( this );
    }

    // Switch the background color between yellow and red.

    public void toggleColor()
    {
        if ( getBackground() == Color.yellow )
            setBackground( Color.red );
        else
```

```
         setBackground( Color.yellow );

      repaint();
   }

   // Override this to return our custom AccessibleContext.

   public AccessibleContext getAccessibleContext()
   {
      return mAccessInfo;
   }

   // Implement this method as the last thing for the
   // AccessibleComponent interface.

   public Accessible getAccessibleAt( Point p )
   {
      return SwingUtilities.getAccessibleAt( this, p );
   }

   // We want this to be focus traversable.

   public boolean isFocusTraversable()
   {
      return true;
   }

   // Paint the component.

   public void paint( Graphics g )
   {
      g.setColor( getBackground() );
      g.fillRect( 0, 0, getWidth(), getHeight() );
      if ( hasFocus() )
      {
         g.setColor( Color.black );
         g.drawRect( 5, 5, getWidth() - 10,
                     getHeight() - 10 );
      }
   }

   // When the focus is gained or lost, repaint to show or
   // hide the focus rectangle.

   public void focusGained( FocusEvent e )
   {
      repaint();
   }

   public void focusLost( FocusEvent e )
   {
      repaint();
   }
}
```

Here is the source code for the AccessibleContext subclass MyAccessibleContext.java:

```
import com.sun.java.accessibility.*;
import com.sun.java.swing.*;
import java.util.*;
import java.awt.*;

public class MyAccessibleContext extends AccessibleContext
{
    // Our custom AccessibleAction.

    private AccessibleAction mAccAction=null;

    // Our custom AccessibleComponent.

    private AccessibleComponent mAccComponent=null;

    // The component with which this AccessibleContext is
    // associated.

    private JComponent mComponent;

    // Create the AccessibleContext, passing in the
    // component.

    public MyAccessibleContext( JComponent c )
    {
        mComponent = c;
    }

    // Allows outside classes to specify the
    // AccessibleActions this class uses.

    public void setAccessibleAction( AccessibleAction aa )
    {
        mAccAction = aa;
    }

    // Overridden to return our custom one.

    public AccessibleAction getAccessibleAction()
    {
        return mAccAction;
    }

    // Allows outside classes to set the AccessibleComponent.

    public void setAccessibleComponent( AccessibleComponent
                                        ac )
    {
        mAccComponent = ac;
    }
```

```
// Overridden to return our custom one.

public AccessibleComponent getAccessibleComponent()
{
    return mAccComponent;
}

// Returns the role this component fills.

public AccessibleRole getAccessibleRole()
{
    return AccessibleRole.PANEL;
}

// Returns a set of AccessibleStates describing the
// current state of the component.

public AccessibleStateSet getAccessibleStateSet()
{
    AccessibleStateSet set = new AccessibleStateSet();

    if ( mComponent.isEnabled() )
    {
        set.add( AccessibleState.ENABLED );
        set.add( AccessibleState.FOCUSABLE );
        if ( mComponent.hasFocus() )
            set.add( AccessibleState.FOCUSED );
    }

    if ( mComponent.isVisible() )
        set.add( AccessibleState.VISIBLE );

    return set;
}

// Implemented since it is abstract.

public int getAccessibleIndexInParent()
{
    return SwingUtilities.getAccessibleIndexInParent(
            mComponent );
}

// Implemented since it is abstract.

public int getAccessibleChildrenCount()
{
    return SwingUtilities.getAccessibleChildrenCount(
            mComponent );
}

// Implemented since it is abstract.

public Accessible getAccessibleChild( int n )
{
    return SwingUtilities.getAccessibleChild( mComponent,
```

```
                                                    n );
        }

        // Implemented since it is abstract.

        public Locale getLocale()
        {
           return mComponent.getLocale();
        }
    }
```

Here is the source code for the class MyAccessibleAction.java which implements the AccessibleAction interface:

```
import com.sun.java.accessibility.*;
import java.util.*;
import com.sun.java.swing.*;
import java.awt.event.*;

public class MyAccessibleAction implements AccessibleAction
{
    private JComponent mComponent;

    // Create the AccessibleAction, passing the component
    // with which it is associated.

    public MyAccessibleAction( JComponent c )
    {
       mComponent = c;
    }

    // This gets all of the component's registered keystroke
    // actions and returns them in a Vector.

    private Vector getAccessibleActions()
    {
       Vector actions = new Vector();
       Action keyAction;

       // Retrieve all keystrokes registered with the
       // component.

       KeyStroke strokes[] =
                   mComponent.getRegisteredKeyStrokes();

       // For each registered keystroke, get the associated
       // action.  If the action has a long description,
       // short description, or name, we will consider it
       // an accessible action.

       for ( int i = 0; i < strokes.length; i++ )
       {
          keyAction =
              (Action)mComponent.getActionForKeyStroke(
              strokes[i] );
```

```
        if ( keyAction.getValue(
            Action.LONG_DESCRIPTION ) != null ||
            keyAction.getValue(
            Action.SHORT_DESCRIPTION ) != null ||
            keyAction.getValue( Action.NAME ) != null )
        {
            actions.addElement( keyAction );
        }
    }

    return actions;
}

// This returns a count of the component's accessible
// actions.

public int getAccessibleActionCount()
{
    Vector actions = getAccessibleActions();

    return actions.size();
}

// This returns the description of the n-th accessible
// action.

public String getAccessibleActionDescription( int n )
{
    Vector actions = getAccessibleActions();

    Action thisAction = (Action)actions.elementAt( n );

    if ( thisAction.getValue(
        Action.LONG_DESCRIPTION ) != null )
    {
        return (String)thisAction.getValue(
            Action.LONG_DESCRIPTION );
    }
    else if ( thisAction.getValue(
            Action.SHORT_DESCRIPTION ) != null )
    {
        return (String)thisAction.getValue(
            Action.SHORT_DESCRIPTION );
    }
    else if ( thisAction.getValue( Action.NAME ) != null )
    {
        return (String)thisAction.getValue( Action.NAME );
    }

    return null;
}

// This executes the n-th accessible action.

public boolean doAccessibleAction( int n )
```

```
{
    Vector actions = getAccessibleActions();

    // Find the n-th accessible action.

    Action thisAction = (Action)actions.elementAt( n );

    // Create an ActionEvent we can use to trigger the
    // action.

    ActionEvent evt = new ActionEvent( mComponent,
                        ActionEvent.ACTION_PERFORMED,
                        null );

    // Trigger the action by passing the ActionEvent to
    // the action's actionPerformed() method.

    thisAction.actionPerformed( evt );

    return true;
    }
}
```

AccessibleContext's Public Methods

void addPropertyChangeListener(PropertyChangeListener listener)

Tells the component to notify the given class when properties change.

void firePropertyChange(String propertyName, Object oldValue, Object newValue)

Causes the AccessibleContext subclass to send a PropertyChangeEvent to all of its registered listeners.

AccessibleAction getAccessibleAction()

Returns a class that implements the AccessibleAction interface, or null. If the return is non-null, it can be used to find out about actions that may be performed on the component, and to trigger those actions.

abstract Accessible getAccessibleChild(int i)

Returns the ith accessible child component within the component.

abstract int getAccessibleChildrenCount()

Returns the number of accessible child components in the component.

AccessibleComponent getAccessibleComponent()

Returns a class that implements the AccessibleComponent interface, or null. If the return is non-null, it can be used to find out all kinds of graphical information about the component.

`String getAccessibleDescription()`

Returns a string that describes the purpose of the component.

`abstract int getAccessibleIndexInParent()`

Returns the component's index within its accessible parent.

`String getAccessibleName()`

Returns a string the user can use to identify the component.

`Accessible getAccessibleParent()`

Returns the component's accessible parent, if it has one. This will frequently be the component's actual parent, but may be set to something else using the setAccessibleParent() method.

`abstract AccessibleRole getAccessibleRole()`

Returns a constant from the AccessibleRole class (or a subclass) that fits the component's purpose into a preset of possibilities.

`AccessibleSelection getAccessibleSelection()`

Returns a class that implements the AccessibleSelection interface, or null. If the return is non-null, it can be used to get and change information about the component's current selection state.

`abstract AccessibleStateSet getAccessibleStateSet()`

Returns a set of AccessibleStates that describe the component's current state.

`AccessibleText getAccessibleText()`

Returns a class that implements the AccessibleText interface, or null. If the return is non-null, it can be used to read the text contents of the component as well as the text attributes.

`AccessibleValue getAccessibleValue()`

Returns a class that implements the AccessibleValue interface, or null. If the return is non-null, it can be used to get and set the component's numeric value, or to find out the component's minimum and maximum values.

```
abstract Locale getLocale()
```

Returns the locale of the component.

```
void removePropertyChangeListener(PropertyChangeListener listener)
```

Tells the component to stop notifying the given class when properties change.

```
void setAccessibleDescription(String s)
```

Specifies the component's descriptive string.

```
void setAccessibleName(String s)
```

Specifies the component's identifying string.

```
void setAccessibleParent(Accessible a)
```

Specifies the accessible class that should be used as the component's accessible parent.

BevelBorder

A BevelBorder is a two-pixel-wide border that makes it appear that the area within is either raised or lowered relative to the surrounding area. A common example of the BevelBorder effect is in a standard button. When the button is not pressed, it uses a raised BevelBorder. When it is pressed, it uses a lowered BevelBorder (see Figure 8-6).

A BevelBorder may be passed to any subclass of JComponent, but it is up to the component and its look-and-feel whether the border will actually be used.

Ancestors

```
java.lang.Object
    |
```

Figure 8-6
Example of both a raised and a lowered BevelBorder.

```
+-com.sun.java.swing.border.AbstractBorder
|
    +-com.sun.java.swing.border.BevelBorder
```

NOTE: *For more information, see the "AbstractBorder" section in this chapter and the "Component Borders" section in Chapter 7, "JFC By Concept."*

Steps in Creating and Using BevelBorder

1. Create a component that supports borders. Typically this will be a JPanel:

   ```
   JPanel borderedPane = new JPanel();
   ```

2. Create a BevelBorder to apply to the component. Variations on the component's background color will be used to draw the border, and all that needs to be set is whether the area inside the border should appear raised or lowered:

   Raised:

   ```
   BevelBorder bevel = new BevelBorder( BevelBorder.RAISED );
   ```

   Lowered:

   ```
   BevelBorder bevel = new BevelBorder( BevelBorder.LOWERED );
   ```

   Remember to import the com.sun.java.swing.border package so Java can find the border-related classes:

   ```
   import com.sun.java.swing.border.*;
   ```

3. Apply the border to the pane:

   ```
   borderedPane.setBorder( bevel );
   ```

   When 'borderedPane' is displayed, its paint() method will tell the border to paint itself.

4. Use a bevel border as part of a TitledBorder. A TitledBorder takes a string and a border (like BevelBorder) and combines them so that the string appears in a break in the given border. The border will appear as a normal bevel border except that it will be moved slightly in from the bordered pane's edge, and it will be interrupted by a string (title) at some point (left end of the top side by default):

   ```
   JPanel pane3 = new JPanel();
   pane3.setBorder( new TitledBorder(
                    new BevelBorder( BevelBorder.RAISED ),
                    "Raised" ) );
   ```

Basic Code Examples

EXAMPLE 8-6 **Different Uses for BevelBorder**

The following code example creates four bordered panes: one with a plain raised bevel, one with a plain lowered bevel, one with a raised bevel as part of a titled border, and one with a lowered bevel as part of a titled border. It illustrates many of the concepts discussed above. Figure 8-7 shows the example as it first comes up.

Here is the source code:

```java
import com.sun.java.swing.*;
import com.sun.java.swing.border.*;
import java.awt.*;

public class MyFrame extends JFrame
{
    public MyFrame()
    {
        setTitle( "BevelBorder1" );

        // Store the content pane for convenience.
        JPanel contentPane = (JPanel)getContentPane();

        // Components will all be added to this panel.
        contentPane.setLayout( new GridLayout( 2, 2, 10,
                                               10 ) );

        // Create a panel with a raised border and add it to
        // the content pane.
        JPanel pane1 = new JPanel();
        pane1.setBorder( new BevelBorder(
                                    BevelBorder.RAISED ) );
        contentPane.add( pane1 );

        // Create a panel with a lowered border and add it to
        // the content pane.
        JPanel pane2 = new JPanel();
        pane2.setBorder( new BevelBorder(
                                    BevelBorder.LOWERED ) );
        contentPane.add( pane2 );

        // Create a panel with a titled border that uses a
```

Figure 8-7

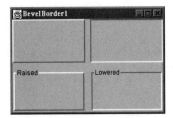

```
// raised border and add it to the content pane.
JPanel pane3 = new JPanel();
pane3.setBorder( new TitledBorder(
                new BevelBorder( BevelBorder.RAISED ),
                "Raised" ) );
contentPane.add( pane3 );

// Create a panel with a titled border that uses a
// lowered border and add it to the content pane.
JPanel pane4 = new JPanel();
pane4.setBorder( new TitledBorder(
                new BevelBorder( BevelBorder.LOWERED ),
                "Lowered" ) );
contentPane.add( pane4 );

    }
}
```

Advanced Issues

EXAMPLE 8-7   **Customizing the Colors in the Bevel**

The colors in a bevel are supposed to represent what the background color of the border's main component looks like when exposed to more or less light. On the display, the standard model for light is that it comes from the upper lefthand corner of the screen. With this in mind, you can see how a bevel works. For a raised bevel, the upper and left sides need to appear to be catching extra light, so they are brighter than the component's background color. Similarly, the lower and right sides need to appear to be in shadow, so they are darker. For a lowered bevel, the opposite is the case with upper and left sides being darker than the background, and the lower and right sides being brighter.

BevelBorder takes this model a step further by having two separate colors for the brighter sides and two for the darker sides. These colors can be set using one of the BevelBorder constructors:

```
public BevelBorder( int type,
                Color highlightOuter,
                Color highlightInner,
                Color shadowOuter,
                Color shadowInner )
```

where 'highlightOuter' is typically darker than 'highlightInner' and 'shadowOuter' is darker than 'shadowInner'. Using the AWT's SystemColor, if you create a component whose background color is SystemColor.control, creating an appropriate BevelBorder might look something like:

```
JPanel pane3 = new JPanel();
pane3.setBackground( SystemColor.control );
```

```
pane3.setBorder( new BevelBorder( BevelBorder.RAISED,
                                  SystemColor.controlHighlight,
                                  SystemColor.controlLtHighlight,
                                  SystemColor.controlDkShadow,
                                  SystemColor.controlShadow ) );
```

To use a component's current background color, you could use:

```
JPanel pane4 = new JPanel();
pane4.setBackground( Color.gray );
Color bkg = pane4.getBackground();
pane4.setBorder( new BevelBorder( BevelBorder.RAISED,
                         bkg.brighter(),
                         bkg.brighter().brighter(),
                         bkg.darker().darker(),
                         bkg.darker() ) );
```

This is, in fact, the default behavior of BevelBorder.

Following is a complete code sample showing the above concepts in practice:

```
import com.sun.java.swing.*;
import com.sun.java.swing.border.*;
import java.awt.*;

public class MyFrame extends JFrame
{
    public MyFrame()
    {
        setTitle( "BevelBorder2" );

        // Store the content pane for convenient access.
        JPanel contentPane = (JPanel)getContentPane();

        // Components will all be added to this panel.
        contentPane.setLayout( new GridLayout( 2, 2, 10, 10 ) );

        // Create a panel with a raised bevel border, but replace
        // the bevel colors.
        JPanel panel = new JPanel();
        panel.setBorder( new BevelBorder( BevelBorder.RAISED,
                    Color.red,
                    Color.green, Color.blue, Color.yellow ) );
        contentPane.add( panel );

        // Create a panel with a lowered bevel border, but replace
        // the bevel colors.
        JPanel pane2 = new JPanel();
        pane2.setBorder( new BevelBorder( BevelBorder.LOWERED,
                    Color.red, Color.green, Color.blue,
                    Color.yellow ) );
        contentPane.add( pane2 );

        // Create a panel that uses the system colors for a control
        // including its correct bevel colors.
```

```
        JPanel pane3 = new JPanel();
        pane3.setBackground( SystemColor.control );
        pane3.setBorder( new BevelBorder( BevelBorder.RAISED,
                        SystemColor.controlHighlight,
                        SystemColor.controlLtHighlight,
                        SystemColor.controlDkShadow,
                        SystemColor.controlShadow ) );
        contentPane.add( pane3 );

        // Create a panel that has a gray background, then imitate what
        // BevelBorder does normally to get the bevel colors.
        JPanel pane4 = new JPanel();
        pane4.setBackground( Color.gray );
        Color bkg = pane4.getBackground();
        pane4.setBorder( new BevelBorder( BevelBorder.RAISED,
                        bkg.brighter(),
                        bkg.brighter().brighter(),
                        bkg.darker().darker(),
                        bkg.darker() ) );
        contentPane.add( pane4 );
    }
}
```

EXAMPLE 8-8 Making a wider bevel

You cannot use BevelBorder itself to create a wider bevel. Instead, you have
to subclass AbstractBorder or BevelBorder or just implement the Border
interface to make your own border class. For this example, we subclass
AbstractBorder.

```
public class WideBevelBorder extends AbstractBorder
```

Implement the Border interface. This includes methods isBorderOpaque(),
getBorderInsets(), and paintBorder(), all discussed below.

We want the border to be opaque, meaning that we guarantee to paint the
whole thing:

```
public boolean isBorderOpaque()
{
    return true;
}
```

The getBorderInsets() method tells any inquiring class how much space of
its component's top, left, bottom, and right sides the border will draw. The
'mWidth' variable comes from the 'width' argument passed to the border's
constructor, which you can see in the full source listing.

```
public Insets getBorderInsets( Component c )
{
    return new Insets( mWidth, mWidth, mWidth, mWidth );
}
```

The paintBorder() method is called indirectly by the component's paint() method, and calls paintRaised() or paintLowered() depending on the border's state passed in via its constructor. Notice the calls to g.translate(). Without these, the border will not work properly if it is used as part of a TitledBorder:

```
public void paintBorder( Component c, Graphics g, int x, int y,
                         int width, int height )
{
    Color oldColor = g.getColor();

    // Figure out the bevel colors based on the main component's
    // background color.
    mLightColor = c.getBackground().brighter();
    mLighterColor = c.getBackground().brighter();
    mDarkColor = c.getBackground().darker();
    mDarkerColor = c.getBackground().darker();

    // Using this border as part of a titled border doesn't work
    // properly without this.
    g.translate( x, y );

    // Choose how to paint the border based on whether the border
    // is raised or lowered.
    if ( mState == BevelBorder.RAISED )
        paintRaised( g, x, y, width, height );
    else
        paintLowered( g, x, y, width, height );

    // Set things back the way the parent component left them.
    g.translate(-x, -y);
    g.setColor(oldColor);
}
```

Create a pane that uses this new border:

```
JPanel pane5 = new JPanel();
pane5.setBorder( new WideBevelBorder( 5,
                     BevelBorder.RAISED ) );
```

Figure 8-8 shows the example as it first comes up. The full code for WideBevelBorder looks like this:

```
import com.sun.java.swing.*;
import com.sun.java.swing.border.*;
import java.awt.*;
```

Figure 8-8

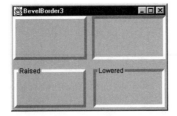

```java
public class WideBevelBorder extends AbstractBorder
{
    Color mLightColor;
    Color mLighterColor;
    Color mDarkColor;
    Color mDarkerColor;
    int mWidth;
    int mState;

    // Constructor that sets the border width and whether it
    // is raised or lowered.
    public WideBevelBorder( int width, int state )
    {
        mWidth = width;
        mState = state;
    }

    // This is an opaque border.
    public boolean isBorderOpaque()
    {
        return true;
    }

    // From the Border interface.
    public Insets getBorderInsets( Component c )
    {
        return new Insets( mWidth, mWidth, mWidth, mWidth );
    }

    // From the Border interface.
    public void paintBorder( Component c, Graphics g, int x,
                             int y, int width, int height )
    {
        Color oldColor = g.getColor();

        // Figure out the bevel colors based on the main
        // component's background color.
        mLightColor = c.getBackground().brighter();
        mLighterColor = c.getBackground().brighter();
        mDarkColor = c.getBackground().darker();
        mDarkerColor = c.getBackground().darker();

        // Using this border as part of a titled border
        // doesn't work properly without this.
        g.translate( x, y );

        // Choose how to paint the border based on whether the
        // border is raised or lowered.
        if ( mState == BevelBorder.RAISED )
            paintRaised( g, x, y, width, height );
        else
            paintLowered( g, x, y, width, height );

        // Set things back the way the parent component left
        // them.
        g.translate(-x, -y);
```

```
      g.setColor(oldColor);
}

// Paint the bevel for a raised border.
public void paintRaised( Graphics g, int x, int y,
                              int width, int height )
{
   g.setColor( mLightColor );

   g.drawLine( 0, 0, width - 1, 0 );
   g.drawLine( 0, 1, 0, height - 1 );

   g.setColor( mDarkerColor );

   g.drawLine( width - 1, 0, width - 1, height - 1 );
   g.drawLine( width - 2, height - 1, 1, height - 1 );

   for ( int i = 1; i < mWidth; i++ )
   {
      g.setColor( mLighterColor );

      g.drawLine( i, i, width - i - 1, i );
      g.drawLine( i, i, i, height - i - 1 );

      g.setColor( mDarkColor );

      g.drawLine( width - i - 1, i + 1, width - i - 1,
                  height - i - 1 );
      g.drawLine( i + 1, height - i - 1, width - i - 1,
                  height - i - 1 );
   }
}

// Paint the bevel for a lowered border.
public void paintLowered( Graphics g, int x, int y,
                              int width, int height )
{
   g.setColor( mDarkColor );

   g.drawLine( 0, 0, width - 1, 0 );
   g.drawLine( 0, 1, 0, height - 1 );

   g.setColor( mLighterColor );

   g.drawLine( width - 1, 0, width - 1, height - 1 );
   g.drawLine( width - 2, height - 1, 1, height - 1 );

   for ( int i = 1; i < mWidth; i++ )
   {
      g.setColor( mDarkerColor );

      g.drawLine( i, i, width - i - 1, i );
      g.drawLine( i, i, i, height - i - 1 );

      g.setColor( mLightColor );
```

```
        g.drawLine( width - i - 1, i + 1, width - i - 1,
                   height - i - 1 );
        g.drawLine( i + 1, height - i - 1, width - i - 1,
                   height - i - 1 );
    }
  }
}
```

Notice that the border is translated relative to the component it is painted on. You have to translate or the border won't work properly as part of a TitledBorder.

BevelBorder's Public Methods

`int getBevelType()`

Returns whether the border is RAISED or LOWERED.

`Insets getBorderInsets(Component c)`

Returns the distance the border will extend in from each side of the component it will draw on.

`Color getHighlightInnerColor(Component c)`

Returns the current inner color for lighter edges.

`Color getHighlightOuterColor(Component c)`

Returns the current outer color for lighter edges.

`Color getShadowInnerColor(Component c)`

Returns the current inner color for darker edges.

`Color getShadowOuterColor(Component c)`

Returns the current outer color for darker edges.

`boolean isBorderOpaque()`

Returns true if all of the border area is drawn. Normally returns true for BevelBorder.

`void paintBorder(Component c,Graphics g,int x,int y,int width,int height)`

Paints the border onto its component.

Box

A Box is a very handy container for use in laying out single rows or columns of components. It uses the BoxLayout, but adds methods that make it more useful. Some of the methods are static and can be used to create filler components for use even in containers that do not use the BoxLayout.

Box is very useful, but is not a subclass of JComponent. Because of this, a Box cannot have a border. When you want a Box with a border, use a JPanel with a BoxLayout instead.

A Box contains two types of components: ones whose preferred size and maximum size are the same, and ones whose preferred size and maximum size are different. All components are initially placed using their preferred size, then any left over whitespace is distributed among the components that have a maximum size larger than their preferred size (see Figure 8-9).

Box allows you to create three types of components to be used for padding. These are glue, struts, and rigid areas:

■ "Glue" is an invisible component that starts out with a size of 0,0, but has no maximum size so it will accept its full share of extra whitespace, if there is any. Glue components can be created to grow in either or both directions. This is useful for making sure the spacing between components grows in proportion with any growth in the container itself.

■ "Strut" is an invisible component that starts out with one dimension set to a particular number of pixels and the other dimension set to 0. The non-zero dimension should stay that size no matter what. The zero dimension has no maximum size, so it will accept full its share of extra whitespace, if there is any. This is useful for forcing the distance between two components to be exactly the same no matter how big or small the container becomes. If you use a strut to force a Box to be at least a certain width or height (using a horizontal strut in a vertical box or a vertical strut in a horizontal box), remember that the strut will act like a glue component in the other direction (in the Box's main direction).

■ "Rigid Area" is an invisible component that takes up exactly the specified area and does not change size no matter what. This is handy for setting an exact width (for a vertical Box) or an exact height (for a horizontal Box) and/or for maintaining an exact spacing between two components.

Figure 8-9
Two buttons spaced evenly using a Box.

The rules are

- A Box lays out components either left to right or top to bottom depending on how it was constructed.
- The components are initially laid out at their preferred size.
- If there is extra white space left over, it is distributed among the components whose maximum size is greater than their preferred size.
- If the components, laid out at their preferred size, do not completely fit into the Box, the components whose minimum size is less than their preferred size get shrunk either until the components all fit, or until all are at their minimum size.
- No component can be larger than its maximum or smaller than its minimum size.
- A horizontal glue component has minimum size of 0,0, preferred size of 0,0, and maximum size of infinite, 0.
- A vertical glue component has minimum size of 0,0, preferred size of 0,0, and maximum size of 0, infinite.
- A normal glue component (created with createGlue()) has minimum size of 0,0, preferred size of 0,0, and maximum size of infinite,infinite.
- A horizontal strut where x is the value set in createHorizontalStrut(x) has minimum size of x,0, preferred size of x,0, and maximum size of x,infinite.
- A vertical strut where y is the value set in createVerticalStrut(y) has minimum size of 0,y, preferred size of 0,y, and maximum size of infinite, y.
- A rigid area where x, and y are the dimensions set in createRigidArea(new Dimension(x,y)) has a minimum size of x,y, preferred size of x,y, and maximum size of x,y.
- Note that glue, strut, and rigid area components are direct subclasses of Component defined internally to Box.

Ancestors

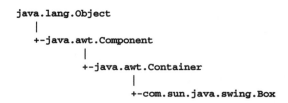

```
java.lang.Object
   |
   +-java.awt.Component
           |
           +-java.awt.Container
                   |
                   +-com.sun.java.swing.Box
```

NOTE: *Box is one of the few Swing components that does not descend from JComponent.*

NOTE: *For more information, see the "BoxLayout" section in this chapter and the "JFC Containers" section in Chapter 7, "JFC by Concept."*

Steps in Creating and Using Box

1. Create a Box. The direction in which the Box will lay out components is specified at construction time. To lay out from left to right:

    ```
    Box horizBox = new Box( BoxLayout.X_AXIS );
    ```

    or:

    ```
    Box horizBox = Box.createHorizontalBox();
    ```

    To lay out from top to bottom:

    ```
    Box vertBox = new Box( BoxLayout.Y_AXIS );
    ```

    or:

    ```
    Box vertBox = Box.createVerticalBox();
    ```

2. Add some components to the box. Assume for this example that the Box is *horizBox* created above. These statements create two buttons that will be stuck next to each other with no space between:

    ```
    JButton ok = new JButton( "Ok" );
    horizBox.add( ok );
    JButton cancel = new JButton( "Cancel" );
    horizBox.add( cancel );
    ```

3. Put glue around the buttons. These statements create two buttons that are equally spaced. Note that a JButton's preferred size and maximum size are the same so it will not grow in size. A glue component's preferred width is 0, so it starts out at 0 pixels wide, but its maximum width is infinite so it gets a fair share of any extra whitespace.

    ```
    horizBox.add( Box.createHorizontalGlue() );
    JButton ok = new JButton( "Ok" );
    horizBox.add( ok );
    horizBox.add( Box.createHorizontalGlue() );
    JButton cancel = new JButton( "Cancel" );
    ```

```
horizBox.add( cancel );
horizBox.add( Box.createHorizontalGlue() );
```

Notice that there are three glue components: one to the left of the first button, one between the two buttons, and one to the right of the second button. These three will split the Box's extra horizontal whitespace between them, causing the buttons to be nicely spaced across the Box.

4. Add a strut. These statements create two buttons just like in step 3, except the glue between the buttons is replaced by a horizontal strut 50 pixels wide. This causes the distance between the buttons to be fixed, no matter how big the Box gets. The two glue components split any remaining horizontal whitespace between them so that the left side of the first button and the right side of the second button are the same distance from the left and right edges of the container.

```
horizBox.add( Box.createHorizontalGlue() );
JButton ok = new JButton( "Ok" );
horizBox.add( ok );
horizBox.add( Box.createHorizontalStrut( 50 ) );
JButton cancel = new JButton( "Cancel" );
horizBox.add( cancel );
horizBox.add( Box.createHorizontalGlue() );
```

5. Use a rigid area to both set a fixed distance between two components, and to make the Box be a fixed size in one direction. These statements create two buttons with a rigid area in between. Since the rigid area's height is greater than the height of the buttons, the Box's preferred height will be set to the height of the rigid area. In this case, the horizontal dimension of the rigid area acts much like the horizontal strut in step 4.

```
horizBox.add( Box.createHorizontalGlue() );
JButton ok = new JButton( "Ok" );
horizBox.add( ok );
horizBox.add( Box.createRigidArea( new Dimension( 50, 200 ) ) );
JButton cancel = new JButton( "Cancel" );
horizBox.add( cancel );
horizBox.add( Box.createHorizontalGlue() );
```

6. Change the preferred size of the components. This is especially useful for JButtons since you normally want them to be the same width, but their preferred size is based on their text. Notice that we use setPreferredSize() rather than setSize() since BoxLayout uses the preferred size. This is just like step 3 above except that the buttons' preferred size is set.

```
horizBox.add( Box.createHorizontalGlue() );
JButton ok = new JButton( "Ok" );
ok.setPreferredSize( new Dimension( 80, 30 ) );
horizBox.add( ok );
horizBox.add( Box.createHorizontalGlue() );
```

```
JButton cancel = new JButton( "Cancel" );
cancel.setPreferredSize( new Dimension( 80, 30 ) );
horizBox.add( cancel );
horizBox.add( Box.createHorizontalGlue() );
```

Basic Code Examples

EXAMPLE 8-9 Options for Using Box

The following code sample illustrates the topics discussed above. It shows a JFrame containing a series of horizontal Boxes, each using a different combination of Box padding components. The horizontal Boxes are contained within a single vertical Box. Figure 8-10 shows the example as it first comes up.

Here is the source code:

```
import com.sun.java.swing.*;
import java.awt.*;
import java.util.*;

public class MyFrame extends JFrame
{
    public MyFrame()
    {
        setTitle( "Box1" );

        // Store the content pane for easier access.
        JPanel contentPane = (JPanel)getContentPane();

        // Components will all be added to this panel.
        contentPane.setLayout( new BorderLayout() );

        // Create a box to put the other boxes in, adding from
        // top to bottom.
        Box mainBox = new Box( BoxLayout.Y_AXIS );

        // Create a box that will contain two components
```

Figure 8-10

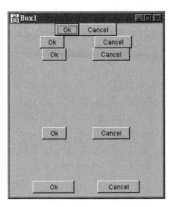

```
    // directly adjacent to each other.
    {  // The '{' '}' are just so we can use the same
       // variables so it is easier to compare examples.
       Box horizBox = new Box( BoxLayout.X_AXIS );

       JButton ok = new JButton( "Ok" );
       horizBox.add( ok );
       JButton cancel = new JButton( "Cancel" );
       horizBox.add( cancel );

       mainBox.add( horizBox );
    }

    // Create a box that will contain two components
    // evenly spaced across the window.  Notice the call
    // to Box.createHorizontalGlue().
    {  // The '{' '}' are just so we can use the same
       // variables so it is easier to compare examples.
       Box horizBox = new Box( BoxLayout.X_AXIS );

       horizBox.add( Box.createHorizontalGlue() );
       JButton ok = new JButton( "Ok" );
       horizBox.add( ok );
       horizBox.add( Box.createHorizontalGlue() );
       JButton cancel = new JButton( "Cancel" );
       horizBox.add( cancel );
       horizBox.add( Box.createHorizontalGlue() );

       mainBox.add( horizBox );
    }

    // Create a box that will contain two components where
    // the distance between the components stays the same
    // no matter what size the container is.  Note the
    // call to Box.createHorizontalStrut().
    {  // The '{' '}' are just so we can use the same
       // variables so it is easier to compare examples.
       Box horizBox = new Box( BoxLayout.X_AXIS );

       horizBox.add( Box.createHorizontalGlue() );
       JButton ok = new JButton( "Ok" );
       horizBox.add( ok );
       horizBox.add( Box.createHorizontalStrut( 50 ) );
       JButton cancel = new JButton( "Cancel" );
       horizBox.add( cancel );
       horizBox.add( Box.createHorizontalGlue() );

       mainBox.add( horizBox );
    }

    // Create a box that will contain two components
    // where the distance between the components stays
    // the same no matter what size the container is and
    // the height of the box is at least 200 pixels.
```

```
                     // Note the call to Box.createRigidArea().
                     {  // The '{' '}' are just so we can use the same
                        // variables so it is easier to compare examples.
                        Box horizBox = new Box( BoxLayout.X_AXIS );

                        horizBox.add( Box.createHorizontalGlue() );
                        JButton ok = new JButton( "Ok" );
                        horizBox.add( ok );
                        horizBox.add( Box.createRigidArea(
                                    new Dimension( 50, 200 ) ) );
                        JButton cancel = new JButton( "Cancel" );
                        horizBox.add( cancel );
                        horizBox.add( Box.createHorizontalGlue() );

                        mainBox.add( horizBox );
                     }

                     // Create a box in which two buttons of a specified
                     // size are evenly spaced.  This is much like one of
                     // the examples above except for the explicit sizing
                     // of the buttons.  Notice the calls to
                     // JButton.setPreferredSize().
                     {  // The '{' '}' are just so we can use the same
                        // variables so it is easier to compare example.
                        Box horizBox = new Box( BoxLayout.X_AXIS );

                        horizBox.add( Box.createHorizontalGlue() );
                        JButton ok = new JButton( "Ok" );
                        ok.setPreferredSize( new Dimension( 80, 30 ) );
                        horizBox.add( ok );
                        horizBox.add( Box.createHorizontalGlue() );
                        JButton cancel = new JButton( "Cancel" );
                        cancel.setPreferredSize( new Dimension( 80, 30 ) );
                        horizBox.add( cancel );
                        horizBox.add( Box.createHorizontalGlue() );

                        mainBox.add( horizBox );
                     }

                     contentPane.add( "Center", mainBox );
                  }
               }
```

Box's Public Methods

```
Component createGlue()
```

Creates a padding component that initially has no size, but can expand to fill empty space both horizontally and vertically.

```
Box createHorizontalBox()
```

This returns a Box component that adds components horizontally from left to right.

`Component createHorizontalGlue()`

Creates a padding component that initially has no size, but can grow to fill empty space horizontally.

`Component createHorizontalStrut(int width)`

Creates a padding component that is exactly the given number of pixels wide, but can grow to fill empty space vertically.

`Component createRigidArea(Dimension d)`

Creates a padding component that is exactly the given size.

`Box createVerticalBox()`

This returns a Box component that adds components vertically from top to bottom.

`Component createVerticalGlue()`

Creates a padding component that initially has no size, but can grow vertically to fill empty space.

`Component createVerticalStrut(int height)`

Creates a padding component that is exactly the given number of pixels tall, but can grow horizontally to fill empty space.

`AccessibleContext getAccessibleContext()`

Returns a subclass of AbstractContext, which gives access to the Box's accessibility information.

`void setLayout(LayoutManager l)`

This is overridden to make it throw an exception since a Box should always use a BoxLayout.

BoxLayout

BoxLayout is a LayoutManager that provides a simple way to layout a row or column of components. You can use the padding components defined in the Box class to provide inter-component spacing.

When you lay out a row, BoxLayout looks for the component with the largest preferred height and tries to make all of the components that height. Any that cannot be made that tall will be vertically positioned according to their alignment property (see java.awt.Container.setAlignmentY()).

Similarly, when you lay out a column, BoxLayout looks for the component with the largest preferred width and tries to make all of the components that width. Any that cannot be made that wide will be horizontally positioned according to their alignment property (see java.awt.Container. setAlignmentX()).

The Box component uses BoxLayout and provides some nice methods that other types of components can use. In particular, it provides static methods to create various types of padding components.

BoxLayout relies heavily on components' minimum, preferred, and maximum sizes when laying its container out. It wants to lay everything out at its preferred size, but it also wants to spread its components out to fill the available space. For example, when you have a container using a horizontal BoxLayout, the following things happen. First, the layout manager tries to lay its components out at their preferred widths. Once done, it sees if the components at their preferred sizes are too wide for the container or do not fill it completely. If they are too wide, any components that are wider than their minimum width are shrunk until all components are at their minimum widths, or they are no longer too wide to fit in the container. If, at their preferred sizes, the components take up less than the container's width, all components that are smaller than their maximum width are stretched until all are at their maximum width or the components take up the full width of the container. A similar set of steps happen for a vertical BoxLayout.

Ancestors

```
java.lang.Object
   |
   +-com.sun.java.swing.BoxLayout
```

NOTE: *For more information, see the "Box" section in this chapter, the "Swing Layout Managers" section in Chapter 7, "JFC by Concept," and Chapter 3, "The JComponent Class."*

Steps in Creating and Using BoxLayout

1. Create a container in which to use BoxLayout:

```
JPanel box1 = new JPanel();
```

2. Set the container's layout manager to be BoxLayout, in this case adding components left to right:

```
box1.setLayout( new BoxLayout( box1, BoxLayout.X_AXIS ) );
```

3. Add some components with varying preferred heights. We accomplish this by using JButtons with different font sizes:

```
JButton a1 = new JButton( "Save" );
box1.add( a1 );
JButton b1 = new JButton( "Discard" );
b1.setFont( new Font( "TimesRoman", Font.PLAIN, 24 ) );
box1.add( b1 );
JButton c1 = new JButton( "Cancel" );
c1.setFont( new Font( "TimesRoman", Font.PLAIN, 18 ) );
box1.add( c1 );
```

The buttons will be directly next to each other since we provided no padding components. They will not grow to fill the available area because their preferred and maximum sizes are the same.

Basic Code Examples

EXAMPLE 8-10 Different Uses for BoxLayout

The following code sample lays out two containers with BoxLayout—one horizontal and the other vertical. Notice that the buttons in the horizontal BoxLayout are flush against the top of the container while the ones in the vertical BoxLayout are centered. This is because we used the default Y alignment (0.0) in the horizontal BoxLayout, but explicitly set the X alignment to 0.5 in the vertical BoxLayout. This shows how the placement of components depends on the components' alignment values.

Also notice that the buttons do not shrink to fit the containers and, if you make the whole frame bigger, they do not stretch to fit them. This is because the buttons' minimum, preferred, and maximum sizes are the same. So, BoxLayout places them at their preferred sizes, but the components give it no leeway in resizing them. Figure 8-11 shows the example as it looks when it first comes up.

Here is the source code:

Figure 8-11

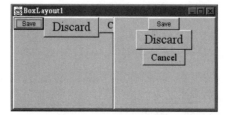

```java
import com.sun.java.swing.*;
import com.sun.java.swing.border.*;
import java.awt.*;

public class MyFrame extends JFrame
{
    public MyFrame()
    {
        setTitle( "BoxLayout1" );

        // Store the content pane for easier access.
        JPanel contentPane = (JPanel)getContentPane();

        // Components will all be added to this panel.
        contentPane.setLayout( new GridLayout() );

        // Create a container for a horizontal BoxLayout.
        JPanel box1 = new JPanel();

        // Set the layout manager.
        box1.setLayout( new BoxLayout( box1,
                        BoxLayout.X_AXIS ) );
        box1.setBorder( new BevelBorder(
                        BevelBorder.RAISED ) );

        // Create three buttons and add them to the
        // container.  We change the font to give the buttons
        // different preferred sizes so we can see
        // BoxLayout's centering feature.
        JButton a1 = new JButton( "Save" );
        box1.add( a1 );
        JButton b1 = new JButton( "Discard" );
        b1.setFont( new Font( "TimesRoman",
                              Font.PLAIN, 24 ) );
        box1.add( b1 );
        JButton c1 = new JButton( "Cancel" );
        c1.setFont( new Font( "TimesRoman",
                              Font.PLAIN, 18 ) );
        box1.add( c1 );

        // Add the container to the content pane.
        contentPane.add( box1 );

        // Create a container for a vertical BoxLayout.
        JPanel box2 = new JPanel();
        box2.setBorder( new BevelBorder(
                        BevelBorder.RAISED ) );

        // Set the layout manager.
        box2.setLayout( new BoxLayout( box2,
                        BoxLayout.Y_AXIS ) );

        // Create three buttons and add them to the container.
        // We change the font to give the buttons different
        // preferred sizes so we can see BoxLayout's
```

```
        // centering feature.
        JButton a2 = new JButton( "Save" );
        a2.setSize( 100, 40 );
        box2.add( a2 );
        JButton b2 = new JButton( "Discard" );
        b2.setFont( new Font( "TimesRoman",
                   Font.PLAIN, 24 ) );
        box2.add( b2 );
        JButton c2 = new JButton( "Cancel" );
        c2.setFont( new Font( "TimesRoman",
                   Font.PLAIN, 18 ) );
        box2.add( c2 );

        // Cause these three components to be centered
        // horizontally.
        a2.setAlignmentX( (float)0.5 );
        b2.setAlignmentX( (float)0.5 );
        c2.setAlignmentX( (float)0.5 );

        // Add the container to the content pane.
        contentPane.add( box2 );
    }
}
```

BoxLayout's Public Methods

`void addLayoutComponent(Component comp,Object constraints)`

Overridden because it is not supported.

`void addLayoutComponent(String name,Component comp)`

Overridden because it is not supported.

`float getLayoutAlignmentX(Container target)`

Returns the container's default alignment for a horizontal BoxLayout, or the accumulated X alignment of the components in a vertical BoxLayout.

`float getLayoutAlignmentY(Container target)`

Returns the container's default alignment for a vertical BoxLayout, or the accumulated Y alignment of the components in a horizontal BoxLayout.

`void invalidateLayout(Container target)`

This should be called when a component being laid out has a change in its layout information, like size or alignment.

```
void layoutContainer(Container target)
```

This actually lays out the container. It should not be called except by the system.

```
Dimension maximumLayoutSize(Container target)
```

Returns the maximum size of the target container.

```
Dimension minimumLayoutSize(Container target)
```

Returns the minimum size at which the layout manager feels the target container can be laid out.

```
Dimension preferredLayoutSize(Container target)
```

Returns the best size for laying out the target container.

```
void removeLayoutComponent(Component comp)
```

Overridden because it is not supported.

ButtonGroup

ButtonGroup is a nongraphical class that is used to make sure only one of a group of related components is selected at a time. These components can be: JToggleButtons, JRadioButtons, or JRadioButtonMenuItems. Adding components to a ButtonGroup does not display them, it just associates them with each other.

Ancestors

```
java.lang.Object
   |
   +-com.sun.java.swing.ButtonGroup
```

NOTE: *For more information, see the "JRadioButton," "JToggleButton," and "JRadioButtonMenuItem" sections in this chapter. Also see the "Components That Can Be Turned On and Off" section in Chapter 7, "JFC by Concept."*

Steps in Creating and Using ButtonGroup

1. Create two or more components that represent mutually exclusive options. In this case, we will create two JRadioButtons that are used to set printing orientation.

```
JRadioButton portrait = new JRadioButton( "Portrait" );
JRadioButton landscape = new JRadioButton( "Landscape" );
```

We can set one of the components to be initially selected:

```
portrait.setSelected( true );
```

2. Create a ButtonGroup:

```
ButtonGroup group = new ButtonGroup();
```

3. Add the components to the ButtonGroup so only one may be selected at a time:

```
group.add( portrait );
group.add( landscape );
```

4. Place the components in a panel:

```
panel.add( portrait );
panel.add( landscape );
```

5. Get an enumeration of the components in the group:

```
for ( Enumeration e  = group.getElements();
        e.hasMoreElements(); )
{
   JRadioButton button = (JRadioButton)e.nextElement();

   // Now you can do something with it.
}
```

Basic Code Examples

EXAMPLE 8-11 Using a ButtonGroup with JRadioButtons

This simple example shows two JRadioButtons associated by using a ButtonGroup, so only one can be selected at a time. Figure 8-12 shows the example after the Landscape option has been selected.

Here is the source code:

Figure 8-12

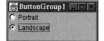

```java
import com.sun.java.swing.*;
import java.awt.*;
import java.util.*;

public class MyFrame extends JFrame
{
    public MyFrame()
    {
        setTitle( "ButtonGroup1" );

        // Store the content pane in a variable for easier
        // access.
        JPanel contentPane = (JPanel)getContentPane();

        // Components will all be added to this panel.
        contentPane.setLayout( new BoxLayout( contentPane,
                                BoxLayout.Y_AXIS ) );

        // Create the two components that will be in the
        // ButtonGroup.
        JRadioButton portrait =
                            new JRadioButton( "Portrait" );
        JRadioButton landscape =
                            new JRadioButton( "Landscape" );

        // Set portrait as the initial orientation.
        portrait.setSelected( true );

        // Create the ButtonGroup.
        ButtonGroup group = new ButtonGroup();

        // Add the two components to the ButtonGroup.
        group.add( portrait );
        group.add( landscape );

        // Place the two components in the content pane.
        contentPane.add( portrait );
        contentPane.add( landscape );

        // List the components in the ButtonGroup.
        for ( Enumeration e  = group.getElements();
            e.hasMoreElements(); )
        {
            JRadioButton button =
                            (JRadioButton)e.nextElement();

            // Just print out the buttons.
            System.out.println( button.getText() );
        }
    }
}
```

ButtonGroup's Public Methods

`void add(AbstractButton b)`

Adds a button to the ButtonGroup.

`Enumeration getElements()`

Returns an enumeration of all buttons in the ButtonGroup.

`ButtonModel getSelection()`

Returns the ButtonGroup's currently selected item. Notice that it returns the selected button's ButtonModel instead of the component itself.

`boolean isSelected(ButtonModel m)`

Returns true if the given ButtonModel is part of the currently selected button.

`void remove(AbstractButton b)`

Removes the given button from the ButtonGroup.

`void setSelected(ButtonModel m,boolean b)`

Specifies whether the button associated with the given ButtonModel is selected.

CompoundBorder

CompoundBorder is simply a border made up of two borders—one inside the other (see Figure 8-13). It can be very handy for creating special border effects.

Ancestors

```
java.lang.Object
    |
    +-com.sun.java.swing.border.AbstractBorder
            |
            +-com.sun.java.swing.border.CompoundBorder
```

Figure 8-13
A TitledBorder
containing an
EtchedBorder around
a BevelBorder.

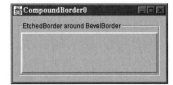

NOTE: *For more information, see the "AbstractBorder," "BevelBorder," "EmptyBorder," "EtchedBorder," "LineBorder," "MatteBorder," "SoftBevelBorder," and "TitledBorder" sections in this chapter. Also see the "Component Borders" section in Chapter 7, "JFC by Concept," and Chapter 3, "The JComponent Class."*

Steps in Creating and Using CompoundBorder

1. Create a container that supports borders. This is typically a JPanel:

   ```
   JPanel panel = new JPanel();
   ```

2. Create a CompoundBorder. In this case, we will create a border that has a TitledBorder that incorporates an EtchedBorder and encloses a BevelBorder:

   ```
   CompoundBorder comp1 = new CompoundBorder( new TitledBorder(
                      new EtchedBorder(), "Etched around Bevel" ),
                      new BevelBorder( BevelBorder.RAISED ) );
   ```

3. Apply the border to the container:

   ```
   panel.setBorder( comp1 );
   ```

Basic Code Examples

EXAMPLE 8-12 Some Common Uses for CompoundBorder

This code sample creates a panel with a CompoundBorder that includes a TitledBorder around a BevelBorder, and another panel that has an EmptyBorder around a TitledBorder. Figure 8-14 shows the example as it looks when it first comes up.

Here is the source code:

```
import com.sun.java.swing.*;
import com.sun.java.swing.border.*;
import java.awt.*;

public class MyFrame extends JFrame
{
    public MyFrame()
```

Figure 8-14

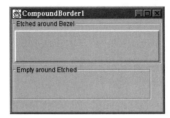

```
{
    setTitle( "CompoundBorder1" );

    // Store the content pane for easier access.
    JPanel contentPane = (JPanel)getContentPane();

    // Components will all be added to this panel.
    contentPane.setLayout( new GridLayout( 2, 1 ) );

    // Create a bordered pane.
    JPanel pane1 = new JPanel();

    // Create the compound border from a titled border
    // incorporating an EtchedBorder, and a BevelBorder.
    // The etched title border will enclose the
    // BevelBorder.
    CompoundBorder comp1 = new CompoundBorder(
            new TitledBorder( new EtchedBorder(),
            "Etched around Bezel" ),
            new BevelBorder( BevelBorder.RAISED ) );

    // Apply the border to the panel.
    pane1.setBorder( comp1 );

    // Add the bordered pane to the content pane.
    contentPane.add( pane1 );

    // Create another panel.
    JPanel pane2 = new JPanel();

    // Create a CompoundBorder that will have an
    // EmptyBorder enclosing an etched TitledBorder.
    CompoundBorder comp2 = new CompoundBorder(
                new EmptyBorder( 10, 10, 10, 10 ),
                new TitledBorder( new EtchedBorder(),
                "Empty around Etched" ) );

    // Apply the border to the panel.
    pane2.setBorder( comp2 );

    // Add the bordered pane to the content pane.
    contentPane.add( pane2 );
}
}
```

Advanced Issues

EXAMPLE 8-13 A Double-Compound Border

This example makes a custom border of two EtchedBorders separated by an EmptyBorder. It does this by making a single CompoundBorder of an EtchedBorder inside of a five pixels wide EmptyBorder, then using that as part of another CompoundBorder that surrounds it all with another EtchedBorder. This gives the effect of a more formal frame around the edge of the main panel. Figure-15 shows the example as it looks when it first comes up.

Here is the source code:

```
import com.sun.java.swing.*;
import com.sun.java.swing.border.*;
import java.awt.*;

public class MyFrame extends JFrame
{
    public MyFrame()
    {
        setTitle( "CompoundBorder2" );

        // Store the content pane in a variable for easier
        // access.
        JPanel contentPane = (JPanel)getContentPane();

        // The double-compound border will be used in the
        // content pane.

        // Create the inside compound border which is made up
        // of an etched border inside of an empty border, 5
        // pixels wide.
        CompoundBorder border1 = new CompoundBorder(
                        new EmptyBorder( 5, 5, 5, 5 ),
                        new EtchedBorder() );

        // Create the double compound border by putting
        // another etched border around 'border1' created
        // above.
        CompoundBorder border2 = new CompoundBorder(
                        new EtchedBorder(), border1 );

        // Apply the double compound border to the content
        // pane.
        contentPane.setBorder( border2 );
    }
}
```

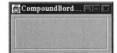

Figure 8-15

CompoundBorder's Public Methods

```
Insets getBorderInsets(Component c)
```

Returns the distance the border will be drawn in from each of the component's sides.

```
Border getInsideBorder()
```

Returns the border that is inside the other border.

```
Border getOutsideBorder()
```

Returns the border that is outside the other border.

```
boolean isBorderOpaque()
```

Returns true if both borders are opaque, or false if they are not.

```
void paintBorder(Component c,Graphics g,int x,int y,int width,int
        height)
```

Paints the CompoundBorder on the component.

DefaultBoundedRangeModel

DefaultBoundedRangeModel is Swing's default implementation of the BoundedRangeModel interface. It is used by JScrollBar to store information about limits and current values. It is not responsible for changing when the JScrollBar changes. Rather, it is told when to change and what its new values are so the current state can be requested and will be up-to-date. When the mouse is clicked within a JScrollBar, the JScrollBar's current look-and-feel class accepts the mouse click and asks the JScrollBar's BoundedRangeModel for information about its maximum and minimum and current values. It also asks the JScrollBar for unit and block increment information. Then the look-and-feel class calculates the new value for the BoundedRangeModel and tells it to update itself.

Ancestors

```
java.lang.Object
    |
    +-com.sun.java.swing.DefaultBoundedRangeModel
```

NOTE: *For more information, see the "JScrollBar" section of this chapter and the "Scrolling" section of Chapter 7, "JFC by Concept."*

Steps to Creating and Using DefaultBoundedRangeModel

A DefaultBoundedRangeModel is created by default when a JScrollBar is created. See the "JScrollBar" section in this chapter for a discussion of how it uses its DefaultBoundedRangeModel.

DefaultBoundedRangeModel's Public Methods

void addChangeListener(ChangeListener l)

Tells the DefaultBoundedRangeModel to notify the given class when any of the model's values change.

int getExtent()

Returns the number of scrollbar units represented by the thumbnail.

int getMaximum()

Returns the scrollbar's maximum possible value in scrollbar units.

int getMinimum()

Returns the scrollbar's minimum possible value in scrollbar units.

int getValue()

Returns the current value in scrollbar units.

boolean getValueIsAdjusting()

Returns true if the DefaultBoundedRangeModel has been told that more value changes are imminent.

void removeChangeListener(ChangeListener l)

Tells the DefaultBoundedRangeModel to stop notifying the given class when the model changes.

void setExtent(int n)

Specifies the length of the thumbnail in scrollbar units.

`void setMaximum(int n)`

Specifies the maximum possible value in scrollbar units.

`void setMinimum(int n)`

Specifies the minimum possible value in scrollbar units.

`void setRangeProperties(int newValue,int newExtent,int newMin,int`
`    newMax,boolean adjusting)`

Sets the value, extent, minimum, maximum, and currently adjusting properties of the DefaultBoundedRangeModel.

`void setValue(int n)`

Specifies the current value in scrollbar units.

`void setValueIsAdjusting(boolean b)`

Tells the DefaultBoundedRangeModel that more value changes are imminent.

`String toString()`

Overridden to provide special string formatting.

DefaultButtonModel

DefaultButtonModel is Swing's default implementation of the ButtonModel interface. A ButtonModel is used to store internal state information about subclasses of AbstractButton. This includes things like:

- Is the button selected?
- Is the mouse currently over the button?
- Is the button enabled?
- Is rollover functionality enabled?

It does not sense these states, they are set either through the button class itself (JButton, JCheckBox, etc.), or through the button's look-and-feel class. For example, the enabled state is typically set by calling the button's setEnabled() method. The button class passes the new state on to the ButtonModel class. Changing the state through the look-and-feel class happens as follows: since the look-and-feel class is handling events, it is notified when the mouse passes over the button, so it asks the button class for access to the ButtonModel class, and sets the rollover state.

You will not typically need to use the DefaultButtonModel class directly. The AbstractButton subclass creates it automatically and provides convenience methods for accessing the state information.

Ancestors

```
java.lang.Object
   |
   +-com.sun.java.swing.DefaultButtonModel
```

NOTE: *For more information, see the "AbstractButton," "JButton," "JCheckBox," "JRadioButton," "JMenuItem," "JCheckBoxMenuItem," and "JRadioButtonMenuItem" sections in this chapter. Also see the "Allowing the User to Trigger Actions" section in Chapter 7, "JFC by Concept," as well as Chapter 4, "Pluggable-Look-and-Feel."*

Steps in Creating and Using DefaultButtonModel

1. Create a component which is a subclass of AbstractButton:

   ```
   JButton button = new JButton( "Ok" );
   ```

2. Get the button's ButtonModel:

   ```
   ButtonModel model = button.getModel();
   ```

3. Make the button disabled. You can either do this through the model:

   ```
   model.setEnabled( false );
   ```

   Or, you can do it through the button's convenience method:

   ```
   button.setEnabled( false );
   ```

   There are similar methods in the model, and similar convenience methods in the button for setting the rest of the button's internal state information.

4. Listen for changes in the state of the model, like when the mouse passes over the button or when the button becomes disabled.

   Tell the button or the model to add a ChangeListener. In this case, it is the current class:

   ```
   button.addChangeListener( this );
   ```

or:

```
model.addChangeListener( this );
```

Make the event-receiving class implement the ChangeListener interface.

```
public class MyFrame extends JFrame implements ChangeListener
{
    .
    .
    .
    public void stateChanged( ChangeEvent e )
    {
        // Do something since you know the state changed.
    }
}
```

Basic Code Examples

Since the DefaultButtonModel is not generally used directly, there is no separate example. See the "JButton" section in this chapter for an example.

DefaultButtonModel's Public Methods

```
void addActionListener(ActionListener l)
```

Tells the button model to notify the given class when the button is pressed.

```
void addChangeListener(ChangeListener l)
```

Tells the button model to notify the given class when the model's state changes in any way.

```
void addItemListener(ItemListener l)
```

Tells the button model to notify the given class when the button becomes selected or deselected.

```
String getActionCommand()
```

Returns the string that will be delivered with any ActionEvents. May be null.

```
int getMnemonic()
```

Returns the key which, when pressed with a special key (Alt on some systems), will cause the button to be clicked or to change its selection state.

```
Object[] getSelectedObjects()
```

This is just used to fill out the ItemSelectable interface the button implements. It returns an array containing the button model if the button is selected, or null otherwise.

```
boolean isArmed()
```

Returns true if the button can be activated by pressing Enter.

```
boolean isEnabled()
```

Returns true if the button is enabled.

```
boolean isPressed()
```

Returns true if the button is currently pressed.

```
boolean isRollover()
```

Returns true if the mouse is currently over the button.

```
boolean isSelected()
```

Returns true if the button is currently selected.

```
void removeActionListener(ActionListener l)
```

Tells the button model to stop notifying the given class when the button is pressed.

```
void removeChangeListener(ChangeListener l)
```

Tells the button model to stop notifying the given class about model changes.

```
void removeItemListener(ItemListener l)
```

Tells the button model to stop notifying the given class when the button changes state.

```
void setActionCommand(String actionCommand)
```

Specifies the string that should be delivered with any ActionEvents.

```
void setArmed(boolean b)
```

Tells the model that the button is armed. Generally only called by the look-and-feel class.

```
void setEnabled(boolean b)
```

Enables/disables the button.

```
void setGroup(ButtonGroup group)
```

Specifies which ButtonGroup (if any) that the button should be part of.

```
void setMnemonic(int aKey)
```

Specifies the key which, when pressed with a special key (Alt on some platforms), causes the button to be pressed or to change its state.

```
void setPressed(boolean b)
```

Tells the button model that the button is pressed. Generally only called by the look-and-feel class.

```
void setRollover(boolean b)
```

Tells the button model that the mouse is over the button. Generally only called by the look-and-feel class.

```
void setSelected(boolean b)
```

Changes the button's selection state.

DefaultCaret

DefaultCaret is the JFC's standard implementation of the Caret interface. It represents the current position in a text component. Text is inserted at the caret position by default. The caret typically appears as a vertical line, and will usually move when the arrow keys are pressed or when the mouse is clicked inside a text component.

DefaultCaret maintains a *mark* and a *dot*. The dot represents the current caret position. The mark represents the start of a selection range. When the mouse is pressed on a position in a text component, the dot and mark move to that position. If the mouse is dragged from that position, the mark stays where the mouse was pressed while the dot moves with the mouse, expanding the selection range. If the selection is set programatically by calling the text component's setSelectionStart() and setSelectionEnd() methods, the mark is moved to the selection start while the dot is moved to the selection end.

DefaultCaret also maintains a *magic* caret position. This is used when moving vertically among lines of different lengths to keep track of where the horizontal position is. Without the magic caret position, when you moved from the end of a long line to a short line, then to another long line, the horizontal position the caret took in the second long line would not be similar to the horizontal position it was at in the first one.

Ancestors

```
java.lang.Object
   |
   +-com.sun.java.swing.text.DefaultCaret
```

NOTE: *For more information, see the "JTextPane," "JTextArea," "JTextField," and "JTextComponent" sections in this chapter. Also see Chapter 5, "JFC Documents and Text Components."*

Steps in Creating and Using DefaultCaret

1. Create the DefaultCaret. You can create a DefaultCaret explicitly, but there no reason to since the various text components create one for you.

2. Access a text component's caret.

   Create a text component:

   ```
   JTextField field = new JTextField();
   ```

   Get the caret:

   ```
   DefaultCaret caret = (DefaultCaret)field.getCaret();
   ```

3. Set the dot and mark.

   Move the dot and the mark to a position:

   ```
   caret.setDot( 10 );
   ```

   Move the dot to another position, leaving the mark where it is:

   ```
   caret.moveDot( 12 );
   ```

4. Track the motion of the caret. The caret generates ChangeEvents when it moves.

   Tell the caret which class should be notified when the caret position changes. In this case it will be the current class:

   ```
   caret.addChangeListener( this );
   ```

   Make the event-receiving class (MyFrame) implement the ChangeListener interface:

```
public class MyFrame extends JFrame implements ChangeListener
{
    .
    .
    .
    public void stateChanged( ChangeEvent e )
    {
        // Now you know the caret position has changed, so you can
        // do whatever you need to do.
    }
}
```

Basic Code Examples

EXAMPLE 8-14 Getting Information from the Caret

This example shows a JTextField and prints information about the character at the caret position, where the dot is, and where the mark is. If you drag the caret to make a selection, you will see that the dot and mark diverge. Figure 8-16 shows the example after a selection has been made.

Here is the source code:

```
import com.sun.java.swing.*;
import com.sun.java.swing.border.*;
import com.sun.java.swing.event.*;
import com.sun.java.swing.text.*;
import java.awt.*;

public class MyFrame extends JFrame implements
        ChangeListener
{
    private JTextField mField;

    public MyFrame()
    {
        setTitle( "DefaultCaret1" );

        // Store the content pane in a variable for easier
        // access.
        JPanel contentPane = (JPanel)getContentPane();

        // Components will all be added to this panel.
        contentPane.setLayout( new BorderLayout() );

        // Leave blank space around the edges of the content
```

Figure 8-16

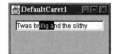

```
      // pane.
      contentPane.setBorder(
                       new EmptyBorder( 10, 10, 10, 10 ) );

      // Create a text field with some text.
      mField = new JTextField(
                       "Twas brillig and the slithy" );

      // Get the text field's caret.
      DefaultCaret caret = (DefaultCaret)mField.getCaret();

      // Make it so this class is notified when the caret
      // position changes.
      caret.addChangeListener( this );

      // Add the text field to the top of the content pane.
      contentPane.add( "North", mField );
   }

   public void stateChanged( ChangeEvent e )
   {
      Caret c = (Caret)e.getSource();
      int pos = c.getDot();

      try
      {
         System.out.println( "The character at the dot is:  " +
                           mField.getText( pos, 1 ) );
      }
      catch ( BadLocationException ex )
      {
         System.out.println( ex );
      }

      System.out.println( "The mark is at:  " +
                        c.getMark() );
      System.out.println( "The dot is at:  " +
                        c.getDot() );
   }
}
```

DefaultCaret's Public Methods

void addChangeListener(ChangeListener l)

Tells the DefaultCaret to notify the given class when the caret position changes.

void deinstall(JTextComponent c)

Called by the text component's look-and-feel class when it is being removed.

`void focusGained(FocusEvent e)`

Part of the FocusListener interface. Called when the text component gets the focus.

`void focusLost(FocusEvent e)`

Part of the FocusListener interface. Called when the text component loses the focus.

`int getBlinkRate()`

Returns the caret blink rate in milliseconds.

`int getDot()`

Returns the caret position.

`Point getMagicCaretPosition()`

Returns the current magic caret position.

`int getMark()`

Returns the position of the selection start if there is a selection, or the caret position if not.

`void install(JTextComponent c)`

Called by the text component's look-and-feel class when it is loaded.

`boolean isSelectionVisible()`

Returns true if the selection (if any) is currently visible.

`boolean isVisible()`

Returns true if the caret can be seen.

`void moveDot(int dot)`

Move the dot position to the given index, leaving the mark where it is.

`void paint(Graphics g):`

Paints the caret.

`void removeChangeListener(ChangeListener l)`

Tells the DefaultCaret to stop notifying the given class when the caret position changes.

```
void setBlinkRate(int rate)
```

Specify the caret blink rate in milliseconds.

```
void setDot(int dot)
```

Sets the dot and mark positions to the given position.

```
void setMagicCaretPosition(Point p)
```

Sets the magic caret position.

```
void setSelectionVisible(boolean vis)
```

Specifies whether text selections will be visible.

```
void setVisible(boolean e)
```

Specifies whether the caret can be seen or not.

DefaultCellEditor

DefaultCellEditor is an editor that can be used with a JTable or a JTree to edit table cells and tree nodes. It can edit both because it implements both the TableCellEditor and TreeCellEditor interfaces. It can edit in one of three ways: as a text field, as a check box, or as a combo box.

If you need greater control, you can implement the TableCellEditor or TreeCellEditor interface.

Ancestors

```
java.lang.Object
    |
    +-com.sun.java.swing.DefaultCellEditor
```

NOTE: *For more information, see the "JTable" and "JTree" sections in this chapter, and the "Trees" and "JFC Tables" sections in Chapter 7, "JFC by Concept."*

Steps in Creating and Using DefaultCellEditor

1. Create a component to be used by the DefaultCellEditor. This should be a JTextField, a JCheckBox, or a JComboBox:

   ```
   JTextField editField = new JTextField();
   ```

   You can set properties for the component, although setting the text will have no effect.

   ```
   editField.setBorder( new BevelBorder( BevelBorder.RAISED ) );
   editField.setBackground( Color.lightGray );
   ```

   The type of editor you use should reflect the type of data in the nodes. If you are using String data, you should use a JTextField or a JComboBox. To use a JCheckBox, the data needs to be Booleans. Using a JCheckBox in a tree cell editor is not common, but it is common in a table cell editor.

2. Create the DefaultCellEditor using the component you just created:

   ```
   DefaultCellEditor editor = new DefaultCellEditor( editField );
   ```

3. Specify how many mouse clicks it takes to start the editor. It is two by default. This can be awkward when editing tree nodes that have child nodes, because a double-click also means expand/collapse the node. In this case, the user can use the node handles to expand/collapse nodes. Make sure you call the JTree's setShowsRootHandles() method so the root node will display its node handle so it can be expanded/collapsed.

   ```
   editor.setClickCountToStart( 1 );
   ```

4. To use a cell editor in a JTree, you have to explicitly make the JTree editable:

   ```
   tree.setEditable( true );
   ```

5. Tell the tree to use your cell editor:

   ```
   tree.setCellEditor( editor );
   ```

6. If you want to know when a cell editing session ends, you can register a CellEditorListener with the DefaultCellEditor. In this case, the listener is the current class:

   ```
   editor.addCellEditorListener( this );
   ```

   Make the listener class (MyFrame) implement the CellEditorListener interface:

   ```
   public class MyFrame extends JFrame implements CellEditorListener
   {
        .
   ```

```
.
.
    public void editingCanceled( ChangeEvent e )
    {
       // This is called when editing ended and changes were not
       // saved.
    }

    public void editingStopped( ChangeEvent e )
    {
       // This is called when editing ended and the edits were
       // saved.
    }
}
```

For a tree cell editor, editing is considered canceled if the user was editing one node, and then clicked on another node. In that case, any changes to the cell go away. Editing is considered stopped if the user pressed enter (in a text field editor). Then, the cell reflects the edits.

Basic Code Examples

EXAMPLE 8-15 Using DefaultCellEditor to Edit Tree Nodes

This example illustrates the use of a DefaultCellEditor to edit a JTree's nodes. The editor uses a JTextField that has its border and background color changed. The editor is activated any time the user clicks on a tree node. Figure 8-17 shows the example while a node is being edited.

Here is the source:

```
import com.sun.java.swing.*;
import com.sun.java.swing.event.*;
import com.sun.java.swing.border.*;
import com.sun.java.swing.tree.*;
import java.awt.*;

public class MyFrame extends JFrame implements CellEditorListener
{
    public MyFrame()
    {
        setTitle( "DefaultCellEditor1" );

        // Store the content pane in a variable for easier access.
        JPanel contentPane = (JPanel)getContentPane();

        // Components will all be added to this panel.
```

Figure 8-17

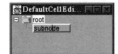

```java
        contentPane.setLayout( new BorderLayout() );

        // Create a root node and give it a single child node.
        DefaultMutableTreeNode root = new DefaultMutableTreeNode(
         "root" );
        DefaultMutableTreeNode subnode = new DefaultMutableTreeNode(
         "subnode" );
        root.add( subnode );

        // Create a JTree with 'root' as its root node.
        JTree tree = new JTree( root );

        // Create the text field that will be used to edit tree nodes.
        JTextField editField = new JTextField();

        // Set its border so it appears raised and its color so
        // everything matches.
        editField.setBorder( new BevelBorder( BevelBorder.RAISED ) );
        editField.setBackground( Color.lightGray );

        // Make a new DefaultCellEditor out of the just-created text
        // field.
        DefaultCellEditor editor = new DefaultCellEditor( editField );

        // Make it so the editor starts whenever the user clicks a
        // node.
        editor.setClickCountToStart( 1 );

        // Make this class listen for the end of edit sessions.
        editor.addCellEditorListener( this );

        // Tell the tree to use our editor.
        tree.setCellEditor( editor );

        // Make the tree editable, or the editor won't be used.
        tree.setEditable( true );

        // Tell the tree to show the node handle on the root node
        // so it can be expanded/collapsed since a double-click
        // won't work.
        tree.setShowsRootHandles( true );

        // Set the tree's background so everything matches.
        tree.setBackground( Color.lightGray );

        // Make the tree take up the content pane's area.
        contentPane.add( "Center", tree );
    }

    // This is called when editing is interrupted.
    public void editingCanceled( ChangeEvent e )
    {
        System.out.println( "Cancelled" );
    }
```

```
// This is called when editing ended successfully.
public void editingStopped( ChangeEvent e )
{
    System.out.println( "Stopped" );
}
}
```

DefaultCellEditor's Public Methods

`void addCellEditorListener(CellEditorListener l)`

Tells the DefaultCellEditor to notify the given class when an editing session ends.

`void cancelCellEditing()`

Tells the DefaultCellEditor to stop editing and discard any changes.

`Object getCellEditorValue()`

Returns the Object that contains the value that the DefaultCellEditor is editing.

`int getClickCountToStart()`

Returns the number of clicks on the tree node or table cell that will activate the DefaultCellEditor.

`Component getComponent()`

Returns the editor component. This is typically the one that was passed to the DefaultCellEditor's constructor.

`Component getTableCellEditorComponent(JTable table,Object value,boolean isSelected,Object columnID,int rowIndex)`

This is the method a JTable calls to get the component that it should display so the user can edit a cell. It should be fully configured when returned.

`Component getTreeCellEditorComponent(JTree tree,Object value,boolean isSelected,boolean expanded,boolean leaf,int row)`

This is the method a JTree calls to get the component that it should display so the user can edit a tree node. It should be fully configured when returned.

`boolean isCellEditable(EventObject anEvent)`

Given an event, returns true if the event will trigger the editor.

```
void removeCellEditorListener(CellEditorListener l)
```

Tells the DefaultCellEditor to stop notifying the given class when editing sessions end.

```
void setClickCountToStart(int count)
```

Sets the number of mouse clicks on an editable tree node or table cell that are required in order to activate the editor.

```
boolean shouldSelectCell(EventObject anEvent)
```

Given an event, return true if the event will cause a node or cell to be selected rather than edited.

```
boolean stopCellEditing()
```

Tells the DefaultCellEditor to stop editing and save changes.

DefaultListModel

DefaultListModel is the JFC's default implementation of the ListModel interface. It is used to store and access all of a JList's data.

Ancestors

```
java.lang.Object
    |
    +-com.sun.java.swing.AbstractListModel
             |
             +-com.sun.java.swing.DefaultListModel
```

NOTE: *For more information, see the "JList" section of this chapter and the "Selecting Items from Lists" section in Chapter 7, JFC by Concept."*

Steps in Creating and Using DefaultListModel

1. You can either explicitly create a DefaultListModel and apply it to a JList, or you can create a JList and have the JList create the DefaultListModel.

   Let the JList create a DefaultListModel:

```
// Specify the items that will go in the list initially.
String listItems[] = new String[3];
listItems[0] = "Item 1";
listItems[1] = "Item 2";
listItems[2] = "Item 3";

// Create the list.
JList myList = new JList( listItems );
```

Create a DefaultListModel and use it to create a JList:

```
// Create the list model.
DefaultListModel model = new DefaultListModel();

// Load it up.
model.addElement( "Item 1" );
model.addElement( "Item 2" );
model.addElement( "Item 3" );

// Create the JList.
JList myList = new JList( model );
```

Create an empty JList, then create a DefaultListModel and tell the JList to use the model:

```
// Create the empty list.
JList myList = new JList();

// Create the list model.
DefaultListModel model = new DefaultListModel();

// Load it up.
model.addElement( "Item 1" );
model.addElement( "Item 2" );
model.addElement( "Item 3" );

// Tell the list to use the model to store its data.
myList.setModel( model );
```

2. Get access to the JList's ListModel:

```
DefaultListModel listModel = (DefaultListModel)myList.getModel();
```

The returned model has to be cast since it is of type ListModel and we need a DefaultListModel so we can use its extra capabilities.

3. Find out how many items are in the list:

```
int count = listModel.getSize();
```

4. Find out what item is at a particular index:

```
String item = (String)listModel.getElementAt( 3 );
```

We cast to a String since that is what we put in the list.

5. Find out where in the list a particular object is. There are four ways to do this. All return -1 if the object is not in the list.

Find out where the object is, starting at the beginning of the list and searching forward:

```
int index = listModel.indexOf( "Item 1" );
```

Find out where the object is, starting at the given index and searching forward:

```
int index = listModel.indexOf( "Item 1", 2 );
```

Find out where the object is, starting at the end of the list and searching backward:

```
int index = listModel.lastIndexOf( "Item 1" );
```

Find out where the object is, starting at the given index and searching backward:

```
int index = listModel.lastIndexOf( "Item 1", 2 );
```

The second and fourth methods are necessary because you may have more than one of the same object in the list.

6. Change the element at a particular index:

```
listModel.setElementAt( "New Item 2", 1 );
```

7. Remove an element. This removes the list item that matches the specified object:

```
listModel.removeElement( "Item 1" );
```

8. Remove the element at a particular index:

```
listModel.removeElementAt( 2 );
```

9. Remove all of the elements in the list:

```
listModel.removeAllElements();
```

10. Tell the list model that you want a particular class to be notified whenever the list contents change:

```
listModel.addListDataListener( myListener );
```

and the listener class has to implement the ListDataListener interface:

```
public void contentsChanged( ListDataEvent e )
{
}

public void intervalAdded( ListDataEvent e )
{
}
```

```
public void intervalRemoved( ListDataEvent e )
{
}
```

11. Add an item to the list. There are two ways to do this.

Add the item to the end of the list:

```
listModel.addElement( "Item 4" );
```

Add the item at the specified index. Items that were previously at that index or beyond are moved down one place:

```
listModel.add( 3, "Item 4" );
```

Basic Code Examples

EXAMPLE 8-16 Using a DefaultListModel

This example sets up a simple GUI that illustrates how a DefaultListModel may be used to add items to a list, remove items from a list, change list items, and monitor changes in the list's items. It has a list that initially contains three items. Below, there is a text field where you can enter text to be put into new items and four buttons. The Insert button creates a new item using the text in the text field, and inserts it before the currently selected item. If no item is selected, it inserts the new item at the start of the list. The Insert After button creates a new item and inserts it after the currently selected item, if any. The Delete button deletes the selected item. The Replace button causes the selected item to change to a new item containing the text from the text field. Figure 8-18 shows the example after a new item has been added.

Important points to notice:

▪ The example includes a ListDataListener that is notified when items are added to, removed from, or changed in the list.

▪ When an item is replaced, we have to call the JList's repaint() method to reflect the change. Additions and removals are automatically reflected.

Figure 8-18

Here is the source:

```java
import com.sun.java.swing.*;
import com.sun.java.swing.event.*;
import java.awt.*;
import java.awt.event.*;

public class MyFrame extends JFrame implements
        ActionListener, ListDataListener
{
    private JList myList;
    private JTextField mField;
    private JButton insert;
    private JButton insertAfter;
    private JButton delete;
    private JButton replace;

    public MyFrame()
    {
        setTitle( "DefaultListModel1" );

        // Store the content pane in a variable for easier
        // access.
        JPanel contentPane = (JPanel)getContentPane();

        // Components will all be added to this panel.
        contentPane.setLayout( new BoxLayout( contentPane,
                            BoxLayout.Y_AXIS ) );

        // Create the empty list.
        myList = new JList();

        // Restrict to single selection.
        myList.setSelectionMode(
                    ListSelectionModel.SINGLE_SELECTION );

        // Create the list model.
        DefaultListModel model = new DefaultListModel();

        // Load it up.
        model.addElement( "Item 1" );
        model.addElement( "Item 2" );
        model.addElement( "Item 3" );

        // Make it so this class listens for changes in the
        // model.
        model.addListDataListener( this );

        // Tell the list to use the model to store its data.
        myList.setModel( model );

        // Create a scroll pane to put the list into in case
        // it gets too big.
        JScrollPane scroller = new JScrollPane( myList );
```

```
// Make the scroll pane take up the upper part of the
// content pane.
contentPane.add( scroller );

// Create a panel to hold the various controls.
Box changeBox = Box.createVerticalBox();

// Create a text field with a label.  The contents of
// the text field will be applied when you insert or
// replace nodes.
JLabel newText = new JLabel( "New item's text:" );
mField = new JTextField( "New item" );

// Make the label and text field line up.
mField.setAlignmentX( 0.0f );
newText.setAlignmentX( mField.getAlignmentX() );

// Add the label and text field to the panel.
changeBox.add( newText );
changeBox.add( mField );

// Leave some space.
changeBox.add( Box.createVerticalGlue() );

// Create four buttons the user can press to insert a
// new item either before the selected item or in the
// list's first position, insert a item after the
// selected item, delete the selected item, or
// replace the selected item.
insert = new JButton( "Insert" );
insert.addActionListener( this );
insert.setActionCommand( "insert" );
changeBox.add( insert );

insertAfter = new JButton( "Insert After" );
insertAfter.addActionListener( this );
insertAfter.setActionCommand( "insertAfter" );
changeBox.add( insertAfter );

delete = new JButton( "Delete" );
delete.addActionListener( this );
delete.setActionCommand( "delete" );
changeBox.add( delete );

replace = new JButton( "Replace" );
replace.addActionListener( this );
replace.setActionCommand( "replace" );
changeBox.add( replace );

// Add the controls panel to the lower part of the
// content pane.
contentPane.add( changeBox );
}

// This is called when one of the buttons is pressed.
```

```java
public void actionPerformed( ActionEvent e )
{
    String command = e.getActionCommand();

    // Get the index of the currently selected item.  It
    // may be -1 if none is selected, or beyond the end
    // of the list if the last item was deleted.
    int index = myList.getSelectedIndex();

    // Get the list data model.
    DefaultListModel model =
                    (DefaultListModel)myList.getModel();

    // If the selected index is beyond the end of the
    // list, treat it like there is no selection.
    if ( index >= myList.getModel().getSize() )
    {
        index = -1;
    }

    if ( command.equals( "insert" ) )
    {
        // If the insert button was pressed - if no item
        // is selected, create a new item and add it as
        // the list's first item.  Otherwise, insert the
        // new item before the selected one.  The new item
        // is created using the text from the text field.
        if ( index == -1 )
            index = 0;
        model.add( index, mField.getText() );
    }
    else if ( index != -1 )
    {
        // If an item is currently selected...
        if ( command.equals( "insertAfter" ) )
        {
            // If the insert after button was pressed, add
            // a new item after the selected one.
            model.add( index + 1, mField.getText() );
        }
        else if ( command.equals( "delete" ) )
        {
            // If the delete button was pressed, delete the
            // selected item.
            model.removeElementAt( index );
        }
        else if ( command.equals( "replace" ) )
        {
            // If the replace button was pressed, replace
            // the selected item.
            model.setElementAt( mField.getText(), index );
        }
    }
    else
    {
```

```
                // Print out a message saying that the button the
                // user pressed requires that an item be selected,
                // and none was.
                System.out.println( "No item is selected" );
            }
        }

        // This is called when the replace button was pressed
        // and we replace the selected item in the list.
        public void contentsChanged( ListDataEvent e )
        {
            System.out.println( "Changed" );

            // Call repaint so the change is reflected in the
            // list.
            myList.repaint();
        }

        public void intervalAdded( ListDataEvent e )
        {
            System.out.println( "Added" );
        }

        public void intervalRemoved( ListDataEvent e )
        {
            System.out.println( "Removed" );
        }
    }
```

DefaultListModel's Public Methods

`void add(int index,Object element)`

Adds the given Object to the list, inserting it at the given index.

`void addElement(Object obj)`

Adds the given Object to the end of the list.

`int capacity()`

Returns the list's internal Vector's capacity.

`void clear()`

Removes all items from the list.

`boolean contains(Object elem)`

Returns true if the given Object is in the list.

`void copyInto(Object anArray[])`

Copies the list items into the given array.

`Object elementAt(int index)`

Returns the list item at the given index.

`Enumeration elements()`

Returns an Enumeration of the list's contents.

`void ensureCapacity(int minCapacity)`

Calls the internal Vector's ensureCapacity() method.

`Object firstElement()`

Returns the first list item.

`Object get(int index)`

Returns the list item at the given index.

`Object getElementAt(int index)`

Returns the list item at the given index.

`int getSize()`

Returns the number of items in the list.

`int indexOf(Object elem)`

Returns the index of the first occurrence of the given Object within the list.

`int indexOf(Object elem,int index)`

Returns the index of the first occurrence of the given `Object`, starting at the given index.

`void insertElementAt(Object obj,int index)`

Inserts the given Object at the given index.

`boolean isEmpty()`

Returns true if the list is empty.

`Object lastElement()`

Returns the last list item.

`int lastIndexOf(Object elem)`

Returns the index of the last occurrence of the given **object** within the list.

`int lastIndexOf(Object elem,int index)`

Returns the last occurrence of the given Object, starting at the given index and working backward.

`Object remove(int index)`

Removes the list item at the given index.

`void removeAllElements()`

Removes all of the items in the list.

`boolean removeElement(Object obj)`

Removes the first occurrence of the given Object from the list.

`void removeElementAt(int index)`

Removes the list item at the given index.

`void removeRange(int fromIndex,int toIndex)`

Removes the list items from 'fromIndex' to 'toIndex', inclusive.

`Object set(int index,Object element)`

Replace the list item at the given index with the new Object.

`void setElementAt(Object obj,int index)`

Replace the list item at the given index with the new Object.

`void setSize(int newSize)`

Set the number of items in the list. Any extra items beyond the new size are dropped.

`int size()`

Returns the number of items in the list.

`Object[] toArray()`

Returns the list items as an array.

```
String toString()
```

Overridden to provide DefaultListModel's own String representation.

```
void trimToSize()
```

Condenses the internal Vector so its size is the same as the number of items in the list.

DefaultListSelectionModel

DefaultListSelectionModel is a class that is used to keep track of which items are selected in JLists, JDirectoryPanes, JFileChoosers, and JTables. It doesn't interact with the user to specify what is selected. It interacts with its component's look-and-feel class which interacts with the user and tells the DefaultListSelectionModel what items are selected.

Ancestors

```
java.lang.Object
   |
   +-com.sun.java.swing.DefaultListSelectionModel
```

NOTE: *For more information, see the "JDirectoryPane," "JList," and "JTable" sections of this chapter. Also see the "File Browsing," "Selecting Items from Lists," and "Swing Tables" sections in Chapter 7, "JFC by Concept."*

Steps in Creating and Using DefaultListSelectionModel

1. Create the DefaultListSelectionModel. Although you can create a DefaultListSelectionModel yourself, JList creates one automatically.

   ```
   JList list = new JList();
   ```

2. Get access to the JList's selection model:

   ```
   ListSelectionModel model = list.getSelectionModel();
   ```

   ListSelectionModel is the interface that DefaultListSelectionModel implements and it defines all of the behavior we need.

3. Listen for changes in the selection state.

Specify which class you want to be notified when the selection state changes. In this case, it is the current class:

```
model.addListSelectionListener( this );
```

Make the event-receiving class (MyFrame) implement the ListSelectionListener interface:

```
public void valueChanged( ListSelectionEvent e )
{
    // Now you know the list selection state has changed.
}
```

4. Add a range of indices to the list of currently selected items. The first index is called the *anchor*, while the second is called the *lead*. The anchor may be less than, greater than, or equal to the lead.

   Make the indices from 5 to 7 (inclusive) selected without deselecting any other already selected items.

   ```
   model.addSelectionInterval( 5, 7 );
   ```

5. Set a range of indices to be the list's only selected items. Again, the first index is the anchor while the second is the lead.

   Make the indices from 5 to 7 (inclusive) selected, deselecting any items that were selected before and are not in the given range:

   ```
   model.setSelectionInterval( 5, 7 );
   ```

6. Make it so a range of indices are not selected.

   Make the items at indices 5 through 7 (inclusive) so they are not selected. If any were previously not selected, they remain that way:

   ```
   model.removeSelectionInterval( 5, 7 );
   ```

7. Get the smallest index that is selected. This returns -1 if no items are selected:

   ```
   int lowIndex = model.getMinSelectionIndex();
   ```

8. Get the largest index that is selected. This returns -1 if no items are selected:

   ```
   int highIndex = model.getMaxSelectionIndex();
   ```

9. Find out if a specific index is currently selected:

   ```
   boolean selected = model.isSelectedIndex( 4 );
   ```

10. Deselect all selected items:

    ```
    model.clearSelection();
    ```

Basic Code Examples

EXAMPLE 8-17 Manipulating the DefaultListSelectionModel

This example contains a JList with 20 items, and a set of controls for changing and monitoring its selection state. There are two text fields that will update to display the anchor and lead settings when the selection is changed, or the user can enter new values into these text fields and press one of the three buttons below the fields to add, remove, or set selections. Figure 8-20 shows the example just after a range has been selected.

Here is the source code:

```java
import com.sun.java.swing.*;
import com.sun.java.swing.event.*;
import java.awt.*;
import java.awt.event.*;

public class MyFrame extends JFrame implements
        ActionListener, ListSelectionListener
{
    private JList list;
    private JTextField anchor;
    private JTextField lead;
    private JButton add;
    private JButton remove;
    private JButton set;

    public MyFrame()
    {
        setTitle( "DefaultListSelecionModel1" );

        // Store the content pane in a variable for easier
        // access.
        JPanel contentPane = (JPanel)getContentPane();
```

Figure 8-19

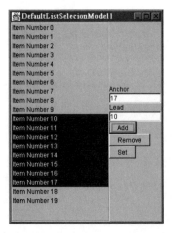

```
// Components will all be added to this panel.
contentPane.setLayout( new BoxLayout( contentPane,
                         BoxLayout.X_AXIS ) );

// Load the lists items in an array.
String items[] = new String[20];

for ( int i = 0; i < 20; i++ )
{
    items[i] = new String( "Item Number " + i );
}

// Use the array to load the items into the list.
list = new JList( items );

// Get the selection model.
ListSelectionModel model = list.getSelectionModel();

// Make it so this class is notified when the
// selection state changes.
model.addListSelectionListener( this );

// Place the list in a scroll pane.
JScrollPane scroller = new JScrollPane( list );

// Add the scroll pane so it becomes the content
// pane's left side.
contentPane.add( scroller );

// Create a panel to hold the text fields and buttons.
JPanel controlPane = new JPanel();
controlPane.setLayout( new BoxLayout( controlPane,
                         BoxLayout.Y_AXIS ) );

// Create the anchor label and text field, and add
// them to the panel.
JLabel l1 = new JLabel( "Anchor" );
anchor = new JTextField();
Dimension dim = anchor.getPreferredSize();
dim.width = 100;
anchor.setMaximumSize( dim );
anchor.setPreferredSize( dim );
l1.setAlignmentX( 0.0f );
anchor.setAlignmentX( 0.0f );
controlPane.add( l1 );
controlPane.add( anchor );

// Create the lead label and text field, and add them
// to the panel.
JLabel l2 = new JLabel( "Lead" );
lead = new JTextField();
dim = lead.getPreferredSize();
dim.width = 100;
lead.setMaximumSize( dim );
lead.setPreferredSize( dim );
```

```
l2.setAlignmentX( 0.0f );
lead.setAlignmentX( 0.0f );
controlPane.add( 12 );
controlPane.add( lead );

// Create the add button, make it so this class will
// be notified when it is pressed, and add it to the
// panel.
add = new JButton( "Add" );
add.addActionListener( this );
controlPane.add( add );

// Create the remove button, make it so this class
// will be notified when it is pressed, and add it to
// the panel.
remove = new JButton( "Remove" );
remove.addActionListener( this );
controlPane.add( remove );

// Create the set button, make it so this class will
// be notified when it is pressed, and add it to the
// panel.
set = new JButton( "Set" );
set.addActionListener( this );
controlPane.add( set );

// Make the control panel so it is the content pane's
// right side.
contentPane.add( controlPane );
}

// This is called when one of the buttons is pressed.
public void actionPerformed( ActionEvent e )
{
    int anchorval = 0;
    int leadval = 0;

    // Put the values of the text field into ints, making
    // sure they are valid.
    try
    {
        anchorval = Integer.parseInt( anchor.getText() );
        leadval = Integer.parseInt( lead.getText() );
    }
    catch ( NumberFormatException ex )
    {
        System.out.println( "Invalid number" );
        return;
    }

    // Get the lists selection model.
    ListSelectionModel model = list.getSelectionModel();

    // Add, remove, or set the selection range based on
    // which button was pressed.
```

```
        if ( e.getSource() == add )
        {
            model.addSelectionInterval( anchorval, leadval );
        }
        else if ( e.getSource() == remove )
        {
            model.removeSelectionInterval( anchorval,
                                           leadval );
        }
        else if ( e.getSource() == set )
        {
            model.setSelectionInterval( anchorval, leadval );
        }
    }

    // This is called when the list selection state changes.
    public void valueChanged( ListSelectionEvent e )
    {
        // Get the selection model.
        ListSelectionModel model = list.getSelectionModel();

        // Get the new anchor and lead indices from the model
        // and put them into the text fields.
        anchor.setText( String.valueOf(
                        model.getAnchorSelectionIndex() ) );
        lead.setText( String.valueOf(
                        model.getLeadSelectionIndex() ) );
    }
}
```

DefaultListSelectionModel's Public Methods

`void addListSelectionListener(ListSelectionListener l)`

Tells the DefaultListSelectionModel to notify the given class whenever the selection changes.

`void addSelectionInterval(int index0,int index1)`

Makes it so the items indicated by the range of indices become selected.

`void clearSelection()`

Makes it so no items are selected.

`Object clone()`

Makes a copy of the DefaultListSelectionModel.

`int getAnchorSelectionIndex()`

Returns the first argument to the last call to the addSelectionInterval() or setSelectionInterval() methods.

`int getLeadSelectionIndex()`

Returns the second argument to the last call to the addSelectionInterval() or setSelectionInterval() methods.

`int getMaxSelectionIndex()`

Returns the index that refers is the last selected item in the list.

`int getMinSelectionIndex()`

Returns the index that refers to the first selected item in the list.

`int getSelectionMode()`

Returns one of: ListSelectionModel.SINGLE_SELECTION, ListSelection-Model.SINGLE_INTERVAL_SELECTION, or ListSelectionModel.MULTI-PLE_INTERVAL_SELECTION.

`boolean getValueIsAdjusting()`

Returns true if the look-and-feel class has told the DefaultListSelectionModel that a series of selections are ongoing.

`void insertIndexInterval(int index,int length,boolean before)`

This is called when items are added to the list data model and yet the same items that were selected before should still be selected. 'length' indices are inserted into the selection model so its indices match the data model's. You normally won't call this.

`boolean isLeadAnchorNotificationEnabled()`

Returns true if the notification of changes in the selection is broad.

`boolean isSelectedIndex(int index)`

Returns true if the item at the given index is selected.

`boolean isSelectionEmpty()`

Returns true if no items are selected.

```
void removeIndexInterval(int index0,int index1)
```

This is called when some items have been removed from the list data model and yet the same items that were selected before should still be selected (if they weren't among the items removed). The range of indices are removed from the selection model so its indices match the data model's. You normally won't call this.

```
void removeListSelectionListener(ListSelectionListener l)
```

Tells the DefaultListSelectionModel to stop notifying the given class when selection changes occur.

```
void removeSelectionInterval(int index0,int index1)
```

Makes it so the items referred to by the given range of indices are not selected.

```
void setAnchorSelectionIndex(int anchor)
```

Specifies the new anchor index.

```
void setLeadAnchorNotifcationEnabled(boolean flag)
```

Specifies whether change notification should be broad or narrow.

```
void setLeadSelectionIndex(int anchor)
```

Specifies the new lead index.

```
void setSelectionInterval(int index0,int index1)
```

Makes it so the items referred to by the given range of indices are all selected and no other items are.

```
void setSelectionMode(int mode)
```

Specifies the selection mode. Should be one of: ListSelectionModel.SINGLE_SELECTION, ListSelectionModel.SINGLE_INTERVAL_SELECTION, or ListSelectionModel.MULTIPLE_INTERVAL_SELECTION.

```
void setValueIsAdjusting(boolean b)
```

This tells the DefaultListSelectionModel that the set of selected items is in the process of changing.

```
String toString()
```

Overridden to provide its own String format.

DefaultMutableTreeNode

A tree node is a single item in a JTree's TreeModel. In a tree that represents
a file system, a tree node might represent either a file or a directory. It does
not control the way the item is displayed, but rather what the item contains and its state. TreeNode is the interface that a tree node class must
implement so it can work with a TreeModel, and therefore with a JTree.
DefaultMutableTreeNode is the default TreeNode implementation that
comes with the JFC. Actually, DefaultMutableTreeNode implements the
MutableTreeNode interface which is an extension of TreeNode.

It is important to notice that the DefaultMutableTreeNode class implements quite a few more methods than are specified in the TreeNode and
MutableTreeNode interfaces. This means that if an application uses
DefaultMutableTreeNodes, you cannot just replace these nodes with a class
that just implements MutableTreeNode—you would also have to implement
the other DefaultMutableTreeNode methods.

Ancestors

```
java.lang.Object
    |
    +-com.sun.java.swing.tree.DefaultMutableTreeNode
```

 NOTE: *For more information, see the "JTree" and "DefaultTreeModel" sections of*
this chapter, the "Trees" section in Chapter 7, "JFC by Concept," and Chapter 11,
"JFC Integration Example 2—Adding Items to and Removing Items from JTrees."

Steps in Creating and Using DefaultMutableTreeNode

1. Create the DefaultMutableTreeNode. There are three constructors:

   One creates a tree node with nothing in it. If you use this, you can use
   the setUserObject() method to put something in the node.

   ```
   DefaultMutableTreeNode myNode = new DefaultMutableTreeNode();
   ```

   One creates a tree node and puts something in it:

   ```
   DefaultMutableTreeNode myNode = new DefaultMutableTreeNode(
                                               "My Node" );
   ```

   One creates a tree node, puts something in it, and specifies whether the
   node can have children. By default, a node is allowed to have children.

```
DefaultMutableTreeNode myNode = new DefaultMutableTreeNode(
                                        "My Node", false );
```

2. Add the tree node into a tree. There are many ways to do this. See "JTree" and "DefaultTreeModel" in this chapter for more information.

3. Add a child node to this node. This will not work if this node does not allow children. Note that if you add a child directly to this node, the TreeModel that this node belongs to (if any) will not know about it and will not automatically update its JTree to reflect the change. If this node is part of a TreeModel, add the new node through the TreeModel. Otherwise, you have to explicitly notify the TreeModel that you have changed it.

```
myNode.add( newNode );
```

'newNode' becomes 'myNode's last child.

4. Get a list of this node's children. This method returns an enumeration:

```
// Use the children() method to get an enumeration of myNode's
// child nodes, and go through them one at a time.
for ( Enumeration e = myNode.children(); e.hasMoreElements(); )
{
   DefaultMutableTreeNode thisNode = (DefaultMutableTreeNode)e.
                                        nextElement();
}
```

5. Get a count of how many children this node has:

```
int numChildren = myNode.getChildCount();
```

6. Get the path from the root node to this node. Note that this method actually returns an array of TreeNodes instead of an actual TreePath.

```
TreeNode nodes[] = myNode.getPath();
```

7. Get the root node of this item's tree:

```
TreeNode root = myNode.getRoot();
```

8. Get the object stored in the node. We created *myNode* with a String, so we get a String out.

```
String text = (String)myNode.getUserObject();
```

9. Get a list of the user objects on the path from the root node to this node:

```
String nodeInfo[] = (String [])myNode.getUserObjectPath();
```

10. Find out if this node has no children:

```
boolean nodeIsLeaf = myNode.isLeaf();
```

11. Find out if another node is an ancestor of this node:

```
boolean nodeIsAncestor = myNode.isNodeAncestor( otherNode );
```

12. Find out if another node is a child of this node:

```
boolean nodeIsChild = myNode.isNodeChild( otherNode );
```

13. Find out if another node is a descendant of this node:

```
boolean nodeIsDescendant = myNode.isNodeDescendant( otherNode );
```

14. Remove a child node from this node. If this node is part of a TreeModel, it is best to remove nodes using the TreeModel instead of directly through the tree node. Otherwise, the TreeModel doesn't know you have changed it and will not automatically update its JTree.

Remove it by specifying the node:

```
myNode.remove( otherNode );
```

Or remove it by index:

```
myNode.remove( nodeIndex );
```

You can also remove all of a node's child nodes:

```
myNode.removeAll();
```

15. Specify whether this node allows children. This can also be set through one of the constructors.

```
myNode.setAllowsChildren( false );
```

16. Change the data stored in this node:

```
myNode.setUserObject( "My Changed Node" );
```

Basic Code Examples

For examples of DefaultMutableTreeNodes in use, see the "JTree" and "DefaultTreeModel" sections in this chapter, as well as Chapter 10, "Integrating JFC Example1—A File Browser," and Chapter 11, "Integrating JFC Example 2—Adding Items to and Removing Items from JTrees."

DefaultMutableTreeNode's Public Methods

```
void add(MutableTreeNode newChild)
```

Adds the new node as this node's last.

`Enumeration breadthFirstEnumeration()`

Gets an enumeration of this node and its subtree. The order of the enumeration is: this node, this node's children, this node's children's children, and so on.

`Enumeration children()`

Gets an enumeration of this node's immediate children.

`Object clone()`

Makes a copy of this node with the same user object, but without any connections to parent or children.

`Enumeration depthFirstEnumeration()`

Gets an enumeration of this node and its subtree in depth-first order.

`boolean getAllowsChildren()`

Returns true if this node is allowed to have child nodes.

`TreeNode getChildAfter(TreeNode aChild)`

Returns this node's child node that comes after the given child node.

`TreeNode getChildAt(int index)`

Returns this node's child at the given index.

`TreeNode getChildBefore(TreeNode aChild)`

Returns this node's child node that comes before the given child.

`int getChildCount()`

Returns the number of children this node has.

`int getDepth()`

Returns the number of tree levels that exist in this node's subtree.

`TreeNode getFirstChild()`

Returns this node's first child node.

`DefaultMutableTreeNode getFirstLeaf()`

Returns this node's first child that is a leaf.

`int getIndex(TreeNode aChild)`

Returns the index of the given child node under this node.

`TreeNode getLastChild()`

Returns this node's last child node.

`DefaultMutableTreeNode getLastLeaf()`

Returns this node's last child that is a leaf.

`int getLeafCount()`

Returns the number of leaf nodes this node has.

`int getLevel()`

Returns the number of tree levels there are above this node.

`DefaultMutableTreeNode getNextLeaf()`

Returns the next leaf node after this node in a special traversal order. Do no traverse entire trees this way—use an enumeration.

`DefaultMutableTreeNode getNextNode()`

Returns the next node after this node in a special traversal order. Do no traverse entire trees this way—use an enumeration.

`DefaultMutableTreeNode getNextSibling()`

Gets the next node, under this node's parent, after this node.

`TreeNode getParent()`

Gets this node's parent node.

`TreeNode[] getPath()`

Gets the path from the root node to this node. Note that an array of TreeNodes is returned, not a TreePath.

`DefaultMutableTreeNode getPreviousLeaf()`

Gets the leaf node before this node in a special traversal order.

`DefaultMutableTreeNode getPreviousNode()`

Gets the node before this node in a special traversal order.

`DefaultMutableTreeNode getPreviousSibling()`

Gets the previous node, under this node's parent, before this node.

`TreeNode getRoot()`

Returns the root node of the tree this node is in.

`TreeNode getSharedAncestor(DefaultMutableTreeNode aNode)`

Gets the nearest node that is an ancestor of both this node and the given node.

`int getSiblingCount()`

Returns how many nodes besides this one that are also children of this node's parent node.

`Object getUserObject()`

Returns the Object that this node represents.

`Object[] getUserObjectPath()`

Returns an array of the user objects of all nodes on a path from the root node to this node.

`void insert(MutableTreeNode newChild,int childIndex)`

Inserts the given node as a child of this node at the given index.

`boolean isLeaf()`

Returns true if this node has no children.

`boolean isNodeAncestor(TreeNode anotherNode)`

Returns true if the given node is in the path from the root node to this node.

`boolean isNodeChild(TreeNode aNode)`

Returns true if the given node is a child of this node.

`boolean isNodeDescendant(DefaultMutableTreeNode anotherNode)`

Returns true if the given node is a descendant of this node (is in the subtree that this node is the root of).

`boolean isNodeRelated(DefaultMutableTreeNode aNode)`

Returns true if the root node of this node's tree is the same as the root node of the given node's tree.

`boolean isNodeSibling(TreeNode anotherNode)`

Returns true if this node and the given node have the same parent node.

`boolean isRoot()`

Returns true if this node is the root node of a tree.

`Enumeration pathFromAncestorEnumeration(TreeNode ancestor)`

Gets an enumeration of the nodes on the path from the given ancestor node to this node.

`Enumeration postorderEnumeration()`

Gets an enumeration of this node's subtree in postorder.

`Enumeration preorderEnumeration()`

Gets an enumeration of this node's subtree in preorder.

`void remove(int childIndex)`

Removes the child of this node at the given index.

`void remove(MutableTreeNode aChild)`

Removes the given node from this node if it is a child of this node.

`void removeAllChildren()`

Removes all of this node's child nodes.

`void removeFromParent()`

Removes this node from its parent node.

`void setAllowsChildren(boolean allows)`

Specifies whether this node is allowed to have child nodes.

`void setParent(MutableTreeNode newParent)`

Adds this node as a child of the given node.

```
void setUserObject(Object userObject)
```

Specifies the Object that this node represents.

```
String toString()
```

Overridden for DefaultMutableTreeNode's own string creation.

DefaultSingleSelectionModel

DefaultSingleSelectionModel is the JFC's default implementation of the SingleSelectionModel interface. It keeps track of which item is selected in simple components that only allow one item to be selected at a time. These include components like JMenuBar (only one menu may be selected at a time), JPopupMenu (only one menu item may be selected at a time), and JTabbedPane (only one tab may be selected at a time). It doesn't actually cause different items to be selected. Instead, it is told by other classes that the selection has changed. For example, when the user clicks on a menu in a JMenuBar, the JMenuBar's look-and-feel class gets the event, figures out which menu should be selected, asks the JMenuBar class for its SingleSelectionModel class, and tells the SingleSelectionModel class what the new selection is. Or, when you programmatically tell a JTabbedPane to cause a tab to become selected, you typically call the JTabbedPane's setSelectedIndex() method which calls the SingleSelectionModel's setSelectedIndex() method, which changes the selection state.

When the selection changes, the SingleSelectionModel class generates a ChangeEvent and sends it to all registered ChangeListeners.

Ancestors

```
java.lang.Object
    |
    +-com.sun.java.swing.DefaultSingleSelectionModel
```

NOTE: *For more information, see the "JMenuBar," "JPopupMenu," and "JTabbedPane" sections in this chapter.*

Steps in Creating and Using DefaultSingleSelectionModel

1. You will typically not have to create a DefaultSingleSelectionModel because components that use it will create one automatically. So, by creating one of these components, you also create a DefaultSingleSelectionModel:

   ```
   JTabbedPane tabbedPane = new JTabbedPane();
   ```

   Or:

   ```
   JMenuBar menuBar = new JMenuBar();
   ```

2. Get access to the DefaultSingleSelectionModel. Not all components that use a SingleSelectionModel actually allow you to get or change it.

   ```
   SingleSelectionModel menuSelectionModel =
     menuBar.getSelectionModel();
   ```

3. Register to be notified when the selection changes. Components that use a SingleSelectionModel will sometimes provide a way to register for these changes through the component class (especially if they don't allow access to the SingleSelectionModel itself).

   Register to be notified when a new menu is selected from a menu bar:

   ```
   menuSelectionModel.addChangeListener( myListener );
   ```

   Register to be notified when a new tab is selected in a tabbed pane:

   ```
   tabbedPane.addChangeListener( myListener );
   ```

4. Change the selection through your program. Directly:

   ```
   menuSelectionModel.setSelectedIndex( 1 );
   ```

   Or, indirectly:

   ```
   tabbedPane.setSelectedIndex( 1 );
   ```

Basic Code Examples

EXAMPLE 8-18 Using a JMenuBar's SingleSelectionModel

This example creates a frame with a menu bar that contains three menus (one menu item in each). The frame also contains three buttons. When you press one of the buttons, it causes one of the menus to become selected. The selection model generates a ChangeEvent, which the example uses to cause the selected menu's popup to display. This example illustrates:

■ Accessing the JMenuBar's selection model

■ Getting the current selection from the selection model

■ Using a ChangeListener to monitor changes in the selection model

Figure 8-20 shows a DefaultSingleSelectionModel in use in a JMenuBar. Here is the source code:

```java
import com.sun.java.swing.*;
import java.awt.*;
import com.sun.java.swing.event.*;
import java.awt.event.*;

public class MyFrame extends JFrame implements
        ActionListener, ChangeListener
{
    private JMenuBar menuBar;

    public MyFrame()
    {
        setTitle( "DefaultSingleSelectionModel1" );

        // Store the content pane in a variable for easier
        // access.
        JPanel contentPane = (JPanel)getContentPane();

        // Components will all be added to this panel.
        contentPane.setLayout( new BorderLayout() );

        // Create the menu bar.
        menuBar = new JMenuBar();

        // Create three menus each with a single item and add
        // them to the menu bar.
        JMenu fileMenu = new JMenu( "File" );
        JMenuItem item1 = new JMenuItem( "Exit" );
        fileMenu.add( item1 );
        menuBar.add( fileMenu );

        JMenu optionsMenu = new JMenu( "Options" );
        JMenuItem item2 = new JMenuItem( "Some Option" );
        optionsMenu.add( item2 );
        menuBar.add( optionsMenu );

        JMenu windowMenu = new JMenu( "Window" );
        JMenuItem item3 = new JMenuItem( "Tile Windows" );
```

Figure 8-20

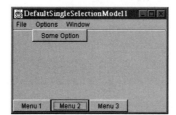

```java
        windowMenu.add( item3 );
        menuBar.add( windowMenu );

        // Make the menu bar the frame's menu bar.
        getRootPane().setMenuBar( menuBar );

        // Make this class listen for selection changes in
        // the menu bar.
        menuBar.getSelectionModel().addChangeListener( this );

        // Create a panel to hold the buttons.
        Box buttonPane = Box.createHorizontalBox();

        // Create three buttons.  Each will trigger a
        // different menu to be selected.
        JButton b1 = new JButton( "Menu 1" );
        b1.setActionCommand( "1" );
        b1.addActionListener( this );
        buttonPane.add( b1 );

        JButton b2 = new JButton( "Menu 2" );
        b2.setActionCommand( "2" );
        b2.addActionListener( this );
        buttonPane.add( b2 );

        JButton b3 = new JButton( "Menu 3" );
        b3.setActionCommand( "3" );
        b3.addActionListener( this );
        buttonPane.add( b3 );

        // Place the button panel at the bottom of the
        // content pane.
        contentPane.add( "South", buttonPane );
    }

    // This is called when one of the buttons is pressed.
    // We use the button's action command string to decide
    // which item in the menu bar should become selected.
    public void actionPerformed( ActionEvent e )
    {
        String command = e.getActionCommand();

        if ( command.equals( "1" ) )
        {
            menuBar.getSelectionModel().setSelectedIndex( 0 );
        }
        else if ( command.equals( "2" ) )
        {
            menuBar.getSelectionModel().setSelectedIndex( 1 );
        }
        if ( command.equals( "3" ) )
        {
            menuBar.getSelectionModel().setSelectedIndex( 2 );
        }
    }
```

```
// This is called when the selection state of the menu
// bar changes, either programmatically (by pressing the
// buttons) or by user interaction.
public void stateChanged( ChangeEvent e )
{
    // The selection model is the source of this event.
    DefaultSingleSelectionModel model =
            (DefaultSingleSelectionModel)e.getSource();

    // We have to catch the array out of bounds exception
    // because when a menu is selected and you move the
    // mouse to another menu item, the previous item
    // becomes unselected, a ChangeEvent is generated,
    // and the selected index is -1 because nothing is
    // selected.
    try
    {
        // Get the menu at the selected index.
        JMenu menu = menuBar.getMenu(
                        model.getSelectedIndex() );

        // Expand the menu's popup.
        menu.setPopupMenuVisible( true );
    }
    catch ( ArrayIndexOutOfBoundsException ex )
    {
    }
}
}
```

DefaultSingleSelectionModel's Public Methods

`void addChangeListener(ChangeListener l)`

Tells the DefaultSingleSelectionModel to notify the given class whenever the selction changes.

`void clearSelection()`

Makes it so that no items are selected.

`int getSelectedIndex()`

Returns the index of the selected item.

`boolean isSelected()`

Returns true if an item is selected.

`void removeChangeListener(ChangeListener l)`

Tells the DefaultSingleSelectionModel to stop notifying the given class when the selection changes.

```
void setSelectedIndex(int index)
```

Specifies which item should become the selected item.

DefaultStyledDocument

DefaultStyledDocument is the AbstractDocument subclass that a JTextPane uses to store its text and attributes. You can use this class to add and remove text, and to change text attributes.

Ancestors

```
java.lang.Object
    |
    +-com.sun.java.swing.text.AbstractDocument
            |
            +-com.sun.java.swing.text.DefaultStyledDocument
```

NOTE: *For more information, see the "JTextPane," "JTextComponent," "Abstract-Document," and "Element" sections in this chapter. Also see Chapter 5, "JFC Documents and Text Components," as well as Chapter 13, "JFC Intergration Example 4 —A Simple Word Processor."*

Steps in Creating and Using DefaultStyledDocument

1. You can either explicitly create a DefaultStyledDocument and apply it to a JTextPane, or you can just use the one that is automatically generated when a JTextPane is created.

   When you create a DefaultStyledDocument, you can either specify a set of Styles (named AttributeSets), or you can use the empty constructor.

   Use the empty constructor:

   ```
   DefaultStyledDocument doc = new DefaultStyledDocument();
   JTextPane textPane = new JTextPane( doc );
   ```

   Specify a set of Styles:

```
// Create an empty StyleContext.
StyleContext styles = new StyleContext();

// Create a title heading style and put it in the StyleContext.
Style heading1 = styles.addStyle( "Heading 1", null );
StyleConstants.setFontFamily( heading1, "TimesRoman" );
StyleConstants.setFontSize( heading1, 36 );
StyleConstants.setBold( heading1, true );

// Modify the previous Style to create a smaller title style.
Style heading2 = styles.addStyle( "Heading 2", heading1 );
StyleConstants.setFontSize( heading2, 14 );

// Create the DefaultStyledDocument with the just-created
// StyleContext.
DefaultStyledDocument doc = new DefaultStyledDocument( styles );

// Create the text pane with the DefaultStyledDocument.
JTextPane mTextPane = new JTextPane( doc );
```

Create a JTextPane, and access its DefaultStyledDocument:

```
JTextPane textPane = new JTextPane();
DefaultStyledDocument doc = textPane.getStyledDocument();
```

2. Add text to the document.

This inserts the string *new text* into the document at position 5 and gives it the attributes in the style whose name is *Heading 1*:

```
Style set = doc.getStyle( "Heading 1" );
doc.insertString( 5, "new text", set );
```

3. Remove text from the document.

This removes the range of 5 characters starting at index 3:

```
doc.remove( 3, 5 );
```

4. Get the number of characters in the document.

```
int length = doc.getLength();
```

5. Get a specific part of the document's text. There are two getText() methods for this.

Get a copy of the text in a range starting at character 3 and having a length of 4:

```
String part = doc.getText( 3, 4 );
```

Read the same range, but load it into a Segment which gives direct access to the document's characters:

```
Segment part = new Segment;
String part = doc.getText( 3, 4, part );
```

If you change the contents of the Segment, the text in the document is changed. You can access the characters directly through the Segment's *array* variable.

6. Listen for changes to the document. You will be notified when text is inserted or deleted, or when attributes change.

Specify a class that will be notified of document changes. In this case it is the current class.

```
doc.addDocumentListener( this );
```

Make the event-receiving class (MyFrame) implement the DocumentListener interface:

```
public class MyFrame extends JFrame implements DocumentListener
{
    public void changedUpdate( DocumentEvent e )
    {
        // Atributes changed.
    }

    public void insertUpdate( DocumentEvent e )
    {
        // Text was inserted.
    }

    public void removeUpdate( DocumentEvent e )
    {
        // Text was deleted.
    }
}
```

7. Get the Element that contains a particular index.

This returns the Element that contains index 7:

```
Element theElement = doc.getCharacterElement( 7 );
```

8. Get the paragraph Element that contains a particular index.

This returns the Element that contains index 50:

```
Element theElement = doc.getParagraphElement( 50 );
```

9. Get the Style associated with a string. This is accessing the document's StyleContext:

```
Style bigStyle = doc.getStyle( "Heading 1" );
```

10. Set the attributes for a range of characters. The new attributes can either replace the previous ones or merge with them. Merging means that any attributes that are not explicitly set in the new AttrbuteSet will keep their current settings.

This creates an AttributeSet that has its color set to red and merges it with the existing attributes for a two-character range starting at index 3:

```
SimpleAttributeSet s = new SimpleAttributeSet();
StyleConstants.setForeground( s, Color.red );
doc.setCharacterAttributes( 3, 2, s, false );
```

Basic Code Examples

For a simple example of DefaultStyledDocument, see the "StyleContext" section in this chapter.

Advanced Issues

For an advanced example of DefaultStyledDocument at work, see Chapter 13, "Integrating JFC Example 4—A Simple Word Processor."

DefaultStyledDocument's Public Methods

`Style addStyle(String nm, Style parent)`

Create a new Style and add it to the DefaultStyledDocument's StyleContext. *'nm'* is the Style's name and may be null. *'parent'* is an existing Style that the new Style will inherit its attributes from. It can then override those attributes or add others. Returns the new Style.

`Color getBackground(AttributeSet attr)`

Returns the background color attribute from the given AttributeSet.

`Element getCharacterElement(int pos)`

Returns the character Element containing the given index.

`Element getDefaultRootElement()`

Returns the DefaultStyledDocument's main root Element. This is typically the only root Element.

`Font getFont(AttributeSet attr)`

Returns the font from the given AttributeSet.

`Color getForeground(AttributeSet attr)`

Returns the foreground color attribute from the given AttributeSet.

```
Style getLogicalStyle(int p)
```

Returns the logical style associated with the paragraph at the given position.

```
Element getParagraphElement(int pos)
```

Returns the paragraph Element that contains the given index.

```
Style getStyle(String nm)
```

Returns the Style that is associated with the given string from the DefaultStyledDocument's StyleContext.

```
void removeStyle(String nm)
```

Removes the Style associated with the given string from the DefaultStyledDocument's StyleContext.

```
void setCharacterAttributes(int offset,int length,AttributeSet s,
       boolean replace)
```

Sets the attributes for the range of '*length*' characters starting at '*offset*'. The new attributes either replace or merge with the existing ones, depending on the value of '*replace*'.

```
void setLogicalStyle(int pos,Style s)
```

Sets the logical style at the given position to the given style.

```
void setParagraphAttributes(int offset,int length,AttributeSet
       s,boolean replace)
```

Specifies the paragraph attributes for the given offset and length.

DefaultTableColumnModel

DefaultTableColumnModel is the JFC's default implementation of the TableColumnModel interface. When a JTable is created, if a TableColumnModel is not given, it creates a DefaultTableColumnModel and uses that.

This class is used to keep track of information about table columns although it doesn't store columns' data. It gives access to TableColumns and keeps track of general characteristics of columns, like column margins and widths. It also contains a ListSelectionModel that it uses to keep track of which columns are currently selected.

The DefaultTableColumnModel has column indices that go pretty much left to right. These do not necessarily correspond to column numbers in the table model. The TableColumns contain model indices.

Ancestors

```
java.lang.Object
   |
   +-com.sun.java.swing.table.DefaultTableColumnModel
```

NOTE: *For more information, see the "JTable" and "TableColumn" sections in this chapter and the "JFC Tables" section in Chapter 7, "JFC by Concept."*

Steps in Creating and Using DefaultTableColumnModel

1. Although DefaultTableColumnModel does have a constructor (an empty constructor), you will normally just let the JTable create it:

   ```
   JTable myTable = new JTable();
   DefaultTableColumnModel columnModel =
                   (DefaultTableColumnModel)myTable.
                   getColumnModel();
   ```

2. Specify the selection mode for the DefaultTableColumnModel:

   ```
   columnModel.getSelectionModel().setSelectionMode(
                           ListSelectionModel.SINGLE_SELECTION );
   ```

3. A DefaultTableColumnModel will generate events when: a column is added, a column is removed, a column is moved, column margins are changed, or the column selection state changes. You can specify a class that will be notified when any of these things happen. In this case the notified class will be the current class:

   ```
   columnModel.addColumnModelListener( this );
   ```

   Make the event-receiving class (MyFrame) implement the TableColumnModelListener interface:

   ```
   public class MyFrame extends JFrame implements
   TableColumnModelListener
   {
       .
       .
       .
   ```

```java
public void columnAdded( TableColumnModelEvent e )
{
    // A column was added.
}

public void columnMarginChanged( ChangeEvent e )
{
    // The margins were changed. Notice that this method gets a
    // ChangeEvent.
}

public void columnMoved( TableColumnModelEvent e )
{
    // A column was moved.
}

public void columnRemoved( TableColumnModelEvent e )
{
    // A column was deleted.
}

public void columnSelectionChanged( ListSelectionEvent e )
{
    // The column selection state changed.  Notice that this
    // method gets a ListSelectionEvent.
}
}
```

4. Get the currently selected columns:

```java
int columnIndices[] = columnModel.getSelectedColumns();
```

You can also get a count of selected columns:

```java
int numSelected = columnModel.getSelectedColumnCount();
```

5. Get the TableColumn associated with a column index:

```java
TableColumn tableCol = columnModel.getColumn( 0 );
```

6. Get all of the columns in the DefaultTableColumnModel:

```java
for ( Enumeration e = columnModel.getColumns();
    e.hasMoreElements(); )
{
    TableColumn tableCol = (TableColumn).nextElement();

    // Now you have a TableColumn, you can do what you need to.
}
```

7. Delete a column given a TableColumn to look for:

```java
columnModel.removeColumn( myTableColumn );
```

Basic Code Examples

EXAMPLE 8-19 Exercising DefaultTableColumnModel

This example creates a simple GUI that exercises some of DefaultTableColumnModel's features. It includes a JTable that starts out with three columns and two rows. It also has an Add Column button that will add a column, a text field whose contents will be used as new columns' headers, and a Remove Column button that deletes the currently selected column. At the bottom, the currently selected column's model index is displayed, and there is a place where you can see and change what the current column margin is. Figure 8-21 shows the example after a column has been added and another column has been moved.

Important points to notice:

- The example implements the TableColumnModelListener interface, and is registered to receive table column model events. It prints a string out when these events occur, except for the selection event which it uses to decide if certain components should be enabled or disabled.

Here is the source code:

```
import com.sun.java.swing.*;
import com.sun.java.swing.border.*;
import com.sun.java.swing.event.*;
import com.sun.java.swing.table.*;
import java.awt.*;
import java.awt.event.*;

public class MyFrame extends JFrame implements
        TableColumnModelListener, ActionListener
{
    private JButton mAddButton;
    private JTextField mId;
    private JButton mRemoveButton;
    private JTextField mMargin;
    private JLabel mIndex;
    private JTable mTable;
```

Figure 8-21

```java
public MyFrame()
{
    setTitle( "DefaultTableColumnModel1" );

    // Store the content pane in a variable for easier
    // access.
    JPanel contentPane = (JPanel)getContentPane();

    // Components will all be added to this panel.
    contentPane.setLayout( new BorderLayout() );

    // Leave a space around the edge.
    contentPane.setBorder(
                new EmptyBorder( 10, 10, 10, 10 ) );

    // Create an array of data and another for column ids.
    Object data[][] = new Object[2][3];
    data[0][0] = "Row 0";
    data[0][1] = "0,1";
    data[0][2] = "0,2";
    data[1][0] = "Row 1";
    data[1][1] = "1,1";
    data[1][2] = "1,2";

    Object headers[] = new Object[3];
    headers[0] = "Column 0";
    headers[1] = "Column 1";
    headers[2] = "Column 2";

    // Use the arrays to create a JTable.
    mTable = new JTable( data, headers );

    // Get the DefaultTableCoulmnModel that the JTable
    // created.
    DefaultTableColumnModel columnModel =
    (DefaultTableColumnModel)mTable.getColumnModel();

    // Make it so this class is notified when things
    // happen to the table column model.
    columnModel.addColumnModelListener( this );

    // Make it so only one column can be selected at a
    // time.
    columnModel.getSelectionModel().setSelectionMode(
                ListSelectionModel.SINGLE_SELECTION );

    // Create a special scroll pane to handle the table.
    JScrollPane scroller =
                JTable.createScrollPaneForTable( mTable );

    // Place the scroll pane over the main area of the
    // content pane.
    contentPane.add( "Center", scroller );
```

```
// Create a pane for the controls.
Box controlPane = Box.createVerticalBox();

// Create a pane for the add controls.
Box addbox = Box.createHorizontalBox();

// Create the add controls and put them in their pane.
mAddButton = new JButton( "Add Column" );
mAddButton.addActionListener( this );
addbox.add( mAddButton );
mId = new JTextField();
mId.setAlignmentY( mAddButton.getAlignmentY() );
addbox.add( mId );

// Add the pane to the control pane.
controlPane.add( addbox );

// Create a pane for the Remove button.
Box delbox = Box.createHorizontalBox();

// Create the Remove button and put it into its pane
// with a padding component that will move it to the
// left.
mRemoveButton = new JButton( "Remove Column" );
mRemoveButton.setEnabled( false );
mRemoveButton.addActionListener( this );
delbox.add( mRemoveButton );
delbox.add( Box.createHorizontalGlue() );

// Add the pane to the control pane.
controlPane.add( delbox );

// Create a pane for the other controls.
Box miscbox = Box.createHorizontalBox();

// Create the index-display label and put it in the
// box.
mIndex = new JLabel( "Selected index is:  NA" );
mIndex.setEnabled( false );
miscbox.add( mIndex );

// Leave some space.
miscbox.add( Box.createHorizontalStrut(100) );

// Create the margin controls and put the default
// margin value in.  Add them to the pane.
JLabel lbl = new JLabel( "Margin:  " );
miscbox.add( lbl );
mMargin = new JTextField( 10 );
mMargin.setText( String.valueOf(
                 columnModel.getColumnMargin() ) );
mMargin.addActionListener( this );
miscbox.add( mMargin );

// Add the pane to the control pane.
```

```
        controlPane.add( miscbox );

        // Put the control pane at the bottom of the content
        // pane.
        contentPane.add( "South", controlPane );
    }

    // Called when a column is added.
    public void columnAdded( TableColumnModelEvent e )
    {
        System.out.println( "Added" );
    }

    // Called when the column margin changes.
    public void columnMarginChanged( ChangeEvent e )
    {
        System.out.println( "Margin" );
    }

    // Called when a column is moved.
    public void columnMoved( TableColumnModelEvent e )
    {
        System.out.println( "Moved" );
    }

    // Called when a column is deleted.
    public void columnRemoved( TableColumnModelEvent e )
    {
        System.out.println( "Removed" );
    }

    // Called when the column selection state changes.
    public void columnSelectionChanged( ListSelectionEvent e )
    {
        // Get the table column model.
        DefaultTableColumnModel model =
            (DefaultTableColumnModel)mTable.getColumnModel();

        // If any items are currently selected, enable the
        // remove button, and load the selected column's
        // model index into mIndex for display.  Otherwise,
        // disable them.
        if ( model.getSelectedColumnCount() > 0 )
        {
            mRemoveButton.setEnabled( true );
            mIndex.setEnabled( true );
            int indices[] = model.getSelectedColumns();

            mIndex.setText( "Selected index is:  " +
                    model.getColumn(
                    indices[0] ).getModelIndex() );
        }
        else
        {
            mRemoveButton.setEnabled( false );
```

```
        mIndex.setEnabled( false );
    }

    // Make sure the enabling/disabling is reflected on
    // the screen.
    repaint();
}

// This is called when one of the buttons is pressed, or
// the user presses return in the margin text field.
public void actionPerformed( ActionEvent e )
{
    // Get the table column model.
    DefaultTableColumnModel model =
        (DefaultTableColumnModel)mTable.getColumnModel();

    // Get the table model.
    DefaultTableModel tableModel =
                    (DefaultTableModel)mTable.getModel();

    if ( e.getSource() == mAddButton )
    {
        // If the Add button was pressed, create a new
        // column with the text in the field next to the
        // button.
        tableModel.addColumn( mId.getText() );
    }
    else if ( e.getSource() == mRemoveButton )
    {
        // If the Remove button was pressed, delete the
        // currently selected column.
        int indices[] = model.getSelectedColumns();
        TableColumn selectedCol =
                        model.getColumn( indices[0] );
        model.removeColumn( selectedCol );
    }
    else if ( e.getSource() == mMargin )
    {
        // If return was pressed in the margin text field,
        // use the field's contents as the new column
        // margin.
        try
        {
            int value = Integer.parseInt(
                            mMargin.getText() );
            model.setColumnMargin( value );
        }
        catch ( NumberFormatException ex )
        {
            System.out.println( mMargin.getText() +
                            " is not a valid number" );
        }
    }
}
}
```

DefaultTableColumnModel's Public Methods

`void addColumn(TableColumn aColumn)`

Adds the given column.

`void addColumnModelListener(TableColumnModelListener x)`

Tells the table column model to notify the given class when changes happen.

`TableColumn getColumn(int columnIndex)`

Returns the TableColumn associated with the given column index.

`int getColumnCount()`

Returns the number of columns.

`int getColumnIndex(Object identifier)`

Returns the column index of the TableColumn associated with the given column identifier.

`int getColumnIndexAtX(int xPosition)`

Returns the index of the column at the given X coordinate.

`int getColumnMargin()`

Returns the current column margin.

`Enumeration getColumns()`

Returns an enumeration of all columns in the table column model.

`boolean getColumnSelectionAllowed()`

Returns true if columns may be selected.

`int getSelectedColumnCount()`

Returns the number of columns that are currently selected.

`int[] getSelectedColumns()`

Returns an array of the column indices of the currently selected columns.

`ListSelectionModel getSelectionModel()`

Returns the table column model's selection model.

```
int getTotalColumnWidth()
```

Returns the width of all columns combined.

```
void moveColumn(int columnIndex,int newIndex)
```

Moves the column at the given column index to the new index.

```
void propertyChange(PropertyChangeEvent evt)
```

Implementation side effect.

```
void removeColumn(TableColumn column)
```

Removes the given column.

```
void removeColumnModelListener(TableColumnModelListener x)
```

Tells the table column model to stop notifying the given class when changes occur.

```
void setColumnMargin(int newMargin)
```

Specifies a new column margin.

```
void setColumnSelectionAllowed(boolean flag)
```

Specifies whether columns may be selected or not.

```
void setSelectionModel(ListSelectionModel newModel)
```

Replaces the current selection model with the given one.

```
void valueChanged(ListSelectionEvent e)
```

Implementation side effect.

DefaultTableModel

DefaultTableModel is the JFC's default subclass of the abstract AbstractTableModel class. If a JTable is created and no TableModel is specified, the JTable creates an instance of DefaultTableModel and uses it to hold the table's data. If you have complex data, you may prefer to extend the AbstractTableModel yourself instead of loading up a DefaultTableModel since you may be able to get better performance that way.

Ancestors

```
java.lang.Object
    |
    +-com.sun.java.swing.table.AbstractTableModel
        |
        +-com.sun.java.swing.table.DefaultTableModel
```

NOTE: *For more information, see the "AbstractTableModel" and "JTable" sections in this chapter. Also see the "JFC Tables" section in Chapter 7, "JFC by Concept."*

Steps in Creating and Using DefaultTableModel

1. Create the DefaultTableModel. There are a total of six constructors.

   Constructor #1:

   ```
   DefaultTableModel()
   ```

   This creates an empty DefaultTableModel with no set number of rows or columns. If you use this constructor, you can use one of the setDataVector() methods to add data. Or, you can add columns using one of the addColumn() methods.

   Constructor #2:

   ```
   DefaultTableModel( int numColumns, int numRows )
   ```

   This creates an empty DefaultTableModel and specifies the number of rows and columns it should start with. Use this if you want to create an empty table with cells that the user (or your program) can modify later.

   Constructor #3:

   ```
   DefaultTableModel( Object columnIDs[], int numRows )
   ```

   This creates an empty DefaultTableModel with a column for each given column ID, and a set number of rows. If the '*columnIDs*' array is null, no columns are created.

   Constructor #4:

   ```
   DefaultTableModel( Object data[][], Object columnIDs[] )
   ```

   This creates a DefaultTableModel with a column for each given column ID. It fills the model with the values in the '*data*' array, with the first index in the array specifying the row, and the second index specifying the column.

Constructor #5:

```
DefaultTableModel( Vector columnIDs, int numRows )
```

This creates an empty DefaultTableModel with a column for every element in the *'columnIDs'* vector and the given number of rows. If the vector is null, no columns are created.

Constructor #6:

```
DefaultTableModel( Vector data, Vector columnIDs )
```

This creates a DefaultTableModel with a column for each element in the *'columnIDs'* vector, and fills it with the contents of the *'data'* vector. The *'data'* vector is actually a vector of vectors where each subvector contains the data for a single row.

Here is a sample of creating a DefaultTableModel:

```
// Allocate the row/column data array.
Object dataValues[][] = new Object[3][4];

// Load values for the table cells.
dataValues[0][0] = "West Region";
dataValues[0][1] = new Integer( 400 );
dataValues[0][2] = new Integer( 600 );
dataValues[0][3] = new Integer( 500 );

dataValues[1][0] = "South Region";
dataValues[1][1] = new Integer( 200 );
dataValues[1][2] = new Integer( 300 );
dataValues[1][3] = new Integer( 400 );

dataValues[2][0] = "East Region";
dataValues[2][1] = new Integer( 400 );
dataValues[2][2] = new Integer( 300 );
dataValues[2][3] = new Integer( 600 );

// Put the column headers into an array.
String headers[] = new String[4];

headers[0] = "Region";
headers[1] = "January";
headers[2] = "February";
headers[3] = "March";

// Create a DefaultTableModel filled with the data above.
DefaultTableModel model = new DefaultTableModel( dataValues,
headers );
```

2. Create a JTable using the DefaultTableModel:

```
JTable myTable = new JTable( model );
```

You can also create an empty JTable and pass the DefaultTableModel to its setModel() method.

3. Listen for changes in the DefaultTableModel. When the model structure changes, or when one or more cells' contents change, the DefaultTableModel generates a TableModelEvent and sends it to all registered TableModelListeners.

   Specify a class that should be notified when the model changes. In this case, it is the current class:

   ```
   model.addTableModelListener( this );
   ```

   Make the event-receiving class (MyFrame) implement the TableModelListener interface:

   ```
   public class MyFrame extends JFrame implements TableModelListener
   {
       .
       .
       .
       public void tableChanged( TableModelEvent e )
       {
           // Now you know the table has changed.  You can query the
           // event for some information about the change.
       }
   }
   ```

4. Add a row to the DefaultTableModel. You can either add a row after the model's last row, or you can insert it.

   There are two methods for adding a row—using an array of Objects or a Vector. The items in the array or Vector will be used to fill the row. If there are more items than there are columns, extra items will be dropped. If there are fewer items than columns, the extra columns will be empty. You can create a completely empty row by passing an empty Vector.

   Create an array with two items and use it to add a row to the table model. The two items in the array will go into the first two columns of the new row.

   ```
   Object items[] = new Object[2];
   items[0] = "Item 0";
   items[1] = "Item 1";
   model.addRow( items );
   ```

   Create a new row that is empty:

   ```
   model.addRow( new Vector() );
   ```

   There are also two methods for inserting a row into the table model. They are just like the addRow() methods except that they specify a row at which to insert the new row.

   Create an array with two items and use it to create a row that is inserted as row three in the table model. The two items in the array will go into the first two columns of the new row.

```
Object items[] = new Object[2];
items[0] = "Item 0";
items[1] = "Item 1";
model.addRow( 3, items );
```

Create a new row that is empty and insert it as row 5:

```
model.addRow( 5, new Vector() );
```

5. Add a column to the DefaultTableModel. There are three methods that you can use to add a column to the model. They all take a column identifier. Two of them allow you to set values for the new column's cells. If you give more values than there are rows in the model, the extras will be dropped. If you give fewer values than there are rows, the extra rows will be empty.

Add an empty column to the model:

```
model.addColumn( "New Column" );
```

Load an array with values for the column's cells, and use it to create a column and add it to the model:

```
Object items[] = new Object[3];
items[0] = "New column, first row";
items[1] = "New column, second row";
items[2] = "New column, third row";
model.addColumn( "New Column", items );
```

Load a Vector with values for the column's cells, and use it to create a column and add a it to the model:

```
Vector items = new Vector();
items.addElement( "New column, first row" );
items.addElement( "New column, second row" );
items.addElement( "New column, third row" );
model.addColumn( "New Column", items );
```

6. Get the current value of a cell in a DefaultTableModel. The following retrieves the value of the cell at row 3, column 2:

```
Object cellValue = model.getValueAt( 3, 2 );
```

7. Set the value of a specific cell. The following sets the value of the cell at row 3, column 2 to "New value":

```
model.setValueAt( "New value", 3, 2 );
```

8. Move one or more rows. The following moves the rows 3 through 5 up to row 1:

```
model.moveRow( 3, 5, 1 );
```

9. Delete a row. The following deletes row 3:

```
model.removeRow( 3 );
```

10. Load a new set of data into a DefaultTableModel. There are two versions of the setDataVector() method that allow you to totally replace the contents of the table model:

The version below loads the table model's cells with the contents of the '*newData*' array and applies the column identifiers in '*columnIDs*' to the columns. '*newData*' 's first index is rows, and its second is columns.

```
public void setDataVector( Object newData[][], Object
                            columnIDs[] )
```

The version below loads the table model's cells with the contents of the 'newData' Vector. This Vector is a Vector of Vectors where every sub-Vector holds the data for one row. The 'columnIDs' Vector holds identifiers to be applied to the columns.

```
public void setDataVector( Vector newData, Vector columnIDs )
```

For either version, the number of column identifiers must be equal to the columns in 'newData'.

11. Get the number of rows in a DefaultTableModel:

```
int numRows = model.getRowCount();
```

12. Set the number of rows in a DefaultTableModel:

```
model.setNumRows( 10 );
```

13. Get the number of columns in a DefaultTableModel:

```
int numColumns = model.getColumnCount();
```

14. Find out if a specific cell can be edited. By default, all cells are editable. The following finds out if the cell at row 3, column 2 is editable:

```
boolean canBeEdited = model.isCellEditable( 3, 2 );
```

If you want some cells in your model to be editable and others not to be, you will need to extend DefaultTableModel and override this method.

Basic Code Examples

EXAMPLE 8-20 Adding rows and columns using DefaultTableModel

This example creates a simple GUI displaying a JTable and a set of controls for adding to that table. The table is initially one row by two columns. There is an Add Column button that you can press to add a column to the table. You can enter '|' delimited values for the column's cells in the text field next to the button. There is an Add Row button that works similarly. The Insert Row button uses the values in the Add Row button's text field and inserts its row before the currently selected row. If there is not a selected row, this but-

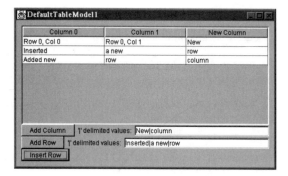

Figure 8-22

ton is disabled. Figure 8-22 shows the example after a row and column have been added, and a row has been inserted.

Important points to notice:

■ The initial DefaultTableModel is created using a vector of vectors for the data and a single vector for the column identifiers. That model is then used to create the JTable.

■ The main class listens for the model's TableModelEvents and prints a string when one is received.

■ The main class has to listen to the table's selection model events in order to keep track of when the Insert Row button should be enabled and disabled.

Here is the source code:

```java
import com.sun.java.swing.*;
import com.sun.java.swing.event.*;
import com.sun.java.swing.border.*;
import com.sun.java.swing.table.*;
import java.awt.*;
import java.awt.event.*;
import java.util.*;

public class MyFrame extends JFrame implements
        ActionListener, ListSelectionListener,
        TableModelListener
{
    private JButton mAddColumn;
    private JButton mAddRow;
    private JButton mInsertRow;
    private JTextField mColumnContents;
    private JTextField mRowContents;
    private JTable mTable;

    public MyFrame()
    {
        setTitle( "DefaultTableModel1" );
```

```
// Store the content pane in a variable for easier
// access.
JPanel contentPane = (JPanel)getContentPane();

// Components will all be added to this panel.
contentPane.setLayout( new BorderLayout() );

// Leave space around the edge of the content pane.
contentPane.setBorder(
                new EmptyBorder( 10, 10, 10, 10 ) );

// Create a vector that will hold row vectors.
Vector data = new Vector();

// Create a row vector and add two items to it.
Vector row0 = new Vector();
row0.addElement( "Row 0, Col 0" );
row0.addElement( "Row 0, Col 1" );

// Add the row vector to the main vector.
data.addElement( row0 );

// Create a vector that will hold the column ids, and
// add the ids.
Vector ids = new Vector();
ids.addElement( "Column 0" );
ids.addElement( "Column 1" );

// Create a DefaultTableModel with the data and
// column id vectors.
DefaultTableModel model =
                new DefaultTableModel( data, ids );

// Create the JTable with the just-created table
// model.
mTable = new JTable( model );

// Listen for when the table model changes.
model.addTableModelListener( this );

// Listen for when the selected row changes.
mTable.getSelectionModel().addListSelectionListener(
                                this );

// Make it so only one row is selected at a time.
mTable.getSelectionModel().setSelectionMode(
                ListSelectionModel.SINGLE_SELECTION );

// Create a special scroll pane for this table.
JScrollPane scroller =
                JTable.createScrollPaneForTable( mTable );

// Add the scroll pane so it takes up the content
// pane's avaliable area.
contentPane.add( "Center", scroller );
```

```
// Create a panel for the buttons, etc.
Box controlPane = Box.createVerticalBox();

// Create a panel for the column addition controls.
Box columnBox = Box.createHorizontalBox();

// Create the controls for adding a column to the
// table model, and add them to their panel.
mAddColumn = new JButton( "Add Column" );
mAddColumn.addActionListener( this );
columnBox.add( mAddColumn );
JLabel colLabel =
          new JLabel( "  '|' delimited values:  " );
columnBox.add( colLabel );
mColumnContents = new JTextField();
columnBox.add( mColumnContents );
mAddColumn.setAlignmentY( colLabel.getAlignmentY() );

// Add the panel to the control panel.
controlPane.add( columnBox );

// Create a panel for the row addition controls.
Box rowBox = Box.createHorizontalBox();

// Create the row addition controls and put them in
// the panel.
mAddRow = new JButton( "Add Row" );
mAddRow.addActionListener( this );
rowBox.add( mAddRow );
JLabel rowLabel =
          new JLabel( "  '|' delimited values:  " );
rowBox.add( rowLabel );
mRowContents = new JTextField();
rowBox.add( mRowContents );
mAddRow.setAlignmentY( rowLabel.getAlignmentY() );

// Put the panel in the control panel.
controlPane.add( rowBox );

// Create a panel for the row insert button.
Box insertBox = Box.createHorizontalBox();

// Create the row insert button and add padding to
// its right so it aligns left.  Disable the button
// initially since no rows are selected.
mInsertRow = new JButton( "Insert Row" );
mInsertRow.addActionListener( this );
mInsertRow.setEnabled( false );
insertBox.add( mInsertRow );
insertBox.add( Box.createHorizontalGlue() );

// Add the panel to the control panel.
controlPane.add( insertBox );
```

```
      // Put the control panel at the bottom of the content
      // pane.
      contentPane.add( "South", controlPane );
   }


   // This is called when one of the buttons is pressed.
   public void actionPerformed( ActionEvent e )
   {
      // Get the table's model.
      DefaultTableModel model =
                  (DefaultTableModel)mTable.getModel();

      if ( e.getSource() == mAddColumn )
      {
         // If the Add Column button was pressed, parse the
         // '|' delimited text field next to it and create
         // a new column with those values.  Add it to the
         // table.
         Vector values =
                  getValues( mColumnContents.getText() );
         model.addColumn( "New Column", values );
      }
      else if ( e.getSource() == mAddRow )
      {
         // If the Add Row button was pressed, parse the
         // '|' delimited text field next to it and create
         // a new row with those values.  Add it to the
         // table.
         Vector values =
                  getValues( mRowContents.getText() );
         model.addRow( values );
      }
      else if ( e.getSource() == mInsertRow )
      {
         // If the Insert Row button was pressed, parse the
         // '|' delimited text field next to the Add Row
         // button and create a new row with those values.
         // Insert it into the table before the currently
         // selected row.
         Vector values =
                  getValues( mRowContents.getText() );
         model.insertRow( mTable.getSelectionModel().
                     getLeadSelectionIndex(),
                     values );
      }
   }


   // This parses a '|' delimited string and returns the
   // items in a vector.
   private Vector getValues( String delimText )
   {
      Vector values = new Vector();
      StringTokenizer st =
                  new StringTokenizer( delimText, "|" );
```

```
            while ( st.hasMoreTokens() )
            {
                values.addElement( st.nextToken().trim() );
            }

            return values;
        }

        // This is called when the row selection state changes.
        // We track this so the Insert Row button is only
        // enabled when a row is selected.
        public void valueChanged( ListSelectionEvent e )
        {
            int selectedRow = mTable.getSelectionModel().
                                getLeadSelectionIndex();

            if ( e.getSource() == mTable.getSelectionModel() )
            {
                if ( selectedRow < 0 )
                {
                    mInsertRow.setEnabled( false );
                }
                else
                {
                    mInsertRow.setEnabled( true );
                }
            }
        }

        // This is called when the table model changes.
        public void tableChanged( TableModelEvent e )
        {
            System.out.println( "Model changed" );
        }

    }
```

DefaultTableModel's Public Methods

```
void addColumn(Object columnIdentifier)
```

Adds an empty column with the given identifier to the model.

```
void addColumn(Object columnIdentifier,Vector columnData)
```

Adds a column containing the data in the *columnData* Vector to the model and gives it the given identifier.

```
void addColumn(Object columnIdentifier,Object columnData[])
```

Adds a column containing the data in the *columnData* array to the model and gives it the given identifier.

```
void addRow(Object rowData[])
```

Adds a row containing the data in the *rowData* array to the model.

```
void addRow(Vector rowData)
```

Adds a row containing the data in the *rowData* Vector to the model.

```
int getColumnCount()
```

Returns the number of columns in the model.

```
String getColumnName(int column)
```

Returns the name of the column at the given index.

```
Vector getDataVector()
```

Returns the contents of the model as a Vector of Vectors.

```
int getRowCount()
```

Returns the number of rows in the model.

```
Object getValueAt(int row,int column)
```

Returns the value in the cell at the given row/column.

```
void insertRow(int row,Vector rowData)
```

Creates a new row containing the values in the given Vector and inserts it at the given row.

```
void insertRow(int row,Object rowData[])
```

Creates a new row containing the values in the given array and inserts it at the given row.

```
boolean isCellEditable(int row,int column)
```

Returns true if the cell at the given row/column can be edited.

```
void moveRow(int startIndex,int endIndex,inttoIndex)
```

Moves the rows from '*startIndex*' through '*endIndex*' to '*toIndex*'.

```
void newDataAvailable(TableModelEvent event)
```

Tells the model that the data vector has been changed directly.

```
void newRowsAdded(TableModelEvent event)
```

Makes sure the model correctly reflects the number of rows in the data vector, and notifies listeners.

```
void removeRow(int row)
```

Removes the row at the given index.

```
void rowsRemoved(TableModelEvent event)
```

Makes sure the model correctly reflects the number of rows in the data vector, and notifies listeners.

```
void setColumnIdentifiers(Object newIdentifiers[])
```

Replaces the model's current column identifiers with the ones in the given array.

```
void setColumnIdentifiers(Vector newIdentifiers)
```

Replaces the model's current column identifiers with the ones in the given Vector.

```
void setDataVector(Object newData[][],Object columnIDs[])
```

Replaces the model's data with the data in the *newData'* array, and replaces its column identifiers with the ones in the *'columnIDs'* array.

```
void setDataVector(Vector newData,Vector columnIDs)
```

Replaces the model's data with the data in the *'newData'* Vector, and replaces its column identifiers with the ones in the *'columnIDs'* Vector.

```
void setNumRows(int newSize)
```

Specifies the number of rows in the model. If this number is less than the current number of rows, the extra rows will be dropped. If it is greater than the current number of rows, extra blank rows will be added.

```
void setValueAt(Object aValue,int row,int column)
```

Sets the value of the cell at the given row/column to the given value.

DefaultTreeModel

A tree model is a class that stores and manages the data associated with a JTree. TreeModel is the interface that a tree model class must implement. DefaultTreeModel is the JFC default implementation of the TreeModel interface. It is very important to recognize that DefaultTreeModel provides much more functionality than is specified in the TreeModel interface. Due to this fact, tree models are not very pluggable—if you create a new implementation of the TreeModel interface it will not necessarily plug into an application that used DefaultTreeModel. Since DefaultTreeModel implements so much useful functionality, you will use it for most, if not all, applications.

Ancestors

```
java.lang.Object
   |
   +-com.sun.java.swing.tree.DefaultTreeModel
```

NOTE: *For more information, see the "JTree," "DefaultMutableTreeNode," and "DefaultTreeSelectionModel" sections in this chapter. Also see the "Trees" section in Chapter 7, "JFC by Concept."*

Steps in Creating and Using DefaultTreeModel

1. Create a root tree node for the DefaultTreeModel. This example just puts a String into the new node:

   ```
   DefaultMutableTreeNode rootNode = new DefaultMutableTreeNode(
                                                      "Root" );
   ```

2. You can create a DefaultTreeModel either implicitly or explicitly. If you create a JTree without specifying a TreeModel, the JTree uses a DefaultTreeModel.

   To create a DefaultTreeModel implicitly:

   ```
   JTree theTree = new JTree( rootNode );
   ```

   JTree creates a DefaultTreeModel behind the scenes and gives it the root node.

   To create a DefaultTreeModel explicitly, there are two constructors. The difference between the two is that one allows you to set how the model decides what is a leaf and what is not. A tree node is either allowed to have child nodes or it is not. By default, not only are nodes that cannot have children considered to be leaves, but so are nodes that can have children but don't. If you use the second constructor and set 'asksAllowsChildren' to true, only nodes that cannot have children are considered leaves. This is useful for situations like a file browser in which you want all directories—even empty ones—to appear to the user as directories, not files.

Constructor 1:

```
DefaultTreeModel model = new DefaultTreeModel( rootNode );
```

Constructor 2:

```
DefaultTreeModel model = new DefaultTreeModel( rootNode, true );
```

You can get the same effect by using the first constructor and calling the setAsksAllowsChildren(true) method.

3. Find out information about nodes in the tree. There are a number of types of information and ways to get it.

Find the node's child at a particular index:

```
TreeNode child = model.getChild( parentNode, 3 );
```

Get the number of children a node has. This only counts its direct children—it doesn't include its children's children:

```
int numChildren = model.getChildCount( parentNode );
```

Get the index of a particular child:

```
int index = model.getIndexOfChild( parentNode, childNode );
```

Given a tree node, get the path from the root node to it. This returns a TreePath which is basically a list of the nodes you have to traverse to get from the root node to the specified node:

```
TreePath path = model.getPathToRoot( thisNode );
```

Get the tree's root node:

```
TreeNode rootNode = model.getRoot();
```

Check if a node is a leaf. If setAsksAllowsChildren() is set to false, this method returns false only if the node allows children and has children. If setAsksAllowsChildren() is true, this method returns false if the node allows children—whether it actually has children or not:

```
boolean isItALeaf = model.isLeaf( node );
```

4. Insert a node under a parent node. This specifies the node to insert, the node which will be its parent, and the index at which to insert the node. You can user the parent node's insert() method, but then you have to notify the TreeModel that it has been changed. If you use the insertNodeInto() method described here, the TreeModel is

automatically notified which causes the JTree to update to reflect the change.

```
model.insertNodeInto( newChildNode, parentNode, 3 );
```

5. Remove a node from its parent. We could use the tree node's removeFromParent() method, but then we would have to notify the tree model that we had done it. Using this method automatically notifies the tree model which then tells the JTree so it can update to reflect the change:

```
model.removeNodeFromParent( node );
```

6. Notify the tree model that something in it has changed. There are a variety of types of change.

Tell the model that a single node has changed:

```
model.nodeChanged( node );
```

Tell the model that some of a node's children have changed. The child nodes are passed in an array containing the child indices:

```
model.nodesChanged( parentNode, childArray );
```

Tell the tree that the tree structure under a node has changed:

```
model.nodeStructureChanged( parentNode );
```

Tell the tree that nodes were inserted under a node. The inserted nodes are passed as an array of their indices sorted in ascending order:

```
model.nodesWereInserted( parentNode, insertedArray );
```

Tell the tree that nodes were removed from under a node. The indices of the removed nodes are stored in an array in ascending order. You must also pass in an array of the removed nodes:

```
model.nodesWereRemoved( parentNode, childIndices, childNodes );
```

Tell the model that the contents of the node at the specified path have changed. This is used when you store a special object in a node, like a File object. When it changes, you call this method:

```
model.valueForPathChanged( treePath, newContents );
```

Tell the model to tell the JTree to totally reload. Use this when widespread changes have been made. It will cause the tree's nodes to be collapsed:

```
model.reload();
```

Tell the model to tell the JTree to reload starting from a specific tree node. The node's subnodes will display collapsed:

```
model.reload( parentNode );
```

Basic Code Examples

EXAMPLE 8-21 Basic DefaultTreeModel Operations

This example displays a simple GUI with a tree that has a single node which is selected. The GUI allows you to create new nodes by entering the node's text string and whether it can have children, then pressing a button to add the new node under the selected node (if it allows children) or after the selected node (as its sibling). You can also delete the selected node. Information about the selected node is displayed as well. There is a check box that allows you to define whether the tree displays nodes that are allowed to have children but do not as leaves. Figure 8-23 shows the example after several nodes have been added.

Important points to notice:

- The selection model is set to allow single selection only.

- Buttons are disabled when their use is not appropriate with the selected item. You cannot delete the root node, for example.

- A TreeSelectionListener is used so the node information can be changed when the user selects a different node.

Here is the source:

```java
import com.sun.java.swing.*;
import com.sun.java.swing.border.*;
import com.sun.java.swing.event.*;
import com.sun.java.swing.tree.*;
import java.awt.*;
import java.awt.event.*;

public class MyFrame extends JFrame implements ItemListener,
        TreeSelectionListener, ActionListener
{
    // The tree.
    private JTree mTree;

    // The text that will be put into the new node.
    private JTextField mNodeText;
```

Figure 8-23

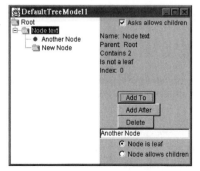

```java
// Specify whether the new node will be a leaf or will
// allow children.
private JRadioButton mNodeIsLeaf;
private JRadioButton mNodeIsExpandable;

// The labels that will be used to display node
// information.
private JLabel mNameLabel;
private JLabel mParentLabel;
private JLabel mCountLabel;
private JLabel mLeafLabel;
private JLabel mIndexLabel;

// Add the new node to the current expandable node.
private JButton mAddBtn;

// Add the new node as the current node's sibling.
private JButton mAddAfterBtn;

// Delete the current node.
private JButton mDeleteBtn;

public MyFrame()
{
    setTitle( "DefaultTreeModel1" );

    // Store the content pane in a variable for easier
    // access.
    JPanel contentPane = (JPanel)getContentPane();

    // Components will all be added to this panel.
    contentPane.setLayout( new GridLayout( 1, 2 ) );

    // Create the root node.
    DefaultMutableTreeNode root =
                new DefaultMutableTreeNode( "Root" );

    // Create the TreeModel using the root node, and set
    // it so empty nodes that allow children do not show
    // up as leaves.
    DefaultTreeModel model =
                new DefaultTreeModel( root, true );

    // Create the JTree using the TreeModel.
    mTree = new JTree( model );

    // Set the tree so only one item may be selected at a
    // time.
    mTree.getSelectionModel().setSelectionMode(
            TreeSelectionModel.SINGLE_TREE_SELECTION );

    // Put the tree in a scroll pane in case it gets too
    // big.
    JScrollPane scroller = new JScrollPane( mTree );
```

```
// Add the scroll pane so it fills the content pane's
// left side.
contentPane.add( scroller );

// Create a container for the right-side components.
Box controlBox = Box.createVerticalBox();

// Create the check box that will toggle how the tree
// defines a leaf.
JCheckBox asksAllowsChildren =
        new JCheckBox( "Asks allows children", true );

// This class will listen for the check box's state
// changes, and will change the tree accordingly.
asksAllowsChildren.addItemListener( this );

// Although the action command will not be delivered
// with the ItemEvent, it can still be gotten from
// the check box and used to see which component
// generated the event.
asksAllowsChildren.setActionCommand(
                            "asksAllowsChildren" );

// Add the check box to its container.
controlBox.add( asksAllowsChildren );

// Leave a gap below the check box.
controlBox.add( Box.createVerticalGlue() );

// Create a panel that will hold the labels that
// contain information about the currently selected
// node.
JPanel details = new JPanel();
details.setLayout( new GridLayout( 7, 1 ) );

// Create the labels whose values will be modified
// when the currently selected node changes.  Add
// each to the panel.
mNameLabel = new JLabel();
details.add( mNameLabel );
mParentLabel = new JLabel();
details.add( mParentLabel );
mCountLabel = new JLabel();
details.add( mCountLabel );
mLeafLabel = new JLabel();
details.add( mLeafLabel );
mIndexLabel = new JLabel();
details.add( mIndexLabel );

// Add the node information panel to the right-hand
// panel.
controlBox.add( details );

// Create the button that will cause a new node to be
// created and will add it to the expandable current
```

```
    // node.
    mAddBtn = new JButton( "Add To" );
    mAddBtn.addActionListener( this );
    controlBox.add( mAddBtn );

    // Create the button that will create a node and add
    // it to the currently selected node's parent.
    mAddAfterBtn = new JButton( "Add After" );
    mAddAfterBtn.addActionListener( this );
    controlBox.add( mAddAfterBtn );

    // Create the button that will delete the currently
    // selected node.
    mDeleteBtn = new JButton( "Delete" );
    mDeleteBtn.addActionListener( this );
    controlBox.add( mDeleteBtn );

    // This text field will hold the text that will be
    // put into a new node when it is created.
    mNodeText = new JTextField( "Node text" );
    controlBox.add( mNodeText );

    // These two radio buttons define whether the new
    // node is a leaf, or can have children.
    mNodeIsExpandable = new JRadioButton(
                        "Node allows children", true );
    mNodeIsLeaf = new JRadioButton( "Node is leaf" );
    ButtonGroup group = new ButtonGroup();
    group.add( mNodeIsLeaf );
    group.add( mNodeIsExpandable );
    controlBox.add( mNodeIsLeaf );
    controlBox.add( mNodeIsExpandable );

    // Add space below the radio buttons.
    controlBox.add( Box.createVerticalGlue() );

    // Add the right hand box to the content pane.
    contentPane.add( controlBox );

    // Make it so this class is notified when the tree's
    // selection changes.
    mTree.addTreeSelectionListener( this );

    // Set the root node selected.
    mTree.setSelectionRow( 0 );
}

// This is called when the "Asks Allows Children" check
// box changes state.
public void itemStateChanged( ItemEvent e )
{
    AbstractButton btn = (AbstractButton)e.getSource();
    String actionCommand = btn.getActionCommand();

    if ( actionCommand.equals( "asksAllowsChildren" ) )
    {
```

```
         // Change the tree model's definition of what a
         // leaf is.
         if ( e.getStateChange() == ItemEvent.SELECTED )
         {
            ((DefaultTreeModel)mTree.getModel()).
                             setAsksAllowsChildren( true );
         }
         else
         {
            ((DefaultTreeModel)mTree.getModel()).
                             setAsksAllowsChildren( false );
         }

         // Redraw the tree to reflect the changes.
         mTree.repaint();
      }
   }


   // This is called when the tree selection changes.
   public void valueChanged( TreeSelectionEvent e )
   {
      // Since a new item is selected, we need to display
      // its node information.
      updateNodeInfo();
   }


   // Change the node information labels so they reflect
   // the selected node's information.
   private void updateNodeInfo()
   {
      // Get the path to the currently selected node.
      TreePath path = mTree.getSelectionPath();

      // Get the actual selected node.
      DefaultMutableTreeNode node =
         (DefaultMutableTreeNode)path.getLastPathComponent();

      // Get the model into a variable for code readability.
      DefaultTreeModel model =
                       (DefaultTreeModel)mTree.getModel();

      // Change the name label's text to reflect the node
      // string.
      mNameLabel.setText( "Name:   " + node );

      // Change the parent label to contain the node
      // parent's string.
      mParentLabel.setText( "Parent:   " +
                              node.getParent() );

      if ( node == model.getRoot() )
      {
         // If the selected node is the root node, disable
         // the "Add After" button and the "Delete" button.
         mAddAfterBtn.setEnabled( false );
         mDeleteBtn.setEnabled( false );
```

```
   }
   else
   {
      // If the selected node is not the root, enable
      // the buttons.
      mAddAfterBtn.setEnabled( true );
      mDeleteBtn.setEnabled( true );
   }

   // If the selected node does not allow children,
   // disable the "Add To" button.  Otherwise enable it.
   if ( node.getAllowsChildren() == false )
      mAddBtn.setEnabled( false );
   else
      mAddBtn.setEnabled( true );

   // Change the count label to reflect the selected
   // node's child count.
   mCountLabel.setText( "Contains " +
                        node.getChildCount() );

   // Change the leaf label to show if the selected node
   // is a leaf.
   if ( node.isLeaf() )
      mLeafLabel.setText( "Is a leaf" );
   else
      mLeafLabel.setText( "Is not a leaf" );

   // Change the index label to reflect the selected
   // node's index under its parent node.
   mIndexLabel.setText( "Index:  " +
      model.getIndexOfChild( node.getParent(), node ) );
}

public void actionPerformed( ActionEvent e )
{
   if ( e.getSource() == mAddBtn )
   {
      // When the "Add To" button is pressed...

      // Get the model into a variable for code
      // readability.

      DefaultTreeModel model =
                   (DefaultTreeModel)mTree.getModel();

      // Create a new node with the text field's
      // contents.
      DefaultMutableTreeNode newNode =
                   new DefaultMutableTreeNode(
                   mNodeText.getText() );

      // Tell the node whether it can have children
      // based on the radio buttons.
      newNode.setAllowsChildren(
```

```
                        mNodeIsExpandable.isSelected() );

   // Get the path to the currently selected node.
   TreePath path = mTree.getSelectionPath();

   // The selected node will be the new node's
   // parent, so get it from the selected path.
   DefaultMutableTreeNode parent =
                    (DefaultMutableTreeNode)path.
                    getLastPathComponent();

   // Insert the new node as the parent's first.
   model.insertNodeInto( newNode, parent, 0 );

   // Find the path to the new node.
   TreePath rootPath = new TreePath(
                    model.getPathToRoot( newNode ) );

   // Use the path to the new node to make sure it is
   // expanded.
   mTree.expandPath( rootPath );

   // Update the displayed node information.
   updateNodeInfo();
}
else if ( e.getSource() == mAddAfterBtn )
{
   // If the "Add After" button was pressed...

   // Put the tree model in a variable for code
   // readability.

   DefaultTreeModel model =
                    (DefaultTreeModel)mTree.getModel();

   // Create the new node based on the text field and
   // the radio buttons.
   DefaultMutableTreeNode newNode =
                    new DefaultMutableTreeNode(
                    mNodeText.getText() );
   newNode.setAllowsChildren(
                    mNodeIsExpandable.isSelected() );

   // Get the path to the selected node.
   TreePath path = mTree.getSelectionPath();

   // Get the selected node from the end of the path.
   DefaultMutableTreeNode node =
                    (DefaultMutableTreeNode)path.
                    getLastPathComponent();

   // Get the selected node's parent node.
   DefaultMutableTreeNode parent =
              (DefaultMutableTreeNode)node.getParent();
```

```
// Find the index of the selected node so we know
// where to add the new node.
int nodeIndex = model.getIndexOfChild( parent,
                                       node );


// Insert the new node after the selected node.
model.insertNodeInto( newNode, parent,
                      nodeIndex + 1 );


// Get the path to the new node.
TreePath rootPath = new TreePath(
              model.getPathToRoot( newNode ) );


// Use the path to make sure it is expanded.
mTree.expandPath( rootPath );


// Change the displayed node information.
updateNodeInfo();
}
else if ( e.getSource() == mDeleteBtn )
{
    // If the "Delete" button is pressed.

    // Put the model in a variable for code
    // readability.
    DefaultTreeModel model =
              (DefaultTreeModel)mTree.getModel();


    // Get the path to the selected node.
    TreePath path = mTree.getSelectionPath();


    // Get the selected node from the end of the path.
    DefaultMutableTreeNode node =
              (DefaultMutableTreeNode)path.
              getLastPathComponent();


    // Remove the node through the model.
    model.removeNodeFromParent( node );


    // Set root as the selected node.
    mTree.setSelectionRow( 0 );


    // Change the displayed node information.
    updateNodeInfo();
    }
  }
}
```

Advanced Issues

See Chapter 10, "Integrating JFC Example 1—A File Browser," and Chapter 11, "Integrating JFC Example 2—Adding Items to and Removing Items from JTrees," for advanced examples of using trees. Also see "JTree."

DefaultTreeModel's Public Methods

```
void addTreeModelListener(TreeModelListener l)
```

Tells the DefaultTreeModel to notify the given class whenever the model changes.

```
boolean asksAllowsChildren()
```

If the model thinks an empty node that allows children is a leaf, this returns false.

```
Object getChild(Object parent,int index)
```

Returns the child at the given index of the specified parent node.

```
int getChildCount(Object parent)
```

Returns the number of child nodes the given parent node has.

```
int getIndexOfChild(Object parent,Object child)
```

Returns the index of the given child node under the given parent node.

```
TreeNode[] getPathToRoot(TreeNode child)
```

Returns the path of nodes from the root node to the given node. Note that the path is returned as an array of tree nodes, not as a TreePath.

```
Object getRoot()
```

Returns the root node.

```
void insertNodeInto(MutableTreeNode newChild,MutableTreeNode
        parent,int index)
```

Adds the given child node as a child of the given parent node, inserted at the given index.

```
boolean isLeaf(Object node)
```

Returns true if the given node is a leaf node.

```
void nodeChanged(TreeNode node)
```

Tells the DefaultTreeModel that the contents of the given node has changed.

```
void nodesChanged(TreeNode node,int childIndices[])
```

Tells the DefaultTreeModel that the children of the given node at the specified indices have changed.

```
void nodeStructureChanged(TreeNode node)
```

Tells the DefaultTreeModel that the structure of the subtree rooted at the given node has changed.

```
void nodesWereInserted(TreeNode node,int childIndices[])
```

Tells the DefaultTreeModel that the child nodes specified by the given indices were inserted into the given node.

```
void nodesWereRemoved(TreeNode node,int childIndices[],Object
        removedChildren[])
```

Tells the DefaultTreeModel that the nodes specified by the given indices were removed from the given node.

```
void reload()
```

Tells the DefaultTreeModel that the entire tree has changed.

```
void reload(TreeNode node)
```

Tells the DefaultTreeModel that the subtree rooted at the given node has changed.

```
void removeNodeFromParent(MutableTreeNode node)
```

Removes the given node from its parent.

```
void removeTreeModelListener(TreeModelListener l)
```

Tells the DefaultTreeModel to stop notifying the given class when the model changes.

```
void setAsksAllowsChildren(boolean newValue)
```

Set to false if you want nodes that are allowed to have children but do not to be treated as leaf nodes.

```
void valueForPathChanged(TreePath path,Object newValue)
```

This changes the given node's user object to the specified new value.

DefaultTreeSelectionModel

DefaultTreeSelectionModel implements the TreeSelectionModel interface and is used to store which tree nodes are currently selected. Other classes can register listeners with this class in order to be notified when the selection state changes.

Ancestors

```
java.lang.Object
    |
    +-com.sun.java.swing.tree.DefaultTreeSelectionModel
```

NOTE: *For more information, see the "JTree" and "DefaultTreeModel" sections in this chapter. Also see the "Trees" section in Chapter 7, "JFC by Concept."*

Steps in Creating and Using DefaultTreeSelectionModel

1. You don't typically create a DefaultTreeSelectionModel yourself. Instead, JTree creates one itself when it is instantiated.

   ```
   JTree myTree = new JTree( someRootNode );
   ```

2. Access the DefaultTreeSelectionModel. You do this by calling JTree's getSelectionModel() method.

   ```
   DefaultTreeSelectionModel selectionModel =
   (DefaultTreeSelectionModel)myTree.getSelectionModel();
   ```

3. Add a class to listen for changes in the tree selection state:

   ```
   selectionModel.addTreeSelectionListener( someListener);
   ```

   Then, in the listener class:

   ```
   public void valueChanged( TreeSelectionEvent e )
   {
       // Do something now we know the selection has changed.
       TreePath paths[] = e.getPaths();
   }
   ```

4. Get all paths that are selected:

   ```
   TreePath paths[] = selectionModel.getSelectionPaths();
   ```

5. Get all rows indices that are selected:

```
int rows[] = selectionModel.getSelectionRows();
```

6. Set the mode in which selection can take place. These can be:

- SINGLE_TREE_SELECTION-Only one node may be selected at a time.

- CONTIGUOUS_TREE_SELECTION-More than one node may be selected at a time, but all selections must be contiguous.

- DISCONTIGUOUS_TREE_SELECTION-More than one node may be selected at a time and they do not have to be contiguous.

```
selectionModel.setSelectionMode(
    TreeSelectionModel.SINGLE_TREE_SELECTION );
```

Basic Code Examples

EXAMPLE 8-22 A Simple GUI That Illustrates DefaultTreeSelectionModel

This example creates a simple tree with a panel that allows the user to change the selection mode, and displays information about the selection state. The left side contains a tree that shows a simple class hierarchy of buttons. The right side has three radio buttons used to change the selection mode, a list box that displays the nodes in the current lead selection path, three labels displaying the different selection rows, and a list box displaying all selected nodes. Figure 8-24 shows the example after the tree has been fully expanded and a number of nodes selected

Important points to notice:

- All of the selection information is updated when the main class is notified of a TreeSelectionEvent.

- When the selection mode is changed, it generates a TreeSelectionEvent, so the information is updated.

- We had to set the JLists' X alignment to match the JLabels'.

- The first node is initially selected so the example starts up with selection information showing.

Here is the source code:

```
import com.sun.java.swing.*;
import com.sun.java.swing.border.*;
import com.sun.java.swing.event.*;
import com.sun.java.swing.tree.*;
import java.awt.*;
import java.util.*;
import java.awt.event.*;
```

Figure 8-24

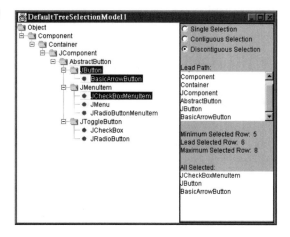

```java
public class MyFrame extends JFrame implements ItemListener,
        TreeSelectionListener
{
    DefaultTreeSelectionModel mModel;
    JRadioButton mSglSel;
    JRadioButton mCtgSel;
    JRadioButton mNonctgSel;
    JList mLeadPath;
    JTree mTheTree;
    JLabel mMinRow;
    JLabel mLeadRow;
    JLabel mMaxRow;
    JList mAllSelected;

    public MyFrame()
    {
        setTitle( "DefaultTreeSelectionModel1" );

        // Store the content pane in a variable for easier
        // access.
        JPanel contentPane = (JPanel)getContentPane();

        // Components will all be added to this panel.
        contentPane.setLayout( new BoxLayout( contentPane,
                            BoxLayout.X_AXIS ) );

        // Call the method that creates the JTree and loads
        // its data.
        JTree mTheTree = buildTree();

        // Get the JTree's selection model.
        mModel = (DefaultTreeSelectionModel)mTheTree.
                                    getSelectionModel();

        // Make it so this class is notified when the
        // selection changes.
```

```
mModel.addTreeSelectionListener( this );

// Initially only one node may be selected at a time.
mModel.setSelectionMode(
    DefaultTreeSelectionModel.SINGLE_TREE_SELECTION );

// Put the JTree in a scroll pane.
JScrollPane scroller = new JScrollPane( mTheTree );

// Add the scroll pane so it takes up the left side
// of the content pane.
contentPane.add( scroller );

// Create the panel that will hold our selection
// information.
JPanel rightPane = new JPanel();
rightPane.setLayout( new BoxLayout( rightPane,
                        BoxLayout.Y_AXIS ) );
rightPane.setBorder(
                    new LineBorder( Color.black, 2 ) );

// Create the radio buttons that control the
// selection mode.
mSglSel = new JRadioButton( "Single Selection" );
mCtgSel = new JRadioButton( "Contiguous Selection" );
mNonctgSel =
        new JRadioButton( "Discontiguous Selection" );

// Single node selection is initially on.
mSglSel.setSelected( true );

// Create a ButtonGroup and put the radio buttons in
// it.
ButtonGroup group = new ButtonGroup();
group.add( mSglSel );
group.add( mCtgSel );
group.add( mNonctgSel );

// Add the radio buttons into the pane.
rightPane.add( mSglSel );
rightPane.add( mCtgSel );
rightPane.add( mNonctgSel );

// Make it so this class is notified when the radio
// buttons change.
mSglSel.addItemListener( this );
mCtgSel.addItemListener( this );
mNonctgSel.addItemListener( this );

// Add some space between the radio buttons and what
// lies below.
rightPane.add( Box.createVerticalGlue() );

// Create a list box for the lead path list and add
// it to the panel.
```

```
JLabel leadPath = new JLabel( "Lead Path:" );
rightPane.add( leadPath );

// Create the list that displays the lead path.
mLeadPath = new JList();

// Give it a preferred size.
mLeadPath.setVisibleRowCount( 4 );

// Load the list box into a scroll pane.
JScrollPane scroller2 = new JScrollPane( mLeadPath );

// Make it so the scroll pane will align with the
// label.
scroller2.setAlignmentX( 0.0f );

// Add the scroll pane to the panel.
rightPane.add( scroller2 );

// Leave some more space.
rightPane.add( Box.createVerticalGlue() );

// Create the three labels that will display the
// minimum, lead, and maximum selection rows.
mMinRow = new JLabel();
mLeadRow = new JLabel();
mMaxRow = new JLabel();

// Add the labels to the panel.
rightPane.add( mMinRow );
rightPane.add( mLeadRow );
rightPane.add( mMaxRow );

// Add some more space...
rightPane.add( Box.createVerticalGlue() );

// Create a label to go with the list of selected
// nodes and add it.
JLabel allSelected = new JLabel( "All Selected:" );
rightPane.add( allSelected );

// Create the list that will hold the selected nodes.
mAllSelected = new JList();

// Give it a preferred size.
mAllSelected.setVisibleRowCount( 4 );

// Add the list to a scroll pane.
JScrollPane scroller3 =
                    new JScrollPane( mAllSelected );

// Make the scroll pane align with the label.
scroller3.setAlignmentX( 0.0f );

// Add the scroll pane to the panel.
```

```
        rightPane.add( scroller3 );

        // Add the info panel so it takes the right side of
        // the content pane.
        contentPane.add( rightPane );

        // Make it so the first node in the tree is initially
        // selected.
        mTheTree.setSelectionRow( 0 );
    }


    // Build all of the nodes and put them together into a
    // tree.
    private JTree buildTree()
    {
        DefaultMutableTreeNode obj, comp, cont, jcomp;
        DefaultMutableTreeNode absbtn, jbtn, arrowbtn;
        DefaultMutableTreeNode jmnuitm, jcbmnuitm, jmnu;
        DefaultMutableTreeNode jrbmnuitm, jtglbtn;
        DefaultMutableTreeNode jchkbx, jrdiobtn;

        obj = new DefaultMutableTreeNode( "Object" );
        comp = new DefaultMutableTreeNode( "Component" );
        cont = new DefaultMutableTreeNode( "Container" );
        jcomp = new DefaultMutableTreeNode( "JComponent" );
        absbtn = new DefaultMutableTreeNode(
                                    "AbstractButton" );
        jbtn = new DefaultMutableTreeNode( "JButton" );
        arrowbtn = new DefaultMutableTreeNode(
                                    "BasicArrowButton" );
        jmnuitm = new DefaultMutableTreeNode( "JMenuItem" );
        jcbmnuitm = new DefaultMutableTreeNode(
                                    "JCheckBoxMenuItem" );
        jmnu = new DefaultMutableTreeNode( "JMenu" );
        jrbmnuitm = new DefaultMutableTreeNode(
                                    "JRadioButtonMenuItem" );
        jtglbtn = new DefaultMutableTreeNode(
                                    "JToggleButton" );
        jchkbx = new DefaultMutableTreeNode( "JCheckBox" );
        jrdiobtn = new DefaultMutableTreeNode(
                                    "JRadioButton" );

        obj.add( comp );
        comp.add( cont );
        cont.add( jcomp );
        jcomp.add( absbtn );
        absbtn.add( jbtn );
        jbtn.add( arrowbtn );
        absbtn.add( jmnuitm );
        jmnuitm.add( jcbmnuitm );
        jmnuitm.add( jmnu );
        jmnuitm.add( jrbmnuitm );
        absbtn.add( jtglbtn );
        jtglbtn.add( jchkbx );
```

```
      jtglbtn.add( jrdiobtn );

   return new JTree( obj );
}

// This is called when the user changes the selection
// mode.  It triggers a change in the selction model.
public void itemStateChanged( ItemEvent e )
{
   if ( e.getSource() == mSglSel )
   {
      mModel.setSelectionMode(
                     DefaultTreeSelectionModel.
                     SINGLE_TREE_SELECTION );
   }
   else if ( e.getSource() == mCtgSel )
   {
      mModel.setSelectionMode(
                     DefaultTreeSelectionModel.
                     CONTIGUOUS_TREE_SELECTION );
   }
   else if ( e.getSource() == mNonctgSel )
   {
      mModel.setSelectionMode(
                     DefaultTreeSelectionModel.
                     DISCONTIGUOUS_TREE_SELECTION );
   }
}

// This is called when the selection changes.
public void valueChanged( TreeSelectionEvent e )
{
   // Put the nodes in the lead selection path into the
   // appropriate list box.
   loadLeadPath();

   // Put the list of selected nodes in its list box.
   loadAllSelected();

   // Make the labels reflect the new selction.
   mMinRow.setText( "Minimum Selected Row:  " +
                     mModel.getMinSelectionRow() );
   mLeadRow.setText( "Lead Selected Row:  " +
                     mModel.getLeadSelectionRow() );
   mMaxRow.setText( "Maximum Selected Row:  " +
                     mModel.getMaxSelectionRow() );

   // Redraw everything.
   validate();
}

// Gets the lead selection path, and loads its nodes
// into the list box.
private void loadLeadPath()
{
```

```
Object nodes[];

// Get the lead selection path.
TreePath leadPath = mModel.getLeadSelectionPath();

// The selection may be empty.  Otherwise get the
// nodes.
if ( leadPath == null )
   nodes = null;
else
   nodes = leadPath.getPath();

// Load the nodes into the list.
if ( nodes != null )
   mLeadPath.setListData( nodes );
else
   mLeadPath.setListData( new Vector() );

// Redraw the list.
mLeadPath.repaint();
}

// Causes all selected nodes to be displayed in the
// list box.
private void loadAllSelected()
{
// Get the number of currently selected nodes.
int count = mModel.getSelectionCount();

// Retrieve the selected paths.
TreePath paths[] = mModel.getSelectionPaths();

// Create a string array that will be loaded with
// node strings and loaded into the list box.
String nodes[] = new String[count];

// For each selected path.
for ( int i = 0; i < count; i++ )
{
   // Get the node at the end of the path.
   DefaultMutableTreeNode node =
            (DefaultMutableTreeNode)paths[i].
            getLastPathComponent();

   // Load the node's string into the array.
   nodes[i] = node.toString();
}

// Replace the list box's data with the new array.
mAllSelected.setListData( nodes );

// Make sure the change is reflected.
mAllSelected.repaint();
}
}
```

DefaultTreeSelectionModel's Public Methods

`void addPropertyChangeListener(PropertyChangeListener listener)`

Tells the DefaultTreeSelectionModel to notify the given class when the selection mode changes.

`void addSelectionPath(TreePath path)`

Specifies a path to add to the current list of selected tree paths.

`void addSelectionPaths(TreePath paths[])`

Specifies a group of paths to add to the current list of selected tree paths.

`void addTreeSelectionListener(TreeSelectionListener x)`

Tells the DefaultTreeSelectionModel to notify the given class when the selection state changes.

`void clearSelection()`

Makes it so that no tree paths are selected.

`Object clone()`

Makes a copy of the DefaultTreeSelectionModel, including the current selections.

`TreePath getLeadSelectionPath()`

Returns the last path that was added to the list of selected paths.

`int getLeadSelectionRow()`

Returns the row number of the last path that was added.

`int getMaxSelectionRow()`

Returns the highest numbered row that is selected.

`int getMinSelectionRow()`

Returns the lowest numbered rwo that is selected.

`RowMapper getRowMapper()`

Returns a RowMapper that can be used to map a tree path to the rows that the nodes in the path are displayed at.

```
int getSelectionCount()
```

Returns the number of selected tree paths.

```
int getSelectionMode()
```

Returns the DefaultTreeSelectionModel's selection mode: SINGLE_TREE_ SELECTION, CONTIGUOUS_TREE_SELECTION, or DISCONTIGUOUS_ TREE_SELECTION.

```
TreePath getSelectionPath()
```

Returns the first of the currently selected tree paths.

```
TreePath[] getSelectionPaths()
```

Returns all of the currently selected tree paths.

```
int[] getSelectionRows()
```

Returns all of the currently selected tree rows.

```
boolean isPathSelected(TreePath path)
```

Returns true if the given tree path is currently selected.

```
boolean isRowSelected(int row)
```

Returns true if the given row is currently selected.

```
boolean isSelectionEmpty()
```

Returns true if at least one tree path is currently selected.

```
void removePropertyChangeListener(PropertyChangeListener listener)
```

Tells the DefaultTreeSelectionModel to stop notifying the given class when the selection mode changes.

```
void removeSelectionPath(TreePath path)
```

Removes the given tree path from the list of currently selected paths.

```
void removeSelectionPaths(TreePath paths[])
```

Removes all of the given tree paths from the list of currently selected paths.

```
void removeTreeSelectionListener(TreeSelectionListener x)
```

Tells the DefaultTreeSelectionModel to stop notifying the given class when the selection changes.

```
void resetRowSelection()
```

Tells the RowMapper to remap the selected paths to rows.

```
void setRowMapper(RowMapper newMapper)
```

Replaces the RowMapper with another one.

```
void setSelectionMode(int mode)
```

Changes the current selection mode to one of SINGLE_TREE_ SELECTION, CONTIGUOUS_TREE_SELECTION, or DISCONTIGUOUS_ TREE_SELECTION.

```
void setSelectionPath(TreePath path)
```

Sets the current selection to consist of only the specified path.

```
void setSelectionPaths(TreePath pPaths[])
```

Sets the current selection to be only the specified paths.

```
String toString()
```

Overridden for DefaultTreeSelectionModel's own string output.

DirectoryModel

DirectoryModel is the Swing class that lets you browse file systems. It has no graphical component (hence the Model) but is the behind-the-scenes worker for both JDirectoryPane and JFileChooser. If you want to build your own file system browser GUI, you should use DirectoryModel's capabilities.

DirectoryModel is oriented around the idea of a current directory. You can get the contents of the current directory, you can "go up" from the current directory, and you can change the current directory. You can get files in other directories, but the emphasis is on the current one.

NOTE: *Many of the JFC components work fine with early JDK 1.1 versions. That is not the case with DirectoryModel because it relies heavily of the java.io.File class, which has some unfortunate bugs, especially on Window systems. For a version of DirectoryModel that works on JDK versions before 1.2, see "WorkingDirectoryModel.java" in Chapter 10, "Integrating JFC Example 1— A File Browser."*

NOTE: *For JFC 1.1, DirectoryModel has been moved to the com.sun.java.swing. preview package. This means that its API is likely to change in the near future.*

Ancestors

```
java.lang.Object
    |
    +-com.sun.java.swing.preview.DirectoryModel
```

NOTE: *For more information, see the "JDirectoryPane," "JFileChooser," "TypedFile," and "FileType" sections in this chapter. Also see the "File Browsing" section in Chapter 7, "JFC by Concept," as well as Chapter 10, "JFC Integration Example 1—A File Browser."*

Steps in Creating and Using DirectoryModel

1. Create the DirectoryModel. There are two constructors.

   Create a DirectoryModel with the user's home directory as the current directory:

   ```
   DirectoryModel dm = new DirectoryModel();
   ```

   Create a DirectoryModel with a specific directory as its current directory:

   ```
   DirectoryModel dm = new DirectoryModel( new File( "." ) );
   ```

2. Find out what the DirectoryModel's current directory is:

   ```
   File currDir = dm.getCurrentDirectory();
   ```

3. Find out if the DirectoryModel's current directory is the root directory for the system (has no parent directory):

   ```
   boolean isNotParentDir = dm.canGoUp();
   ```

   canGoUp() returns false if the DirectoryModel's current directory is the system's root.

4. Change the DirectoryModel's current directory to its current directory's parent:

```
dm.goUp();
```

5. Change the DirectoryModel's current directory:

```
dm.setCurrentDirectory( new File( "/usr/lib" ) );
```

The above would work on a UNIX system but would need to be something like:

```
dm.setCurrentDirectory( new File( "C:\\windows\\system" ) );
```

on a Windows system.

6. Get a list of the contents of a directory. There are two methods for this task.

```
File newDir = new File( "C:\\windows" );
Vector files = dm.getTypedFilesForDirectory( newDir );
```

The above makes a list of all of the contents of the c:\windows directory and returns them in a Vector. Each element of the Vector is a TypedFile, which is a subclass of File.

Or you can use:

```
Vector files = dm.getTypedFiles();
```

which returns a list of the contents of the DirectoryModel's current directory.

7. Specify which types of files and directories that the DirectoryModel recognizes. When the DirectoryModel sees a file in the directory it is trying to read, it attempts to figure out the file's type. When it figures it out, it packs the associated File class and the type into a TypedFile instance. The file type can be useful in finding out if a file is actually a directory, or is a hidden file, or is a special type that your application understands. The known file types are stored in instances of class FileType and may be selected from six predefined types plus any types you have defined yourself.

The predefined types are:

```
FileType.SharedGenericFile;
FileType.SharedFolder;
FileType.SharedHidden;
FileType.SharedComputer;
FileType.SharedFloppyDrive;
FileType.SharedHardDrive;
```

You use the setKnownFileTypes() method by first loading an array with the types you want, then passing that array to the method:

```
FileType types[] = new FileType[5];
types[0] = FileType.SharedGenericFile;
```

```
types[1] = FileType.SharedFolder;
types[2] = FileType.SharedComputer;
types[3] = FileType.SharedFloppyDrive;
types[4] = FileType.SharedHardDrive;
dm.setKnownFileTypes( types );
```

This will make it so that the DirectoryModel will recognize all files and directories except hidden ones.

You can also add to the list by calling the addKnownFileType() method.

8. Specify which FileType the Directory's getTypedFiles() and getTypedFilesForDirectory() methods will return. By default, these methods return all files in the given directory (the FileType is null). If you specify a FileType, only files of that type will be returned.

```
dm.setShownType( new MyFileType() );
```

Basic Code Examples

EXAMPLE 8-23 Creating a Recursive File Finder with DirectoryModel

This nongraphical example shows how to recursively search a directory tree to find all occurrences of files with a specific name.

Important points to notice:

- The starting directory and file name are passed in from the command line. For this example, only exact file name matches are supported-no wildcards.

- The findFileInDirectory() method is recursive. It looks at all of the files in a particular directory, checking for matches, and calls itself on any directories in that directory.

- The DirectoryModel's current directory is set before findFileInDirectory() is called. For recursive calls, the old current directory is saved then restored after the call.

- Directories are recognized by getting the FileType of an item in a directory and calling the FileType's isContainer() method.

Here is the source:

```
import com.sun.java.swing.*;
import com.sun.java.swing.preview.*;
import java.util.*;
import java.io.*;

public class Test
{
    public Test( String args[] )
    {
        // Create a File from the starting directory string.
        File startDir = new File( args[0] );
```

```
        // Create a DirectoryModel whose current directory is
        // the specified starting directory.
        DirectoryModel dm = new DirectoryModel( startDir );

        // Start finding the target file (args[1]).
        findFileInDirectory( dm, args[1] );
    }


    // This method is recursive.  The DirectoryModel 'dm'
    // has a preset current directory.  This method gets a
    // list of all files and directories in that current
    // directory.  If a file matches the specified file
    // name, the absolute path of the file is printed.
    // For each directory in the current directory, this
    // method is called again.
    private void findFileInDirectory( DirectoryModel dm,
                                      String fileName )
    {
        // Get the contents of the DirectoryModel's current
        // directory.  We have to clone it because it is just
        // a reference to the Vector which gets changed in
        // recursive calls as the DirectoryModel's current
        // directory changes.
        Vector files = (Vector)dm.getTypedFiles().clone();

        // Store the number of files/directories in this
        // directory.
        int size = files.size();

        // For each file/directory in this directory...
        for ( int i = 0; i < size; i++ )
        {
            // Put the next file/directory in a TypedFile for
            // more readable code.  The contents of the 'files'
            // Vector are all TypedFiles.
            TypedFile thisFile =
                        (TypedFile)files.elementAt( i );

            // If this item can contain other files (it is a
            // directory), save the DirectoryModel's current
            // directory so we can restore it.  Then set its
            // current directory to this item and call this
            // method again.  Upon return, restore the old
            // current directory.
            if ( thisFile.getType().isContainer() )
            {
                File currDir = dm.getCurrentDirectory();
                dm.setCurrentDirectory( thisFile );
                findFileInDirectory( dm, fileName );
                dm.setCurrentDirectory( currDir );
            }
            else
            {
                // The item is a file.  Compare it to the
                // target string.  If they match, print out
```

```
            // the complete path to the file.
            if ( thisFile.getName().equals( fileName ) )
            {
                System.out.println(
                            thisFile.getAbsolutePath() );
            }
        }
    }
}

// The main() method.  This makes sure there are two
// arguments, then creates an instance of this class.
public static void main( String args[] )
{
    if ( args.length == 2 )
    {
        new Test( args );
    }
    else
    {
        System.out.println( "\nUsage:\n" +
                "\tjava Test <start dir> <file name>\n" );
    }
}
}
```

Advanced Issues

You can also see DirectoryModel in use in Chapter 10, "Integrating JFC Example 1—A File Browser."

DirectoryModel's Public Methods

```
void addKnownFileType(FileType type)
```

Specifies a new file type that the DirectoryModel can apply to files it reads from the file system.

```
void addListDataListener(ListDataListener l)
```

Tells the DirectoryModel to notify the given class when properties change.

```
void addPropertyChangeListener(PropertyChangeListener listener)
```

Tells the DirectoryModel to notify the given class whenever a DirectoryModel change takes place, like when the current directory or list of known file types changes.

`boolean canGoUp()`

Returns true if the current directory is not the root for its file system.

`Enumeration enumerateKnownFileTypes()`

Gets an enumeration of the known file types.

`File getCurrentDirectory()`

Returns the DirectoryModel's current directory.

`Object getElementAt(index n)`

Returns the nth file (of the type being shown) in the DirectoryModel's current directory.

`FileType getHiddenRule()`

Returns the file type that is used to decide if a file is hidden or not.

`Vector getKnownFileTypes()`

Gets a Vector containing all of the file types that the DirectoryModel recognizes.

`FileType getShownType()`

Returns the type of file that the getTypedFiles() and getTypedFilesForDirectory() methods return. Can be null if all types should be returned.

`int getSize()`

Returns the number of files (of the type being shown) in the DirectoryModel's current directory.

`TypedFile getTypedFile(String path)`

Returns a TypedFile representing the file at the given path.

`TypedFile getTypedFile(String path,String name)`

Returns a TypedFile representing the file at the given path and file name.

`Vector getTypedFiles()`

Returns the files in the DirectoryModel's current directory. The files are returned as TypedFiles. The types of files returned depends on the setShownType() method.

`Vector getTypedFilesForDirectory(File dir)`

Returns the files in the given directory. The files are returned as TypedFiles. The types of files returned depends on the setShownType() method.

`void goUp()`

Tells the DirectoryModel to go up one level from its current directory and make that its new current directory.

`boolean isKnownFileType(FileType t)`

Returns true if the given FileType is curently recognized by the DirectoryModel.

`boolean isKnownFileType(FileType t)`

Returns true if the given file type has been specified to the DirectoryModel as a recognized file type.

`void removeListDataListener(ListDataListener l)`

Tells the DirectoryModel to stop notifying the given class when properties change.

`void removePropertyChangeListener(PropertyChangeListener listener)`

Tells the DirectoryModel to stop notifying the given class when the DirectoryModel's properties changes.

`void setCurrentDirectory(File dir)`

Tells the DirectoryModel to make the given directory its current directory.

`void setHiddenRule(FileType rule)`

Specifies which FileType to use to decide whether a file is hidden or not.

`void setKnownFileTypes(FileType types[])`

Specifies which file types the DirectoryModel recognizes.

`void setShownType(FileType t)`

Specifies which type of file will be returned by the getTypedFiles() and getTypedFilesForDirectory() methods. If set to null, all file types are returned.

Element

Element is an interface for which the JFC has no standard implementation. Element is typically implemented by Document class inner classes like AbstractDocument's LeafElement class.

An Element refers to a range of characters, and contains attributes that apply to those characters. An Element can have child Elements. For instance, in a DefaultStyledDocument, there are "section" Elements that can contain multiple "paragraph" Elements that can contain multiple "content" Elements. Attributes in lower level Elements override attributes set in their parents or in higher levels. Higher level attributes are only used when they are not defined in lower levels. An example of this would be when a lower level Element contains font family and size attributes, but no color attributes. If a higher level Element contained font family attributes and color attributes, the lower level's font family attribute would be used, but the higher level's color attribute would be used.

Basically, Elements are how attributes are stored for text.

NOTE: *For more information, see the "DefaultStyledDocument," "PlainDocument," "AbstractDocument," "SimpleAttributeSet," "StyleConstants," and "JTextPane" sections in this chapter. Also see Chapter 5, "JFC Documents and JFC Components," and Chapter 13, "JFC Integration Example 4—A Simple Word Processor."*

Element's Public Methods

`AttributeSet getAttributes()`

Gets the attributes associated with this Element.

`Document getDocument()`

Returns the Document that the element is a part of.

`Element getElement(int i)`

Returns this Element's ith child Element.

`int getElementCount()`

Returns the number of child Elements in this Element.

`int getElementIndex(int offset)`

Returns the index of this Element's child Element that is closest to the given offset in the Document's text.

`int getEndOffset()`

Returns the index in the Document's text just after where the Element ends.

`String getName()`

Returns the Element's name. This is likely to be something like "content" or "paragraph."

`Element getParentElement()`

Returns the Element's parent Element or null if this is the root Element.

`int getStartOffset()`

Returns the index in the Document's text at which the Element starts.

`boolean isLeaf()`

Returns true if the Element has no child Elements.

EmptyBorder

An empty border does not do any drawing, it just takes up space around the edges of its parent component (see Figure 8-25).

Ancestors

```
java.lang.Object
    |
    +-com.sun.java.swing.border.AbstractBorder
            |
            +-com.sun.java.swing.border.EmptyBorder
```

NOTE: *For more information, see the "AbstractBorder" and "JPanel" sections in this chapter, and the "Component Borders" section in Chapter 7, "JFC by Concept."*

Figure 8-25
A button whose default border has been replaced with an EmptyBorder.

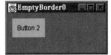

Steps in Creating and Using EmptyBorder

1. Create a component that supports borders. This will typically be a JPanel:

   ```
   JPanel panel = new JPanel();
   ```

2. Create an empty border. There are two constructors, and they accept top, left, bottom, and right arguments in pixels. This example shows the construction of a border that will force a three-pixel-wide empty area on all four sides of its panel:

   ```
   EmptyBorder empty1 = new EmptyBorder( 3, 3, 3, 3 );
   ```

3. Apply the border to the component:

   ```
   panel.setBorder( empty1 );
   ```

4. Set the component's layout:

   ```
   panel.setLayout( new BorderLayout() );
   ```

5. Create and add a component to the panel:

   ```
   panel.add( new JButton( "empty border, 3, 3, 3, 3" ) );
   mPanel.add( panel );
   ```

At this point, there will be a panel whose area is filled with a button, except for a three-pixel-wide strip around the panel's edge.

Basic Code Examples

EXAMPLE 8-24 Basic EmptyBorder

This sample creates three panels with varying width empty borders and one panel with a titled border that incorporates an empty border. Each panel uses a BorderLayout and contains a button in its "Center" area so you can see the widths of the EmptyBorders. Figure 8-26 shows the example as it looks initially.

Figure 8-26

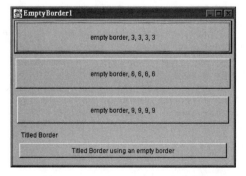

Here is the source code:

```java
import com.sun.java.swing.*;
import com.sun.java.swing.border.*;
import java.awt.*;

public class MyFrame extends JFrame
{
    public MyFrame()
    {
        setTitle( "EmptyBorder1" );

        // Store the content pane in a variable for easy
        // access.
        JPanel contentPane = (JPanel)getContentPane();

        // Components will all be added to this panel.
        contentPane.setLayout( new GridLayout( 4, 1 ) );

        // Create a panel with an empty border whose width is
        // 3 pixels all the way around.
        JPanel panel1 = new JPanel();
        EmptyBorder empty1 = new EmptyBorder( 3, 3, 3, 3 );
        panel1.setBorder( empty1 );

        // Set the content pane's layout manager.
        panel1.setLayout( new BorderLayout() );

        // Create a button and add it to the content pane.
        panel1.add(
                new JButton( "empty border, 3, 3, 3, 3" ) );
        contentPane.add( panel1 );

        // Create a panel with an empty border whose width is
        // 6 pixels all the way around.
        JPanel pane2 = new JPanel();
        EmptyBorder empty2 = new EmptyBorder( 6, 6, 6, 6 );
        pane2.setBorder( empty2 );

        // Set the layout manager.
        pane2.setLayout( new BorderLayout() );

        // Create and add a component to the content pane.
        pane2.add(
                new JButton( "empty border, 6, 6, 6, 6" ) );
        contentPane.add( pane2 );

        // Create a panel with an empty border whose width
        // is 9 pixels all around.
        JPanel pane3 = new JPanel();
        EmptyBorder empty3 = new EmptyBorder( 9, 9, 9, 9 );
        pane3.setBorder( empty3 );

        // Set the panel's layout manager.
```

```
                           pane3.setLayout( new BorderLayout() );

                           // Create and add a component.
                           pane3.add(
                                   new JButton( "empty border, 9, 9, 9, 9" ) );
                           contentPane.add( pane3 );

                           // Create a panel that uses a titled border including
                           // an empty border.
                           JPanel pane4 = new JPanel();
                           TitledBorder title1 = new TitledBorder(
                                               new EmptyBorder( 9, 9, 9, 9 ),
                                               "Titled Border" );
                           pane4.setBorder( title1 );

                           // Set the panel's layout manager.
                           pane4.setLayout( new BorderLayout() );

                           // Create and add a component.
                           pane4.add( new JButton(
                                   "Titled Border using an empty border" ) );
                           contentPane.add( pane4 );
                       }
                   }
```

Advanced Issues

EXAMPLE 8-25 Giving an Internal Frame a Transparent Border

This example shows how to use an EmptyBorder to give an internal frame a
transparent border. Figure 8-27 shows the example as it initially looks.

Important points to notice:

Figure 8-27

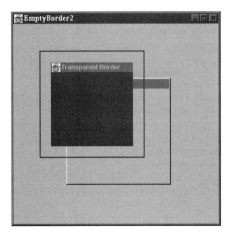

■ We subclassed JInternalFrame to create our custom internal frame, because otherwise the border will have its background painted so you cannot see through. We overrode the internal frame's isOpaque() method so it returns false instead of true. The custom internal frame is in a private class just to make the example cleaner-it could just as easily have been in a source file all its own.

■ We added an EtchedBorder outside of the EmptyBorder so you could see its edge.

■ We also put a standard JInternalFrame onto the deskptop pane where our custom one is. This was just so there would be something to see through the transparent border.

Here is the source code:

```
import com.sun.java.swing.*;
import com.sun.java.swing.border.*;
import java.awt.*;

public class MyFrame extends JFrame
{
    public MyFrame()
    {
        setTitle( "EmptyBorder2" );

        // Store the content pane in a variable for easier
        // access.
        JPanel contentPane = (JPanel)getContentPane();

        // Components will all be added to this panel.
        contentPane.setLayout( new BorderLayout() );

        // Create a desktop pane to add our internal frames
        // to.
        JDesktopPane desktop = new JDesktopPane();
        desktop.setBackground( contentPane.getBackground() );

        // Add the desktop pane to the content pane so it
        // completely covers it.
        contentPane.add( "Center", desktop );

        // Create our custom internal frame.
        MyInternalFrame inFrame =
                new MyInternalFrame( "Transparent Border" );
        inFrame.getContentPane().setBackground(
                                            Color.darkGray );

        // Set the border to be an etched border around a
        // wide empty border.
        inFrame.setBorder( new CompoundBorder(
                    new EtchedBorder(),
                    new EmptyBorder( 20, 20, 20, 20 ) ) );
```

```
        inFrame.setBounds( 50, 50, 200, 200 );

        // Make the frame resizable so we can see that the
        // resize cursor works eveywhere on the wide border.
        inFrame.setResizable( true );

        // Add our custom internal frame to the desktop pane.
        desktop.add( inFrame );

        // Create and add a standard internal frame so we
        // have something to see through our transparent
        // border.
        JInternalFrame frame2 =
                    new JInternalFrame( "Normal Frame" );
        frame2.setBounds( 100, 100, 200, 200 );
        desktop.add( frame2 );
    }

    // Create a custom internal frame so we can change
    // isOpaque() to return false.  Otherwise, you can't
    // see through the empty border.
    private class MyInternalFrame extends JInternalFrame
    {
        public MyInternalFrame( String title )
        {
            super( title );
        }

        public boolean isOpaque()
        {
            return false;
        }
    }
}
```

EmptyBorder's Public Methods

`Insets getBorderInsets(Component c)`

Returns the width of the EmptyBorder on each side.

`boolean isBorderOpaque()`

Returns false since it doesn't paint its area.

`void paintBorder(Component c,Graphics g,int x,int y,int width,int
    height)`

Paints the border by not painting at all.

EtchedBorder

An etched border makes it look like there is a groove dug around the border's parent component's edge (see Figure 8-28). It is particularly appealing when used as part of a TitledBorder.

Ancestors

```
java.lang.Object
    |
    +-com.sun.java.swing.border.AbstractBorder
        |
        +-com.sun.java.swing.border.EtchedBorder
```

NOTE: *For more information, see the "AbstractBorder" and "JPanel" sections in this chapter and the "Component Borders" section in Chapter 7, "JFC by Concept."*

Steps in Creating and Using EtchedBorder

1. Create a container that supports borders. This will typically be a JPanel:

    ```
    JPanel panel = new JPanel();
    ```

2. Create an EtchedBorder. You can either use the default constructor:

    ```
    EtchedBorder etch1 = new EtchedBorder();
    ```

    or you can customize the highlight and shadow colors used to draw the groove:

    ```
    EtchedBorder etch2 = new EtchedBorder( Color.gray.brighter(),
                                           Color.gray.darker() );
    ```

    where the first argument is the highlight color and the second is the shadow color.

    You can also specify the etch type to be either RAISED or LOWERED.

3. Apply the border to the container:

    ```
    panel.setBorder( etch1 );
    ```

Figure 8-28
A panel with an
EtchedBorder.

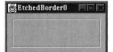

Basic Code Examples

EXAMPLE 8-26 Basic EtchedBorder

The following example creates: a panel with a default EtchedBorder, a panel with an EtchedBorder using custom highlight/shadow colors, and a panel with a TitledBorder that incorporates an EtchedBorder. Figure 8-29 shows the example as it looks initially.

Here is the source code:

```
import com.sun.java.swing.*;
import com.sun.java.swing.border.*;
import java.awt.*;

public class MyFrame extends JFrame
{
    public MyFrame()
    {
        setTitle( "EtchedBorder1" );

        // Store the content pane in a variable for easy
        // access.
        JPanel contentPane = (JPanel)getContentPane();

        // Components will all be added to this panel.
        contentPane.setLayout( new GridLayout( 3, 1 ) );

        // Use an EmptyBorder on the content pane so it is
        // easier to see the EtchedBorders.
        contentPane.setBorder(
                        new EmptyBorder( 5, 5, 5, 5 ) );

        // Create a panel with a default Etched border.
        JPanel pane1 = new JPanel();
        EtchedBorder etch1 = new EtchedBorder();
        pane1.setBorder( etch1 );
        contentPane.add( pane1 );

        // Create a panel with an etched border with custom
        // colors.
        JPanel pane2 = new JPanel();
        EtchedBorder etch2 = new EtchedBorder(
                        Color.gray.brighter(),
                        Color.gray.darker() );
```

Figure 8-29
Sample
EtchedBorders.

```
        pane2.setBorder( etch2 );
        contentPane.add( pane2 );

        // Create a panel with a titled border that
        // incorporates an etched border.
        JPanel pane3 = new JPanel();
        TitledBorder titled1 = new TitledBorder(
                            new EtchedBorder(),
                            "Titled Incorporating Etched" );
        pane3.setBorder( titled1 );
        contentPane.add( pane3 );
    }
}
```

Advanced Issues

EXAMPLE 8-27 Making a Wider-Grooved EtchedBorder

This example shows how to make an etched border that has a wider groove. It does this not by using EtchedBorder, but by creating a three-part compound border. The border uses an empty border to provide the extra width, and surrounds it with a raised and a lowered bevel border to give the etched effect. Figure 8-30 shows the example as it looks when it first comes up.

Here is the source code:

```
import com.sun.java.swing.*;
import com.sun.java.swing.border.*;
import java.awt.*;

public class MyFrame extends JFrame
{
    public MyFrame()
    {
        setTitle( "EtchedBorder2" );

        // Store the content pane in a variable for easier
        // access.
        JPanel contentPane = (JPanel)getContentPane();

        // Components will all be added to this panel.
        contentPane.setLayout( new BorderLayout() );

        // Leave a gap around the inside of the content pane
        // so we can see the wider groove properly.
```

Figure 8-30

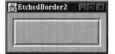

```
contentPane.setBorder(
                new EmptyBorder( 10, 10, 10, 10 ) );

// Create a pane that will use the wide-etched border.
JPanel pane = new JPanel();

// Create the first part of the compound border by
// making a new border with a 2-pixel wide empty
// border around a raised bevel border.
CompoundBorder border1 = new CompoundBorder(
            new EmptyBorder( 2, 2, 2, 2 ),
            new BevelBorder( BevelBorder.RAISED ) );

// Complete the border by putting a lowered bevel
// border around the other compound border.
CompoundBorder border2 = new CompoundBorder(
            new BevelBorder( BevelBorder.LOWERED ),
            border1 );

// Tell the pane to use our special border.
pane.setBorder( border2 );

// Add the pane so it fills the content pane (except
// for the content pane's border).
contentPane.add( "Center", pane );
    }
}
```

EtchedBorder's Public Methods

`Insets getBorderInsets(Component c)`

Returns the width of the EtchedBorder on each side.

`int getEtchType()`

Returns RAISED or LOWERED.

`Color getHighlightColor()`

Returns the color used for the border's highlight.

`Color getShadowColor()`

Returns the color used for the border's shadow.

`boolean isBorderOpaque()`

Returns true because the EtchedBorder paints its entire area.

```
void paintBorder(Component c,Graphics g,int x,int y,int width,int
    height)
```

Paints the EtchedBorder onto the given component.

EventListenerList

EventListenerList is a class that makes it more convenient to manage event listeners within a component. All components are initially created with the ability to multicast (send to many registered listeners) some particular types of events. A JButton, for example, generates an ActionEvent when it is pressed, so it is designed to maintain a list of ActionListeners to which it will send the event. However, there are times when a component will need to notify listeners of an event type that it was not initially designed to multicast. When this happens, you will want to use an EventListenerList to manage your event listeners.

Ancestors

```
java.lang.Object
    |
    +-com.sun.java.swing.event.EventListenerList
```

NOTE: *For more information, see "A Quick Review of the JDK 1.1 Event Model" in Chapter 7, "JFC by Concept."*

Steps in Creating and Using EventListenerList

1. Make sure the JFC event package is imported:

```
import com.sun.java.swing.event.*;
```

2. Create the component that needs to manage the event listeners. This example extends JPanel, but it could extend anything:

```
public class MyComponent extends JPanel
{
    .
    .
    .
}
```

3. Declare an instance of EventListenerList within the class and initialize it. For this example, we want our JPanel to generate ActionEvents, so we will be managing ActionListeners:

```
public class MyComponent extends JPanel

{
    private EventListenerList mActionListenerList;

    public MyComponent()
    {
        mActionListenerList = new EventListenerList();
        .
        .
        .
    }
    .
    .
    .
}
```

4. Implement a method to add an EventListener to the list. It is
important that this method's name follows the add<event
type>Listener() template so that introspection can reveal the types
of events your class generates. Notice that the type of the event
listener is passed into EventListenerList's add() method:

```
public void addActionListener( ActionListener listener )
{
    mActionListenerList.add( ActionListener.class, listener );
}
```

5. Implement a method to remove an EventListener from the list. It is
important that this method's name follows the remove<event
type>Listener() template so introspection can recognize it. Again, the
type of the event listener is passed—this time to EventListenerList's
remove() method:

```
public void removeActionListener( ActionListener listener )
{
    mActionListenerList.remove( ActionListener.class, listener );
}
```

6. Implement a method that will multicast the event to all of the
EventListenerList's registered listeners. The getListenerList() method
gets an array of the EventListenerList's registered listeners. The array
actually contains two values for each registered listener: the class type
of the listener, and the listener itself. We process the list from the last to
the first. For each registered listener we first check to make sure the
listener wants this type of event (you can put different types of event
listeners in the same list), then we call one of methods that is specified
within that type of event listener. In this case, the listeners are all
ActionListeners and the only method defined in the ActionListener
interface is actionPerformed(), so we call that method.

```
protected void fireActionEvent( ActionEvent newEvent )
{
```

```
// Get the listener class type / listener class instance
// pairs.
Object[] listeners = mActionListenerList.getListenerList();

// We step through the pairs from last to first.  The first is
// the pair is the class type, then is the class instance.
// This is why we step through the list two at a time.
for ( int i = listeners.length-2; i >= 0; i -= 2 )
{
    // Make sure this listener is the right type.
    if ( listeners[i] == ActionListener.class )
    {
        // Call the ActionListener method.
        ((ActionListener)listeners[i+1]).actionPerformed(
                                                    newEvent );
    }
}
}
```

7. Cause the event to be generated by creating the event and passing it to the fire"Event() method. We are generating ActionEvents, so that is what we will give to the fireActionEvent() method. In this example, the only important part in creating the ActionEvent is that the source is set to this instance of MyComponent:

```
// Something happened and we want MyComponent to generate
// an ActionEvent.  This is within the MyComponent class.
ActionEvent myEvent = new ActionEvent( this, 0,
                                        "MyComponent action" );

// Cause the event to be distributed to this class'
// ActionListeners.
fireActionEvent( myEvent );
```

Now all of the ActionListeners' actionPerformed() methods are called with an ActionEvent that tells them that the event came from this class.

Basic Code Examples

EXAMPLE 8-28 Managing Event Listeners with EventListenerList

This example implements the concepts discussed above. It creates a new class based on JPanel. This class contains a JCheckBox. When the check box becomes selected, the new class is notified of the fact, generates an ActionEvent, and sends it to registered ActionListeners. The EventListenerList is used within the new class to manage the registered ActionListeners.

Important points to notice:

■ This example includes the MyComponent class, which is the new class containing the EventListenerList, and the MyFrame class that

Figure 8-31
The MyComponent
panel with the
JCheckBox.

contains an instance of MyComponent and acts as an ActionListener
for that instance.

■ Figure 8-31 shows the MyComponent panel with the JCheckBox in it,
and the box has been checked.

Here is the source for MyFrame.java (the source for MyComponent.java
follows it):

```java
import com.sun.java.swing.*;
import java.awt.*;
import java.awt.event.*;

public class MyFrame extends JFrame implements
        ActionListener
{
    public MyFrame()
    {
        setTitle( "EventListenerList1" );

        // Store the content pane in a variable for easier
        // access.
        JPanel contentPane = (JPanel)getContentPane();

        // Components will all be added to this panel.
        contentPane.setLayout( new BorderLayout() );

        // Create a new instance of MyComponent.
        MyComponent comp = new MyComponent();

        // Make it so this class is notified when 'comp'
        // generates and ActionEvent.
        comp.addActionListener( this );

        // Place the compoenent at the top of the content
        // pane.
        contentPane.add( "North", comp );
    }

    // This will be called when the MyComponent's checkbox
    // becomes selected.
    public void actionPerformed( ActionEvent e )
    {
        // Print out the action command string that
        // MyComponent added to the event.
        System.out.println( e.getActionCommand() );
    }
}
```

And here is the source for MyComponent.java:

```java
import com.sun.java.swing.*;
import com.sun.java.swing.event.*;
import java.awt.event.*;
import java.awt.*;

// This class implements ItemListener so it can catch the
// checkbox's state changes.
public class MyComponent extends JPanel implements
        ItemListener
{
    // We use an EventListenerList to manage this component's
    // ActionEvents.
    private EventListenerList mActionListenerList;

    public MyComponent()
    {
        // Initialize the listener list.
        mActionListenerList = new EventListenerList();

        setLayout( new BorderLayout() );

        // Create a checkbox and place it at the top of this
        // component.
        JCheckBox chk = new JCheckBox( "Click me" );
        chk.setHorizontalAlignment( SwingConstants.CENTER );
        add( "North", chk );

        // Cause this class to listen for when the checkbox's
        // state changes.
        chk.addItemListener( this );
    }

    // This is called when this class' checkbox state
    // changes.
    public void itemStateChanged( ItemEvent e )
    {
        if ( e.getStateChange() == ItemEvent.SELECTED )
        {
            // If the checkbox's state has just become
            // selected, generate an ActionEvent and send it
            // off.
            ActionEvent myEvent = new ActionEvent( this, 0,
                    "MyComponent checkbox is selected" );

            // Cause the event to be distributed to this
            // class' ActionListeners.
            fireActionEvent( myEvent );
        }
    }

    // Register an ActionListener with our listener list.
    public void addActionListener( ActionListener listener )
    {
```

```
        mActionListenerList.add( ActionListener.class,
                                 listener );
    }

    // Un-register an ActionListener from our listener list.
    public void removeActionListener(
                                ActionListener listener )
    {
        mActionListenerList.remove( ActionListener.class,
                                 listener );
    }

    // Cause the passed-in ActionEvent to be sent to our
    // registered ActionListeners.
    protected void fireActionEvent( ActionEvent newEvent )
    {
        // Get the listener class type / listener class
        // instance pairs.
        Object[] listeners =
                    mActionListenerList.getListenerList();

        // We step through the pairs from last to first.  The
        // first is the pair is the class type, then is the
        // class instance.  This is why we step through the
        // list two at a time.
        for ( int i = listeners.length-2; i >= 0; i -= 2 )
        {
            // Make sure this listener is the right type.
            if ( listeners[i] == ActionListener.class )
            {
                // Call the ActionListener method.
                ((ActionListener)listeners[i+1]).
                                    actionPerformed( newEvent );
            }
        }
    }
}
```

Advanced Issues

You can see "EventListenerList" in action in Chapter 11, "Integrating JFC Example 2—Adding Items to and Removing Items from JTrees," and Chapter 12, "Integrating JFC Example 3—A Simple Paint Program."

EventListenerList's Public Methods

```
void add(Class t,EventListener l)
```

Adds the given event listener to the EventListenerList along with its class type.

```
int getListenerCount()
```

Returns the number of event listeners in the EventListenerList.

```
int getListenerCount(Class t)
```

Returns the number of event listeners of the passed-in class type in the EventListenerList.

```
Object[] getListenerList()
```

Returns an array containing all event listeners in the EventListenerList.

```
void remove(Class t,EventListener l)
```

Removes an event listener from the EventListenerList.

```
String toString()
```

Overridden to provide EventListenerList's own formatted String.

FileType

FileType is an interface that you can implement to cause a DirectoryModel or JFileChooser to recognize your own types of file. By default, they recognize the following types:

```
FileType.SharedComputer
FileType.SharedFloppyDrive
FileType.SharedFolder
FileType.SharedGenericFile
FileType.SharedHardDrive
FileType.SharedHidden
```

FileType is most often used with DirectoryModels and with the TypedFiles that DirectoryModel returns. A DirectoryModel has a set of FileTypes that it recognizes. When it reads the contents of a directory, it checks each file against its known FileTypes to decide the file's type. It creates a TypedFile for each file, which is just a File with its FileType added.

A FileType has a special string that describes it, an icon that can be used for that type of file in a file browser, and a method that a File can be passed to which tells if the File is of that type.

A DirectoryModel will normally get all files, no matter what type, when it reads a directory. You can make it get only a single type using DirectoryModel's setShownType() method.

NOTE: *For JFC 1.1, FileType has been moved to the com.sun.java.swing.preview package. This means its API is likely to change in the near future.*

Ancestors

FileType is an interface with no parent interface.

NOTE: *For more information, see the "TypedFile," "DirectoryModel," "JFileChooser," and "JDirectoryPane" sections in the chapter. Also see the "File Browsing" section in Chapter 7, "JFC by Concept," as well as Chapter 13, "JFC Integration Example 4—A Simple Word Processor."*

Steps in Implementing FileType

1. Create a new class:

   ```
   public class MyFileType implements FileType
   {
       .
       .
       .
   }
   ```

2. Add a getPresentationName() method. This method returns a string that describes what the file type represents:

   ```
   public String getPresentationName()
   {
       return "Java source files (*.java)";
   }
   ```

3. Add a getIcon() method. This returns an icon that can be used next to this type of file in a file browser:

   ```
   public Icon getIcon()
   {
       return new ImageIcon( "javasource.gif" );
   }
   ```

4. Add a isContainer() method. This returns true if this type of file can be expanded (contains other files). This will typically return true only for directories.

   ```
   public boolean isContainer()
   {
       return false;
   }
   ```

5. Add a testFile() method. This is called with a File argument and returns true if the File matches this FileType, or false if not:

```
public boolean testFile( File file )
{
    String name = file.getAbsolutePath();

    if ( name.endsWith( "java" ) )
        return true;

    return false;
}
```

Basic Code Examples

EXAMPLE 8-29 Implement a FileType That Recognizes Files by Extension

This example shows how to implement the FileType interface so a Directory-Model can recognize your custom file types. When you run it, it prints out the files in the current directory and their types.

Important points to notice:

■ The FileType implementor class (MyFileType) accepts a file extension and a description of the file type through its constructor. The extension is used in the testFile() method to see if a file is of this type. The description is returned from the getPresentationName() method.

■ MyFileType is defined as an inner class to make this example more self-contained. There is no reason why it could not be a stand-alone class.

■ The new FileType is added to the DirectoryModel through its setKnownFileTypes() method.

■ The isContainer() method returns false since files of our custom type are not able to hold other files.

Here is the source:

```
import com.sun.java.swing.*;
import com.sun.java.swing.preview.*;
import java.io.*;
import java.util.*;

public class Test
{
    public Test()
    {
        // Create a DirectoryModel instance with its current
        // directory set to the current directory ".".
        DirectoryModel dm = new DirectoryModel(
                                        new File( "." ) );

        // Tell the DirectoryModel which file types to
```

```
            // recognize.
            FileType types[] = new FileType[1];

            // This instance of MyFileType recognizes files that
            // have a "java" extension.
            types[0] = new MyFileType( "java", "Java source" );

            dm.setKnownFileTypes( types );

            // Get a list of the files/directories in the
            // DirectoryModel's current directory.
            Vector files = dm.getTypedFiles();

            // Print out the files/directories and their types.
            for ( int i = 0; i < files.size(); i++ )
            {
               // Get the TypedFile from the list.
               TypedFile thisFile =
                                 (TypedFile)files.elementAt(i);

               // Print out the name of the file and its type.
               System.out.println( "Name:  " +
                   thisFile.getAbsolutePath() +
                   "\n    Type:  "
                   + thisFile.getType().getPresentationName() );
            }
      }

   // This implementation of FileType accepts a file
   // extension and corresponding string description
   // through the constructor.
   private class MyFileType implements FileType
   {
         // Storage for the file extension and description.
         private String mExt;
         private String mName;

         public MyFileType( String ext, String name )
         {
            // Store the extension and description.
            mExt = ext;
            mName = name;
         }

         // Return this file type's description.
         public String getPresentationName()
         {
            return mName;
         }

         // Return an icon that can be placed next to files
         // of this type in a file browser.
         public Icon getIcon()
         {
            return new ImageIcon( "javasource.gif" );
         }
```

```
    // Return false because this file type is not able
    // to contain others.
    public boolean isContainer()
    {
        return false;
    }

    // If the file's name ends with "java", the file is
    // of this type.
    public boolean testFile( File file )
    {
        String name = file.getAbsolutePath();

        if ( name.endsWith( mExt ) )
            return true;

        return false;
    }
}

    // The main() method.  This just creates an instance of
    // this class.
    public static void main( String args[] )
    {
        new Test();
    }
}
```

File Type's Public Methods

```
Icon getIcon():
```

Returns the icon associated with the FileType.

```
String getPresentationName():
```

Returns the descriptive String associated with the FileType.

```
boolean isContainer():
```

Returns true if this type of file can contain other files (e.g. directories).

```
boolean testFile(File file):
```

Returns true if the given File is this type of file.

ImageIcon

The AWT's asynchronous loading of images is useful for large images that take a while to load because it allows other things to be going on while the image is loading. For smaller images it is rather cumbersome since what you

Figure 8-32
A JButton containing an ImageIcon.

really want from icon-type images is to have them guaranteed to be completely loaded before your applet/application gets going. The ImageIcon class makes it easy to load small images and have them available when needed.

ImageIcons are used frequently in the JFC for images on buttons, checkboxes, radio buttons, etc. (as shown in Figure 8-32). ImageIcon is designed for use with small images (hence the Icon in the name), but will work for any image you want to load all-at-once.

Ancestors

```
java.lang.Object
   |
   +-com.sun.java.swing.ImageIcon
```

NOTE: *For more information, see the "JLabel," "AbstractButton," "JButton," "JCheckBox," "JRadioButton," "JMenuItem," "JCheckBoxMenuItem," and "JRadioButtonMenuItem" sections in this chapter.*

Steps in Creating and Using ImageIcon

1. Create an ImageIcon. The image source may be a preloaded image, a file name, or a URL. You may also specify a descriptive string that can be used as a nongraphical alternative to the image. There are nine constructors:

```
ImageIcon()
ImageIcon( byte imageData[] )
ImageIcon( byte imageData[], String description )
ImageIcon( Image preloadedImage )
ImageIcon( Image preloadedImage, String description )
ImageIcon( String filename )
ImageIcon( String filename, String description )
ImageIcon( URL location )
ImageIcon( URL location, String description )
```

To create an ImageIcon from a string:

```
ImageIcon myIcon = new ImageIcon( "pushme.gif" );
```

2. Retrieve the ImageIcon's image. Do this if you want to use Image's extended capabilities. ImageIcon doesn't do any special processing for this call—it just returns the image it stores internally.

```
Image myImage = myIcon.getImage();
```

3. Use the ImageIcon in a component. Several JFC components have constructors and other methods that take an ImageIcon:

```
JButton myButton = new JButton( "Ok", myIcon );
myButton.setPressedIcon( new ImageIcon( "stopit.gif" ) );
```

4. Paint the ImageIcon onto a component at a particular spot. This call requires a component and an instance of Graphics, and the coordinates refer to where the ImageIcon's upper-left corner will be:

```
myIcon.paintIcon( this, g, 10, 10 );
```

5. Find the ImageIcon's width and height:

```
int height = myIcon.getIconHeight();
int width = myIcon.getIconWidth();
```

Basic Code Examples

EXAMPLE 8-30 Using an ImageIcon

The following code sample creates a custom component that accepts an image icon, uses the image icon's size as its own preferred size, and paints the image icon. Notice that the component is looking for Icon rather than ImageIcon. It can do this since Icon is the interface that ImageIcon implements. Figure 8-33 shows the ImageIcon drawn on its component.

Here is the source code:

```
import com.sun.java.swing.*;
import java.awt.*;

public class MyFrame extends JFrame
{
    public MyFrame()
    {
        setTitle( "ImageIcon1" );

        // Store the content pane in a variable for easier
        // access.
        JPanel contentPane = (JPanel)getContentPane();

        // Components will all be added to this panel.
        contentPane.setLayout( new BoxLayout( contentPane,
                                BoxLayout.X_AXIS ) );

        // Create the image icon that will be added to the
        // custom component.
```

Figure 8-33

```
ImageIcon myIcon = new ImageIcon( "silvstar.gif" );

// Create the custom component.
MyComponent comp = new MyComponent( myIcon );

// Add the new component to the buffered panel.
contentPane.add( comp );
}


// This custom component doesn't do anything except set
// its preferred size to the size of the icon that gets
// passed in, and then draw that icon.
private class MyComponent extends JComponent
{
    // We use Icon instead of ImageIcon just to show that
    // we can since Icon is the interface that ImageIcon
    // implements.
    Icon icon;

    public MyComponent( Icon myIcon )
    {
        // Store the image icon.
        icon = myIcon;

        // Use the icon's size to set the preffered size
        // for the component.  This is especially handy
        // when you use BoxLayout.
        setPreferredSize( new Dimension(
                            myIcon.getIconWidth(),
                            myIcon.getIconHeight() ) );
    }

    // Just paint the icon into the component's space.
    public void paint( Graphics g )
    {
        icon.paintIcon( this, g, 0, 0 );
    }
}
}
```

Advanced Issues

EXAMPLE 8-31 Using ImageIcon with a Larger Image

This example shows that ImageIcon can be used when working with a larger image. ImageIcon encapsulates the ImageObserver functionality so you don't have to deal with it. The big difference between handling an image this way and handling it through the normal Image methods is that the image loads in the foreground. That is, it doesn't let anything else happen while it is loading (unless you specifically make it multithreaded). Figure 8-34 shows the larger-than-usual ImageIcon displayed in its component.

Important things to notice:

Figure 8-34

■ The example contains a custom component called MyComponent. This is done so that we can override the paint() method and paint the Icon.

■ The custom component stores the ImageIcon as an Icon. It can do this because Icon is the interface that ImageIcon implements.

Here is the source:

```
import com.sun.java.swing.*;
import java.awt.*;

public class MyFrame extends JFrame
{
    public MyFrame()
    {
        setTitle( "ImageIcon2" );

        // Store the content pane in a variable for easier
        // access.
        JPanel contentPane = (JPanel)getContentPane();

        // Components will all be added to this panel.
        contentPane.setLayout( new BorderLayout() );

        // Load this larger image via ImageIcon.  This
        // command does not return until the image is
        // completely loaded.
        ImageIcon bigImage = new ImageIcon( "parrots.jpg" );

        // Create an instance of our custom component that is
        // made to display an Icon.
        MyComponent myComp = new MyComponent( bigImage );

        // Add the custom component to the content pane so it
        // covers the whole thing.
        contentPane.add( "Center", myComp );
    }

    // This component is designed to accept an Icon through
    // the constructor, and display it whenever the
    // component is painted.
```

```
private class MyComponent extends JComponent
{
   // Store the Icon so the paint() method has access to
   // it.
   private Icon mImage;

   public MyComponent( Icon image )
   {
      // Save the Icon.
      mImage = image;

      // Set the component's preferred size to the
      // Icon's size.
      setPreferredSize( new Dimension(
                     image.getIconWidth(),
                     image.getIconHeight() ) );
   }

   // Use Icon's paintIcon() method to paint the icon
   // flush against the component's top and left sides.
   public void paint( Graphics g )
   {
      mImage.paintIcon( this, g, 0, 0 );
   }
}
}
```

ImageIcon's Public Methods

`String getDescription()`

Returns the ImageIcon's description string.

`int getIconHeight()`

Returns the ImageIcon's height in pixels.

`int getIconWidth()`

Returns the ImageIcon's width in pixels.

`Image getImage()`

Returns the ImageIcon's internal copy of the image.

`int getImageLoadStatus()`

Returns the current status of the ImageIcon. May be: ABORTED, ERRORED, or COMPLETE.

```
ImageObserver getImageObserver()
```

Returns the ImageObserver that is being used to track the progress of loading the image.

```
void paintIcon(Component c,Graphics g,int x,int y)
```

Paints the ImageIcon onto the given component, with its upper-left corner at the given x,y coordinates.

```
void setDescription(String description)
```

Specifies the description string that will go with the ImageIcon.

```
void setImage(Image image)
```

Replaces the ImageIcon's internal image.

```
void setImageObserver(ImageObserver observer)
```

Specifies an ImageObserver of your own to use in tracking the progress of loading the image.

JApplet

JApplet is the JFC equivalent to the AWT's Applet class. If you want to use JFC components in applets, you should use JApplet. JApplet works the same as Applet except that, like the other JFC window components, it gives access to its display area through a JRootPane. If you want to add components or a menu to a JApplet, get the JApplet's JRootPane and add them there.

Ancestors

```
java.lang.Object
   |
   +-java.awt.Component
           |
           +-java.awt.Container
                   |
                   +-java.awt.Panel
                           |
                           +-java.applet.Applet
                                   |
                                   +-com.sun.java.swing.JApplet
```

NOTE: *For more information, see the "JRootPane" section in this chapter. Also see the "Windows" section in Chapter 7, "JFC by Concept."*

Steps in Creating and Using JApplet

1. Create an HTML page in which to embed the JApplet.

This HTML will display the applet defined by the MyApplet class and will make it 200 pixels by 250 pixels:

```
<HTML>
<HEAD>
<TITLE>My Applet</TITLE>
</HEAD>
<BODY>
<!-identify object to run as applet ->
<applet code="MyApplet.class" width=200 height=250></applet>
</BODY>
</HTML>
```

2. Create a class that extends JApplet.

Here is a skeleton:

```
import com.sun.java.swing.*;

public class MyApplet extends JApplet
{
}
```

Since JApplet is a descendent of java.applet.Applet, it still uses the same five methods to interact with the browser:

- public void init()—The browser calls this to initialize the applet.
- public void paint(Graphics g)—The browser calls this to paint the applet's area.
- public void start()—The browser calls this when the page in which the applet is embedded is viewed.
- public void stop()—The browser calls this when the page stops being viewed.
- public void destroy()—The browser calls this when it is being closed or when it decides the applet should be removed from memory.

All of these methods are optional although an applet without any of them is not very useful.

3. Add a menu bar to the JApplet.

Create the menu bar:

```
JMenuBar mbar = new JMenuBar();
```

Create a menu and add it to the menu bar:

```
JMenu options = new JMenu( "Options" );
mbar.add( options );
```

Create a menu item and add it to the menu:

```
JMenuItem menuItem = new JMenuItem( "A Menu Item" );
options.add( menuItem );
```

Apply the menu bar to the JApplet through its JRootPane. JApplet has a convenience method for adding a menu bar to its JRootPane, so you can either call:

```
getRootPane().setMenuBar( mbar );
```

Or:

```
setJMenuBar( mbar );
```

4. Add a component to the JApplet.

Create a component:

```
JButton ok = new JButton( "Ok" );
```

Add the component to the JApplet through its JRootPane. Components are added to the JRootPane via its content pane. JApplet includes a convenience method for getting its JRootPane's content pane, so you can add the component by calling:

```
getRootPane().getContentPane().add( ok );
```

Or:

```
getContentPane().add( ok );
```

Basic Code Example

EXAMPLE 8-32 Creating a Basic JApplet

This example shows a very simple JApplet with the accompanying HTML code. The JApplet has a menu bar and a status bar that you can turn on and off from the menu. Figure 8-35 shows the example running inside the AppletViewer.

Here is the HTML code in which the applet is embedded:

```
<HTML>
<HEAD>
<TITLE>My Applet</TITLE>
</HEAD>
<BODY>
<!-identify object to run as applet ->
<applet code="MyApplet.class" width=200 height=250></applet>
</BODY>
</HTML>
```

Figure 8-35

Here is the applet's source code:

```
import com.sun.java.swing.*;
import com.sun.java.swing.border.*;
import java.awt.*;
import java.awt.event.*;

public class MyApplet extends JApplet implements
        ItemListener
{
    private JPanel mStatusBar;

    public void init()
    {
        // Use the system's native look-and-feel.
        String lf = UIManager.getSystemLookAndFeelClassName();

        if ( lf != null )
        {
            try
            {
                UIManager.setLookAndFeel( lf );
            }
            catch ( Exception ex )
            {
                ex.printStackTrace();
            }
        }

        // Create a menu bar.
        JMenuBar mbar = new JMenuBar();

        // Make the applet window use the menu bar.
        setJMenuBar( mbar );

        // Create a menu.
        JMenu options = new JMenu( "Options" );

        // Add the menu to the menu bar.
        mbar.add( options );
```

```java
        // Create a menu item for turning the status bar
        // on/off.
        JCheckBoxMenuItem useStatusBar =
                    new JCheckBoxMenuItem( "Status Bar" );

        // Make it so this class is notified when the menu
        // item changes state.
        useStatusBar.addItemListener( this );

        // Add the menu item to the menu.
        options.add( useStatusBar );

        // Store the content pane in a variable for easy
        // access.
        JPanel contentPane = (JPanel)getContentPane();

        // Create a status bar panel.
        mStatusBar = new JPanel();

        // Give the status bar a border.
        mStatusBar.setBorder( new BevelBorder(
                                    BevelBorder.RAISED ) );

        // Put some text in the status bar.
        JLabel sbLabel = new JLabel( "Status Bar" );

        // Set the status bar's layout manager.
        mStatusBar.setLayout( new BoxLayout( mStatusBar,
                        BoxLayout.X_AXIS ) );

        // Add the label to the status bar.
        mStatusBar.add( sbLabel );

        // Place the status bar at the bottom of the content
        // pane.
        contentPane.add( "South", mStatusBar );

        // Set the menu item so the status bar is initially
        // visible.
        useStatusBar.setSelected( true );
    }

    // This is called when the menu item changes state.
    public void itemStateChanged( ItemEvent e )
    {
        // Cast the source of the event so we can work with
        // its methods.
        JCheckBoxMenuItem item =
                    (JCheckBoxMenuItem)e.getSource();

        // Make the status bar's visibility reflect the menu
        // item's setting.
        mStatusBar.setVisible( item.isSelected() );
```

```
        // Update the display.
        repaint();
    }
}
```

Advanced Issues

Future versions of Netscape Navigator will ship with the JFC built in. Until that time, if you want to use the JFC in your applets, you need to place the swingall.jar file in Netscape's Program\Java\Classes directory.

Versions of Navigator up to 4.04 also require a JDK 1.1 patch that you can download from Netscape's web site.

JApplet's Public Methods

`void addNotify()`

Overridden to handle an applet's special situation.

`AccessibleContext getAccessibleContext()`

Returns a subclass of AccessibleContext that gives access to the JApplet's accessibility information.

`Container getContentPane()`

Convenience method to get the JApplet's JRootPane's content pane.

`Component getGlassPane()`

Convenience method to get the JApplet's JRootPane's glass pane.

`JMenuBar getJMenuBar()`

Convenience method to get the JApplet's JRootPane's menu bar.

`JLayeredPane getLayeredPane()`

Convenience method to get the JApplet's JRootPane's layered pane.

`JRootPane getRootPane()`

Returns the JApplet's root pane.

```
void removeNotify()
```

Overridden for JApplet's special case.

```
void setContentPane(Container contentPane)
```

Convenience method for replacing the JApplet's JRootPane's content pane.

```
void setGlassPane(Component glass)
```

Convenience method for replacing the JApplet's JRootPane's glass pane.

```
void setJMenuBar(JMenuBar menuBar)
```

Convenience method for replacing the JApplet's JRootPane's menu bar.

```
void setLayeredPane(JLayeredPane layered)
```

Convenience method for replacing the JApplet's JRootPane's layered pane.

```
void setLayout(LayoutManager layout)
```

Overridden since layout should be set for the content pane instead.

```
void update(Graphics g)
```

Overridden to just call paint(g).

JButton

A JButton is a control that you push to make something happen. It typically consists of a text label and/or icon that describes its function, an empty area around the text/icon, and a border (as shown in Figure 8-36). By default, the border is a special border that reflects the status of the button (pressed or not). When pressed, a JButton generates an ActionEvent that your application can use to trigger an appropriate response.

Figure 8-36
A standard text-only
Jbutton.

Ancestors

```
java.lang.Object
    |
   +—java.awt.Component
            |
           +—java.awt.Container
                    |
                   +—com.sun.java.swing.JComponent
                            |
                           +—com.sun.java.swing.AbstractButton
                                    |
                                   +—com.sun.java.swing.JButton
```

NOTE: *For more information, see the "AbstractButton" and "ImageIcon" sections in this chapter, and the "Allowing the User to Trigger Actions" section in Chapter 7, "JFC by Concept."*

NOTE: *If a button is not double-buffered, it will appear to flash when pressed. For a button to be double-buffered, its container (or its container's parent, etc.) must be double-buffered. This is normally taken care of by the parent frame whose default content pane is a double-buffered JPanel. If the parent frame's content pane has been replaced with something else, you will need to place a double-buffered JPanel yourself. See "Double Buffering" in Chapter 7, "JFC by Concept."*

Steps in Creating and Using JButton

1. Create the button. There are four constructors, but you will normally use one of the following three:

   Create a button with text on it:

   ```
   JButton textButton = new JButton( "Text only" );
   ```

   Create a button with an icon on it:

   ```
   JButton iconButton = new JButton(
                       new ImageIcon( "picture.gif" ) );
   ```

   Create a button with both text and an icon.

   ```
   JButton comboButton = new JButton( "text with icon",
                       new ImageIcon( "picture.gif" ) );
   ```

2. Catch the button's events. This is not strictly required, but if you don't catch events the button is pretty but doesn't do much.

Define which class will receive the events. In this case, it's the class that the button resides in:

```
textButton.addActionListener( this );
```

Make the receiving class implement the ActionListener interface:

```
public class MyFrame extends JFrame implements ActionListener
{
    .
    .
    .
    public void actionPerformed( ActionEvent e )
    {
        // Do your stuff here.
    }
}
```

3. Set the accelerator key that allows the user to depress the button using the keyboard rather than the mouse (optional). This method is inherited from AbstractButton:

```
textButton.setMnemonic( 'T' );
```

This causes the first *T* (either upper or lowercase) to be underlined on the button. The button won't be depressed when the user presses T, but rather when the user presses T and the platform-specific modifier key (e.g. Alt on Windows). You can specify an accelerator key for icon-only buttons even though the button will not be able to advertise what the key is. In these cases, it is customary to place a JLabel next to the button and advertise the accelerator key there (see "JLabel.setDisplayedMnemonic(char)").

4. Set the font to be used to display the button's text (optional). This method is inherited from Component:

```
textButton.setFont( new Font( "Helvetica", Font.ITALIC, 24 ) );
```

5. For buttons with icons, you can specify icons to be displayed when the button is pressed or disabled or when the mouse passes over the button (optional). These methods are inherited from AbstractButton:

To specify the icon to be displayed when the button is pressed:

```
comboButton.setPressedIcon( new ImageIcon( "pressed.gif" ) );
```

By default, when a button is disabled its icon's colors change to shades of gray. To specify a particular icon to be used when the button is disabled:

```
comboButton.setDisabledIcon( new ImageIcon( "disabled.gif" ) );
```

To specify the icon to use when the mouse "rolls over" the button:

```
combobutton.setRolloverEnabled( true );
comboButton.setRolloverIcon( new ImageIcon( "rolledover.gif" ) );
```

Notice that rollover has to be enabled or the setRolloverIcon() will have no effect.

6. Change the text color (optional). This method is inherited from Component. Changing the text color by changing the foreground color works with the *Windows* look-and-feel, because it happens to use the foreground color to draw button text. This is not guaranteed to work with all look-and-feels:

```
textButton.setForeground( Color.red );
```

7. Change how the text and icon are placed on a button that has both. By default, the icon is placed to the left of the text. These methods are inherited from AbstractButton:

To make the text display to the left of the icon:

```
comboButton.setHorizontalTextPosition( JButton.LEFT );
```

To make the text display above the icon:

```
comboButton.setHorizontalTextPosition( JButton.CENTER );
comboButton.setVerticalTextPosition( JButton.TOP );
```

Notice that the text has to be moved to the center as well as up.

8. Add a tool tip (optional). This provides text that will appear in its own little window when the user places the mouse over the button:

```
iconButton.setToolTipText( "This is an icon button" );
```

This method is inherited from JComponent.

9. Change the button's border (optional). This generally looks bad since it makes it so that the border does not change when the button is pressed.

If you want to make the edge of the button blend in with its container, you can use an EmptyBorder:

```
iconButton.setBorder( new EmptyBorder( 5, 5, 5, 5 ) );
```

This can also be achieved by telling the button not to paint its border:

```
iconButton.setBorderPainted( false );
```

Basic Code Examples

EXAMPLE 8-33 Basic JButton

This example puts the above topics together in a working class. Figure 8-37 shows the result.

Here is the source code:

```
import com.sun.java.swing.*;
import com.sun.java.swing.event.*;
```

Figure 8-37

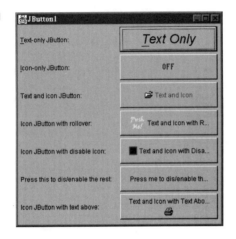

```
import com.sun.java.swing.border.*;
import java.awt.*;
import java.awt.event.*;

public class MyFrame extends JFrame implements
        ActionListener, ChangeListener
{
    JButton mTextBtn;
    JButton mIconBtn;
    JButton mComboBtn;
    JButton mBtnWithRollover;
    JButton mBtnWithDisable;
    JButton mDisableBtn;
    JButton mTextOverIconBtn;

    public MyFrame()
    {
        JLabel l;

        setTitle( "JButton1" );

        // Store the content pane in a variable for easier
        // access.
        JPanel contentPane = (JPanel)getContentPane();

        // Components will all be added to this panel.
        contentPane.setLayout( new GridLayout( 7, 2, 5, 5 ) );

        // Give the content pane an empty border so the
        // labels and buttons are moved away from the edge of
        // the frame.
        contentPane.setBorder(
                        new EmptyBorder( 5, 5, 5, 5 ) );

        // Notice that the first two buttons have
        // accelerators that are echoed in their JLabels.
```

```
// Text-only button.  The font is extra large, the
// button responds to accelerator key 'T', and that
// key is also advertised in the accompanying label.
l = new JLabel( "Text-only JButton:  " );
l.setDisplayedMnemonic( 'T' );
contentPane.add( l );

mTextBtn = new JButton( "Text Only" );
mTextBtn.setMnemonic( 'T' );
mTextBtn.setFont( new Font( "Helvetica",
                    Font.ITALIC, 24 ) );
contentPane.add( mTextBtn );

// Icon-only button.  A pressed icon is defined so
// the icon changes when the button is pressed.  The
// button responds to accelerator key 'I' and the
// key is also advertised in the accompanying label.
l = new JLabel( "Icon-only JButton:  " );
l.setDisplayedMnemonic( 'I' );
contentPane.add( l );

mIconBtn = new JButton( new ImageIcon( "off.gif" ) );
mIconBtn.setMnemonic( 'I' );
mIconBtn.setPressedIcon( new ImageIcon( "on.gif" ) );
mIconBtn.addActionListener( this );
mIconBtn.setActionCommand( "cmd1" );
contentPane.add( mIconBtn );

// Button with text and an icon.  Notice that the
// text color is red.
contentPane.add(
        new JLabel( "Text and icon JButton:  " ) );

mComboBtn = new JButton( "Text and Icon",
                    new ImageIcon( "open.gif" ) );
mComboBtn.setForeground( Color.red );
mComboBtn.addActionListener( this );
mComboBtn.setActionCommand( "cmd2" );
contentPane.add( mComboBtn );

// Text + icon button with a separate icon that
// replaces the normal one when the mouse passes over
// the button.
contentPane.add(
    new JLabel( "Icon JButton with rollover:  " ) );

mBtnWithRollover =
        new JButton( "Text and Icon with Rollover",
                    new ImageIcon( "pushme.gif" ) );
mBtnWithRollover.setRolloverIcon(
            new ImageIcon( "pushme_maybe.gif" ) );
mBtnWithRollover.setRolloverEnabled( true );
mBtnWithRollover.addChangeListener( this );
contentPane.add( mBtnWithRollover );
```

```
            // Text+icon button with a separate icon that
            // replaces the normal one when the button is
            // depressed.
            contentPane.add( new JLabel(
                       "Icon JButton with disable icon:  " ) );

            mBtnWithDisable = new JButton(
                          "Text and Icon with Disable Icon",
                          new ImageIcon( "enabled.gif" ) );
            mBtnWithDisable.setDisabledIcon(
                             new ImageIcon( "disabled.gif" ) );
            contentPane.add( mBtnWithDisable );

            // Simple button that disables the rest just to show
            // what they look like disabled.  Notice that the
            // events from this button are being caught.
            contentPane.add( new JLabel(
                    "Press this to dis/enable the rest:  " ) );

            mDisableBtn = new JButton(
                          "Press me to dis/enable the others" );
            mDisableBtn.addActionListener( this );
            contentPane.add( mDisableBtn );

            // Text+icon button illustrating how the text and
            // icon relative positions can be changed.
            contentPane.add( new JLabel(
                          "Icon JButton with text above:  " ) );

            mTextOverIconBtn = new JButton(
                             "Text and Icon with Text Above",
                             new ImageIcon( "print.gif" ) );
            mTextOverIconBtn.setHorizontalTextPosition(
                                          JButton.CENTER );
            mTextOverIconBtn.setVerticalTextPosition(
                                          JButton.TOP );
            contentPane.add( mTextOverIconBtn );
    }

    // Called when the mDisableBtn control is pressed.
    // Required since the enable state of the other buttons
    // is switched when mDisableBtn is pressed.
    public void actionPerformed( ActionEvent e )
    {
        // Doesn't do much, just shows the getActionCommand()
        // method.
        if ( e.getActionCommand().equals( "cmd1" ) )
           System.out.println( e.getSource() );

        // Disable/enable the others when the disable button
        // is pressed.
        if ( e.getSource() == mDisableBtn )
        {
           mTextBtn.setEnabled( ! mTextBtn.isEnabled() );
           mIconBtn.setEnabled( ! mIconBtn.isEnabled() );
```

```
                          mComboBtn.setEnabled( ! mComboBtn.isEnabled() );
                          mBtnWithRollover.setEnabled(
                                          ! mBtnWithRollover.isEnabled() );
                          mBtnWithDisable.setEnabled(
                                          ! mBtnWithDisable.isEnabled() );
                          mTextOverIconBtn.setEnabled(
                                          ! mTextOverIconBtn.isEnabled() );
          }
      }

      public void stateChanged( ChangeEvent e )
      {
          System.out.println( "Got a ChangeEvent" );
      }
  }
```

Advanced Issues

EXAMPLE 8-34 Intercepting Right-Clicks on a Button

The default JButton action upon receiving a right mouse click (with the *Windows* look-and-feel, anyway) is to treat it just like a left click and depress the button. In this example we make it so that the right click does not depress the button, but rather causes a popup menu to come up.

There are at least three ways to accomplish this:

- Create your own UI for JButton since it is the look-and-feel that actually defines the default right click action on a JButton. This has the drawback that the modified functionality would only work with your new look-and-feel, so it would go away if another look-and-feel was plugged in.

- Overlay the button with an invisible component that would intercept all events and pass through all except right clicks. This is cumbersome and confusing to maintain.

- Subclass JButton and override the processMouseEvent() method. This is the best solution because it works with any look-and-feel and is easy to program.

Figure 8-38 shows the button having just been right-clicked. Important points to notice:

- We use the third way described above.

Figure 8-38

- When you override the processMouseEvent() method, you catch all mouse events before they can be applied to the button. So we catch the right clicks and pass the rest to JButton for normal processing.
- In our processMouseEvent() method, if the popup menu is not created already, we create it.
- The menu items don't do anything in this example, but there is no reason why they couldn't.
- Other than its handling of right-clicks, this new button acts like a regular JButton.

Here is the source for a subclass of JButton called ButtonWithPopup, followed by the source of the sample class that uses it:

```
import com.sun.java.swing.*;
import java.awt.event.*;
import java.awt.*;

public class ButtonWithPopup extends JButton
{
    JPopupMenu mMenu;
    JMenuItem mOption1;
    JMenuItem mOption2;
    JMenuItem mOption3;

    // We just implement a single constructor for this
    // example.
    public ButtonWithPopup( String title )
    {
        super( title );
    }

    // Override processMouseEvent() so we catch mouse events
    // before JButton and its UI can get them.  If the event
    // is a right click, show the popup menu.  Otherwise,
    // pass it through for JButton to handle.
    protected void processMouseEvent( MouseEvent e )
    {

        // Check to see if the click is a right-click.
        if ( (e.getModifiers() & InputEvent.BUTTON3_MASK)
            != 0 )
        {
            // If the popup menu has not been created, create
            // it.
            if ( mMenu == null )
            {
```

```
                            mMenu = new JPopupMenu();
                            mOption1 = mMenu.add(
                                        new JMenuItem( "Option 1" ) );
                            mOption2 = mMenu.add(
                                        new JMenuItem( "Option 2" ) );
                            mOption3 = mMenu.add(
                                        new JMenuItem( "Option 3" ) );
                    }

                    // Display the popup menu with its upper-left
                    // corner at the point where the mouse was clicked.
                    mMenu.show( (JComponent)e.getSource(), e.getX(),
                                e.getY() );
                }
                else
                {
                    // Pass the event through for default processing.
                    super.processMouseEvent( e );
                }
        }
}
```

Here is the sample class MyFrame that uses ButtonWithPopup

```
import com.sun.java.swing.*;
import java.awt.*;
import java.util.*;

public class MyFrame extends JFrame
{
    JPanel mPanel;

    public MyFrame()
    {
        setTitle( "JButton2" );

        // Store the content pane in a variable for easier
        // access.
        mPanel = (JPanel)getContentPane();

        // Components will all be added to this panel.
        mPanel.setLayout( new GridLayout( 1, 1 ) );

        ButtonWithPopup b1 = new ButtonWithPopup(
                            "Right-click for a JPopupMenu" );
        mPanel.add( b1 );
    }
}
```

JButton's Public Methods

`AccessibleContext getAccessibleContext()`

Returns a subclass of AccessibleContext, which gives access to the JButton's accessibility information.

`String getUIClassID()`

Returns an identifying string that the look-and-feel uses to assign a UI class to the JButton.

`boolean isDefaultButton()`

Returns true if the JButton is its root pane's default button.

`void updateUI()`

Called by the currently plugged-in look-and-feel to suggest to the component that it ask the UIManager for a new UI class.

JCheckBox

A JCheckBox is a control that may be turned on and off by the user to designate some kind of property being selected or not selected. It typically consists of a background rectangle (normally the color of its parent container), and a text string and/or icon. The JCheckBox will normally show its current state visually. This is done either by placing an check mark in a box, or by changing the icon (if there is one) associated with the check box (see Figure 8-39).

A JCheckBox generates ItemEvents when its state changes. It is normal practice to catch the ItemEvents to trigger any activities related to changes in the JCheckBox's state. If you don't need to know exactly when the state changes, you don't need to catch these events—you can just ask the JCheckBox for its state when you actually need to know.

Ancestors

```
java.lang.Object
    |
    +—java.awt.Component
        |
        +—java.awt.Container
```

Figure 8-39
A typical JCheckBox.

```
                        |
      +—com.sun.java.swing.JComponent
                   |
         +—com.sun.java.swing.AbstractButton
                      |
            +—com.sun.java.swing.JToggleButton
                         |
               +—com.sun.java.swing.JCheckBox
```

NOTE: *For more information, see the "JCheckBox" and "ImageIcon" sections in this chapter, and the "Components That Can Be Turned On and Off" section in Chapter 7, "JFC by Concept."*

Steps in Creating and Using JCheckBox

1. Create a new check box. There are seven constructors, but all are variations on:

   ```
   JCheckBox( String boxText, Icon boxIcon, boolean selected )
   ```

   where *'boxText'* is the text that appears in the control, *'boxIcon'* is the icon that displays when the check box is not selected, and *'selected'* is the check box's initial state.

   Create a check box with no text or icon:

   ```
   JCheckBox b1 = new JCheckBox();
   ```

   Create a check box with an icon but no text:

   ```
   JCheckBox b2 = new JCheckBox( new ImageIcon( "off.gif" ) );
   ```

   Create a check box with text and an icon, and which starts out selected (by default, a check box starts out not selected):

   ```
   JCheckBox b3 = new JCheckBox( "This has text",
                                 new ImageIcon( "pushme.gif" ),
                                 true );
   ```

2. Explicitly make the control selected. We could just as well have done this in the constructor:

   ```
   b6.setSelected( true );
   ```

3. For a check box that uses an icon, it is best to use another icon to designate that the control is selected, otherwise it will be difficult to

tell the check box's state. The icon that is specified in the constructor will be used when the control is not selected:

```
b3.setSelectedIcon( new ImageIcon( "stopit.gif" ) );
```

4. Move the text to a new position relative to the button. By default, the text is to the right of the button. Of course, this won't have much meaning if the check box doesn't use text:

Put the text left of the button:

```
b5.setHorizontalTextPosition( JCheckBox.LEFT );
```

Put the text above the button:

```
b7.setVerticalTextPosition( JCheckBox.TOP );
b7.setHorizontalTextPosition( JCheckBox.CENTER );
```

Notice that you have to move the text to the center as well as up.

5. Align the text/button to one edge of the control. By default, it is aligned left and centered vertically:

Align it to the center:

```
b6.setHorizontalAlignment( JCheckBox.CENTER );
```

6. Change the text color. setForeground() is inherited from Component. This only works if the look-and-feel currently plugged in uses the foreground color to draw the check box's text. This is true for the *Windows* look-and-feel, but is not guaranteed to be true for all look-and-feels:

```
b9.setForeground( Color.red );
```

7. Change the font. setFont() is inherited from Component. Again, the current look-and-feel determines whether it will use the component's font or one of its own choosing. This works for the *Windows* look-and-feel, but is not guaranteed to work for all look-and-feels:

```
b10.setFont( new Font( "TimesRoman", Font.ITALIC, 24 ) );
```

8. Give the control an accelerator key. If the check box doesn't use text, the accelerator will work, but it will not be visually clear what the key is. The character is case insensitive ('a' is the same as 'A'):

```
b11.setMnemonic( 'a' );
```

9. Give the control a tool tip. The given text will appear in its own little window when the user places the mouse over the check box. This is inherited from JComponent:

```
b12.setToolTipText( "Tool tips are terrific!" );
```

10. Give the control an icon to use when it is disabled. By default, when the JCheckBox is disabled, its regular icon shows up in shades of gray. This method only has an effect if the check box uses an icon:

```
mDisableTest.setDisabledIcon( new ImageIcon( "disabled.gif" ) );
```

11. Specify an icon to display when the mouse passes over the control. Notice that rollover has to be explicitly enabled.

```
b3.setRolloverEnabled( true );
b3.setRolloverIcon( new ImageIcon( "pushme_maybe.gif" ) );
```

12. Specify the control's background color. This method is inherited from Component. By default it takes the color of its parent container.

```
b3.setBackground( Color.green );
```

13. Define a class to capture events from the check box. There are two ways to know when the state of the check box has changed—with ItemEvents or ActionEvents.

To use ItemEvents, specify a class to listen for these events. In this case, the listening class will be the class that contains the check box:

```
b14.addItemListener( this );
```

Make sure the listening class implements the ItemListener interface. In this example, when the state of the check box changes, it causes another check box 'mDisableTest' to be enabled/disabled:

```
public class MyFrame extends JFrame implements ItemListener
{
    .
    .
    .
    public void itemStateChanged( ItemEvent e )
    {
        if ( e.getStateChange() == ItemEvent.SELECTED )
            mDisableTest.setEnabled( true );
        else
            mDisableTest.setEnabled( false );
    }
}
```

To use ActionEvents, specify a class to listen for these events:

```
b14.addActionListener( this );
```

Specify a string to be passed as part of the ActionEvent that gets generated (useful for identifying which component generated the event):

```
b14.setActionCommand( "b14" );
```

Make sure the listening class implements the ActionListener interface. In this example, a string is printed out each time check box b14 changes state:

```
public class MyFrame extends JFrame implements ActionListener
{
    .
```

```
            .
            .
    public void actionPerformed( ActionEvent e )
    {
        if ( e.getActionCommand() == "b14" )
            System.out.println( "b14 changed state" );
    }
}
```

It is generally more convenient to use an ItemListener rather than an ActionListener since ItemEvents contain the component's new state, while you have to query the component for its new state when you use Action-Events.

Basic Code Examples

EXAMPLE 8-35 Shows the Standard JCheckBox Options

This example shows the options for displaying check boxes. It reflects the steps discussed above. Notice that one of the check boxes (b14) controls whether another (mDisableTest) is enabled.

Figure 8-40 shows the various JCheckBoxes created in this example.

Here is the source code:

```
import com.sun.java.swing.*;
import com.sun.java.swing.border.*;
import java.awt.*;
import java.awt.event.*;

public class MyFrame extends JFrame implements ItemListener,
        ActionListener
{
    JCheckBox mDisableTest;

    public MyFrame()
    {
        setTitle( "JCheckBox1" );
```

Figure 8-40

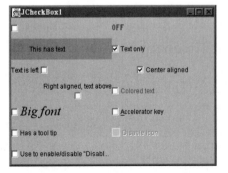

```
// Store the content pane in a variable for easier
// access.
JPanel contentPane = (JPanel)getContentPane();

// Components will all be added to this panel.
contentPane.setLayout( new GridLayout( 7, 2 ) );

// No text or icon.
JCheckBox b1 = new JCheckBox();
contentPane.add( b1 );

// Icon only plus a different icon for when the
// control is selected.
JCheckBox b2 = new JCheckBox( new ImageIcon(
                                "off.gif" ) );
b2.setSelectedIcon( new ImageIcon( "on.gif" ) );
contentPane.add( b2 );

// Text, icon, and selected icon.
JCheckBox b3 = new JCheckBox( "This has text",
                      new ImageIcon( "pushme.gif" ),
                      true );

// Set the icon that should be displayed when the
// check box is not selected and the mouse passes
// over.  Notice that rollover has to be enabled for
// this to work.
b3.setRolloverIcon(
            new ImageIcon( "pushme_maybe.gif" ) );
b3.setRolloverSelectedIcon(
            new ImageIcon( "pushme_maybe.gif" ) );
b3.setRolloverEnabled( true );

// Set the icon that will be displayed when the check
// box is selected.
b3.setSelectedIcon( new ImageIcon( "stopit.gif" ) );

// Set the control's background color.
b3.setBackground( Color.green );

contentPane.add( b3 );

// Default text only checkbox.
JCheckBox b4 = new JCheckBox( "Text only", true );
contentPane.add( b4 );

// Text to the left of the button.
JCheckBox b5 = new JCheckBox( "Text is left" );
b5.setHorizontalTextPosition( JCheckBox.LEFT );
contentPane.add( b5 );

// Align the control to the center.  Make it selected
// after creation.
JCheckBox b6 = new JCheckBox( "Center aligned" );
b6.setHorizontalAlignment( JCheckBox.CENTER );
```

```
        b6.setSelected( true );
        contentPane.add( b6 );

        // Put the text above the button.
        JCheckBox b7 = new JCheckBox(
                        "Right aligned, text above" );
        b7.setHorizontalAlignment( JCheckBox.RIGHT );
        b7.setVerticalTextPosition( JCheckBox.TOP );
        b7.setHorizontalTextPosition( JCheckBox.CENTER );
        contentPane.add( b7 );

        // Red text.
        JCheckBox b9 = new JCheckBox( "Colored text" );
        b9.setForeground( Color.red );
        contentPane.add( b9 );

        // Change the font.
        JCheckBox b10 = new JCheckBox( "Big font" );
        b10.setFont( new Font( "TimesRoman",
                                Font.ITALIC, 24 ) );
        contentPane.add( b10 );

        // Give the control an accelerator.
        JCheckBox b11 = new JCheckBox( "Accelerator key" );
        b11.setMnemonic( 'a' );
        contentPane.add( b11 );

        // Give the control a tool tip.
        JCheckBox b12 = new JCheckBox( "Has a tool tip" );
        b12.setToolTipText( "Tool tips are terrific!" );
        contentPane.add( b12 );

        // Add a special icon for when the control is
        // disabled.  Rollover icon doesn't work.
        mDisableTest = new JCheckBox( "Disable icon",
                        new ImageIcon( "enabled.gif" ) );
        mDisableTest.setDisabledIcon(
                        new ImageIcon( "disabled.gif" ) );
        mDisableTest.setEnabled( false );
        contentPane.add( mDisableTest );

        JCheckBox b14 = new JCheckBox(
                "Use to enable/disable \"Disable icon\"" );
        b14.addItemListener( this );
        b14.setActionCommand( "b14" );
        b14.addActionListener( this );
        contentPane.add( b14 );
    }

// Implementation on ItemListener interface.  Called by
// any JCheckBoxes that have this class registered to
// receive state change events.
public void itemStateChanged( ItemEvent e )
{
    if ( e.getStateChange() == ItemEvent.SELECTED )
```

```
                              mDisableTest.setEnabled( true );
                        else
                           mDisableTest.setEnabled( false );
                  }


                  // Implementation of the ActionListener interface.
                  // Called by any JCheckBoxes that have this class
                  // registered to receive action events.
                  public void actionPerformed( ActionEvent e )
                  {
                     if ( e.getActionCommand() == "b14" )
                        System.out.println( "b14 was clicked" );
                  }
            }
```

Advanced Issues

EXAMPLE 8-36 Creating a Check Box Whose Border Changes with Its State

This example shows you how to make a check box with a border (since it is not supported directly), and makes it so the border changes as the check box's state changes.

Figure 8-41 shows the border as left arrows since the check box is not selected. When it is selected, the border changes to right arrows.

Important things to notice:

▪ We use two MatteBorders, each with a different icon, to represent the changes in state.

▪ We create a subclass of JComponent into which we place the check box. This is how we can use a border with a check box.

▪ The custom class uses an ItemListener so it is notified of changes in the check box's state. The itemStateChanged() method has to call the component's repaint() method so the border change can be seen.

Here is the source:

```
import com.sun.java.swing.*;
import com.sun.java.swing.border.*;
import java.awt.*;
import java.awt.event.*;

public class MyFrame extends JFrame
{
```

Figure 8-41

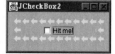

```
public MyFrame()
{
    setTitle( "JCheckBox2" );

    // Store the content pane in a variable for easier
    // access.
    JPanel contentPane = (JPanel)getContentPane();

    // Components will all be added to this panel.
    contentPane.setLayout( new BorderLayout() );

    // Give the content pane an empty border so there
    // will be a gap between the edge of the frame and
    // the edge of our special component.
    contentPane.setBorder(
                new EmptyBorder( 10, 10, 10, 10 ) );

    // Create the check box that will be part of the
    // special component.
    JCheckBox box = new JCheckBox( "Hit me!" );
    box.setHorizontalAlignment( JCheckBox.CENTER );

    // Create the custom component with the just-created
    // check box.
    BorderedCheckBox borderedBox =
                        new BorderedCheckBox( box );

    // Add the custom component to the content pane.
    contentPane.add( "North", borderedBox );
}

// This class is just a component that places its check
// box it its center, and surrounds it with a border.
// This class listens for changes in the check box.
// When the state of the check box changes, the border
// changes.
private class BorderedCheckBox extends JComponent
        implements ItemListener
{
    // The two borders that will reflect the check box's
    // two states.
    private MatteBorder mUnselectedBorder;
    private MatteBorder mSelectedBorder;

    public BorderedCheckBox( JCheckBox box )
    {
        setLayout( new BorderLayout() );

        // Place the check box in the component's center.
        add( "Center", box );

        // Make it so that this class will be notified
        // when the check box's state changes.
        box.addItemListener( this );
```

```
        // Create the two borders here.  We could just
        // create them over and over when the state
        // changed, but this is more efficient.
        mUnselectedBorder =
                    new MatteBorder( 15, 15, 15, 15,
                    new ImageIcon( "left.gif" ) );
        mSelectedBorder =
                    new MatteBorder( 15, 15, 15, 15,
                    new ImageIcon( "right.gif" ) );

        // Apply the unselected border to the component.
        setBorder( mUnselectedBorder );
    }

    // When the check box's state changes, this method is
    // called.
    public void itemStateChanged( ItemEvent e )
    {
        // If the check box's state is now selected, apply
        // the border with the right arrows.  Otherwise,
        // apply the border with the left arrows.
        if ( e.getStateChange() == ItemEvent.SELECTED )
        {
            setBorder( mSelectedBorder );
        }
        else
        {
            setBorder( mUnselectedBorder );
        }

        // Repaint the component so the border change can
        // be seen.
        repaint();
    }
  }
}
```

JCheckBox's Public Methods

AccessibleContext getAccessibleContext()

Returns a subclass of AccessibleContext, which gives access to all of the JCheckBox's accessibility information.

String getUIClassID()

Returns the indentifying string that the look-and-feel uses to assign a UI class to the JCheckBox.

void updateUI()

Generally called by the current look-and-feel to suggest that the JCheckBox ask the UIManager for its UI class.

JCheckBoxMenuItem

A JCheckBoxMenuItem is, not surprisingly a check box that resides in a menu. It has two states: on and off, and when you click it, its state changes and an event is generated to announce the change.

Although this component is like a JCheckBox in operation, it is slightly different in appearance (at least for the "windows" look-and-feel). It looks like a standard menu item except that when the item is selected, a check mark appears to the component's left (see Figure 8-42). Also, even though a JCheckBoxMenuItem can have an icon, the state of the component is not reflected in the icon. For a normal check box with an icon, the icon looks one way when the component is selected and another way when it is not. For a JCheckBoxMenuItem, the icon is there for looks—the component's state is shown by the presence or absence of a check mark.

Ancestors

```
java.lang.Object
   |
   +—java.awt.Component
          |
          +—java.awt.Container
                 |
                 +—com.sun.java.swing.JComponent
                        |
                        +—com.sun.java.swing.AbstractButton
                               |
                               +—com.sun.java.swing.JMenuItem
                                      |
                                      +—com.sun.java.swing.JCheckBoxMenuItem
```

Figure 8-42
A menu with two JCheckBoxMenuItems.

NOTE: *For more information, see the "AbstractButton," "JCheckBox," and "ImageIcon" sections in this chapter, and the "Components That Can Be Turned On and Off" section in Chapter 7, "JFC by Concept."*

Steps in Creating and Using JCheckBoxMenuItem

1. Create a menu bar and a menu. A JCheckBoxMenuItem normally resides in a JMenu and a JMenu is usually attached to a menu bar, although there is no reason why a JCheckBoxMenuItem cannot be in a JPopupMenu.

   Create the menu bar:

   ```
   JMenuBar mbar = new JMenuBar();
   ```

   Add the menu bar to the current frame, internal frame, etc.:

   ```
   getRootPane().setMenuBar( mbar );
   ```

   Create a menu:

   ```
   JMenu options = new JMenu( "Options" );
   ```

   Add the menu to the menu bar:

   ```
   mbar.add( options );
   ```

2. Create a JCheckBoxMenuItem. There are six constructors, but they are all variations on:

   ```
   JCheckBoxMenuItem( String text, Icon icon, boolean selected )
   ```

   where *'text'* is the string that appears as part of the component, *'icon'* is the icon that appears with the text, and *'selected'* is the component's initial state. The default state is deselected.

   Create a JCheckBoxMenuItem with only a string:

   ```
   JCheckBoxMenuItem cbmi1 = new JCheckBoxMenuItem( "Disabled" );
   ```

   Create one with a string and an icon:

   ```
   JCheckBoxMenuItem cbmi2 = new JCheckBoxMenuItem( "Toolbar",
                               new ImageIcon( "print.gif" ) );
   ```

   Create one with a string, an icon, and an initial state of selected:

   ```
   JCheckBoxMenuItem cbmi3 = new JCheckBoxMenuItem( "Timed Save",
                               new ImageIcon( "save.gif" ), true );
   ```

   If you want to change the text, icon, or state after construction, use setText(), setIcon(), or setState().

3. Capture the JCheckBoxMenuItem's events that reflect changes in the component's state. These can either be ActionEvents or ItemEvents. It is slightly better to use ItemEvents since the new state is delivered with the event.

Specify which class will receive the JCheckBoxMenuItem's events. For this example, the class that contains the component will receive the events:

```
cbmi1.addItemListener( this );
```

Make the event-receiving class implement the ItemListener interface:

```
public class MyFrame extends JFrame implements ItemListener
{
    .
    .
    .
    public void itemStateChanged( ItemEvent e )
    {
        // The new state can be retrieved using the event's
        // getStateChange() method.
    }
}
```

4. A JCheckBoxMenuItem can change its appearance in much the same ways that a JCheckBox can.

Change the font. The effect of this depends on the current look-and-feel. In the "windows" look-and-feel, the component font is used for the JCheckBoxMenuItem's text, but this is not guaranteed to be the case:

```
cbmi1.setFont( new Font( "TimesRoman", Font.ITALIC, 16 ) );
```

Change the relative positioning of the text and the icon. These two lines of code will cause the text to appear above the icon:

```
cbmi2.setHorizontalTextPosition( SwingConstants.CENTER );
cbmi2.setVerticalTextPosition( SwingConstants.TOP );
```

Set the icon that replaces the normal icon when the component is disabled:

```
cbmi3.setDisabledIcon( new ImageIcon( "off.gif" ) );
```

Set the icon that replaces the normal icon when the component is pressed:

```
cbmi3.setPressedIcon( new ImageIcon( "off.gif" ) );
```

Change the text color. This works for the *Windows* look-and-feel, but may not work for others:

```
cbmi3.setForeground( Color.red );
```

Even set a tool tip:

```
cbmi3.setToolTipText( "Wow, this is a check box in a menu!" );
```

5. Set the JCheckBoxMenuItem's background color. By default, it takes the menu's background color.

```
cbmi3.setBackground( Color.green );
```

Basic Code Examples

EXAMPLE 8-37 Standard Uses for JCheckBoxMenuItem

The following example creates a menu bar with one menu. The menu contains three JCheckBoxMenuItems. The first one controls whether the other two are disabled, and all three illustrate the appearance changes discussed above. There is also a button in the frame's main panel which, when pressed, pops up the menu and automatically clicks the last item there. Figure 8-43 shows this example with the menu open and two items selected.

Here is the source code:

```
import com.sun.java.swing.*;
import com.sun.java.swing.border.*;
import java.awt.*;
import java.awt.event.*;

public class MyFrame extends JFrame implements
        ActionListener, ItemListener
{
    JCheckBoxMenuItem cbmi1;
    JCheckBoxMenuItem cbmi2;
    JCheckBoxMenuItem cbmi3;
    JMenu options;

    public MyFrame()
    {
        setTitle( "JCheckBoxMenuItem1" );

        // Store the content pane in a variable for easier
        // access.
        JPanel mPanel = (JPanel)getContentPane();
```

Figure 8-43

```
// Set the layout so we can place a button later.
mPanel.setLayout( new BoxLayout( mPanel,
                    BoxLayout.Y_AXIS ) );

// Force the button to keep from being overlain by
// the menu's popup so we can see it at all times.
mPanel.add( Box.createRigidArea(
            new Dimension( 50, 100 ) ) );

// Create a button that, when clicked will cause the
// menu's popup to appear and will auto-click one of
// the menu items.
JButton click = new JButton( "Click" );
click.addActionListener( this );
click.setActionCommand( "click" );
mPanel.add( click );

// Create the menu bar and add it to the frame.
JMenuBar mbar = new JMenuBar();
getRootPane().setMenuBar( mbar );

// Create a menu and add it to the menu bar.
options = new JMenu( "Options" );
mbar.add( options );

// Create a menu check box and change its font.  We
// will listen for its events so that when this menu
// check box's state changes the other items on the
// menu will be disabled.
cbmi1 = new JCheckBoxMenuItem( "Disabled" );
cbmi1.setBorder( new BevelBorder(
                    BevelBorder.LOWERED ) );
cbmi1.setFont( new Font( "TimesRoman",
                        Font.ITALIC, 16 ) );
cbmi1.addItemListener( this );

// Add the menu check box to the menu.
options.add( cbmi1 );

// Create another menu check box with text and an
// icon and cause the text to appear above the icon
// instead of to its right.
cbmi2 = new JCheckBoxMenuItem( "Toolbar",
                    new ImageIcon( "print.gif" ) );
cbmi2.setHorizontalTextPosition(
                    SwingConstants.CENTER );
cbmi2.setVerticalTextPosition( SwingConstants.TOP );

// Add the menu check box to the menu.
options.add( cbmi2 );

// Create a menu check box with text and an icon and
// give it an initial state of selected.  Also
```

```
    // specify the icons to use when the component
    // is disabled or pressed, change the text color,
    // and specify a tool tip.
    cbmi3 = new JCheckBoxMenuItem( "Timed Save",
                    new ImageIcon( "save.gif" ), true );
    cbmi3.setDisabledIcon( new ImageIcon( "off.gif" ) );
    cbmi3.setPressedIcon( new ImageIcon( "off.gif" ) );
    cbmi3.setToolTipText(
                "Wow, this is a check box in a menu!" );
    cbmi3.setBackground( Color.green );
    cbmi3.setForeground( Color.red );

    // Add the menu check box to the menu.
    options.add( cbmi3 );
}


// When the "Click" button is pressed, it causes the
// Options menu to pop-up and automates a click on the
// last item on the menu.
public void actionPerformed( ActionEvent e )
{
    if ( e.getActionCommand().equals( "click" ) )
    {
        options.setPopupMenuVisible( true );
        cbmi3.doClick();
    }
}


// If the "Disabled" check box on the "Options" menu
// changes, either enable or disable the other two menu
// items depending on how the state changed.
public void itemStateChanged( ItemEvent e )
{
    // See if this is the disabling check box.
    if ( e.getSource() == cbmi1 )
    {
        // The ItemEvent has the check box menu item's new
        // state, so use it to decide whether to disable
        // or enable the others.
        if ( e.getStateChange() == ItemEvent.SELECTED )
        {
            cbmi2.setEnabled( false );
            cbmi3.setEnabled( false );
        }
        else
        {
            cbmi2.setEnabled( true );
            cbmi3.setEnabled( true );
        }
    }
}
}
```

JCheckBoxMenuItem's Public Methods

`AccessibleContext getAccessibleContext()`

Returns a subclass of AccessibleContext that gives access to the JCheckBoxMenuItem's accessibility information.

`Object[] getSelectedObjects()`

Fills out the ItemSelectable interface—returns an array of length 1, with the JCheckBoxMenuItem in it or null, depending on whether the JCheckBoxMenuItem is selected.

`boolean getState()`

Returns true if the JCheckBoxMenuItem is currently selected.

`String getUIClassID()`

Returns the identifying string that the look-and-feel uses to assign a UI class to the JCheckBoxMenuItem.

`void requestFocus()`

Asks to have the JCheckBoxMenuItem become the component with the focus.

`void setState(boolean b)`

Specifies whether the JCheckBoxMenuItem is currently selected.

`void setUI(CheckBoxMenuItemUI ui)`

Specifies the look-and-feel class the JCheckBoxMenuItem should use.

`void updateUI()`

Generally called by the look-and-feel to tell the JCheckBoxMenuItem that the look-and-feel class has changed.

JColorChooser

JColorChooser is a control that you can display to give the user the chance to select a color (see Figure 8-44). It includes the capability to set hue, saturation, and brightness, but can be operated with the mouse. JColorChooser can be added to a container like any other JComponent but is more frequently dis-

Figure 8-44
A typical
JColorChooser.

Figure 8-44
A typical
JColorChooser.

played within a dialog. It has several methods for displaying itself within a dialog.

JColorChooser has an HSV tab that has six parts:

- A text field that displays the current hue, and in which the user can explicitly set the hue value.

- A text field that displays the current saturation, and in which the user can explicitly set the saturation value.

- A text field that displays the current brightness, and in which the user can explicitly set the brightness value.

- A ring of color that the user can click on to choose a hue. The user can drag the mouse around on this ring to get constantly changing hue values.

- A square within the hue ring that the user can click on to change the saturation and brightness. The user can drag the mouse around this area to get constantly changing saturation/brightness values.

- A rectangle that shows the current color. This changes when the hue, saturation, or brightness change.

- It also has an RGB tab that allows the user to explicitly set red, green, and blue values.

Ancestors

```
java.lang.Object
    |
    +—java.awt.Component
            |
            +—java.awt.Container
                    |
                    +—com.sun.java.swing.JComponent
                            |
                            +—com.sun.java.swing.preview.JColorChooser
```

NOTE: *For JFC 1-1, JColorChooser has been moved to the com.sun.java.swing,preview package. This means that it may have bugs and its API is likely to change in future versions.*

NOTE: *For more information, see the "JDialog" and "JInternalFrame" sections in this chapter, and the "Windows" section in Chapter 7, "JFC by Concept."*

Steps in Creating and Using JColorChooser

1. Create a JColorChooser. There are two constructors—one that creates a JColorChooser whose initial color is white, and another that creates a JColorChooser with the specified color.

   Create a default JColorChooser (initial color is white):

   ```
   JColorChooser myChooser = new JColorChooser();
   ```

   Create a JColorChooser whose initial color is blue:

   ```
   JColorChooser myChooser = new JColorChooser( Color.blue );
   ```

   If you are going to use JColorChooser's showDialog() method to display the color chooser, you do not need to create a JColorChooser of your own—it creates one for you.

2. There are three ways to display a JColorChooser. You can add it to a container just like any other JComponent. You can create a JColorChooser dialog and listen for the buttons to be pressed. Or, you can create a dialog and wait for its return value.

   Create an internal frame, and put the color chooser into it:

   ```
   JInternalFrame intFrame = new JInternalFrame( "Choose a Color" );
   intFrame.getContentPane().add( "Center", myChooser );
   ```

   Create a dialog and listen for its buttons to be pressed:

   ```
   JDialog dialog = JColorChooser.createDialog( parent, "Choose a
                   Color", true, myChooser, okListener,
                   cancelListener );
   ```

   Notice that createDialog() is a static method. *'parent'* is the dialog's parent frame. *'okListener'* is the class that should be notified when the dialog's OK button is pressed. *'cancelListener'* is the class that should be notified when the dialog's Cancel button is pressed. The dialog also has a Reset button, but there is no ActionEvent associated with that.

The *true* means the dialog is modal so none of the application's other windows may be accessed until the dialog has been closed. '*myChooser*' is a precreated JColorChooser.

Create a dialog and wait for it to return:

```
Color newColor = JColorChooser.showDialog( parent, "Choose a
                                    Color", Color.blue );
```

Again, this is a static method. *parent* is the parent frame, and you also specify a title for the dialog and an initial color for the dialog's color chooser. Using showDialog() differs from createDialog() in that it doesn't accept a JColorChooser (it creates its own), and you get the user-selected color by waiting for showDialog() to return it to you. It returns null if the dialog's Cancel button is pressed.

3. Get the color chooser's current color:

Get the color as a java.awt.Color:

```
Color newColor = myChooser.getColor();
```

4. Set the color chooser's color. You can set the color as a java.awt.Color, as an integer, or as an RGB triplet:

Set the color with a java.awt.Color:

```
myChooser.setColor( Color.red );
```

Set the color with an integer:

```
myChooser.setColor( 65535 );
```

Set the Color with an RGB triplet:

```
myChooser.setColor( 0, 255, 0 );
```

5. When you use JColorChooser.createDialog(), you need a class to listen for when the dialog buttons' are pressed. You can tell which button was pressed because the resulting event's action command string is *OK* for the dialog's OK button or '*cancel*' for the dialog's Cancel button. So, you would make a class implement the ActionListener interface:

```
public class MyClass implements ActionListener
{
   .
   .
   .
   public void actionPerformed( ActionEvent e )
   {
      if ( e.getActionCommand().equals( "OK" ) )
      {
         // The dialog's "Ok" button was pressed, so get its
         // color chooser's current color and apply it to
```

```
            // something.
        }
        else if ( e.getActionCommand().equals( "cancel" ) )
        {
            // The dialog's "Cancel" button was pressed.
        }
    }
}
```

This is the class that should be passed as '*okListener*' and '*cancelListener*' to the createDialog() method.

6. If you are placing the JColorChooser as a standard component (not using the createDialog() or showDialog() methods), you may want to know whenever its color changes. To do this, you will want to listen for the color chooser's *color* property to change. To do this, you make a class that implements the PropertyChangeListener interface. Then you tell the color chooser that your PropertyChangeListener class should be notified when the color chooser's properties change. In this case, the listener will be the class MyFrame in which the color chooser is defined:

```
public class MyFrame extends JFrame implements
    PropertyChangeListener
{
    public MyFrame()
    {
        .
        .
        .
        // Create the color chooser and specify the class that
        // should be notified when the chooser's color changes.
        JColorChooser myChooser = new JColorChooser();
        myChooser.addPropertyChangeListener( this );
        .
        .
        .
    }
    .
    .
    .
    // This method is called when the color chooser's properties
    // change.
    public void propertyChange( PropertyChangeEvent e )
    {
        // See if the changed property is the "color" property.
        if ( e.getPropertyName().equals( "color" ) )
        {
            // The chooser's color has changed, so now you can get
            // it apply it to something.
        }
    }
}
```

Basic Code Examples

EXAMPLE 8-38 Different Ways to use JColorChooser

This example illustrates the different ways you can create and display a color chooser, and how to get the results when the color is changed. It starts out showing a JColorChooser in an internal frame. It also has two buttons that show the two ways to display a JColorChooser in a dialog. Whenever the color changes in the internal frame's chooser, or when the dialogs' OK buttons are pressed, the new color is applied to the background of the main frame's content pane and to the main desktop pane. Figure 8-45 shows the example as it starts out, with just one JColorChooser in its internal frame.

Here is the source:

```
import com.sun.java.swing.*;
import com.sun.java.swing.preview.*;
import java.awt.*;
import java.awt.event.*;
import java.beans.*;

public class MyFrame extends JFrame implements ActionListener,
        PropertyChangeListener
{
    private JColorChooser mChooser;
    private JColorChooser mIntFrameChooser;
    private JDesktopPane mDesktop;

    public MyFrame()
    {
        setTitle( "JColorChooser1" );

        // Store the content pane in a variable for easier
        // access.
        JPanel contentPane = (JPanel)getContentPane();

        // Components will all be added to this panel.
        contentPane.setLayout( new BorderLayout() );

        // Create a desktop pane into which we can put an
```

Figure 8-45

```
// internale frame, and make it cover the content
// pane's main area.
mDesktop = new JDesktopPane();
mDesktop.setBackground( contentPane.getBackground() );
contentPane.add( "Center", mDesktop );

// Create en internal frame that will have a color
// chooser in it.
JInternalFrame intFrame = new JInternalFrame(
                              "Choose a Color",
                              true, true );

// Locate and size the internal frame relative to the
// desktop pane.
intFrame.setBounds( 5, 5, 250, 250 );

// Create the internal frame's color chooser and give
// it the content pane's background color as its
// initial color.
mIntFrameChooser = new JColorChooser(
                mDesktop.getBackground() );

// We need to know when the color chooser's color is
// changed by the user.  A PropertyChangeEvent is
// generated when that happens, so we will catch that.
mIntFrameChooser.addPropertyChangeListener( this );

// Make the color chooser take up the internal
// frame's main area.
intFrame.getContentPane().add( "Center",
                               mIntFrameChooser );

// Add the internal frame to the desktop pane.
mDesktop.add( intFrame );

// Create a container for the buttons.  Use horizontal
// glue components to space the buttons evenly.
Box btnBox = Box.createHorizontalBox();

btnBox.add( Box.createHorizontalGlue() );

// Create a button to spawn a color chooser dialog
// using the createDialog() method.  Make MyFrame
// listen for when the button is pressed.
JButton useCreateDialog =
            new JButton( "Use createDialog" );
useCreateDialog.addActionListener( this );
useCreateDialog.setActionCommand(
                        "Use createDialog" );

// Add the button to our button pane.
btnBox.add( useCreateDialog );
```

```
            btnBox.add( Box.createHorizontalGlue() );

            // Create a button to spawn a color chooser dialog
            // using the showDialog() method.  Make MyFrame
            // listen for when the button is pressed.
            JButton useShowDialog =
                            new JButton( "Use showDialog" );
            useShowDialog.addActionListener( this );
            useShowDialog.setActionCommand( "Use showDialog" );

            // Add the button to the button pane.
            btnBox.add( useShowDialog );

            btnBox.add( Box.createHorizontalGlue() );

            // Cause the pane containing  the buttons to display
            // across the bottom of the content pane.
            contentPane.add( "South", btnBox );
        }


    // This method will be called when either of the main
    // frame's buttons is pressed, or when the "Ok" or
    // "Cancel" buttons in the dialog created with the
    // createDialog() method are pressed.
    public void actionPerformed( ActionEvent e )
    {
        // We use the action command string to figure out
        // which button caused the action event.
        String command = e.getActionCommand();

        if ( command.equals( "Use createDialog" ) )
        {
            // Create the color chooser that the dialog will
            // use.  We get the initial color from the content
            // pane's background color since that is what the
            // new color will be applied to.
            mChooser = new JColorChooser(
                        getContentPane().getBackground() );

            // Use JColorChooser's createDialog() method to
            // make a dialog containing the just-created color
            // chooser.
            JDialog dlg = JColorChooser.createDialog( this,
                        "Color Chooser in Dialog", true,
                        mChooser, this, this );

            // Make the dialog visible.
            dlg.show();
        }
        else if ( command.equals( "Use showDialog" ) )
        {
            // Create and show a color chooser dialog using
            // JColorChooser's showDialog() method.  The
```

```
                     // initial color is the content pane's initial
                     // color.  When the dialog is closed, the result
                     // is returned.
                     Color newColor = JColorChooser.showDialog( this,
                                   "Using showDialog",
                                   getContentPane().getBackground() );

                     // Apply the new color as the content pane's
                     // background.
                     getContentPane().setBackground( newColor );
                     mDesktop.setBackground( newColor );

                     // Make the content pane reflect its new color.
                     getContentPane().repaint();
                  }
                  else if ( command.equals( "OK" ) )
                  {
                     // This section of code runs when the dialog
                     // created with createDialog() has its "Ok" button
                     // pressed.

                     // Get the new color from the dialog's color
                     // chooser.
                     Color newColor = mChooser.getColor();

                     // Apply the new color as the content pane's
                     // background color.
                     getContentPane().setBackground( newColor );
                     mDesktop.setBackground( newColor );

                     // Make the content pane reflect the change.
                     getContentPane().repaint();
                  }
               }

               // This method is called when the internal frame's color
               // chooser's color is changed.
               public void propertyChange( PropertyChangeEvent e )
               {
                  if ( e.getPropertyName().equals( "color" ) )
                  {
                     // Get the new color from the property change
                     // event.
                     Color newColor = (Color)e.getNewValue();

                     // Apply the new color to the content pane.
                     getContentPane().setBackground( newColor );
                     mDesktop.setBackground( newColor );

                     // Make the content pane reflect the change.
                     getContentPane().repaint();
                  }
               }
            }
         }
```

JColorChooser's Public Methods

```
void addChooserPanel(String name, ColorChooserPanel panel)
```

Associates the given panel with the given name and adds it to the JColorChooser.

```
JDialog createDialog(Component c,String title,boolean
       modal,JColorChooser chooserPane,ActionListener
       okListener,ActionListener cancelListener)
```

Creates a JDialog that contains a JColorChooser, an OK button, a Cancel button, and a Reset button. You are responsible for showing the JDialog. You specify which classes should be notified when the JDialog's OK and Cancel buttons are pressed.

```
Color getColor()
```

Returns the color that the JColorChooser is currently showing as a Color.

```
ColorChooserUI getUI()
```

Returns the UI class being used with the JColorChooser.

```
String getUIClassID()
```

Returns the String that the current look-and-feel uses to find the look-and-feel class for the JColorChooser.

```
ColorChooserPanel removeChooserPanel(String name)
```

Removes the ColorChooserPanel associated with the given name.

```
void setColor(Color c)
```

Tells the JColorChooser to display the given `color`.

```
void setColor(int c)
```

Tells the JColorChooser to display the given integer combined color.

```
void setColor(int r,int g,int b)
```

Tells the JColorChooser to display the given RGB color.

```
void setUI(ColorChooserUI ui )
```

Specifies the UI class to use with the JColorChooser.

```
Color showDialog(Component component,String title,Color initialColor)
```

Creates a JDialog with the given initial color. This method will not return until the user gets rid of the dialog. The user's selected color is the return value.

```
void updateUI()
```

Suggests that the JColorChooser check with the UIManager for a new UI class.

JComboBox

A JComboBox is a control that offers the capability to choose an item from a list or to enter a value of your own (see Figure 8-46). Aside from being able to enter your own value, the main benefits of using a combo box over a set of radio buttons are that it is more compact and it is easier to change the items that can be selected.

A JComboBox typically consists of several parts:

- A text field containing the current value. This may or may not be editable. If it is editable, the user can enter values not in the JComboBox's list. You can replace this part with your own component if you need custom functionality.

- A popup window that displays the available choices. If the user clicks on one of these items, it becomes the new current selection. When a selection has been made, the popup window disappears. You can specify a custom component to be used for displaying these items if you need special behavior.

- An arrow button to the right of the text field. This, when pressed, causes the popup window to appear.

When a JComboBox's selection is changed, it generates an ItemEvent which your application can catch if it needs to.

Ancestors

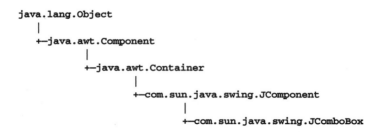

```
java.lang.Object
    |
    +-java.awt.Component
            |
            +-java.awt.Container
                    |
                    +-com.sun.java.swing.JComponent
                            |
                            +-com.sun.java.swing.JComboBox
```

Figure 8-46
A typical JComboBox.

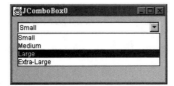

NOTE: *For more information, see the "Selecting Items from Lists" section in Chapter 7, "JFC by Concept."*

Steps in Creating and Using a JComboBox

1. Create the combo box. There is an alternate constructor that accepts a ComboBoxModel, but since JComboBox has most of the methods you need for building and maintaining the list, you will normally use the empty constructor or one of the constructors that allow you to load items. Create an empty JComboBox:

```
JComboBox combo = new JComboBox();
```

2. Add items to the list in the order they should appear in the list:

```
combo.addItem( "First item" );
combo.addItem( "Second item" );
```

Once you add the combo box to a container, it is completely ready to display.

3. Define which class will accept events that tell when the value has changed, and make sure that class (MyFrame in this case) implements ItemListener:

Tell the combo box which class should be notified when the selection changes. In this case, it is the class that contains the combo box.

```
combo.addItemListener( this );
```

Make the class that will receive the events (MyFrame) implement the interface:

```
public class MyFrame extends JFrame implements ItemListener
{
   .
   .
   .
   public void itemStateChanged( ItemEvent e )
   {
      // Notice the use of ItemEvent's getStateChange() method
      // to get the new state.
      if ( e.getStateChange() == ItemEvent.SELECTED )
```

```
                System.out.println( (String)(e.getItem()) +
                                        " was selected" );
            else
              System.out.println( (String)(e.getItem()) +
                                            " was de-selected" );
      }
    }
```

4. Make the current value editable (optional). By default, the current value can only be changed by selecting an item from the list. You can make it so that the item can be selected from the list OR can be typed in by the user.

```
combo.setEditable( true );
```

Note that when a JComboBox is not editable, when it has the focus you can type a letter and the next item that starts with that letter will be automatically selected. This will not work when the combo box is editable.

5. Create a cell renderer to customize the way items in the list appear (optional). This is the same as with a ListBox, in fact it uses a ListCellRenderer.

Tell the combo box what renderer to use:

```
combo.setRenderer( new MyCellRenderer() );
```

Create the class that implements ListCellRenderer. Note that our renderer extends JLabel—it will be drawn to look like a JLabel, and the JLabel functions setText() and setIcon() are called to customize the look:

```
class MyCellRenderer extends JLabel implements
  ListCellRenderer
{
    ImageIcon mSelected;
    ImageIcon mNotSelected;
    JComboBox mMyMaster;

    MyCellRenderer()
    {
       // Load the icons that will be displayed with the list
       // strings.
       mSelected = new ImageIcon( "on.gif" );
       mNotSelected = new ImageIcon( "off.gif" );
    }

    // Required for classes that implement ListCellRenderer.
    // This method configures this class so it will display
    // properly.
    public Component getListCellRendererComponent( JList list,
                                        Object value,
                                        int index,
                                        boolean isSelected,
```

```
                                              boolean cellHasFocus )
    {
        // If an item is selected use one icon, otherwise use
        // the other.
        if ( isSelected )
            setIcon( mSelected );
        else
            setIcon( mNotSelected );

        // Set the renderer's text so it will draw.
        setText( (String)value );

        return this;
    }
}
```

Basic Code Examples

EXAMPLE 8-39 A Simple JComboBox

This example shows how to use a simple, non-editable combo box to choose from a list of strings. It prints a string when the combo box's selection state changes (when an item is selected or deselected). Notice that the ItemEvents come in pairs—the previously selected item gets deselected, then the new item gets selected. Figure 8-47 shows the example with the list expanded.

Here is the source code:

```
import com.sun.java.swing.*;
import com.sun.java.swing.border.*;
import java.awt.*;
import java.awt.event.*;

public class MyFrame extends JFrame implements ItemListener
{
    public MyFrame()
    {
        setTitle( "JComboBox1" );

        // Store the content pane in a variable for easier
        // access.
        JPanel contentPane = (JPanel)getContentPane();

        // The combo box will be added to this panel.
        contentPane.setLayout( new BorderLayout() );
```

Figure 8-47

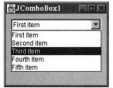

```
            // Give the content pane a border so the combo box is
            // away from the edge of the frame.
            contentPane.setBorder(
                        new EmptyBorder( 10, 10, 10, 10 ) );

            // Create the combo box — not editable.
            JComboBox combo = new JComboBox();

            // Add items to the combo box.
            combo.addItem( "First item" );
            combo.addItem( "Second item" );
            combo.addItem( "Third item" );
            combo.addItem( "Fourth item" );
            combo.addItem( "Fifth item" );

            // Make it so this class is notified when the combo
            // box's selection changes.
            combo.addItemListener( this );

            // Add the combo box to the content pane.
            contentPane.add( "North", combo );
        }

    // This method is called when the combo box's selection
    // is changed.  It looks at the affected item and its
    // new state and prints out a string describing the
    // change.
    public void itemStateChanged( ItemEvent e )
    {
        // Notice the use of ItemEvent's getStateChange()
        // method to get the new state.
        if ( e.getStateChange() == ItemEvent.SELECTED )
            System.out.println( (String)(e.getItem()) +
                                " was selected" );
        else
            System.out.println( (String)(e.getItem()) +
                                " was de-selected" );
    }
}
```

Advanced Issues

EXAMPLE 8-40 Using a Custom Editor in a JComboBox

This example shows how to create a custom ComboBoxEditor that only accepts digits. The ComboBoxEditor is in a class called MyEditor which is a subclass of JTextField. This is about the easiest ComboBoxEditor you can write because JTextField already implements half of the ComboBoxEditor interface. It has the following methods that are part of the interface: addActionListener(), removeActionListener(), and selectAll(). So, we just have to implement: getItem(), setItem(), and getEditorComponent(). Figure

Figure 8-48

8-48 shows the example after the user has typed in "36" and dropped down the combo box's list.

Important points to notice:

- MyEditor overrides the processKeyEvent() method to screen characters before they are displayed. It looks at each character and only passes through the digits, the Enter key, and some editing keys.
- The main frame class listens for ItemEvents from the combo box and prints out items as they are selected.

Here is the source code for MyFrame.java (followed by the source for MyEditor.java):

```java
import com.sun.java.swing.*;
import java.awt.*;
import java.awt.event.*;

public class MyFrame extends JFrame implements ItemListener
{
    JComboBox mCombo;

    public MyFrame()
    {
        setTitle( "JComboBox2" );

        // Store the content pane in a variable for easier
        // access.
        JPanel contentPane = (JPanel)getContentPane();

        // Components will all be added to this panel.
        contentPane.setLayout( new BorderLayout() );

        // Create the combo box.
        mCombo = new JComboBox();

        // Load some items into the combo box.
        mCombo.addItem( "8" );
        mCombo.addItem( "9" );
        mCombo.addItem( "10" );
        mCombo.addItem( "12" );
        mCombo.addItem( "14" );
```

```
        mCombo.addItem( "16" );
        mCombo.addItem( "18" );
        mCombo.addItem( "20" );

        // Make it so the user can type in his/her own stuff.
        mCombo.setEditable( true );

        // Create an instance of the custom editor, and tell
        // the combo box to use it.
        mCombo.setEditor( new MyEditor() );

        // Add it to the container.
        contentPane.add( "North", mCombo );

        // Listen for changes in the combo box.
        mCombo.addItemListener( this );
    }

    // Respond to change events from the combo box.  In this
    // case, just print out when items are selected.
    public void itemStateChanged( ItemEvent e )
    {
        if ( e.getStateChange() == ItemEvent.SELECTED )
        {
            System.out.println( "+++"+
                                    mCombo.getSelectedItem() );
        }
    }
}
```

Here is the source code for MyEditor.java:

```
import com.sun.java.swing.*;
import com.sun.java.swing.event.*;
import java.awt.*;
import java.awt.event.*;

public class MyEditor extends JTextField implements
        ComboBoxEditor
{
    // Return the component that is being used as an editor.
    public Component getEditorComponent()
    {
        return this;
    }

    // Return the contents of the editor.
    public Object getItem()
    {
        return getText();
    }

    // Load the object into the editor.
    public void setItem( Object obj )
    {
```

```
            setText( obj.toString() );
    }

    // Intercept key events and only pass through the ones
    // we want.
    protected void processKeyEvent( KeyEvent e )
    {
        // We only pay attention to digits and <Enter> and
        // only when they have no modifiers.  We also accept
        // delete and backspace.
        if ( e.getModifiers() == 0 )
        {
            int keyChar = e.getKeyChar();
            int keyCode = e.getKeyCode();

            // Check to see if the key stroke is a digit or
            // <Enter>.
            if ( keyChar >= '0' && keyChar <= '9' ||
                 keyChar == '\n' ||
                 keyCode == KeyEvent.VK_BACK_SPACE ||
                 keyCode == KeyEvent.VK_DELETE )
            {
                // If it is a digit or <Enter>, process it as
                // usual.
                super.processKeyEvent( e );
            }
        }
    }
}
```

JComboBox's Public Methods

void actionPerformed(ActionEvent e)

Don't worry about this method, JComboBox has to receive ActionEvents, so this has to be public.

void addActionListener(ActionListener l)

Tells the JComboBox to notify the given class when ActionEvents occur.

void addItem(Object anObject)

Adds the given item to the end of the list.

void addItemListener(ItemListener aListener)

Tells the JComboBox to notify the given class when the JComboBox's selection changes.

`void configureEditor(ComboBoxEditor anEditor,Object anItem)`

Loads the given object into the editor.

`void contentsChanged(ListDataEvent e)`

Ignore this method.

`AccessibleContext getAccessibleContext()`

Returns a subclass of AccessibleContext that gives access to the JComboBox's accessibility information.

`String getActionCommand()`

Returns the String to be delivered with the JComboBox's ActionEvents.

`ComboBoxEditor getEditor()`

Returns the ComboBoxEditor that is being used to allow the user to enter new items and modify the state of existing ones.

`Object getItemAt(int index)`

Returns the list item at the given index.

`int getItemCount()`

Returns the number of items in the list.

`JComboBox.KeySelectionManager getKeySelectionManager()`

Returns the key selection manager for the list. The return value is an instance of KeySelectionManager which is an inner class of JComboBox.

`int getMaximumRowCount()`

Returns the number of items that the JComboBox can display before it adds a scrollbar.

`ComboBoxModel getModel()`

Returns the JComboBox's data model.

`ListCellRenderer getRenderer()`

Returns the ListCellRenderer being used to draw items in the list.

`int getSelectedIndex()`

Returns the index of the currently selected item (if any).

```
Object getSelectedItem()
```

Returns the currently selected item (if any).

```
Object[] getSelectedObjects()
```

Returns the currently selected item in an array. Required for the ItemSelectable interface.

```
ComboBoxUI getUI()
```

Returns the look-and-feel class that the JComboBox is currently using.

```
String getUIClassID()
```

Returns the string that identifies the look-and-feel class that the JComboBox is currently using.

```
void hidePopup()
```

Makes the list collapse if it is currently expanded.

```
void insertItemAt(Object anObject,int index)
```

Inserts the given Object into the list at the given index.

```
void intervalAdded(ListDataEvent e)
```

Tells the JComboBox that items have been added to the list.

```
void intervalRemoved(ListDataEvent e)
```

Tells the JComboBox that items have been removed from the list.

```
boolean isEditable()
```

Specifies whether the user can enter his/her own values into the JComboBox.

```
boolean isFocusTraversable()
```

Overridden so it returns false.

```
boolean isLightWeightPopupEnabled()
```

Returns false if the JComboBox's drop-down list is always a peered component.

```
boolean isOpaque()
```

Overridden to return true.

```
void processKeyEvent(KeyEvent e)
```

Overridden for special processing of KeyEvents.

```
void removeActionListener(ActionListener l)
```

Tells the JComboBox to stop notifying the given class when ActionEvents occur.

```
void removeAllItems()
```

Removes all items from the list.

```
void removeItem(Object anObject)
```

Removes the first occurrence of the given Object from the list.

```
void removeItemAt(int anIndex)
```

Removes the list item at the given index.

```
void removeItemListener(ItemListener aListener)
```

Tells the JComboBox to stop notifying the given class when the JComboBox's selection state changes.

```
boolean selectWithKeyChar(char keyChar)
```

Returns true if the JComboBox will iterate through a non-editable list everytime you press a character key that is the same as the first letter of a list item.

```
void setActionCommand(String cmd)
```

Specifies the String that the JComboBox should deliver with its ActionEvents.

```
void setEditable(boolean aFlag)
```

Specifies whether the user can enter his/her own values.

```
void setEditor(ComboBoxEditor anEditor)
```

Specifies the ComboBoxEditor that will be used to allow the user to enter his/her own values.

```
void setEnabled(boolean b)
```

Specifies whether the JComboBox is enabled or disabled.

```
void setKeySelectionManager(JComboBox.KeySelectionManager aManager)
```

Sets the class that is used to convert a keystroke into a selection in the list. By default, this works when the combo box is not editable and the user presses a key. In that case, the next item in the list that starts with the entered character will become selected. The argument type is an inner class within JComboBox.

```
void setLightWeightPopupEnabled(boolean enabled)
```

If true, the JComboBox's drop-down list will be a Swing component if it will fit in the parent window.

```
void setMaximumRowCount(int count)
```

Sets the maximum number of rows the JComboBox can display before adding a scrollbar.

```
void setModel(ComboBoxModel aModel)
```

Specifies the data model that the JComboBox should use.

```
void setRenderer(ListCellRenderer aRenderer)
```

Specifies the ListCellRenderer that the JComboBox should use to draw its list items.

```
void setSelectedIndex(int anIndex)
```

Specifies that the list item at the given index should become the selected item.

```
void setSelectedItem(Object anObject)
```

Specifies that the first occurrence of the given item in the list should become the selected item.

```
void setUI(ComboBoxUI ui)
```

Tells the JComboBox what its new look-and-feel class is.

```
void showPopup()
```

Causes the list to be expanded just as if the user had pressed the arrow button.

```
void updateUI()
```

Tells the JComboBox that the look-and-feel class has changed.

JComponent

NOTE: *For a complete discussion of "JComponent," see Chapter 3, "The JComponent Class."*

JDesktopPane

A JDesktopPane is used to manage a set of JInternalFrames (see Figure 8-49). Like a workstation desktop, it manages how its child windows act when they are resized, minimized, etc. As a descendant of JLayeredPane, JDesktopPane also keeps track of which windows go on top of other windows. Since it uses a layout manager designed for managing its JInternalFrames, it is not much good for adding buttons to.

Ancestors

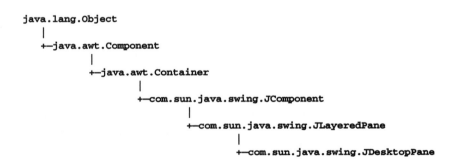

```
java.lang.Object
   |
   +—java.awt.Component
          |
          +—java.awt.Container
                 |
                 +—com.sun.java.swing.JComponent
                        |
                        +—com.sun.java.swing.JLayeredPane
                               |
                               +—com.sun.java.swing.JDesktopPane
```

Figure 8-49
A frame with a
JDesktopPane that
contains three
JInternalFrames. One
is minimized.

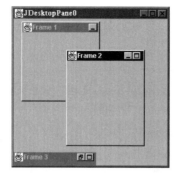

NOTE: *For more information, see the "JInternalFrame," "JLayeredPane," and "JRootPane" sections in this chapter. Also see the "Windows" section in Chapter 7, "JFC by Concept."*

NOTE: *If the JDesktopPane is not double-buffered, it will flash when its internal frames are moved around. Double-buffering will normally be handled automatically because the JDesktopPane is a child of a frame's default content pane (see example) which uses double-buffering by default. If the content pane is replaced by a pane that does not do double buffering, you set double-buffering on with the setDoubleBuffered() method that JDesktopPane inherits from JComponent.*

Steps in Creating and Using JDesktopPane

1. Create a JDesktopPane. There is only one constructor:

   ```
   JDesktopPane desktop = new JDesktopPane();
   ```

2. Create a JInternalFrame. Any JInternalFrame is supported.

   ```
   JInternalFrame frame1 = new JInternalFrame( "Frame 1", true,
                                    true, true, true );
   ```

3. Specify where the internal frame will appear within the JDesktopPane and how big it will initially be:

   ```
   frame1.setBounds( 100, 100, 200, 150 );
   ```

4. Set the internal frame's layer. This defines how the internal frame will display when overlapping another one. An internal frame with a higher layer will display on top of one with a lower layer. If two

overlapping internal frames have the same layer, the one that was last active will be on top (the active internal frame is always on top of others in the same layer).

```
frame1.setLayer( new Integer( 10 ) );
```

Or, you can do this using a method JDesktopPane inherits from JLayeredPane:

```
desktop.setLayer( frame1, 10 );
```

Notice that the JInternalFrame method requires an Integer while the JDesktopPane method takes a component and an int.

There is a series of predefined layers that you can use with their layer values in parentheses:

```
FRAME_CONTENT_LAYER (-30000)
DEFAULT_LAYER (0)
PALETTE_LAYER (100)
MODAL_LAYER (200)
POPUP_LAYER (300)
DRAG_LAYER (400)
```

5. Add the internal frame to the desktop pane:

```
desk.add( frame1 );
```

Basic Code Examples

EXAMPLE 8-41 Basic JDesktopPane

The following example creates a desktop pane, adds it to a frame, and displays two internal frames in it. The internal frames have different layers. Figure 8-50 shows the example after the internal frame with the lower layer number has been selected.

Here is the source code:

```
import com.sun.java.swing.*;
import java.awt.*;
```

Figure 8-50

```java
import java.util.*;

public class MyFrame extends JFrame
{
    public MyFrame()
    {
        setTitle( "JDesktopPane1" );

        // Store the content pane in a variable for easier
        // access.

        JPanel contentPane = (JPanel)getContentPane();

        // The desktop pane will overlay this panel.

        contentPane.setLayout( new BorderLayout() );

        // Create the desktop pane.

        JDesktopPane desk = new JDesktopPane();
        desk.setBackground( contentPane.getBackground() );

        // Overlay the content pane with the desktop pane.

        contentPane.add( "Center", desk );

        // Create and internal frame for the desktop pane to
        // manage.  This internal frame has its layer set to
        // 10, so it will always be on top of other children
        // of the JDesktopPane that have lower layers.

        JInternalFrame frame1 = new JInternalFrame(
                                "Frame 1", true, true,
                                 true, true );
        frame1.setBounds( 50, 50, 200, 120 );
        frame1.setIconifiable( true );
        frame1.setLayer( new Integer( 10 ) );
        desk.add( frame1 );

        // Create another internal frame that has layer set
        // to 5.  This means it will always be under the
        // other internal frame where they overlap.

        JInternalFrame frame2 =
                new JInternalFrame( "Frame 2", true, true,
                                     true, true );
        frame2.setFrameIcon( new ImageIcon( "open.gif" ) );
        frame2.setBounds( 30, 30, 200, 120 );
        frame2.setIconifiable( true );
        frame2.setLayer( new Integer( 5 ) );
        desk.add( frame2 );
    }
}
```

JDesktopPane's Public Methods

`AccessibleContext getAccessibleContext()`

Returns a subclass of AccessibleContext. This gives access to all of the JDesktopPanel's accessibility information.

`JInternalFrame[] getAllFrames()`

Returns all JInternalFrames that are in the JDesktopPane.

`JInternalFrame[] getAllFramesInLayer(int layer)`

Returns all of the JDesktopPane's JInternalFrames that are at the given layer.

`DesktopManager getDesktopManager()`

Returns the class that implements the DesktopManager interface and is responsible for the look-and-feel specific management of the JDesktopPane's JInternalFrames.

`DesktopPaneUI getUI()`

Returns the JDesktopPane's current look-and-feel class.

`String getUIClassID()`

Returns the string that identifies the JDesktopPane's current look-and-feel class.

`boolean isOpaque()`

Returns true since the JDesktopPane draws its background rectangle.

`void setDesktopManager(DesktopManager d)`

Specifies a class that implements the DesktopManager interface and which will be used to take care of the look-and-feel specific management of the JDesktopPane's JInternalFrames.

`void setUI(DesktopPaneUI ui)`

Specifies the JDesktopPane's look-and-feel class.

`void updateUI()`

Tells the JDesktopPane that its look-and-feel class has been changed.

JDialog

A dialog is a window that is used to get user input about a specific thing (see Figure 8-51). This includes:

- Simple windows that inform the user of an error and require the user to respond before the application can continue.
- Floating tool palettes that the user clicks on to specify some kind of tool (paint brush, etc.).
- More complicated windows that gather all information about a specific topic (like all personnel information about an employee) and allow the user to simply view it or to change some or all of the displayed information.

A dialog is associated with a frame, but floats independently of it. A dialog can require the user to close it before continuing with the application (modal), or it can stay visible, allowing the user to work in the application's other windows (nonmodal). Modal dialogs are used when a piece of information or recognition of some event is needed before the application can successfully go on. The appearance of the dialog's border and title bar are defined by the operating system.

Ancestors

```
java.lang.Object
    |
    +—java.awt.Component
            |
            +—java.awt.Container
                    |
                    +—java.awt.Window
                            |
                            +—java.awt.Dialog
                                    |
                                    +—com.sun.java.swing.JDialog
```

NOTE: *For more information, see the "JRootPane," "JOptionPane," "JFileChooser," and "JColorChooser" sections in this chapter. Also see the "Windows" section in Chapter 7, "JFC by Concept."*

Figure 8-51
A typical JDialog.

Steps in Creating and Using JDialog

1. Create a dialog. There are five constructors, but they are all variations on:

   ```
   JDialog( JFrame parent, String title, boolean modal )
   ```

   where 'parent' is the dialog's parent frame, 'title' is the string that will appear in the dialog's title bar, and 'modal' tells whether the calling class will wait until the dialog is gone (hidden or destroyed) before allowing the user to work in the application's other windows. By default, the title is an empty string, and dialogs are nonmodal.

   Create a nonmodal dialog with title set to "Dialog Title." In this case the dialog is to be associated with its parent frame, so 'this' is passed in.

   ```
   JDialog myDialog;
   myDialog = new JDialog( this, "Dialog Title" );
   ```

2. Place and size the dialog. The origin given to setBounds() is relative to the display, not to the parent frame:

   ```
   myDialog.setBounds( 100, 100, 300, 200 );
   ```

3. Set the dialog's layout manager. Note that as with JInternalFrame, JWindow, and JFrame, we want to use the content pane to hold components:

   ```
   myDialog.getContentPane().setLayout( new BorderLayout() );
   ```

4. Add a button. In a real case you will probably subclass JDialog and do all of your component creation and layout within that class.

   ```
   JButton destroy = new JButton( "Destroy" );
   myDialog.getContentPane().add( "South", destroy );
   ```

5. Cause a class to recognize and process button events from the button created above. In this case we make the "Destroy" button generate a command string when it is pressed. When the command string is received, we destroy the dialog. Notice that the dispose() method is called to destroy the JDialog.

   Specify the button's command string:

   ```
   destroy.setActionCommand( "Destroy me" );
   ```

   Tell the button which class should be notified when it is pressed. In this example the receiving class will be the dialog's parent frame (MyFrame):

   ```
   destroy.addActionListener( this );
   ```

Make the receiving class able to receive action events:

```
public class MyFrame extends JFrame implements ActionListener
{
    .
    .
    .
    public void actionPerformed( ActionEvent e )
    {
        if ( e.getActionCommand().equals( "Destroy me" ) )
        {
            // Destroy the dialog.
            myDialog.dispose();
        }
    }
}
```

6. If we just wanted the button to cause the dialog to disappear rather than be destroyed, we would call setVisible() instead of dispose:

```
myDialog.setVisible( false );
```

When you want the dialog to reappear:

```
myDialog.setVisible( true );
```

Or:

```
myDialog.show();
```

7. Show the dialog initially. As discussed above, you can use either show() or setVisible(true) to make a dialog appear. However, the dialog cannot appear before its parent frame has been created, so you cannot call JDialog.show() or JDialog.setVisible() before the parent frame's show() or setVisible(true) method has been called. To make a dialog appear as soon as the parent frame appears, implement a WindowListener so we know when the window becomes visible. Note that a dialog automatically disappears when its parent frame is iconified, then reappears when the parent frame is restored.

Specify a class that will receive the parent frame's window events. In this case, the parent frame will receive its own events:

```
this.addWindowListener( this );
```

Make the receiving class able to receive window events by implementing the WindowListener interface:

```
public class MyFrame extends JFrame implements WindowListener
{
    .
    .
    .
```

```
                    public void windowActivated( WindowEvent e )
                    {
                    }

                    public void windowClosed( WindowEvent e )
                    {
                    }

                    public void windowClosing( WindowEvent e )
                    {
                    }

                    public void windowDeactivated( WindowEvent e )
                    {
                    }

                    public void windowDeiconified( WindowEvent e )
                    {
                    }

                    public void windowIconified( WindowEvent e )
                    {
                    }

                    public void windowOpened( WindowEvent e )
                    {
                        myDialog.setVisible( true );
                    }
                }
```

If you want to catch less that all of these events, you may want to have a class that extends WindowAdapter. See the next example or "A Quick Review of the JDK 1.1 Event Model" in Chapter 7, "JFC by Concept," for more information on event adapters.

Basic Code Examples

EXAMPLE 8-42 Basic JDialog

This example creates a frame with a dialog. The dialog will appear when the frame appears initially. The Show button on the parent frame causes the dialog to appear if it is hidden. The Hide button on the dialog causes the dialog to become invisible. The Destroy button on the dialog causes the dialog to be completely disposed of so it cannot be re-shown. Figure 8-52 shows the example in its initial state.

Here is the source code:

```
import com.sun.java.swing.*;
import java.awt.*;
import java.awt.event.*;
```

Figure 8-52

```java
public class MyFrame extends JFrame implements
        ActionListener
{
    JDialog myDialog;
    JButton show;

    public MyFrame()
    {
        setTitle( "JDialog1" );

        // Store the content pane in a variable for easier
        // access.
        JPanel contentPane = (JPanel)getContentPane();

        contentPane.setLayout( new BorderLayout() );

        // Create the button on the parent frame that will
        // cause the dialog to appear.
        show = new JButton( "Show" );

        // Make this class listen so that when this button is
        // pressed, it can tell the dialog to show itself.
        show.addActionListener( this );
        show.setActionCommand( "Show me" );

        // Add the button.
        contentPane.add( "South", show );

        // Create the dialog.  We will show it initially when
        // the parent frame first appears.
        myDialog = new JDialog( this, "Dialog Title" );

        // Size and locate the dialog.
        myDialog.setBounds( 100, 100, 200, 100 );

        // Set the dialog's layout so we can stick buttons
        // into it.
        myDialog.getContentPane().setLayout(
                                    new BorderLayout() );

        // Create a button that will cause the dialog to hide.
        JButton hide = new JButton( "Hide" );

        // Make this class listen so that when the dialog's
        // button is pressed, the dialog will disappear.
        hide.addActionListener( this );
```

```
        hide.setActionCommand( "Hide me" );

        // Add the button to the dialog.
        myDialog.getContentPane().add( "South", hide );

        // Create a button that will destroy the dialog.
        JButton destroy = new JButton( "Destroy" );

        // Make this class listen so that when the dialog's
        // button is pressed, the dialog will be destroyed.
        destroy.addActionListener( this );
        destroy.setActionCommand( "Destroy me" );

        // Add the button to the dialog.
        myDialog.getContentPane().add( "North", destroy );

        // Make a class to listen so we can know when the
        // dialog is destroyed so it can disable the "Show"
        // button.
        myDialog.addWindowListener( new MyWindowAdapter() );

        // Make it so that when the dialog is showing the
        // "Show" button is disabled.
        myDialog.addComponentListener(
                                new MyComponentAdapter() );

        // Make this class accept window events se we know
        // when the parent frame is opened and so we know
        // when the dialog was destroyed.
        addWindowListener( new MyWindowAdapter() );
    }

    public void actionPerformed( ActionEvent e )
    {
        // If the "Show" button on the frame is pressed, show
        // the dialog.  If the "Hide" button on the dialog is
        // pressed, hide the dialog.  If the "Destroy" button
        // is pressed, dispose of the dialog.  Doing this
        // will trigger the dialog to send the WindowClose
        // event which will make the "Show" button disabled
        // since we can't show a destroyed dialog.
        if ( e.getActionCommand().equals( "Show me" ) )
        {
            myDialog.setVisible( true );
        }
        else if ( e.getActionCommand().equals( "Hide me" ) )
        {
            myDialog.setVisible( false );
        }
        else if ( e.getActionCommand().equals(
                                        "Destroy me" ) )
        {
            myDialog.dispose();
        }
    }
```

```
private class MyWindowAdapter extends WindowAdapter
{
   public void windowClosed( WindowEvent e )
   {
      // If the dialog was destroyed, disable the parent
      // frame's button used to show the dialog since
      // showing a destroyed dialog generates an error.
      // dispose() destroys the JDialog for good.
      if ( e.getSource() == myDialog )
      {
         show.setEnabled( false );
         show.setToolTipText( "Dialog can't be shown " +
                              "— it has been destroyed" );
      }
   }

   // When the parent frame first appears, make the
   // dialog appear.
   public void windowOpened( WindowEvent e )
   {
      myDialog.setVisible( true );
   }
}

private class MyComponentAdapter extends ComponentAdapter
{
   // When the dialog is hidden, enable the parent
   // frame's "Show" button so we can make the dialog
   // visible again.
   public void componentHidden( ComponentEvent e )
   {
      if ( e.getSource() == myDialog )
         show.setEnabled( true );
   }

   // When the dialog is made visible, make the parent
   // frame's "Show" button diabled since it only has
   // meaning when the dialog is not visible.
   public void componentShown( ComponentEvent e )
   {
      if ( e.getSource() == myDialog )
         show.setEnabled( false );
   }
}
}
```

Advanced Issues

EXAMPLE 8-43 Transferring Data between a JDialog and a Listener

Dialogs frequently have fields for user input, an OK button for telling the parent application that input into the dialog is complete, and a Cancel button for telling the application that input has been made but should be discarded. This example will demonstrate how to transfer a dialog's user input back to the parent application when OK is pressed. Figure 8-53 shows the example just after a string has been entered in the dialog and OK has been pressed.

Important points to notice:

▨ The dialog class is a subclass of JDialog called MyDialog.java. It is created by and communicates with a class called MyFrame.java.

▨ The dialog has a text field and an OK button. When the button is pressed, the current contents of the text field are sent back to MyFrame where they are displayed.

▨ The dialog tells MyFrame that its OK button has been pressed by generating an ItemEvent. MyFrame then calls the dialog's getSelectedObjects() method to get the text field's contents.

▨ See Chapter 7, "JFC by Concept," for a discussion of EventListenerLists.

Here is the full source for MyDialog.java, followed by the source for MyFrame.java:

```java
import com.sun.java.swing.*;
import com.sun.java.swing.border.*;
import com.sun.java.swing.event.*;
import java.awt.*;
import java.awt.event.*;

// This dialog has a textfield and a button.  When the
// button is pressed it generates an ItemEvent which goes
// out to any registered ItemListeners.
public class MyDialog extends JDialog implements
        ActionListener, ItemSelectable
{
    // The text field.
    JTextField text;

    // The "Ok" button.
    JButton ok;

    // The class that will help manage item listeners.
    EventListenerList mItemListenerList;

    // In the real world, this would have more constructors
```

Figure 8-53

```
        // to match JDialog.
        public MyDialog( JFrame parent, String title )
        {
            super( parent, title );

            // Initialize the class that will help manage the
            // item listeners.
            mItemListenerList = new EventListenerList();

            // Store the content pane for easier access.
            JPanel pane = (JPanel)getContentPane();

            // Give the content pane an empty border just to
            // inset everything in from the frame's edge.
            pane.setBorder( new EmptyBorder( 10, 10, 10, 10 ) );

            pane.setBackground( Color.lightGray );

            pane.setLayout( new BoxLayout( pane,
                                      BoxLayout.Y_AXIS ) );

            // Create and add the textfield and the button.
            text = new JTextField();
            pane.add( text );

            // Expand the text field's maximum width so it will
            // take up extra horizontal whitespace.
            Dimension size = text.getMaximumSize();
            size.width = 10000;
            text.setMaximumSize( size );

            // Add a padding component so the text field and
            // button go to opposite ends of the frame.
            pane.add( Box.createVerticalGlue() );

            // Create the "Ok" button, make it so the layout
            // manager will center it horizontally, and add it to
            // the content pane.
            ok = new JButton( "Ok" );
            ok.setAlignmentX( 0.5f );
            pane.add( ok );

            // Make it so this class knows when the button has
            // been pressed.
            ok.addActionListener( this );
        }

        // When the button is pressed, generate an item changed
        // event and send it to registered listeners.
        public void actionPerformed( ActionEvent e )
        {
            if ( e.getSource() == ok )
                fireItemEvent( new ItemEvent( this, 0,
                            text.getText(),
                            ItemEvent.ITEM_STATE_CHANGED ) );
```

```
   }

   // ItemSelectable interface methods:  ————————
   public Object[] getSelectedObjects()
   {
      String val[];
      val = new String[1];
      val[0] = text.getText();
      return val;
   }


   // Register an ItemListener with our listener list.
   public void addItemListener( ItemListener listener )
   {
      mItemListenerList.add( ItemListener.class, listener );
   }


   // Un-register an ItemListener from our listener list.
   public void removeItemListener( ItemListener listener )
   {
      mItemListenerList.remove( ItemListener.class,
                                listener );
   }


   // Cause the passed-in ItemEvent to be sent to our
   // registered ItemListeners.
   protected void fireItemEvent( ItemEvent newEvent )
   {
      // Get the listener class type / listener class
      // instance pairs.
      Object[] listeners =
                  mItemListenerList.getListenerList();

      // We step through the pairs from last to first.  The
      // first is the pair is the class type, then is the
      // class instance.  This is why we step through the
      // list two at a time.
      for ( int i = listeners.length-2; i >= 0; i -= 2 )
      {
         // Make sure this listener is the right type.
         if ( listeners[i] == ItemListener.class )
         {
            // Call the ItemListener method.
            ((ItemListener)listeners[i+1]).itemStateChanged(
                                          newEvent );
         }
      }
   }
}
```

Here is the source for MyFrame.java:

```
import com.sun.java.swing.*;
import java.awt.*;
```

```java
import java.awt.event.*;

public class MyFrame extends JFrame implements ItemListener
{
    MyDialog myDialog;
    JButton show;
    JLabel label;

    public MyFrame()
    {
        setTitle( "JDialog2" );

        // Store the content pane for easier access.
        JPanel mPanel = (JPanel)getContentPane();

        mPanel.setLayout( new BorderLayout() );

        // Create the dialog.  We will show it initially when
        // the parent frame first appears.
        myDialog = new MyDialog( this, "Dialog Title String" );

        // We chose to use ItemEvents for MyDialog to use to
        // notify listeners that its state has changed.
        // ActionEvents could have been used also.
        myDialog.addItemListener( this );

        // Size and locate the dialog.
        myDialog.setBounds( 100, 150, 200, 120 );

        // Create a class that can be used with the frame and
        // the dialog to listen for window events.
        MyWinAdapter winListener = new MyWinAdapter();

        // Listen for when the user wants to close the dialog.
        myDialog.addWindowListener( winListener );

        // We need to know when the parent frame has been
        // created so we can show the dialog initially.
        addWindowListener( winListener );

        // Create a label that will reflect changes in the
        // dialog.
        label = new JLabel( "The value is:  " );
        label.setHorizontalTextPosition( JLabel.CENTER );
        label.setVerticalTextPosition( JLabel.CENTER );

        mPanel.add( "Center", label );
    }

    private class MyWinAdapter extends WindowAdapter
    {
        // If the user clicks the close button on either the
        // dialog or the main frame, exit.
        public void windowClosing( WindowEvent e )
```

```
        {
           System.exit( 0 );
        }

        // When the parent frame first appears, make the
        // dialog appear.
        public void windowOpened( WindowEvent e )
        {
           if ( e.getSource() == MyFrame.this )
           {
              myDialog.setVisible( true );
           }
        }
     }

     // When the button on the dialog is pressed, we get this
     // event and can use ItemSelectable's
     // getSelectedObjects() method to retrieve the
     // value.  You could have used an ActionEvent instead
     // and passed the changed string value via the action
     // command.
     public void itemStateChanged( ItemEvent e )
     {
        String newval =
                   (String)(myDialog.getSelectedObjects()[0]);
        label.setText( "The value is:  " + newval );
     }
  }
```

JDialog's Public Methods

```
AccessibleContext getAccessibleContext()
```

Returns a subclass of AccessibleContext which gives access to the JDialog's accessibility information.

```
Container getContentPane()
```

Returns the root pane's content pane.

```
int getDefaultCloseOperation()
```

Returns a constant that describes what will happen to the JDialog when the user closes it. The constant will be one of: DISPOSE_ON_CLOSE, DO_NOTHING_ON_CLOSE, or HIDE_ON_CLOSE.

```
Component getGlassPane()
```

Returns the root pane's glass pane.

`JMenuBar getJMenuBar()`

Returns the root panel's menu bar.

`JLayeredPane getLayeredPane()`

Returns the root pane's layered pane.

`JRootPane getRootPane()`

Returns the JDialog's root pane.

`void setContentPane(Container content)`

Replaces the root pane's content pane with a new container.

`void setDefaultCloseOperation(int closeOp)`

Specifies what happens to the JDialog when the user closes it. It should be one of: DISPOSE_ON_CLOSE, DO_NOTHING_ON_CLOSE, or HIDE_ON_CLOSE.

`void setGlassPane(Component glass)`

Replaces the root pane's glass pane with a new component.

`void setJMenuBar(JMenuBar mb)`

Replaces the root panel's menu bar with a new one.

`void setLayeredPane(JLayeredPane layered)`

Replaces the root pane's layered pane.

`void setLayout(LayoutManager manager)`

Overridden to throw an exception. You should lay out the content pane instead.

`void setLocationRelativeTo(Component c)`

Sets the dialog's location relative to the given component.

`void update(Graphics g)`

Overridden to just call paint(g).

JDirectoryPane

JDirectoryPane is a pane that displays the contents of a directory and allows the user to browse downward through the file system by double-clicking on a subdirectory (see Figure 8-54). When listing the contents of a directory, JDirectoryPane always puts the subdirectories first, followed by the files. This pane is like the right-hand pane in the Windows 95 Explorer. You can make the JDirectoryPane's current directory change to a directory above its current directory, but this must be triggered through method calls—it cannot happen through the JDirectoryPane user interface alone. A JDirectoryPane generates ActionEvents when a file or directory is selected or is double-clicked.

NOTE: *For JFC 1.1, JDirectoryPane has been moved to the com.sun.java.swing.preview package. This means it may have bugs and its API may change in the near future.*

NOTE: *JDirectoryPane relies on the DirectoryModel class, which in turn relies on the java.io.File class. java.io.File has bugs in JDK 1.1.5 and before that are particularly apparent on Windows systems. For these earlier JDKs, you can replace DirectoryModel with WorkingDirectoryModel.java from Chapter 11, "Integrating JFC Example 1—A File Browser." To do so, you will have to subclass JDirectoryPane so you can call the protected setModel() method.*

Ancestors

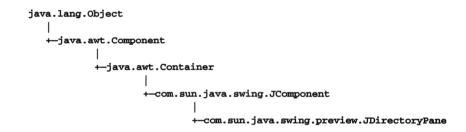

```
java.lang.Object
    |
    +—java.awt.Component
          |
          +—java.awt.Container
                |
                +—com.sun.java.swing.JComponent
                      |
                      +—com.sun.java.swing.preview.JDirectoryPane
```

NOTE: *For more information, see the "DirectoryModel," "TypedFile," "FileType," "JFileChooser," and "DefaultListSelectionModel" sections in this chapter. Also see the "File Browsing" section in Chapter 7, "JFC by Concept."*

Figure 8-54
A typical
JDirectoryPane.

Steps in Creating and Using JDirectoryPane

1. Create the JDirectoryPane. There are three constructors:

   Create a JDirectoryPane with current directory set to the user's home directory:

   ```
   JDirectoryPane myPane = new JDirectoryPane();
   ```

   Create a JDirectoryPane with current directory set to the specified File (which should represent a directory):

   ```
   JDirectoryPane myPane = new JDirectoryPane( new File(
                                        "C:\\windows" ) );
   ```

   Create a JDirectoryPane with current directory set the the specified path (which should be a valid path):

   ```
   JDirectoryPane myPane = new JDirectoryPane( "C:\\windows" );
   ```

2. Add the JDirectoryPane to a container. You will normally want to place it within a JScrollPane since directory listings can get pretty long. In this case, we will add it to a frame's content pane which is assumed to be using a BorderLayout:

   ```
   JScrollPane scroller = new JScrollPane( myPane );
   getContentPane().add( "Center", scroller );
   ```

   When the frame is displayed, the JDirectoryPane is ready to be used in a limited (down-browsing only) fashion.

3. Since JDirectoryPane uses a DirectoryModel to do the actual interactions with the file system, it has the DirectoryModel functionality built in. Most of what you need has been included in JDirectoryPane through convenience methods that call the equivalent DirectoryModel methods behind the scenes.

   See if the JDirectoryPane's current directory has a parent directory:

   ```
   boolean hasParent = myPane.canGoUp();
   ```

Cause the JDirectoryPane to display the parent directory of its current directory and make that its current directory:

```
myPane.goUp();
```

See what the JDirectoryPane's current directory is:

```
File currentDir = myPane.getCurrentDirectory();
```

Explicitly change the JDirectoryPane's current directory (causing it to be the displayed directory):

```
myPane.setCurrentDirectory( new File( "C:\\windows" ) );
```

Get a file from the filesystem. This file's location has nothing to do with the JDirectoryPane's current directory. If you use a relative path like MyFrame.java, it will try to find that file in the application's current directory, which is likely to be the directory in which it was started. Notice that this returns a TypedFile. TypedFile is a subclass of File and includes a FileType member that has information about the type of file it is.

```
TypedFile thisFile = myPane.getTypedFile(
                                      "C:\\windows\\ Tiles.bmp" );
```

There is a similar method that splits the file name up into path and name:

```
TypedFile thisFile = myPane.getTypedFile( "C:\\windows",
                                          "Tiles.bmp" );
```

Get a listing of all of the files in the JDirectoryPane's current directory:

```
Vector dirContents = myPane.getTypedFiles();
```

Get a listing of the contents of a specific directory:

```
Vector dirContents = myPane.getTypedFilesForDirectory(
                                  new File( "C:\\windows" ) );
```

4. Get the selected file or the first selected file if more than one is selected:

```
TypedFile thisFile = myPane.getSelectedFile();
```

5. Get all of the files that are selected:

```
Vector selectedFiles = myPane.getSelectedFiles();
```

6. When the JDirectoryPane displays a file name, it also displays an icon. This icon comes from the FileType associated with the file or, if there is none, is supplied by the current look-and-feel. If you want to create your own FileType with its own icon, you can do so. Then you can make the JDirectoryPane use it by calling the addKnownFileType() method:

```
myPane.addKnownFileType( new MyFileType() );
```

The next time the JDirectoryPane goes looking for files, it will use your type in its efforts to figure out the files' types. For information on creating your own FileType, see Chapter 7, "JFC by Class."

7. Listen for changes in the JDirectoryPane. JDirectoryPane generates an ActionEvent when one of its items is selected or is double-clicked. You can set action command strings for each of these so you can differentiate between a selection and a double-click.

Tell the JDirectoryPane which class should be notified when a selection or a double-click occurs. In this case the event-receiver will be the class in which the JDirectoryPane resides:

```
myPane.addActionListener( this );
```

Specify the string to be delivered with the ActionEvent when an item is selected:

```
myPane.setActionCommand( "selected" );
```

Specify the string to be delivered with the ActionEvent when a file item is double-clicked:

```
myPane.setDoubleClickCommand( "double_click" );
```

Specify the string to be delivered with the ActionEvent when a directory item is double-clicked:

```
myPane.setDoubleClickContainerCommand(
                                "container double_click" );
```

Make the event-receiving class (MyFrame.java in this case) implement the ActionListener interface so it can receive ActionEvents:

```
public class MyFrame extends JFrame implements ActionListener
{
   .
   .
   .
   public void actionPerformed( ActionEvent e )
   {
      // Do something depending on the meaning of the event.
      if ( e.getActionCommand().equals( "selected" ) )
      {
      }
      else if ( e.getActionCommand().equals( "double-click" ) )
      {
      }
   }
}
```

Basic Code Examples

EXAMPLE 8-44 Browsing the File System with JDirectoryPane

This example shows how to display a JDirectoryPane, how to make it change directories, and how to respond to its events. It includes a directory pane showing the current directory, a text field that always reflects the name of the current directory and into which the user can enter a new current directory, and a button that will move the current directory up a level. Figure 8-55 shows the example browsing the JDK 1.1.4 directories.

Important points to notice:

- In order to keep the text field up-to-date when the user changes the directory by double-clicking a subdirectory, we catch PropertyChangeEvents. We use the one named "currentDirectory".

- When the directory changes, we check the new directory to see if it is the root directory, and if so, we disable the "Go up a level" button.

- Files that end in .java and .exe (case insensitive) will display special icons because we have implemented a custom FileType called MyFileType.

- When an ActionEvent is received, from whatever source, its action command string is printed out.

Here is the source code for the main class MyFrame (the source for the custom FileType class follows it):

```java
import com.sun.java.swing.*;
import com.sun.java.swing.preview.*;
import java.awt.*;
import java.io.*;
import java.awt.event.*;
import java.util.*;
import java.beans.*;

public class MyFrame extends JFrame implements
        ActionListener, PropertyChangeListener
{
```

Figure 8-55

```
// The button to go up a level.
JButton mUpButton;

// The text field that holds and can set the current
// directory.
JTextField mDirField;

// The pane that holds the contents of the current
// directory.
JDirectoryPane mDirPane;

public MyFrame()
{
    setTitle( "JDirectoryPane1" );

    // Store the content pane for easier access.
    JPanel panel = (JPanel)getContentPane();

    // Components will all be added to this panel.
    panel.setLayout( new BorderLayout() );

    // Create the JDirectoryPane.
    mDirPane = new JDirectoryPane();

    // Specify the string that is delivered with
    // ActionEvents when an item is single-clicked.
    mDirPane.setActionCommand( "selection" );

    // Specify the string that is delivered with
    // ActionEvents when an item is double-clicked.
    mDirPane.setDoubleClickCommand( "double-click" );

    // Make it so this class is notified of the
    // JDirectoryPane's ActionEvents.
    mDirPane.addActionListener( this );

    // Make it so this class is notified of changes to
    // the directory model's current directory.
    mDirPane.getModel().addPropertyChangeListener( this );

    // Tell the directory model of new file types so it
    // can display them properly.
    mDirPane.addKnownFileType( new MyFileType( "java",
                "Java source",
                new ImageIcon( "javasource.gif" ) ) );
    mDirPane.addKnownFileType( new MyFileType( "exe",
                "Executable file",
                new ImageIcon( "delete.gif" ) ) );

    // Create a scroll pane to allow the user to see all
    // of the JDirectoryPane even when it gets big.
    JScrollPane scroller = new JScrollPane( mDirPane );

    // Put the scroll pane in the content pane's main
    // area.
```

```
        panel.add( "Center", scroller );

        // Create a text field that will reflect the current
        // directory and will also allow the user to type in
        // a new current directory.
        mDirField = new JTextField(
            mDirPane.getCurrentDirectory().getAbsolutePath() );

        // Make this class be notified of the text field's
        // ActionEvents.
        mDirField.addActionListener( this );

        // Place the text field at the top of the content
        // pane.
        panel.add( "North", mDirField );

        // Create a button that will allow the user to browse
        // up to the parent directory of the one being
        // displayed.
        mUpButton = new JButton( "Go up a level" );

        // Specify an action command string to help tell
        // which component generated a received ActionEvent.
        mUpButton.setActionCommand( "Go up" );

        // Make it so this class is notified when the button
        // is pressed.
        mUpButton.addActionListener( this );

        // Call the method that disables the button if we are
        // at the root directory.
        checkButton();

        // Place the button at the bottom of the content pane.
        panel.add( "South", mUpButton );
    }

    // This method checks to see if the directory model's
    // current directory is the root directory.  If so, it
    // disables the "Go up" button.
    private void checkButton()
    {
        if ( mDirPane.getModel().canGoUp() )
            mUpButton.setEnabled( true );
        else
            mUpButton.setEnabled( false );
    }

    // This is called when an item in the JDirectoryPane is
    // single- or double-clicked, the user presses <enter>
    // in the text field, or the "Go up" button is pressed.
    public void actionPerformed( ActionEvent e )
    {
        String command = e.getActionCommand();
```

```
      // We do this to keep from getting exceptions when
      // an ActionEvent doesn't have a command string.
      if ( command == null )
         command = "";

      // Print out the command string
      System.out.println( "Action command:  " + command );

      if ( e.getSource() == mDirField )
      {
         // If the text field changed, we apply the new
         // value as the current directory.
         File newDir = new File( mDirField.getText() );

         if ( newDir.isDirectory() )
            mDirPane.setCurrentDirectory( newDir );
         else
            mDirField.setText(
                     mDirPane.getCurrentDirectory().
                     getAbsolutePath() );
      }
      else if ( command.equals( "Go up" ) )
      {
         // If the "Go up" button was pressed, we tell the
         // directory pane to change its current directory.
         mDirPane.goUp();
      }
   }

   public void propertyChange( PropertyChangeEvent e )
   {
      // When the user changes directories by
      // double-clicking a sub-directory, a
      // PropertyChangeEvent is generated.
      if ( e.getPropertyName().equals(
                              "currentDirectory" ) )
      {
         // Disable the "Go up" button if the new directory
         // is root.
         checkButton();

         // Load the new directory name into the text field.
         mDirField.setText(
                     mDirPane.getCurrentDirectory().
                     getAbsolutePath() );
      }
   }
}
```

Here is the source for the custom FileType called MyFileType:

```
import com.sun.java.swing.*;
import com.sun.java.swing.preview.*;
```

```java
import java.io.*;

// This implementation of FileType accepts a file extension
// and corresponding string description through the
// constructor.
public class MyFileType implements FileType
{
  // Storage for the file extension and description.
  private String mExt;
  private String mName;
  private Icon mIcon;

  public MyFileType( String ext, String name, Icon icon )
  {
    // Store the extension and description.
    mExt = ext.toLowerCase();
    mName = name;

    mIcon = icon;
  }

  // Return this file type's description.
  public String getPresentationName()
  {
    return mName;
  }

  // Return an icon that can be placed next to files of
  // this type in a file browser.
  public Icon getIcon()
  {
    return mIcon;
  }

  // Return false because this file type is not able to
  // contain others.
  public boolean isContainer()
  {
    return false;
  }

  // If the file's name ends with ".java", the file is of
  // this type.
  public boolean testFile( File file )
  {
    String name = file.getAbsolutePath().toLowerCase();

    if ( name.endsWith( "." + mExt ) )
      return true;

    return false;
  }
}
```

JDirectoryPane's Public Methods

```
void addActionListener(ActionListener l)
```

Tells the JDirectoryPane to notify the given class whenever an item is single or double-clicked.

```
void addKnownFileType(FileType type)
```

Tells the JDirectoryPane about a new file type so the JDirectoryPane can display it properly.

```
boolean canGoUp()
```

Returns false if the current directory is the root directory.

```
void clearSelection()
```

Makes it so that no items in the JDirectoryPane are selected.

```
Enumeration enumerateKnownFileTypes()
```

Gets an enumeration of all of the FileTypes that the JDirectoryPane recognizes.

```
AccessibleContext getAccessibleContext()
```

Returns a subclass of AccessibleContext. This gives access to all of the JDirectoryPanel's accessibility information.

```
String getActionCommand()
```

Returns the action command string that will be delivered with ActionEvents resulting from an item being single-clicked.

```
File getCurrentDirectory()
```

Returns the current directory.

```
ActionListener getDefaultActionListener()
```

This is part of the way a JDirectoryPane listens for double-clicks.

```
String getDoubleClickCommand()
```

Returns the action command string that will be delivered with ActionEvents resulting from a file item being double-clicked.

```
String getDoubleClickContainerCommand()
```

Returns the action command string that will be delivered with ActionEvents resulting from a directory item being double-clicked.

`Action getGoUpAction()`

Returns the Action that causes the parent directory to be loaded.

`FileType getHiddenRule()`

Returns the FileType that is used to determine if a file is hidden or not.

`Vector getKnownFileTypes()`

Gets a Vector loaded with the FileTypes that the JDirectoryPane recognizes.

`ListSelectionModel getListSelectionModel()`

Returns the JDirectoryPane's list selection model that keeps track of what items are currently selected.

`DirectoryModel getModel()`

Returns the JDirectoryPane's DirectoryModel.

`TypedFile getSelectedFile()`

Returns the first item that is currently selected.

`Vector getSelectedFiles()`

Returns all of the currently selected items.

`TypedFile getTypedFile(String path)`

Returns the file at the specified path.

`TypedFile getTypedFile(String path, String name)`

Returns the file at the specified path with the given name.

`Vector getTypedFiles()`

Returns a Vector of TypedFiles containing the contents of the JDirectoryPane's current directory.

`Vector getTypedFilesForDirectory(File dir)`

Returns a Vector of TypedFiles containing the contents of the specified directory.

`DirectoryPaneUI getUI()`

Returns the look-and-feel class that the JDirectory is currently using.

`String getUIClassID()`

Returns the string that identifies the look-and-feel class that the JDirectoryPane is currently using.

`void goUp()`

Tells the JDirectory pane to move up a level so its current directory is the next one up.

`boolean isKnownFileType(FileType t)`

Returns true if the given FileType is recognized by the JDirectoryPane.

`boolean isSelectionEmpty()`

Returns true if there are no items currently selected in the JDirectoryPane.

`void performDoubleClick()`

This is called by the look-and-feel.

`void removeActionListener(ActionListener l)`

Tells the JDirectoryPane to stop notifying the given class when items are clicked.

`void setActionCommand(String command)`

Sets the action command string to be delivered with ActionEvents resulting from an item being single-clicked.

`void setCurrentDirectory(File dir)`

Changes the JDirectoryPane's current directory to the given one.

`void setDoubleClickCommand(String command)`

Sets the action command string to be delivered with ActionEvents resulting from a file item being double-clicked.

`void setDoubleClickContainerCommand(String command)`

Sets the action command string to be delivered with ActionEvents resulting from a directory item being double-clicked.

```
void setHiddenRule(FileType rule)
```

Specifies which FileType should be used to decide if a file is hidden or not.

```
void setKnownFileTypes(FileType types[])
```

Replaces the FileTypes that the JDirectoryPane understands with a new list.

```
void setUI(DirectoryPaneUI ui)
```

Gives the JDirectoryPane a new look-and-feel class.

```
void updateUI()
```

Tells the JDirectoryPane that its look-and-feel class has been changed.

JEditorPane

JEditorPane is a general pane that can be used to display different text file types, edit different file types, and follow hyperlinks within text (see Figure 8-56). JEditorPane itself does not contain the intelligence to read these file types—each supported type must have its own EditorKit. The JFC ships with EditorKits for plain text, HTML, and Rich Text Format (RTF). These EditorKits are not fully featured for HTML and RTF, but can be useful in controlled situations.

A JEditorPane can have multiple EditorKits installed with each one assigned to a specific MIME type. For a particular URL, JEditorPane finds out the MIME type and uses the associated EditorKit. The EditorKit is able to read the input stream and load it into the JEditorPane. The EditorKit also

Figure 8-56
A typical JEditorPane displaying HTML.

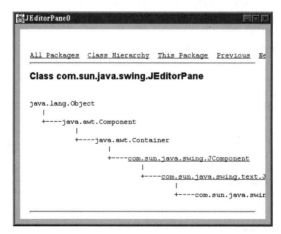

includes a set of actions that can be used to navigate the JEditorPane contents and modify it (if the JEditorPane is editable).

Ancestors

```
java.lang.Object
    |
    +—java.awt.Component
              |
              +—java.awt.Container
                        |
                        +—com.sun.java.swing.JComponent
                                  |
                                  +—com.sun.java.swing.text.JTextComponent
                                            |
                                            +—com.sun.java.swing.JEditorPane
```

Steps in Creating and Using JEditorPane

1. Create a JEditorPane. There are three constructors.

   One creates the component without specifying a URL to read:

   ```
   JEditorPane myPane = JEditorPane();
   ```

   One creates the component and gives it a URL:

   ```
   JEditorPane myPane = new JEditorPane( destURL );
   ```

   One creates the component and specifies the URL as a string:

   ```
   JEditorPane myPane = JEditorPane( destString );
   ```

2. Create a scroll pane to put the JEditorPane into so the user can scroll around pages that are too big to fit in the container. You can associate the JEditorPane with the scroll pane via the scroll pane's constructor.

   ```
   JScrollPane scroller = new JScrollPane( myPane );
   ```

3. Give the JEditorPane a page to display. This method throws an IOException if the page string is invalid.

   ```
   try
   {
      myPane.setPage(
               "file:///d:\\swing-0.7\\doc\\api\\packages.html" );
   }
   catch ( IOException ex )
   {
      System.out.println( "Invalid destination string" );
   }
   ```

4. Make it so the JEditorPane follows hyperlinks. By default, the JEditorPane generates a HyperlinkEvent when a hyperlink is activated, but the link's URL does not display. So, we have to catch the event and make the new page display.

Specify a class that will be notified when hyperlinks are clicked. In this case, it is the current class:

```
myPane.addHyperlinkListener( this );
```

Make the event-receiving class (MyFrame) implement the HyperlinkListener interface and feed the new URL back to the JEditorPane:

```
public void hyperlinkUpdate( HyperlinkEvent e )
{
    if (e.getEventType() == HyperlinkEvent.EventType.ACTIVATED)
    {
        // When a hyperlink is activated, we call the setPage()
        // method with the URL from the HyperlinkEvent.
        try
        {
            myPane.setPage( e.getURL() );
        }
        catch ( IOException ex )
        {
            System.out.println( ex );
        }
    }
}
```

Basic Code Examples

EXAMPLE 8-45 Browsing HTML in JEditorPane

This example contains a text field and a subclass of JEditorPane. When the user enters a destination into the text field and presses Enter, the HTML pane tries to display the destination page. Also, when the page changes either by a user entry into the text field or by a click on a hyperlink, the text field is updated to reflect the change. Figure 8-57 shows the example navigating through the JavaSoft site.

Important points to notice:

■ We subclassed JEditorPane so we could override the setPage(URL page) method. The subclass is called MyEditorPane. The setPage(URL page) method is called whenever the displayed page is being replaced. When this method is called, our subclass generates an ActionEvent so the main frame class (MyFrame) can display the new page's URL in the text field.

Figure 8-57

■ The JEditorPane subclass also implements the HyperlinkListener interface so hyperlinks will work.

■ The main frame class implements the ActionListener for two reasons: so it can listen for when Enter is pressed in the text field and use the field's contents as a new URL for the JEditorPane subclass, and so it can listen for when the page changes in the JEditorPane subclass and update the text field with the new URL.

Here is the source code for MyFrame.java (followed by the source for MyEditorPane.java):

```java
import com.sun.java.swing.*;
import com.sun.java.swing.event.*;
import java.awt.*;
import java.awt.event.*;
import java.io.*;

public class MyFrame extends JFrame implements
        ActionListener
{
    JTextField mDestination;
    MyEditorPane mPane;

    public MyFrame()
    {
        setTitle( "JEditorPane2" );

        // Store the content pane in a variable for easier
        // access.
        JPanel contentPane = (JPanel)getContentPane();

        // Components will all be added to this panel.
        contentPane.setLayout( new BorderLayout() );

        // Create a text field into which the user can type
        // new destinations.
```

```
        mDestination = new JTextField();

        // Catch the text field's action events so we know
        // when return was pressed.
        mDestination.addActionListener( this );

        // Add the text field to the top edge of the content
        // pane.
        contentPane.add( "North", mDestination );

        // Create an Editor pane.
        mPane = new MyEditorPane();

        // Make this class be notified when the Editor page
        // changes so we can reflect the change in the text
        // field.
        mPane.addActionListener( this );

        // Create a scroll pane so the user can scroll around
        // pages that are bigger than the frame.
        JScrollPane scroller = new JScrollPane( mPane );

        // Add the scroll pane so it fills all of the content
        // pane below the text field.
        contentPane.add( "Center", scroller );
    }

    // This is called either when <enter> is pressed in the
    // text field, or when the Editor page is changed in the
    // browser window.
    public void actionPerformed( ActionEvent e )
    {
        if ( e.getSource() == mPane )
        {
            // This event means the Editor page changed, so we
            // put the name of the new page into the text
            // field.
            mDestination.setText( e.getActionCommand() );
        }
        else
        {
            // When return is pressed in the text field, get
            // the field's string and try to load it into the
            // Editor pane.
            try
            {
                mPane.setPage( mDestination.getText() );
            }
            catch ( IOException ex )
            {
                System.out.println( ex );
            }
        }
    }
}
```

Here is the source code for MyEditorPane.java:

```java
import com.sun.java.swing.*;
import com.sun.java.swing.event.*;
import java.io.*;
import java.net.*;
import java.util.*;
import java.awt.event.*;

public class MyEditorPane extends JEditorPane implements
        HyperlinkListener
{
    // Store all registered ActionListeners.
    protected EventListenerList mActionListenerList;

    public MyEditorPane()
    {
        // call the equivalent constructor in JEditorPane.
        super();

        // Make it so this class is notified when the user
        // clicks a hyperlink.
        addHyperlinkListener( this );

        // Initialize the listener list.
        mActionListenerList = new EventListenerList();
    }

    public void setPage( URL page ) throws IOException
    {
        // This is called whenever the page is being changed,
        // no matter whether setPage( URL ) or
        // setPage( String ) was called, or if the page was
        // changed following a link.
        super.setPage( page );

        // Generate an event that tells our ActionListeners
        // that the page has changed.  Pass the new page's
        // name through as the command string.
        fireActionEvent( new ActionEvent( this,
                        ActionEvent.ACTION_PERFORMED,
                        page.toString() ) );
    }

    // Register an ActionListener with our listener list.
    public void addActionListener( ActionListener listener )
    {
        mActionListenerList.add( ActionListener.class,
                                    listener );
    }

    // Un-register an ActionListener from our listener list.
    public void removeActionListener(
                                    ActionListener listener )
```

```
      {
         mActionListenerList.remove( ActionListener.class,
                                     listener );
      }

      // Cause the passed-in ActionEvent to be sent to our
      // registered ActionListeners.
      protected void fireActionEvent( ActionEvent newEvent )
      {
         if ( mActionListenerList == null )
            return;

         // Get the listener class type / listener class
         // instance pairs.
         Object[] listeners =
                  mActionListenerList.getListenerList();

         // We step through the pairs from last to first.  The
         // first is the pair is the class type, then is the
         // class instance.  This is why we step through the
         // list two at a time.
         for ( int i = listeners.length-2; i >= 0; i -= 2 )
         {
            // Make sure this listener is the right type.
            if ( listeners[i] == ActionListener.class )
            {
               // Call the ActionListener method.
               ((ActionListener)listeners[i+1]).
                                 actionPerformed( newEvent );
            }
         }
      }

      // Called when something happens with respect to a
      // hyperlink.  We only use the ACTIVATED events.
      public void hyperlinkUpdate( HyperlinkEvent e )
      {
         if ( e.getEventType() ==
              HyperlinkEvent.EventType.ACTIVATED )
         {
            // When a hyperlink is activated, we call the
            // setPage() method with the URL from the
            // HyperlinkEvent.
            try
            {
               setPage( e.getURL() );
            }
            catch ( IOException ex )
            {
               System.out.println( ex );
            }
         }
      }
   }
}
```

JEditorPane's Public Methods

synchronized void addHyperlinkListener(HyperlinkListener listener)

Tells the JEditorPane to notify the given class when events happen regarding a hyperlink.

static EditorKit createEditorKitForContentType(String type)

Called automatically when the editor pane gets a type of data it recognizes but does not have the associated EditorKit loaded.

void fireHyperlinkUpdate(HyperlinkEvent e)

Tells registered HyperlinkListeners that a link event has happened.

AccessibleContext getAccessibleContext()

Returns a subclass of AccessibleContext. This gives access to all of the JEditorPanel's accessibility information.

final String getContentType()

Returns the content type the editor handles.

final EditorKit getEditorKit()

Returns the EditorKit that the JEditorPane is currently using. This can change when a different type of data is read.

EditorKit getEditorKitForContentType(String type)

Returns the JEditorPane's EditorKit associated with the given type.

URL getPage()

Returns the URL of the page currently being displayed.

boolean getScrollableTracksViewportWidth()

Returns true if the JEditorPane's width is not allowed to extend beyond the width of its JScrollPane (if it is in a JScrollPane).

String getUIClassID()

Returns the identifying string that the look-and-feel uses to assign a UI class to the JEditorPane.

```
boolean isManagingFocus()
```

Overridden to return true so pressing Tab doesn't make the JEditorPane lose focus.

```
static void registerEditorKitForContentType(String type,String
        classname)
```

This registers the name of an EditorKit's that should be loaded when the given type of data is encountered.

```
synchronized void removeHyperlinkListener(HyperlinkListener listener)
```

Tells the JEditorPane to stop notifying the given class when hyperlink events happen.

```
final void setContentType(String type)
```

Specifies the type of data the JEditorPane understands.

```
final void setEditorKit(EditorKit kit)
```

Installs the given EditorKit for use with the JEditorPane's default type of data.

```
void setEditorKitForContentType(String type,EditorKit k)
```

Associates the given EditorKit with the given data type.

```
void setPage(URL page)
```

Tells the JEditorPane to display the page at given URL.

```
void setPage(String url)
```

Tells the JEditorPane to convert the given string to a URL and to display the page there.

JFileChooser

JFileChooser is used to implement a standard dialog for selecting files from the file system. It can be placed within a container, but is more commonly displayed within its own dialog box. The layout of JFileChooser is different for each look-and-feel (see Figure 8-58). Look-and-feels that are platform-native look-and-feels (windows and motif), look like the standard file dialogs for their platforms.

Figure 8-58
A typical motif look-
and-feel JFileChooser.

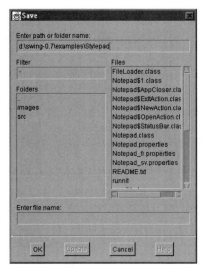

NOTE: *For JFC 1.1, JFileChooser has been moved into the com.sun.java.swing.preview package. Its API is not complete, and is likely to change in the near future.*

Ancestors

```
java.lang.Object
    |
    +—java.awt.Component
            |
            +—java.awt.Container
                    |
                    +—com.sun.java.swing.JComponent
                            |
                            +—com.sun.java.swing.preview.JFileChooser
```

NOTE: *For more information, see the "DirectoryModel," "JDirectoryPane," "TypedFile," "FileType," and "JDialog" sections in this chapter. Also see the "File Browsing" section in Chapter 7, "JFC by Concept."*

Steps in Creating and Using JFileChooser

1. JFileChooser has three constructors:

   Create a JFileChooser with its current directory set to the user's home directory:

```
JFileChooser chooser = new JFileChooser();
```

Create a JFileChooser with its current directory specified by a File object which represents a directory:

```
JFileChooser chooser = new JFileChooser( new File(
                                       "C:\\windows" ) );
```

Create a JFileChooser with its current directory specified by a path that represents a directory:

```
JFileChooser chooser = new JFileChooser( "C:\\windows" );
```

This creates the JFileChooser—it doesn't display it.

2. Display the JFileChooser as a dialog box. This dialog displays modally and you can use the return value to tell if the user pressed the dialog's OK or Cancel button. This method requires the parent frame to be passed in. If the user has selected a file, the method will return 0. Otherwise, it will return -1.

```
returnVal = chooser.showDialog( this );

if ( returnVal == 0 )
{
    // The user pressed "Ok", so get the selected file(s)...
}
```

3. You may have noticed that the JFileChooser has a combo box that allows the user to filter which types of files are shown. By default, it contains "All Types (*.*)" which means all files will be displayed, no matter what type they are. It is possible to add your own types to this. This will not only make it so the user can choose to only show your types of files. It has the side effect of causing your types of files to display with the icon you specify—even if the user is using the "All Types (*.*)" filter. There are several ways to specify your own types.

Let the JFileChooser create a FileType on-the-fly. You just specify the presentation name (like "Executable Files (*.exe)"), the extension (like "exe"), and the icon to display next to files of that type:

```
chooser.addChoosableFileType( "Executable Files (*.exe)", "exe",
                              new ImageIcon( "exe.gif" ) );
```

Or you can create multiple extensions to go with the type:

```
String exts[] = new String[2];
exts[0] = "exe";
exts[1] = "bat";
chooser.addChoosableFileType( "Executable Files (*.exe, *.bat),
                              exts, new ImageIcon( "exe.gif" )
);
```

Or, you can create your own FileType and add that:

```
chooser.addChoosableFileType( new MyFileType() );
```

4. Get the selected file(s). You will want to call one of these methods when you get a return value of 0 from the showDialog() method. Both methods return TypedFiles which are subclasses of File that include information about the file's type.

Get the selected file, or the first selected if multiple are selected:

```
TypedFile thisFile = chooser.getSelectedFile();
```

5. As a container of a JDirectoryPane, you have access to a number of methods that you can use to manipulate which directory the JFileChooser displays. There are two that are particularly useful, but for more, see the JDirectoryPane section in this chapter.

To use the JDirectoryPane methods, you first have to get the JDirectoryPane:

```
JDirectoryPane dirPane = chooser.getDirectoryPane();
```

Find out the JFileChooser's current directory:

```
File thisDir = dirPane.getCurrentDirectory();
```

Set the JFileChooser's current directory:

```
dirPane.setCurrentDirectory new File("C:\\windows" );
```

JFileChooser Public Methods

```
void addChoosableFileType(FileType type)
```

Adds a FileType that the JFileChooser can put in its filter combo box.

```
void addChooseableFileType(String presentationName,String
        extension,Icon icon)
```

Creates a file type with the given presentation name and icon which tests files by their extension, and places it in the JFileChooser's filter combo box.

```
void addChooseableFileType(String presentationName,String
        extensions[],Icon icon)
```

Creates a file type with the given presentation name and icon which tests files against a set of extensions, and places it into the JFileChooser's filter dialog.

```
Enumeration enumerateChoosableFileTypes()
```

Returns and enumeration of the FileTypes that are in the filter combo box.

`Component getAccessory()`

Returns the "accessory" component.

`String getCancelCommand()`

Returns the action command string that is distributed with the ActionEvent generated when the cancel button is pressed.

`String getCancelTitle()`

Returns the string that appears on the Cancel button.

`Vector getChoosableFileTypes()`

Returns a Vector of the FileTypes in the filter combo box.

`JDirectoryPane getDirectoryPane()`

Returns the JFileChooser's directory pane.

`String getLocationTitle()`

Returns the title for the current directory component.

`String getOkayCommand()`

Returns the action command string that is distributed with the ActionEvent generated when the OK button is pressed.

`String getOkayTitle()`

Returns the string that appears on the OK button.

`String getPrompt()`

Returns the String next to the place where the user enters the filename.

`TypedFile getSelectedFile()`

Returns the selected file. This is typically called after the showDialog() method returns a 0.

`String getTypesTitle()`

Returns the String next to the filters combo box.

```
String getUIClassID()
```

Returns the string that identifies the JFileChooser to the look-and-feel.

```
boolean isChoosableFileType(FileType t)
```

Returns true if the given FileType is already in the JFileChooser's filter combo box.

```
void performCancel()
```

Called by the UI class.

```
void performOkay()
```

Called by the UI class.

```
void setAccessory(Component c)
```

Specifies the "accessory" component.

```
void setCancelCommand(String cancelCommand)
```

Specifies the string that will be distributed with ActionEvents generated when the Cancel button is pressed.

```
void setCancelTitle(String cancelTitle)
```

Specifies the string that displays on the Cancel button.

```
void setChoosableFileTypes(FileType types[])
```

Replaces the existing FileTypes in the JFileChooser's filter combo box with a new list.

```
void setLocationTitle(String locationTitle)
```

Sets the String to display next to the current directory component.

```
void setOkayCommand(String okayCommand)
```

Specifies the string that will be distributed with ActionEvents generated when the OK button is pressed.

```
void setOkayTitle(String okayTitle)
```

Specifies the string that displays on the OK button.

```
void setPrompt(String prompt)
```

Specify the String to display next to the place where the user enters the filename.

```
void setTypesTitle(String prompt)
```

Specify the String to display next to the filters combo box.

```
int showDialog(Component parent)
```

Displays a dialog containing this JFileChooser.

```
void updateUI()
```

Tells the JFileChooser that its look-and-feel class has been changed.

JFrame

A JFrame is a standard window. It retains the look-and-feel of the host operating system and is maintained by the operating system's window manager (see Figure 8-59). This is in contrast to a JInternalFrame whose look and feel are completely defined by their own UIs and which are typically maintained by a JDesktopPane. An application's main window is normally a JFrame and applets can create a separate JFrame that floats free of the host browser.

JFrame has only one child—its JRootPane. Menu bars and other components are put into the JFrame through this child. See JRootPane for a complete discussion.

A JFrame can automatically close when its close button is pressed or Close is selected from its system menu, but to make those actions cause the application to exit, you will need to listen to the JFrame's WindowEvents to make it do what the user expects.

Figure 8-59
A standard JFrame with nothing in it.

Ancestors

```
java.lang.Object
     |
    +—java.awt.Component
            |
           +—java.awt.Container
                   |
                  +—java.awt.Window
                          |
                         +—java.awt.Frame
                                 |
                                +—com.sun.java.swing.JFrame
```

NOTE: *Notice that JFrame is not a subclass of JComponent, so does not get JComponent's special properties. However, these properties are available in the JRootPane's components. JFrame does, however, inherit capabilities from java.awt.Window and java.awt.Frame. For more information, see the "JRootPane" section in this chapter, and the "Windows" section in Chapter 7, "JFC by Concept."*

Steps in Creating and Using JFrame

1. Create a JFrame. There are two constructors: one that specifies a title for the frame, and one that doesn't.

   Create a JFrame with a title:

   ```
   JFrame mf = new JFrame( "Test Frame" );
   ```

2. Set the frame's size:

   ```
   mf.setSize( 400, 300 );
   ```

   This causes the JFrame to appear in the display's upper-left corner. Use setBounds() if you want to specify not only the size, but also the origin:

   ```
   mf.setBounds( 100, 100, 400, 300 );
   ```

3. Create a menu bar and menus to go with it. This is optional, and is part of the frame's JRootPane. This example creates a menu bar with a File menu that has an Exit item:

   ```
   // Create the menu bar.
   JMenuBar mb = new JMenuBar();

   // Create the menu.
   JMenu menu = new JMenu( "File" );
   ```

```
// Add the menu to the menu bar.
mb.add( menu );

// Create the menu item.
JMenuItem item = new JMenuItem( "Exit" );

// Add the menu item to the menu.
menu.add( item );

// Add the menu bar to the frame's root pane.
mf.getRootPane().setMenuBar( mb );
```

4. Tell the JFrame what to do when the user closes it using the close button or the system menu. The default behavior is for the JFrame to hide, but you can also tell it to appear to ignore the close, or dispose of itself. The possible settings are constants in the WindowConstants interface.

```
mf.setDefaultCloseOperation(
                    WindowConstants.DO_NOTHING_ON_CLOSE );
```

5. Catch the frame's close event. This event is generated when its close button is pressed or the system menu's Close item is selected. Depending on the default close operation, closing the frame may make it disappear, or may appear to have no effect. Either way, closing an application's main frame will not exit the application—you have to catch the close event to make it do so.

Create a listener class. Here we extend WindowAdapter so we only have to implement the method from WindowListener that we need:

```
private class WinExitAdapter extends WindowAdapter
{
    public void windowClosing( WindowEvent e )
    {
        // Exit the application.
        System.exit( 0 );
    }
}
```

Specify that an instance of the listener class should listen to the frame's events:

```
mf.addWindowListener( new WinExitAdapter() );
```

6. Specify whether the JFrame can be resized. This method is inherited from java.awt.Frame (the default is true):

```
mf.setResizable( false );
```

7. Make the frame visible:

```
mf.show();
```

8. Destroy the JFrame. This method is inherited from java.awt.Window:

```
mf.dispose();
```

Basic Code Examples

EXAMPLE 8-46 Basic JFrame

This example illustrates the concepts discussed above. It creates a frame with a menu bar which contains a menu labeled File which in turn contains an item labeled Exit. The frame causes the application to exit when the Exit menu item in the File menu is chosen, the Close button is pressed, or the system menu's close item is selected. Figure 8-60 shows the example just before the user clicks on the Exit menu item.

Here is the source code:

```java
import com.sun.java.swing.*;
import java.awt.event.*;
import java.awt.*;

public class Test implements ActionListener
{
    public Test()
    {
        // Use the system's native look-and-feel.
        String lf = UIManager.getSystemLookAndFeelClassName();

        if ( lf != null )
        {
            try
            {
                UIManager.setLookAndFeel( lf );
            }
            catch ( Exception ex )
            {
                ex.printStackTrace();
            }
        }

        // Create the frame.
        JFrame mf = new JFrame( "JFrame1" );
```

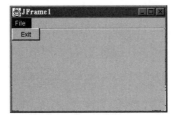

Figure 8-60

```java
        // Make the JFrame keep its initial size.
        mf.setResizable( false );

        // Set the frame's size.
        mf.setSize( 300, 200 );

        // Create a menu bar with a File menu that has an
        // Exit item.
        JMenuBar mb = new JMenuBar();
        JMenu menu = new JMenu( "File" );
        mb.add( menu );
        JMenuItem item = new JMenuItem( "Exit" );
        menu.add( item );

        // Make the just-created menu bar into the frame's
        // menu bar.
        mf.getRootPane().setMenuBar( mb );

        // Listen to the Exit item so we can exit when it is
        // chosen.
        item.addActionListener( this );

        // Listen to the frame so we can exit if the close
        // button is pressed.
        mf.addWindowListener( new WinExitAdapter() );

        // Show the frame.
        mf.show();
    }

    // The only component generating action events is the
    // Exit item, so if we get an action event, we exit.
    public void actionPerformed( ActionEvent e )
    {
        System.exit( 0 );
    }

    // An instance of this class is listening to the frame
    // created above.  When that frame is closed using the
    // close button or the close item on the system menu, go
    // ahead and exit.
    private class WinExitAdapter extends WindowAdapter
    {
        public void windowClosing( WindowEvent e )
        {
            System.exit( 0 );
        }
    }

    // Main routine.
    public static void main( String args[] )
    {
        new Test();
    }
}
```

JFrame's Public Methods

`AccessibleContext getAccessibleContext()`

Returns a subclass of AccessibleContext, which gives access to the JFrame's accessibility information.

`Container getContentPane()`

Gets the root pane's content pane.

`int getDefaultCloseOperation()`

Returns a constant that describes what will happen to the JFrame when the user closes it. The constant will be one of: DISPOSE_ON_CLOSE, DO_NOTHING_ON_CLOSE, or HIDE_ON_CLOSE.

`Component getGlassPane()`

Gets the root pane's glass pane.

`JMenuBar getJMenuBar()`

Gets the root pane's menu bar.

`JLayeredPane getLayeredPane()`

Gets the root pane's layered pane.

`JRootPane getRootPane()`

Gets the JFrame's root pane.

`void setContentPane(Container content)`

Replaces the root pane's content pane with another container.

`void setDefaultCloseOperation(int closeOp)`

Specifies what happens to the JFrame when the user closes it. It should be one of: DISPOSE_ON_CLOSE, DO_NOTHING_ON_CLOSE, or HIDE_ON_CLOSE.

`void setGlassPane(Component glass)`

Replaces the root pane's glass pane with another component.

`void setJMenuBar(JMenuBar menu)`

Replaces the root pane's menu bar with another JMenuBar.

```
void setLayeredPane(JLayeredPane layered)
```

Replaces the root pane's layered pane with another one.

```
void setLayout(LayoutManager manager)
```

Overridden to throw an exception. You should lay out the content pane instead.

```
void update(Graphics g)
```

Calls paint(g).

JInternalFrame

A JInternalFrame is a window, typically with a border, that can contain other components and can be dragged around like a normal frame except that it cannot go outside of its parent container (see Figure 8-61). Unlike JFrames, the look is totally controlled by the JFC.

JInternalFrames are generally added to a JDesktopPane which manages what happens when the internal frames are resized or minimized.

Ancestors

```
java.lang.Object
    |
    +—java.awt.Component
            |
            +—java.awt.Container
                    |
                    +—com.sun.java.swing.JComponent
                            |
                            +—com.sun.java.swing.JInternalFrame
```

Figure 8-61
A basic
JInternalFrame.

NOTE: *For more information, see the "JDesktopPane," "JRootPane," and "JLayeredPane" sections in this chapter. Also see the "Windows" section in Chapter 7, "JFC by Concept."*

NOTE: *If the container that holds an internal frame is not double-buffered, the display will flash when the internal frame is dragged around. This is normally taken care of since a frame's content pane is a double-buffering JPanel by default, so all of its children (and their children, etc.) will be double-buffered. However, if the content pane is replaced, you may need to set double-buffering on in the JDesktopPane.*

Steps in Creating and Using JInternalFrame

1. Create the internal frame. There are six constructors, but all are variations of:

```
JInternalFrame( String title, boolean resizable,
                boolean closable, boolean maximizable,
                boolean iconifiable )
```

Where 'title' is the string that will go in the internal frame's title bar, 'resizable' says whether the internal frame can be resized, 'closable' says whether the internal frame will have a Close button in the title bar, 'maximizable' says whether the internal frame can be maximized either with a maximize button in the title bar or by double-clicking the title bar itself, and 'iconifiable' says whether the internal frame can be minimized. By default, an internal frame is not resizable, closable, maximizable, or iconifiable.

Create an internal frame that is resizable, maxable, and iconable, but not closable:

```
JInternalFrame inFrame = new JInternalFrame( "My Window",
                             true, false, true, true );
```

2. Add the internal frame to a container (required). You will normally want to add the internal frame to a JDesktopPane. If you add it to a JPanel, the internal frame will be placed and sized based on the JPanel's layout manager, and even if you move the internal frame, it will revert to its original position whenever the JPanel changes size or is re-laid out.

Create a JDesktopPane and add it to a container. In this case, mainPanel is using a BorderLayout:

```
JDesktopPane desktopPane = new JDesktopPane();
mainPanel.add( "Center", desktopPane );
```

Now, set the internal frame's size and position. The origin is relative to the container into which the internal frame is added:

```
inFrame.setBounds( 50, 50, 150, 200 );
```

Add the internal frame to the JDesktopPane:

```
desktopPane.add( inFrame );
```

The JDesktopPane handles its own layout (it uses a null layout manager), so any components added to it should be placed using setBounds().

3. Capture messages that notify you when the internal frame changes size, etc. (optional). The first step is to tell the internal frame which class will be listening (for this example it is the class that contains the internal frame):

```
inFrame.addComponentListener( this );
```

Make the event-receiving class (MyFrame in this case) implement the ComponentListener interface:

```
public class MyFrame extends JFrame implements ComponentListener
{
    .
    .
    .
    public void componentHidden( ComponentEvent e )
    {
    }

    public void componentMoved( ComponentEvent e )
    {
    }

    public void componentResized( ComponentEvent e )
    {
    }

    public void componentShown( ComponentEvent e )
    {
    }
}
```

If you are only going to implement one or two of the methods from the ComponentListener interface, you may want to create a ComponentAdapter class instead. See "A Quick Review of the JDK 1.1 Event Model" in Chapter 7, "JFC by Concept."

4. Add components to the internal frame (optional but usually done).

Set the content pane's layout manager (see JRootPane for a discussion of content panes). By default, the layout of a

JInternalFrame's content pane is BorderLayout, but we set it explicitly as an example.

```
inFrame.getContentPane().setLayout( new BorderLayout() );
```

Create and add a component:

```
JButton btn1 = new JButton( "Bottom button" );
inFrame.getRootPane().getContentPane().add( "South", btn1 );
```

This is the same as:

```
JButton btn1 = new JButton( "Bottom button" );
inFrame.getContentPane().add( "South", btn1 );
```

5. Set the internal frame's layer relative to other components in the JDesktopPane (optional). Components with higher layer numbers go on top of ones with lower layer numbers. JDesktopPane has a number of constants that may be used instead of actual numbers:

```
inFrame.setLayer( new Integer( 5 ) );
```

The layer constants are all of type Integer and their values are:

FRAME_CONTENT_LAYER	-30000
DEFAULT_LAYER	0
PALETTE_LAYER	100
MODAL_LAYER	200
POPUP_LAYER	300
DRAG_LAYER	400

6. Create and add a menu bar (optional). We use the setMenuBar() method which is the same as using getRootPane().setMenuBar():

```
// Create the menu bar.
JMenuBar mbar = new JMenuBar();

// Create a menu.
JMenu filemenu = new JMenu( "File" );

// Add the menu to the menu bar.
mbar.add( filemenu );

// Create a menu item.
JMenuItem closeitem = new JMenuItem( "Close" );

// Add the menu item to the menu.
filemenu.add( closeitem );

// Make the internal frame use this menu bar as its main menu
// bar.
inFrame.setMenuBar( mbar );
```

7. Change the internal frame's border. By default it uses a raised BevelBorder. Here we make it use a lowered BevelBorder for a slightly different look:

```
inFrame.setBorder( new BevelBorder( BevelBorder.LOWERED ) );
```

8. Programatically close, iconify, deiconify, maximize, or minimize the internal frame.

Close it:

```
inFrame.setClosed( true );
```

Iconify it:

```
inFrame.setIcon( true );
```

De-iconify it:

```
inFrame.setIcon( false );
```

Maximize it:

```
inFrame.setMaximum( true );
```

Minimize it:

```
inFrame.setMaximum( false );
```

9. You can track when a JInternalFrame is opened, closing, closed, activated, de-activated, iconified, or de-iconified by using an InternalFrameListener.

Basic Code Examples

EXAMPLE 8-47 Basic JInternalFrame

The following code sample illustrates many of the topics discussed above. It creates a JFrame containing a JDesktopPane, which has a single JInternalFrame. The JInternalFrame has a menu bar and a button, and appears sunken because of a change to its border. The JFrame also has two buttons: Show and Hide. When the Show button is pressed, the JInternalFrame becomes visible. When the Hide button is pressed, the JInternalFrame becomes invisible. The main class also catches the JInternalFrame's Component Events and prints a descriptive string when a Component-Event arrives. Figure 8-62 shows the example with the JInternalFrame visible.

NOTE: *If you hide the JInternalFrame then press the "Show" button, you will get a stack overflow exception. This is a known bug in JFC 1.1 (bug #4116835) for which there is currently no workaround.*

Here is the source code:

Figure 8-62

```java
import com.sun.java.swing.*;
import com.sun.java.swing.border.*;
import java.awt.*;
import java.awt.event.*;

public class MyFrame extends JFrame implements
        ComponentListener, ActionListener
{
    private JInternalFrame mInFrame;

    public MyFrame()
    {
        setTitle( "JInternalFrame1" );

        // Store the content pane in a variable for easier
        // access.
        JPanel contentPane = (JPanel)getContentPane();

        // Components will all be added to this panel.
        contentPane.setLayout( new BorderLayout() );

        // Create a JInternalFrame that is resizable and
        // maximizable, but not iconifiable or closable.
        mInFrame = new JInternalFrame( "My Window",
                                    true, false, true, false );

        // Create a desktop pane for the internal frame to
        // float around in.
        JDesktopPane desktopPane = new JDesktopPane();
        desktopPane.setBackground(
                        contentPane.getBackground() );

        // Add the desktop pane so it covers all of the
        // buffered pane.
        contentPane.add( "Center", desktopPane );

        // Place the internal frame relative to the desktop
        // pane's origin.
        mInFrame.setBounds( 50, 10, 150, 200 );
```

```
        // Add the internal frame to the desktop pane.
        desktopPane.add( mInFrame );

        // Make this class listen for changes to the internal
        // frame.
        mInFrame.addComponentListener( this );

        // Set the layout manager for the internal frame.
        mInFrame.getContentPane().setLayout(
                                    new BorderLayout() );

        // Add a button to the internal frame.
        JButton btn1 = new JButton( "Bottom button" );
        mInFrame.getContentPane().add( "South", btn1 );

        // Set the internal frame's layer in the desktop
        // pane.  This doesn't matter since there is only
        // one internal pane here.
        mInFrame.setLayer( new Integer( 5 ) );

        // Create a menu and add it to the internal frame's
        // root pane.
        JMenuBar mbar = new JMenuBar();
        JMenu filemenu = new JMenu( "File" );
        mbar.add( filemenu );
        JMenuItem closeitem = new JMenuItem( "Close" );
        filemenu.add( closeitem );
        mInFrame.setMenuBar( mbar );

        // Give the internal frame a lowered look instead of
        // the default raised look.
        mInFrame.setBorder( new BevelBorder(
                            BevelBorder.LOWERED ) );

        // Create a "Hide" button that, when pressed, makes
        // the internal frame invisible.
        JButton hide = new JButton( "Hide" );
        hide.setActionCommand( "hide" );
        hide.addActionListener( this );
        contentPane.add( "North", hide );

        // Create a "Show" button that, when pressed, makes
        // the internal frame visible.
        JButton show = new JButton( "Show" );
        show.setActionCommand( "show" );
        show.addActionListener( this );
        contentPane.add( "South", show );
    }

    // This is called when the hide or show button is
    // pressed.
    public void actionPerformed( ActionEvent e )
    {
        if ( e.getActionCommand().equals( "hide" ) )
        {
```

```
            // If the hide button was pressed, tell the
            // internal frame that it is invisible and then
            // repaint to the change is reflected.
            mInFrame.setVisible( false );
            repaint();
        }
        else if ( e.getActionCommand().equals( "show" ) )
        {
            // If the show button is pressed, make the
            // internal frame visible.
            mInFrame.setVisible( true );
            repaint();
        }
    }


    // ComponentListener methods ──────────
    public void componentHidden( ComponentEvent e )
    {
        System.out.println( "Hid" );
    }

    public void componentMoved( ComponentEvent e )
    {
        System.out.println( "Moved" );
    }

    public void componentResized( ComponentEvent e )
    {
        System.out.println( "Resized" );
    }

    public void componentShown( ComponentEvent e )
    {
        System.out.println( "Shown" );
    }
}
```

JInternalFrame's Public Methods

void addInternalFrameListener(InternalFrameListener l)

Tells the JInternalFrame to notify the given class when it opens, closes (or is closing), activates, de-activates, is iconified, or is de-iconified.

void dispose()

Disposes of the JInternalFrame.

AccessibleContext getAccessibleContext()

Returns a subclass of AccessibleContext, which gives access to the JInternalFrame's accessibility information.

```
Color getBackground()
```

Overridden to return the content panel's background color.

```
Container getContentPane()
```

Returns the root pane's content pane.

```
int getDefaultCloseOperation()
```

Returns a constant that describes what will happen to the JInternalFrame when the user closes it. The constant will be one of: DISPOSE_ON_CLOSE, DO_NOTHING_ON_CLOSE, or HIDE_ON_CLOSE.

```
JDesktopIcon getDesktopIcon()
```

Returns the JDesktopIcon that will represent the JInternalFrame when it is iconified.

```
JDesktopPane getDesktopPane()
```

Gets the JDesktopPane that this JInternalFrame has been added to.

```
Color getForeground()
```

Overridden to return the content panel's foreground color.

```
Icon getFrameIcon()
```

Returns the icon that is displayed in the JInternalFrame's title bar.

```
Component getGlassPane()
```

Returns the root pane's glass pane.

```
int getLayer()
```

Returns this JInternalFrame's layer value.

```
JLayeredPane getLayeredPane()
```

Returns the root pane's layered pane.

```
JMenuBar getMenuBar()
```

Returns the root pane's menu bar.

`JRootPane getRootPane()`

Returns this JInternalFrame's root pane.

`String getTitle()`

Gets the string that is displayed in this JInternalFrame's title bar.

`InternalFrameUI getUI()`

Returns this JInternalFrame's current look-and-feel class.

`String getUIClassID()`

Returns the identifying string that the look-and-feel uses to assign a UI class to the JInternalFrame.

`final String getWarningString()`

Returns null.

`boolean isClosable()`

Returns true if this JInternalFrame has a Close button.

`boolean isClosed()`

Returns true if this JInternalFrame has been closed.

`boolean isIcon()`

Returns true if this JInternalFrame is currently iconified.

`boolean isIconifiable()`

Returns true if this JInternalFrame can be iconified.

`boolean isMaximizable()`

Returns true if this JInternalFrame can be maximized.

`boolean isMaximum()`

Returns true if this JInternalFrame is currently maximized.

`boolean isOpaque()`

Returns true if this JInternalFrame paints its entire area.

```
boolean isResizable()
```

Returns true if this JInternalFrame can be resized.

```
boolean isSelected()
```

Returns true if this JInternalFrame is the selected JInternalFrame within its JDesktopPane.

```
void moveToBack()
```

Moves this JInternalFrame behind all others with the same layer value in its JDesktopPane.

```
void moveToFront()
```

Moves this JInternalFrame in front of all others with the same layer value in its JDesktopPane.

```
void pack()
```

Lays out the content panel's contents at their preferred sizes.

```
void removeInternalFrameListener(InternalFrameListener l)
```

Tells the JInternalFrame to stop notifying the given class when it opens, closes (or is closing), activates, de-activates, is iconified, or is de-iconified.

```
void reshape(int x, int y, int width, int height)
```

Moves and resizes the JInternalFrame.

```
void setBackground(Color color)
```

Overridden to set the content panel's color.

```
void setClosable(boolean b)
```

Specifies whether this JInternalFrame has a close button.

```
void setClosed(boolean close)
```

Specifies whether the JInternalFrame is closed or not.

```
void setContentPane(Container c)
```

Replaces the root pane's content pane with another container.

```
void setDefaultCloseOperation(int closeOp)
```

Specifies what happens to the JInternalFrame when the user closes it. It should be one of: DISPOSE_ON_CLOSE, DO_NOTHING_ON_CLOSE, or HIDE_ON_CLOSE.

```
void setDesktopIcon(JInternalFrame.JDesktopIcon d)
```

Specifies the JDesktopIcon that will represent this JInternalFrame when it is iconified.

```
void setForeground(Color color)
```

Overridden to set the content panel's foreground color.

```
void setFrameIcon(Icon icon)
```

Specifies which icon to display in the JInternalFrame's title bar.

```
void setGlassPane(Component glass)
```

Replaces the root pane's glass pane with another component.

```
void setIcon(boolean isIcon)
```

Specifies whether the JInternalFrame should be iconified or not.

```
void setIconifiable(boolean b)
```

Specifies whether this JInternalFrame has a minimize button.

```
void setLayer(Integer layer)
```

Sets this JInternalFrame's layer value.

```
void setLayeredPane(JLayeredPane layered)
```

Replaces the root pane's layered pane with another one.

```
void setLayout(LayoutManager layout)
```

Overridden since layout should be set for the content pane instead.

```
void setMaximizable(boolean b)
```

Specifies whether this JInternalFrame will have a maximize button.

```
void setMaximum(boolean isMaximized)
```

Specifies whether the JInternalFrame is maximized or minimized.

`void setMenuBar(JMenuBar m)`

Replaces the root pane's menu bar.

`void setResizable(boolean b)`

Specifies whether this JInternalFrame can be resized.

`void setSelected(boolean isSelected)`

Specifies whether the JInternalFrame is its JDesktopPanel's active window.

`void setTitle(String title)`

Sets the string that this JInternalFrame displays in its title bar.

`void setUI(InternalFrameUI ui)`

Gives this JInternalFrame a new look-and-feel class.

`void setVisible(boolean isVisible)`

Overridden to generate opened event the first time.

`void show()`

Makes the JInternalFrame visible and moves it to the front.

`void toBack()`

Moves this JInternalFrame to the back.

`void toFront()`

Moves this JInternalFrame to the front.

`void updateUI()`

Tells this JInternalFrame that the look-and-feel class has been changed.

JLabel

JLabel is a component that places static text on a user interface (see Figure 8-63). It is typically used to define what an associated control (like a text field)

Figure 8-63
A label with text but
no icon.

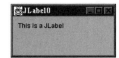

is used for. In the JFC, a label can be text only, text and an icon, or an icon only. Even though a JLabel doesn't respond to accelerator keys, it can be used to show an associated component's accelerator key.

A JLabel typically consisits of a background rectangle (generally the color of its container), and a text string and/or an icon. JLabel can generate mouse events if required.

Ancestors

```
java.lang.Object
    |
    +—java.awt.Component
            |
            +—java.awt.Container
                    |
                    +—com.sun.java.swing.JComponent
                            |
                            +—com.sun.java.swing.JLabel
```

NOTE: *For more information, see the "ImageIcon" section in this chapter.*

Steps in Creating and Using JLabel

1. Create the JLabel using one of the constructors. There are six constructors, but all are variations on:

   ```
   JLabel( String text, Icon icon, int horizontalAlignment )
   ```

   where 'text' is the label text, 'icon' is the icon that can accompany the text, and 'horizontalAlignment' specifies where within the control the text is aligned.

   Create a text-only label:

   ```
   JLabel myLabel = new JLabel( "Simple label:  " );
   ```

   Create a label that has text and an icon and in which the text is aligned to the left edge of the component:

```
JLabel myLabel = new JLabel( "Label with icon",
                    new ImageIcon( "picture.gif" ),
                    JLabel.LEFT );
```

2. Define an accelerator key character. This character will be underlined on the label. The label will not respond to any key strokes—the underlined character is used to direct the user to press an accelerator key for a component associated with the label. This is helpful when a label is associated with a component like a text field that cannot advertise its own accelerator key.

```
myLabel.setDisplayedMnemonic( 'i' );
```

You will still have to define the associated component's accelerator character. For text fields, see JTextField.setFocusAccelerator(char).

3. Add a tool tip. This is a string that shows up when you stop the mouse over the label.

```
myLabel.setToolTipText( "This is a label" );
```

4. Capture events that can be associated with the label. For example, JLabel can see mouse events.

Define which class will receive the events. In this case, it is the class in which the JLabel is defined:

```
myLabel.addMouseListener( this );
```

Make the receiving class implement the event listener:

```
public class MyFrame extends JFrame implements MouseListener
{
    .
    .
    .
    public void mousePressed( MouseEvent e )
    {
    }

    public void mouseReleased( MouseEvent e )
    {
    }

    public void mouseEntered( MouseEvent e )
    {
    }

    public void mouseExited( MouseEvent e )
    {
    }

    public void mouseClicked( MouseEvent e )
    {
    }
}
```

If you only care about a couple of the MouseListener methods, you may want to create a MouseAdapter class so you can implement only the methods that you need to. For more information, see "A Quick Review of the JDK 1.1 Event Model" in Chapter 7, "JFC by Concept."

5. For labels with icons, when the label is disabled, the default behavior is for the icon's colors to be grayed out. If you want to set your own icon to be displayed when the label is disabled:

```
myLabel.setDisabledIcon( new ImageIcon( "disabled.gif" ) );
```

6. You can also change the alignment of the label. This can be done either using an alignment parameter in the constructor, or by changing the alignment after the label has been created. Horizontal alignment can be LEFT, RIGHT, or CENTER. Vertical alignment can be TOP, BOTTOM, or CENTER. By default, horizontal position is LEFT and vertical position is CENTER.

```
myLabel.setHorizontalAlignment( JLabel.CENTER );
myLabel.setVerticalAlignment( JLabel.BOTTOM );
```

7. If your label has both text and an icon, you can change the text and icon's relative positions in the label. By default, the icon is to the left of the text, aligned horizontally LEFT and vertically in the CENTER.

To move the text above the icon, you have to move the text to the CENTER horizontally and to the TOP vertically:

```
myLabel.setHorizontalTextPosition( JLabel.CENTER );
myLabel.setVerticalTextPosition( JLabel.TOP );
```

8. To change the text color, use the setForeground() method inherited from Component. This works for the Windows look-and-feel since it uses the foreground color to draw text. It is not guaranteed to work with all look-and-feels:

```
myLabel.setForeground( Color.blue );
```

9. To change the label's font, you can use the setFont() method. This works with the Windows look-and-feel, but is not guaranteed to work with every look-and-feel:

```
myLabel.setFont( new Font( "Helvetica", Font.PLAIN, 24 ) );
```

Basic Code Examples

EXAMPLE 8-48 Standard Ways to Use JLabel

This example illustrates many of the techniques listed above, creating a variety of JLabels with different fonts, colors, alignments, etc. There is also a button in this example which, when pushed, causes one of the JLabels to be disabled/enabled. This exercises the setDisabledIcon() method. You may also

Figure 8-64

notice that the example listens to the first JLabel's MouseEvents and MouseMotionEvents and prints out a number from 1 to 7 depending on the type of event. Figure 8-64 shows how the example looks initially.

Here is the source code:

```
import com.sun.java.swing.*;
import com.sun.java.swing.border.*;
import java.awt.*;
import java.awt.event.*;

public class MyFrame extends JFrame implements
        ActionListener, MouseListener, MouseMotionListener
{
    JLabel mDisableLabel;
    ImageIcon mEnabled;
    ImageIcon mDisabled;

    public MyFrame()
    {
        setTitle( "JLabel1" );

        // Load the icons in advance.
        mEnabled = new ImageIcon( "enabled.gif" );
        mDisabled = new ImageIcon( "disabled.gif" );

        // Use a buffered panel to make it resize smoothly
        // and not flash when the button is pressed.
        JPanel contentPane = (JPanel)getContentPane();

        // Components will all be added to this panel.
        contentPane.setLayout( new GridLayout( 9, 1 ) );
        contentPane.setBorder(
                    new EmptyBorder( 10, 10, 10, 10 ) );

        // Just a regular label.
        JLabel l1 = new JLabel( "Basic Label" );
        l1.addMouseListener( this );
        l1.addMouseMotionListener( this );
```

```
        contentPane.add( l1 );

        // A label aligned to the right side of the container.
        JLabel l2 = new JLabel(
                    "Right-aligned Label", JLabel.RIGHT );
        contentPane.add( l2 );

        // Note that the first 'c' is underlined.
        JLabel l3 = new JLabel( "Accelerated Label" );
        l3.setDisplayedMnemonic( 'c' );
        contentPane.add( l3 );

        // This label has a different font.
        JLabel l4 = new JLabel( "Big Font Label" );
        l4.setForeground( Color.red );
        l4.setFont( new Font( "Helvetica", Font.BOLD, 18 ) );
        contentPane.add( l4 );

        // A label with an icon using default alignment.
        JLabel l5 = new JLabel( "Image Label Center",
                                mEnabled, JLabel.LEFT );
        contentPane.add( l5 );

        // A label aligned above its icon.
        JLabel l6 = new JLabel( "Image Label Top", mEnabled,
                                JLabel.LEFT );
        l6.setVerticalTextPosition( JLabel.TOP );
        l6.setHorizontalTextPosition( JLabel.CENTER );
        contentPane.add( l6 );

        // 50 pixel gap between the text and the icon.
        JLabel l7 = new JLabel( "Big Image Gap", mEnabled,
                                JLabel.LEFT );
        l7.setIconTextGap( 50 );
        l7.setToolTipText(
                    "My, what a lovely icon-text gap!");
        contentPane.add( l7 );

        // With the JButton below, this illustrates how the
        // icon can be disabled along with the text.
        mDisableLabel = new JLabel( "Disable-able label",
                                    mEnabled,
                        JLabel.LEFT );
        mDisableLabel.setDisabledIcon( mDisabled );
        contentPane.add( mDisableLabel );

        // JButton to toggle the above label's enabled state.
        JButton b1 = new JButton( "Enable/Disable" );
        b1.addActionListener( this );
        contentPane.add( b1 );
    }

    // Catches the button press and toggles one label's
    // state.
    public void actionPerformed( ActionEvent e )
```

```
{
    mDisableLabel.setEnabled(
                         ! mDisableLabel.isEnabled() );
    repaint();
}

// Mouse event and mouse motion handlers.  They show
// that mouse events can be generated by a JLabel.
// JLabel '11' is the only one actually being listened
// to.
public void mousePressed( MouseEvent e )
{
    System.out.println( "1" );
}

public void mouseReleased( MouseEvent e )
{
    System.out.println( "2" );
}

public void mouseEntered( MouseEvent e )
{
    System.out.println( "3" );
}

public void mouseExited( MouseEvent e )
{
    System.out.println( "4" );
}

public void mouseClicked( MouseEvent e )
{
    System.out.println( "5" );
}

public void mouseDragged( MouseEvent e )
{
    System.out.println( "6" );
}

public void mouseMoved( MouseEvent e )
{
    System.out.println( "7" );
}
}
```

JLabel's Public Methods

```
AccessibleContext getAccessibleContext()
```

Returns a subclass of AccessibleContext, which gives access to the JLabel's accessibility information.

`Icon getDisabledIcon()`

Returns the icon (if any) that this JLabel displays when it is disabled.

`char getDisplayedMnemonic()`

Returns which character in the JLabel's text string is underlined, indicating the accelerator key for an associated component.

`int getHorizontalAlignment()`

Returns how the text/icon are aligned horizontally within the JLabel's rectangle. May be LEFT, CENTER, or RIGHT.

`int getHorizontalTextPosition()`

Returns the JLabel's text's horizontal position relative to its icon. May be LEFT, CENTER, or RIGHT.

`Icon getIcon()`

Returns the JLabel's normal icon.

`int getIconTextGap()`

Returns the size of the gap between the text and icon in pixels.

`Component getLabelFor()`

Returns the component this JLabel is associated with, if any.

`String getText()`

Returns the JLabel's text string.

`LabelUI getUI()`

Returns the JLabel's current look-and-feel class.

`String getUIClassID()`

Returns the identifying string that the look-and-feel uses to assign a UI class to the JLabel.

`int getVerticalAlignment()`

Returns how the text/icon are vertically aligned within the JLabel's rectangular area. May be TOP, CENTER, or BOTTOM.

`int getVerticalTextPosition()`

Returns the text's vertical position relative to the icon. May be TOP, CENTER, or BOTTOM.

```
void setDisabledIcon(Icon disabledIcon)
```

Specifies the icon that the JLabel will display when disabled.

```
void setDisplayedMnemonic(char aKey)
```

Specifies the character that will be underlined in the JLabel's text string, indicating the accelerator key for an associated component.

```
void setDisplayedMnemonic(int keycode)
```

Specifies the keycode for the associated component's accelerator key.

```
void setFont(Font font)
```

Specifies the font the JLabel will use to display its text string. Overridden to cause the JLabel to repaint.

```
void setHorizontalAlignment(int alignment)
```

Specifies the text/icon's horizontal alignment within the JLabel's rectangular area. May be LEFT, CENTER, or RIGHT.

```
void setHorizontalTextPosition(int x)
```

Specifies the text string's horizontal position relative to the icon. May be LEFT, CENTER, or RIGHT.

```
void setIcon(Icon icon)
```

Specifies the icon that the JLabel will normally display.

```
void setIconTextGap(int iconTextGap)
```

Specifies the gap between the text and icon in pixels.

```
void setLabelFor(Component c)
```

Tells the JLabel that the given component is associated with it. This means the JLabel is almost certainly used to decsribe the given component.

```
void setText(String text)
```

Specifies the JLabel's text string.

```
void setUI(LabelUI ui)
```

Gives the JLabel a new look-and-feel class.

```
void setVerticalAlignment(int alignment)
```

Specifies the text/icon's vertical alignment within the JLabel's rectangular area. May be TOP, CENTER, or BOTTOM.

```
void setVerticalTextPosition(int textPosition)
```

Specifies the text string's vertical position relative to the icon. May be TOP, CENTER, or BOTTOM.

```
void updateUI()
```

Tells the JLabel that the look-and-feel class has been changed.

JLayeredPane

JLayeredPane is a panel that can control how its child components behave when they overlap. It can specify a layer for each component so that some components always appear above others. JLayeredPane is not all that useful by itself, but is used behind the scenes in JRootPanes, and JDesktopPane is a JLayeredPane subclass.

Ancestors

```
java.lang.Object
   |
   +—java.awt.Component
           |
           +—java.awt.Container
                   |
                   +—com.sun.java.swing.JComponent
                           |
                           +—com.sun.java.swing.JLayeredPane
```

JLayeredPane's Public Methods

```
AccessibleContext getAccessibleContext()
```

Returns a subclass of AccessibleContext which gives access to the JLayeredPane's accessibility information.

`int getComponentCountInLayer(int layer)`

Returns the number of components in the given layer.

`Component[] getComponentsInLayer(int layer)`

Returns all components in a given layer.

`int getIndexOf(Component c)`

Returns the component index for the given component.

`int getLayer(Component c)`

Returns the layer at which the given component is being drawn.

`int getLayer(JComponent c)`

Returns the layer at which the given component is being drawn.

`JLayeredPane getLayeredPaneAbove(Component c)`

Finds the first layered pane above the JLayeredPane in the display hierarchy.

`int getPosition(Component c)`

Returns the given component's relative position within its layer.

`int highestLayer()`

Returns the highest layer in use.

`boolean isOptimizedDrawingEnabled()`

Overridden. Returns false.

`int lowestLayer()`

Returns the lowest layer currently in use.

`void moveToBack(Component c)`

Moves the given component behind the other components in its layer.

`void moveToFront(Component c)`

Moves the given component ahead of the other components in its layer.

void paint(Graphics g)

Overridden for special painting.

void putLayer(JComponent c, int layer)

Specifies the layer number for the given component.

void remove(int n)

Removes the nth component from the JLayeredPane.

void setLayer(Component c, int layer)

Specifies the layer number for the given component, but must be called before the component is added.

void setLayer(Component c, int layer, int position)

Specifies the layer number and position within the layer for the given component, but must be called before the component is added.

void setPosition(Component c, int position)

Specifies the given component's position within its layer.

JList

JList is a graphical area that displays a list of objects and allows the user to select from the list (see Figure 8-65). It does not do scrolling, so if your list is likely to be too big for the available space, you will want to use a JScrollPane. By default JList handles only strings, but you can make it handle other data types like text with icons, etc., by making your own cell renderer. This is described later in this section.

A JList will generate events when its selection changes, or when any of its items change.

Figure 8-65
A JList within a
JScrollPane.

Ancestors

```
java.lang.Object
    |
    +-java.awt.Component
            |
            +-java.awt.Container
                    |
                    +-com.sun.java.swing.JComponent
                            |
                            +-com.sun.java.swing.JList
```

NOTE: *For more information, see the "DefaultListModel" and "DefaultListSelectionModel" in this chapter and the "Selecting Items from Lists" section in Chapter 7, "JFC by Concept."*

Steps in Creating and Using JList

1. Load up the initial list data and create the list box. This can be done in one of three ways:

   Load a Vector:

   ```
   Vector v = new Vector();
   v.addElement( "One" );
   v.addElement( "Two" );
   v.addElement( "Three" );
   JList listBox = new JList( v );
   ```

   Load an object array:

   ```
   String arr[] = new String[3];
   arr[0] = "One";
   arr[1] = "Two";
   arr[2] = "Three";
   JList listBox = new JList( arr );
   ```

   Or, create a ListModel and load the data into it:

   ```
   DefaultListModel model = new DefaultListModel();
   model.addElement( "One" );
   model.addElement( "Two" );
   model.addElement( "Three" );
   JList listBox = new JList( model );
   ```

   All three methods will work. Using an array is not as flexible since you cannot add more items indefinitely. It is not necessary to load the list items before passing the Vector/array/ListModel into the constructor. They can be loaded afterward. If you add items later, it is important to call the validate() method so the list will recognize the new items and take them into account. You can also use the empty constructor JList(), then load the data using setListData(Vector), setListData(Object [ ]), or setModel(ListModel).

2. Create a cell renderer. This is required if you want list items that are not just Strings. A cell renderer accepts a list item and configures it for display. Cell renderers extend components like JLabel. This does not mean you can put a bunch of JButtons in a list and then be able to click on them as if they were real buttons. They will look like buttons in the list, but they will not respond to clicks like buttons do. In fact, the list items as they appear on the screen are not separate components—they just appear to be.

First, make a class that implements ListCellRenderer. This particular example assumes the data are Strings. It causes all selected items to be drawn with one icon and non-selected items to be drawn with another icon:

```java
class MyCellRenderer extends JLabel implements ListCellRenderer
{
    ImageIcon mSelected;
    ImageIcon mNotSelected;

    MyCellRenderer()
    {
        // Load the icons that will be displayed with the list
        // strings.
        mSelected = new ImageIcon( "enabled.gif" );
        mNotSelected = new ImageIcon( "disabled.gif" );
    }

    // Required for classes that implement ListCellRenderer.  If
    // this item is selected, use the selected icon.  Otherwise,
    // use the other one.
    public Component getListCellRendererComponent( JList list,
                                     Object value,
                                     int index,
                                     boolean isSelected,
                                     boolean cellHasFocus )
    {
        if ( isSelected )
        {
            setBackground( SystemColor.textHighlight );
            setForeground( SystemColor.textHighlightText );
            setIcon( mSelected );
        }
        else
        {
            setBackground( getContentPane().getBackground() );
            setForeground( SystemColor.textText );
            setIcon( mNotSelected );
        }

        // Set the renderer's text so it will draw.
        setText( (String)value );
```

```
      return this;
   }

}
```

Then, tell the list box to use your cell renderer:

```
listBox.setCellRenderer( new MyCellRenderer() );
```

3. Assign a class to listen for changes in the list box's selections. Notice that the events come from the JList's selection model.

First, tell the list box which class will be listening for events. In this example, the listener will be the class in which the list box is defined (MyFrame):

```
listBox.getSelectionModel().addListSelectionListener( this );
```

Then, make sure the listening class implements the ListSelectionListner interface:

```
public class MyFrame extends JFrame implements
            ListSelectionListener
{
   .
   .
   .
   public void valueChanged( ListSelectionEvent e )
   {
      // This is called when the selection changes, so
      // do what you need to do here.
   }
}
```

4. Use a JScrollPane to make it so the user can scroll through the list if it gets too big for its display area:

```
JScrollPane scrollPane = new JScrollPane( mListBox );
```

5. Specify how many items should be visible at a time. This affects the JList's preferred size.

```
mListBox.setVisibleRowCount( 3 );
```

6. You can also listen for changes to the list itself. That is, if items get added to the list or removed from it, you can be notified. These events come from the JList's ListModel, accessible through the getModel() method. You do this by making a class implement the ListDataListener interface, and add that class to the ListModel as a listener.

Specify a class that will be notified when the ListModel changes. In this case it is the class in which the JList is defined:

```
mListBox.getModel().addListDataListener( this );
```

Make the event-receiving class implement the ListDataListener interface:

```java
public class MyFrame extends JFrame implements ListDataListener
{
    .
    .
    .
    public void contentsChanged( ListDataEvent e )
    {
        // The list contents changed.
    }

    public void intervalAdded( ListDataEvent e )
    {
        // One or more items were added.
    }

    public void intervalRemoved( ListDataEvent e )
    {
        // One or more items were removed.
    }
}
```

Basic Code Examples

EXAMPLE 8-49 BASIC JLIST

This example puts the concepts discussed above into a working program. It starts with three strings added to the list and has a button that, when pressed, will add another item. Unimaginatively, it is always the same item. The main class (MyFrame) listens for changes in the list's selection and its contents. It uses a custom ListCellRenderer to draw an icon next to each string in the list. There are two icons—one for the selected item and one for the rest. Figure 8-66 shows the example after some items have been added.

Important points to notice:

■ The addNotify() method is overridden so the list will display properly the first time.

■ The validate() method is called when an item is added so the display will reflect the list contents.

Figure 8-66

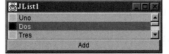

■ The custom ListCellRenderer is created as an inner class, but it could just as well have been in its own source file.

Here is the source:

```
import com.sun.java.swing.*;
import com.sun.java.swing.event.*;
import java.awt.*;
import java.awt.event.*;

public class MyFrame extends JFrame implements
        ActionListener, ListSelectionListener,
        ListDataListener
{
    DefaultListModel mModel;
    JList mListBox;

    public MyFrame()
    {
        setTitle( "JList1" );

        // Store the content pane in a variable for easier
        // access.
        JPanel contentPane = (JPanel)getContentPane();

        // Components will all be added to this panel.
        contentPane.setLayout( new BorderLayout() );

        // Load the initial three items into the data model.
        mModel = new DefaultListModel();
        mModel.addElement( "Uno" );
        mModel.addElement( new String( "Dos" ) );
        mModel.addElement( new String( "Tres" ) );

        // Create the list box with a model full of data.
        mListBox = new JList( mModel );

        // Tell the list box how to draw the items.
        mListBox.setCellRenderer( new MyCellRenderer() );

        mListBox.setBackground( Color.gray );

        // We only want the list to have 3 items visible at
        // a time.
        mListBox.setVisibleRowCount( 3 );

        // Tell the list box's selection model to send events
        // to this class.
        mListBox.getSelectionModel().addListSelectionListener(
                                    this );

        // Specify that this class will be notified of
        // changes within the list.
        mListBox.getModel().addListDataListener( this );
```

```
      // Put the list in a scroll pane so we can keep
      // growing it.
      JScrollPane scrollPane = new JScrollPane( mListBox );

      contentPane.add( "North", scrollPane );

      // Create a button that, when pressed, will add an
      // element to the list box.
      JButton b1 = new JButton( "Add" );
      b1.addActionListener( this );
      contentPane.add( "South", b1 );
   }

   // Override this so the list draws properly the first
   // time.
   public void addNotify()
   {
      super.addNotify();
      mListBox.validate();
   }

   // When the button is pressed, add the string "Quatro"
   // to the end of the list.
   public void actionPerformed( ActionEvent e )
   {
      mModel.addElement( "Quatro" );

      // Make sure the just-added item is visible.
      mListBox.ensureIndexIsVisible( mModel.getSize() - 1 );

      // Tell the list box to make sure it is laid out
      // properly.
      mListBox.validate();
   }

   // Respond to selection events in the list box.
   public void valueChanged( ListSelectionEvent e )
   {
      // Print out all items currently selected.
      System.out.println( "Selected:" );

      Object arr[] = mListBox.getSelectedValues();

      for ( int i = 0; i < arr.length; i++ )
         System.out.println( "    "+(String)(arr[i]) );
   }

   // This method is called if items in the list change.
   public void contentsChanged( ListDataEvent e )
   {
      System.out.println( "Changed" );
   }

   // This method is called if items are added to the Jlist.
```

```
public void intervalAdded( ListDataEvent e )
{
    System.out.println( "Added" );
}

// This method is called if items are removed from the
// list.
public void intervalRemoved( ListDataEvent e )
{
    System.out.println( "Removed" );
}

// Private class to draw the item's strings as labels.
class MyCellRenderer extends JLabel implements
      ListCellRenderer
{
    ImageIcon mSelected;
    ImageIcon mNotSelected;

    MyCellRenderer()
    {
        // Load the icons that will be displayed with the
        // list strings.
        mSelected = new ImageIcon( "enabled.gif" );
        mNotSelected = new ImageIcon( "disabled.gif" );
    }

    // Required for classes that implement
    // ListCellRenderer.  If this item is selected, use
    // the selected icon.  Otherwise, use the other one.
    public Component getListCellRendererComponent(
                            JList list,
                            Object value,
                            int index,
                            boolean isSelected,
                            boolean cellHasFocus )
    {
        if ( isSelected )
        {
            setBackground( SystemColor.textHighlight );
            setForeground( SystemColor.textHighlightText );
            setIcon( mSelected );
        }
        else
        {
            setBackground(
                        getContentPane().getBackground() );
            setForeground( SystemColor.textText );
            setIcon( mNotSelected );
        }

        // Set the renderer's text so it will draw.
        setText( (String)value );

        return this;
```

```
                }

                public boolean isOpaque()
                {
                    return true;
                }
            }
        }
```

JList's Public Methods

`void addListSelectionListener(ListSelectionListener listener)`

Tells the JList to notify the given class when the JList's selection state changes.

`void addSelectionInterval(int anchor,int lead)`

Adds the items between the two given item indices to the current list of selected items.

`void clearSelection()`

Makes it so that no items are selected.

`void ensureIndexIsVisible(int index)`

Makes sure that the item at the given index is visible if the JList is being scrolled.

`AccessibleContext getAccessibleContext()`

Returns a subclass of AccessibleContext which gives access to the JList's accessibility information.

`int getAnchorSelectionIndex()`

Returns the 'anchor' argument from the previous addSelectionInterval() or setSelectionInterval() call.

`Rectangle getCellBounds(int index1,int index2)`

Returns the rectangle that bounds the list items from index1 to index2.

`ListCellRenderer getCellRenderer()`

Returns the ListCellRenderer that the JList is currently using to draw its items.

```
int getFirstVisibleIndex()
```

Returns the index of the topmost list item that is visible.

```
int getFixedCellHeight()
```

Returns the cell height.

```
int getFixedCellWidth()
```

Returns the cell width.

```
int getLastVisibleIndex()
```

Returns the index of the bottom-most list item that is visible.

```
int getLeadSelectionIndex()
```

Returns the 'lead' argument from the previous addSelectionInterval() or setSelectionInterval() call.

```
int getMaxSelectionIndex()
```

Returns the index of the bottom-most selected item.

```
int getMinSelectionIndex()
```

Returns the index of the topmost selected item.

```
ListModel getModel()
```

Returns the JList's data model class.

```
Dimension getPreferredScrollableViewportSize()
```

Returns the size required to display the number of rows set in the setVisibleRowCount() method (or its default value if not explicitly set).

```
Object getPrototypeCellValue()
```

Returns the fake list item value (if any) that was used to calculate the fixed cell width and height.

```
int getScrollableBlockIncrement(Rectangle visibleRect,int
        orientation,int direction)
```

Overridden to provide scrolling information.

```
boolean getScrollableTracksViewportHeight()
```

Overridden to return false.

```
boolean getScrollableTracksViewportWidth()
```

Overridden to return false.

```
int getScrollableUnitIncrement(Rectangle visibleRect,int
        orientation,int direction)
```

Overridden to provide scrolling information.

```
int getSelectedIndex()
```

Returns the index of the topmost selected item.

```
int[] getSelectedIndices()
```

Returns the indices of all of the selected items.

```
Object getSelectedValue()
```

Returns the topmost selected item.

```
Object[] getSelectedValues()
```

Returns all of the selected items.

```
Color getSelectionBackground()
```

Returns the color used to draw selected items' backgrounds.

```
Color getSelectionForeground()
```

Returns the color used to draw selected items' foregrounds.

```
int getSelectionMode()
```

Returns the current selection mode. Valid values are constants from List-SelectionModel: MULTIPLE_INTERVAL_SELECTION, SINGLE_INTER-VAL_SELECTION, and SINGLE_SELECTION.

```
ListSelectionModel getSelectionModel()
```

Returns the JList's selection model.

```
ListUI getUI()
```

Returns the JList's current look-and-feel class.

```
String getUIClassID()
```

Returns the identifying string that the look-and-feel uses to assign a UI class to the JList.

```
boolean getValueIsAdjusting(boolean b)
```

Returns true if the list feels it is in the middle of a change.

```
int getVisibleRowCount()
```

Returns the number of rows that the JList wants to have visible at once.

```
Point indexToLocation(int index)
```

Returns the upper left coordinate of the list item at the given index.

```
boolean isOpaque()
```

Returns true since the JList paints its entire area.

```
boolean isSelectedIndex(int index)
```

Returns true if the item at the given index is selected.

```
boolean isSelectionEmpty()
```

Returns true if no items are currently selected.

```
int locationToIndex(Point location)
```

Returns the index of the list item that is at the specified point.

```
void removeListSelectionListener(ListSelectionListener listener)
```

Tells the JList to stop notifying the given class when the selection state changes.

```
void removeSelectionInterval(int index0,int index1)
```

Removes the list items from index0 to index1 inclusive from the current list of selected items.

```
void setCellRenderer(ListCellRenderer cellRenderer)
```

Specifies the ListCellRenderer that will be used to draw the list items.

```
void setFixedCellHeight(int height)
```

Specifies the cell height to be applied to all list items.

```
void setFixedCellWidth(int width)
```

Specifies the cell width to be applied to all list items.

```
void setListData(Object listData[])
```

Replaces the items in the list with a whole new set of items.

```
void setListData(Vector listData)
```

Replaces the items in the list with a whole new set of items.

```
void setModel(ListModel model)
```

Replaces the current list data model with a new one.

```
void setPrototypeCellValue(Object prototypeCellValue)
```

You can use this to give the JList a fake list item that it can use to calculate the fixed cell width and height.

```
void setSelectedIndex(int index)
```

Specify that the item at the given index should be the JList's only selected item.

```
void setSelectedIndices(int indices[])
```

Specifies that the items represented by the given array of indices will be the only selected items in the JList. Any existing selected items will be deselected.

```
void setSelectedValue(Object anObject,boolean shouldScroll)
```

Specifies that the given list item should become the JList's only selected item. You can also set shouldScroll to force the newly selected item to become visible if the JList is being scrolled.

```
void setSelectionBackground(Color color)
```

Specifies the color used to draw selected items' backgrounds.

```
void getSelectionForeground(Color color)
```

Specifies the color used to draw selected items' foregrounds.

```
void setSelectionInterval(int anchor,int lead)
```

Makes the items from anchor to lead inclusive the JList's only selected items.

```
void setSelectionMode(int mode)
```

Specifies the current selection mode. Valid values are constants from List-SelectionModel: MULTIPLE_INTERVAL_SELECTION, SINGLE_INTER-VAL_SELECTION, and SINGLE_SELECTION.

```
void setSelectionModel(ListSelectionModel selectionModel)
```

Replaces the current ListSelectionModel.

```
void setUI(ListUI ui)
```

Gives the JList a new look-and-feel class.

```
void setValueIsAdjusting(boolean b)
```

Generally called by the UI class to tell the list that it is in the middle of a change.

```
void setVisibleRowCount(int visibleRowCount)
```

Sets the number of rows that should be visible at one time. This affects the vertical size of the JList.

```
void updateUI()
```

Tells the JList that its look-and-feel class has been changed.

JMenu

A JMenu is a standard menu that is either attached to a menu bar or is a sub-menu to another JMenu (see Figure 8-67). A JMenu restricts what may be added to it to components that implement the MenuElement interface, so normally all items in a menu are JMenuItems or are descended from JMe-nuItem (JMenu itself, JCheckBoxMenuItem, and JRadioButtonMenuItem).

Figure 8-67
A typical JMenu.

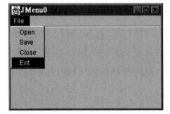

Ancestors

```
java.lang.Object
    |
    +--java.awt.Component
           |
           +--java.awt.Container
                   |
                   +--com.sun.java.swing.JComponent
                           |
                           +--com.sun.java.swing.AbstractButton
                                   |
                                   +--com.sun.java.swing.JMenuItem
                                           |
                                           +--com.sun.java.swing.JMenu
```

NOTE: *For more information, see the "JMenuBar," "JMenuItem," "JCheckBoxMenuItem," "JRadioButtonMenuItem," "AbstractAction," and "JRootPane" sections in this chapter. Also see the "Menus" section in Chapter 7, "JFC by Concept."*

Steps in Creating and Using JMenu

1. Create a menu bar and add it to the frame/internal frame/etc. JMenus are typically put into JMenuBars. JMenuBars normally go at the top of a frame or internal frame, just beneath the title bar, but they can be added as components into any container. Here we add the menu bar to a JFrame via its root pane, which is the normal way to do it:

   ```
   JMenuBar mbar = new JMenuBar();
   getRootPane().setMenuBar( mbar );
   ```

2. Create a menu. There are three constructors:

   Create an empty menu. This constructor does not provide a string that will show up in the menu bar so you will probably want to call the menu's setText() method to specify this string.

   ```
   JMenu blankmenu = new JMenu();
   ```

   Create a normal menu with a string that will show up in the menu bar.

   ```
   JMenu filemenu = new JMenu( "File" );
   ```

   Create a tear-off menu with a string that will appear in the menu bar:

   ```
   JMenu filemenu = new JMenu( "File", true );
   ```

3. Change/set a menu's text string:

   ```
   blankmenu.setText( "Options" );
   ```

4. Give the menu an icon that will be displayed with its string (if any) in the menu bar:

```
blankmenu.setIcon( new ImageIcon( "on.gif" ) );
```

5. Set the menu's font. This works with the Windows look and feel, but is not guaranteed to work with others:

```
filemenu.setFont( new Font( "TimesRoman", Font.BOLD, 18 ) );
```

6. Set the menu's text color and background. These apply only to the menu's string in the menu bar, not to items in the menu. It works with the Windows look and feel, but is not guaranteed to work with others:

```
filemenu.setForeground( Color.green );
filemenu.setBackground( Color.red );
```

7. Create items and add them to the menu. Normally, the things you add to a JMenu will be JMenuItems, but you can add just about any kind of component you want, as long as it implements the MenuElement interface.

Create a new JMenuItem and add it:

```
JMenuItem open = new JMenuItem( "Open" );
filemenu.add( open );
```

Create a menu that will be a submenu of the current one:

```
JMenu submenu = new JMenu( "Sub Menu" );
filemenu.add( submenu );
```

Add a separator between menu items:

```
filemenu.addSeparator();
```

8. Set the menu's accelerator. Pressing this with a special key (Alt on many platforms) causes the menu to expand.

```
filemenu.setMnemonic( 'f' );
```

9. Create an Action and add it to the menu as a JMenuItem.

Create a subclass of AbstractAction, and give it a text string:

```
private class CopyAction extends AbstractAction
{
   public CopyAction( String text )
   {
      super( text );
   }

   public void actionPerformed( ActionEvent e )
   {
      // Do something now you know the "Copy" menu item was
      // pressed.
   }
}
```

Create an instance of the action and add it to the JMenu:

```
// Create a JMenu.
JMenu editMenu = new JMenu( "Edit" );

// Create an instance of the action.
CopyAction copyAction = new CopyAction( "Copy" );

// Add the action to the JMenu.  This causes a JMenuItem to be
// created and added to the JMenu.  The created JMenuItem is
// returned from the add() method.
JMenuItem copyMenuItem = editMenu.add( copyAction );
```

Basic Code Examples

EXAMPLE 8-50 Variations on JMenu

This example takes the concepts discussed above and puts them into a working class. It has a menu bar with two menus. The menus' attributes have been changed. The first menu has two regular menu items, one submenu, and a separator in it. The second menu just has a single menu item. There is a MenuListener attached to the first menu and it prints out a string when a MenuEvent happens. Figure 8-62 shows the example with the first opened up.

Here is the source code:

```
import com.sun.java.swing.*;
import com.sun.java.swing.event.*;
import com.sun.java.swing.border.*;
import java.awt.*;
import java.awt.event.*;

public class MyFrame extends JFrame implements MenuListener
{
    public MyFrame()
    {
        setTitle( "JMenu1" );

        // Store the content pane in a variable for easier
        // access.
        JPanel contentPane = (JPanel)getContentPane();
```

Figure 8-68

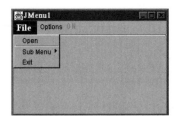

```java
// Create a menu bar and add it to the frame.
JMenuBar mbar = new JMenuBar();
getRootPane().setMenuBar( mbar );

// Create a file menu.
JMenu filemenu = new JMenu( "File" );

// Change the menu's font.
filemenu.setFont( new Font( "TimesRoman",
                            Font.BOLD, 18 ) );

// Change the menu's text color.
filemenu.setForeground( Color.green );

// Change the menu's background color.
filemenu.setBackground( Color.red );

// Make it so this class is notified when menu events
// are generated by this menu.
filemenu.addMenuListener( this );

// Add the menu to the menu bars.
mbar.add( filemenu );

// Create and add a simple JMenuItem.
JMenuItem open = new JMenuItem( "Open" );
filemenu.add( open );

// Add a separator between menu items.
filemenu.addSeparator();

// Create a sub menu with one item in it and add it
// to the menu.
JMenu submenu = new JMenu( "Sub Menu" );
filemenu.add( submenu );
JMenuItem subitem1 = new JMenuItem( "Sub Item 1" );
submenu.add( subitem1 );

// Create and add another simple menu item.
JMenuItem exit = new JMenuItem( "Exit" );
filemenu.add( exit );

// Create a menu with no icon or string, then set its
// icon and string.
JMenu blankmenu = new JMenu();
blankmenu.setText( "Options" );
blankmenu.setIcon( new ImageIcon( "on.gif" ) );

// Create a simple menu item and add it to the menu.
JMenuItem preferences =
                new JMenuItem( "Preferences" );
blankmenu.add( preferences );

// Add the menu to the menu bar.
```

```
        mbar.add( blankmenu );
    }

    // The MenuListener interface methods——
    public void menuCanceled( MenuEvent e )
    {
        System.out.println( "Cancelled" );
    }

    public void menuDeselected( MenuEvent e )
    {
        System.out.println( "Deselected" );
    }

    public void menuSelected( MenuEvent e )
    {
        System.out.println( "Selected" );
    }
}
```

JMenu's Public Methods

`JMenuItem add(Action a)`

Given an Action, this method creates a JMenuItem from the Action, places the JMenuItem into the menu, and returns it.

`Component add(Component c)`

Adds a component to the JMenu.

`JMenuItem add(JMenuItem menuItem)`

Adds a JMenuItem to the JMenu.

`void add(String s)`

Pass a String to the JMenu and let it create a menu item from it.

`void addMenuListener(MenuListener l)`

Tells the JMenu to notify the given class when it generates a MenuEvent.

`void addSeparator()`

Places a menu separator after the previously added item.

`AccessibleContext getAccessibleContext()`

Returns a subclass of AccessibleContext which gives access to the JMenu's accessibility information.

```
Component getComponent()
```

Returns the JMenu.

```
int getDelay()
```

Returns the delay in milliseconds between clicking the menu in the menu bar and the popup displaying.

```
JMenuItem getItem(int pos)
```

Returns the item at the given index.

```
int getItemCount()
```

Returns the number of items in the JMenu.

```
Component getMenuComponent(int n)
```

Returns the nth component in the menu.

```
int getMenuComponentCount()
```

Returns the number of components in the menu.

```
Component[] getMenuComponents()
```

Returns the components in the menu.

```
JPopupMenu getPopupMenu()
```

Returns the JPopupMenu used to display the menu when it is expanded.

```
MenuElement[] getSubElements()
```

Returns all of the JMenu's sub-menus.

```
String getUIClassID()
```

Returns the identifying string that the look-and-feel uses to assign a UI class to the JMenu.

```
JMenuItem insert(Action a, int pos)
```

Given an Action, this method creates a JMenuItem and places it in the menu at the given position. The generated JMenuItem is returned.

```
JMenuItem insert(JMenuItem mi,int pos)
```

Inserts the given menu item into the JMenu at the given index.

```
void insert(String s,int pos)
```

Create a menu item containing the given string, and insert it at the given position.

```
void insertSeparator(int index)
```

Inserts a menu separator into the JMenu at the given index.

```
boolean isMenuComponent(Component c)
```

Returns true if the given component is in the JMenu's sub-menu hierarchy.

```
boolean isPopupMenuVisible()
```

Returns true if the menu is popped up.

```
boolean isSelected()
```

Returns true if the menu is currently the selected menu.

```
boolean isTearOff()
```

Returns true if the menu is a tear-off menu.

```
boolean isTopLevelMenu()
```

Returns true if the JMenu is attached directly to a menu bar.

```
void menuSelectionChanged(boolean newState)
```

Gives the JMenu a new selection state. This is from the MenuElement interface.

```
String paramString()
```

Get a string representing the state of the menu.

```
void processKeyEvent(KeyEvent e, MenuElement path[],
     MenuSelectionManager manager)
```

Part of the MenuElement interface.

```
void processMouseEvent(MouseEvent event, MenuElement path[],
     MenuSelectionManager manager)
```

Part of the MenuElement interface.

`void remove(int pos)`

Removes the menu item at the given index.

`void remove(JMenuItem item)`

Removes the given menu item from the JMenu.

`void removeAll()`

Removes all of the JMenu's items.

`void removeMenuListener(MenuListener l)`

Tells the JMenu to stop notifying the given class when it generates MenuEvents.

`void setAccelerator(KeyStroke key)`

Specifies the KeyStroke that will trigger the menu.

`void setDelay(int d)`

Specifies the delay in milliseconds between the time the menu is clicked and the time it pops up.

`void setMenuLocation(int x,int y)`

Specifies the location of the popup menu.

`void setModel(ButtonModel newModel)`

Replaces the JMenu's ButtonModel.

`void setPopupMenuVisible(boolean b)`

Causes the menu to pop up.

`void setSelected(boolean b)`

Specifies whether this JMenu should be the selected menu.

`void setUI(MenuUI ui)`

Gives the JMenu a new look-and-feel class.

`void updateUI()`

Tells the JMenu that its look-and-feel class has been changed.

JMenuBar

A JMenuBar is typically a horizontal bar that runs across the top of a frame just under the title bar and has one or more menus attached to it (see Figure 8-69). Menus under a JMenuBar appear as text in the menu bar. When a menu's text is clicked, the menu pops up then goes away when a selection has been made.

JMenuBar does not restrict the types of components that may be added to it, so although only JMenus are normally added, any kind of component is acceptable. JMenuBar uses a BoxLayout.

Ancestors

```
java.lang.Object
    |
    +—java.awt.Component
            |
            +—java.awt.Container
                    |
                    +—com.sun.java.swing.JComponent
                            |
                            +—com.sun.java.swing.JMenuBar
```

NOTE: *For more information, see the "JMenu," "DefaultSingleSelectionModel," "JRootPane," and "BoxLayout" sections of this chapter. Also see the "Menus" section of Chapter 7, "JFC by Concept."*

Steps in Creating and Using JMenuBar

1. Create the menu bar. There is only one constructor:

   ```
   JMenuBar mbar = new JMenuBar();
   ```

2. Add things to the menu bar. Any component that implements the MenuElement interface may be added although JMenu components are most commonly used.

Figure 8-69
A typical JMenuBar.

Create a JMenu and put some menu items into it:

```
JMenu filemenu = new JMenu( "File" );
JMenuItem open = new JMenuItem( "Open" );
JMenuItem exit = new JMenuItem( "Exit" );
filemenu.add( open );
filemenu.add( exit );
```

Add the menu to the menu bar:

```
mbar.add( filemenu );
```

3. Place the menu bar. Normally, you will want the menu bar to be snug under the title bar of a JFrame or a JInternalFrame. These components use their root pane to hold menu bars (see JRootPane in this chapter for more information):

```
myFrame.getRootPane().setMenuBar( mbar );
```

Components with JRootPanes typically have a setMenuBar() or setJMenuBar() convenience method. Using this method, the above line of code could be replaced with:

```
myFrame.setJMenuBar( mbar );
```

You don't have to put the menu bar in the traditional spot. Since it is just a component, you can put it pretty much wherever a component can be put. For example, if the container 'mPanel' uses a vertical BoxLayout, the following would place a menu bar within the container:

```
JMenuBar midbar = new JMenuBar();
mPanel.add( midbar );
```

It is even possible to add a menu bar to another menu bar. If you do so, you will want to use an EmptyBorder on the added menu bar so it will blend in.

4. Change the menu bar's border:

```
mbar.setBorder( new BevelBorder( BevelBorder.RAISED ) );
```

Basic Code Examples

EXAMPLE 8-51 Basic JMenuBar

This example creates two menu bars, placing one as the frame's main menu and the other as a component in the body of the frame. The frame's menu bar has been given a raised BevelBorder, while the other menu bar has a lowered BevelBorder. Figure 8-70 shows the example with one of the menus on the other menu bar expanded.

Here is the source code:

```
import com.sun.java.swing.*;
import com.sun.java.swing.border.*;
```

Figure 8-70

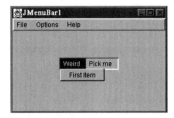

```java
import java.awt.*;

public class MyFrame extends JFrame
{
    JMenu filemenu;

    public MyFrame()
    {
        setTitle( "JMenuBar1" );

        // Store the content pane in a variable for easier
        // access.
        JPanel contentPane = (JPanel)getContentPane();

        // Set the layout so we can add a menu bar inside of
        // this pane.
        contentPane.setLayout( new BoxLayout( contentPane,
                               BoxLayout.Y_AXIS ) );

        // Create the first menu bar.
        JMenuBar mbar = new JMenuBar();

        // Add the menu bar to the frame via its root pane.
        getRootPane().setMenuBar( mbar );

        // Set the menu bar background.
        mbar.setBackground( Color.lightGray );

        // Give the menu bar a different border.
        mbar.setBorder(
                   new BevelBorder( BevelBorder.RAISED ) );

        // Create a menu.
        filemenu = new JMenu( "File" );

        // Add the menu to the menu bar.
        mbar.add( filemenu );

        // Create items to add to the menu and then add them.
        JMenuItem open = new JMenuItem( "Open" );
        filemenu.add( open );
        JMenuItem close = new JMenuItem( "Close" );
        filemenu.add( close );
        filemenu.addSeparator();
        JMenuItem exit = new JMenuItem( "Exit" );
```

```
filemenu.add( exit );

// Create another menu.
JMenu optionsmenu = new JMenu( "Options" );

// Add this second menu to the menu bar.
mbar.add( optionsmenu );

// Create an item for the options menu and add it.
JMenuItem preferences =
                    new JMenuItem( "Preferences" );
optionsmenu.add( preferences );

// Create a help menu.
JMenu helpmenu = new JMenu( "Help" );

// Add the help menu to the menu bar.
mbar.add( helpmenu );

// Create an item for the help menu and add it.
JMenuItem about = new JMenuItem( "About" );
helpmenu.add( about );

// Add this padding component to the frame's main
// panel to provide a little vertical spacing between
// the main menu and the menu we are about to place
// inside the main panel.
contentPane.add( Box.createRigidArea(
                    new Dimension( 50, 50 ) ) );

// Create another menu bar.
JMenuBar midbar = new JMenuBar();

// Set the menu bar's background.
midbar.setBackground( Color.lightGray );

// Give it a border different from the main menu
// bar's.
midbar.setBorder(
            new BevelBorder( BevelBorder.LOWERED ) );

// Add the new menu bar into the main panel.
contentPane.add( midbar );

// Create a menu and add it to this new menu bar.
JMenu weirdmenu1 = new JMenu( "Weird" );
midbar.add( weirdmenu1 );

// Create an item for this menu and add it.
JMenuItem item1 = new JMenuItem( "First Item" );
weirdmenu1.add( item1 );

// Create another menu and add it to the menu bar.
JMenu weirdmenu2 = new JMenu( "Pick me" );
midbar.add( weirdmenu2 );
```

```
                 // Create an item for the menu and add it.
                 JMenuItem item2 = new JMenuItem( "Another Item" );
                 weirdmenu2.add( item2 );
            }
    }
```

JMenuBar's Public Methods

`JMenu add(JMenu c)`

Adds the given JMenu to the end of the JMenuBar.

`AccessibleContext getAccessibleContext()`

Returns a subclass of AccessibleContext which gives access to the JMenuBar's accessible information.

`Component getComponent()`

Part of the MenuElement interface. Returns the JMenuBar.

`Component getComponentAtIndex(int i)`

Returns the component at the given index.

`int getComponentIndex(Component c)`

Returns the index at which the given component is currently.

`JMenu getHelpMenu()`

Returns the current help menu.

`Insets getMargin()`

Gets the space on each side of the JMenuBar between the border and the JMenus.

`JMenu getMenu(int index)`

Returns the component at the given index if it is a JMenu.

`int getMenuCount()`

Returns the number of JMenus in the JMenuBar.

`SingleSelectionModel getSelectionModel()`

Returns the JMenuBar's selection model.

`MenuElement[] getSubElements()`

Part of the MenuElement interface. Returns all of the MenuBar's menus.

`JMenuItem getShortcutMenuItem(MenuShortcut m)`

Returns the menu item associated with the given menu shortcut.

`Enumeration getShortcuts()`

Returns all menu shortcuts.

`MenuBarUI getUI()`

Returns the JMenuBar's current look-and-feel class.

`String getUIClassID()`

Returns the identifying string that the look-and-feel uses to assign a UI class to the JMenuBar.

`boolean isBorderPainted()`

Returns true if the JMenuBar will tell its border to paint itself.

`boolean isManagingFocus()`

Overridden to return true.

`boolean isOpaque()`

Returns true if the JMenuBar paints its entire area.

`boolean isSelected()`

Returns true if one of the JMenus within the JMenuBar is currently selected.

`void menuSelectionChanged(boolean newState)`

From the MenuElement interface, this just returns.

`void processKeyEvent(KeyEvent e, MenuElement path[],
        MenuSelectionManager manager)`

Part of the MenuElement interface.

```
void processMouseEvent(MouseEvent event, MenuElement path[],
    MenuSelectionManager manager)
```

Part of the MenuElement interface.

```
void remove(int index)
```

Removes the menu component at the given index.

```
void setBorderPainted(boolean s)
```

Specifies whether the JMenuBar should paint its border or not.

```
void setHelpMenu(JMenu menu)
```

Specifies a menu to use as the help menu.

```
void setMargin(Insets margin)
```

Sets the space on each side of the JMenuBar between the border and the JMenus.

```
void setSelected(Component sel)
```

Specifies that the given component should become the selected component.

```
void setSelectionModel(SingleSelectionModel model)
```

Replaces the current selection model with the given one.

```
void setUI(MenuBarUI ui)
```

Gives the JMenuBar a new look-and-feel class.

```
void updateUI()
```

Tells the JMenuBar that its look-and-feel class has been changed.

JMenuItem

A JMenuItem, as the name suggests, is a component that acts as an item in a menu. It is a child of AbstractButton, so it has many of the characteristics of a button. If you click it, it generates an ActionEvent just as a button does (see Figure 8-71).

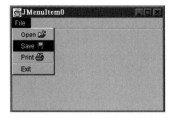

Figure 8-71
A JMenu with several
JMenuItems.

Ancestors

```
java.lang.Object
    |
    +—java.awt.Component
            |
            +—java.awt.Container
                    |
                    +—com.sun.java.swing.JComponent
                            |
                            +—com.sun.java.swing.AbstractButton
                                    |
                                    +—com.sun.java.swing.JMenuItem
```

NOTE: *For more information, see the "AbstractButton,"
"DefaultButtonModel," "JMenu," "JMenuBar," "JCheckBoxMenuItem,"
and "JCheckBoxRadioButtonMenuItem" sections in this chapter. Also see the
"Menus" section in Chapter 7, "JFC by Concept."*

Steps in Creating and Using JMenuItem

1. Create a menu bar with a menu. JMenuItems are kept inside
   JMenus that are attached to JMenuBars, so we have to create the
   menu bar and the menu so we have somewhere to add the menu
   item. JMenuItems may also be added to JPopupMenus, but for this
   example, we stick to regular menus:

```
// Create the menu bar.
JMenuBar mbar = new JMenuBar();

// Create a menu.
JMenu filemenu = new JMenu( "File" );

// Add the menu to the menu bar.
mbar.add( filemenu );

// Add the menu bar to its frame.
myFrame.getRootPane().setMenuBar( mbar );
```

2. Create a menu item. There are several constructors including:

An empty constructor. You will have to use setText() and/or setIcon() to give this menu item meaning:

```
JMenuItem blankitem = new JMenuItem();
```

A constructor to create a menu item that contains a text string:

```
JMenuItem textitem = new JMenuItem( "Open" );
```

A constructor to create a menu item that contains an icon:

```
JMenuItem iconitem = new JMenuItem( new ImageIcon( "off.gif" ) );
```

A constructor to create a menu item that contains a text string and an icon:

```
JMenuItem text_and_iconitem = new JMenuItem( "Close",
                              new ImageIcon( "left.gif" ) );
```

A constructor to create a menu item that contains a text string and can be triggered using an accelerator keycode:

```
JMenuItem text_with_shortcut = new JMenuItem( "Exit",
  KeyEvent.VK_X);
```

3. Add the menu item into a menu. JMenu uses a GridbagLayout and handles all of the layout settings internally.

```
filemenu.add( textitem );
```

4. Have the menu item generate events and then specify a class to receive them.

Tell the menu item which class will be receiving its events. The usual event to catch for a JMenuItem is an ActionEvent that is generated when the JMenuItem is pressed. For this example, the class that contains the menu item will be receiving the events:

```
textitem.addActionListener( this );
```

If you want to have the event deliver a command string:

```
textitem.setActionCommand( "Open item pressed" );
```

Make the receiving class implement the ActionListener interface. Here the receiving class is called MyFrame:

```
public class MyFrame extends JFrame implements ActionListener
{
    .
    .
    .
    public actionPerformed( ActionEvent e )
    {
        if ( e.getActionCommand().equals( "Open item pressed" ) )
```

```
        {
            // Do something here.
        }
    }
}
```

5. Change the menu item's font. This works with the Windows look and feel, but may not work with others:

```
textitem.setFont( new Font( "Helvetica", Font.ITALIC, 16 ) );
```

6. Change the text color and the item's background color. These work with the "windows" look and feel, but may not work with others:

```
textitem.setForeground( Color.blue );    // sets text color
textitem.setBackground( Color.green );
```

7. Move the item's text relative to the item's icon. This only applies to menu items that use both text and an icon. By default, the text is left of the icon, but this command will move the text to the icon's right:

```
text_and_iconitem.setHorizontalTextPosition( SwingConstants.RIGHT
);
```

8. Set the menu item's accelerator:

```
textitem.setMnemonic( 't' );
```

Basic Code Examples

EXAMPLE 8-52 Different uses for JMenuItem

This example illustrates the concepts discussed above, including changing the menu item font, using icons, and setting menu item colors. It has two menus with a variety of JMenuItems on them. The main class prints out a string when the Open item on the File menu is selected, and closes the application when Exit is chosen. Figure 8-72 shows the example with the menu expanded.

Here is the source code:

```
import com.sun.java.swing.*;
import com.sun.java.swing.border.*;
```

Figure 8-72

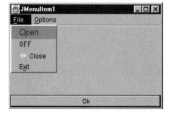

```java
import java.awt.*;
import java.awt.event.*;

public class MyFrame extends JFrame implements
        ActionListener
{
    public MyFrame()
    {
        setTitle( "JMenuItem1" );

        // Store the content pane as a variable for easier
        // access.
        JPanel contentPane = (JPanel)getContentPane();

        // Add a button since the menmonics won't work
        // if there are no components.
        JButton b = new JButton( "Ok" );
        contentPane.add( "South", b );

        // Create the menu bar and add it to the frame.
        JMenuBar mbar = new JMenuBar();
        getRootPane().setMenuBar( mbar );

        // Create a file menu and add it to the menu bar.
        JMenu filemenu = new JMenu( "File" );
        filemenu.setMnemonic( 'f' );
        mbar.add( filemenu );

        // Create a menu item that contains a text string.
        JMenuItem textitem = new JMenuItem( "Open" );

        // Change the item's font.
        textitem.setFont( new Font( "Helvetica",
                                    Font.ITALIC, 16 ) );

        // Set the item's text color.
        textitem.setForeground( Color.blue );

        // Set the items background.
        textitem.setBackground( Color.green );

        // Add the item to the menu.
        filemenu.add( textitem );

        // Make this class listen for action events from the
        // menu item.
        textitem.addActionListener( this );

        // Assign a string to be delivered with the item's
        // action events.
        textitem.setActionCommand( "Open item pressed" );

        // Create a menu item with an icon but no text and
        // add it to the menu.
```

```
        JMenuItem iconitem =
                new JMenuItem( new ImageIcon( "off.gif" ) );
        filemenu.add( iconitem );

        // Create a menu item with both text and icon.
        JMenuItem text_and_iconitem =
                        new JMenuItem( "Close",
                        new ImageIcon( "left.gif" ) );

        // Make it so the text appears right of the icon.
        text_and_iconitem.setHorizontalTextPosition(
                                SwingConstants.RIGHT );

        // Add the item to the menu.
        filemenu.add( text_and_iconitem );

        // Create a simple menu item and add it to the menu.
        JMenuItem exit = new JMenuItem( "Exit",
                        KeyEvent.VK_X );
        filemenu.add( exit );

        // Make it so this class is notified when the exit
        // item is pressed, and define the string that will
        // be delivered with its events.
        exit.addActionListener( this );
        exit.setActionCommand( "Exit" );

        // Create a second menu and add it to the menu bar.
        JMenu optionsmenu = new JMenu( "Options" );
        optionsmenu.setMnemonic( 'o' );
        mbar.add( optionsmenu );

        // Give this second menu a simple menu item.
        JMenuItem preferences =
                        new JMenuItem( "Preferences" );
        preferences.setMnemonic( 'p' );
        optionsmenu.add( preferences );
    }

    // Catch events from any menu items that named this
    // class as their action listener.
    public void actionPerformed( ActionEvent e )
    {
        if ( e.getActionCommand().equals(
                                "Open item pressed" ) )
        {
            System.out.println( "File-Open chosen" );
        }
        else if ( e.getActionCommand().equals( "Exit" ) )
        {
            System.exit( -1 );
        }
    }
}
```

JMenuItem's Public Methods

`KeyStroke getAccelerator()`

Returns the KeyStroke that triggers the JMenuItem directly.

`AccessibleContext getAccessibleContext()`

Returns a subclass of AccessibleContext, which gives access to the JMenuItem's accessibility information.

`Component getComponent()`

Part of the MenuElement interface. Returns the JMenuItem.

`MenuElement[] getSubElements()`

Part of the MenuElement interface. Returns all of the JMenuItem's submenus.

`String getUIClassID()`

Returns the identifying string that the look-and-feel uses to assign a UI class to the JMenuItem.

`void menuSelectionChanged(boolean newState)`

From the MenuElement interface, this changes the JMenuItem's state.

```
void processKeyEvent(KeyEvent e, MenuElement path[],
    MenuSelectionManager manager)
```

Part of the MenuElement interface.

```
void processMouseEvent(MouseEvent event, MenuElement path[],
    MenuSelectionManager manager)
```

Part of the MenuElement interface.

`void setAccelerator(KeyStroke key)`

Specifies the KeyStroke that will directly trigger the JMenuItem.

`void setArmed(boolean b)`

If set to true, then Enter will trigger the JMenuItem.

`void setEnabled(boolean b)`

Specifies whether the JMenuItem is enabled or disabled.

`void setShortcut(MenuShortcut s)`

Assigns the given menu shortcut to trigger the JMenuItem.

`void setUI(MenuItemUI ui)`

Gives the JMenuItem a new look-and-feel class.

`void updateUI()`

Tells the JMenuItem that the look-and-feel class has been changed.

JOptionPane

JOptionPane is a flexible class used to easily display simple dialogs that give the user information or prompt for a simple response. JOptionPane makes it so you can pop up basic but varied dialogs without having to lay them out yourself. Figure 8-73 shows one of the many uses for JOptionPane.

You can create a JOptionPane and then later display it within a JDialog or a JInternalFrame. More often you will use JOptionPane's many static methods that create the JOptionPane and display it—all in a single method call.

Ancestors

```
java.lang.Object
   |
   +—java.awt.Component
             |
             +—java.awt.Container
                        |
                        +—com.sun.java.swing.JComponent
                                   |
                                   +—com.sun.java.swing.JOptionPane
```

Figure 8-73

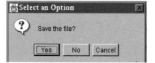

NOTE: *For more information, see the "JDialog" and "ImageIcon" sections in this chapter. Also see the "Windows" section in Chapter 7, JFC by Concept."*

Steps in Creating and Using JOptionPane

1. Create and display a JOptionPane. JOptionPane can be used to create variations on four types of dialogs:

- Message dialogs—These display a simple message, an OK button, and an icon and are used to inform the user that something has occurred. A message dialog could be used to tell the user that a file has finished transmitting.

- Confirmation dialogs—These display a message, an icon, and a series of buttons. They are used to display a question and allow the user to respond in one of several ways. A confirmation dialog could be used to tell the user that the printer is out of paper and allow him/her to retry or abort the print job.

- Input dialogs—These have an input field, frequently text, into which the user can enter data and then press one of a set of buttons to save the entered data or cancel. An input dialog could be used to ask for the output file name when you send a print job to file.

- Option dialogs—These are dialogs that are not directed at a specific use and can be configured however you want.

Details of how to create and display each of these types of dialog follow.

MESSAGE DIALOGS   Message dialogs can be displayed inside JDialogs or JInternalFrames. You can either create a JOptionPane and display the dialog yourself, or you can call one of the static methods to take care of it for you. The dialog's message and icon are determined by the method you call and the parameters you pass in.

Message dialogs have three configurable items that are important: the displayed message, the displayed icon, and the dialog title. You always specify the message, but the icon and title can either be specified or you can choose one of the predefined message types and allow the look-and-feel to select the icon and title.

One method will fill most of your message dialog needs. It is defined as:

```
public static void showMessageDialog(Component parentComponent,
        Object message)
```

'parentComponent' is the component that the dialog considers its source. The dialog will typically display just below this component. If the component is null, the dialog will be centered on the screen. 'message' is the Object that contains the message text. It is usually a String if the message will fit on one line, or an array of Strings where each item in the array will display on its own line.

Using the method above, the default dialog title is "Message," and the default icon is the one that the look-and-feel associates with the INFORMATION_MESSAGE type.

The following line of code uses this method. Figure 8-74 shows the result.

```
JOptionPane.showMessageDialog( parent,
                                    "Your file transfer is complete" );
```

You can change the title and/or the icon using the following method:

```
public static void showMessageDialog(Component parentComponent,
                                    Object message, String title,
                                    int messageType)
```

'title' is the String that will display in the dialog's title bar. 'messageType' is used mainly to tell the look-and-feel which icon to use and can be one of these: ERROR_MESSAGE, INFORMATION_MESSAGE, PLAIN_MESSAGE, QUESTION_MESSAGE, or WARNING_MESSAGE.

The following line of code uses this method. Figure 8-75 shows the result.

```
JOptionPane.showMessageDialog( src, "Your computer is on fire!",
                               "Urgent Warning",
                               JOptionPane.WARNING_MESSAGE );
```

In addition to the methods mentioned, there is another that also allows you to set the icon if you don't want to use the predefined ones.

You can display the JOptionPane within a JInternalFrame instead of a JDialog by calling the equivalent showInternalMessageDialog(…) methods.

The showMessageDialog(…) and showInternalMessageDialog(…) methods are static methods and the dialogs they create are disposed of as soon as the user presses OK. If you want to create a message dialog and be able to access it before and/or after it is displayed, you can create a JOptionPane using

Figure 8-74

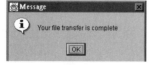

Figure 8-75

a constructor, create the dialog from that, and then you can do what you wish with that dialog.

Here is a sample that will create a message dialog much like the one above:

```
JOptionPane myPane = new JOptionPane( "Your computer is on fire!",
                                      JOptionPane.WARNING_MESSAGE,
                                      JOptionPane.OK_OPTION );
JDialog paneDialog = myPane.createDialog( parent, "Urgent Warning" );
paneDialog.show();
```

If you would rather display your JOptionPane in a JInternalFrame, you can call createInternalFrame(…) instead of createDialog(…).

CONFIRMATION DIALOGS   Confirmation dialogs can be displayed inside JDialogs or JInternalFrames. You can either create a JOptionPane and display the dialog yourself, or you can call one of the static methods to take care of it for you. The message, the icon, and the buttons that the dialog uses are all determined by the method you call and the parameters you pass in.

The simplest way to create a confirmation dialog is using the following line of code:

```
retval = JOptionPane.showConfirmDialog( parent, "Save the file?" );
```

This displays a dialog with the given message, a Yes button, a No button, a Cancel button, a default icon, and a default title. Figure 8-76 shows how it looks.

Notice that the JOptionPane.showConfirmDialog() method returns a value. That value tells you which button the user pushed, or if the user closed the dialog without pushing a button. The possible results from this particular dialog are YES_OPTION, NO_OPTION, CANCEL_OPTION, and CLOSED_OPTION.

You can specify certain combinations of buttons if you don't want the default set of Yes/No/Cancel. There are a number of predefined button sets that you can use: YES_NO_CANCEL_OPTION, YES_NO_OPTION, and OK_CANCEL_OPTION.

Like a message dialog, you can set the message type, which is used to select the displayed icon. The default icon is the one associated with QUESTION_MESSAGE. The following line of code shows an example of changing the button option and the message type. Figure 8-77 shows how the dialog looks.

```
retval = JOptionPane.showConfirmDialog( parent,
                        "You are about to overwrite a file",
                                        "File Overwrite",
```

Figure 8-76

Figure 8-77

```
JOptionPane.OK_CANCEL_OPTION,
JOptionPane.WARNING_MESSAGE
);
```

The JOptionPane.showConfirmDialog() method above will return OK_OPTION, CANCEL_OPTION, or CLOSED_OPTION.

In addition to the methods discussed, there is another method that allows you to specify your own icon if the predefined ones are not sufficient.

You can display the JOptionPane within a JInternalFrame instead of a JDialog by calling the equivalent showInternalConfirmDialog(…) methods.

The showConfirmDialog(…) and showInternalConfirmDialog(…) methods are static methods, and the dialogs they create are disposed of as soon as the user presses OK. If you want to create a confirmation dialog and be able to access it before and/or after it is displayed, you can create a JOptionPane using a constructor, create the dialog from that, and then you can do what you wish with that dialog.

Here is a sample that will create a confirmation dialog much like the one above:

```
JOptionPane myPane = new JOptionPane( "Your computer is on fire!",
                                JOptionPane.WARNING_MESSAGE,
                                JOptionPane.OK_OPTION );
JDialog paneDialog = myPane.createDialog( parent, "Urgent Warning" );
paneDialog.show();
retval = ((Integer)myPane.getValue()).intValue();
```

Since information about which button the user pressed is not a return value when you display the dialog this way, you have to call the JOptionPane's getValue() method which, in this case, returns an Integer that contains OK_OPTION or CANCEL_OPTION. The getValue() method returns null if the dialog was closed without pressing OK or Cancel.

If you would rather display your JOptionPane in a JInternalFrame, you can call the createInternalFrame(…) instead of createDialog(…).

INPUT DIALOGS An input dialog displays a message, an icon, a text field, and buttons corresponding to the OK_CANCEL_OPTION. The user is expected to enter text into the text field in response to a question asked by the message string. Then the user presses one of the buttons to exit the dialog and save/apply the input, or to exit the dialog and cancel the operation.

Input dialogs can be displayed inside JDialogs or JInternalFrames. You can either create a JOptionPane and display the dialog yourself, or you can call one of the static methods to take care of it for you.

The following line of code can take care of most of your input dialog needs:

```
String response = JOptionPane.showInputDialog(
                                "Enter the output file name" );
```

This causes an input dialog to be displayed in the center of the screen. Notice that it returns a string when the user exits. This string is the user's input into the text field, or null if the user canceled the operation or closed the dialog without pressing a button. The dialog is created with a default title, OK and Cancel buttons, and the icon associated with a QUESTION_MESSAGE. Figure 8-78 shows the input dialog that results from the above code.

If you want the user to select among a predefined set of values, you can pass an array holding the acceptable values, and an initial value to one of the showInputDialog(...) methods. The look-and-feel decides how to display the acceptable values, but all of the JFC look-and-feels put them into a combo box. Here is an example of how to create this type of input dialog:

```
// Load the acceptable values in an array.
String choices[] = new String[3];
choices[0] = "8.5\" x 11.0\"";
choices[1] = "11.0\" x 17.0\"";
choices[2] = "17.0\" x 17.0\"";

// Create and display the input dialog.
String response = (String)JOptionPane.showInputDialog( src,
                        "Enter the paper size",
                        "Paper Size",
                        JOptionPane.QUESTION_MESSAGE,
                        new ImageIcon( "delete.gif" ),
                        choices, choices[0] );
```

This method requires that you set the icon, but if you want to use the icon associated with the message type (in this case, QUESTION_MESSAGE), you can enter null for the icon. This method returns the value that the user selected or null if the user presses Cancel or closes the dialog without pressing a button. Figure 8-79 shows the dialog created by the preceding code.

Figure 8-78

Figure 8-79

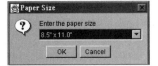

You can display the JOptionPane within a JInternalFrame instead of a JDialog by calling the equivalent showInternalInputDialog(…) methods.

The showInputDialog(…) and showInternalInputDialog(…) methods are static methods, and the dialogs they create are disposed of as soon as the user presses OK. If you want to create an input dialog and be able to access it before and/or after it is displayed, you can create a JOptionPane using a constructor, create the dialog from that, and then you can do what you wish with that dialog. To do so, you have to take advantage of the fact that the message in a JOptionPane does not have to be a single Object. If we have a long string to display, we can break it up into an array of Strings with the array elements displaying one above the other. Similarly, we can make a message array that has a String and a JTextField or a String and a JComboBox. Here is an example of how to duplicate the input dialog shown in Figure 8-83:

```
// Create the paper size combo box.
JComboBox paperSizes = new JComboBox();
paperSizes.addItem( "8.5\" x 11.0\"" );
paperSizes.addItem( "11.0\" x 17.0\"" );
paperSizes.addItem( "17.0\" x 17.0\"" );

// Load the prompt string and the combo box as elements in the
// Object array that will be passed as the JOptionPane's message.
Object messages[] = new Object[2];
messages[0] = "Enter the paper size";
messages[1] = paperSizes;

// Create the JOptionPane with the message array.
JOptionPane myPane = new JOptionPane( messages,
                                JOptionPane.QUESTION_MESSAGE,
                                JOptionPane.OK_CANCEL_OPTION );

// Create a JDialog from the just-created JOptionPane.
JDialog paneDialog = myPane.createDialog( src, "Paper Size" );

// Display the JDialog.
paneDialog.show();

// If the user exited the dialog by pressing "Ok", get the value that
// was selected from the combo box.
if ( myPane.getValue() != null )
{
   retval = ((Integer)myPane.getValue()).intValue();
   if ( retval == JOptionPane.OK_OPTION )
      System.out.println( "User selected:  " +
      paperSizes.getSelectedItem() );
}
```

If you would rather display your JOptionPane in a JInternalFrame, you can call the createInternalFrame(…) instead of createDialog(…).

OPTION DIALOGS   These are dialogs that are not directed at specific uses, but give you access to JOptionPane's full range of capabilities. You can specify messages that are Strings or components or arrays of different types of Objects. You can define exactly which buttons you want to display, what their text strings are, and which is the default button. You can use one of the predefined icons, or you can use one of you own.

The following code shows how to create and display a dialog that contains a String, a JTextArea, an icon, and two custom buttons. Figure 8-80 shows the dialog that this code generates.

```
// Define the array of Strings that will be used to make the dialog's
// buttons
String choices[] = new String[2];
choices[0] = "I agree";
choices[1] = "I don't agree";

// Create the text area.
JTextArea area = new JTextArea(
        "This agreement states that you will not be naughty but\n" +
        "will rather be nice.  Upon failure to uphold the\n" +
        "agreement, you will not receive any good presents, but\n" +
        "instead will receive a single lump of coal" );
area.setColumns( 50 );
area.setRows( 3 );

// Create a scroll pane to allow the user to scroll around the
// agreement.
JScrollPane scroller = new JScrollPane( area );

// Put the prompt string and the text area scroller into the messages
// array.
Object messages[] = new Object[2];
messages[0] = "Read the agreement and press a button";
messages[1] = scroller;

JOptionPane myPane = new JOptionPane( messages,
        JOptionPane.QUESTION_MESSAGE,
        JOptionPane.OK_CANCEL_OPTION,
        null,
        choices, choices[0] );

// Use the just-created JOptionPane to create a JDialog to hold it.
JDialog paneDialog = myPane.createDialog( src, "Santa Agreement" );
```

Figure 8-80

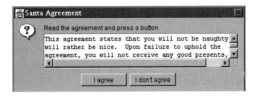

```
// Display the option pane dialog.
paneDialog.show();

// If the user exited the dialog by pressing a button, print the
// button string.
if ( myPane.getValue() != null )
{
    System.out.println( "User selected:  " + myPane.getValue() );
}
```

Basic Code Examples

EXAMPLE 8-53 Many Uses for JOptionPane

This example contains 14 buttons that, when pressed, display 14 different uses for JOptionPane. There are four confirmation dialogs, four message dialogs, four input dialogs, and two option dialogs. At the bottom are three radio buttons so you can change the look-and-feel to see what the different dialogs look like under different look-and-feels. The buttons that end with "- Separate" display dialogs created by using JOptionPane constructors. The rest display dialogs created using JOptionPane's static methods. Figure 8-81 shows the example as it comes up initially.

Here is the source code:

```
import com.sun.java.swing.*;
import java.awt.*;
import java.awt.event.*;

public class MyFrame extends JFrame implements
        ActionListener, ItemListener
{
```

Figure 8-81

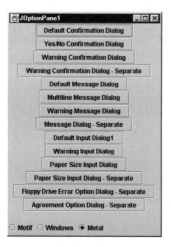

```
// The buttons that trigger the different dialogs.
private JButton confirm1;
private JButton confirm2;
private JButton confirm3;
private JButton confirm4;
private JButton message1;
private JButton message2;
private JButton message3;
private JButton message4;
private JButton input1;
private JButton input2;
private JButton input3;
private JButton input4;
private JButton option1;
private JButton option2;

// The radio buttons that let you switch look-and-feel.
private JRadioButton mMotif;
private JRadioButton mWindows;
private JRadioButton mMetal;

public MyFrame()
{
   setTitle( "JOptionPane1" );

   // Store the content pane in a variable for easier
   // access.
   JPanel contentPane = (JPanel)getContentPane();

   // Components will all be added to this panel.
   contentPane.setLayout( new BorderLayout() );

   // Create a panel to hold the dialog buttons.
   JPanel buttonPane = new JPanel();
   buttonPane.setLayout( new BoxLayout( buttonPane,
                         BoxLayout.Y_AXIS ) );

   // Create the buttons that trigger the display of the
   // different dialogs and make this class listen for
   // when they are pressed.
   confirm1 = new JButton(
                  "Default Confirmation Dialog" );
   confirm1.addActionListener( this );
   buttonPane.add( confirm1 );

   confirm2 = new JButton(
                  "Yes/No Confirmation Dialog" );
   confirm2.addActionListener( this );
   buttonPane.add( confirm2 );

   confirm3 = new JButton(
                  "Warning Confirmation Dialog" );
   confirm3.addActionListener( this );
   buttonPane.add( confirm3 );
```

```
confirm4 = new JButton(
        "Warning Confirmation Dialog - Separate" );
confirm4.addActionListener( this );
buttonPane.add( confirm4 );

message1 = new JButton( "Default Message Dialog" );
message1.addActionListener( this );
buttonPane.add( message1 );

message2 = new JButton( "Multiline Message Dialog" );
message2.addActionListener( this );
buttonPane.add( message2 );

message3 = new JButton( "Warning Message Dialog" );
message3.addActionListener( this );
buttonPane.add( message3 );

message4 = new JButton( "Message Dialog - Separate" );
message4.addActionListener( this );
buttonPane.add( message4 );

input1 = new JButton( "Default Input Dialog1" );
input1.addActionListener( this );
buttonPane.add( input1 );

input2 = new JButton( "Warning Input Dialog" );
input2.addActionListener( this );
buttonPane.add( input2 );

input3 = new JButton( "Paper Size Input Dialog" );
input3.addActionListener( this );
buttonPane.add( input3 );

input4 = new JButton(
            "Paper Size Input Dialog - Separate" );
input4.addActionListener( this );
buttonPane.add( input4 );

option1 = new JButton(
    "Floppy Drive Error Option Dialog - Separate" );
option1.addActionListener( this );
buttonPane.add( option1 );

option2 = new JButton(
            "Agreement Option Dialog - Separate" );
option2.addActionListener( this );
buttonPane.add( option2 );

// Make the buttons display horizontally centered.
confirm1.setAlignmentX( 0.5f );
confirm2.setAlignmentX( 0.5f );
confirm3.setAlignmentX( 0.5f );
confirm4.setAlignmentX( 0.5f );
message1.setAlignmentX( 0.5f );
message2.setAlignmentX( 0.5f );
```

```
        message3.setAlignmentX( 0.5f );
        message4.setAlignmentX( 0.5f );
        input1.setAlignmentX( 0.5f );
        input2.setAlignmentX( 0.5f );
        input3.setAlignmentX( 0.5f );
        input4.setAlignmentX( 0.5f );
        option1.setAlignmentX( 0.5f );
        option2.setAlignmentX( 0.5f );

        // Add the button panel to the contant pane's main
        // area.
        contentPane.add( "Center", buttonPane );

        // Create the three radio buttons that control the
        // look-and-feel and make it so this class is
        // notified when their states change.
        mMotif = new JRadioButton( "Motif" );
        mMotif.addItemListener( this );
        mWindows = new JRadioButton( "Windows" );
        mWindows.addItemListener( this );
        mMetal = new JRadioButton( "Metal" );
        mMetal.addItemListener( this );

        // Create a button group for the radio buttons and
        // add them to it.
        ButtonGroup group = new ButtonGroup();
        group.add( mMotif );
        group.add( mWindows );
        group.add( mMetal );

        // Make it so the Metal look-and-feel is initially
        // selected.
        mMetal.setSelected( true );

        // Create a horizontal box to put the radio buttons
        // in.
        Box lfpanel = Box.createHorizontalBox();

        lfpanel.add( mMotif );
        lfpanel.add( mWindows );
        lfpanel.add( mMetal );

        // Place the radio buttons' panel at the bottom of
        // the content pane.
        contentPane.add( "South", lfpanel );
    }

    // This is called when one of the dialog-triggering
    // buttons is pressed.
    public void actionPerformed( ActionEvent e )
    {
        JButton src = (JButton)e.getSource();
        int retval;

        if ( src == confirm1 )
```

```
   {
      // Display a basic confirmation dialog and print
      // out which button was pressed to exit the dialog.
      retval = JOptionPane.showConfirmDialog( src,
                              "Save the file?" );
      printResponse( retval );
   }
   else if ( src == confirm2 )
   {
      // Display a confirmation dialog with "Yes" and
      // "No" buttons and print out which button was
      // pressed to exit the dialog.
      retval = JOptionPane.showConfirmDialog(
                        src, "Save the file?",
                        "File Saving",
                        JOptionPane.YES_NO_OPTION );
      printResponse( retval );
   }
   else if ( src == confirm3 )
   {
      // Display a confirmation dialog that has "Ok" and
      // "Cancel" buttons and uses the warning icon.
      retval = JOptionPane.showConfirmDialog( src,
                  "You are about to overwrite a file",
                  "File Overwrite",
                  JOptionPane.OK_CANCEL_OPTION,
                  JOptionPane.WARNING_MESSAGE );
      printResponse( retval );
   }
   else if ( src == confirm4 )
   {
      // Use a JOptionPane constructor to create a
      // confirmation dialog, then display it and print
      // out the button that was used to exit the dialog.
      JOptionPane myPane = new JOptionPane(
                  "You are about to overwrite a file",
                  JOptionPane.WARNING_MESSAGE,
                  JOptionPane.OK_CANCEL_OPTION );

      // Create the JDialog to hold the JOptionPane.
      JDialog paneDialog = myPane.createDialog( src,
                        "File Overwrite" );

      // Display the dialog.
      paneDialog.show();

      // If the user pressed a button to exit the
      // dialog, print the button that was used.
      if ( myPane.getValue() != null )
      {
         retval =
               ((Integer)myPane.getValue()).intValue();
         printResponse( retval );
      }
   }
```

```
else if ( src == message1 )
{
   // Display a basic message dialog.
   JOptionPane.showMessageDialog( src,
               "Your file transfer is complete" );
}
else if ( src == message2 )
{
   // Display a multiline message dialog.

   // Define the multiple lines of text as an array
   // of strings.
   String message[] = new String[3];

   message[0] = "Your computer is about to crash,";
   message[1] = "and there is nothing you can";
   message[2] = "do about it";

   // Pass the array of strings as the dialog's
   // message.
   JOptionPane.showMessageDialog( src, message );
}
else if ( src == message3 )
{
   // Display a message dialog that uses the warning
   // icon.
   JOptionPane.showMessageDialog( src,
                  "Your computer is on fire!",
                  "Urgent Warning",
                  JOptionPane.WARNING_MESSAGE );
}
else if ( src == message4 )
{
   // Use a JOptionPane constructor to create a
   // message dialog.

   // Define a single "Ok" button to display.
   String choices[] = new String[1];
   choices[0] = "Ok";

   // Create the JOptionPane.
   JOptionPane myPane = new JOptionPane(
                  "This dialog will hang around",
                  JOptionPane.INFORMATION_MESSAGE,
                  JOptionPane.OK_OPTION,
                  null, choices );

   // Use the JOptionPane to create a dialog
   // containing it.
   JDialog paneDialog = myPane.createDialog( src,
                  "Information message" );

   // Display the dialog.
   paneDialog.show();
}
```

```
else if ( src == input1 )
{
   // Display a simple input dialog.
   String response = JOptionPane.showInputDialog(
                     "Enter the output file name" );

   // Print the text from the dialog's text field.
   System.out.println( "User entered:  " +
                       response );
}
else if ( src == input2 )
{
   // Display an input dialog that uses the warning
   // icon.
   String response = JOptionPane.showInputDialog(
        src,
        "This is you last chance to enter the code!",
        "Urgent Warning",
        JOptionPane.WARNING_MESSAGE );

   // Print the text from the dialog's text field.
   System.out.println( "User entered:  " + response );
}
else if ( src == input3 )
{
   // Display an input field that uses a combo box.

   // Load the combo box choices.
   String choices[] = new String[3];
   choices[0] = "8.5\" x 11.0\"";
   choices[1] = "11.0\" x 17.0\"";
   choices[2] = "17.0\" x 17.0\"";

   // Create the dialog and display it.
   String response =
           (String)JOptionPane.showInputDialog( src,
                     "Enter the paper size",
                     "Paper Size",
                     JOptionPane.QUESTION_MESSAGE,
                     null, choices, choices[0] );

   // Print out the user's selection.
   System.out.println( "User selected:  " +
                       response );
}
else if ( src == input4 )
{
   // Use a JOptionPane constructor to create a paper
   // size input dialog.

   // Create and load the paper size combo box.
   JComboBox paperSizes = new JComboBox();
   paperSizes.addItem( "8.5\" x 11.0\"" );
   paperSizes.addItem( "11.0\" x 17.0\"" );
   paperSizes.addItem( "17.0\" x 17.0\"" );
```

```
                          // Load the prompt string and the combo box as the
                          // JOptionPane's message array.
                          Object messages[] = new Object[2];
                          messages[0] = "Enter the paper size";
                          messages[1] = paperSizes;

                          // Create the JOptionPane and use the question
                          // icon.
                          JOptionPane myPane = new JOptionPane( messages,
                                        JOptionPane.QUESTION_MESSAGE,
                                        JOptionPane.OK_CANCEL_OPTION );

                          // Create the JDialog that holds the JOptionPane.
                          JDialog paneDialog = myPane.createDialog( src,
                                                        "Paper Size" );

                          // Display the dialog.
                          paneDialog.show();

                          // If the user exited the dialog by pressing a
                          // button, check which button it was.  If it was
                          // "Ok", print the combo box's current value.
                          if ( myPane.getValue() != null )
                          {
                             retval =
                                    ((Integer)myPane.getValue()).intValue();
                             if ( retval == JOptionPane.OK_OPTION )
                             {
                                System.out.println( "User selected:  " +
                                            paperSizes.getSelectedItem() );
                             }
                          }
                       }
                       else if ( src == option1 )
                       {
                          // Create an option dialog by using a JOptionPane
                          // constructor.

                          // Load the button strings.
                          String choices[] = new String[3];
                          choices[0] = "Abort";
                          choices[1] = "Retry";
                          choices[2] = "Fail";

                          // Create the JOptionPane with the error icon and
                          // the defined buttons.
                          JOptionPane myPane = new JOptionPane(
                                          "Drive A: is not ready",
                                          JOptionPane.ERROR_MESSAGE,
                                          JOptionPane.OK_CANCEL_OPTION,
                                          null,
                                          choices, choices[0] );

                          // Create the JDialog that holds the JOptionPane.
                          JDialog paneDialog = myPane.createDialog( src,
```

```
                              "Floppy Drive Error" );

    // Display the dialog.
    paneDialog.show();

    // Print out the button that was pressed.
    System.out.println( myPane.getValue() );
}
else if ( src == option2 )
{
    // Create an option dialog that displays a text
    // area.  Use a JOptionPane constructor to do it.

    // Load the button strings.
    String choices[] = new String[2];
    choices[0] = "I agree";
    choices[1] = "I don't agree";

    // Create the text area that holds the agreement.
    JTextArea area = new JTextArea(
        "This agreement states that you will not be " +
        "naughty but\n" +
        "will rather be nice.  Upon failure to " +
        "uphold the\n" +
        "agreement, you will not receive any good " +
        "presents, but\n" +
        "instead will receive a single lump of coal" );
    area.setColumns( 50 );
    area.setRows( 3 );

    // Put the text area in a scroll pane.
    JScrollPane scroller = new JScrollPane( area );

    // Make the messages array and put the prompt
    // string and text area scroller into it.
    Object messages[] = new Object[2];
    messages[0] =
            "Read the agreement and press a button";
    messages[1] = scroller;

    // Create the JOptionPane with the message array
    // and button strings.
    JOptionPane myPane = new JOptionPane( messages,
                JOptionPane.QUESTION_MESSAGE,
                JOptionPane.OK_CANCEL_OPTION,
                null,
                choices, choices[0] );

    // Create the JDialog to hold the JOptionPane.
    JDialog paneDialog = myPane.createDialog( src,
                    "Santa Agreement" );

    // Display the dialog.
    paneDialog.show();
```

```
            // If the user exited the dialog by pressing a
            // button, print which button.
            if ( myPane.getValue() != null )
            {
                System.out.println( "User selected:  " +
                                        myPane.getValue() );
            }
        }

        // We have to repaint since a bug makes a button
        // appear in the wrong place after the option
        // dialog is dismissed.
        doLayout();
        repaint();
    }

    // This is a simple utility to convert the standard
    // button options to strings and print them.
    private void printResponse( int response )
    {
        switch ( response )
        {
            case JOptionPane.YES_OPTION:
                System.out.println( "User chose YES/OK" );
                break;

            case JOptionPane.NO_OPTION:
                System.out.println( "User chose NO" );
                break;

            case JOptionPane.CANCEL_OPTION:
                System.out.println( "User chose CANCEL" );
                break;

            case JOptionPane.CLOSED_OPTION:
                System.out.println( "User CLOSED the dialog" );
                break;

            default:
                System.out.println( "Unrecognized:  " +
                                        response );
        }
    }

    // This is called when one of the look-and-feel radio
    // buttons is pressed.
    public void itemStateChanged( ItemEvent e )
    {
        String l_f_name;

        // We ignore de-select events.
        if ( e.getStateChange() == ItemEvent.SELECTED )
        {
            // Based on the radio button that generated the
            // event, set the look-and-feel class' name.
```

```
if ( e.getSource() == mMotif )
{
    l_f_name = "com.sun.java.swing.plaf." +
               "motif.MotifLookAndFeel";
}
else if ( e.getSource() == mWindows )
{
    l_f_name = "com.sun.java.swing.plaf." +
               "windows.WindowsLookAndFeel";
}
else
{
    l_f_name = "com.sun.java.swing.plaf." +
               "metal.MetalLookAndFeel";
}

try
{
    // Try to set the look-and-feel.
    UIManager.setLookAndFeel( l_f_name );

    // Propagate the new look-and-feel to all
    // components in the frame.
    SwingUtilities.updateComponentTreeUI( this );

    // Re-pack the frame since the different
    // look-and-feels require different amounts
    // of space.
    pack();
}
catch ( Exception ex )
{
    System.out.println( ex );
}
        }
    }
}
```

JOptionPane's Public Methods

`JDialog createDialog(Component c,String title)`

Creates a JDialog and places this JOptionPane within it. Uses the given title as the JDialog title.

`JInternalFrame createInternalFrame(Component component,String title)`

Creates a JInternalFrame and places this JOptionPane within it. Uses the given title as the JInternalFrame title.

`static JDesktopPane getDesktopPaneForComponent(Component c)`

A static convenience method that looks through the display hierarchy to find the given component's nearest ancestor which is a JDesktopPane, if there is one.

```
static Frame getFrameForComponent(Component component)
```

A static convenience method that looks through the display hierarchy to find the given 'component's nearest ancestor which is a Frame, if there is one.

```
Icon getIcon()
```

Returns the icon that this JOptionPane is displaying.

```
Object getInitialSelectionValue()
```

Returns the JOptionPane's default selection value.

```
Object getInitialValue()
```

Gets the JOptionPane's initially selected option.

```
Object getInputValue()
```

Returns the value that the user has entered.

```
int getMaxCharactersPerLineCount()
```

Returns the maximum number of characters per line in a message.

```
int getMaxCharactersPerLineCount()
```

Returns the maximum number of characters per line in a message.

```
Object getMessage()
```

Returns the message object.

```
int getMessageType()
```

Returns the type of message being displayed.

```
Object[] getOptions()
```

Returns an array of all of the options.

```
int getOptionType()
```

Returns the option configuration for the JOptionPane.

```
static Frame getRootFrame()
```

Returns the JOptionPane's root frame.

```
Object[] getSelectionValues()
```

Returns an array filled with all available selection values.

```
OptionPaneUI getUI()
```

Returns the JOptionPane's current look-and-feel class.

```
String getUIClassID()
```

Returns the ID string that the plugged-in look-and-feel uses to assign a UI class to the JOptionPane.

```
Object getValue()
```

Returns the value selected by the user.

```
boolean getWantsInput()
```

Typically used for communication with the UI class.

```
void selectInitialValue()
```

Tells the JOptionPane to make the initial value selected.

```
void setIcon(Icon newIcon)
```

Specifies the icon to use in the JOptionPane. If it is null, the icon associated with the message type is used.

```
void setInitialSelectionValue(Object newValue)
```

Specifies the initial selection value to be the given Object.

```
void setInitialValue(Object newInitialValue)
```

Specifies the initial value to be the given Object.

```
void setInputValue(Object newValue)
```

Sets the input value.

```
void setMessage(Object newMessage)
```

Specifies the message object to display.

```
void setMessageType(int newType)
```

Specifies the message type for the JOptionPane.

```
void setOptions(Object newOptions[])
```

Specifies the set of options for the JOptionPane.

```
void setOptionType(int newType)
```

Specifies the option configuration.

```
static void setRootFrame(Frame newRootFrame)
```

Specifies the JOptionPane's root frame.

```
void setSelectionValues(Object newValues[])
```

Specifies the set of selection values.

```
void setUI(OptionPaneUI ui)
```

Gives the JOptionPane a new look-and-feel class.

```
void setValue(Object newValue)
```

Sets the value.

```
void setWantsInput(boolean newValue)
```

Typically used for communication with the UI class.

```
static int showConfirmDialog(Component component,Object message)
```

Creates and displays a JOptionPane within a JDialog, using the given message Object and the default confirmation dialog buttons and icon.

```
static int showConfirmDialog(Component component,Object
        message,String title,int optionType)
```

Creates and displays a JOptionPane within a JDialog, using the given message Object and dialog title, the buttons associated with the given option type, and the default icon for confirmation dialogs.

```
static int showConfirmDialog(Component component,Object
        message,String title,int optionType,int messageType)
```

Creates and displays a JOptionPane within a JDialog, using the given message Object and dialog title, the buttons associated with the given option type, and the icon associated with the given message type.

```
static int showConfirmDialog(Component component,Object
        message,String title,int optionType,int messageType,Icon icon)
```

Creates and displays a JOptionPane within a JDialog, using the given message Object and dialog title, the buttons associated with the given option type, and the given icon.

```
static Object showInputDialog(Component component,Object
        message,String title,int messageType,Icon icon,Object
        selectionValues[],Object initialSelectionValue)
```

Creates and displays a JOptionPane within a JDialog, using the given message, the given dialog title, the buttons associated with the given message type, and a combo box containing the list of selection values. The dialog is placed near the specified component.

```
static String showInputDialog(Component component,Object message)
```

Creates and displays a JOptionPane within a JDialog, using the given message, the default input field (usually a JTextField), and the default buttons and icon associated with input dialogs. The dialog is placed near the specified component.

```
static String showInputDialog(Component component,Object
        message,String title,int messageType)
```

Creates and displays a JOptionPane within a JDialog, using the given message, the default input field (usually a JTextField), the given dialog title, and the buttons and icon associated with the given message type. The dialog is placed near the specified component.

```
static String showInputDialog(Object message)
```

Creates and displays a JOptionPane within a JDialog, using the given message, the default input field (usually a JTextField), and the default buttons and icon associated with input dialogs. The dialog is centered relative to the screen.

```
static int showInternalConfirmDialog(Component component,Object
        message)
```

Creates and displays a JOptionPane within a JInternalFrame, using the given message and the default buttons and icon associated with confirmation dialogs. The frame is placed near the given component.

```
static int showInternalConfirmDialog(Component component,Object
        message,String title,int optionType)
```

Creates and displays a JOptionPane within a JInternalFrame, using the given message, the given frame title, the buttons specified by the given option type, and the icon associated with confirmation dialogs. The frame is placed near the given component.

```
static int showInternalConfirmDialog(Component component,Object
        message,String title,int optionType,int messageType)
```

Creates and displays a JOptionPane within a JInternalFrame, using the given message, the given frame title, the buttons specified by the given option type, and the icon associated with given message type. The frame is placed near the given component.

```
static int showInternalConfirmDialog(Component component,Object
        message,String title,int optionType,int messageType,Icon icon)
```

Creates and displays a JOptionPane within a JInternalFrame, using the given message, the given frame title, the buttons specified by the given option type, and the given icon. The frame is placed near the given component.

```
static Object showInternalInputDialog(Component component,Object
        message,String title,int messageType,Icon icon,Object
        selectionValues[],Object initialSelectionValue)
```

Creates and displays a JOptionPane within a JInternalFrame, using the given message, the given frame title, the buttons associated with the given message type, the given icon, and a combo box containing the list of selection values. The frame is placed near the specified component.

```
static String showInternalInputDialog(Component component,Object
        message)
```

Creates and displays a JOptionPane within a JInternalFrame, using the given message, the default input field (usually a JTextField), and the default buttons and icon associated with input dialogs. The frame is placed near the specified component.

```
static String showInternalInputDialog(Component component,Object
        message,String title,int messageType)
```

Creates and displays a JOptionPane within a JInternalFrame, using the given message, the default input field (usually a JTextField), the given frame title, and the buttons and icon associated with the given message type. The frame is placed near the specified component.

```
static void showInternalMessageDialog(Component component,Object
        message)
```

Creates and displays a JOptionPane within a JInternalFrame, using the given message, an OK button, and the default icon for message dialogs. The frame is placed near the given component.

```
static void showInternalMessageDialog(Component component,Object
        message,String title,int messageType)
```

Creates and displays a JOptionPane within a JInternalFrame, using the given message, an OK button, and the icon associated with the given message type. The frame is placed near the given component.

```
static void showInternalMessageDialog(Component component,Object
        message,String title,int messageType,Icon icon)
```

Creates and displays a JOptionPane within a JInternalFrame, using the given message, an OK button, and the given icon. The frame is placed near the given component.

```
static int showInternalOptionDialog(Component component,Object
        message,String title,int optionType,int messageType,Icon
        icon,Object options[],Object initialValue)
```

Creates and displays a JOptionPane within a JInternalFrame. See the Option dialog discussion.

```
static void showMessageDialog(Component component,Object message)
```

Creates and displays a JOptionPane within a JDialog, using the given message, an OK button, and the default icon for message dialogs. The dialog is placed near the given component.

```
static void showMessageDialog(Component component,Object
        message,String title,int messageType)
```

Creates and displays a JOptionPane within a JDialog, using the given message, an OK button, and the icon associated with the given message type. The dialog is placed near the given component.

```
static void showMessageDialog(Component component,Object
        message,String title,int messageType,Icon icon)
```

Creates and displays a JOptionPane within a JInternalFrame, using the given message, an OK button, and the given icon. The dialog is placed near the given component.

```
static int showOptionDialog(Component component,Object message,String
        title,int optionType,int messageType,Icon icon,Object
        options[],Object initialValue)
```

Creates and displays a JOptionPane within a JInternalFrame. See the Option dialog discussion.

```
void updateUI()
```

Tells the JOptionPane that its look-and-feel class has been changed.

JPanel

JPanel is a general panel that you can add components to, or draw into (see Figure 8-82). It is essentially a non-abstract version of JComponent, so it has all of the capabilities defined there. The most common use for JPanel is in grouping other components.

Ancestors

```
java.lang.Object
    |
    +—java.awt.Component
         |
         +—java.awt.Container
              |
              +—com.sun.java.swing.JComponent
                   |
                   +—com.sun.java.swing.JPanel
```

NOTE: *For more information, see Chapter 3, "The JComponent Class," and the "JFC Containers" and "Component Borders" sections in Chapter 7, "JFC by Concept."*

Figure 8-82
An empty JPanel with a border.

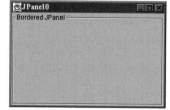

Steps in Creating and Using JPanel

1. Create a JPanel. There are four constructors:

   Create a JPanel with double-buffering turned on:

   ```
   JPanel()
   ```

   Create a JPanel with double-buffering set explicitly:

   ```
   JPanel( boolean isBuffered )
   ```

   Create a JPanel with double-buffering on and the layout manager explicitly set:

   ```
   JPanel( LayoutManager mgr )
   ```

   Create a JPanel with both double-buffering and the layout manager explicitly set:

   ```
   JPanel( LayoutManager mgr, boolean isBuffered )
   ```

   Create a default JPanel:

   ```
   JPanel myPanel = new JPanel();
   ```

   For a discussion of double-buffering, see the "Double Buffering" section in Chapter 7, "JFC by Concept."

2. Add the JPanel to a container. By default, a JRootPane's content pane is a JPanel, but you can replace it with a JPanel of your own if you wish. Usually, the default content pane is left alone and other panes are added:

   Set the content pane's layout manager:

   ```
   getContentPane().setLayout( new GridLayout( 3, 1 ) );
   ```

   Add the JPanel:

   ```
   getContentPane().add( myPanel );
   ```

3. Set the JPanel's layout manager:

   ```
   myPanel.setLayout( new BoxLayout( myPanel, BoxLayout.X_AXIS ) );
   ```

4. Add some components to the JPanel:

   Create the components:

   ```
   JButton ok = new JButton( "Ok" );
   JButton cancel = new JButton( "Cancel" );
   ```

   Add the components:

   ```
   myPanel.add( ok );
   myPanel.add( cancel );
   ```

5. Give the JPanel a border:

Create the border:

```
TitledBorder myBorder = new TitledBorder( "Two Buttons" );
```

Add the border:

```
myPanel.setBorder( myBorder );
```

Basic Code Examples

EXAMPLE 8-54 Using JPanel to Layout Controls

This example shows how to use nested JPanels to lay out controls in a frame. It also illustrates the use of borders in JPanels. Figure 8-83 shows the example as it comes up initially.

Important points to notice:

- There are a total of five JPanels in the example, including the content pane. It holds two subpanels—one for holding components used in getting first and last name input, and one that contains the OK and Cancel buttons.
- The subpanel that gets name input has two subpanels of its own. One holds the JLabel and JTextField for entering first names, and the other holds the JLabel and JTextField for entering last names. These are in separate subpanels so the vertical gaps between them can grow.
- The labels and text fields do not align vertically by default, so we have to tell the labels to change their vertical alignments.
- EmptyBorders are used to provide insets to keep components from running up against each other and to keep components from butting up against the frame's edges.
- This example doesn't do anything. It just shows some of JPanel's uses.

Here is the source:

```
import com.sun.java.swing.*;
import com.sun.java.swing.border.*;
import java.awt.*;
import java.awt.event.*;

public class MyFrame extends JFrame
{
    public MyFrame()
    {
        Dimension compSize;

        setTitle( "JPanel1" );

        // Store the content pane in a variable so we don't
        // have to keep calling getContentPane().
```

```
JPanel contentPane = (JPanel)getContentPane();

// Set the layout manager that the content pane will
// use to lay out its two panels.
contentPane.setLayout( new BoxLayout( contentPane,
                        BoxLayout.Y_AXIS ) );

// Create the first panel.
JPanel namePanel = new JPanel();

// Give the panel a titled border.
namePanel.setBorder(
                new TitledBorder( "Name Entry" ) );

// Set the layout manager that this panel will use to
// lay out its two sub panels.
namePanel.setLayout( new BoxLayout( namePanel,
                        BoxLayout.Y_AXIS ) );

// Create the first name label and text field.
JLabel firstLbl = new JLabel( "First Name:" );
JTextField firstField = new JTextField();

// Make the label and text field align vertically.
firstLbl.setAlignmentY( 0.5f );

// Create the panel that will hold the first name
// label and text field.
JPanel firstPanel = new JPanel();

// Set the panel's border so its contents will be
// indented 20 pixels from both the left and right
// sides.
firstPanel.setBorder(
                new EmptyBorder( 0, 20, 0, 20 ) );

// Set the first name panel's layout manager.
firstPanel.setLayout( new BoxLayout( firstPanel,
                        BoxLayout.X_AXIS ) );

// Add the panel's two components.
firstPanel.add( firstLbl );
firstPanel.add( firstField );

// Create the last name label and text field.
JLabel lastLbl = new JLabel( "Last Name:" );
JTextField lastField = new JTextField();

// Make the label and text field align vertically.
lastLbl.setAlignmentY( 0.5f );

// Create the panel that will hold the last name
// components.
JPanel lastPanel = new JPanel();

// Set the panel's border so its controls will be
```

```
                    // inset from the left and right sides.
                    lastPanel.setBorder(
                                    new EmptyBorder( 0, 20, 0, 20 ) );

                    // Set the panel's layout manager.
                    lastPanel.setLayout( new BoxLayout( lastPanel,
                                    BoxLayout.X_AXIS ) );

                    // Add the last name label and text field to the
                    // panel.
                    lastPanel.add( lastLbl );
                    lastPanel.add( lastField );

                    // Add the first and last name panels to the name
                    // panel.  Use 'glue' padding components so the first
                    // and last name panels will be vertically spaced
                    // properly.
                    namePanel.add( Box.createVerticalGlue() );
                    namePanel.add( firstPanel );
                    namePanel.add( Box.createVerticalGlue() );
                    namePanel.add( lastPanel );
                    namePanel.add( Box.createVerticalGlue() );

                    // Add the name panel to the content pane.
                    contentPane.add( namePanel );

                    // Create a panel to hold the two buttons.
                    JPanel buttonPanel = new JPanel();

                    // Set the border so the buttons will be inset 20
                    // pixels from the panel's top and bottom.
                    buttonPanel.setBorder(
                                    new EmptyBorder( 20, 0, 20, 0 ) );

                    // Specify a BoxLayout for the panel so we can easily
                    // space out the buttons.
                    buttonPanel.setLayout( new BoxLayout( buttonPanel,
                                    BoxLayout.X_AXIS ) );

                    // Create the two buttons.
                    JButton ok = new JButton( "Ok" );
                    JButton cancel = new JButton( "Cancel" );

                    // Add the buttons to the panel.  Use 'glue'
                    // components around the buttons so they are properly
                    // horizontally spaced.
                    buttonPanel.add( Box.createHorizontalGlue() );
                    buttonPanel.add( ok );
                    buttonPanel.add( Box.createHorizontalGlue() );
                    buttonPanel.add( cancel );
                    buttonPanel.add( Box.createHorizontalGlue() );

                    // Add the button panel to the content pane.
                    contentPane.add( buttonPanel );
                }
        }
```

NOTE: *You can see JPanel in use as a drawing canvas in Chapter 12, "Integrating JFC Example 3—A Simple Paint Program."*

JPanel's Public Methods

`AccessibleContext getAccessibleContext()`

Returns a subclass of AccessibleContext, which gives access to the JPanel's accessibility information.

`void paintComponent(Graphics g)`

This paints the main area of the JPanel—the part inside the border.

JPasswordField

JPasswordField is a text field that echoes a constant character like '*' when the user types into it (see Figure 8-84). As the name implies, this is useful for taking in passwords without them being echoed to the screen for anyone to see. JPasswordField generates an ActionEvent when the user signals that editing is complete. This usually means the user pressed Enter.

Ancestors

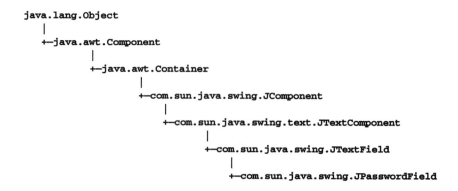

```
java.lang.Object
    |
    +—java.awt.Component
         |
         +—java.awt.Container
              |
              +—com.sun.java.swing.JComponent
                   |
                   +—com.sun.java.swing.text.JTextComponent
                        |
                        +—com.sun.java.swing.JTextField
                             |
                             +—com.sun.java.swing.JPasswordField
```

NOTE: *For more information, see the "JTextField," "JTextArea," and "JTextPane" sections in this chapter. Also see the "Text Entry and Editing" section in Chapter 7, "JFC by Concept," as well as Chapter 5, "JFC Documents and Text Components."*

Figure 8-84
A typical
JPasswordField with a
JLabel next to it.

Steps in Creating and Using JPasswordField

1. Create the JPasswordField. There are five constructors:
   Create an empty JPasswordField:

   ```
   JPasswordField()
   ```

   Create an empty JPasswordField with the specified number of columns:

   ```
   JPasswordField( int numColumns )
   ```

   Create a JPassword with the specified initial value:

   ```
   JPasswordField( String value )
   ```

   Create a JPassword with the specified initial value and number of columns:

   ```
   JPasswordField( String value, int numColumns )
   ```

   Create a JPasswordField with the specified text storage model, initial value, and number of columns:

   ```
   JPasswordField( Document doc, String value, int numColumns )
   ```

   For example, you can use the following:

   ```
   JPasswordField myPass = new JPasswordField( "si6_uynq", 15 );
   ```

   to create a JPasswordField with the initial value "si6_uynq" and a width of 15 columns.

2. Place the JPasswordField in a container. It will normally be placed with a JLabel that indicates it is a field used for password entry:

   ```
   JLabel prompt = new JLabel( "Enter password:" );
   JPasswordField myPass = new JPasswordField( 15 );
   myContainer.add( prompt );
   myContainer.add( myPass );
   ```

3. Set the echo character. It is '*' by default:

   ```
   myPass.setEchoChar( '?' );
   ```

4. Get the current text in the JPasswordField:

   ```
   String thePassword = myPass.getText();
   ```

5. Set the JPasswordField's text. You can do this through the constructor, but if you want to do it post-construction:

```
myPass.setText( "Fake password" );
```

Even though you set the text, it will still show up as all '*'s, or whatever the echo character is.

6. Listen for the user to press the Enter key to signal the end of input. This comes across as an ActionEvent.

Specify which class should be notified when this happens. In this case, it is the class that contains the JPasswordField:

```
myPass.addActionListener( this );
```

Make the event-receiving class (MyFrame) implement the ActionListener interface:

```
public class MyFrame extends JFrame implements ActionListener
{
    .
    .
    .
    public void actionPerformed( ActionEvent e )
    {
        // Password entry is complete, so get the password and
        // do something with it.
    }
}
```

7. Set the font. This will work with the "windows" look-and-feel, but is not guarateed to work with others:

```
myPass.setFont( new Font( "Courier", Font.PLAIN, 16 ) );
```

8. Set the echo character's color. The "windows" look-and-feel uses the component's foreground color as the text color, but other look-and-feels may or may not:

```
myPass.setForeground( Color.red );
```

9. Set the component's background color:

```
myPass.setBackground( Color.lightGray );
```

10. Change the JPasswordField's border. The default is a BevelBorder that makes the text entry area appear sunken into its container. You can specify another border to make it look raised or outlined. Or, you can use an EmptyBorder to blend it in with the surrounding area.

```
myPass.setBorder( new BevelBorder( BevelBorder.RAISED ) );
```

11. Specify a key accelerator that will cause the JPasswordField to get focus. Since the JPasswordField has no way of advertising its accelerator, it is customary to have an accompanying label that does.

```
JLabel passPrompt = new JLabel( "Password:" );
passPrompt.setDisplayedMnemonic( 'p' );
JPasswordField myPass = new JPasswordField();
myPass.setFocusAccelerator( 'p' );
```

JLabel's setDisplayedMnemonic() and JPasswordField's setFocusAccelerator() methods treat the 'p' as case insensitive. So, the 'P' in Password: will be underlined, and myPass will get the focus if Alt-p is pressed (the Alt works on Windows, but will be different on other platforms).

Basic Code Examples

EXAMPLE 8-55 Various Ways To Use JPasswordField

This example illustrates the concepts discussed above and puts them together in a working class. It displays five JPasswordFields with different attributes set differently. The main class listens to each of the JPasswordFields and prints out their field's contents when Enter is pressed while editing. Each JPasswordField has an accompanying JLabel and the two are placed in their own JPanel. 'glue' components are used to vertically space these JPanels. Figure 8-85 shows the example as it comes up initially.

Important points to notice:

- The first JPasswordField is just an empty one.
- The second JPasswordField changes the font and the echo character.
- The third JPasswordField makes the text the same color as the field's background so you can't even see the echo character.
- The fourth JPasswordField uses an EmptyBorder and changes the background color to make the field blend into its container.
- The fifth JPasswordField uses an accelerator character.
- We have to change the JLabels' Y alignments so they align vertically with the JPasswordFields.

Here is the source:

```
import com.sun.java.swing.*;
import com.sun.java.swing.border.*;
import java.awt.*;
import java.awt.event.*;

public class MyFrame extends JFrame implements
        ActionListener
{
```

Figure 8-85

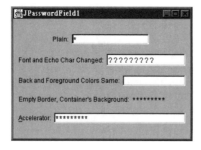

```
public MyFrame()
{
    setTitle( "JPasswordField1" );

    // Store the content pane in a variable for easier
    // access.
    JPanel contentPane = (JPanel)getContentPane();

    // Components will all be added to this panel.
    contentPane.setLayout( new BoxLayout( contentPane,
                           BoxLayout.Y_AXIS ) );

    contentPane.setBorder(
                new EmptyBorder( 10, 10, 10, 10 ) );

    // Add padding so the fields are properly vertically
    // spaced.
    contentPane.add( Box.createVerticalGlue() );

    // A plain JPasswordField with a JLabel.
    {
        // The '{' '}' pairs are just so we can reuse the
        // same variables so the differences between the
        // components can be seen better.
        JPanel passPanel = new JPanel();
        passPanel.setLayout( new BoxLayout( passPanel,
                             BoxLayout.X_AXIS ) );

        JLabel passLbl = new JLabel( "Plain:  " );
        passLbl.setAlignmentY( 0.5f );

        JPasswordField pwf = new JPasswordField();

        pwf.addActionListener( this );

        passPanel.add( passLbl );
        passPanel.add( pwf );
        contentPane.add( passPanel );
    }

    // Add padding so the fields are properly vertically
    // spaced.
    contentPane.add( Box.createVerticalGlue() );
```

```
// Pass an initial value to the constructor, change
// the font, and change the echo character.
{
   // The `{` `}` pairs are just so we can reuse the
   // same variables so the differences between the
   // components can be seen better.
   JPanel passPanel = new JPanel();
   passPanel.setLayout( new BoxLayout( passPanel,
                              BoxLayout.X_AXIS ) );

   JLabel passLbl = new JLabel(
                 "Font and Echo Char Changed:   " );
   passLbl.setAlignmentY( 0.5f );

   JPasswordField pwf =
                 new JPasswordField( "Password" );
   pwf.addActionListener( this );
   pwf.setFont( new Font( "Courier",
                         Font.PLAIN, 16 ) );
   pwf.setEchoChar( '?' );

   passPanel.add( passLbl );
   passPanel.add( pwf );

   contentPane.add( passPanel );
}

// Add padding so the fields are properly vertically
// spaced.
contentPane.add( Box.createVerticalGlue() );

// Set the background and foreground color to be the
// same.
{
   // The `{` `}` pairs are just so we can reuse the
   // same variables so the differences between the
   // components can be seen better.
   JPanel passPanel = new JPanel();
   passPanel.setLayout( new BoxLayout( passPanel,
                              BoxLayout.X_AXIS ) );

   JLabel passLbl = new JLabel(
               "Back and Foreground Colors Same:   " );
   passLbl.setAlignmentY( 0.5f );

   JPasswordField pwf =
                    new JPasswordField( "Password" );
   pwf.addActionListener( this );
   pwf.setBackground( Color.white );
   pwf.setForeground( Color.white );

   passPanel.add( passLbl );
   passPanel.add( pwf );

   contentPane.add( passPanel );
```

```
}

// Add padding so the fields are properly vertically
// spaced.
contentPane.add( Box.createVerticalGlue() );

// Give it an empty border and the same background
// color as the panel so it blends in.
{
    // The '{' '}' pairs are just so we can reuse the
    // same variables so the differences between the
    // components can be seen better.
    JPanel passPanel = new JPanel();
    passPanel.setLayout( new BoxLayout( passPanel,
                         BoxLayout.X_AXIS ) );

    JLabel passLbl = new JLabel(
          "Empty Border, Container's Background:  " );
    passLbl.setAlignmentY( 0.5f );

    JPasswordField pwf =
                 new JPasswordField( "Password" );
    pwf.addActionListener( this );
    pwf.setBorder( new EmptyBorder( 0, 0, 0, 0 ) );
    pwf.setBackground( passPanel.getBackground() );

    passPanel.add( passLbl );
    passPanel.add( pwf );

    contentPane.add( passPanel );
}

// Add padding so the fields are properly vertically
// spaced.
contentPane.add( Box.createVerticalGlue() );

// Use accelerators.
{
    // The '{' '}' pairs are just so we can reuse the
    // same variables so the differences between the
    // components can be seen better.
    JPanel passPanel = new JPanel();
    passPanel.setLayout( new BoxLayout( passPanel,
                         BoxLayout.X_AXIS ) );

    JLabel passLbl = new JLabel(
                     "Accelerator:  " );
    passLbl.setAlignmentY( 0.5f );

    JPasswordField pwf =
                 new JPasswordField( "Password" );
    pwf.addActionListener( this );
    passLbl.setDisplayedMnemonic( 'a' );
    pwf.setFocusAccelerator( 'a' );
```

```
                              passPanel.add( passLbl );
                              passPanel.add( pwf );

                              contentPane.add( passPanel );
                       }

                       // Add padding so the fields are properly vertically
                       // spaced.
                       contentPane.add( Box.createVerticalGlue() );
                }


                // This method is called when <enter> is pressed in one
                // of the JPasswordFields.  It just prints out the
                // contents of whichever field was being edited at the
                // time.
                public void actionPerformed( ActionEvent e )
                {
                       JPasswordField field = (JPasswordField)e.getSource();
                       System.out.println( field.getText() );
                }
        }
```

JPasswordField's Public Methods

```
boolean echoCharIsSet()
```

Returns true if the JPasswordField has a set echo character.

```
AccessibleContext getAccessibleContext()
```

Returns a subclass of AccessibleContext that gives access to the JPass-wordField's accessibility information.

```
char getEchoChar()
```

Returns the character that is displayed instead of the actually typed characters.

```
String getUIClassID()
```

Returns the identifying string that the look-and-feel uses to assign a UI class to the JPasswordField.

```
void setEchoChar(char c)
```

Specifies the character to display when a character is entered into the JPasswordField.

Figure 8-88
A typical
JPopupMenu.

JPopupMenu

A JPopupMenu is a single menu that can appear without a menu bar (see Figure 8-88). It is usually associated with an action on a component and will typically appear where the action took place. If a JPopupMenu does not extend outside its Window, it will display as a lightweight component. Otherwise, it will be a preferred component.

Ancestors

```
java.lang.Object
    |
    +—java.awt.Component
            |
            +—java.awt.Container
                    |
                    +—com.sun.java.swing.JComponent
                            |
                            +—com.sun.java.swing.JPopupMenu
```

NOTE: *For more information, see the "JMenu," "JMenuBar," "JMenuItem," "JCheckBoxMenuItem," and "JRadioButtonMenuItem" sections in this chapter. Also see the "Menus" section in Chapter 7, "JFC by Concept."*

Steps in Creating and Using JPopupMenu

1. Create a JPopupMenu:

   ```
   JPopupMenu mMenu = new JPopupMenu();
   ```

2. Add menu items to the popup menu. These are usually JMenuItems, JCheckBoxMenuItems, JRadioButtonMenuItems, or JMenus, but can be any Component that implements the MenuElement interface.

   Create and add a JMenuItem:

```
JMenuItem item1 = new JMenuItem( "A JMenuItem" );
mMenu.add( item1 );
```

Create and add a JCheckBoxMenuItem:

```
JCheckBoxMenuItem item2 = new JCheckBoxMenuItem(
  "A JCheckBoxMenuItem" );
mMenu.add( item2 );
```

Create and add a pair of grouped JRadioButtonMenuItems:

```
// Create the items.
JRadioButtonMenuItem item3 = new JRadioButtonMenuItem(
                            "One JRadioButtonMenuItem" );
JRadioButtonMenuItem item4 = new JRadioButtonMenuItem(
                            "Another JRadioButtonMenuItem" );

// Set the item to be initially selected.
item3.setSelected( true );

// Create a ButtonGroup to make it so only one of the two items
// can be selected at a time.
ButtonGroup group1 = new ButtonGroup();

// Add the two items to the ButtonGroup.
group1.add( item3 );
group1.add( item4 );

// Add the two items to the menu.
mMenu.add( item3 );
mMenu.add( item4 );
```

Add a separator:

```
mMenu.addSeparator();
```

3. Show the JPopupMenu at a particular location. For example, you might show the menu in response to a mouse click:

```
mMenu.show( clickedComponent, clickX, clickY );
```

You have to pass in the component over which the JPopupMenu will show up, and its upper-left hand corner's position within that component.

Basic Code Examples

EXAMPLE 8-58 Basic JPopupMenu

This example shows how to create and trigger the appearance of a JPopupMenu. It causes a JPopupMenu to appear when a button is pressed and released. It also shows how to add items to the menu as discussed above. Figure 8-87 shows the example just after the button has been clicked.

Here is the source code:

Figure 8-87

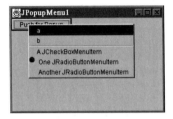

```
import com.sun.java.swing.*;
import java.awt.*;
import java.awt.event.*;

public class MyFrame extends JFrame
{
    JPopupMenu mMenu;

    public MyFrame()
    {
        setTitle( "JPopupMenu1" );

        // Store the content pane in a variable for easy
        // access.
        JPanel mPanel = (JPanel)getContentPane();

        // Components will all be added to this panel.
        mPanel.setLayout( new BoxLayout( mPanel,
                          BoxLayout.Y_AXIS ) );

        // Create a button which, when pressed and released,
        // causes a popup menu to appear.
        JButton b1 = new JButton( "Push for Popup" );
        mPanel.add( b1 );

        // We have to catch its mouse released event so we
        // can trigger the appearance of the popup.
        b1.addMouseListener( new MyListener() );

        // Create a JPopupmenu.
        mMenu = new JPopupMenu();

        // Add a pair of generic menu items.
        mMenu.add( new JMenuItem( "a" ) );
        mMenu.add( new JMenuItem( "b" ) );

        // Add a menu separator.
        mMenu.addSeparator();

        // Set the menu's background so it looks decent.
        mMenu.setBackground( Color.lightGray );

        // Create a check box menu item and add it to the
        // popup menu.
        JCheckBoxMenuItem item2 =
```

```
                          new JCheckBoxMenuItem( "A JCheckBoxMenuItem" );
        mMenu.add( item2 );

        // Create a pair of radio button menu items.
        JRadioButtonMenuItem item3 =
                              new JRadioButtonMenuItem(
                              "One JRadioButtonMenuItem" );
        JRadioButtonMenuItem item4 =
                              new JRadioButtonMenuItem(
                              "Another JRadioButtonMenuItem" );

        // Specify which item is initially selected.
        item3.setSelected( true );

        // Group the two radio button menu items so that only
        // one may be selected at a time.
        ButtonGroup group1 = new ButtonGroup();
        group1.add( item3 );
        group1.add( item4 );

        // Add the radio button menu items to the popup menu.
        mMenu.add( item3 );
        mMenu.add( item4 );
    }

    // Catch the button's events so we can trigger the
    // appearance of the popup menu.
    private class MyListener extends MouseAdapter
    {
        public void mouseReleased( MouseEvent e )
        {
            mMenu.show( (JComponent)e.getSource(), e.getX(),
                    e.getY() );
        }
    }
}
```

JPopupMenu's Public Methods

`JMenuItem add(Action a)`

Creates a JMenuItem from the given Action and adds it as the next item in the JPopupMenu.

`Component add(Component c)`

Adds a component as the next item in the JPopupMenu.

`JMenuItem add(JMenuItem menuItem)`

Adds a menu item as the next item in the JPopupMenu.

```
void addPopupMenuListener(PopupMenuListener l)
```

Tells the JPopupMenu to notify the given class when the menu becomes visible, invisible, or is canceled.

```
void addSeparator()
```

Adds a separator item as the next item in the JPopupMenu.

```
AccessibleContext getAccessibleContext()
```

Returns a subclass of AccessibleContext which gives access to the JPopupMenu's accessibility information.

```
Component getComponent()
```

Part of the MenuElement interface. Returns the JPopupMenu

```
Component getComponentAtIndex(int i)
```

Returns the component at the given index within the JPopupMenu.

```
int getComponentIndex(Component c)
```

Returns the index for the given component within the JPopupMenu.

```
static boolean getDefaultLightWeightPopupEnabled()
```

Returns true if the popup can be displayed as a lightweight component.

```
Component getInvoker()
```

Returns the component relative to which the JPopupMenu is being located.

```
String getLabel()
```

Returns the String associated with the JPopupMenu.

```
Insets getMargin()
```

Returns the gap in pixels between the JPopupMenu's border and its menu items.

```
SingleSelectionModel getSelectionModel()
```

Returns the JPopupMenu's selection model which keeps track of which item is selected.

`MenuElement[] getSubElements()`

Part of the MenuElement interface. Returns all of the JPopupMenu's menus.

`PopupMenuUI getUI()`

Returns the JPopupMenu's current look-and-feel class.

`String getUIClassID()`

Returns the identifying string that the look-and-feel uses to assign a UI class to the JPopupMenu.

`void insert(Action a,int index)`

Given an Action, create a JMenuItem and insert it at the given position.

`void insert(Component component,int index)`

Inserts the given component into the JPopupMenu at the given index.

`boolean isBorderPainted()`

Returns true if the JPopupMenu allows its border to be painted.

`boolean isLightWeightPopupEnabled()`

Returns true if the JPopupMenu can be shown as a lightweight component.

`boolean isVisible()`

Returns true if the JPopupMenu can be seen.

`void menuSelectionChanged(boolean newState)`

From the MenuElement interface.

`void pack()`

Causes the JPopupMenu to re-lay out its items.

`void processKeyEvent(KeyEvent e, MenuElement path[],
     MenuSelectionManager manager)`

Part of the MenuElement interface.

`void processMouseEvent(MouseEvent event, MenuElement path[],
     MenuSelectionManager manager)`

Part of the MenuElement interface.

```
void removePopupMenuListener(PopupMenuListener l)
```

Tells the JPopupMenu to stop notifying the given class when the menu becomes visible, invisible, or is canceled.

```
void setBorderPainted(boolean b)
```

Specifies whether the JPopupMenu should paint its border or not.

```
void setDefaultLightWeightPopupEnabled(boolean enable)
```

Specifies whether the JPopupMenu can be displayed as a lightweight component by default.

```
void setInvoker(Component invoker)
```

Sets the component relative to which the JPopupMenu should be located.

```
void setLabel(String label)
```

Specifies the String associated with the JPopupMenu.

```
void setLightWeightPopupEnabled(boolean state)
```

Specifies whether the JPopupMenu can display as a lightweight component.

```
void setLocation(int x,int y)
```

Specifies the location of the JPopupMenu's upper-left corner relative to its invoking component.

```
void setPopupSize(Dimension d)
```

Specifies the size of the popup.

```
void setPopupSize(int width,int height)
```

Specifies the size of the popup.

```
void setSelected(Component sel)
```

Specifies that the given component is now the JPopupMenu's selected item.

void setSelectionModel(SingleSelectionModel model)

Replaces the JPopupMenu's selection model.

void setUI(PopupMenuUI ui)

Gives the JPopupMenu a new look-and-feel class.

void setVisible(boolean b)

Specifies whether the JPopupMenu should be visible or not.

void show(Component invoker,int x,int y)

Displays the JPopupMenu at the given point relative to the given component.

void updateUI()

Tells the JPopupMenu that the look-and-feel class has been changed.

JProgressBar

JProgressBar is a component used to visually display the progress of a task (see Figure 8-88). It doesn't display any numbers or text, but rather a bar that gets longer as the task becomes more complete. When the bar extends the full length of the JProgressBar, then the task is complete.

A JProgressBar generates a ChangeEvent when its value changes.

Ancestors

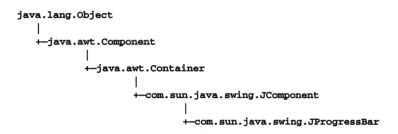

```
java.lang.Object
    |
    +—java.awt.Component
            |
            +—java.awt.Container
                    |
                    +—com.sun.java.swing.JComponent
                            |
                            +—com.sun.java.swing.JProgressBar
```

Figure 8-88
A typical horizontal
JProgressBar.

NOTE: *For more information, see the "JOptionPane" and "DefaultBoundedRangeModel" sections in this chapter.*

Steps in Creating and Using JProgressBar

1. Create the JProgressBar. There is only one constructor.

   ```
   JProgressBar bar1 = new JProgressBar();
   ```

2. Specify the progress bar's orientation. There are only two orientations: horizontal and vertical. The orientation is horizontal by default, so you don't need to call this method unless you want a vertical orientation.

   ```
   bar1.setOrientation( JProgressBar.VERTICAL );
   ```

   A vertical JProgressBar always grows from bottom to top and a horizontal JProgressBar grows from left to right.

3. Change the bar's color. A progress bar consists of a panel, a border, and the bar itself. The "basic" look-and-feel uses the foreground color to draw the bar, so by changing the component's foreground color, we change the bar's color. This may not work with all look-and-feels.

   ```
   bar1.setForeground( Color.red );
   ```

4. Change the border. The default border is a lowered BevelBorder.

   ```
   bar1.setBorder( new BevelBorder(BevelBorder.RAISED) );
   ```

   This gives the JProgressBar a raised look instead.

5. Add the JProgressBar to a container. A JProgressBar generally looks best when it is longer than it is wide. For this example, assume the panel where the progress bar will go uses a BorderLayout and is called contentPane.

   ```
   contentPane.add( "West", bar1 );
   ```

   This places the JProgressBar along the left edge of the container—a good location for a vertical bar.

6. A JProgressBar needs a task whose progress it can display. You will have to decide what the task's minimum progress value is, what its maximum progress value is, and when the value changes. By default, the minimum is 0 and the maximum is 100 since progress bars often display percent completed.

Set the minimum value:

```
bar1.setMinimum( -100 );
```

Set the maximum value:

```
bar1.setMaximum( 100 );
```

Set the current value:

```
bar1.setValue( -50 );
```

7. You can also choose to be notified when a JProgressBar's value changes. To do this, you specify a ChangeListener.

Tell the JProgressBar which class to notify when its value changes. For this example, the listener is the class in which the progress bar is defined:

```
mBar1.addChangeListener( this );
```

Make the event-receiving class implement the ChangeListener interface. The class in this case is MyFrame.

```
import com.sun.java.swing.event.*;
    .
    .
    .
public class MyFrame extends JFrame implements ChangeListener
{
    .
    .
    .
    public void stateChanged( ChangeEvent e )
    {
        // Use getSource() to identify which component changed and
        // then take appropriate action.
    }
}
```

Basic Code Examples

EXAMPLE 8-57 Basic JProgressBar

This example lays out two progress bars: one horizontal and one vertical. Each progress bar has a Timer associated with it that causes its value to change, just to show the progress bar in motion. The vertical bar has its color changed to red and its border changed to raised. A ChangeListener is also attached to the horiziontal bar so changes in the value can be tracked and printed. Figure 8-89 shows the example when it is part way through.

Here is the source code:

```
import com.sun.java.swing.*;
import com.sun.java.swing.event.*;
```

Figure 8-89

```java
import com.sun.java.swing.border.*;
import java.awt.*;
import java.awt.event.*;

public class MyFrame extends JFrame implements
        ActionListener, ChangeListener
{
    // Define these as instance variables so the event
    // listener functions can see them.

    // The two progress bars.
    JProgressBar mBar1;
    JProgressBar mBar2;

    // The progress bars' current values.
    private int mBar1Value = 0;
    private int mBar2Value = 0;

    // The timers that make the progress bars go (since we
    // don't have a real task).
    private Timer mBar1Timer;
    private Timer mBar2Timer;

    public MyFrame()
    {
        setTitle( "JProgressBar1" );

        // Store the content pane in a variable for easier
        // access.
        JPanel contentPane = (JPanel)getContentPane();

        // Components will all be added to this panel.
        contentPane.setLayout( new BorderLayout() );

        // Create the horizontal progress bar.
        mBar1 = new JProgressBar();

        // Make it so this class will be notified when the
        // progress bar's value changes.
        mBar1.addChangeListener( this );
```

```
                           // Add the progress bar to the content pane's top
                           // side.
                           contentPane.add( "North", mBar1 );

                           // Create a vertical progress bar.
                           mBar2 = new JProgressBar();
                           mBar2.setOrientation( JProgressBar.VERTICAL );

                           // Change the progress bar's border to make it look
                           // raised instead of lowered.
                           mBar2.setBorder( new BevelBorder(
                                             BevelBorder.RAISED ) );

                           // Change the color of the bar itself.
                           mBar2.setForeground( Color.red );

                           // Add the progress bar to the content pane's left
                           // edge.
                           contentPane.add( "West", mBar2 );

                           // Create the timers that will be used to control
                           // changing the progress bars' values.
                           mBar1Timer = new Timer( 100, this );
                           mBar2Timer = new Timer( 200, this );

                           // Start the timers.  As the run, they will generate
                           // ActionEvents.  Each ActionEvent will cause the
                           // associated progress bar's value to be incremented
                           // by one.
                           mBar1Timer.start();
                           mBar2Timer.start();
                      }

// Catch ActionEvents from the two timers and change the
// current value of the associated progress bar.  If the
// value goes beyond the progress bar's maximum, stop
// the timer.
public void actionPerformed( ActionEvent e )
{
    if ( e.getSource() == mBar1Timer )
    {
        mBar1Value++;
        if ( mBar1Value > mBar1.getMaximum() )
            mBar1Timer.stop();
        else
        {
            mBar1.setValue( mBar1Value );
        }
    }
    else if ( e.getSource() == mBar2Timer )
    {
        mBar2Value++;
        if ( mBar2Value > mBar2.getMaximum() )
            mBar2Timer.stop();
        else
```

```
                    {
                        mBar2.setValue( mBar2Value );
                    }
                }
            }

            // This is called when the progress bar being listened
            // to (mBar1) gets a value change.
            public void stateChanged( ChangeEvent e )
            {
                if ( e.getSource() == mBar1 )
                    System.out.println( "—"+mBar1.getValue() );
            }
        }
```

Advanced Issues

EXAMPLE 8-58 Putting a JProgressBar in Its Own Dialog

This example is much like Example 8-57, "Basic JProgressBar" except that there is only a single progress bar, and it appears in a dialog. The main frame has a single Start button which, when pressed, displays a dialog with a progress bar. It also starts a Timer which makes the progress bar go and disables the Start button. When the progress bar's value reaches its maximum, the timer stops, the progress bar is reset, the dialog is disposed of, and the Start button is re-enabled so it can go again. Figure 8-90 shows the example with the dialog up and running.

Here is the source code:

```
import com.sun.java.swing.*;
import com.sun.java.swing.event.*;
import com.sun.java.swing.border.*;
import java.awt.*;
import java.awt.event.*;

public class MyFrame extends JFrame implements ActionListener
{
    // Define these as instance variables so the event listener
    // functions
    // can see them.
```

Figure 8-90

```
    // The progress bar.
    JProgressBar mBar1;

    // The progress bar's current value.
    private int mBar1Value = 0;

    // The timer that makes the progress bar go (since we don't
    // have a real task).
    private Timer mBar1Timer;

    // The dialog that will hold the progress bar.
    JDialog mProgressDlg;

    // The start button.
    JButton mStartButton;

    public MyFrame()
    {
        setTitle( "JProgressBar2" );

        // Store the content pane in a variable for easier access.
        JPanel contentPane = (JPanel)getContentPane();

        // Components will all be added to this panel.
        contentPane.setLayout( new BorderLayout() );

        // Create a buuton that can be used to start the timer.
        // Place the button along the content pane's bottom edge.
        mStartButton = new JButton( "Start" );
        mStartButton.setActionCommand( "Start" );
        mStartButton.addActionListener( this );
        contentPane.add( "South", mStartButton );

        // Create a horizontal progress bar.
        mBar1 = new JProgressBar();

        // Create the timer that will be used to control changing
        // the progress bar's value.
        mBar1Timer = new Timer( 100, this );

    }

    // Catch ActionEvents from the timer and change the current
    // value of the associated progress bar.  If the value goes
    // beyond the progress bar's maximum, stop the timer.
    // Also catch the event in which the start button is pressed
    // so the timer can be started and the progress bar
    // displayed.

    public void actionPerformed( ActionEvent e )
    {
        if ( e.getSource() == mBar1Timer )
        {
            // This catches timer events and causes the progress bar's
            // value to be incremented.
```

```
    mBar1Value++;
    if ( mBar1Value > mBar1.getMaximum() )
    {
        // The progress bar has reached it maximum, so we stop
the
        // timer, get rid of the dialog that holds the progress
        // bar, reset the progress bar, and re-enable the start
        // button so the progress bar can be restarted.
        mBar1Timer.stop();
        mProgressDlg.dispose();
        mBar1Value = 0;
        mBar1.setValue( 0 );
        mStartButton.setEnabled( true );
    }
    else
    {
        mBar1.setValue( mBar1Value );
    }
}
else if ( e.getActionCommand().equals( "Start" ) )
{
    // Disable the start button so the progress bar can't be
    // restarted while it is running.
    mStartButton.setEnabled( false );

    // Create the option dialog that holds the progress bar.
    JOptionPane pane = new JOptionPane( mBar1 );
    mProgressDlg = pane.createDialog( getContentPane(),
                    "Tracking Progress" );

    // Start the timer.  As it runs, it will generate
    // ActionEvents.
    // Each ActionEvent will cause the progress bar's value
    // to be incremented by one.
    mBar1Timer.start();

    // Show the dialog.
    mProgressDlg.show();
}
}
}
```

JProgressBar's Public Methods

```
void addChangeListener(ChangeListener l)
```

Tells the JProgressBar to notify the given class whenever the JProgressBar's value changes.

```
AccessibleContext getAccessibleContext()
```

Returns a subclass of AccessibleContext, which gives access to the JProgressBar's accessibility information.

```
int getMaximum()
```

Gets the JProgressBar's maximum value.

```
int getMinimum()
```

Gets the JProgressBar's minimum value.

```
BoundedRangeModel getModel()
```

Returns the BoundedRangeModel that holds the JProgressBar's minimum, maximum, and current values, among other things.

```
int getOrientation()
```

Returns whether the JProgressBar is horizontal or vertical.

```
ProgressBarUI getUI()
```

Returns the JProgressBar's current look-and-feel class.

```
String getUIClassID()
```

Returns the identifying string that the look-and-feel uses to assign a UI class to the JProgressBar.

```
int getValue()
```

Gets the JProgressBar's current value.

```
boolean isBorderPainted()
```

Returns true if the JProgressBar will tell its border to paint itself.

```
void removeChangeListener(ChangeListener l)
```

Tells the JProgressBar to stop notifying the given class when JProgressBar's value changes.

```
void setBorderPainted(boolean b)
```

Specifies whether the JProgressBar will let its border paint itself.

```
void setMaximum(int n)
```

Specifies the JProgressBar's maximum value.

```
void setMinimum(int n)
```

Specifies the JProgressBar's minimum value.

```
void setModel(BoundedRangeModel newModel)
```

Replaces the JProgressBar's BoundedRangeModel.

```
void setOrientation(int newOrientation)
```

Specifies whether the JProgressBar is horizontal or vertical.

```
void setUI(ProgressBarUI ui)
```

Gives the JProgressBar a new look-and-feel class.

```
void setValue(int n)
```

Specifies the JProgressBar's value.

```
void update(Graphics g)
```

Overridden so it doesn't fill the background rectangle.

```
void updateUI()
```

Tells the JProgressBar that its look-and-feel class has been changed.

JRadioButton

A JRadioButton is normally used as one of a group of radio buttons of which only one may be selected at a time (see Figure 8-91). JRadioButtons are grouped using a ButtonGroup and are usually used to select from a set of mutually exclusive options.

A JRadioButton consists of a background rectangle (usually the color of its container), and text and/or an icon. If it includes an icon, the icon is used to visually reflect the JRadioButton's current state, so you will need to specify an alternate icon to represent its other state.

Figure 8-91
A typical set of
JRadioButtons.

A JRadioButton generates an ItemEvent when its state changes.

Ancestors

```
java.lang.Object
|
+—java.awt.Component
    |
    +—java.awt.Container
        |
        +—com.sun.java.swing.JComponent
            |
            +—com.sun.java.swing.AbstractButton
                |
                +—com.sun.java.swing.JToggleButton
                    |
                    +—com.sun.java.swing.JRadioButton
```

NOTE: *For more information, see the "AbstractButton," "DefaultButtonModel,"*
"JButton," "JCheckBox," and "JRadioButtonMenuItem" sections in this chapter.
Also see the "Components That Can Be Turned On and Off" section in Chapter 7,
"JFC by Concept."

Steps in Creating and Using JRadioButton

1. Create a radio button. There are multiple constructors, but all are
   variations of:

   ```
   JRadioButton( String text, Icon icon, boolean selected )
   ```

   where 'text' is the string that goes with the radio button, 'icon' is the
   picture that displays when the radio button is not selected, and
   'selected' is the radio button's initial state. All arguments are optional.
   If no icon is specified, a circular checkbox is used to indicate the state
   of the control (it is different depending on the current look-and-feel).

   Create a radio button with text and no icon:

   ```
   JRadioButton b2 = new JRadioButton( "Text only" );
   ```

   Create a radio button with text and an icon and that is initially
   selected. Here we create an icon for use when the button is selected,
   then generate another icon using GrayFilter for when the button is
   not selected:

   ```
   Icon open_on = new ImageIcon( "open.gif" );
   Icon open_off = new ImageIcon( GrayFilter.createDisabledImage(
           ((ImageIcon)open_on).getImage() ) );
   ```

```
JRadioButton b1b = new JRadioButton( "Open mode", open_off,
                                      true );
```

Notice that the icon that represents the not selected state is passed to the constructor. The one that represents the selected state must be passed separately with the setSelectedIcon() method.

2. Set the radio button's state. This can be done either in the constructor as shown above, or using the setSelected() method:

```
b1.setSelected( true );
```

3. Set the radio button's selected icon. This is only needed if the radio button was created with an icon. 'open_on' was created as part of step 1 above:

```
b1b.setSelectedIcon( open_on );
```

4. Create more radio buttons that will be grouped with the first so the user can choose between them. Notice that these items are also given icons. The basic radio button-creating statements are shown here:

```
Icon save_on = new ImageIcon( "save.gif" );
Icon save_off = new ImageIcon( GrayFilter.createDisabledImage(
                    ((ImageIcon)save_on).getImage() ) );
JRadioButton b2b = new JRadioButton( "Save mode", save_off );
b2b.setSelectedIcon( save_on );

Icon print_on = new ImageIcon( "print.gif" );
Icon print_off = new ImageIcon( GrayFilter.createDisabledImage(
                    ((ImageIcon)print_on).getImage() ) );
JRadioButton b3b = new JRadioButton( "Print mode", print_off );
b3b.setSelectedIcon( print_on );
```

5. Create a ButtonGroup and add the radio buttons to it. A ButtonGroup associates radio buttons and makes it so only one radio button in the group may be selected at a time:

```
ButtonGroup bg1b = new ButtonGroup();
bg1b.add( b1b );
bg1b.add( b2b );
bg1b.add( b3b );
```

6. Change where the text draws relative to the control. Here we make it so the text is displayed above the button/icon:

```
b1b.setHorizontalTextPosition( JRadioButton.CENTER );
b1b.setVerticalTextPosition( JRadioButton.TOP );
```

Notice that both the text's horizontal and vertical positions must be set for this to work.

7. Add a tool tip. This is text that displays in its own little window when the user stops the mouse over the radio button:

```
b1b.setToolTipText( "Set mode to OPEN" );
```

8. Change the text color. This works for "windows" look-and-feel, but is not guaranteed to work with others:

```
b1b.setForeground( Color.red );
```

9. Change the font. Again, this works with the "windows" look-and-feel, but is not guaranteed to work with others:

```
b1b.setFont( new Font( "TimesRoman", Font.ITALIC, 18 ) );
```

10. Specify an icon to use when the radio button is disabled. This is only useful when an icon was specified in the constructor:

```
b1b.setDisabledIcon( new ImageIcon( "disabled.gif" ) );
```

11. Assign an accelerator key to the radio button. When the specified key is pressed in combination with a special key which is platform-dependent (Alt on Windows), it is like clicking on the radio button.

The key is case-insensitive:

```
b1b.setMnemonic( 'o' );
```

12. Catch events that tell when a radio button's state has changed.

Specify which class will receive the events. In this case, it will be the class that contains the radio button:

```
dis1.addItemListener( this );
```

Make the event-receiving class implement the ItemListener interface. In this case, the receiving class is called MyFrame. When the radio button's state changes, it goes through all of the registered ItemListeners and calls their itemStateChanged() methods. The radio button's new state is included as part of the ItemEvent passed to itemStateChanged(). It can be extracted using ItemEvent's getStateChange() method. The new value will be either ItemEvent.SELECTED or ItemEvent.DESELECTED:

```
public class MyFrame extends JFrame implements ItemListener
{
    .
    .
    .
    public void itemStateChanged( ItemEvent e )
    {
        // Use e.getSource() to find out which component generated
        // the event, and use e.getStateChange() to find out
        // whether the component is now selected or not
    }
}
```

13. Catch actions that happen to the radio button. These events do not just happen when the button's state changes. They also happen when

an already selected item is clicked (it does not change state). First, specify a class that will receive the events:

```
b1.addActionListener( this );
```

Define the string that will be delivered with ActionEvents from this radio button:

```
b1.setActionCommand( "Radio button b1" );
```

Make the event receiving class (in this case, MyFrame) implement the ActionListener interface. Use the ActionEvent's getActionCommand() method to get the string that was defined in the setActionCommand() method above. The command string helps to identify which component generated the event:

```
public void actionPerformed( ActionEvent e )
    {
    // Here we just print out the command string.
    System.out.println( "Action:  " + e.getActionCommand() );
    }
```

If you want the state when you get an ActionEvent, you have to call the event source's isSelected() method.

Basic Code Examples

EXAMPLE 8-59 Variations on JRadioButton

This example illustrates the topics discussed above. It has four rows of JRadioButtons, each row representing a separate ButtonGroup. The bottom row can be used to enable/disable the rest—the example knows when these buttons' state has changed because it catches their ItemEvents. It also catches ActionEvents from the first row of buttons and prints out the button's action command string. Notice that the second button on the second row uses a rollover icon that shows up when it is not selected and the mouse is over it. Figure 8-92 shows the example in its initial state.

Here is the source code:

```
import com.sun.java.swing.*;
import com.sun.java.swing.border.*;
import java.awt.*;
import java.awt.event.*;

public class MyFrame extends JFrame implements ItemListener,
      ActionListener
{
    JRadioButton b1, b2, b3, b1a, b2a, b3a, b1b, b2b, b3b;

    public MyFrame()
    {
```

Figure 8-92

```
setTitle( "JRadioButton1" );

// Store the content pane in a variable for easier
// access.
JPanel contentPane = (JPanel)getContentPane();

// Components will all be added to this panel.
contentPane.setLayout( new GridLayout( 4, 3 ) );

// Leave some space around the edge.
contentPane.setBorder(
                new EmptyBorder( 10, 10, 10, 10 ) );

// Button with no text or image.  When clicked, an
// action event is generated.
b1 = new JRadioButton();
b1.setSelected( true );
b1.addActionListener( this );
b1.setActionCommand( "Nameless button" );
contentPane.add( b1 );

// Button with text but no image.  When clicked, an
// action event is generated.
b2 = new JRadioButton( "Text Only" );
b2.addActionListener( this );
b2.setActionCommand( "Text-only button" );
contentPane.add( b2 );

// Button with no text but an image.  When clicked,
// an action event is generated.
b3 = new JRadioButton( new ImageIcon( "open.gif" ) );
b3.addActionListener( this );
b3.setActionCommand( "Image-only button" );
contentPane.add( b3 );

// Associate the previous three buttons so only one
// may be selected at a time.
ButtonGroup bg1 = new ButtonGroup();
bg1.add( b1 );
bg1.add( b2 );
bg1.add( b3 );
```

```
// The following three buttons have the same selected
// and non-selected icons and are in a button group
// so only one can show its selected icon at a time.
// The second of the group also has a rollover icon
// defined.
b1a = new JRadioButton(
                new ImageIcon( "silvstar.gif" ) );
b1a.setSelected( true );
b1a.setSelectedIcon(
                new ImageIcon( "goldstar.gif" ) );
contentPane.add( b1a );

b2a = new JRadioButton(
                new ImageIcon( "silvstar.gif" ) );
b2a.setSelectedIcon(
                new ImageIcon( "goldstar.gif" ) );
b2a.setRolloverIcon( new ImageIcon( "beermug.gif" ) );
b2a.setRolloverEnabled( true );
contentPane.add( b2a );

b3a = new JRadioButton(
                new ImageIcon( "silvstar.gif" ) );
b3a.setSelectedIcon(
                new ImageIcon( "goldstar.gif" ) );
contentPane.add( b3a );

ButtonGroup bg1a = new ButtonGroup();
bg1a.add( b1a );
bg1a.add( b2a );
bg1a.add( b3a );

// The following three buttons use icons with color
// for their selected icons, but use the gray filter
// version of the same icons when they are not
// selected.  Note that the text goes above the icon
// here, the font has been changed, the color has
// been changed, the buttons have tool tips, and they
// all have keyboard accelerators.
Icon open_on = new ImageIcon( "open.gif" );
Icon open_off = new ImageIcon(
                GrayFilter.createDisabledImage(
                ((ImageIcon)open_on).getImage() ) );
Icon save_on = new ImageIcon( "save.gif" );
Icon save_off = new ImageIcon(
                GrayFilter.createDisabledImage(
                ((ImageIcon)save_on).getImage() ) );
Icon print_on = new ImageIcon( "print.gif" );
Icon print_off = new ImageIcon(
                GrayFilter.createDisabledImage(
                ((ImageIcon)print_on).getImage() ) );

b1b = new JRadioButton( "Open mode", open_off, true );
b1b.setHorizontalTextPosition( JRadioButton.CENTER );
b1b.setVerticalTextPosition( JRadioButton.TOP );
b1b.setForeground( Color.red );
```

```
        b1b.setMnemonic( 'o' );
        b1b.setToolTipText( "Set mode to OPEN" );
        b1b.setFont( new Font( "TimesRoman",
                              Font.ITALIC, 18 ) );
        b1b.setSelectedIcon( open_on );
        b1b.setDisabledIcon(
                            new ImageIcon( "disabled.gif" ) );
        contentPane.add( b1b );

        b2b = new JRadioButton( "Save mode", save_off );
        b2b.setToolTipText( "Set mode to SAVE" );
        b2b.setMnemonic( 's' );
        b2b.setFont( new Font( "TimesRoman",
                              Font.ITALIC, 18 ) );
        b2b.setForeground( Color.red );
        b2b.setHorizontalTextPosition( JRadioButton.CENTER );
        b2b.setVerticalTextPosition( JRadioButton.TOP );
        b2b.setSelectedIcon( save_on );
        contentPane.add( b2b );

        b3b = new JRadioButton( "Print mode", print_off );
        b3b.setToolTipText( "Set mode to PRINT" );
        b3b.setMnemonic( 'p' );
        b3b.setFont( new Font( "TimesRoman",
                              Font.ITALIC, 18 ) );
        b3b.setForeground( Color.red );
        b3b.setHorizontalTextPosition( JRadioButton.CENTER );
        b3b.setVerticalTextPosition( JRadioButton.TOP );
        b3b.setSelectedIcon( print_on );
        contentPane.add( b3b );

        ButtonGroup bg1b = new ButtonGroup();
        bg1b.add( b1b );
        bg1b.add( b2b );
        bg1b.add( b3b );

        // These buttons allow you to see how item events can
        // be generated.  When dis1 is selected, all of the
        // buttons above get enabled.  When it is de-selected,
        // they are all disabled.
        JRadioButton dis1 = new JRadioButton( "Enabled" );
        dis1.setSelected( true );
        dis1.addItemListener( this );
        contentPane.add( dis1 );

        JRadioButton dis2 = new JRadioButton( "Disabled" );
        contentPane.add( dis2 );

        ButtonGroup dis_gp = new ButtonGroup();
        dis_gp.add( dis1 );
        dis_gp.add( dis2 );
    }

// Catches events from 'dis1' defined just above.  If
// the button is selected, all specified controls are
```

```
    // enabled.   Otherwise, they are all disabled.
    public void itemStateChanged( ItemEvent e )
    {
        if ( e.getStateChange() == ItemEvent.SELECTED )
        {
            b1.setEnabled( true );
            b2.setEnabled( true );
            b3.setEnabled( true );
            b1a.setEnabled( true );
            b2a.setEnabled( true );
            b3a.setEnabled( true );
            b1b.setEnabled( true );
            b2b.setEnabled( true );
            b3b.setEnabled( true );
        }
        else
        {
            b1.setEnabled( false );
            b2.setEnabled( false );
            b3.setEnabled( false );
            b1a.setEnabled( false );
            b2a.setEnabled( false );
            b3a.setEnabled( false );
            b1b.setEnabled( false );
            b2b.setEnabled( false );
            b3b.setEnabled( false );
        }
    }

    // Illustrates catching actions from JRadioButtons
    // instead of item events.  Note that an action is
    // generated even when the state does not change (when
    // you click on an item that is already selected.
    public void actionPerformed( ActionEvent e )
    {
        System.out.println( "Action:   " +
                                 e.getActionCommand() );
    }
}
```

Advanced Issues

EXAMPLE 8-60 Using JRadioButtons as a Level Control

This example puts up ten radio buttons as a scale from one to ten. As the mouse passes over one of the radio buttons, it becomes the selected one. Using this you can change the value of the overall control just by moving the mouse around. Figure 8-93 shows the example as it appears initially.

Important things to notice:

■ The value represented by a radio button is stored in its action command string for convenience.

Figure 8-93

- Only the first and last radio buttons have text assigned to them, which is placed below the button.
- The example tracks mouse events on each of the ten JRadioButtons and, when the mouse enters one, it becomes the selected one.

Here is the source code:

```
import com.sun.java.swing.*;
import java.awt.*;
import java.awt.event.*;

public class MyFrame extends JFrame
{
    public MyFrame()
    {
        setTitle( "JRadioButton2" );

        // Store the content pane in a variable for easier access.
        JPanel contentPane = (JPanel)getContentPane();

        // Components will all be added to this panel.
        contentPane.setLayout( new BoxLayout( contentPane,
         BoxLayout.X_AXIS ) );

        // This variable will hold each radio button in turn.  We don't
        // need separate variables for each, because we are using the
        // action command string to identify each one.
        JRadioButton radioButton;

        // Create the button group that the radio buttons will belong
        // to and that will make it so only one can be selected at a
        // time.
        ButtonGroup buttonGroup = new ButtonGroup();

        // Create the 10 radio buttons.
        for ( int i = 0; i < 10; i++ )
        {
            // Create this button.
            radioButton = new JRadioButton();

            if ( i == 0 )
            {
                // If it's the first, give it a label of '1' which will
                // appear
                // just below the button itself.  The first is also the
                // initially
                // selected one.
                radioButton.setSelected( true );
                radioButton.setText( "1" );
                radioButton.setHorizontalTextPosition(
```

```
JRadioButton.CENTER );
      radioButton.setVerticalTextPosition( JRadioButton.BOTTOM
);
   }
   else if ( i == 9 )
   {
      // If it's the last button, give it a label of '10' which
      // will
      // appear below the button.
      radioButton.setText( "10" );
      radioButton.setHorizontalTextPosition(
JRadioButton.CENTER );
      radioButton.setVerticalTextPosition( JRadioButton.BOTTOM
);
   }

   // Don't paint the focus, because it doesn't look right for
   // this
   // type of radio button use.
   radioButton.setFocusPainted( false );

   // Set the action command.  This will be our way of
   // identifying
   // the selected button.  We add 1 since the value to the
   // user
   // is 1-based while 'i' is 0-based.
   radioButton.setActionCommand( String.valueOf( i + 1 ) );

   // Make it so that mouse events are caught.  We only use
   // mouseEntered().
   radioButton.addMouseListener( new MyMouseAdapter() );

   // Add the radio button to the group.
   buttonGroup.add( radioButton );

   // Add the button to the container.
   contentPane.add( radioButton );
   }
}

// This class catches mouse entered events, and when the mouse
// enters
// one of the radio buttons, it becomes the selected one.
private class MyMouseAdapter extends MouseAdapter
{
   public void mouseEntered( MouseEvent e )
   {
      JRadioButton thisButton = (JRadioButton)e.getSource();
      thisButton.setSelected( true );

      // Print out the value of the selected button.
      System.out.println( thisButton.getActionCommand() );
   }
}
}
```

JRadioButton's Public Methods

`AccessibleContext getAccessibleContext()`

Returns a subclass of AccessibleContext, which gives access to the JRadioButton's accessibility information.

`String getUIClassID()`

Returns the identifying string that the look-and-feel uses to assign a UI class to the JRadioButton.

`void updateUI()`

Tells the JRadioButton that the look-and-feel class has been changed.

JRadioButtonMenuItem

A JRadioButtonMenuItem is, as the name suggests, a radio button that occurs on a menu (see Figure 8-94). It will normally occur as one of a group of radio buttons, of which only one may be chosen at a time. The one that is currently selected will have a mark to its left designating that it is selected. This component will almost always have a text string describing it and will often also have an icon. Unlike a JRadioButton, the icon does not change based on whether the component is selected.

A JRadioButtonMenuItem generates an ItemEvent when its state changes.

Ancestors

```
java.lang.Object
    |
    +—java.awt.Component
        |
        +—java.awt.Container
            |
            +—com.sun.java.swing.JComponent
                |
                +—com.sun.java.swing.AbstractButton
                    |
                    +—com.sun.java.swing.JMenuItem
                        |
                        +—com.sun.java.swing.JRadioButtonMenuItem
```

Figure 8-94

A typical set of
JRadioButton-
MenuItems.

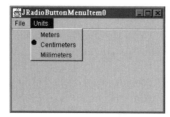

NOTE: *For more information, see the "JMenu," "JMenuBar," "JMenuItem," "JCheckBoxMenuItem," "AbstractButton," and "DefaultButtonModel" sections in this chapter. Also see the "Components That Can Be Turned On and Off" section in Chapter 7, "JFC by Concept."*

Steps in Creating and Using JRadioButtonMenuItem

1. Create a menu to add the item into. This can be a JMenu or a JPopupMenu. For this example, we will use a JMenu, so we will also need to create a JMenuBar to hold the JMenu.

   Create the JMenuBar:

   ```
   JMenuBar mbar = new JMenuBar();
   ```

   Attach the menu bar to the frame:

   ```
   getRootPane().setMenuBar( mbar );
   ```

   Create the JMenu and give it a text string that will show up in the menu bar:

   ```
   JMenu plainMenu = new JMenu( "Plain" );
   ```

   Add the menu to the menu bar:

   ```
   mbar.add( plainMenu );
   ```

2. Create a JRadioButtonMenuItem. There are four constructors.

   Create a JRadioButtonMenuItem with no text or icon. To make it useful, you will want to call its setText() and/or setIcon() methods to give it a text string and/or icon.

   ```
   JRadioButtonMenuItem()
   ```

   Create a JRadioButtonMenuItem with a text string and no icon. This is the most commonly used constructor:

   ```
   JRadioButtonMenuItem( String text )
   ```

Create a JRadioButtonMenuItem with an icon but no text string:

```
JRadioButtonMenuItem( Icon icon )
```

Create a JRadioButtonMenuItem with both a text string and an icon:

```
JRadioButtonMenuItem( String text, Icon icon )
```

Use a constructor to create a JRadioButtonMenuItem with text only:

```
JRadioButtonMenuItem mItem1 = new JRadioButtonMenuItem( "1" );
```

Use a constructor to create a JRadioButtonMenuItem with text and an icon:

```
JRadioButtonMenuItem mItem4 = new JRadioButtonMenuItem( "Cut",
                                new ImageIcon( "cut.gif" ) );
```

3. Collect a set of JRadioButtonMenuItems into a ButtonGroup so that only one of the set may be selected at a time.

Create a ButtonGroup:

```
ButtonGroup itemGroup = new ButtonGroup();
```

Add the items into the group:

```
itemGroup.add( mItem1 );
itemGroup.add( mItem2 );
itemGroup.add( mItem3 );
```

4. Choose which item will be selected at the start. The selected item will change as the user interacts, but this is the way you set it programmatically. By default, none of the items in the group is selected until you set it programmatically or the user selects one.

```
mItem1.setSelected( true );
```

5. Catch the items' events. It is best to use ItemEvents since they not only tell you when the item's state changes, but also what state it has changed to. You can use ActionEvents, but you will get an event even when an already-selected item is clicked (state doesn't change). Also, with ActionEvents you have to query the source component to get the new state.

Tell the JRadioButtonMenuItem what class wants to receive its ItemEvents. In this case, the class that will be listening is the class in which the JRadioButtonMenuItem is defined:

```
mItem1.addItemListener( this );
```

Make the event-receiving class (MyFrame.java in this example) implement the ItemListener interface:

```
public class MyFrame extends JFrame implements ItemListener
{
```

.
.
.

```
public void itemStateChanged( ItemEvent e )
{
    // Use e.getSource() to find out which JRadioButtonMenuItem
    // this event came from, and e.getStateChange() to find the
    // new state.
}
}
```

6. Change the text and icon positions relative to each other. This doesn't apply if the JRadioButtonMenuItem doesn't use both text and an icon. By default, the icon is to the left of the text.

Move the icon to the right of the text:

```
mItem7.setHorizontalTextPosition( AbstractButton.LEFT );
```

Move the text so it is positioned above the icon. Notice that you have to position the text in both the horizontal and vertical directions:

```
mItem9.setHorizontalTextPosition( AbstractButton.CENTER );
mItem9.setVerticalTextPosition( AbstractButton.TOP );
```

7. Change the text color. This works for the Windows look-and-feel since it uses the foreground color for the text color. It may not work for other look-and-feels.

```
mItem11.setForeground( Color.blue );
```

8. Change the font. Again, this works for the Windows look-and-feel, but may not work with others:

```
mItem10.setFont( new Font( "TimesRoman", Font.ITALIC, 18 ) );
```

9. Change where, within the space of the component, the text goes. By default, it aligns to the left. If there is an icon it will move with the text.

```
mItem12.setHorizontalAlignment( AbstractButton.RIGHT );
```

Basic Code Examples

EXAMPLE 8-61 Basic JRadioButtonMenuItem

This example has four menus. One shows a normal group of text-only JRadioButtonMenuItems. The next has a set of items that have both text and icons. The third has items with text and icons, but changes the positions of the text and icons. The last menu has icons showing different text effects. The first menu also has an ItemListener receiving its menu items' events and printing out what happens when the selection changes. Figure 8-95 shows the example with one menu expanded.

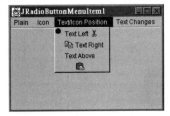

Figure 8-95

Here is the source code:

```java
import com.sun.java.swing.*;
import java.awt.*;
import java.awt.event.*;

public class MyFrame extends JFrame implements ItemListener
{
    JRadioButtonMenuItem mItem1;
    JRadioButtonMenuItem mItem2;
    JRadioButtonMenuItem mItem3;
    JRadioButtonMenuItem mItem4;
    JRadioButtonMenuItem mItem5;
    JRadioButtonMenuItem mItem6;
    JRadioButtonMenuItem mItem7;
    JRadioButtonMenuItem mItem8;
    JRadioButtonMenuItem mItem9;
    JRadioButtonMenuItem mItem10;
    JRadioButtonMenuItem mItem11;
    JRadioButtonMenuItem mItem12;

    public MyFrame()
    {
        setTitle( "JRadioButtonMenuItem1" );

        // Store the content pane in a variable for easier
        // access.
        JPanel contentPane = (JPanel)getContentPane();

        // Create the menu bar and attach it to the frame.
        JMenuBar mbar = new JMenuBar();
        getRootPane().setMenuBar( mbar );

        // Create the first menu and attach it to the menu
        // bar.
        JMenu plainMenu = new JMenu( "Plain" );
        mbar.add( plainMenu );

        // Create a text-only radio button.
        mItem1 = new JRadioButtonMenuItem( "1" );

        // Make it the initially selected item for its group.
        mItem1.setSelected( true );
```

```
// Make this class listen for the item's state
// changes.
mItem1.addItemListener( this );

// Add the item to the menu.
plainMenu.add( mItem1 );

// Create another text-only radio button.
mItem2 = new JRadioButtonMenuItem( "2" );

// Make this class listen for its state changes.
mItem2.addItemListener( this );

// Add the item to the menu.
plainMenu.add( mItem2 );

// Create another text-only radio button.
mItem3 = new JRadioButtonMenuItem( "3" );

// Make this class listen for its state changes.
mItem3.addItemListener( this );

// Add the item to the menu.
plainMenu.add( mItem3 );

// Create a button group into which we will add the
// three items we just created.
ButtonGroup itemGroup = new ButtonGroup();

// Add the three items into the group.
itemGroup.add( mItem1 );
itemGroup.add( mItem2 );
itemGroup.add( mItem3 );

// Create the second menu and add it to the menu bar.
JMenu iconMenu = new JMenu( "Icon" );
mbar.add( iconMenu );

// Create a text+icon radio button.
JRadioButtonMenuItem mItem4 =
                new JRadioButtonMenuItem( "Cut",
                new ImageIcon( "cut.gif" ) );

// Make this item the initially selected one.
mItem4.setSelected( true );

// Add the item into the menu.
iconMenu.add( mItem4 );

// Create another text+icon radio button.
JRadioButtonMenuItem mItem5 =
                new JRadioButtonMenuItem( "Copy",
                new ImageIcon( "copy.gif" ) );

// Add the item into the menu.
```

```
                         iconMenu.add( mItem5 );

                         // Create another text+icon radio button.
                         JRadioButtonMenuItem mItem6 =
                                         new JRadioButtonMenuItem( "Paste",
                                         new ImageIcon( "paste.gif" ) );

                         // Add the item to the menu.
                         iconMenu.add( mItem6 );

                         // Create a button group where we will put the three
                         // radio button menu items we just created.
                         ButtonGroup itemGroup2 = new ButtonGroup();

                         // Add the items into the group.
                         itemGroup2.add( mItem4 );
                         itemGroup2.add( mItem5 );
                         itemGroup2.add( mItem6 );

                         // Create another menu and add it to the menu bar.
                         JMenu textIconSwapMenu =
                                         new JMenu( "Text/Icon Position" );
                         mbar.add( textIconSwapMenu );

                         // Create a text+icon radio button.
                         JRadioButtonMenuItem mItem7 =
                                         new JRadioButtonMenuItem( "Text Left",
                                         new ImageIcon( "cut.gif" ) );

                         // Make it the initially selected item.
                         mItem7.setSelected( true );

                         // Make it so the text is to the left of the icon.
                         mItem7.setHorizontalTextPosition(
                                                     AbstractButton.LEFT );

                         // Add the item into the menu.
                         textIconSwapMenu.add( mItem7 );

                         // Create another text+icon radio button.
                         JRadioButtonMenuItem mItem8 =
                                         new JRadioButtonMenuItem( "Text Right",
                                         new ImageIcon( "copy.gif" ) );

                         // Make the text be right of the icon.  This is
                         // actually the default.
                         mItem8.setHorizontalTextPosition(
                                                     AbstractButton.RIGHT );

                         // Add the item into the menu.
                         textIconSwapMenu.add( mItem8 );

                         // Create another text+icon radio button.
                         JRadioButtonMenuItem mItem9 =
                                         new JRadioButtonMenuItem( "Text Above",
```

```
                              new ImageIcon( "paste.gif" ) );

// Set the text position so it is above the icon.
mItem9.setHorizontalTextPosition(
                                AbstractButton.CENTER );
mItem9.setVerticalTextPosition( AbstractButton.TOP );

// Add the item into the menu.
textIconSwapMenu.add( mItem9 );

// Create a button group into which the three just
// created items will be added.
ButtonGroup itemGroup3 = new ButtonGroup();

// Add the items into the button group.
itemGroup3.add( mItem7 );
itemGroup3.add( mItem8 );
itemGroup3.add( mItem9 );

// Create one more menu and add it to the menu bar.
JMenu textChangeMenu = new JMenu( "Text Changes" );
mbar.add( textChangeMenu );

// Create a text-only radio button.
JRadioButtonMenuItem mItem10 =
            new JRadioButtonMenuItem( "Big text" );

// Make the item the initially selected one.
mItem10.setSelected( true );

// Change the item's font.
mItem10.setFont( new Font( "TimesRoman",
                                Font.ITALIC, 18 ) );

// Add the item to the menu.
textChangeMenu.add( mItem10 );

// Create another text-only radio button.
JRadioButtonMenuItem mItem11 =
            new JRadioButtonMenuItem( "Blue Text" );

// Change the text color by changing the foreground
// color.
mItem11.setForeground( Color.blue );

// Add the item into the menu.
textChangeMenu.add( mItem11 );

// Create a third text-only radio button.
JRadioButtonMenuItem mItem12 =
            new JRadioButtonMenuItem( "Text Right" );

// Align the text to the right.
mItem12.setHorizontalAlignment(
                                AbstractButton.RIGHT );
```

```
        // Add the item into the menu.
        textChangeMenu.add( mItem12 );

        // Create a button group to hold the three items we
        // just created.
        ButtonGroup itemGroup4 = new ButtonGroup();

        // Add the items into the group.
        itemGroup4.add( mItem10 );
        itemGroup4.add( mItem11 );
        itemGroup4.add( mItem12 );
    }

    // The three JRadioButtonMenuItems in the first menu
    // will have their item events listened to by this
    // class.  When one of their states changes, this method
    // is called and the change will be printed out.
    public void itemStateChanged( ItemEvent e )
    {
        if ( e.getSource() == mItem1 )
        {
            if ( e.getStateChange() == ItemEvent.SELECTED )
                System.out.println( "Item 1 selected" );
            else
                System.out.println( "Item 1 de-selected" );
        }
        else if ( e.getSource() == mItem2 )
        {
            if ( e.getStateChange() == ItemEvent.SELECTED )
                System.out.println( "Item 2 selected" );
            else
                System.out.println( "Item 2 de-selected" );
        }
        else if ( e.getSource() == mItem3 )
        {
            if ( e.getStateChange() == ItemEvent.SELECTED )
                System.out.println( "Item 3 selected" );
            else
                System.out.println( "Item 3 de-selected" );
        }
    }
}
```

JRadioButtonMenuItem's Public Methods

```
AccessibleContext getAccessibleContext()
```

Returns a subclass of AccessibleContext, which gives access to the JRadioButtonMenuItem's accessible information.

```
String getUIClassID()
```

Returns the identifying string that the look-and-feel uses to assign a UI class to the JRadioButtonMenuItem.

```
void requestFocus()
```

Asks to have the focus shifted to the JRadioButtonMenuItem.

```
void setAction(Action action)
```

Specifies the Action that the JRadioButtonMenuItem will trigger.

```
void setUI(RadioButtonMenuItemUI ui)
```

Gives the JRadioButtonMenuItem a new look-and-feel class.

```
void updateUI()
```

Tells the JRadioButtonMenuItem that the look-and-feel class has been changed.

JRootPane

A JRootPane is a container that JInternalFrames, JApplets, JFrames, JDialogs, and JWindows use to provide a uniform way to work with all of them. A JRootPane has four main parts: the content pane that will generally hold all of the components you want to place in the container; the layered pane that is used to manage the content pane and menu bar; the glass pane that is very useful for laying a transparent component over the entire window to deflect events, etc.; and the menu bar.

A JRootPane is the sole child of the listed containers, but you do not actually add components to it. You can access the four parts and add things to them, or you can replace any of the four parts with parts of your own. For example, you can replace the default content pane by calling the root pane's set-ContentPane() method.

The only one of JRootPane's four parts that does not have a default component is the menu bar. If you want to use a menu bar through a JRootPane, you have to create it and apply it to the JRootPane using the setMenuBar() method.

Containers like JFrame that use a JRootPane will often have convenience methods of their own that call the equivalent JRootPane method. For example, JFrame has a getContentPane() method that is the same as calling get-RootPane().getContentPane().

Although JRootPanes are normally used only in the context of JFrames, JApplets, JWindows, JDialogs, and JInternalFrames, you can make your own component use a JRootPane.

Ancestors

```
java.lang.Object
    |
    +—java.awt.Component
            |
            +—java.awt.Container
                    |
                    +—com.sun.java.swing.JComponent
                            |
                            +—com.sun.java.swing.JRootPane
```

NOTE: *For more information, see the "JFrame," "JWindow," "JDialog," "JApplet," "JInternalFrame," "JPanel," "JMenuBar," and "OverlayLayout" sections in this chapter. Also see the "Windows" and "JFC Containers" sections in Chapter 7, "JFC by Concept."*

Steps in Creating and Using JRootPane

1. Create a container that uses JRootPane (JInternalFrame, JWindow, JApplet, JFrame, JDialog):

   ```
   JInternalFrame myIntFrame = new JInternalFrame( "Title" );
   ```

   The JRootPane is automatically created.

2. You can replace a JRootPane's various panes with ones of your own. If you want components to be added to your custom panel instead of adding them to the default content pane, you can replace the default content pane with your own:

   ```
   myIntFrame.getRootPane().setContentPane( new MyCustomPane() );
   ```

   JInternalFrame has a convenience method called setContentPane() that is equivalent to getRootPane().setContentPane(). Using this method, you could have replaced the above with:

   ```
   myIntFrame.setContentPane( new MyCustomPane() );
   ```

   Now your custom pane is the content pane and will be returned when getRootPane().getContentPane() is called.

3. Create a control and add it to the new content pane:

   ```
   JButton btn = new JButton( "Ok" );
   myIntFrame.getRootPane().getContentPane().add( "Center", btn );
   ```

   This is the same as:

   ```
   JButton btn = new JButton( "Ok" );
   pane.getContentPane().add( "Center", btn );
   ```

4. Add a menu bar to the root pane:

Create a menu bar with a menu and an item in the menu:

```
JMenuBar mbar = new JMenuBar();
JMenu fileMenu = new JMenu( "File" );
mbar.add( fileMenu );
JMenuItem exitItem = new JMenuItem( "Exit" );
fileMenu.add( exitItem );
```

Add the menu bar to the root pane:

```
getRootPane().setMenuBar( mbar );
```

which is equivalent to

```
setMenuBar( mbar );
```

for some root pane parents or

```
setJMenuBar( mbar );
```

for others.

Basic Code Examples

EXAMPLE 8-62 Basic JRootPane

This example illustrates how to use a frame's JRootPane to add components to the frame. It adds a JButton and a JDesktopPane to the content pane, and the JDesktopPane in turn contains an internal frame. In addition, it creates a JMenuBar and adds it to the JRootPane. Notice the use of getContentPane() instead of getRootPane().getContentPane(). Also notice that components are only added to the content pane, never to the root pane or the frame itself. Figure 8-96 shows the example as it looks initially.

Here is the source code:

```
import com.sun.java.swing.*;
import java.awt.*;
import java.util.*;

public class MyFrame extends JFrame
{
    JPanel mPanel;

    public MyFrame()
    {
        setTitle( "JRootPane1" );

        // Store the content pane in a variable for easier
        // access.
```

Figure 8-96

```
mPanel = (JPanel)getContentPane();

// Set the content pane's layout.
mPanel.setLayout( new BorderLayout() );

// Create a desktop pane to go over the content pane
// and manage the internal frame.
JDesktopPane dp = new JDesktopPane();

// Overlay the desktop pane on the content pane.
mPanel.add( "Center", dp );

// Create a simple internal frame.
JInternalFrame myIntFrame =
                       new JInternalFrame( "Title" );

// Add a button so we watch the internal frame go
// under it.
JButton btn = new JButton( "Ok" );

mPanel.add( "South", btn );

// Set the internal frame's size/location.
myIntFrame.setBounds( 50, 20, 200, 100 );

// Add the internal frame to the desktop pane.
dp.add( myIntFrame );

// Create a menu bar and add a menu with some items
// in it.
JMenuBar mbar = new JMenuBar();
JMenu fileMenu = new JMenu( "File" );
mbar.add( fileMenu );
JMenuItem exitItem = new JMenuItem( "Exit" );
fileMenu.add( exitItem );

// Add the menu bar to the root pane.
getRootPane().setMenuBar( mbar );
    }
  }
```

JRootPane's Public Methods

`AccessibleContext getAccessibleContext()`

Returns a subclass of AccessibleContext, which gives access to the JRoot-Pane's accessibility information.

`Container getContentPane()`

Returns the JRootPane's content pane.

`JButton getDefaultButton()`

Returns the default button for the JRootPane.

`Component getGlassPane()`

Returns the JRootPane's glass pane.

`JLayeredPane getLayeredPane()`

Returns the JRootPane's layered pane.

`JMenuBar getMenuBar()`

Returns the JRootPane's menu bar (may be null).

`void setContentPane(Container content)`

Replaces the JRootPane's content pane with another container.

`void setDefaultButton(JButton btn)`

Specifies which button will be the JRootPanel's default button.

`void setGlassPane(Component glass)`

Replaces the JRootPane's glass pane with another component.

`void setLayeredPane(JLayeredPane layered)`

Replaces the JRootPane's layered pane with another one.

`void setMenuBar(JMenuBar menu)`

Tells the JRootPane to use the given menu bar.

JScrollBar

A JScrollBar is a component that shows the relationship between a maximum possible value, a minimum possible value, a current value, and how the current value can change. It has four parts: the two end buttons, the scrolling area, and the thumbnail (see Figure 8-97). One end of the scroll bar represents the minimum possible value. The other end represents the maximum possible value. The thumbnail represents the current value. Clicking on one of the end buttons makes the current value move in that direction in a preset small increment. Clicking between the thumbnail and one of the end buttons makes the current value move in that direction in a preset larger increment. Since scroll bars are frequently used to scroll around a picture that is too big for the screen to hold, the size of the thumbnail may vary to reflect the amount of the picture that is visible relative to the overall size of the picture.

Although a scroll bar is a graphical representation, the values that it uses (minimum, maximum, current value) are not in pixels. If you tell the scroll bar that its minimum is 1 and its maximum is 100, its scrolling area will not be 100 pixels long. Rather, the scroll bar will be sized according to its preferred size or the size forced on it by the layout manager. You can have a scroll bar whose minimum is -1000 and maximum is $+1000$ and the component itself may be 150 pixels and can change size as its container changes size.

There are several terms that are used in JScrollBar's methods that are not very clear. These are explained here:

Extent	The number of scroll bar units represented by the thumbnail.
Unit increment	The number of scroll bar units by which the current value should change when one of the end buttons is pressed.
Block increment	The number of scroll bar units by which the current value should change when the scrolling area is clicked between the thumbnail and one of the end buttons.

Ancestors

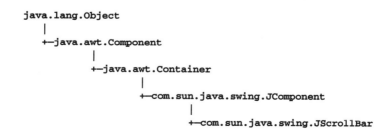

```
java.lang.Object
    |
    +—java.awt.Component
           |
           +—java.awt.Container
                  |
                  +—com.sun.java.swing.JComponent
                         |
                         +—com.sun.java.swing.JScrollBar
```

Figure 8-97
A typical horizontal
JScrollBar.

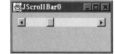

NOTE: *For more information, see the "DefaultBoundedRangeModel," "JScroll-Pane," and "JViewport" sections in this chapter. Also see the "Scrolling" section in Chapter 7, "JFC by Concept."*

Steps in Creating and Using JScrollBar

1. Create a JScrollBar. There are three constructors.

This one creates a vertical scroll bar. As it is, the scroll bar is unusable because the minimum, maximum, and extents all default to zero. This causes the unit and block increments to be zero as well. You will have to call setValues() or at least setMaximum(), setBlockIncrement(), and setUnitIncrement() in order to have a functional scroll bar.

```
JScrollBar()
```

This next one creates a scroll bar with the specified orientation. Just as with the empty constructor above, the scroll bar created with this constructor is not of much use as it is. orientation must be either JScrollBar.HORIZONTAL or JScrollBar.VERTICAL:

```
JScrollBar( int orientation )
```

This last constructor creates a fully useful scroll bar:

```
JScrollBar( int orientation, int value, int extent, int minimum,
            maximum )
```

where orientation tells whether it will be horizontal or vertical, 'extent' is the number of units the thumbnail represents, 'minimum' is the value represented by the scroll bar's left (for a horizontal scroll bar) or top (for a vertical scroll bar) end, and 'maximum' is the value represented by the scroll bar's right (for horizontal scroll bars) or bottom (for vertical scroll bars) end.

To create a horizontal scroll bar with minimum of 0, maximum of 100, extent of 25, and value of 10:

```
JScrollBar scroll1 = new JScrollBar( JScrollBar.HORIZONTAL, 10,
                                     25, 0, 100 );
```

This can also be accomplished using the following:

```
JScrollBar scroll2 = new JScrollBar( JScrollBar.HORIZONTAL );
scroll2.setMinimum( 0 );
```

```
scroll2.setMaximum( 100 );
scroll2.setValue( 10 );
scroll2.setVisibleAmount( 25 );
scroll2.setBlockIncrement( 25 );
```

or:

```
JScrollBar scroll3 = new JScrollBar( JScrollBar.HORIZONTAL );
scroll3.setValues( 10, 25, 0, 100 );
scroll3.setBlockIncrement( 25 );
```

2. Specify a listener for your scroll bar. A scroll bar can be quite attractive, but it is of little but aesthetic value if nothing results from moving the scroll bar's thumbnail around.

JScrollBars generate AdjustmentEvents when their states change.

State which class will listen to changes in the scroll bar. For this example, the listener is the class that contains the scroll bar:

```
scroll1.addAdjustmentListener( this );
```

Make the event-receiving class implement the AdjustmentListener interface. In this case, the receiving class is called MyFrame:

```
public class MyFrame extends JFrame implements AdjustmentListener
{
    .
    .
    .
    public void adjustmentValueChanged( AdjustmentEvent e )
    {
        System.out.println( "-"+e.getValue()+"|"+
                            e.getAdjustmentType() );
    }
}
```

Notice that when the adjustment event was received, the event's getValue() method was called. This saves you the trouble of having to call the scroll bar's getValue() method.

3. Change the scroll bar's settings. This is useful if the thing represented by the scroll bar can be changed in other ways than by using the scroll bar itself. When a scroll bar is used as part of a JScrollPane, the size of the component being scrolled may change, or a rectangle in the component being scrolled may be forced to a visible position. These kinds of situations are handled within the JScrollPane using calls to the scroll bars' value-setting methods. All arguments to these methods are in scroll bar units, not in pixels. Note that none of these methods try to re-calculate any of the other settings—you have to do that yourself:

Change the value represented by the thumbnail:

```
scroll2.setValue( 10 );
```

Change the size of the thumbnail:

```
scroll2.setVisibleAmount( 25 );
```

Change the amount the thumbnail moves when you click one of the
end arrows:

```
scroll2.setUnitIncrement( 1 );
```

Change the amount the thumbnail moves when you click between the
thumbnail and an end arrow:

```
scroll2.setBlockIncrement( 4 );
```

Change the value represented by the left (for horizontal scroll bars) or
top (for vertical scroll bars) end:

```
scroll2.setMinimum( 0 );
```

Change the value represented by the right (for horizontal scroll bars)
or bottom (for vertical scroll bars) end:

```
scroll2.setMaximum( 100 );
```

Change the value, size of the thumbnail, maximum and minimum all
at once:

```
scroll2.setValues( 10, 25, 0, 100 );
```

4. Listen for changes in the JScrollBar's BoundedRangeModel. This is
   more flexible than just catching AdjustmentEvents because you get
   all changes, not just changes in the value.

   Get the JScrollBar's BoundedRangeModel:

```
BoundedRangeModel model = scroll1.getModel();
```

   Specify the class that will receive the ChangeEvents from the
   BoundedRangeModel. In this case, it is the current class.

```
model.addChangeListener( this );
```

   Make the event-receiving class (MyFrame) implement the
   ChangeListener interface:

```
public class MyFrame extends JFrame implements ChangeListener
{
    .
    .
    .
    public void stateChanged( ChangeEvent e )
    {
        // Now you know the model has changed, you can get the
        // model since it is the event's source, and ask it
        // what the change was.
    }
}
```

Basic Code Examples

EXAMPLE 8-63 Using JScrollBar

This example uses three different ways to create scroll bars that have the same characteristics. This illustrates JScrollBar's most important methods and the automatic settings that happen behind the scenes. The example contains three horizontal scrollbars that act the same despite the fact that the were created differently.

The first scrollbar has both an AdjustmentListener and a ChangeListener attached so that when the scrollbar changes, the main class is alerted and prints out a string. Figure 8-98 shows the example after the scrollbars have been moved around.

Here is the source code:

```
import com.sun.java.swing.*;
import com.sun.java.swing.event.*;
import java.awt.*;
import java.awt.event.*;

public class MyFrame extends JFrame implements
        AdjustmentListener, ChangeListener
{
    public MyFrame()
    {
        setTitle( "JScrollBar1" );

        // Store the content pane in a variable for easier
        // access.
        JPanel contentPane = (JPanel)getContentPane();

        // Components will all be added to this panel.
        contentPane.setLayout( new GridLayout( 3, 1 ) );

        // Create a scroll bar with all settings.
        JScrollBar scroll1 = new JScrollBar(
                        JScrollBar.HORIZONTAL,
                        10, 25, 0, 100 );

        // Add the scroll bar to the buffered panel.
        contentPane.add( scroll1 );

        // Make this class listen for changes in the scroll
        // bar's value.
        scroll1.addAdjustmentListener( this );
```

Figure 8-98

```
        // Make this class listen for changes in the bounded
        // range model.  This does basically the same thing
        // as adding and AdjustmentListener, but delivers the
        // bounded range model with the event.
        BoundedRangeModel model = scroll1.getModel();

        model.addChangeListener( this );

        // Create another scroll bar and explicitly call the
        // methods required to duplicate the settings
        // automatically generated in 'scroll1' above.
        JScrollBar scroll2 =
                    new JScrollBar( JScrollBar.HORIZONTAL );
        scroll2.setMinimum( 0 );
        scroll2.setMaximum( 100 );
        scroll2.setValue( 10 );
        scroll2.setVisibleAmount( 25 );
        scroll2.setBlockIncrement( 25 );

        // Add the scroll bar to the buffered panel.
        contentPane.add( scroll2 );

        // Create another scroll bar that uses another way to
        // duplicate 'scroll1's settings.
        JScrollBar scroll3 =
                    new JScrollBar( JScrollBar.HORIZONTAL );
        scroll3.setValues( 10, 25, 0, 100 );
        scroll3.setBlockIncrement( 25 );
        contentPane.add( scroll3 );
    }

    // When the scroll bar being listened to changes, an
    // AdjustmentEvent is generated.
    public void adjustmentValueChanged( AdjustmentEvent e )
    {
        // Print out the scroll bar's new value and the type
        // of adjustment made.
        System.out.println( "—"+e.getValue()+"|"+
                                e.getAdjustmentType() );
    }

    public void stateChanged( ChangeEvent e )
    {
        System.out.println( "___"+e );
    }
}
```

JScrollBar's Public Methods

```
void addAdjustmentListener(AdjustmentListener l)
```

Tells the JScrollBar to notify the given class when the JScrollBar's value changes.

`AccessibleContext getAccessibleContext()`

Returns a subclass of AccessibleContext, which gives access to the JScrollBar's accessibility information.

`int getBlockIncrement()`

Returns the amount in scroll bar units that the thumbnail will move when the scroll bar is clicked between the thumbnail and one of the end arrows.

`int getBlockIncrement(int direction)`

Returns the amount that the thumbnail will be incremented when the mouse is clicked between the thubmnail and the end arrow in the given direction.

`int getMaximum()`

Returns the JScrollBar's maximum value in scroll bar units.

`Dimension getMaximumSize()`

Overridden so the JScrollBar can decrease in size in the scrolling direction but not in the other direction.

`int getMinimum()`

Returns the JScrollBar's minimum value in scroll bar units.

`Dimension getMinimumSize()`

Overridden so the JScrollBar can increase in size in the scrolling direction but not in the other direction.

`BoundedRangeModel getModel()`

Returns the JScrollBar's BoundedRangeModel.

`int getOrientation()`

Returns the JScrollBar's orientation: HORIZONTAL or VERTICAL.

`ScrollBarUI getUI()`

Returns the JScrollBar's current look-and-feel class.

`String getUIClassID()`

Returns the identifying string that the look-and-feel uses to assign a UI class to the JScrollBar.

`int getUnitIncrement()`

Returns the amount, in scroll bar units, that the thumbnail moves when the user clicks one of the end arrows.

`int getUnitIncrement(int direction)`

Returns the amount the thumbnail will be incremented when the scroll-bar's end arrow is pressed.

`int getValue()`

Returns the current value, in scroll bar units, represented by the position of the thumbnail.

`boolean getValueIsAdjusting()`

Returns true if the scrollbar feels it is in the middle of a change.

`int getVisibleAmount()`

Returns the JScrollBar's extent.

`void removeAdjustmentListener(AdjustmentListener l)`

Tells the JScrollBar to stop notifying the given class when the JScrollBar's value changes.

`void setBlockIncrement(int n)`

Specifies how far, in scroll bar units, the thumbnail should move when the user clicks between the thumbnail and an end arrow.

`void setEnabled(boolean x)`

Specifies whether the JScrollBar is enabled or disabled.

`void setMaximum(int n)`

Specifies the JScrollBar's maximum value in scroll bar units.

`void setMinimum(int n)`

Specifies the JScrollBar's minimum value in scroll bar units.

`void setModel(BoundedRangeModel newModel)`

Replaces the JScrollBar's BoundedRangeModel with another one.

```
void setOrientation(int n)
```

Specifies whether the JScrollBar will be HORIZONTAL or VERTICAL.

```
void setUnitIncrement(int n)
```

Specifies how far the thumbnail should move, in scroll bar units, when the user clicks an end arrow.

```
void setValue(int n)
```

Specifies the JScrollBar's current value.

```
void setValueIsAdjusting(boolean b)
```

Generally called by the UI class to tell the scrollbar it is in the midst of a change.

```
void setValues(int newValue,int newExtent,int newMinimum,int
        newMaximum)
```

Specifies the JScrollBar's value, extent, minimum, and maximum values, all in scroll bar units.

```
void setVisibleAmount(int n)
```

Specifies the JScrollBar extent.

```
void updateUI()
```

Tells the JScrollBar that the look-and-feel class has been changed.

JScrollPane

JScrollPane is a component that helps you scroll around panels that are too big to be seen all at once. It incorporates two scroll bars and automatically adjusts itself for changes in the size of the panel being scrolled.

Figure 8-99
A JScrollPane being used to scroll around a large image.

Ancestors

```
java.lang.Object
    |
    +—java.awt.Component
            |
            +—java.awt.Container
                    |
                    +—com.sun.java.swing.JComponent
                            |
                            +—com.sun.java.swing.JScrollPane
```

NOTE: *For more information, see the "JScrollBar" and "JViewport" sections in this chapter, and the "Scrolling" section in Chapter 7, "JFC by Concept."*

Steps in Creating and Using JScrollPane

1. Create the panel that will be scrolled. For this example, we will create a JPanel and add 100 JButtons to it to make it bigger than the available viewing area:

```
JPanel mControlPane;
int mControlNum = 0;

mControlPane = new JPanel();
mControlPane.setLayout( new GridLayout( 10, 10, 10, 10 ) );

JButton btn;

for ( int i = 0; i < 100; i++ )
{
   btn = new JButton( String.valueOf( mControlNum ) );
   mControlPane.add( btn );
   mControlNum++;
}
```

Each button has a number on it and they go from 0 to 99. The details of this panel and the controls on it are not important. The important thing is that it is pretty big, so we use a JScrollPane to scroll around in it.

2. Create the JScrollPane. There are four constructors.

This one just creates a JScrollPane. You will have to add the component to be scrolled later using JScrollPane's setViewportView() method.

```
JScrollPane()
```

This one creates a JScrollPane and specifies the component to be scrolled.

```
JScrollPane( Component viewComponent )
```

This one creates a JScrollPane and specifies the scrollbar policies for the horizontal and vertical scrollbars. Since no component-to-be-scrolled is passed in, you will have to call the setViewportView() method.

```
JScrollPane( int vertBarPolicy, int horizBarPolicy )
```

Scrollbar policies define when each scrollbar will be visible. The possible policies are:

- HORIZONTAL_SCROLLBAR_ALWAYS
- HORIZONTAL_SCROLLBAR_AS_NEEDED
- HORIZONTAL_SCROLLBAR_NEVER
- VERTICAL_SCROLLBAR_ALWAYS
- VERTICAL_SCROLLBAR_AS_NEEDED
- VERTICAL_SCROLLBAR_NEVER

This one creates a JScrollPane and specifies the component to scroll as well as the scrollbar policies.

```
JScrollPane( Component viewComponent, int vertBarPolicy, int
             horizBarPolicy )
```

Create a JScrollPane:

```
JScrollPane scrollPane = new JScrollPane();
```

3. Set the component to scroll. Only necessary if it was not specified in the constructor:

```
scrollPane.setViewportView( mControlPane );
```

4. Set the scrollbar policies. This is necessary only if you didn't set the policies in the constructor and you do not want to use the default policies. The default is as-needed on both horizontal and vertical scrollbars.

```
scrollPane.setHorizontalScrollBarPolicy(
                        JScrollPane.HORIZONTAL_SCROLLBAR_ALWAYS );
scrollPane.setVerticalScrollBarPolicy(
                        JScrollPane.VERTICAL_SCROLLBAR_ALWAYS );
```

5. Add a panel to use for row headers or column headers. A row header is a panel that shows up on the left side of the scrolling area and only scrolls up and down. This is like a spreadsheet where the actual rows of data can be scrolled from side to side but the letters that identify the rows do not scroll from side to side, so they are always visible. A

column header is the same except that it shows up at the top of the scrolling area and cannot scroll up and down.

A row header panel is displayed at its preferred size. You will need to make sure it is the same height as the main scrolling panel so you have a row header for each actual row and no rows left over. The same goes for column header panels, except that you want to make sure the widths are the same instead of the heights.

Create a panel to use as a row or column header, then add it using:

```
scrollPane.setRowHeaderView( rowHeaderPanel );
```

for row headers, or:

```
scrollPane.setColumnHeaderView( rowHeaderPanel );
```

for column headers.

6. When a component that is being scrolled changes size, it should call its revalidate() method. This will ultimately result in the revalidate() working its way up to the JScrollPane.

```
panelBeingScrolled.revalidate();
```

Basic Code Examples

EXAMPLE 8-64 Basic JScrollPane

This example shows how to use a JScrollPane to scroll around a panel. It creates a panel with 100 buttons and allows the user to scroll around the panel and also to add more buttons so the size of the panel being scrolled gets larger. It also creates a panel for row headers so the user always knows which row he/she is on. Figure 8-100 shows the example after some scrolling has gone on. Notice that while the row headers ("Row 0", "Row 1", etc.) are scrolling up with their rows, they they do not scroll sideways.

Here is the source code:

```
import com.sun.java.swing.*;
import java.awt.*;
```

Figure 8-100

```java
import java.awt.event.*;

public class MyFrame extends JFrame implements
      ActionListener
{
   // This is the panel that will be scrolled.
   JPanel mControlPane;

   // This is a counter so each new button created will
   // take the next number.
   int mControlNum = 0;

   public MyFrame()
   {
      setTitle( "JScrollPane1" );

      // Store the content pane in a variable for easier
      // access.
      JPanel contentPane = (JPanel)getContentPane();

      // Components will all be added to this panel.
      contentPane.setLayout( new BorderLayout() );

      // Create the button that will allow the user to add
      // more buttons.  Put it at the bottom of the frame,
      // and make it so this class receives notification
      // when the button is pressed.
      JButton addBtn = new JButton( "Add" );
      contentPane.add( "South", addBtn );
      addBtn.addActionListener( this );

      // Create the panel that will be scrolled.
      mControlPane = new JPanel();
      mControlPane.setLayout(
                  new GridLayout( 10, 10, 10, 10 ) );

      // Create 100 buttons, giving them consecutive
      // numbers as button labels, and add them to the
      // control pane.
      JButton btn;

      for ( int i = 0; i < 100; i++ )
      {
         btn = new JButton( String.valueOf( mControlNum ) );
         mControlPane.add( btn );
         mControlNum++;
      }

      // Create the row headers.
      JPanel rowHeaders = new JPanel();
      rowHeaders.setLayout(
                  new GridLayout( 10, 1, 10, 10 ) );

      for ( int i = 0; i < 10; i++ )
      {
```

```
                    btn = new JButton( "Row " + String.valueOf( i ) );
                    rowHeaders.add( btn );
                }

                // Create the JScrollPane.
                JScrollPane scrollPane = new JScrollPane();

                // Tell the scroll pane which component to scroll.
                scrollPane.setViewportView( mControlPane );

                // Set the panel to use for row headers.
                scrollPane.setRowHeaderView( rowHeaders );

                // Add the scroll pane into the content pane.
                contentPane.add( "Center", scrollPane );
            }

            // When the "Add" button is pressed, create a new button,
            // give it the next number, and add it to the control
            // pane.
            public void actionPerformed( ActionEvent e )
            {
                JButton btn =
                        new JButton( String.valueOf( mControlNum ) );
                mControlPane.add( btn );
                mControlNum++;
                mControlPane.revalidate();
            }
        }
```

JScrollPane's Public Methods

`JScrollBar createHorizontalScrollBar()`

Creates the horizontal scroll bar. This is called by the look-and-feel class.

`JScrollBar createVerticalScrollBar()`

Creates the horizontal scroll bar. This is called by the look-and-feel class.

`AccessibleContext getAccessibleContext()`

Returns a subclass of AccessibleContext which gives access to the JScroll-Pane's accessibility information.

`JViewport getColumnHeader()`

Returns the viewport that handles any column headers.

`Component getCorner(String key)`

Returns the component (if any) that sits in the corner between the horizontal and vertical scrollbars.

`JScrollBar getHorizontalScrollBar()`

Returns the horizontal scroll bar.

`int getHorizontalScrollBarPolicy()`

Returns the constant that tells whether the horizontal scroll bar will be displayed: as needed, always, or never.

`JViewport getRowHeader()`

Returns the viewport that handles any row headers.

`ScrollPaneUI getUI()`

Returns the JScrollPane's current look-and-feel class.

`String getUIClassID()`

Returns the identifying string that the look-and-feel uses to assign a UI class to the JScrollPane.

`JScrollBar getVerticalScrollBar()`

Returns the vertical scroll bar.

`int getVerticalScrollBarPolicy()`

Returns the constant that tells whether the vertical scroll bar will be displayed: as needed, always, or never.

`JViewport getViewport()`

Returns the main viewport.

`Border getViewportBorder()`

Returns the border being used on the viewport.

`boolean isOpaque()`

Returns true if the JScrollPane paints its entire area.

`boolean isValidateRoot()`

Returns true since it is responsible for trapping any revalidate() calls coming up the display hierarchy.

```
void setColumnHeader(JViewport x)
```

Specifies the viewport that will be used as the column header viewport.

```
void setColumnHeaderView(Component view)
```

Specifies a component that will be placed in a JViewport, then used as the JScrollPane's column header viewport.

```
void setCorner(String key,Component x)
```

Specifies the component to put in the corner between the horizontal and vertical scrollbars.

```
void setHorizontalScrollBarPolicy(int x)
```

Specifies the constant that tells whether the horizontal scroll bar will be displayed: as needed, always, or never.

```
void setRowHeader(JViewport x)
```

Specifies the viewport that will be used as the row header viewport.

```
void setRowHeaderView(Component view)
```

Specifies a component that will be placed in a JViewport, then used as the JScrollPane's row header viewport.

```
void setUI(ScrollPaneUI ui)
```

Gives the JScrollPane a new look-and-feel class.

```
void setVerticalScrollBarPolicy(int x)
```

Specifies the constant that tells whether the vertical scroll bar will be displayed: as needed, always, or never.

```
void setViewport(JViewport x)
```

Specifies the viewport that will be used as the main viewport.

```
void setViewportView(Component view)
```

Specifies the component that will be put into a JViewport, then used as the JScrollPane's main viewport.

```
void updateUI()
```

Tells that JScrollPane that the look-and-feel class has been changed.

JSlider

A JSlider is much like a scroll bar in that it has a minimum value, a maximum value, and a current value and the current value can be changed by dragging a part of the component from side to side or up and down (see Figure 8-101). It is different in that the "thumbnail" is of a fixed size and units on a JSlider can be displayed using tick marks and labels.

A JScrollBar can be used for anything a JSlider is used for, but a JSlider is more visually helpful.

Ancestors

```
java.lang.Object
    |
    +—java.awt.Component
        |
        +—java.awt.Container
            |
            +—com.sun.java.swing.JComponent
                |
                +—com.sun.java.swing.JSlider
```

NOTE: *For more information, see the "DefaultBoundedRangeModel" section in this chapter.*

Steps in Creating and Using JSlider

1. Create the slider. There are two constructors, but you will usually use:

   ```
   JSlider( orientation, minimum, maximum, value )
   ```

   For example,

   ```
   JSlider mySlider = new JSlider( JSlider.HORIZONTAL,
                        0, 100, 50 );
   ```

   creates a horizontal slider whose minimum value is 0, its maximum value is 100, and its starting value is 50.

2. Make it so that the events that are generated when the slider moves are caught. The JSlider generates ChangeEvents when its value

Figure 8-101
A typical horizontal slider.

changes. You only have to do this if you want to track the changes. If you just want to move the slider around and later get the value (when OK is pressed, for example), you can just call getValue().

Assign a class to receive the events. In this case it is the class containing the slider:

```
mySlider.addChangeListener( this );
```

Make the event-receiving class (MyFrame, in this case) implement the ChangeListener interface and do something when events come:

```
public class MyFrame extends JFrame implements ChangeListener
{
    .
    .
    .
    public void stateChanged( ChangeEvent e )
    {
        // Print out the new value.
        System.out.println( String.valueOf(
                        ((JSlider)(e.getSource())).getValue() ) );
    }
}
```

3. Explicitly set the value after construction. It is sometimes necessary to set the current value programmatically after the slider has been created:

```
mySlider.setValue( 37 );
```

4. Add tick marks. JSlider supports both major and minor tick marks. For example, the slider created above might have major tick marks at intervals of 25, and minor tick marks at intervals of 5. Not only do you set the tick spacings, but you also have to tell it to paint the tick marks.

```
mySlider.setMajorTickSpacing( 25 );
mySlider.setMinorTickSpacing( 5 );
mySlider.setPaintTicks( true );
```

These values are in JSlider units, not pixels. So, the number of major and minor tick marks on a JSlider will not change as the JSlider component is stretched or shrunk.

5. Add labels. By default, no labels print on the JSlider. If you set major tick marks and pass 'true' to the setPaintLabels() method, the JSlider values corresponding to the major tick marks will display next to those tick marks.

```
mySlider.setMajorTickSpacing( 25 );
mySlider.setPaintLabels( true );
```

The labels will print whether the tick marks are printed or not.

The labels on a JSlider are actually JLabels. If printing the default labels at major tick mark locations is not sufficient, you can assign a JLabel to be placed at any JSlider value. The labels are stored in a Dictionary, so you can create a Hashtable with slider values and the labels to display at those positions.

Create a Hashtable:

```
Hashtable labels3 = new Hashtable();
```

Load slider value/label pairs:

```
labels3.put( new Integer( 0 ), new JLabel( "Zero" ) );
labels3.put( new Integer( 5 ), new JLabel( "Five" ) );
labels3.put( new Integer( 10 ), new JLabel( "Ten" ) );
```

Tell the slider to use the custom labels:

```
mSlider3.setLabelTable( labels3 );
```

6. Invert the slider. This means reverse the maximum and minimum ends:

```
mSlider3.setInverted( true );
```

Basic Code Examples

EXAMPLE 8-65 Using JSlider

This example shows five horizontal JSliders, illustrating various capabilities. The first one shows how you can use ChangeEvents to track changes in the JSlider's value. The second one places default labels, and forces snap-to-grid. The third illustrates the use of custom text labels. The fourth shows how to use image labels. The fifth shows what inverting the slider looks like. Figure 8-102 shows the example as it initially comes up.

Here is the source code:

```
import com.sun.java.swing.*;
import com.sun.java.swing.border.*;
import com.sun.java.swing.event.*;
```

Figure 8-102

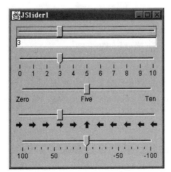

```java
import java.awt.*;
import java.awt.event.*;
import java.util.*;

public class MyFrame extends JFrame implements
        ChangeListener, ActionListener
{
    JSlider mSlider1;
    JTextField mValue;

    public MyFrame()
    {
        setTitle( "JSlider1" );

        // Store the content pane in a variable for easier
        // access.
        JPanel mPanel = (JPanel)getContentPane();

        // Components will all be added to this panel.
        mPanel.setLayout( new BoxLayout( mPanel,
                        BoxLayout.Y_AXIS ) );

        // Leave some space around the edge.
        mPanel.setBorder(
                    new EmptyBorder( 10, 10, 10, 10 ) );

        // Create a slider with minimum of 0, maximum of 10,
        // and initial value of 3.
        mSlider1 = new JSlider(
                        JSlider.HORIZONTAL, 0, 10, 3 );

        // Make the slider snap to integer positions (ticks
        // not set).
        mSlider1.setSnapToTicks( true );

        // Add the slider to the panel.
        mPanel.add( mSlider1 );

        // Make this class receive events when the slider
        // moves.
        mSlider1.addChangeListener( this );

        // Create a text field where the slider's current
        // value will be displayed as it changes.
        mValue = new JTextField();
        mValue.setText( String.valueOf(
                            mSlider1.getValue() ) );

        // Make it so this class listens for when the text
        // field changes, and change the slider value to
        // match.
        mValue.addActionListener( this );

        // Add the text field to the content pane.
        mPanel.add( mValue );
```

```
// Leave space between the text field and the next
// slider.
mPanel.add( Box.createVerticalGlue() );

// Create another slider.
JSlider slider2 =
        new JSlider( JSlider.HORIZONTAL, 0, 10, 3 );

// Tell the slider to paint labels and ticks.
slider2.setPaintLabels( true );
slider2.setPaintTicks( true );

// Place major ticks.
slider2.setMajorTickSpacing( 1 );

// Make the slider snap to the tick marks.
slider2.setSnapToTicks( true );

// Add the slider to the content pane.
mPanel.add( slider2 );

// Leave space between sliders.
mPanel.add( Box.createVerticalGlue() );

// Create a new slider.
JSlider slider3 =
        new JSlider( JSlider.HORIZONTAL, 0, 10, 5 );

// Tell the slider to paint labels.
slider3.setPaintLabels( true );

// Create a hashtable to hold our special labels.
Hashtable labels3 = new Hashtable();

// Assign text labels to the 0, 5, and 10 values.
labels3.put( new Integer( 0 ), new JLabel( "Zero" ) );
labels3.put( new Integer( 5 ), new JLabel( "Five" ) );
labels3.put( new Integer( 10 ), new JLabel( "Ten" ) );

// Apply the hashtable as the slider's label table.
slider3.setLabelTable( labels3 );

// Add the slider to the content pane.
mPanel.add( slider3 );

// Leave space before the next slider.
mPanel.add( Box.createVerticalGlue() );

// Create another slider.
JSlider slider4 =
        new JSlider( JSlider.HORIZONTAL, 0, 10, 3 );

// Create a hash table for our special labels.
Hashtable labels = new Hashtable();
```

```
   // Assign the labels for the values 0-5.
   for ( int i = 0; i < 5; i++ )
   {
      labels.put( new Integer( i ),
            new JLabel( new ImageIcon( "right.gif" ) ) );
   }

   // Assign a label for the value 5.
   labels.put( new Integer( 5 ),
              new JLabel( new ImageIcon( "up.gif" ) ) );

   // Assign labels for values 6-10.
   for ( int i = 6; i <= 10; i++ )
   {
      labels.put( new Integer( i ),
            new JLabel( new ImageIcon( "left.gif" ) ) );
   }

   // Tell the slider to use the labels.
   slider4.setLabelTable( labels );

   // Tell the slider to paint labels.
   slider4.setPaintLabels( true );

   // Add the slider to the content pane.
   mPanel.add( slider4 );

   // Leave space before the next slider.
   mPanel.add( Box.createVerticalGlue() );

   // Create another slider.
   JSlider slider5 =
       new JSlider( JSlider.HORIZONTAL, -100, 100, 0 );

   // Make the major tick marks at increments of 50 and
   // the minor ones at 10.
   slider5.setMajorTickSpacing( 50 );
   slider5.setMinorTickSpacing( 10 );

   // Tell the slider to paint ticks and labels.
   slider5.setPaintTicks( true );
   slider5.setPaintLabels( true );

   // Invert the slider.
   slider5.setInverted( true );

   // Add the slider to the content pane.
   mPanel.add( slider5 );
}

// Every time the first slider's position changes, this
// method is called and causes the text field to
// reflect the changed value of the slider.
public void stateChanged( ChangeEvent e )
{
```

```
            if ( e.getSource() == mSlider1 )
            {
                mValue.setText( String.valueOf(
                                        mSlider1.getValue() ) );
            }
        }

        // When the user presses <Enter> in the text field, the
        // integer value there is applied to the first slider as
        // its new value.
        public void actionPerformed( ActionEvent e )
        {
            String val = mValue.getText();

            try
            {
                int intvalue = Integer.parseInt( val );
                mSlider1.setValue( intvalue );
            }
            catch ( NumberFormatException ex )
            {
                System.out.println( ex );
            }
        }
    }
```

JSlider's Public Methods

```
void addChangeListener(ChangeListener l)
```

Tells the JSlider to notify the given class when the JSlider changes.

```
Hashtable createStandardLabels(int increment)
```

Creates a Hashtable that can be passed to the setLabelTable() method. It creates a JLabel for the minimum value, then increments that value and creates another, and so on until the maximum value is reached.

```
Hashtable createStandardLabels(int increment,int start)
```

Creates a Hashtable that can be passed to the setLabelTable() method. It creates a JLabel for the given start value, then increments that value and creates another, and so on until the maximum value is reached.

```
AccessibleContext getAccessibleContext()
```

Returns a subclass of AccessibleContext that gives access to the JSlider's accessibility information.

```
int getExtent()
```

Returns the number of slider units the arrow represents.

`boolean getInverted()`

Returns true if the JSlider's maximum and minimum ends are swapped.

`Dictionary getLabelTable()`

Returns the set of labels being used on the JSlider.

`int getMajorTickSpacing()`

Returns the distance between major tick marks, in slider units.

`int getMaximum()`

Returns the JSlider's maximum value in slider units.

`int getMinimum()`

Returns the JSlider's minimum value in slider units.

`int getMinorTickSpacing()`

Returns the distance between minor tick marks, in slider units.

`BoundedRangeModel getModel()`

Returns the BoundedRangeModel that is storing and tracking the JSlider's maximum, minimum, and current value.

`int getOrientation()`

Returns the JSlider orientation. This will be either JSlider.HORIZONTAL or JSlider.VERTICAL.

`boolean getPaintLabels()`

Returns true if the JSlider's labels are being painted.

`boolean getPaintTicks()`

Returns true if the JSlider's tick marks are being painted.

`boolean getSnapToTicks()`

Returns true if the slider is not allowed to rest between tick marks.

`SliderUI getUI()`

Returns the JSlider's current UI class.

`String getUIClassID()`

Returns the identifying string that the look-and-feel uses to assign a UI class to the JSlider.

`int getValue()`

Returns the JSlider's current value in slider units.

`boolean getValueIsAdjusting()`

Returns true if the JSlider feels the slider is being dragged.

`void removeChangeListener(ChangeListener l)`

Tells the JSlider to stop notifying the given class when the JSlider changes.

`void setExtent(int n)`

Specifies the number of slider units that the arrow represents.

`void setInverted(boolean b)`

Specifies whether the JSlider's maximum and minimum ends should be swapped.

`void setLabelTable(Dictionary labels)`

Provides the set of values/labels to use on the JSlider.

`void setMajorTickSpacing(int n)`

Specifies the distance between major tick marks, in slider units.

`void setMaximum(int n)`

Specifies the JSlider's maximum value in slider units.

`void setMinimum(int n)`

Specifies the JSlider's minimum value in slider units.

`void setMinorTickSpacing(int n)`

Specifies the distance between the minor tick marks, in slider units.

`void setModel(BoundedRangeModel newModel)`

Replaces the JSlider's BoundedRangeModel with the given one.

`void setOrientation(int n)`

Tells the JSlider whether it is horizontal or vertical.

`void setPaintLabels(boolean b)`

Specifies whether the JSlider will paint its labels.

`void setPaintTicks(boolean b)`

Specifies whether the JSlider will paint its tick marks.

`void setSnapToTicks(boolean b)`

Specifies whether the slider can rest between tick marks.

`void setUI(SliderUI ui)`

Gives the JSlider a new UI class.

`void setValue(int n)`

Specifies a new value for the JSlider, in slider units.

`void setValueIsAdjusting(boolean b)`

Tells the JSlider that the slider is being dragged. Typically called by the UI class.

`String toString()`

Overridden to provide a special string format.

`void updateUI()`

Tells the JSlider to ask the UIManager for a new UI class.

JSplitPane

A JSplitPane is a container that holds two components separated horizontally or vertically by a divider and allows the user to move the divider so that one of the components gets more space and another gets less (see Figure 8-103). This is much like the concept of frames in HTML.

Figure 8-103
A typical JSplitPane.

Ancestors

```
java.lang.Object
     |
    +—java.awt.Component
          |
         +—java.awt.Container
               |
              +—com.sun.java.swing.JComponent
                    |
                   +—com.sun.java.swing.JSplitPane
```

NOTE: *For more information, see the "JFC Containers" section in Chapter 7, "JFC by Concept."*

Steps in Creating and Using JSplitPane

1. Create the JSplitPane. There are a total of five constructors that can be broken into two categories: ones that get the two components to be split, and ones that don't.

   These constructors get the components to be split, so the components must have already been created:

   ```
   JSplitPane( int orientation, boolean useContinuousLayout,
           Component component1, Component component2 )

   JSplitPane( int orientation, Component component1, Component
           component2 )
   ```

   where 'orientation' is HORIZONTAL_SPLIT (divider is vertical) or VERTICAL_SPLIT (divider is horizontal), 'useContinuousLayout' is whether the components should be re-laid out as the divider is being dragged, and component1 and component2 are the components to be divided. useContinuousLayout is false by default, so the components will not be redrawn until the divider is released.

The following constructors do not get the components to be separated, so the components must be set using setLeftComponent(), setRightComponent(), setTopComponent(), and setBottomComponent():

```
JSplitPane()

JSplitPane( int orientation )

JSplitPane( int orientation, boolean useContinuousLayout )
```

'orientation' is HORIZONTAL_SPLIT by default.

2. Create the components to be separated. In this case, we will use two Box components and put a button in each:

```
Box comp1 = new Box( BoxLayout.X_AXIS );
comp1.add( new JButton( "This is a button" ) );
Box comp2 = new Box( BoxLayout.X_AXIS );
comp2.add( new JButton( "This is a wider button" ) );
```

3. Add the components to the split pane:

In the constructor:

```
JSplitPane pane = new JSplitPane( JSplitPane.HORIZONTAL_SPLIT,
                                  comp1, comp2 );
```

or after construction:

```
pane.setLeftComponent( comp1 );
pane.setRightComponent( comp2 );
```

Once the two components are added, the split pane will try to lay them out at their preferred sizes. The divider can be dragged around, but is not allowed to be dragged such that it causes one of the two components to be less than its minimum size.

4. If you want the two components to be dynamically re-laid out as you drag the divider, you need to set continuous layout to true either via one of the constructors, or using setContinuousLayout(true). Using continuous layout will slow performance somewhat.

5. Set the divider location. This is from the left if the divider is vertical, and from the top if the divider is horizontal:

```
pane.setDividerLocation( 100 );
```

The argument to setDividerLocation() is in pixels.

6. If you need to put the divider back to where it would naturally go call:

```
pane.resetToPreferredSizes();
```

This will normally cause the divider to sit snug up against the left (or top) component after that component has been drawn at its preferred size.

7. Enable one-touch expansion. This puts two arrows on the divider so that if you click on one arrow, the divider moves all the way to the far side of the split pane in the arrow's direction. The other arrow will cause it to move to the other end. The effect is that one of the split components suddenly takes up the whole split pane's area.

```
pane.setOneTouchExpandable( true );
```

Basic Code Examples

EXAMPLE 8-66 Basic JSplitPane

This example illustrates many of the concepts discussed above. It contains a single split pane with a vertical divider. Each of the two components being separated has a button in it. When the example is run, you can see where the divider begins, and how it is not allowed to be dragged to a point where one of the separated components is less than its minimum size. Notice that one-touch expansion is enabled. Figure 8-104 shows the example as it comes up initially.

Here is the source code:

```
import com.sun.java.swing.*;
import com.sun.java.swing.border.*;
import java.awt.*;

public class MyFrame extends JFrame
{
    public MyFrame()
    {
        setTitle( "JSplitPane1" );

        // Store the content pane in a variable for easier
        // access.
        JPanel mPanel = (JPanel)getContentPane();

        // Components will all be added to this panel.
```

Figure 8-104

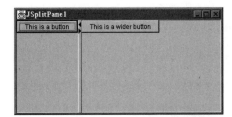

```
mPanel.setLayout( new BorderLayout() );

// Create the left-hand pane and put a button into it.
Box comp1 = new Box( BoxLayout.X_AXIS );

comp1.add( new JButton( "This is a button" ) );

// Create the right-hand pane and put a wider button
// into it.
Box comp2 = new Box( BoxLayout.X_AXIS );

comp2.add( new JButton( "This is a wider button" ) );

// Create the split pane, specifying the orientation
// of the split plus the two components that will be
// separated.
JSplitPane pane = new JSplitPane(
                   JSplitPane.HORIZONTAL_SPLIT,
                   comp1, comp2 );

// Enable one-touch expansion.
pane.setOneTouchExpandable( true );

// Add the split pane to the buffered pane.
mPanel.add( "Center", pane );
    }
}
```

JSplitPane's Public Methods

`AccessibleContext getAccessibleContext()`

Returns a subclass of AccessibleContext that gives access to the JSplit-Pane's accessibility information.

`Component getBottomComponent()`

Returns the lower component if the divider is horizontal, or the right component if the divider is vertical.

`int getDividerLocation()`

Returns the distance, in pixels, between the divider and the left side (if the divider is vertical), or the divider and the top (if the divider is horizontal).

`int getDividerSize()`

Returns the width of the divider.

`int getLastDividerLocation()`

Returns the divider's previous position.

```
Component getLeftComponent()
```

Returns the left component if the divider is vertical, or the upper component if the divider is horizontal.

```
int getMaximumDividerLocation()
```

Returns the maximum distance the divider can be from the left (if the divider is vertical) or top (if the divider is horizontal).

```
int getMinimumDividerLocation()
```

Returns the minimum distance the divider can be from the left (if the divider is vertical) or top (if the divider is horizontal).

```
int getOrientation()
```

Returns the current orientation, either VERTICAL_SPLIT or HORIZONTAL_SPLIT.

```
Component getRightComponent()
```

This is the same as the getBottomComponent() method.

```
Component getTopComponent()
```

This is the same as the getLeftComponent() method.

```
SplitPaneUI getUI()
```

Returns the JSplitPane's current look-and-feel class.

```
String getUIClassID()
```

Returns the identifying string that the look-and-feel uses to assign a UI class to the JSplitPane.

```
boolean isContinuousLayout()
```

Returns true if the JSplitPane's two components are constantly redrawn as the divider is dragged.

```
boolean isOneTouchExpandable()
```

Returns true if one touch expansion is enabled.

```
void remove(Component component)
```

Removes the given component from the JSplitPane.

```
void remove(int index)
```

Removes the component corresponding to the given index.

```
void removeAll()
```

Removes both of the JSplitPane's components.

```
void resetToPreferredSizes()
```

Resets the JSplitPane so it tries to draw both components at their preferred sizes and places the divider snug up against the left (or top) component.

```
void setBottomComponent(Component comp)
```

Sets the component that will be below or to the right of the divider, depending on orientation.

```
void setContinuousLayout(boolean newContinuousLayout)
```

Specifies whether the two components should be constantly redrawn while the divider is being dragged.

```
void setDividerLocation(double location)
```

Sets the divider location as a fraction of the width or height, depending on orientation. Must be between 0 and 1.0.

```
void setDividerLocation(int location)
```

Sets the distance in pixels between the divider and the top or left side, depending on orientation.

```
void setDividerSize(int newSize)
```

Specifies the width of the divider.

```
void setLastDividerLocation(int newLastLocation)
```

Specifies the previous location for the divider.

```
void setLeftComponent(Component comp)
```

Sets the component that will be left or above the divider, depending on the orientation.

void setOneTouchExpandable(boolean newValue)

Specifies whether one touch expansion is enabled or disabled.

void setOrientation(int orientation)

Specifies the JSplitPane's orientation.

void setRightComponent(Component comp)

Sets the right or bottom component, depending on the orientation.

void setTopComponent(Component comp)

Sets the top or left component, depending on the orientation.

void setUI(SplitPaneUI ui)

Gives the JSplitPane a new look-and-feel class.

void updateUI()

Tells the JSplitPane that the look-and-feel class has been changed.

JTabbedPane

A JTabbedPane is a component that allows you to display lots of components in a single area without the user interface becoming cluttered (see Figure 8-105). When you create a dialog, one of the common problems is that once you have everything in the dialog that you want, it is too busy or full to be usable. What you want is to be able to break it all up into categories and display one category at a time while allowing the user to switch between categories. A JTabbedPane lets you do this. One category is shown

Figure 8-105
A typical JTabbedPane as part of a dialog.

at a time, but there are tabs like file folder tabs across the top of the tabbed pane that let the user change to another category.

A JTabbedPane generates a ChangeEvent when the user selects a tab.

Ancestors

```
java.lang.Object
    |
    +—java.awt.Component
            |
            +—java.awt.Container
                    |
                    +—com.sun.java.swing.JComponent
                            |
                            +—com.sun.java.swing.JTabbedPane
```

NOTE: *For more information, see the "DefaultSingleSelectionModel," "Image-Icon," and "JPanel" sections in this chapter, and the "JFC Containers" section in Chapter 7, "JFC by Concept."*

Steps in Creating and Using JTabbedPane

1. Create the JTabbedPane that will control the pages that will be selected from.

   There are two one constructors. The first creates a JTabbedPane with tabs across the top:

   ```
   JTabbedPane()
   ```

   The second allows you to specify where the tabs go:

   ```
   JTabbedPane(int tabside)
   ```

   'tabside' may be: TOP, BOTTOM, LEFT or RIGHT.

   So, we use:

   ```
   JTabbedPane tabbedPane = new JTabbedPane();
   ```

2. Add the tabbed pane to an existing container (our container happens to be using a BorderLayout):

   ```
   myContainer.add( "Center", tabbedPane );
   ```

3. Create components to add as pages to be selected from:

   ```
   JPanel panel1 = new JPanel();
   JPanel panel2 = new JPanel();
   ```

4. Add the components to the tabbed pane. There are three versions of the addTab() method. One supplies the tab's panel and a text string for the tab; another supplies the tab's panel, the tab text, and a tab icon; and the other supplies the panel, the tab text, the tab icon, and a tool tip string.

Add a component to the JTabbedPane and specify the tab text:

```
tabbedPane.addTab( "First Panel", panel1 );
```

Add a component to the JTabbedPane and specify the tab text, the tab icon, and the tool tip text:

```
tabbedPane.addTab( "Second Panel", new ImageIcon( "open.gif" ),
                            panel2, "Tool tip" );
```

5. Choose which page will be displayed initially. This is required or it looks odd when it first comes up:

```
tabbedPane.setSelectedIndex( 0 );
```

6. Make it so a class listens for when a different tab is selected. First, tell the JTabbedPane which class will receive these events. In this case, the class that contains 'tabbedPane' will receive the events.

```
tabbedPane.addChangeListener( this );
```

Make the receiving class (MyFrame, in this case) implement the ChangeListener interface:

```
public class MyFrame extends JFrame implements ChangeListener
{
    .
    .
    .
    public void stateChanged( ChangeEvent e )
    {
        // Do whatever action you want now you know a new page
        // is being displayed.
    }
}
```

7. Find out which tab is selected. This method returns the index of the currently selected tab:

```
tabbedPane.getSelectedIndex();
```

8. Get the component represented by a particular tab. The tab is referred to by its index (1, in this case):

```
Component currentComponent = tabbedPane.getComponentAt( 1 );
```

9. Get the icon of the tab at a particular index:

```
Icon icon = tabbedPane.getIconAt( 1 );
```

10. Get the title string of the tab at a particular index:

```
String title = tabbedPane.getTitleAt( 1 );
```

11. Get the number of tabs in the JTabbedPane:

```
int numTabs = tabbedPane.getTabCount();
```

12. Find the index of the tab with the specified title text:

```
int theTab = tabbedPane.indexOfTab( "Tab 1" );
```

13. Insert a new tab at the specified index. This method takes the new tab's title text, icon, component, tool tip, and insertion index. The title and icon may be null.

```
JPanel newTab = new JPanel();
tabbedPane.insertTab( "Tab - X", new ImageIcon( "tabx.gif" ),
                      newTab, "This is tab - x", 3 );
```

This creates a new JPanel and adds it to the JTabbedPane at index 3.

14. Remove the tab at the specified index:

```
tabbedPane.removeTabAt( 1 );
```

15. Replace the component associated with the tab at the specified index:

```
JPanel replacementTab = new JPanel();
tabbedPane.setComponentAt( 1, replacementTab );
```

16. Set the icon of the tab at the specified index:

```
tabbedPane.setIconAt( 3, new ImageIcon( "new.gif" ) );
```

17. Set the title string of the tab at the specified index:

```
tabbedPane.setTitleAt( 2, "Replacement Title" );
```

Basic Code Examples

EXAMPLE 8-67 Basic JTabbedPane

This example creates a JTabbedPane with three tabs. It illustrates the concepts described above including creating and adding tabs and listening for changes in tab selection. Figure 8-108 shows the example as it comes up initially.

Here is the source code:

```
import com.sun.java.swing.*;
import com.sun.java.swing.event.*;
import java.awt.*;

public class MyFrame extends JFrame implements
        ChangeListener
```

Figure 8-108

```
        {
            JTabbedPane mTabbedPane;
            JPanel mPanel1;
            JPanel mPanel2;
            JPanel mPanel3;

            public MyFrame()
            {
                setTitle( "JTabbedPane1" );

                // Store the content pane in a variable for easier
                // access.
                JPanel contentPane = (JPanel)getContentPane();

                // Components will all be added to this panel.
                contentPane.setLayout( new BorderLayout() );

                // Create the tabbed pane.
                mTabbedPane = new JTabbedPane();

                // Create one of the panels that will be accessed via
                // the tabbed pane.
                mPanel1 = new JPanel();
                mPanel1.setLayout( new BorderLayout() );
                JLabel l = new JLabel( "This is panel 1" );
                l.setFont( new Font( "TimesRoman", Font.BOLD, 36 ) );
                mPanel1.add( "Center", l );

                // Add the new panel to the tabbed pane and give it
                // tab text of "Panel 1".
                mTabbedPane.addTab( "Panel 1", mPanel1 );

                // Create the tabbed pane's second panel.
                mPanel2 = new JPanel();
                mPanel2.setLayout( new BorderLayout() );
                l = new JLabel( "This is panel 2" );
                l.setFont( new Font( "TimesRoman", Font.BOLD, 36 ) );
                mPanel2.add( "Center", l );

                // Add the second panel to the tabbed pane.  It has
                // both tab text and and icon.
                mTabbedPane.addTab( "Panel 2",
                                    new ImageIcon( "open.gif" ),
                                    mPanel2 );
```

```
// Create the third panel for the tabbed pane.
mPanel3 = new JPanel();
mPanel3.setLayout( new BorderLayout() );
l = new JLabel( "This is panel 3" );
l.setFont( new Font( "TimesRoman", Font.BOLD, 36 ) );
mPanel3.add( "Center", l );

// Add the third panel to the tabbed pane.  This also
// has both text and icon for the tab.
mTabbedPane.addTab( "Panel 3",
                    new ImageIcon( "print.gif" ),
                    mPanel3 );

// Add the tabbed pane so it fills the content pane.
contentPane.add( "Center", mTabbedPane );

// You must choose one of the tabs to be selected
// initially.
mTabbedPane.setSelectedIndex( 0 );

// We can use a change listener so we know when the
// user has chosen a new tab.
mTabbedPane.addChangeListener( this );
}

// This method is called when a new tab is selected.
public void stateChanged( ChangeEvent e )
{
    System.out.println( e );
}
}
```

Advanced Issues

EXAMPLE 8-68 Using Actions to Switch between Tabs

This example shows how to switch between a JTabbedPane's panels using
the keyboard. Each panel has an associated key stroke (Alt-1, Alt-2, Alt-3)
which, when pressed, brings that panel to the front. Figure 8-107 shows the
example after Alt-2 has been pressed.

Figure 8-107

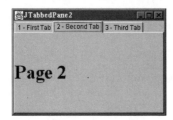

Important points to notice:

■ The keyboard action is registered to the JTabbedPane rather than to the individual panels.

■ Each panel's tab index (0-2 since there are three panels) is passed into the MyAction instance so that when the key stroke happens and actionPerformed() is called, it knows which panel to move to the front.

Here is the source code:

```java
import com.sun.java.swing.*;
import java.awt.*;
import java.awt.event.*;

public class MyFrame extends JFrame
{
    // Make this an instance variable so actionPerformed()
    // can see it.
    JTabbedPane tabbedPane;

    public MyFrame()
    {
        setTitle( "JTabbedPane2" );

        // Store the content pane in a variable for easier
        // access.
        JPanel contentPane = (JPanel)getContentPane();

        // Components will all be added to this panel.
        contentPane.setLayout( new BorderLayout() );

        // Create a tabbed pane.
        tabbedPane = new JTabbedPane();

        // Add the tabbed pane to the content pane so it
        // fills the entire area.
        contentPane.add( "Center", tabbedPane );

        // Create the panel that will be used as the first in
        // the tabbed set.
        JPanel tab1 = new JPanel();

        // Add a label to the center of the panel, just to
        // differentiate it.
        tab1.setLayout( new BorderLayout() );
        JLabel lb1 = new JLabel( "Page 1" );
        tab1.add( "Center", lb1 );
        lb1.setFont( new Font( "TimesRoman",
                               Font.BOLD, 36 ) );

        // Add the panel to the JTabbedPane and give it a
        // string to put on its tab.
        tabbedPane.addTab( "1 - First Tab", tab1 );
```

```
// Make it so that when the user presses Alt-1 this
// tab will come to the front.
tabbedPane.registerKeyboardAction( new MyAction( 0 ),
        KeyStroke.getKeyStroke( KeyEvent.VK_1,
        ActionEvent.ALT_MASK, false ),
        JComponent.WHEN_IN_FOCUSED_WINDOW );

// Create the panel that will be used as the second
// tab in the set.
JPanel tab2 = new JPanel();

// Add a label to the panel's center to differentiate
// it.
tab2.setLayout( new BorderLayout() );
JLabel lb2 = new JLabel( "Page 2" );
tab2.add( "Center", lb2 );
lb2.setFont( new Font( "TimesRoman",
                            Font.BOLD, 36 ) );

// Add the panel to the tabbed pane and give it a tab
// string.
tabbedPane.addTab( "2 - Second Tab", tab2 );

// Make it so that when the user presses Alt-2 this
// panel comes to the front.
tabbedPane.registerKeyboardAction( new MyAction( 1 ),
        KeyStroke.getKeyStroke( KeyEvent.VK_2,
        ActionEvent.ALT_MASK, false ),
        JComponent.WHEN_IN_FOCUSED_WINDOW );

// Create the panel that will be used as the third in
// the set.
JPanel tab3 = new JPanel();

// Add a label to the panel's center to differentiate
// it.
tab3.setLayout( new BorderLayout() );
JLabel lb3 = new JLabel( "Page 3" );
tab3.add( "Center", lb3 );
lb3.setFont( new Font( "TimesRoman",
                            Font.BOLD, 36 ) );

// Add the panel to the tabbed pane, giving it a tab
// string.
tabbedPane.addTab( "3 - Third Tab", tab3 );

// Make it so that when the user presses Alt-3, this
// panel will come to the front.
tabbedPane.registerKeyboardAction( new MyAction( 2 ),
        KeyStroke.getKeyStroke( KeyEvent.VK_3,
        ActionEvent.ALT_MASK, false ),
        JComponent.WHEN_IN_FOCUSED_WINDOW );

// Set it so that the first panel is initially at the
// front.
```

```
            tabbedPane.setSelectedIndex( 0 );
    }

    // We have associated an instance of this class with
    // each of the tabbed panel's tabs.  One recognizes
    // Alt-1, one Alt-2, and the other Alt-3.  When one of
    // those sequences is pressed, the corresponding panel
    // comes to the front.
    private class MyAction extends AbstractAction
    {
        private int mIndex;

        // Create the class instance and give it the panel's
        // tab index.
        public MyAction( int panelIndex )
        {
            mIndex = panelIndex;
        }

        // When the key sequence with which this instance is
        // associated is pressed, make the corresponding
        // panel come to the front.
        public void actionPerformed( ActionEvent e )
        {
            tabbedPane.setSelectedIndex( mIndex );
        }
    }
}
```

JTabbedPane's Public Methods

void addChangeListener(ChangeListener l)

Tells the JTabbedPane to notify the given class when a new tab is selected.

void addTab(String title,Component component)

Adds a new tab to the JTabbedPane, specifying the tab's text string and the component to display when the tab is selected.

void addTab(String title,Icon icon,Component component)

Adds a new tab to the JTabbedPane, specifying the tab's text string and icon, and the component to display when the tab is selected.

void addTab(String title,Icon icon,Component component,String tip)

Adds a new tab to the JTabbedPane, specifying the tab's text string, icon, tool tip, and the component that will be displayed when the tab is selected.

`AccessibleContext getAccessibleContext()`

Returns a subclass of AccessibleContext that gives access to the JTabbed-Pane's accessibility information.

`Color getBackgroundAt(int n)`

Returns the nth tab's background color.

`Rectangle getBoundsAt(int n)`

Returns the nth tab's bounding rectangle.

`Component getComponentAt(int index)`

Returns the tab component at the given index.

`Icon getDisabledIconAt(int n)`

Returns the icon that the nth tab displays when it is diabled.

`Color getForegroundAt(int n)`

Returns the nth tab's foreground color.

`Icon getIconAt(int index)`

Returns the icon associated with the tab at the given index.

`SingleSelectionModel getModel()`

Returns the selection model that stores the information about which tab is currently selected.

`Component getSelectedComponent()`

Returns the Component associated with the currently selected tab.

`int getSelectedIndex()`

Returns the index of the currently selected tab.

`int getTabCount()`

Returns the number of tabs in the JTabbedPane.

`void getTabPlacement(int place)`

Returns the side on which the tabs are being drawn: TOP, BOTTOM,

LEFT, or RIGHT.

```
int getTabRunCount()
```

Returns the number of rows or columns of tabs there are depending on where the tabs are placed.

```
String getTitleAt(int index)
```

Returns the text string associated with the tab at the given index.

```
String getToolTipText(MouseEvent event)
```

Returns the tooltip to be used upon the occurrence of the given event.

```
TabbedPaneUI getUI()
```

Returns the JTabbedPane's current look-and-feel class.

```
String getUIClassID()
```

Returns the identifying string that the look-and-feel uses to assign a UI class to the JTabbedPane.

```
int indexOfComponent(Component c)
```

Returns the index of the tab that the given Component is associated with.

```
int indexOfTab(Icon icon)
```

Returns the index of the tab on which the given Icon is displayed.

```
int indexOfTab(String title)
```

Returns the index of the tab whose associated text string matches the given text string.

```
void insertTab(String title,Icon icon,Component component,String
                tip,int index)
```

Creates a new tab, specifying the text string, icon, tool tip, and the component to display when the tab is selected, and inserts it into the JTabbedPane at the given index.

```
boolean isEnabledAt(int n)
```

Returns true if the nth tab is enabled.

```
void removeChangeListener(ChangeListener l)
```

Tells the JTabbedPane to stop notifying the given class when a new tab is selected.

```
void removeTabAt(int index)
```

Removes the tab at the given index.

```
void setBackgroundAt(int n, Color color)
```

Specifies the background color for the nth tab.

```
void setComponentAt(int index,Component component)
```

Replaces the component associated with the tab at the given index with the new component.

```
void setDisabledIconAt(int n, Icon icon)
```

Specifies the icon that the nth tab should display when disabled.

```
void setEnabledAt(int n, boolean state)
```

Specifies whether the nth tab is enabled.

```
void setForegroundAt(int n, Color color)
```

Specifies the foreground color that the nth tab should use.

```
void setIconAt(int index,Icon icon)
```

Specifies the icon to display on the tab at the given index.

```
void setModel(SingleSelectionModel model)
```

Replaces the JTabbedPane's selection model.

```
void setSelectedComponent(Component c)
```

Specifies that the tab associated with the given Component should become the JTabbedPanel's selected tab.

```
void setSelectedIndex(int index)
```

Specifies that the tab at the given index should become the JTabbedPane's selected tab.

```
void setTabPlacement(int place)
```

Specifies on which side the tabs should draw: TOP, BOTTOM, LEFT, or RIGHT.

```
void setTitleAt(int index, String title)
```

Specifies the text string that should be displayed on the tab at the given index.

```
void setUI(TabbedPaneUI ui)
```

Gives the JTabbedPane a new look-and-feel class.

```
void updateUI()
```

Tells the JTabbedPane that the look-and-feel class has been changed.

JTableHeader

JTableHeader is a companion component to JTable and contains the graphical representation of the table's column headers. It does not display by default when you display its JTable. You can get a JTable's JTableHeader component by calling the getTableHeader() method. The JTableHeader is automatically displayed and scrolls with its JTable when you place the JTable into a JScroll-Pane created using JTable's static createScrollPaneForTable() method.

A JTableHeader draws itself using iinformation from the TableColumn-Model associated with its JTable, as well as from the TableColumns that describe individual column attributes.

Ancestors

```
java.lang.Object
   |
   +—java.awt.Component
          |
          +—java.awt.Container
                 |
                 +—com.sun.java.swing.JComponent
                        |
                        +—com.sun.java.swing.table.JTableHeader
```

NOTE: *For more information, see the "TableColumn," "JTable," and "Default-TableColumnModel" sections in this chapter. Also see the "JFC Tables" section in Chapter 7, "JFC by Concept."*

Steps in Creating and Using JTableHeader

1. You will normally not create a JTableHeader yourself, but will instead let a JTable create the JTableHeader. Once the JTableHeader is created, you can either let it act in its standard way, or you can get it and display it yourself.

    Get a JTable's JTableHeader:

    ```
    JTableHeader header = myTable.getTableHeader();
    ```

2. Change the TableCellRenderer used to draw a column's header. Each header is drawn using a class that implements the TableCellRenderer interface. The renderer is stored in each column's TableColumn.

    Get a column's TableColumn:

    ```
    // Get the TableColumnModel for the table.
    TableColumnModel columnModel = myTable.getColumnModel();

    // Get the TableColumn at the given index.
    TableColumn col = columnModel.getColumn( 0 );
    ```

    Create a new cell renderer. In this case, it will be a custom renderer:

    ```
    CustomRenderer rend=new CustomRenderer();
    ```

    Tell the TableColumn to use the renderer:

    ```
    col.setHeaderRenderer( rend );
    ```

3. Disable column reordering. By default, the user can move columns around.

    ```
    header.setReorderingAllowed( false );
    ```

4. Set a tool tip for the entire JTableHeader:

    ```
    header.setToolTipText( "Table Header" );
    ```

Basic Code Examples

EXAMPLE 8-69 Basic Use of JTableHeader

This example creates a JTable with a special scroll pane for scrolling tables and headers, and changes its JTableHeader so that columns cannot be moved. It also applies a new cell renderer to one of the columns. Figure 8-108 shows the example as it comes up.

Here is the source code:

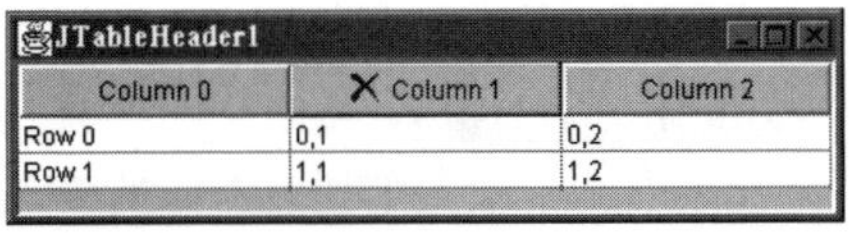

Figure 8-108

```
import com.sun.java.swing.*;
import com.sun.java.swing.table.*;
import java.awt.*;

public class MyFrame extends JFrame
{
    private JTable mTable;

    public MyFrame()
    {
        setTitle( "JTableHeader1" );

        // Store the content pane in a variable for easier
        // access.

        JPanel contentPane = (JPanel)getContentPane();

        // Components will all be added to this panel.

        contentPane.setLayout( new BorderLayout() );

        // Create an array of adat and another for column ids.

        Object data[][] = new Object[2][3];
        data[0][0] = "Row 0";
        data[0][1] = "0,1";
        data[0][2] = "0,2";
        data[1][0] = "Row 1";
        data[1][1] = "1,1";
        data[1][2] = "1,2";

        Object headers[] = new Object[3];
        headers[0] = "Column 0";
        headers[1] = "Column 1";
        headers[2] = "Column 2";

        // Use the arrays to create a JTable.

        mTable = new JTable( data, headers );

        // Create a special scroll pane to handle the table.

        JScrollPane scroller =
                   JTable.createScrollPaneForTable( mTable );

        // Place the scroll pane over the main area of the
        // content pane.

        contentPane.add( "Center", scroller );
```

```
            // Get the TableColumnModel.

            TableColumnModel columnModel =
                                   mTable.getColumnModel();

            // Find the column index associated with the given
            // identifier.

            int colIndex =
                    columnModel.getColumnIndex( "Column 1" );

            // Find the TableColumn at the given column index.

            TableColumn col = columnModel.getColumn( colIndex );

            // Create a cell renderer of a button with and icon.

            ButtonIconRenderer rend = new ButtonIconRenderer(
                            new ImageIcon( "delete.gif" ) );

            // Apply the cell renderer as the TableColumn's
            // header renderer.

            col.setHeaderRenderer( rend );

            // Disable column reordering.

            mTable.getTableHeader().setReorderingAllowed( false );
        }

        private class ButtonIconRenderer implements
                                              TableCellRenderer
        {
            private JButton mButton;

            public ButtonIconRenderer( Icon icon )
            {
                mButton = new JButton( icon );
            }

            public Component getTableCellRendererComponent(
                            JTable table,
                            Object value,
                            boolean isSelected,
                            boolean hasFocus,
                            int row,
                            int column )
            {
                mButton.setText( value.toString() );

                return mButton;
            }
        }
    }
}
```

JTableHeader's Public Methods

NOTE: *Note: Since JTableHeader interacts heavily with other classes, many of these methods are used for those interactions.*

```
void columnAdded(TableColumnModelEvent e)
```

JTableHeader implements the TableColumnModelListener interface, and this is part of it.

```
int columnAtPoint(Point point)
```

Returns the index of the column at the given point.

```
void columnMarginChanged(ChangeEvent e)
```

JTableHeader implements the TableColumnModelListener interface, and this is part of it.

```
void columnMoved(TableColumnModelEvent e)
```

JTableHeader implements the TableColumnModelListener interface, and this is part of it.

```
void columnRemoved(TableColumnModelEvent e)
```

JTableHeader implements the TableColumnModelListener interface, and this is part of it.

```
void columnSelectionChanged(ListSelectionEvent e)
```

JTableHeader implements the TableColumnModelListener interface, and this is part of it.

```
AccessibleContext getAccessibleContext()
```

Returns a subclass of AccessibleContext that is the entry point to accessible information about the JTableHeader.

```
TableColumnModel getColumnModel()
```

Returns the TableColumnModel with which the header is associated.

```
int getDraggedColumn()
```

Returns the index of the column that is being dragged, or -1 if no drag is in progress.

`int getDraggedDistance()`

Returns the distance the column that is being dragged has been dragged.

`Rectangle getHeaderRect(int n)`

Returns the bounding rectangle for the nth column header component.

`boolean getReorderingAllowed()`

Returns true if the columns may be reordered.

`boolean getResizingAllowed()`

Returns true if the columns may be resized.

`int getResizingColumn()`

Returns the index of the column currently being resized, or -1 if no column is being resized.

`JTable getTable()`

Returns the JTable that the JTableHeader is associated with.

`String getToolTipText(MouseEvent event)`

This allows the JTableHeader's individual header renderers to display their own tool tips.

`TableHeaderUI getUI()`

Returns the UI class associated with the JTableHeader.

`String getUIClassID()`

Returns the string ID that the plugged-in look-and-feel uses to identify which UI class should be associated with the JTableHeader.

`boolean getUpdateTableInRealTime()`

Returns true if the display will update constantly as a column is dragged.

`boolean isOpaque()`

Returns true if the JTableHeader fills its entire space.

`void resizeAndRepaint()`

Tells the JTableHeader to make sure it is sized properly.

```
void setColumnModel(TableColumnModel newModel)
```

Associates the JTableHeader with a new TableColumnModel.

```
void setDraggedColumn(int columnIndex)
```

Specifies that a column is being dragged.

```
void setDraggedDistance(int distance)
```

Specifies how far the column being dragged has gone.

```
void setReorderingAllowed(boolean b)
```

Specifies whether columns may be reordered.

```
void setResizingAllowed(boolean b)
```

Specifies whether columns may be resized.

```
void setResizingColumn(int columnIndex)
```

Specifies that the given column is being resized.

```
void setTable(JTable aTable)
```

Associates the JTableHeader with a new JTable.

```
void setUI(TableHeaderUI ui)
```

Gives the JTableHeader a new UI class.

```
void setUpdateTableInRealTime(boolean flag)
```

Specifies whether the display should update constantly while a column is being dragged.

```
void updateUI()
```

Tells the JTableHeader to check with the UIManager for a new UI class.

JTable

JTable is a component that helps you create spreadsheet-like controls that have columns and rows (see Figure 8-109). It also helps deal with column headers, configuring each column as a separate entity, and moving columns around.

JTable is quite complicated to work with. Visually, it consists of:

Figure 8-109
A typical JTable.

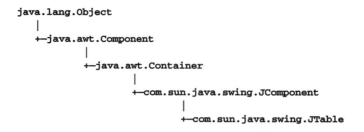

- Rows of data
- Columns of data
- Column headers
- An editor, if you want cells to be editable

It does not include row headers—you have to add those yourself if you need them.

Internally, JTable includes several classes:

- A TableModel, usually a subclass of AbstractTableModel, which stores the table's data.
- A TableColumnModel, usually DefaultTableColumnModel, which controls the behavior of the table's columns and gives access to the TableColumns.
- A ListSelectionModel, usually DefaultListSelectionModel, which keeps track of the JTable's currently selected row(s).
- A TableCellRenderer, usually an instance of DefaultCellRenderer.
- A TableCellEditor (if needed), usually an instance of DefaultCellEditor.
- Multiple TableColumns, which store graphical information about each column.
- A JTableHeader which displays column headers.

Ancestors

```
java.lang.Object
   |
   +—java.awt.Component
          |
          +—java.awt.Container
                 |
                 +—com.sun.java.swing.JComponent
                        |
                        +—com.sun.java.swing.JTable
```

NOTE: *For more information, see the "AbstractTableModel," "DefaultTableModel," "DefaultTableColumnModel," "DefaultListSelectionModel," "TableColumn," "JTable-Header," "DefaultCellEditor," and "JScrollPane" sections in this chapter. Also see the "JFC Tables" section in Chapter 7, "JFC by Concept."*

Steps in Creating and Using JTable

1. Create the JTable. There are a seven constructors representing a wide variety of ways to create a JTable. Each JTable that is created has classes associated with it that implement the TableModel, TableColumnModel, and ListSelectionModel interfaces. Generally, any of these classes that you don't pass in to the constructor will have default versions created for you.

   Notice that even though some constructors take column names, the column names don't show up by default because they are displayed in a JTableHeader, which is a separate component.

   Constructor #1:

   ```
   JTable()
   ```

   This constructor creates an empty JTable with no rows or columns. If you use this constructor, you will have to add the data separately via the TableModel. In use it looks like:

   ```
   JTable mtTable = new JTable();
   ```

   Constructor #2:

   ```
   JTable( int numColumns, int numRows )
   ```

   This constructor creates an empty JTable with 'numColumns' columns and 'numRows' rows. If you use this constructor, you will either have to add the data separately, or assign cell editors to the columns so the user can supply it. In use it looks like:

   ```
   JTable myTable = new JTable( 5, 10 );
   ```

   Constructor #3:

   ```
   JTable( Object dataValues[][], Object columnNames[] )
   ```

   This constructor takes a two dimensional array of values that will be used to fill the JTable's TableModel, plus an array of column names. The dimensions of the 'dataValues' array will be used to set the dimensions of the JTable's TableModel. The first index in 'dataValues' is the row and the second is the column. In use it looks like:

   ```
   String values[][] = new String[2][3];

   values[0][0] = "Row 1";
   values[0][1] = "50";
   values[0][2] = "100";

   values[1][0] = "Row 2";
   values[1][1] = "80";
   values[1][2] = "70";
   ```

```
String columnHeaders[] = new String[3];

columnHeaders[0] = "Row Name";
columnHeaders[1] = "Value 1";
columnHeaders[2] = "Value 2";

JTable myTable = new JTable( values, columnHeaders );
```

Constructor #4:

```
JTable( TableModel tm )
```

This constructor takes a pre-built TableModel and uses its properties
(rows and columns) to build the JTable. Columns are built up from
the column information in the TableModel. There are a number of
ways to create a TableModel. One use is:

```
String values[][] = new String[2][3];

values[0][0] = "Row 1";
values[0][1] = "50";
values[0][2] = "100";

values[1][0] = "Row 2";
values[1][1] = "80";
values[1][2] = "70";

String columnHeaders[] = new String[3];

columnHeaders[0] = "Row Name";
columnHeaders[1] = "Value 1";
columnHeaders[2] = "Value 2";

DefaultTableModel tableModel = new DefaultTableModel( values,
                                        columnHeaders );

JTable myTable = new JTable( tableModel );
```

Constructor #5:

```
JTable( TableModel tm, TableColumnModel tcm )
```

This constructor takes pre-built TableModel and TableColumnModel
and uses them to build the JTable. There is a wide variety of ways to
create a TableModel and a TableColumnModel. Here is one use:

```
String values[][] = new String[2][3];

values[0][0] = "Row 1";
values[0][1] = "50";
values[0][2] = "100";

values[1][0] = "Row 2";
values[1][1] = "80";
values[1][2] = "70";
```

```
String columnHeaders[] = new String[3];

columnHeaders[0] = "Row Name";
columnHeaders[1] = "Value 1";
columnHeaders[2] = "Value 2";

DefaultTableModel tableModel = new DefaultTableModel( values,
                                    columnHeaders );

DefaultTableColumnModel tableColumnModel =
                            new DefaultTableColumnModel();

JTable myTable = new JTable( tableModel, tableColumnModel );
```

Constructor #6:

```
JTable( TableModel tm, TableColumnModel tcm, ListSelectionModel
        lsm )
```

This constructor is just like #5, except it specifies a custom ListSelectionModel. One use could be:

```
String values[][] = new String[2][3];

values[0][0] = "Row 1";
values[0][1] = "50";
values[0][2] = "100";

values[1][0] = "Row 2";
values[1][1] = "80";
values[1][2] = "70";

String columnHeaders[] = new String[3];

columnHeaders[0] = "Row Name";
columnHeaders[1] = "Value 1";
columnHeaders[2] = "Value 2";

DefaultTableModel tableModel = new DefaultTableModel( values,
                                    columnHeaders );

DefaultTableColumnModel tableColumnModel =
                            new DefaultTableColumnModel();

DefaultListSelectionModel listSelectionModel =
                            new DefaultListSelectionModel();

JTable myTable = new JTable( tableModel, tableColumnModel,
                                    listSelectionModel );
```

Constructor #7:

```
JTable( Vector dataVectors, Vector columnNames )
```

This constructor takes 'dataVectors' which is a Vector of Vectors, each sub-Vector of which contains a row of data. The 'columnNames' Vector is just the names for the JTable's columns. In use it looks like:

```
Vector dataRows = new Vector();

Vector firstRow = new Vector();

firstRow.addElement( "Row 1" );
firstRow.addElement( "50" );
firstRow.addElement( "100" );

Vector secondRow = new Vector();

secondRow.addElement( "Row 2" );
secondRow.addElement( "80" );
secondRow.addElement( "70" );

dataRows.addElement( firstRow );
dataRows.addElement( secondRow );

Vector columnHeaders = new Vector();

columnHeaders.addElement( "Row Name" );
columnHeaders.addElement( "Value 1" );
columnHeaders.addElement( "Value 2" );

    JTable myTable = new JTable( dataRows, columnHeaders );
```

2. If desired, create a JScrollPane that can be used to scroll around the JTable. This is handled differently from most scroll panes. JTable has column headers that need to be scrolled differently from the rest of the table (side-to-side only). Also, it is preferrable that, when scrolling around a JTable, the scrolling unit increment should be the height of a row in the vertical scroll bar, and the width of a column in the horizontal scroll bar. JTable has a static method that you can use to create a JScrollPane that handles all of this for you:

```
JScrollPane scroller = JTable.createScrollPaneForTable( myTable );
```

This also causes the column headers to display because the created JScrollPane uses the JTable's JTableHeader as its column header component.

3. Place the JTable within a container. This is just like adding any other component. Assuming the container is using a BorderLayout, you could either place the JTable itself:

```
myContainer.add( "Center", myTable );
```

or, if you are using a JScrollPane, you could place that:

```
myContainer.add( "Center", scroller );
```

4. Control whether grid lines should be drawn so cell locations are more apparent. It is true by default.

```
myTable.setShowGrid( false );
```

5. Set the grid's color. Only useful if the grid is being drawn.

```
myTable.setGridColor( Color.blue );
```

6. Specify the value for a specific cell in the JTable. The cell can be specified using a row index and a column index:

```
myTable.setValueAt( newValue, 3, 4 );
```

7. Tell the JTable to start editing a particular cell. This will cause the TableCellEditor for that cell to start going. You can specify the cell by row index and column index:

```
myTable.editCellAt( 3, 4 );
```

8. Get the value of a particular cell. You can specify the cell by row index and column index:

```
myTable.getValueAt( 3, 4 );
```

9. Change the spacing between cells. This takes a Dimension so you can have different vertical and horizontal spacing.

```
myTable.setIntercellSpacing( new Dimension( 10, 5 ) );
```

10. Get the JTable's JTableHeader component:

```
JTableHeader header = myTable.getTableHeader();
```

11. Find out which row a point is in:

```
int row = myTable.rowAtPoint( point );
```

12. Make it so individual cells can be selected. The setCellSelectionEnabled() method makes it so that when you click on a cell, both the row and column that the cell is in are selected, although only the intersection is highlighted.

```
myTable.setCellSelectionEnabled( true );
```

13. Find out which cells are currently selected. The actual selected cells are not stored anywhere. The selected rows are stored in the JTable's ListSelectionModel, while the selected columns are stored in the JTable's TableColumnModel's ListSelectionModel. To find out the selected cells, you just get the selected rows and selected columns and the intersection makes up the set of selected cells.

14. To set the selection mode for rows and columns, you have to go to the row and column ListSelectionModels stored in the JTable (rows) and the TableColumnModel (columns). This is also where you can get

information about which rows/columns are currently selected, as well as register for notification when the selection state changes.

15. To add new rows and columns and to insert new rows, you should go to the JTable's TableModel. All of the JTable's data is stored there, and the other classes like JTable and JTableHeader will be automatically updated.

16. TableColumns store how cells in a column will be drawn and edited, as well as how table headers will be drawn. To change any of these settings, go to the individual TableColumns in the TableColumnModel.

17. The TableColumnModel contains information about the columns in general, including their margins and whether they can be reordered. Go to the TableColumnModel (usually, DefaultTableColumnModel) to see or change these settings.

Basic Code Examples

EXAMPLE 8-70 Simple Uses of JTable

This example displays a preloaded JTable and its JTableHeader in a JScroll-Pane. All cells in the table are editable. The first column displays strings and uses the default cell editor. The next three columns use special cell renderers and cell editors that display strings right-aligned and allow editing strings right-aligned. The last column contains Boolean values and uses a cell renderer that displays the Boolean values as a checkbox, and uses a checkbox editor. Figure 8-110 shows the example while one of the number cells is being edited.

Here is the source code:

```
import com.sun.java.swing.*;
import com.sun.java.swing.table.*;
import java.awt.*;
import java.util.*;

public class MyFrame extends JFrame
{
    // This is the JTable.
    private JTable myTable;

    public MyFrame()
    {
        setTitle( "JTable1" );
```

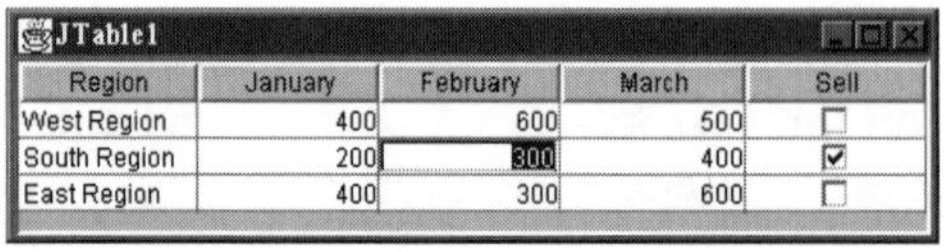

Figure 8-110

```
// Store the content pane in a variable for easier
// access.
JPanel contentPane = (JPanel)getContentPane();

// Components will all be added to this panel.
contentPane.setLayout( new BorderLayout() );

// Use a two-dimensional array to hold the row/column
// data.
Object dataValues[][] = new Object[3][5];

dataValues[0][0] = "West Region";
dataValues[0][1] = new Integer( 400 );
dataValues[0][2] = new Integer( 600 );
dataValues[0][3] = new Integer( 500 );
dataValues[0][4] = new Boolean( false );

dataValues[1][0] = "South Region";
dataValues[1][1] = new Integer( 200 );
dataValues[1][2] = new Integer( 300 );
dataValues[1][3] = new Integer( 400 );
dataValues[1][4] = new Boolean( true );

dataValues[2][0] = "East Region";
dataValues[2][1] = new Integer( 400 );
dataValues[2][2] = new Integer( 300 );
dataValues[2][3] = new Integer( 600 );
dataValues[2][4] = new Boolean( false );

// Put the column headers into an array.
String headers[] = new String[5];

headers[0] = "Region";
headers[1] = "January";
headers[2] = "February";
headers[3] = "March";
headers[4] = "Sell";

// Create the JTable with the just-created arrays.
myTable = new JTable( dataValues, headers );

// Make it so columns and rows may be selected at the
// same time.
myTable.setCellSelectionEnabled( true );

// Create a cell renderer that will display strings
// right-aligned.
RightTextRenderer renderer = new RightTextRenderer();

// Get the table column model.
TableColumnModel colModel = myTable.getColumnModel();

// Get the columns where the numbers will be and apply
// the right-aligned renderer to them.
```

```
        colModel.getColumn( 1 ).setCellRenderer( renderer );
        colModel.getColumn( 2 ).setCellRenderer( renderer );
        colModel.getColumn( 3 ).setCellRenderer( renderer );

        // Create a cell editor in which strings will be
        // right-aligned.
        JTextField editorField = new JTextField();
        editorField.setHorizontalAlignment(
                                    JTextField.RIGHT );
        DefaultCellEditor editor =
                    new DefaultCellEditor( editorField );

        // Apply the right-aligned editor to the columns with
        // the numbers.
        colModel.getColumn( 1 ).setCellEditor( editor );
        colModel.getColumn( 2 ).setCellEditor( editor );
        colModel.getColumn( 3 ).setCellEditor( editor );

        // Create a cell renderer that will look like a
        // centered check box.
        CheckBoxRenderer cbRenderer = new CheckBoxRenderer();

        // Apply the checkbox renderer to the column that has
        // boolean values.
        colModel.getColumn( 4 ).setCellRenderer( cbRenderer );

        // Create a cell editor that will work like a
        // centered checkbox.
        JCheckBox checkbox = new JCheckBox();
        checkbox.setHorizontalAlignment( JCheckBox.CENTER );
        DefaultCellEditor cbEditor =
                    new DefaultCellEditor( checkbox );

        // Apply the checkbox editor to the column with the
        // boolean values.
        colModel.getColumn( 4 ).setCellEditor( cbEditor );

        // Create a special scrollpane that will scroll the
        // table and headers together.
        JScrollPane scroller =
                JTable.createScrollPaneForTable( myTable );

        // Add the scrollpane to the main area on the content
        // pane.
        contentPane.add( "Center", scroller );
    }

    // This is a custom cell renderer that displays Boolean
    // values as center-aligned check boxes.
    private class CheckBoxRenderer extends JCheckBox
            implements TableCellRenderer
    {
        private Color mDefaultForeground;
        private Color mDefaultBackground;
```

```java
public CheckBoxRenderer()
{
   super();
   setHorizontalAlignment( JCheckBox.CENTER );

   // Set initial colors so se can invert when
   // selected.
   mDefaultForeground = getForeground();
   mDefaultBackground = SystemColor.window;
   setOpaque( true );
}


// This method is required, and returns the control
// fully configured for this cell.
public Component getTableCellRendererComponent(
                        JTable table,
                        Object value,
                        boolean isSelected,
                        boolean hasFocus,
                        int row,
                        int column )
{
   Boolean b = (Boolean)value;

   if ( b != null )
      setSelected( b.booleanValue() );

   if ( isSelected )
   {
      setBackground( mDefaultForeground );
      setForeground( mDefaultBackground );
   }
   else
   {
      setBackground( mDefaultBackground );
      setForeground( mDefaultForeground );
   }

   return this;
}
}

// This is a custom cell renderer that displays text
// right-aligned.
private class RightTextRenderer extends JLabel
      implements TableCellRenderer
{
   private Color mDefaultForeground;
   private Color mDefaultBackground;

   public RightTextRenderer()
   {
      super();
      setHorizontalAlignment( JLabel.RIGHT );
```

```
            // Store the colors so we can invert them when
            // the cell is selected.
            mDefaultForeground = getForeground();
            mDefaultBackground = SystemColor.window;
            setOpaque( true );
        }

        // This is required and returns a fully configured
        // label.
        public Component getTableCellRendererComponent(
                              JTable table,
                              Object value,
                              boolean isSelected,
                              boolean hasFocus,
                              int row,
                              int column )
    {
        if ( value != null )
          setText( value.toString() );
         else
          setText( "" );


        if ( isSelected )
        {
            setBackground( mDefaultForeground );
            setForeground( mDefaultBackground );
        }
        else
        {
            setBackground( mDefaultBackground );
            setForeground( mDefaultForeground );
        }

        return this;
        }
    }
}
```

Advanced Issues

EXAMPLE 8-71 Using Row Headers

This example illustrates the addition of row headers to a JTable. The main class is a subclass of JTable called MyTable. It creates a table the dimensions of the passed-in data array and gives it lettered column headers and numbered row headers like a spreadsheet. If you click a row header, the entire row is selected. Cell selection is enabled in the main table. Figure 8-111 shows the example after the table has been scrolled in both directions.

Figure 8-111

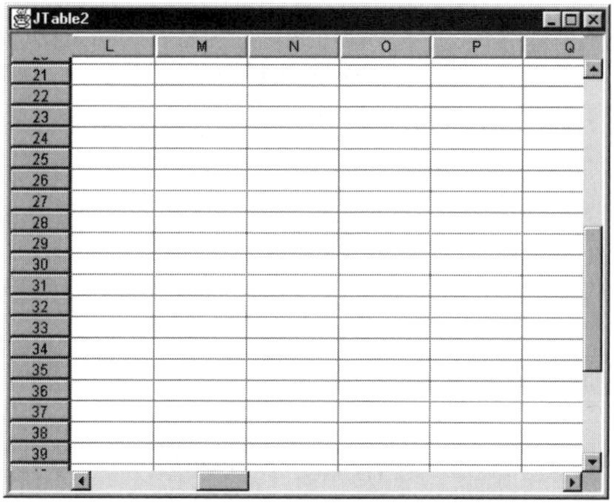

Figure 8-111

Important points to notice:

- MyTable includes an inner class called RowHeader, which is a subclass of JTable. RowHeader has a single column and uses a cell renderer based on a JButton.

- MyTable overrides the createScrollPaneForTable() static method to add the RowHeader as the ScrollPane's row header view.

- We have to explicitly set the preferred size of the RowHeader so we can use it to explicitly set the size of the row header view.

Here is the source code for the main frame class MyFrame (the MyTable source will follow):

```
import com.sun.java.swing.*;
import com.sun.java.swing.table.*;
import java.awt.*;

public class MyFrame extends JFrame
{
    public MyFrame()
    {
        setTitle( "JTable2" );

        // Store the content pane in a variable for easier
        // access.

        JPanel contentPane = (JPanel)getContentPane();

        // Components will all be added to this panel.

        contentPane.setLayout( new BorderLayout() );

        // Allocate a data array to load into the table.

        Object data[][] = new Object[50][50];
```

```
        // Create an instance of our custom table.

        MyTable table = new MyTable( data );

        // Make it so the columns don't try to all fit in the
        // visible area.

        table.setAutoResizeMode( JTable.AUTO_RESIZE_OFF );

        // Create a crollpane that will cause the row and
        // column headers to be displayed.

        JScrollPane scroller =
                MyTable.createScrollPaneForTable( table );

        // Make the scrollpane cover the content pane's main
        // area.

        contentPane.add( "Center", scroller );
    }
}
```

Here is the source code for MyTable.java:

```
import com.sun.java.swing.*;
import com.sun.java.swing.event.*;
import com.sun.java.swing.table.*;
import java.awt.*;
import java.awt.event.*;

public class MyTable extends JTable
{
    private RowHeader mRowHeaders;

    public MyTable( Object data[][] )
    {
        // Get the parent class (JTable) to create the main
        // table with default column headers.
        super( data, new Object[data[0].length] );

        // Create the row header component.
        mRowHeaders = new RowHeader( this );

        // Make it so the intersections of selected rows and
        // columns will be highlighted.
        setCellSelectionEnabled( true );
    }

    // Returns the row header component.
    public RowHeader getRowHeaders()
    {
        return mRowHeaders;
    }
```

```
                    // Overridden to add the row header component.
                    public static JScrollPane createScrollPaneForTable(
                                                        MyTable table )
                    {
                       // Get the row header component.
                       RowHeader rowHeaders = table.getRowHeaders();

                       // Create the scrollpane that will hold the table and
                       // its column headers.
                       JScrollPane scrollPane =
                                   JTable.createScrollPaneForTable( table );

                       // Create a viewport for the row headers.
                       JViewport view = new JViewport();

                       // Put the row headers in the viewport.
                       view.add( rowHeaders );

                       // Make the viewport's preferred size match the row
                       // header component's.
                       view.setPreferredSize(
                                       rowHeaders.getPreferredSize() );

                       // Use the row header view as the scrollpane's row
                       // header view.
                       scrollPane.setRowHeader( view );

                       return scrollPane;
                    }

                    // This is the definition of the row header component.
                    private class RowHeader extends JTable implements
                            ListSelectionListener
                    {
                       private JTable mParentTable;

                       public RowHeader( JTable parentTable )
                       {
                          // Create a JTable with the same number of rows as
                          // the parent table and one column.
                          super( new Object[parentTable.getRowCount()][1],
                                 new Object[1] );

                          // Store the parent table.
                          mParentTable = parentTable;

                          // Set the values of the row headers starting at 1.
                          for ( int i = 0; i < mParentTable.getRowCount();
                                i++ )
                          {
                             setValueAt( new Integer( i + 1 ), i, 0 );
                          }

                          // Create a button cell renderer.
                          ButtonRenderer rend = new ButtonRenderer();
```

```
        // Get the only table column.
        TableColumn col = getColumnModel().getColumn( 0 );

        // Use the cell renderer in the column.
        col.setCellRenderer( rend );

        // Set the row headers preferred width to that of
        // the button.
        Dimension dim = getPreferredSize();
        dim.width = 50;
        setPreferredSize( dim );

        // Listen for changes in the row header selection.
        getSelectionModel().addListSelectionListener(
                                                this );

        setBackground( SystemColor.control );
    }

    // Overridden to return false since the headers are
    // not editable.
    public boolean isCellEditable( int row, int col )
    {
        return false;
    }

    // This is called when the selection changes in the
    // row headers.
    public void valueChanged( ListSelectionEvent e )
    {
        // If the selection change resulted in any rows
        // being selected.

        // Clear the parent table's row selections.
        mParentTable.clearSelection();

        // Get the selected row headers.
        int rows[] = getSelectedRows();

        // For each selected row header, select the
        // corresponding row in the parent table.
        for ( int i = 0; i < rows.length; i++ )
        {
            mParentTable.addRowSelectionInterval(
                            rows[i], rows[i] );
        }

        // Reflect the change to the display.
        repaint();
    }
}

// This is a custom cell renderer that displays
// cells as buttons.
```

```
private class ButtonRenderer extends JButton
        implements TableCellRenderer
{
    public ButtonRenderer()
    {
        super();
    }

    // Required.  This configures the button for the
    // current cell, and returns it.
    public Component getTableCellRendererComponent(
                        JTable table,
                        Object value,
                        boolean isSelected,
                        boolean hasFocus,
                        int row,
                        int column )
    {
        if ( value != null )
            setText( value.toString() );

        return this;
    }
}
}
```

JTable's Public Methods

```
void addColumn(TableColumn aColumn)
```

Adds a column to the end of the JTable. The column's properties have been used to build a TableColumn that is used directly.

```
void addColumnSelectionInterval(int index0,int index1)
```

Says that the columns from 'index0' to 'index1' should be added to the list of selected columns as long as column selection is allowed and multiple selection is allowed.

```
void addRowSelectionInterval(int index0,int index1)
```

Says that the rows from 'index0' to 'index1' should be added to the list of selected rows as long as row selection is allowed and multiple selection is allowed.

```
void clearSelection()
```

Makes it so not columns or rows are selected.

```
void columnAdded(TableColumnModelEvent e)
```

Part of the TableColumnModelListener interface that allows the JTable to be notified when the model changes.

```
int columnAtPoint(Point point)
```

Finds the column in which the given point falls and returns its index.

```
void columnMarginChanged(ChangeEvent e)
```

Part of the TableColumnModelListener interface that allows the JTable to be notified when the model changes.

```
void columnMoved(TableColumnModelEvent e)
```

Part of the TableColumnModelListener interface that allows the JTable to be notified when the model changes.

```
void columnRemoved(TableColumnModelEvent e)
```

Part of the TableColumnModelListener interface that allows the JTable to be notified when the model changes.

```
void columnSelectionChanged(ListSelectionEvent e)
```

Part of the TableColumnModelListener interface that allows the JTable to be notified when the model changes.

```
int convertColumnIndexToModel(int viewColumnIndex)
```

Given a column index, this returns the index from the model.

```
int convertColumnIndexToView(int modelColumnIndex)
```

Given the model index of a column, this returns the corresponding index in the TableColumnModel.

```
void createDefaultColumnsFromModel()
```

This will clear the table and reload its cells from the JTable's TableModel.

```
static JScrollPane createScrollPaneForTable(JTable aTable)
```

This creates a JScrollPane that has the JTable as its main viewport and the JTable's JTableHeader as its column header viewport. The return value is the created JScrollPane.

```
boolean editCellAt(int rowIndex,int columnIndex)
```

Tells the JTable to activate the editor in the cell at the given row and column.

`boolean editCellAt(int rowIndex,int columnIndex,EventObject e)`

Just like the previous method except editing may be rejected depending on 'e'.

`void editingCanceled(ChangeEvent e)`

Tells the JTable that a cell editing session ended and the change was not saved.

`void editingStopped(ChangeEvent e)`

Tells the JTable that a cell editing session ended successfully.

`AccessibleContext getAccessibleContext()`

Returns a subclass of the abstract AccessibleContext class or null if the table doesn't have any accessible support.

`boolean getAutoCreateColumnsFromModel()`

This returns true if the JTable will automatically recreate its columns from its TableModel when the TableModel is replaced or is changed.

`int getAutoResizeMode()`

Returns the resize mode for the columns.

`TableCellEditor getCellEditor()`

Returns the TableCellEditor currently associated with the JTable.

`Rectangle getCellRect(int row,int column,boolean includeSpacing)`

Returns a rectangle that holds the bounds of the cell at the given column and row. Intercell spacing is included if desired.

`boolean getCellSelectionEnabled()`

Returns true if both rows and columns can be selected at the same time (although only the cells where the row/column selections intersect will be highlighted).

`TableColumn getColumn(Object identifier)`

Returns the TableColumn with the given identifier.

`Class getColumnClass(int column)`

Returns the class type of the column at the given column index.

```
int getColumnCount()
```

Returns the number of columns in the JTable.

```
TableColumnModel getColumnModel()
```

Returns the JTable's current TableColumnModel.

```
String getColumnName(int column)
```

Returns the name of the column at the given column index.

```
boolean getColumnSelectionAllowed()
```

Returns true if clicking on a column header selects the whole column.

```
TableCellEditor getDefaultEditor(Class columnClass)
```

This returns the TableCellEditor that is used by default in columns of the given type.

```
int getEditingColumn()
```

Returns the index of the column currently being edited, if any.

```
int getEditingRow()
```

Returns the index of the row currently being edited, if any.

```
TableCellRenderer getDefaultRenderer(Class columnClass)
```

This returns the TableCellRenderer that is used by default in columns of the given type.

```
Component getEditorComponent()
```

This returns the TableCellEditor's component if editing is currently going on.

```
Color getGridColor()
```

Returns the color that is used to draw the grid lines (if they are being drawn).

```
Dimension getIntercellSpacing()
```

Returns the current horizontal spacing between columns and vertical spacing between rows.

```
TableModel getModel()
```

Returns the JTable's current TableModel.

```
Dimension getPreferredScrollableViewportSize()
```

Returns the preferred size for the JTable when it is being scrolled.

```
int getRowCount()
```

Returns the current number of rows in the JTable.

```
int getRowHeight()
```

Returns the standard row height in pixels.

```
boolean getRowSelectionAllowed()
```

Returns true if a row becomes selected when a cell is clicked.

```
int getScrollableBlockIncrement(Rectangle visibleRect,int
        orientation,int direction)
```

Returns the amount that the JTable will scroll when the scrollbar with the given orientation is pressed between the thumbnail and the end arrow in the given direction.

```
boolean getScrollableTracksViewportHeight()
```

Returns true if the JTable will attempt to always fit its height to the visible rectangle's.

```
boolean getScrollableTracksViewportWidth()
```

Returns true if the JTable will attempt to always fit its width to the visible rectangle's.

```
int getScrollableUnitIncrement(Rectangle visibleRect,int
        orientation,int direction)
```

Returns the amount that the JTable will scroll when the scrollbar with the given orientation is pressed on the end arrow in the given direction.

```
int getSelectedColumn()
```

Returns the index of the last column selected.

```
int getSelectedColumnCount()
```

Returns the number of currently selected columns.

`int[] getSelectedColumns()`

Returns the indices of all currently selected columns.

`int getSelectedRow()`

Returns the index of the last row selected.

`int getSelectedRowCount()`

Returns the number of currently selected rows.

`int[] getSelectedRows()`

Returns the indices of all currently selected rows.

`Color getSelectionBackground()`

Returns the background color used for selected cells.

`Color getSelectionForeground()`

Returns the foreground color used for selected cells.

`ListSelectionModel getSelectionModel()`

Returns the JTable's current selection model.

`boolean getShowHorizontalLines()`

Returns true if horizontal grid lines are visible.

`boolean getShowVerticalLines()`

Returns true if vertical grid lines are visible.

`JTableHeader getTableHeader()`

Returns the JTableHeader component made up from the JTable's header information.

`String getToolTipText(MouseEvent event)`

This is overridden so cell and header renderers can display their own tool tips.

`TableUI getUI()`

Returns the JTable's current UI class.

```
String getUIClassID()
```

Returns the string that identifies the JTable so the look-and-feel knows which UI class to assign to it.

```
Object getValueAt(int rowIndex,int columnIndex)
```

Returns the value of the cell at the given row and column.

```
boolean isCellEditable(int rowIndex,int columnIndex)
```

Returns true if the cell at the given row and column is editable.

```
boolean isCellSelected(int row,int column)
```

Returns true if the cell at the given row and column is currently selected.

```
boolean isColumnSelected(int column)
```

Returns true if the column with the given index is currently selected.

```
boolean isEditing()
```

Returns true if a cell is currently being edited.

```
boolean isOpaque()
```

Returns true if the JTable paints all of its area.

```
boolean isRowSelected(int row)
```

Returns true if the given row is currently selected.

```
void moveColumn(int column,int targetColumn)
```

Moves the column at 'column' to the position of 'targetColumn'.

```
Component prepareEditor(TableCellEditor editor,int row,int column)
```

Configures the cell editor for the given cell.

```
void removeColumn(TableColumn aColumn)
```

Removes the given TableColumn from the JTable.

```
void removeColumnSelectionInterval(int index0,int index1)
```

Makes it so the columns from 'index0' to 'index1' are no longer selected.

`void removeEditor()`

Called when editing is finished.

`void removeRowSelectionInterval(int index0,int index1)`

Makes it so the rows from 'index0' to 'index1' inclusive are not selected.

`int rowAtPoint(Point point)`

Returns the index of the row in which the given point falls.

`void selectAll()`

Selects all cells in the JTable.

`void setAutoCreateColumnsFromModel(boolean createColumns)`

Specifies whether the JTable should automatically create TableColumns from its TableModel when the TableModel is replaced or changed.

`void setAutoResizeMode(int mode)`

Sets the columns' resize mode. The possible values are AUTO_RESIZE_ALL_COLUMNS, AUTO_RESIZE_LAST_COLUMN, and AUTO_RESIZE_OFF.

`void setCellEditor(TableCellEditor anEditor)`

Specifies the TableCellEditor to use for the JTable.

`void setCellSelectionEnabled(boolean newstate)`

Specifies whether rows and columns can be selected at the same time.

`void setColumnModel(TableColumnModel newModel)`

Replaces the JTable's TableColumnModel.

`void setColumnSelectionAllowed(boolean flag)`

Specifies whether column selection is allowed.

`void setColumnSelectionInterval(int index0,int index1)`

Tells the JTable that the columns from 'index0' to 'index1' should now be the only columns selected.

`void setDefaultEditor(Class columnClass,TableCellEditor editor)`

Sets the TableCellEditor to use by default for TableColumns that do not have an editor set.

```
void setDefaultRenderer(Class columnClass,TableCellRenderer renderer)
```

Sets the TableCellRenderer to use by default for TableColumns that do not have a renderer set.

```
void setEditingColumn(int aColumn)
```

Tells the JTable that a cell in the given column is being edited.

```
void setEditingRow(int aRow)
```

Tells the JTable that a cell in the given row is being edited.

```
void setGridColor(Color newColor)
```

Specifies the color that will be used to draw the grid, if it is drawn.

```
void setIntercellSpacing(Dimension newSpacing)
```

Specifies the spacing horizontally between columns and vertically between rows.

```
void setModel(TableModel newModel)
```

Replaces the JTable's TableModel with the given one.

```
void setPreferredScrollableViewportSize(Dimension size)
```

Specifies the JTable's preferred viewport size when scrolling.

```
void setRowHeight(int newHeight)
```

Specifies the pixel height to be used for rows.

```
void setRowSelectionAllowed(boolean flag)
```

Specifies whether entire rows may be selected.

```
void setRowSelectionInterval(int index0,int index1)
```

Tells the JTable that the rows from 'index0' to 'index1' should now be the only selected rows.

```
void setSelectionBackground(Color col)
```

Specifies the background color to use in selected cells.

`void setSelectionForeground(Color col)`

Specifies the foreground color to use in selected cells.

`void setSelectionMode(int selectionMode)`

Sets the ListSelectionModel mode for both rows and columns to one of SINGLE_SELECTION, SINGLE_INTERVAL_SELECTION, or MULTIPLE_INTERVAL_SELECTION.

`void setSelectionModel(ListSelectionModel newModel)`

Replaces the JTable's selection model with a new one.

`void setShowGrid(boolean b)`

Specifies whether the cell grid lines should be shown.

`void setShowHorizontalLines(boolean show)`

Specifies whether horizontal grid lines should be displayed.

`void setShowVerticalLines(boolean show)`

Specifies whether vertical grid lines should be displayed.

`void setTableHeader(JTableHeader newHeader)`

Replaces the current JTableHeader component with a new one.

`void setUI(TableUI ui)`

Gives the JTable a new look-and-feel class.

`void setValueAt(Object aValue,int rowIndex,int columnIndex)`

Finds the cell at the given row and column, and sets its value to the given value.

`void sizeColumnsToFit(boolean lastColumnOnly)`

This will attempt to squeeze column widths so all can be seen.

`void tableChanged(TableModelEvent e)`

Tells the JTable that its model has changed.

`void updateUI()`

Tells the JTable that the look-and-feel class has been changed.

```
void valueChanged(ListSelectionEvent e)
```

Tells the JTable that the selection state has changed.

JTextArea

JTextArea is a component used for entering multiple lines of text using a single font and color. For more advanced control of text attributes, use JTextPane.

Ancestors

```
java.lang.Object
    |
    +—java.awt.Component
            |
            +—java.awt.Container
                    |
                    +—com.sun.java.swing.JComponent
                            |
                            +—com.sun.java.swing.text.JTextComponent
                                    |
                                    +—com.sun.java.swing.JTextArea
```

NOTE: *For more information, see the "JTextComponent," "PlainDocument," "JTextPane," "JTextField," and "DefaultCaret" sections in this chapter. Also see Chapter 5, "JFC Documents and Text Components."*

Steps in Creating and Using JTextArea

1. Create the JTextArea. There are six constructors.

   Create an empty JTextArea:

   ```
   JTextArea area1 = new JTextArea();
   ```

   Create an empty JTextArea, specifying the number of rows and columns that should be able to be seen:

Figure 8-112
A typical JTextArea.

```
JTextArea0                        _ □ ×
Twas brillig and the slithy toves
Did gyre and gimbel in the wabe.
All mimsy were the borogoves
And the mome raths outgrabe.
```

```
JTextArea area2 = new JTextArea( 4, 50 );
```

Create a JTextArea, specifying its initial contents:

```
JTextArea area3 = new JTextArea( "Horatio Hornblower" );
```

Create a JTextArea, specifying its initial contents and number of rows and columns:

```
JTextArea area4 = new JTextArea( "Horatio Hornblower", 4, 50 );
```

Create a JTextArea, specifying the Document class that will track its contents.

```
PlainDocument doc = new PlainDocument();
JTextArea area5 = new JTextArea( doc );
```

Create a JTextArea, specifying the initial contents, the Document class that will track its contents, and the number of visible rows and columns:

```
PlainDocument doc = new PlainDocument();
JTextArea area5 = new JTextArea( doc, "My text", 4, 50 );
```

This last two constructors don't get much use normally, but may be useful in transferring a complete document from one text component to another. The document will normally be a PlainDocument since that is what the JTextArea uses.

2. Listen for when text is inserted into or removed from the JTextArea.

To be notified about text insertion and deletion, you need to get access to the JTextArea's document and tell it to notify you:

```
Document doc = area1.getDocument();
```

Tell the document to notify a class of changes. In this case the class to be notified is the current class:

```
doc.addDocumentListener( this );
```

Make the event-receiving class (MyFrame) implement the DocumentListener interface:

```
public class MyFrame extends JFrame implements DocumentListener
{
    .
    .
    .
    public void changedUpdate( DocumentEvent e )
    {
        // Called when attributes change, which won't happen much
        // in a PlainDocument.
    }

    public void insertupdate( DocumentEvent e )
    {
        // Called when text is inserted.
    }
```

```
public void removeUpdate( DocumentEvent e )
{
    // Called when text is removed.
}
}
```

3. Track a position in the JTextArea's text. This is useful if you want to track the start of a word as characters are added and removed in front of it. You tell the JTextArea's document to create a Position instance at a particular index, then at any time you can check that Position instance to see what index it is at.

   Get the JTextArea's document:

   ```
   Document doc = area1.getDocument();
   ```

   Create a Position instance that starts out at index 5.

   ```
   Position pos = doc.createPosition( 5 );
   ```

   You can get the Position's current index location using its getOffset() method. So, if a character is inserted at index 3, the Position created above would return 6 if you called its getOffset() method.

4. Set the accelerator key. This key, when pressed with a special key (Alt on many systems), causes the JTextArea to get the keyboard focus.

   ```
   area1.setFocusAccelerator( 'a' );
   ```

5. Track the caret as it moves. The caret is the thing, usually a flashing vertical line, that marks the current position in the JTextArea where text is inserted.

   Get the JTextArea's Caret:

   ```
   Caret caret = area1.getCaret();
   ```

   Specify a class that will be notified when the caret moves. In this case it is the current class:

   ```
   caret.addChangeListener( this );
   ```

   Make the event-receiving class (MyFrame) implement the ChangeListener interface:

   ```
   public class MyFrame extends JFrame implements ChangeListener
   {
       .
       .
       .
       public void stateChanged( ChangeEvent e )
       {
           // The caret has moved, so do what you need to do.
       }
   }
   ```

6. Get the contents of the JTextArea.

```
String contents = area1.getText();
```

You can also just get part of the contents by specifying an offset and a length. The following gets 5 characters starting at index 3:

```
String part = field1.getText( 3, 5 );
```

7. Set the contents of the JTextArea:

```
area1.setText( "Replacement text" );
```

8. Insert text at a specific index. This inserts "new text" at index 5:

```
area1.insert( "new text",5 );
```

9. Add text to the end of the JTextArea:

```
area1.append( "Added text" );
```

10. Replace a range of text with a new string. The following replaces the characters between indices 2 and four (starting before 2 and going to before 4) with the string "new text":

```
area1.replaceRange( "new text", 2, 4 );
```

11. Set the JTextArea's font. JTextArea uses only one font for its entire contents.

```
area1.setFont( new Font( "TimesRoman", Font.ITALIC, 16 ) );
```

12. Get the JTextArea's currently selected text (if any):

```
String selection = area1.getSelectedText();
```

13. Set the text and background colors. You can set the colors of both selected and unselected text.

Set the color for unselected text. Most look-and-feels use the foreground color, but it is not guaranteed:

```
area1.setForeground( Color.gray );
```

Set the background color for unselected text. Most look-and-feels use the background color, but it is not guaranteed:

```
area1.setBackground( Color.yellow );
```

Set the color for selected text:

```
area1.setSelectedTextColor( Color.red );
```

Set the background color for selected text:

```
area1.setSelectionColor( Color.black );
```

14. Specify an action to go with a certain keystroke. Each JTextArea has a Keymap which associates a KeyStroke with an Action. When the KeyStroke happens, the Action is triggered.

Create an Action class. This one deletes the JTextArea's currently selected text and puts it into the clipboard:

```
private class CutAction extends AbstractAction
{
    public void actionPerformed(ActionEvent e)
    {
        JTextArea ta = (JTextArea)e.getSource();

        // Move the selected text to the clipboard.
        ta.cut();
    }
}
```

Get the JTextArea's Keymap:

```
Keymap map = area1.getKeymap();
```

Get the Ctrl-C KeyStroke:

```
KeyStroke cut = KeyStroke.getKeyStroke( KeyEvent.VK_C,
                    ActionEvent.CTRL_MASK, false );
```

Create an instance of the Action:

```
CutAction cutAction = new CutAction();
```

Associate the KeyStroke and Action via the Keymap:

```
map.addActionForKeyStroke( cut, cutAction );
```

Put the changed Keymap back into the JTextArea:

```
area1.setKeymap( map );
```

Be warned that some KeyStrokes are used by the JTextArea itself.

Basic Code Examples

EXAMPLE 8-72 Basic Use of JTextArea

This example illustrates the use of a JTextArea. It contains a single JTextArea whose text color and background have been changed, for both selected and unselected text. It associates a "cut" action with the Ctrl-C key stroke, so highlighted text is moved into the clipboard. It changes the Caret color and also adds a DocumentListener to listen for changes in the JTextArea's contents. Below the JTextArea is a button which, when pressed, prints the JTextArea's contents to standard out. Figure 8-113 shows the example.

Figure 8-113

Here is the source code:

```
import com.sun.java.swing.*;
import com.sun.java.swing.text.*;
import com.sun.java.swing.border.*;
import com.sun.java.swing.event.*;
import java.awt.*;
import java.awt.event.*;

public class MyFrame extends JFrame implements
        ActionListener, DocumentListener
{
    private JTextArea mArea;

    public MyFrame()
    {
        setTitle( "JTextArea1" );

        // Store the content pane in a variable for easier
        // access.
        JPanel contentPane = (JPanel)getContentPane();

        // Components will all be added to this panel.
        contentPane.setLayout( new BorderLayout() );

        // Leave a blank area around the edges of the content
        // pane.
        contentPane.setBorder(
                    new EmptyBorder( 10, 10, 10, 10 ) );

        // Create a JTextArea with text.
        mArea = new JTextArea(
            "Twas brillig and the slithy toves\nDid gyre" );

        // Set the JTextArea's font.
        mArea.setFont( new Font( "TimesRoman",
                                    Font.PLAIN, 14 ) );

        // Set the text color.
        mArea.setForeground( Color.white );
```

```
        // Set the background color.
        mArea.setBackground( Color.black );

        // Set the color of selected text.
        mArea.setSelectedTextColor( Color.blue );

        // Set the color of selected text's background.
        mArea.setSelectionColor( Color.yellow );

        // Make it so this class is notified when text is
        // added or removed from the text area.
        mArea.getDocument().addDocumentListener( this );

        // Set the color of the caret so it shows up against
        // the black background.
        mArea.setCaretColor( Color.lightGray );

        // Get the text area's keymap.
        Keymap map = mArea.getKeymap();

        // Get the Ctrl-C keystroke.
        KeyStroke cut = KeyStroke.getKeyStroke( KeyEvent.VK_C,
                        ActionEvent.CTRL_MASK, false );

        // Create an instance of the action that will cut
        // selected text.
        CutAction cutAction = new CutAction();

        // Put the keystroke/action pair into the keymap.
        map.addActionForKeyStroke( cut, cutAction );

        // Put the keymap back in the text area.
        mArea.setKeymap( map );

        // Put the text area in a scroll pane.
        JScrollPane scroller = new JScrollPane( mArea );

        // Add the scroll pane so it takes most of the
        // content pane's area.
        contentPane.add( "Center", scroller );

        // Create a button that will cause a listing of the
        // text area's contents.
        JButton b = new JButton( "Press to Dump Contents" );

        // Make it so this class is notified when the button
        // is pressed.
        b.addActionListener( this );

        // Put the button at the bottom of the content pane.
        contentPane.add( "South", b );
    }

    // This is called when the button is pressed.
```

```java
public void actionPerformed( ActionEvent e )
{
    // Print out the text area's contents.
    System.out.println( mArea.getText() );
}


// This is called when the text area's document's
// attributes change.  This doesn't happen much in a
// PlainDocument.
public void changedUpdate( DocumentEvent e )
{
    System.out.println( "Changed" );
}


// This is called when text is inserted in the text area.
public void insertUpdate( DocumentEvent e )
{
    System.out.println( "Inserted" );
}


// This is called when text is removed from the text
// area.
public void removeUpdate( DocumentEvent e )
{
    System.out.println( "Removed" );
}


// This action cuts the selected text (if any) from a
// JTextArea.
private class CutAction extends AbstractAction
{
    public void actionPerformed(ActionEvent e)
    {
        JTextArea ta = (JTextArea)e.getSource();
        ta.cut();
    }
}
}
```

JTextArea's Public Methods

`void append(String str)`

Adds the given text to the end of the JTextArea's contents.

`AccessibleContext getAccessibleContext()`

Returns a subclass of AccessibleContext that gives access to the JTextArea's accessibility information.

`int getColumns()`

Returns the number of columns wide the JTextArea has been set to.

`int getLineCount()`

Returns the number of lines of text in the JTextArea.

`int getLineEndOffset(int n)`

Returns the offset to the end of the nth line.

`int getLineOffset(int offset)`

Returns the line in which the given offset falls.

`int getLineStartOffset(int n)`

Returns the offset to the start of the nth line.

`boolean getLineWrap()`

Returns true if line wrapping is enabled.

`Dimension getMinimumSize()`

Overridden so JTextArea can use its contents and settings to calculate the appropriate value.

`Dimension getPreferredScrollableViewportSize()`

Returns the JTextArea's preferred viewport size when being scrolled.

`int getRows()`

Returns the number of rows tall the JTextArea has been set to.

`boolean getScrollableTracksViewportWidth()`

Returns true if the JTextArea's width is forced to match the viewport width.

`int getScrollableUnitIncrement(Rectangle visibleRect, int orientation, int direction)`

Returns the scrolling unit increment for the given scroll bar orientation and scrolling direction.

```
int getTabSize()
```

Returns the number of characters in a tab.

```
String getUIClassID()
```

Returns the string that the look-and-feel uses to assign a UI class to the JTextArea.

```
void insert(String str,int pos)
```

Inserts the given string at the given position.

```
boolean isManagingFocus()
```

Overridden to return true.

```
void replaceRange(String str,int start,int end)
```

Replaces the range from 'start' to 'end' with the given string.

```
void setColumns(int columns)
```

Specifies the number of columns wide that the JTextArea would like to be displayed at.

```
void setFont(Font f)
```

Specifies the font to use when drawing the JTextArea's contents.

```
void setRows(int rows)
```

Specifies the number of rows tall the JTextArea would like to display at.

```
void setTabSize(int size)
```

Specifies the number of characters in a tab.

JTextComponent

JTextComponent is an abstract class that is the parent class for the JTextField, JTextArea, JTextPane, and JEditorPane classes. It defines much of the most useful behavior for those classes.

Ancestors

```
java.lang.Object
    |
    +—java.awt.Component
        |
        +—java.awt.Container
            |
            +—com.sun.java.swing.JComponent
                |
                +—com.sun.java.swing.text.JTextComponent
```

NOTE: *JTextComponent is in the com.sun.java.swing.text package.*

For more information, see the "JTextField," "JTextPane," "JTextArea," and "JEditorPane" sections in this chapter. Also see the "Text Entry and Editing" section in Chapter 7, "JFC by Concept," as well as Chapter 5, "JFC Documents and Text Components."

Basic Code Examples

EXAMPLE 8-73 Demonstrates Some of JTextComponent's Capabilities

This example has a preloaded JTextArea. You can press Ctrl-C to cut selected text into the clipboard, Ctrl-Insert to copy selected text into the clipboard, or Shift-Insert to paste text from the clipboard into the JTextArea at the caret position. The example also tracks a character, word, and sentence. There are three JRadioButtons that specify whether the displayed character, word, and sentence are before, at, or after the caret's position. Figure 8-114 shows the example as it first comes up.

NOTE: *The JTextArea's AccessibleText class is used to find the previous/current/next character/word/sentence. This has a bug that will cause exceptions and erratic behavior.*

Figure 8-114

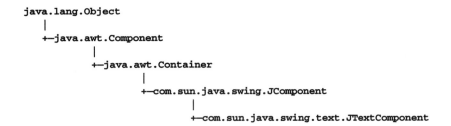

Important points to notice:

- A JTextArea is used since JTextComponent is abstract.

- A ChangeListener is used so we can keep track of when the caret changes position. This is needed in order to update the character, word, and sentence displays.

- We modify the JTextArea's Keymap to associate the Ctrl-C, Ctrl-Insert, and Shift-Insert with three custom Actions that execute the cut, copy, and paste operations.

Here is the source code:

```java
import com.sun.java.swing.*;
import com.sun.java.swing.event.*;
import com.sun.java.swing.border.*;
import com.sun.java.swing.text.*;
import com.sun.java.accessibility.*;
import java.awt.*;
import java.awt.event.*;

public class MyFrame extends JFrame implements ItemListener
{
    private JTextArea mArea1;
    private JRadioButton mBefore;
    private JRadioButton mAt;
    private JRadioButton mAfter;
    private JLabel mChar;
    private JLabel mWord;
    private JLabel mSentence;

    public MyFrame()
    {
        setTitle( "JTextComponent1" );

        // Store the content pane in a variable for easier
        // access.
        JPanel contentPane = (JPanel)getContentPane();

        // Components will all be added to this panel.
        contentPane.setLayout( new BorderLayout() );

        // Create the text area and load it up.
        mArea1 = new JTextArea(
            "Twas brillig and the slithy toves did gyre \n" +
            "and gimbel in the wabe.  \n" +
            "All mimsy were the borogoves and \n" +
            "the mome raths outgrabe." );

        // Make 4 rows visible.
        mArea1.setRows( 4 );

        // Set the background color for selected text.
        mArea1.setSelectionColor( Color.red );
```

```
// Set the caret to the start of the text.
mArea1.setCaretPosition( 0 );

// Make it so our CaretListener class is notified
// when the caret moves so we can update the CHAR,
// WORD, SENTENCE.
mArea1.getCaret().addChangeListener(
                            new CaretListener() );

// Make it so 'Ctrl-C' triggers a cut, 'Ctrl-Insert'
// triggers a copy, and 'Shift-Insert' triggers a
// paste.
Keymap map = mArea1.getKeymap();

KeyStroke cut = KeyStroke.getKeyStroke( KeyEvent.VK_C,
                ActionEvent.CTRL_MASK, false );
CutAction cutAction = new CutAction();
map.addActionForKeyStroke( cut, cutAction );

KeyStroke copy =
        KeyStroke.getKeyStroke( KeyEvent.VK_INSERT,
                ActionEvent.CTRL_MASK, false );
CopyAction copyAction = new CopyAction();
map.addActionForKeyStroke( copy, copyAction );

KeyStroke paste =
        KeyStroke.getKeyStroke( KeyEvent.VK_INSERT,
                ActionEvent.SHIFT_MASK, false );
PasteAction pasteAction = new PasteAction();
map.addActionForKeyStroke( paste, pasteAction );

// Load the changed keymap back into the text area.
mArea1.setKeymap( map );

// Add the text area at the top of the content pane.
contentPane.add( "North", mArea1 );

// Create a panel to show text parts.
JPanel partsPanel = new JPanel();
partsPanel.setBorder( new TitledBorder( "Parts" ) );

// Lay the radio buttons out above the labels.
partsPanel.setLayout( new BoxLayout( partsPanel,
                        BoxLayout.Y_AXIS ) );

// Create the panel for the radio buttons.
Box whichPanel = Box.createVerticalBox();

// Create the radio buttons and make it so this class
// is notified when their states change.
mBefore = new JRadioButton( "Before Index" );
mBefore.addItemListener( this );
mAt = new JRadioButton( "At Index" );
mAt.addItemListener( this );
```

```java
      mAfter = new JRadioButton( "After Index" );
      mAfter.addItemListener( this );

      // Put the radio buttons in a group.
      ButtonGroup group = new ButtonGroup();
      group.add( mBefore );
      group.add( mAt );
      group.add( mAfter );

      // Add the radio buttons to their panel.
      whichPanel.add( mBefore );
      whichPanel.add( mAt );
      whichPanel.add( mAfter );

      // Add the radio button panel to the parts pane.
      partsPanel.add( whichPanel );

      // Create a panel for the labels.
      Box textPanel = Box.createVerticalBox();

      // Create the labels.
      mChar = new JLabel();
      mWord = new JLabel();
      mSentence = new JLabel();

      // Add the labels to their panel.
      textPanel.add( mChar );
      textPanel.add( mWord );
      textPanel.add( mSentence );

      // Add the labels' panel to the parts pane.
      partsPanel.add( textPanel );

      // Add the parts pane to the content pane.
      contentPane.add( "Center", partsPanel );

      // Make it so the At index methods are used initially.
      mAt.setSelected( true );
   }

   // This is called when the radio buttons change state.
   public void itemStateChanged( ItemEvent e )
   {
      // Update the CHAR, WORD, SENTENCE display.
      updateParts();
   }

   private void updateParts()
   {
      // Get the caret;s current position.
      int caretPos = mArea1.getCaretPosition();

      AccessibleContext ac = mArea1.getAccessibleContext();
      AccessibleText at = ac.getAccessibleText();
```

```
            if ( at != null && mAt.isSelected() )
            {
               // Display the At values if At is selected.
               mChar.setText( "CHARACTER:  " + at.getAtIndex(
                       AccessibleText.CHARACTER, caretPos ) );
               mWord.setText( "WORD:  " + at.getAtIndex(
                       AccessibleText.WORD, caretPos ) );
               mSentence.setText( "SENTENCE:  " + at.getAtIndex(
                       AccessibleText.SENTENCE, caretPos ) );
            }
            else if ( at != null && mBefore.isSelected() )
            {
               // Display the Before values if Before is selected.
               mChar.setText( "CHARACTER:  " +
                       at.getBeforeIndex(
                       AccessibleText.CHARACTER, caretPos ) );
               mWord.setText( "WORD:  " + at.getBeforeIndex(
                       AccessibleText.WORD, caretPos ) );
               mSentence.setText( "SENTENCE:  " +
                       at.getBeforeIndex(
                       AccessibleText.SENTENCE, caretPos ) );
            }
            else if ( at != null && mAfter.isSelected() )
            {
               // Display the After values if After is selected.
               mChar.setText( "CHARACTER:  " + at.getAfterIndex(
                       AccessibleText.CHARACTER, caretPos ) );
               mWord.setText( "WORD:  " + at.getAfterIndex(
                       AccessibleText.WORD, caretPos ) );
               mSentence.setText( "SENTENCE:  " +
                       at.getAfterIndex(
                       AccessibleText.SENTENCE, caretPos ) );
            }

            // Reflect the changes on the display.
            mChar.invalidate();
            getContentPane().validate();
         }

         // This Action is triggered by Ctrl-C and cuts the
         // selected text into the clipboard.
         private class CutAction extends AbstractAction
         {
            public void actionPerformed( ActionEvent e )
            {
               mArea1.cut();
            }
         }

         // This Action is triggered by Ctrl-Insert and copies
         // the selected text into the clipboard.
         private class CopyAction extends AbstractAction
         {
            public void actionPerformed( ActionEvent e )
```

```
        {
            mArea1.copy();
        }
    }

    // This Action is triggered by Shift-Insert and pastes
    // the clipboard text into the text component at the
    // caret position.
    private class PasteAction extends AbstractAction
    {
        public void actionPerformed( ActionEvent e )
        {
            mArea1.paste();
        }
    }

    private class CaretListener implements ChangeListener
    {
        public void stateChanged( ChangeEvent e )
        {
            updateParts();
        }
    }
}
```

JTextComponent's Public Methods

`void addCaretListener(CaretListener l)`

Tells the text component to notify the given class when the caret changes.

`static Keymap addKeymap( String nm, Keymap parent)`

Adds a new Keymap as a child of '**parent**' and names it '**nm**'.

`void copy()`

Puts the text component's selected range (if any) into the system clipboard, leaving the text component unchanged.

`void cut()`

Puts the text component's selected range (if any) into the system clipboard, removing the selcted text from the text component.

`AccessibleContext getAccessibleContext()`

Returns a subclass of AccessibleContext, which gives access to the JTextComponent's accessibility information.

```
Action[] getActions()
```

Returns an array of all Actions associated with the text component. These are typically Actions assigned to specific key strokes like page up, etc.

```
Caret getCaret()
```

Returns the text component's current Caret class instance.

```
Color getCaretColor()
```

Returns the color being used to draw the text component's caret.

```
int getCaretPosition()
```

Returns the index at within the text component at which the caret currently resides.

```
Color getDisabledTextColor()
```

Returns the color in which to draw text when the text component is disabled.

```
Document getDocument()
```

Returns the text component's Document, which is where the text and associated information is stored.

```
char getFocusAccelerator()
```

Returns the character which, when pressed with a special key (Alt on some systems), causes the text component to get the keyboard focus.

```
Highlighter getHighlighter()
```

Returns the Highlighter that the text component is using to keep track of what text is highlighted, and to paint the highlights.

```
Keymap getKeymap()
```

Returns the text component's current mapping of KeyStrokes to Actions.

```
static Keymap getKeymap(String nm)
```

Returns the Keymap associated with 'nm'.

```
Insets getMargin()
```

Returns the space (on each side of the text component) between the edge of the component and the area in which text can be displayed.

`Dimension getPreferredScrollableViewportSize()`

Returns the text component's preferred viewport size when it is being scrolled.

`int getScrollableBlockIncrement(Rectangle visibleRect,int orientation,int direction)`

Given the size of the scroll area, the scrolling orientation, and the scroll direction, returns the amount the text component should be scrolled in that condition.

`boolean getScrollableTracksViewportHeight()`

Returns true if the height of the text component will match the height of its scroll pane's visible area, thus inhibiting vertical scrolling.

`boolean getScrollableTracksViewportWidth()`

Returns true if the width of the text component will match the width of its scroll pane's visible area, thus inhibiting horizontal scrolling.

`int getScrollableUnitIncrement(Rectangle visibleRect, int orientation,int direction)`

Given the size of the scroll area, the scrolling orientation, and the scroll direction, returns the amount the text component should be scrolled in those conditions.

`String getSelectedText()`

Returns the currently selected string, if any.

`Color getSelectedTextColor()`

Returns the color in which selected text is drawn.

`Color getSelectionColor()`

Returns the color in which selected text is highlighted.

`int getSelectionEnd()`

Returns the index immediately following where the current selection (if any) stops. This depends on the direction of selection. That is, if the selection was made by dragging the mouse from right to left, this method returns the index of the left-most selected character. Otherwise, it returns the index immediately following the right-most selected character.

`int getSelectionStart()`

Returns the index where the current text selection starts (if any).

`String getText()`

Returns the complete contents of the text component.

`String getText(int offs,int len)`

Returns a segment of the text component's contents, starting at the given offset and having the given length.

`TextUI getUI()`

Returns the text component's look-and-feel class.

`boolean isEditable()`

Returns true if the user can edit the text component's contents.

`boolean isFocusTraversable()`

Returns true if the text component can get the keyboard focus.

`boolean isOpaque()`

Returns true if the text component will draw its entire area.

`static void loadKeymap(Keymap map, JTextComponent.KeyBinding bindings[], Action actions[] )`

Loads the given Keymap with the given key binding/Action pairs.

`Rectangle modelToView(int pos)`

Converts the given index in the model to a rectangular area in the view.

`void moveCaretPosition(int pos)`

Moves the caret to the given position, causing a highlight from the previous position to the new one.

`void paste()`

Inserts the current contents of the system clipboard into the text component at the caret position.

`void read(Reader in,Object desc)`

Causes the text component to take its contents from the given reader. The 'desc' parameter is a description of the type of stream the reader represents. This information may or may not be used.

```
void removeCaretListener(CaretListener l)
```

Tells the text component to stop notifying the given class when the caret changes.

```
static Keymap removeKeymap(String nm)
```

Removes the Keymap associated with 'nm'.

```
void replaceSelection(String content)
```

Replaces the text component's currently selected text (if any) with the given string.

```
void select(int selectionStart,int selectionEnd)
```

Causes the text between the given indices to be selected.

```
void selectAll()
```

Causes the entire contents of the text component to be selected.

```
void setCaret(Caret c)
```

Replaces the text component's **caret** class instance.

```
void setCaretColor(Color c)
```

Specifies the color used to draw the caret.

```
void setCaretPosition(int position)
```

Specifies a new caret position.

```
void setDisabledTextColor(Color c)
```

Specifies the color that should be used to draw the text when the text component is disabled.

```
void setDocument(Document doc)
```

Replaces the text component's document, where its contents and associated information is stored.

```
void setEditable(boolean b)
```

Specifies whether the user can edit the text component's contents.

void setFocusAccelerator(char aKey)

Specifies the character which, when pressed with a special key (Alt on some systems), causes the text component to get the keyboard focus.

void setHighlighter(Highlighter h)

Replaces the Highlighter class instance that the text component uses to keep track of which text is highlighted and to draw the highlights.

void setKeymap(Keymap map)

Replaces the text component's Keymap which it uses to keep track of which KeyStrokes are associated with which Actions.

void setMargin(Insets m)

Specifies the space, on each side of the text component, between the edge of the component and the area in which its contents may be drawn.

void setOpaque(boolean o)

Tells the text component to draw its background rectangle.

void setSelectedTextColor(Color c)

Specifies the color that should be used to draw selected text.

void setSelectionColor(Color c)

Specifies the color that should be used to highlight the selected text.

void setSelectionEnd(int selectionEnd)

Specifies the index at which the current selection should end.

void setSelectionStart(int selectionStart)

Specifies the index at which the current selection should start.

void setText(String t)

Replaces the text component's string contents.

void setUI(TextUI ui)

Specifies the look-and-feel class the text component will use.

```
void updateUI()
```

Tells the text component that the look-and-feel class has changed.

```
int viewToModel(Point pt)
```

Converts the given point in the view to an index in the model.

```
void write(Writer out)
```

Causes the text component to write its contents out to the given writer.

JTextField

JTextField is the component used to edit single-line text strings (see Figure 8-115). It is often used in dialogs to get simple text input.

Ancestors

```
java.lang.Object
    |
    +--java.awt.Component
        |
        +--java.awt.Container
            |
            +--com.sun.java.swing.JComponent
                |
                +--com.sun.java.swing.text.JTextComponent
                    |
                    +--com.sun.java.swing.JTextField
```

NOTE: *For more information, see the "JTextComponent," "JTextArea," "JTextPane," "PlainDocument," and "DefaultCaret" sections in this chapter, Chapter 5, "JFC Documents and Text Components," and the "Text Entry and Editing" section in Chapter 7, "JFC by Concept."*

Figure 8-115
A typical JTextField
with a JLabel.

Steps in Creating and Using JTextField

1. Create the JTextField. There are five constructors.

   Create an empty JTextField:

   ```
   JTextField field1 = new JTextField();
   ```

   Create an empty JTextField, specifying the number of columns that should be able to be seen:

   ```
   JTextField field2 = new JTextField( 20 );
   ```

   Create a JTextField, specifying its initial contents:

   ```
   JTextField field3 = new JTextField( "Horatio Hornblower" );
   ```

   Create a JTextField, specifying its initial contents and number of columns:

   ```
   JTextField field4 = new JTextField( "Horatio Hornblower", 20 );
   ```

   Create a JTextField, specifying the initial contents, the Document that will track its contents, and the number of visible columns:

   ```
   PlainDocument doc = new PlainDocument();
   JTextField field5 = new JTextField( doc, "My text", 20 );
   ```

   This last constructor doesn't get much use normally, but may be useful in transferring a complete document from one text component to another. The document will normally be a PlainDocument since that is what the JTextField uses.

2. Listen for when the user presses Enter. You will often want to be notified when the user has finished input into a JTextField. For most UI's, when Enter is pressed, the JTextField generates an ActionEvent.

   Tell the JTextField which class it should notify when the user presses Enter. In this case it is the current class:

   ```
   field1.addActionListener( this );
   ```

   Give the JTextField a command string that will be delivered with its ActionEvents. If none is specified, then the contents of the JTextField will be delivered:

   ```
   field1.setActionCommand( "text field" );
   ```

   Make the event-receiving class (MyFrame) implement the ActionListener interface:

   ```
   public class MyFrame extends JFrame implements ActionListener
   {
       .
       .
       .
   ```

```
public void actionPerformed( ActionEvent e )
{
    // The command string delivered with the ActionEvent
    // contains the new value of the JTextField.
    System.out.println( "Value is:  " + e.getActionCommand() );
}
}
```

3. Listen for when text is inserted into or removed from the JTextField. You will be notified after the fact, so you cannot use these events to keep the JTextField from displaying invalid characters.

To be notified about text insertion and deletion, you need to get access to the JTextField's document and tell it to notify you:

```
Document doc = field1.getDocument();
```

Tell the document to notify a class of changes. In this case the class to be notified is the current class:

```
doc.addDocumentListener( this );
```

Make the event-receiving class (MyFrame) implement the DocumentListener interface:

```
public class MyFrame extends JFrame implements DocumentListener
{
    .
    .
    .
    public void changedUpdate( DocumentEvent e )
    {
        // Called when attributes change, which won't happen much
        // in a PlainDocument.
    }

    public void insertupdate( DocumentEvent e )
    {
        // Called when text is inserted.
    }

    public void removeUpdate( DocumentEvent e )
    {
        // Called when text is removed.
    }
}
```

4. Track a position in the JTextField's text. This is useful if you want to track the start of a word as characters are added and removed in front of it. You tell the JTextField's document to create a Position instance at a particular index, then at any time you can check that Position instance to see what index it is at.

Get the JTextField's document:

```
Document doc = field1.getDocument();
```

Create a Position instance that starts out at index 5.

```
Position pos = doc.createPosition( 5 );
```

You can get the Position's current index location using its getOffset() method. So, if a character is inserted at index 3, the Position created above would return 6 if you called its getOffset() method.

5. Change the JTextField's border. The look-and-feel defines a JTextField's border, often as a lowered BevelBorder. You can set the border to a new one to achieve a different effect. For example, if you want the field to blend into its container, you might give it an EmptyBorder and change its background color to match its container's.

```
field1.setBorder( new EmptyBorder( 0, 0, 0, 0 ) );
field1.setBackground( parentContainer.getBackground() );
```

6. Set the accelerator key. This key, when pressed with a special key (Alt on many systems), causes the JTextField to get the keyboard focus.

```
field1.setFocusAccelerator( 'a' );
```

7. Track the caret as it moves. The caret is the thing, usually a flashing vertical line, that marks the current position in the JTextField where text is inserted.

Get the JTextField's Caret:

```
Caret caret = field1.getCaret();
```

Specify a class that will be notified when the caret moves. In this case it is the current class:

```
caret.addChangeListener( this );
```

Make the event-receiving class (MyFrame) implement the ChangeListener interface:

```
public class MyFrame extends JFrame implements ChangeListener
{
    .
    .
    .
    public void stateChanged( ChangeEvent e )
    {
        // The caret has moved, so do what you need to do.
    }
}
```

8. Get the contents of the JTextField.

```
String contents = field1.getText();
```

You can also just get part of the contents by specifying an offset and a length. The following gets 5 characters starting at index 3:

```
String part = field1.getText( 3, 5 );
```

9. Set the contents of the JTextField:

```
field1.setText( "Replacement text" );
```

10. Insert text at a specific index. This is done via the JTextField's document.

Get the document:

```
Document doc = field1.getDocument();
```

Insert the text. This inserts "new text" at index 5:

```
doc.insertString( 5, "new text", null );
```

The last argument is null because attributes don't do much in a PlainDocument.

11. Set the JTextField's font. JTextField uses only one font for its entire contents.

```
field1.setFont( new Font( "TimesRoman", Font.ITALIC, 16 ) );
```

12. Get the JTextField's currently selected text (if any):

```
String selection = field1.getSelectedText();
```

13. Set the text and background colors. You can set the colors of both selected and unselected text.

Set the color for unselected text. Most look-and-feels use the foreground color, but it is not guaranteed:

```
field1.setForeground( Color.gray );
```

Set the background color for unselected text. Most look-and-feels use the background color, but it is not guaranteed:

```
field1.setBackground( Color.yellow );
```

Set the color for selected text:

```
field1.setSelectedTextColor( Color.red );
```

Set the background color for selected text:

```
field1.setSelectionColor( Color.black );
```

14. Specify an action to go with a certain keystroke. Each JTextField has a Keymap which associates a KeyStroke with an Action. When the KeyStroke happens, the Action is triggered.

Create an Action class. This one deletes the JTextField's currently selected text and puts it into the clipboard:

```
private class CutAction extends AbstractAction
{
   public void actionPerformed(ActionEvent e)
   {
      JTextField tf = (JTextField)e.getSource();

      // Move the selected text to the clipboard.
      tf.cut();
   }
}
```

Get the JTextField's Keymap:

```
Keymap map = field1.getKeymap();
```

Get the Ctrl-C KeyStroke:

```
KeyStroke cut = KeyStroke.getKeyStroke( KeyEvent.VK_C,
             ActionEvent.CTRL_MASK, false );
```

Create an instance of the Action:

```
CutAction cutAction = new CutAction();
```

Associate the KeyStroke and Action via the Keymap:

```
map.addActionForKeyStroke( cut, cutAction );
```

Put the changed Keymap back into the JTextField:

```
field1.setKeymap( map );
```

Be warned that some KeyStrokes are used by the JTextField itself.

15. Make the text right-aligned in the JTextField. It is left-aligned by default:

```
field1.setHorizontalAlignment( JTextField.RIGHT );
```

Basic Code Examples

EXAMPLE 8-74 Variations on JTextField

This example illustrates many of the concepts discussed above. It has six JTextFields, each with a descriptive label. Figure 8-116 shows the example as it looks when it first comes up.

Important points to notice:

■ We have to set the label and text field Y alignments to match so they align vertically.

■ The fourth text field uses a custom subclass of AbstractAction along with the text field's Keymap to make Ctrl-C cut selected text. Notice that KeyEvent.VK_C was used instead of just 'c'.

Figure 8-116

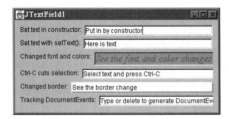

Here is the source code:

```
import com.sun.java.swing.*;
import com.sun.java.swing.border.*;
import com.sun.java.swing.text.*;
import com.sun.java.swing.event.*;
import java.awt.*;
import java.util.*;
import java.awt.event.*;

public class MyFrame extends JFrame implements
        DocumentListener
{
    JPanel mPanel;

    public MyFrame()
    {
        setTitle( "JTextField1" );

        // Store the content pane in a variable for easier
        // access.
        mPanel = (JPanel)getContentPane();

        // Components will all be added to this panel.
        mPanel.setLayout( new BoxLayout( mPanel,
                        BoxLayout.Y_AXIS ) );

        // Leave empty space around the edge of the content
        // pane.
        mPanel.setBorder( new EmptyBorder( 10, 10, 10, 10 ) );

        // The first label/text field combination.
        {
            Box pane = Box.createHorizontalBox();

            JLabel lbl =
                    new JLabel( "Set text in constructor:   " );
            pane.add( lbl );

            // Create the JTextField, specifying text in the
            // constructor.
            JTextField t1 =
                    new JTextField( "Put in by constructor" );

            // Add the text field to the box.
```

```
    pane.add( t1 );

    // Add the box to the content pane, and pad
    // between it and the next.
    mPanel.add( pane );
    mPanel.add( Box.createVerticalGlue() );
}

// The second label/text field combination.
{
    Box pane = Box.createHorizontalBox();

    JLabel lbl =
            new JLabel( "Set text with setText():  " );
    pane.add( lbl );

    // Create an empty text field.
    JTextField t1 = new JTextField();

    // Set the text field's contents.
    t1.setText( "Here is text" );

    // Add the text field to the box.
    pane.add( t1 );

    // Add the box to the content pane and leave some
    // space between it and the next.
    mPanel.add( pane );
    mPanel.add( Box.createVerticalGlue() );
}

// The third label/text field combination.
{
    Box pane = Box.createHorizontalBox();

    JLabel lbl =
            new JLabel( "Changed font and colors:  " );
    pane.add( lbl );

    // Create the text field and give it some text.
    JTextField t1 = new JTextField(
                "See the font and color changes" );

    // Set the font.
    t1.setFont( new Font( "TimesRoman",
                        Font.ITALIC, 18 ) );

    // Set the text color.
    t1.setForeground( Color.red );

    // Set the background color.
    t1.setBackground( Color.green );

    // Add the text field to the box.
    pane.add( t1 );
```

```java
    // Add the box to the content pane and leave some
    // space.
    mPanel.add( pane );
    mPanel.add( Box.createVerticalGlue() );
}

// The fourth label/text field combination.
{
    Box pane = Box.createHorizontalBox();

    JLabel lbl =
            new JLabel( "Ctrl-C cuts selection:   " );
    pane.add( lbl );

    // Create a text field and give it some text.
    JTextField t1 = new JTextField(
                    "Select text and press Ctrl-C" );

    // Get the text field's keymap.
    Keymap map = t1.getKeymap();

    // Get the Ctrl-C keystroke.
    KeyStroke cut = KeyStroke.getKeyStroke(
                    KeyEvent.VK_C,
                    ActionEvent.CTRL_MASK, false );

    // Create an instance of the action that will cut
    // selected text.
    CutAction cutAction = new CutAction();

    // Put the keystroke/action pair into the keymap.
    map.addActionForKeyStroke( cut, cutAction );

    // Put the keymap back in the text field.
    t1.setKeymap( map );

    // Add the text field to the box.
    pane.add( t1 );

    // Add the box to the content pane and leave some
    // space.
    mPanel.add( pane );
    mPanel.add( Box.createVerticalGlue() );
}

// The fifth label/text field combination.
{
    Box pane = Box.createHorizontalBox();

    JLabel lbl = new JLabel( "Changed border:   " );
    pane.add( lbl );

    // Create a text field and give it some text.
    JTextField t1 = new JTextField(
                        "See the border change" );
```

```
                     // Change the border.
                     t1.setBorder( new BevelBorder(
                                           BevelBorder.RAISED ) );

                     // Add the text field to the box.
                     pane.add( t1 );

                     // Add the box to the content pane and leave some
                     // space.
                     mPanel.add( pane );
                     mPanel.add( Box.createVerticalGlue() );
                 }

                 // The sixth label/text field combination.
                 {
                     Box pane = Box.createHorizontalBox();

                     JLabel lbl =
                            new JLabel( "Tracking DocumentEvents:  " );
                     pane.add( lbl );

                     // Create a text field and give it some text.
                     JTextField t1 = new JTextField(
                         "Type or delete to generate DocumentEvents" );

                     // Make it so this class is notified when text is
                     // inserted into or removed from the text field.
                     t1.getDocument().addDocumentListener( this );

                     // Add the text field to the box.
                     pane.add( t1 );

                     // Add the box to the content pane.
                     mPanel.add( pane );
                 }
             }

             // This is called when attributes change in the document.
             // This won't generally happen in a PlainDocument.
             public void changedUpdate( DocumentEvent e )
             {
                 System.out.println( "Changed:  " + e );
             }

             // This is called when text is inserted into a document.
             public void insertUpdate( DocumentEvent e )
             {
                 System.out.println( "Inserted" );
             }

             // This is called when text is deleted from a document.
             public void removeUpdate( DocumentEvent e )
             {
                 System.out.println( "Removed" );
```

```
        }

        // This action cuts the selected text (if any) from a
        // JTextField.
        private class CutAction extends AbstractAction
        {
            public void actionPerformed(ActionEvent e)
            {
                JTextField tf = (JTextField)e.getSource();
                tf.cut();
            }
        }
    }
```

Advanced Issues

EXAMPLE 8-75 Making a Digit-Only Text Field

This example shows how to extend JTextField to make a text field that only accepts digits as input. All other characters are ignored. Figure 8-117 shows the example after some keys have been pressed.

Important points to notice:

■ The key to this is overriding the processKeyEvent() method in the JTextField subclass. This lets us catch key strokes before the component can display them or add them to its contents. What we do is check each key stroke that comes to the component. If the key stroke is a digit or Enter (so we can trigger ActionEvents), we let JTextField process it as usual. All other key strokes are ignored.

■ The custom JTextField is a private class within the main frame class MyFrame. It could as easily have been a public class in its own .java file.

Here is the source code:

```
import com.sun.java.swing.*;
import com.sun.java.swing.border.*;
import com.sun.java.swing.text.*;
import java.awt.*;
import java.awt.event.*;

public class MyFrame extends JFrame implements
        ActionListener
{
    public MyFrame()
    {
```

Figure 8-117

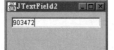

```
                      setTitle( "JTextField2" );

                      // Store the content pane in a variable for easier
                      // access.
                      JPanel contentPane = (JPanel)getContentPane();

                      // Components will all be added to this panel.
                      contentPane.setLayout( new BorderLayout() );

                      // Leave blank space around the edge of the content
                      // pane.
                      contentPane.setBorder(
                                  new EmptyBorder( 10, 10, 10, 10 ) );

                      // Create our custom text field.
                      MyTextField field = new MyTextField();

                      // Listen for when <Enter> is pressed.
                      field.addActionListener( this );

                      // Place the text field at the top of the content
                      // pane.
                      contentPane.add( "North", field );
                  }

                  // This is called when the user presses <Enter> in the
                  // text field.
                  public void actionPerformed( ActionEvent e )
                  {
                      System.out.println( "Contents:  " +
                                          e.getActionCommand() );
                  }

                  private class MyTextField extends JTextField
                  {
                      // Override this method so we can catch key events
                      // before the characters are drawn.  We ignore all
                      // key strokes except digits and <Enter>.  We let
                      // the superclass process those key strokes as usual.
                      protected void processKeyEvent( KeyEvent e )
                      {
                          // We only pay attention to digits and <Enter> and
                          // only when they have no modifiers.
                          if ( e.getModifiers() == 0 )
                          {
                              int keyChar = e.getKeyChar();

                              // Check to see if the key stroke is a digit or
                              // <Enter>.
                              if ( keyChar >= '0' && keyChar <= '9' ||
                                  keyChar == '\n' )
                              {
                                  // If it is a digit or <Enter>, process it
                                  // as usual.
                                  super.processKeyEvent( e );
```

```
                              }
                         }
                     }
                 }
             }
```

JTextField's Public Methods

`void addActionListener(ActionListener l)`

Tells the JTextField to notify the given class when the user presses Enter.

`AccessibleContext getAccessibleContext()`

Returns a subclass of AccessibleContext that gives access to the JTextField's accessibility information.

`Action[] getActions()`

Returns an array containing all of the Actions associated with the JTextField.

`int getColumns()`

Returns the number of columns wide the JTextField should be.

`int getHorizontalAlignment()`

Returns the JTextField's current text alignment.

`BoundedRangeModel getHorizontalVisibility()`

Returns the BoundedRangeModel that defines how the text scrolls when it is too long to all be seen at once.

`Dimension getMinimumSize()`

Overridden to return the minimum size the JTextField thinks it should be displayed at.

`Dimension getPreferredSize()`

Overridden to return the size at which the JTextField would like to be displayed.

`int getScrollOffset()`

Returns the offset to the first visible character.

`String getUIClassID()`

Returns the string that the look-and-feel uses to assign a UI class to use with the JTextField.

`void postActionEvent()`

Causes an ActionEvent to be generated and sent to all ActionListeners.

`void removeActionListener(ActionListener l)`

Tells the JTextField to stop notifying the given class when the user presses Enter.

`void scrollRectToVisible(Rectangle r)`

Overridden for JTextField's horizontal scrolling.

`void setActionCommand(String command)`

Specifies the string to be delivered with ActionEvents that the JTextField generates. If this is not set, then the contents of the JTextField will be delivered.

`void setColumns(int columns)`

Specifies the number of columns to display. Affects what getPreferredSize() returns.

`void setFont(Font f)`

Specifies the font to use for the JTextField's contents.

`void setHorizontalAlignment(int align)`

Specifies whether the text is left-aligned, center-aligned, or right-aligned within the JTextField. Must be: LEFT, CENTER, or RIGHT.

`void setScrollOffset(int scrollOffset)`

Causes the JTextField to be scrolled to 'scroll offset.'

JTextPane

JTextPane is a text component that you can use to display complex documents that use word wrapping, multiple fonts, and icons (see Figure 8-118). JTextPane stores its contents and associated information in a class that implements the StyledDocument interface—usually DefaultStyledDocument.

Figure 8-118
A typical JTextPane.

Ancestors

```
java.lang.Object
    |
    +—java.awt.Component
            |
            +—java.awt.Container
                    |
                    +—com.sun.java.swing.JComponent
                            |
                            +—com.sun.java.swing.text.JTextComponent
                                    |
                                    +—com.sun.java.swing.JEditorPane
                                            |
                                            +—com.sun.java.swing.JTextPane
```

NOTE: *For more information, see the "JTextComponent," "JTextArea," "JTextField," "DefaultStyledDocument," "SimpleAttributeSet," "DefaultCaret," and "Element" sections in this chapter. Also see Chapter 13, "JFC Integration Example 4—A Simple Word Processor," as well as Chapter 5, "JFC Documents and Text Components."*

Steps in Creating and Using JTextPane

1. Create a JTextPane. There are two constructors.

   Create an empty JTextPane that will create its own DefaultStyledDocument:

   ```
   JTextPane pane = new JTextPane();
   ```

   Create a StyledDocument and tell the new JTextPane to use it instead of creating its own:

   ```
   // Create a DefaultStyledDocument.
   DefaultStyledDocument doc = new DefaultStyledDocument();

   // Create an attribute set for the text we are about to add.
   SimpleAttributeSet set = new SimpleAttributeSet();
   StyleConstants.setFontFamily( set, "TimesRoman" );
   StyleConstants.setForeground( set, Color.red );

   // Add some text.  We have to catch BadLocationException.
   try
   ```

```
{
    doc.insertString( 0, "This is TimesRoman text", set );
}
catch ( BadLocationException ex )
{
    System.out.println( ex );
}

// Create the JTextPane.
JTextPane pane = new JTextPane( doc );
```

2. Set the character attributes that will be used for insertions at the current caret position, or for any currently selected text.

```
// Create the attribute set to use.
SimpleAttributeSet newSet = new SimpleAttributeSet();
StyleConstants.setFontFamily( newSet, "Courier" );
StyleConstants.setFontSize( newSet, 20 );

// Apply the attribute set.
pane.setCharacterAttributes( newSet, true );
```

The setCharacterAttributes() method's second parameter defines how the new set of attributes interacts with the existing set at the position (or range) where we are setting attributes. If true, the new attributes totally replace the old ones. If false, all of the new attributes are used, but any attributes that are not set in the new attribute set but are set in the old attribute set will also be used.

3. Set the attributes to be used for a paragraph. Paragraph attributes are overridden by character attributes, so a specific paragraph attribute will only be used if it hasn't been defined as a character attribute.

```
// Create the attribute set to use.
SimpleAttributeSet newSet = new SimpleAttributeSet();
StyleConstants.setFontFamily( newSet, "Courier" );
StyleConstants.setForeground( Color.red );

// Apply the attribute set.
pane.setParagraphAttributes( newSet, true );
```

The new attributes are applied to the paragraph at the current caret position, or to all paragraphs that the selection touches if there is a current selection.

4. Insert a component into the document. JTextPane gives you the ability to insert working components into your documents.

```
// Create the component.
JButton newButton = new JButton( "Button" );

// Change the vertical alignment to fit is with text on the same
// line.
newButton.setAlignmentY( 0.5f );

// Insert the component at the caret or as a replacement for
```

```
// selected text, if any.
mPane.insertComponent( newButton );
```

The added button is a real JButton. It will press in, and if you want to know when it is pressed, just add an ActionListener as usual.

5. Insert an icon into the JTextPane. When an icon is placed on the same line as text, the icon appears at the cursor position, but the text is aligned with the bottom of the icon. So, if the icon is large, you may want to put it on a line by itself.

```
// Create the icon.
ImageIcon icon = new ImageIcon( "parrots.jpg" );

// Insert the icon.
mPane.insertIcon( icon );
```

6. Insert text into the JTextPane. If you want to insert a text string at a specific position in the JTextPane, you can do so through its Document. You can either specify attributes for it to use, or it will use defaults.

```
// Get the character attributes at the insertion position.
StyledDocument doc = mPane.getStyledDocument();
Element elemAtPos = doc.getCharacterElement( 5 );
AttributeSet setAtPos = elemAtPos.getAttributes();

// Insert the text.
doc.insertString( 5, " new text ", setAtPos );
```

7. Listen for when text is inserted into or removed from, or when attributes change in the JTextPane.

To be notified about text insertion and deletion, you need to get access to the JTextPane's document and tell it to notify you:

```
Document doc = mPane.getDocument();
```

Tell the document to notify a class of changes. In this case the class to be notified is the current class:

```
doc.addDocumentListener( this );
```

Make the event-receiving class (MyFrame) implement the DocumentListener interface:

```
public class MyFrame extends JFrame implements DocumentListener
{
    .
    .
    .
    public void changedUpdate( DocumentEvent e )
    {
        // Called when attributes change.
    }

    public void insertupdate( DocumentEvent e )
```

```
{
    // Called when text is inserted.
}

public void removeUpdate( DocumentEvent e )
{
    // Called when text is removed.
}
}
```

8. Track a position in the JTextPane's text. This is useful if you want to track the start of a word as characters are added and removed in front of it. You tell the JTextPane's document to create a Position instance at a particular index, then at any time you can check that Position instance to see what index it is at.

Get the JTextPane's document:

```
Document doc = mPane.getDocument();
```

Create a Position instance that starts out at index 5.

```
Position pos = doc.createPosition( 5 );
```

You can get the Position's current index location using its getOffset() method. So, if a character is inserted at index 3, the Position created above would return 6 if you called its getOffset() method.

9. Set the accelerator key. This key, when pressed with a special key (Alt on many systems), causes the JTextPane to get the keyboard focus.

```
mPane.setFocusAccelerator( 'a' );
```

10. Track the caret as it moves. The caret is the thing, usually a flashing vertical line, that marks the current position in the JTextPane where text is inserted.

Get the JTextPane's Caret:

```
Caret caret = mPane.getCaret();
```

Specify a class that will be notified when the caret moves. In this case it is the current class:

```
caret.addChangeListener( this );
```

Make the event-receiving class (MyFrame) implement the ChangeListener interface:

```
public class MyFrame extends JFrame implements ChangeListener
{
    .
    .
    .
    public void stateChanged( ChangeEvent e )
    {
        // The caret has moved, so do what you need to do.
```

```
        }
    }
```

11. Get the contents of the JTextPane.

```
String contents = mPane.getText();
```

You can also just get part of the contents by specifying an offset and a length. The following gets 5 characters starting at index 3:

```
String part = mPane.getText( 3, 5 );
```

12. Set the contents of the JTextPane:

```
mPane.setText( "Replacement text" );
```

13. Get the JTextPane's currently selected text (if any):

```
String selection = mPane.getSelectedText();
```

14. Specify an action to go with a certain keystroke. Each JTextPane has a Keymap that associates a KeyStroke with an Action. When the KeyStroke happens, the Action is triggered.

Create an Action class. This one deletes the JTextPane's currently selected text and puts it into the clipboard:

```
private class CutAction extends AbstractAction
{
    public void actionPerformed(ActionEvent e)
    {
        JTextPane tp = (JTextPane)e.getSource();

        // Move the selected text to the clipboard.
        tp.cut();
    }
}
```

Get the JTextPane's Keymap:

```
Keymap map = mPane.getKeymap();
```

Get the Ctrl-C KeyStroke:

```
KeyStroke cut = KeyStroke.getKeyStroke( KeyEvent.VK_C,
                    ActionEvent.CTRL_MASK, false );
```

Create an instance of the Action:

```
CutAction cutAction = new CutAction();
```

Associate the KeyStroke and Action via the Keymap:

```
map.addActionForKeyStroke( cut, cutAction );
```

Put the changed Keymap back into the JTextPane:

```
mPane.setKeymap( map );
```

Be warned that some KeyStrokes are used by the JTextPane itself.

Basic Code Examples

EXAMPLE 8-76 Using JTextPane

This example illustrates many of the concepts that make JTextPane useful. It has a JTextPane and a panel with a set of attribute controls. You can type text into the text pane and it will take on the proper attributes. You can change attribute settings and then press the Apply Attributes button to put them into effect. Figure 8-119 shows the example after it has been in use for a while.

Important ponts to notice:

■ Remember to press the Apply Attributes button or your attribute changes will not be used.

■ Attributes may be applied as paragraph attributes or character attributes. Paragraph attributes will be used as defaults for the paragraph the caret is in or for all paragraphs touched by the current selection range if there is one. Character attributes are applied to the current caret position or to all selected text if there is any.

■ Attributes may be merged in or they may replace the existing ones.

■ When you apply attributes, only attributes that are actually set will be applied. If font family is set to Not Set, no font family will be put in the created attribute set.

■ You can cut selected text by pressing Ctrl-C or by choosing Cut from the Edit menu.

■ You can paste text from the clipboard by pressing Shift-Insert or by choosing Paste from the Edit menu.

Figure 8-119

■ You can insert a button or an icon from the Insert menu. They are inserted at the caret position.

■ A single action is used both to create the Cut menu item and to respond to Ctrl-C. Paste is handled similarly.

■ We track the movement of the caret and print out the selected text if there is any.

■ We add an ActionListener to any inserted button. When an inserted button is pressed, the contents of the text pane are printed out.

■ We track changes to the document and print out Changed, Inserted, or Removed, depending on what happened.

Here is the source code:

```
import com.sun.java.swing.*;
import com.sun.java.swing.text.*;
import com.sun.java.swing.event.*;
import java.awt.*;
import java.awt.event.*;

public class MyFrame extends JFrame implements
        DocumentListener, ActionListener, ChangeListener
{
    private JTextPane mPane;
    private JComboBox mFontFamilyBox;
    private JComboBox mFontSizeBox;
    private JComboBox mColorBox;
    private JRadioButton mUseAsCharAttr;
    private JRadioButton mUseAsParaAttr;
    private JCheckBox mMerge;
    public static final String NOT_SET = "Not Set";

    public MyFrame()
    {
        setTitle( "JTextPane1" );

        // Create the menu bar.
        JMenuBar mbar = new JMenuBar();

        // Create the "Insert: menu.
        JMenu insert = new JMenu( "Insert" );

        // Create the "Button" item, and make this class
        // listen for when it is pressed.
        JMenuItem button = new JMenuItem( "Button" );
        button.setActionCommand( "button" );
        button.addActionListener( this );

        // Add the button item to the menu.
        insert.add( button );

        // Create the "Icon" item, and make this class listen
        // for when it is pressed.
```

```java
JMenuItem icon = new JMenuItem( "Icon" );
icon.setActionCommand( "icon" );
icon.addActionListener( this );

// Add the item to the menu.
insert.add( icon );

// Add the menu to the menu bar.
mbar.add( insert );

// Create the "Edit" menu.
JMenu edit = new JMenu( "Edit" );

// Create a "Cut" action that will be triggered by
// its menu item and by a key stroke (see farther
// down).
CutAction cutAction = new CutAction();

// Add the action to the menu.
edit.add( cutAction );

// Create the "Paste" action.
PasteAction pasteAction = new PasteAction();

// Add the action as a menu item.
edit.add( pasteAction );

// Add the menu to the menu bar.
mbar.add( edit );

// Set the menu bar as the frame's menu bar.
getRootPane().setMenuBar( mbar );

// Store the content pane in a variable for easier
// access.
JPanel contentPane = (JPanel)getContentPane();

// Components will all be added to this panel.
contentPane.setLayout( new BorderLayout() );

// Create the JTextPane.
mPane = new JTextPane();

// Make this class listen for changes in the text
// pane's document so we can see when they happen.
mPane.getDocument().addDocumentListener( this );

// Make it so this class is notified when the caret
// changes position.
mPane.getCaret().addChangeListener( this );

// Get the text pane's keymap so we can set
// keystrokes to trigger the cut and paste actions.
Keymap map = mPane.getKeymap();
```

```
    // Get the keystroke for 'Ctrl-C'
    KeyStroke cut = KeyStroke.getKeyStroke( KeyEvent.VK_C,
                    ActionEvent.CTRL_MASK, false );

    // Associate the cut keystroke and action via the
    // keymap.
    map.addActionForKeyStroke( cut, cutAction );

    // Get the 'Ctrl-Insert' keystroke.
    KeyStroke paste = KeyStroke.getKeyStroke(
                    KeyEvent.VK_INSERT,
                    ActionEvent.SHIFT_MASK, false );

    // Associate the paste keystroke and action via the
    // keymap.
    map.addActionForKeyStroke( paste, pasteAction );

    // Put the changed keymap back in the text pane.
    mPane.setKeymap( map );

    // Make the text pane take up the content pane's main
    // area.
    contentPane.add( "Center", mPane );

    // Create the attribute control panel and put it at
    // the top of the content pane.
    contentPane.add( "North", createAttribPane() );
}

// This loads up all of the attribute controls and puts
// them in a panel which is returned.
private JPanel createAttribPane()
{
    JPanel attribPane = new JPanel();
    attribPane.setLayout( new GridLayout( 5, 2 ) );

    JLabel l1 = new JLabel( "Font Family:" );
    attribPane.add( l1 );
    mFontFamilyBox = new JComboBox();
    mFontFamilyBox.addItem( NOT_SET );
    mFontFamilyBox.addItem( "TimesRoman" );
    mFontFamilyBox.addItem( "Courier" );
    attribPane.add( mFontFamilyBox );

    JLabel l2 = new JLabel( "Font Size:" );
    attribPane.add( l2 );
    mFontSizeBox = new JComboBox();
    mFontSizeBox.addItem( NOT_SET );
    mFontSizeBox.addItem( "10" );
    mFontSizeBox.addItem( "18" );
    mFontSizeBox.addItem( "36" );
    attribPane.add( mFontSizeBox );

    JLabel l3 = new JLabel( "Foreground Color:" );
    attribPane.add( l3 );
```

```
        mColorBox = new JComboBox();
        mColorBox.addItem( NOT_SET );
        mColorBox.addItem( Color.black );
        mColorBox.addItem( Color.red );
        mColorBox.addItem( Color.green );
        mColorBox.addItem( Color.blue );
        attribPane.add( mColorBox );

        mUseAsCharAttr =
            new JRadioButton( "Use as character attributes" );
        mUseAsParaAttr =
            new JRadioButton( "Use as paragraph attributes" );
        ButtonGroup group = new ButtonGroup();
        group.add( mUseAsCharAttr );
        group.add( mUseAsParaAttr );
        mUseAsCharAttr.setSelected( true );
        attribPane.add( mUseAsCharAttr );
        attribPane.add( mUseAsParaAttr );

        mMerge = new JCheckBox( "Merge attributes" );
        attribPane.add( mMerge );

        // The current attribute settings are applied using
        // this button.
        JButton apply = new JButton( "Apply Attributes" );
        apply.setActionCommand( "apply" );
        apply.addActionListener( this );
        attribPane.add( apply );

        return attribPane;
    }

    // This is called when attributes are changed in the
    // text pane.
    public void changedUpdate( DocumentEvent e )
    {
        System.out.println( "Changed" );
    }

    // This is called when text is inserted into the text
    // pane.
    public void insertUpdate( DocumentEvent e )
    {
        System.out.println( "Inserted" );
    }

    // This is called when text is deleted from the document.
    public void removeUpdate( DocumentEvent e )
    {
        System.out.println( "Removed" );
    }

    // This is called when the "Apply" button is pressed,
    // the "Button" menu item is pressed, the "Icon" menu
    // item is pressed, or when an inserted button is
```

```java
// pressed.
public void actionPerformed( ActionEvent e )
{
    String command = e.getActionCommand();
    if ( command == null )
        command = "";

    if ( command.equals( "apply" ) )
    {
        // Get the attribute settings, create an
        // attrribute set that contains those settings,
        // and apply them either as character or paragraph
        // attributes.

        // Create a new attribute set.
        SimpleAttributeSet set = new SimpleAttributeSet();

        // Get the selected font family.  If there is not
        // one, don't put a font family into the attribute
        // set.
        String familyValue =
                (String)mFontFamilyBox.getSelectedItem();
        if ( ! familyValue.equals( NOT_SET ) )
        {
            StyleConstants.setFontFamily( set,
                                            familyValue );
        }

        // Get the selected font size.  If there is not
        // one, don't put a font size in the attribute set.
        String sizeValue =
                (String)mFontSizeBox.getSelectedItem();
        if ( ! sizeValue.equals( NOT_SET ) )
        {
            StyleConstants.setFontSize( set,
                        Integer.parseInt( sizeValue ) );
        }

        // Get the selected color.  If it is a string, it
        // is NOT_SET, so don't put a foreground color
        // into the attribute set.
        if ( mColorBox.getSelectedItem() instanceof Color )
        {
            Color colorValue =
                    (Color)mColorBox.getSelectedItem();
            StyleConstants.setForeground( set, colorValue );
        }

        // Use the attribute set as character or paragraph
        // attributes depending on the radio button
        // settings.  Notice that the merge or not merge
        // parameters are gotten from the check box's
        // selection state.
        if ( mUseAsCharAttr.isSelected() )
        {
```

```
                    mPane.setCharacterAttributes( set,
                                        ! mMerge.isSelected() );
    }
    else
    {
        mPane.setParagraphAttributes( set,
                                    ! mMerge.isSelected() );
    }

    // Make the text pane repaint to reflect the
    // change properly.
    mPane.repaint();

    // Give the focus to the text pane so we can start
    // using the new attributes.
    mPane.requestFocus();
}
else if ( command.equals( "button" ) )
{
    // If the Insert-Button menu item was pressed,
    // create a button and insert it into the text
    // pane.

    // Create the button.
    JButton newButton = new JButton( "Button" );

    // Make it so the button aligns better with the
    // text on the same line.
    newButton.setAlignmentY( 0.5f );

    // Give it a proper background.
    newButton.setBackground( SystemColor.control );

    // Make it so we can know when it was pressed.
    newButton.setActionCommand( "new button" );
    newButton.addActionListener( this );

    // Insert the button.
    mPane.insertComponent( newButton );
}
else if ( command.equals( "icon" ) )
{
    // If the Insert-Icon menu item was pressed,
    // create an icon and insert it.

    // Create the icon.
    ImageIcon icon = new ImageIcon( "parrots.jpg" );

    // Insert it.
    mPane.insertIcon( icon );
}
else if ( command.equals( "new button" ) )
{
    // If an inserted button was pressed, print the
    // document contents.
```

```
            System.out.println( mPane.getText() );
        }
    }

    // This is called when the caret moves.  It causes the
    // current selection to be printed if there is one.
    public void stateChanged( ChangeEvent e )
    {
        if ( mPane.getSelectedText() != null )
            System.out.println( "Selection:  " +
                                mPane.getSelectedText() );
    }

    // This action is used to create the Edit-Cut menu item,
    // and is also associated with pressing 'Ctrl-C'.
    private class CutAction extends AbstractAction
    {
        public CutAction()
        {
            super( "Cut" );
        }

        public void actionPerformed( ActionEvent e )
        {
            mPane.cut();
        }
    }

    // This action is used to create the Edit-Paste menu
    // item and is also associated with pressing
    // 'Shift-Insert'.
    private class PasteAction extends AbstractAction
    {
        public PasteAction()
        {
            super( "Paste" );
        }

        public void actionPerformed( ActionEvent e )
        {
            mPane.paste();
        }
    }
}
```

JTextPane's Public Methods

```
Style addStyle(String nm, Style parent)
```

Adds a new style to the JTextPane's StyleContext. name is how you refer to the style later, although it may be null. parent may be null or may be an existing style that the new style will copy.

`AttributeSet getCharacterAttributes()`

Returns the AttributeSet that is in effect at the caret position.

`AttributeSet getInputAttributes()`

Returns the input attributes for the JTextPane.

`Style getLogicalStyle()`

Returns the style that is attached to the paragraph where the caret is.

`AttributeSet getParagraphAttributes()`

Specifies the attributes that will serve as the current paragraph's default attributes.

`boolean getScrollableTracksViewportWidth()`

Overridden to return true.

`Style getStyle(String nm)`

Returns the style associated with the given string.

`StyledDocument getStyledDocument()`

Returns the JTextPane's document.

`String getUIClassID()`

Returns the ID string that the look-and-feel uses to assign a UI class to the JTextPane.

`void insertComponent(Component c)`

Inserts the given component at the caret position, replacing selected text if there is any.

`void insertIcon(Icon g)`

Inserts the given icon at the caret position, replacing selected text if there is any.

`void removeStyle(String nm)`

Removes the style associated with the name from the JTextPane's StyleContext.

```
void replaceSelection(String content)
```

Replaces the current selection with the given string.

```
void setCharacterAttributes(AttributeSet attr,boolean replace)
```

Sets the current character attributes. This goes into effect at the current caret position for any text inserted there and also applies to any current text selection. replace should be true if you want the new attributes to replace the existing ones or false if you want any existing attributes that are not defined in the new attributes to remian.

```
void setDocument(Document doc)
```

Replaces the JTextPane's document with a new one.

```
void setEditorKit(EditorKit kit)
```

Replaces the current editor kit with the given one.

```
void setLogicalStyle(Style s)
```

Specifies the style to apply to the current paragraph.

```
void setParagraphAttributes(AttributeSet attr,boolean replace)
```

Sets the current paragraph (the paragraph where the caret is) attributes. Paragraph attributes are the defaults for a paragraph. 'replace' should be true if you want the new attributes to replace the existing ones or false if you want any existing attributes that are not defined in the new attributes to remain.

```
void setStyledDocument(StyledDocument doc)
```

Replaces the JTextPane's document.

JToggleButton

JToggleButton is like a cross between a JButton and a JCheckBox. In appearance it is exactly like a JButton (see Figure 8-120). However, when you press it, it stays down until you press it again. In this way it is like a JCheckBox—it has a selected and an unselected state. This kind of control is useful for things like buttons on a toolbar that show if bold is turned on. You can also use JToggleButtons in a ButtonGroup so they behave like JRadioButtons. This is useful for situations like showing which of a set of drawing tools is currently active.

Ancestors

```
java.lang.Object
    |
    +—java.awt.Component
            |
            +—java.awt.Container
                    |
                    +—com.sun.java.swing.JComponent
                            |
                            +—com.sun.java.swing.AbstractButton
                                    |
                                    +—com.sun.java.swing.JToggleButton
```

NOTE: *For more information, see the "JToolBar," "AbstractButton," "JButton," "JCheckBox," "JRadioButton," and "DefaultButtonModel" sections in this chapter. Also see the "Components That Can be Turned On and Off" section in Chapter 7, "JFC by Concept."*

Steps in Creating and Using JToggleButton

1. Create the JToggleButton. There are seven constructors, but all are variations on:

```
JToggleButton( String text, Icon icon, boolean selected )
```

where 'text' is the text that appears on the button, 'icon' is the icon that appears on the button, and 'selected' is the initial state of the button.

Create a text-only JToggleButton:

```
JToggleButton textOnly = new JToggleButton( "Text Only" );
```

Create an icon-only JToggleButton:

```
JToggleButton iconOnly = new JToggleButton( new ImageIcon(
                                            "left.gif" ) );
```

Create a JToggleButton with text and an icon and whose initial state is selected:

Figure 8-120
A set of
JToggleButtons with
one depressed.

```
JToggleButton iconAndText = new JToggleButton( "Text and Icon",
                            new ImageIcon( "left.gif" ), true );
```

2. Make it so a class will be notified when the JToggleButton's state changes. For this example, we want to receive ItemEvents so we can get the state change from the event.

Tell the button which class should be notified when its state changes. In this case, the class MyFrame that contains the toggle button will receive its events:

```
textonly.addItemListener( this );
```

Make it so that the event-receiver class (MyFrame) implements the ItemListener interface:

```
public class MyFrame extends JFrame implements ItemListener
{
   .
   .
   .
   public void itemStateChanged( ItemEvent e )
   {
      // Use the event's getStateChange() method, then do what
      // needs to be done in response to the state change.
   }
}
```

3. For JToggleButtons with both text and an icon, you can change their relative positions. By default, the icon is left of the text.

Move the text to the left of the icon:

```
textAndIcon.setHorizontalTextPosition( JToggleButton.LEFT );
```

Move the text above the icon. Notice that you must move the text both to the center and to the top.

```
textAndIcon.setHorizontalTextPosition( JToggleButton.CENTER );
textAndIcon.setVerticalTextPosition( JToggleButton.TOP );
```

4. Change the text/icon position relative to the button itself. By default the text/icon is centered both horizontally and vertically.

Make the text/icon snug against the toggle button's upper left corner:

```
alignBtn.setHorizontalAlignment( JToggleButton.LEFT );
alignBtn.setVerticalAlignment( JToggleButton.TOP );
```

5. Specify a separate icon for the toggle button to display while it is pressed. This is the icon that will display when the mouse is pressed on the button—not while the button is selected but the mouse is not pressed.

```
textAndIcon.setPressedIcon( new ImageIcon( "left2.gif" ) );
```

6. Specify the icon that should replace the JToggleButton's icon while it is in a disabled state:

```
textAndIcon.setDisabledIcon( new ImageIcon( "left6.gif" ) );
```

7. Specify the icon that should be displayed when the button is selected:

```
textAndIcon.setSelectedIcon( new ImageIcon( "left5.gif" ) );
```

8. Specify the icon that should be displayed when the button is not selected and the mouse passes over it. Notice that rollover has to be enabled for this icon to work.

```
textAndIcon.setRolloverIcon( new ImageIcon( "left3.gif" ) );
textAndIcon.setRolloverEnabled( true );
```

9. Set the tool tip text. This will be displayed in its own little window when the mouse pauses over the button.

```
textAndIcon.setToolTipText( "This button has text and an icon" );
```

10. Define an accelerator key which, when pressed with a special platform-specific key (Alt on Windows), causes the button to be clicked (changes its state). The key character is case insensitive.

```
textAndIcon.setMnemonic( 't' );
```

11. Set the button's text color. This works with the Windows look-and-feel, but is not guaranteed to work with all look-and-feels.

```
textAndIcon.setForeground( Color.red );
```

12. Set the button's background color. It will typically take the color of its container. This will change the background color for the Windows look-and-feel, but is not guaranteed to work with others since they may hard code the background.

```
textAndIcon.setBackground( SystemColor.control );
```

13. Remove the default padding around the button's text/icon. This is particularly useful for icon-only buttons.

```
left.setMargin( new Insets( 0, 0, 0, 0 ) );
```

14. Place buttons in a ButtonGroup so only one may be selected at a time. This makes JToggleButtons act like JRadioButtons.

```
JToggleButton left = new JToggleButton( new ImageIcon(
                                        "left.gif" ), true );
JToggleButton right = new JToggleButton( new ImageIcon(
                                         "right.gif" ) );
ButtonGroup group1 = new ButtonGroup();
group1.add( left );
group1.add( right );
```

Basic Code Examples

EXAMPLE 8-77 Basic Uses of JToggleButton

This example takes the concepts discussed above and puts them together in a working class. It includes: three JToggleButtons in a JToolBar, two JToggleButtons in the same ButtonGroup, one JToggleButton that uses a variety of icons, one that shows text/icon alignment, and one that disables/enables the one with all of the icons. The last JToggleButton has its ItemEvents caught, which is how we know when to enable/disable the other button. Figure 8-121 shows the example after some of the buttons have been pressed.

Here is the source:

```
import com.sun.java.swing.*;
import java.awt.*;
import java.awt.event.*;

public class MyFrame extends JFrame implements ItemListener
{
    JToggleButton textAndIcon;

    public MyFrame()
    {
        setTitle( "JToggleButton1" );

        // Store the content pane in a variable for easier
        // access.
        JPanel contentPane = (JPanel)getContentPane();

        // Components will all be added to this panel.
        contentPane.setLayout( new BorderLayout() );

        // Create a container for the toolbar.
        Box topBox = Box.createHorizontalBox();

        // Create an icon-only button.
        JToggleButton bold = new JToggleButton(
                            new ImageIcon( "bold.gif" ) );

        // Strip off the default space around the icon.
        bold.setMargin( new Insets( 0, 0, 0, 0 ) );
```

Figure 8-121

```
// Create another icon-only button and removed the
// default padding.
JToggleButton italic = new JToggleButton(
                    new ImageIcon( "italic.gif" ) );
italic.setMargin( new Insets( 0, 0, 0, 0 ) );

// Create a third icon-only button and remove the
// padding.
JToggleButton underline = new JToggleButton(
                    new ImageIcon( "underline.gif" ) );
underline.setMargin( new Insets( 0, 0, 0, 0 ) );

// Create the tool bar that will hold the three
// icon-only buttons.
JToolBar toolbar = new JToolBar();

// Add the buttons to the toolbar.
toolbar.add( bold );
toolbar.add( italic );
toolbar.add( underline );

// Add the tool bar to the container.
topBox.add( toolbar );

// Put the container at the top of the frame.
contentPane.add( "North", topBox );

// Create a container to hold the rest of the buttons.
JPanel pane = new JPanel();
pane.setLayout( new GridLayout( 4, 1 ) );

// Create a container to hold two toggle-radio
// buttons.
Box box2 = Box.createHorizontalBox();

// Create the two icon-only buttons with arrows and
// remove their default padding.
JToggleButton left = new JToggleButton(
                new ImageIcon( "left.gif" ), true );
left.setMargin( new Insets( 0, 0, 0, 0 ) );
JToggleButton right = new JToggleButton(
                new ImageIcon( "right.gif" ) );
right.setMargin( new Insets( 0, 0, 0, 0 ) );

// Add the buttons to the container.
box2.add( left );
box2.add( right );

// Create a button group that will make it so only
// one of the two can be selected at a time.
ButtonGroup group1 = new ButtonGroup();

// Add the buttons to the group.
group1.add( left );
group1.add( right );
```

```
// Add the container.
pane.add( box2 );

// Create a toggle button with text and an icon.
textAndIcon = new JToggleButton( "Text and Icon",
            new ImageIcon( "left.gif" ), true );

// Cause the text to appear above the icon.
textAndIcon.setHorizontalTextPosition(
                            JToggleButton.CENTER );
textAndIcon.setVerticalTextPosition(
                            JToggleButton.TOP );

// Set the icon that the button will display while
// the mouse is pressed on it.
textAndIcon.setPressedIcon(
                new ImageIcon( "left2.gif" ) );

// Set the icon that will be displayed while the
// button is selected.
textAndIcon.setSelectedIcon(
                new ImageIcon( "left5.gif" ) );

// Set the icon that will display when the button is
// not selected and the mouse passes over it.
textAndIcon.setRolloverIcon(
                new ImageIcon( "left3.gif" ) );

textAndIcon.setRolloverSelectedIcon(
                new ImageIcon( "left4.gif" ) );

// Enable rollover so the rollover icon works.
textAndIcon.setRolloverEnabled( true );

// Set the button's accelerator key.
textAndIcon.setMnemonic( 't' );

// Set the button's tool tip.
textAndIcon.setToolTipText(
                "This button has text and an icon" );

// Set the string that will be delivered with any
// action events the button generates.
textAndIcon.setActionCommand( "Text and Icon" );

// Set the icon that will display while the button is
// disabled.
textAndIcon.setDisabledIcon(
                new ImageIcon( "left6.gif" ) );

// Set the button's text color.
textAndIcon.setForeground( Color.red );

// Set the background color of the button.
textAndIcon.setBackground( Color.green );
```

```
    // Add the button to its container.
    pane.add( textAndIcon );

    // Create a toggle button.
    JToggleButton alignBtn =
                new JToggleButton( "Check Alignment",
                new ImageIcon( "right.gif" ), true );

    // Make the text/icon go to the upper-left corner of
    // the button.
    alignBtn.setHorizontalAlignment( JToggleButton.LEFT );
    alignBtn.setVerticalAlignment( JToggleButton.TOP );

    // Add the button to its container.
    pane.add( alignBtn );

    // Create a toggle button that will set the
    // disable/enable state of the text and icon button
    // so we can test its disable icon.
    JToggleButton disableBtn = new JToggleButton(
            "If this is down, one other is disabled" );

    // We want to be notified when this button's state
    // changes so we can enable/disable the other button.
    disableBtn.addItemListener( this );

    // Add the button to its container.
    pane.add( disableBtn );

    // Add the container to the content pane.
    contentPane.add( "Center", pane );
}

// This method is called when the enable/disable
// button's state changes.  We change the "Text and
// Icon" button's enable state to match.
public void itemStateChanged( ItemEvent e )
{
    if ( e.getStateChange() == ItemEvent.SELECTED )
       textAndIcon.setEnabled( false );
    else
       textAndIcon.setEnabled( true );
}
}
```

JToggleButton's Public Methods

```
AccessibleContext getAccessibleContext()
```

Returns a subclass of AccessibleContext, which gives access to the JToggleButton's accessibility information.

```
String getUIClassID()
```

Returns the string that identifies the JToggleButton's current look-and-feel class.

```
void updateUI()
```

Tells the JToggleButton that the look-and-feel class has been changed.

JToolBar

A JToolBar is a container for a series of icon buttons, generally at the top of an application, which can be used as shortcuts to tasks like saving a file, opening a new file, cutting, pasting, etc. (see Figure 8-122). The icon buttons often have a tool tip associated with them that tells the user what the icon button is for. A tool bar may also be in a separate window (JDialog, JInternalFrame, etc.). In this case, its buttons typically represent tools like paintbrushes or text tools from which the user can select.

Ancestors

```
java.lang.Object
    |
    +—java.awt.Component
        |
        +—java.awt.Container
            |
            +—com.sun.java.swing.JComponent
                |
                +—com.sun.java.swing.JToolBar
```

NOTE: *For more information, see the "JButton," "JToggleButton," and "BoxLayout" sections of this chapter. Also see the "JFC Containers" section in Chapter 7, "JFC by Concept."*

Figure 8-122
A typical JToolBar containing four buttons.

Steps in Creating and Using JToolBar

1. Create the tool bar. There is only one constructor:

   ```
   JToolBar mToolBar = new JToolBar();
   ```

2. Add the tool bar into a container. It is most common to use a BorderLayout. If you do so, the user can drag the tool bar around interactively and drop (dock) it along any edge of the container.

   ```
   mPanel.add( "North", mToolBar );
   ```

3. Create a component to add to the tool bar and add it:

   ```
   JButton newBtn = new JButton( new ImageIcon( "new.gif" ) );
   mToolBar.add( newBtn );
   mToolBar.add( b );
   ```

   By default, a JButton puts extra padding around the icon. Get rid of it by calling the setMargin() method:

   ```
   newBtn.setMargin( new Insets( 0, 0, 0, 0 ) );
   ```

4. Add a tool tip to the component. This is not required but is especially useful when you use icon buttons with no text.

   ```
   b.setToolTipText( "This button does something interesting" );
   ```

5. Make it so that the JButton's action events get caught so we know when it is pressed. Specify a class that will receive events from the button and make that class implement ActionListener. In this case, the event-receiving class is MyFrame, the class that contains the tool bar.

   Tell the JButton which class will be listening for its action events:

   ```
   newBtn.addActionListener( this );
   ```

   Define a string that will be delivered with the action events from this JButton. This string allows the event receiver to know which JButton was pressed.

   ```
   newBtn.setActionCommand( "New" );
   ```

   An alternative is to let the event-receiver differentiate between event-sources using the ActionEvent's getSource() method. In that case, the source component has to be visible to the actionPerformed() method.

   Make the receiving class capable of receiving action events from the button:

   ```
   public class MyFrame extends JFrame implements ActionListener
   {
       .
       .
       .
   ```

```
    public void actionPerformed( ActionEvent e )
    {
        // Do whatever needs to be done when the button is
        // pushed.
    }
}
```

6. Change the JToolBar's layout manager. By default, JToolBar uses a BoxLayout. If you need your JToolBar to hold buttons in two columns, you could use a GridLayout:

```
mToolBar.setLayout( new GridLayout( 3, 2 ) );
```

7. Create a JButton in the JToolBar by adding an Action. When you create an Action and add it to a JToolBar, the JToolBar automatically creates a JButton and returns it. The Action is then able to respond when the JButton is pressed.

   Create a subclass of AbstractAction and give it an icon:

```
private class CopyAction extends AbstractAction
{
    public CopyAction( Icon icon )
    {
        super( "", icon );
    }

    public void actionPerformed( ActionEvent e )
    {
        // Do something now you know the "Copy" menu item was
        // pressed.
    }
}
```

   Create an instance of the action and add it to the JMenu:

```
// Create a JToolBar.
JToolBar toolbar = new JToolBar();

// Create an instance of the action.
CopyAction copyAction = new CopyAction( new ImageIcon(
                                        "copy.gif" ) );

// Add the action to the JToolBar.  This causes a JButton to be
// created and added to the JToolBar.  The created JButton is
// returned from the add() method.
JButton copyButton = toolbar.add( copyAction );
```

8. Make the JToolBar so it stays in its original position ñ is not dockable:

```
toolbar.setFloatable( false );
```

   The JFC's dockable toolbar behavior can be confusing, so you may want to use setFloatable(false) always.

Basic Code Examples

EXAMPLE 8-78 Basic JToolBar

This example illustrates how to create a tool bar, how to add icon-buttons to the tool bar, how to add a tool separator, and how to respond to events when the icon-buttons are pressed. The example includes seven JButtons in a JToolBar. Each button has a tool tip and is being listened to by an Action-Listener. Notice how the extra padding between the buttons' icons and their borders has been removed. Also notice that the JToolBar uses a lowered BevelBorder. Figure 8-123 shows the example as in is when it first starts up.

Here is the source code:

```
import com.sun.java.swing.*;
import com.sun.java.swing.border.*;
import java.awt.*;
import java.awt.event.*;

public class MyFrame extends JFrame implements
        ActionListener
{
    JToolBar mToolBar;

    public MyFrame()
    {
        setTitle( "JToolBar1" );

        // Store the content pane in a variable for easier
        // access.
        JPanel contentPane = (JPanel)getContentPane();

        // The tool bar will be added in the north position.
        contentPane.setLayout( new BorderLayout() );

        // Create an empty tool bar.
        mToolBar = new JToolBar();

        // Play with the tool bar's border.
        mToolBar.setBorder( new BevelBorder(
                            BevelBorder.LOWERED ) );

        // Add icon-buttons to the tool bar one at a time and
        // set their tool tips.
```

Figure 8-123
A basic JToolBar example.

```
// Create an icon button.
JButton newBtn =
        new JButton( new ImageIcon( "new.gif" ) );

// Add the icon button to the tool bar.
mToolBar.add( newBtn );

// Give the icon button a tool tip.
newBtn.setToolTipText( "New" );

// Trim off the excess padding JButton applies by
// default.
newBtn.setMargin( new Insets( 0, 0, 0, 0 ) );

// Make this class (MyFrame) a listener for the
// JButton's action events.
newBtn.addActionListener( this );
newBtn.setActionCommand( "New" );

// Another button, just like the first.
JButton openBtn =
        new JButton( new ImageIcon( "open.gif" ) );
mToolBar.add( openBtn );
openBtn.setToolTipText( "Open" );
openBtn.setMargin( new Insets( 0, 0, 0, 0 ) );
openBtn.addActionListener( this );
openBtn.setActionCommand( "Open" );

// Another button, just like the first.
JButton saveBtn =
        new JButton( new ImageIcon( "save.gif" ) );
mToolBar.add( saveBtn );
saveBtn.setToolTipText( "Save" );
saveBtn.setMargin( new Insets( 0, 0, 0, 0 ) );
saveBtn.addActionListener( this );
saveBtn.setActionCommand( "Save" );

// Add a little space between the previous button and
// the next one.
mToolBar.addSeparator();

// Another button, just like the first.
JButton cutBtn =
        new JButton( new ImageIcon( "cut.gif" ) );
mToolBar.add( cutBtn );
cutBtn.setToolTipText( "Cut" );
cutBtn.setMargin( new Insets( 0, 0, 0, 0 ) );
cutBtn.addActionListener( this );
cutBtn.setActionCommand( "Cut" );

// Another button, just like the first.
JButton copyBtn =
        new JButton( new ImageIcon( "copy.gif" ) );
mToolBar.add( copyBtn );
```

```
copyBtn.setToolTipText( "Copy" );
copyBtn.setMargin( new Insets( 0, 0, 0, 0 ) );
copyBtn.addActionListener( this );
copyBtn.setActionCommand( "Copy" );

// Another button, just like the first.
JButton pasteBtn =
        new JButton( new ImageIcon( "paste.gif" ) );
mToolBar.add( pasteBtn );
pasteBtn.setToolTipText( "Paste" );
pasteBtn.setMargin( new Insets( 0, 0, 0, 0 ) );
pasteBtn.addActionListener( this );
pasteBtn.setActionCommand( "Paste" );

// Add space between the previous and next buttons.
mToolBar.addSeparator();

// Another button, just like the first.
JButton printBtn =
        new JButton( new ImageIcon( "print.gif" ) );
mToolBar.add( printBtn );
printBtn.setToolTipText( "Print" );
printBtn.setMargin( new Insets( 0, 0, 0, 0 ) );
printBtn.addActionListener( this );
printBtn.setActionCommand( "Print" );

// Add the tool bar to the panel.
contentPane.add( "North", mToolBar );
}

// This event is called by the tool bar buttons when
// they are pressed.  The method differentiates between
// button by using their action command strings
// (defined above).
public void actionPerformed( ActionEvent e )
{
    System.out.println(
            "Toolbar button pressed.  Command string:  " +
            e.getActionCommand() );
}
}
```

Advanced Issues

EXAMPLE 8-79 JToolBar as a Tool Palette

This example shows how to create a floating tool palette by placing a JToolBar within a JInternalFrame. It changes the JToolBar's layout manager so it can have three rows of two JButtons each. Each JButton has a tool tip and is listened to by an ActionListener. The main class contains an inner class called ToolFrame, which subclasses JInternalFrame and holds the JToolBar. Figure 8-124 shows the example pretty much as it looks when it first starts up.

Figure 8-124
Creating a floating
tool palette.

Here is the source:

```java
import com.sun.java.swing.*;
import com.sun.java.swing.border.*;
import java.awt.*;
import java.awt.event.*;

public class MyFrame extends JFrame
{
    public MyFrame()
    {
        setTitle( "JToolBar2" );

        // Store the content pane in a variable for easier
        // access.
        JPanel mPanel = (JPanel)getContentPane();

        // Set the layout so we can place a JDesktopPane to
        // totally fill the contant pane.
        mPanel.setLayout( new BorderLayout() );

        // Create a desktop pane to hold the tool palette.
        JDesktopPane desktop = new JDesktopPane();
        desktop.setBackground( mPanel.getBackground() );

        // Make the desktop pane fill the content pane.
        mPanel.add( "Center", desktop );

        // Create the tool palette (ToolFrame is an inner
        // class defined below).
        ToolFrame toolframe = new ToolFrame( "Tools" );

        // Add the tool palette to the desktop.
        desktop.add( toolframe );
    }

    // This class holds an internally defined set of buttons
    // as a tool palette.  It tries to size itself to
    // exactly fit around the tool buttons when they are at
    // their best size.
    private class ToolFrame extends JInternalFrame
            implements ActionListener, ComponentListener
```

```
                    {

          public ToolFrame( String title )
          {
              super( title );

              JToolBar mToolBar;
              JButton newBtn;
              JButton openBtn;
              JButton saveBtn;
              JButton cutBtn;
              JButton copyBtn;
              JButton pasteBtn;

              // It should be closable and minimizable.
              setClosable( true );
              setIconifiable( true );
              setResizable( true );

              // Store the content pane for easier access.
              JPanel buffPane = (JPanel)getContentPane();

              addComponentListener( this );

              // Set the content pane's layout manager.
              buffPane.setLayout( new BorderLayout() );

              // Create the JToolBar.
              mToolBar = new JToolBar();

              // Set its layout to handle six buttons, 3x2.
              mToolBar.setLayout( new GridLayout( 3, 2 ) );

              // Change the tool bar's border.
              mToolBar.setBorder( new BevelBorder(
                                BevelBorder.LOWERED ) );

              // Put the tool bar so it fills the content pane.
              buffPane.add( "Center", mToolBar );

              // Add icon-buttons to the tool bar one at a time
              // and set their tool tips.
              newBtn = new JButton( new ImageIcon( "new.gif" ) );
              mToolBar.add( newBtn );
              newBtn.setToolTipText( "New" );
              newBtn.setMargin( new Insets( 0, 0, 0, 0 ) );
              newBtn.addActionListener( this );
              newBtn.setActionCommand( "New" );

              // Another button, just like the first.
              openBtn =
                    new JButton( new ImageIcon( "open.gif" ) );
              mToolBar.add( openBtn );
              openBtn.setToolTipText( "Open" );
              openBtn.setMargin( new Insets( 0, 0, 0, 0 ) );
```

```
openBtn.addActionListener( this );
openBtn.setActionCommand( "Open" );

// Another button, just like the first.
saveBtn =
     new JButton( new ImageIcon( "save.gif" ) );
mToolBar.add( saveBtn );
saveBtn.setToolTipText( "Save" );
saveBtn.setMargin( new Insets( 0, 0, 0, 0 ) );
saveBtn.addActionListener( this );
saveBtn.setActionCommand( "Save" );

// Another button, just like the first.
cutBtn = new JButton( new ImageIcon( "cut.gif" ) );
mToolBar.add( cutBtn );
cutBtn.setToolTipText( "Cut" );
cutBtn.setMargin( new Insets( 0, 0, 0, 0 ) );
cutBtn.addActionListener( this );
cutBtn.setActionCommand( "Cut" );

// Another button, just like the first.
copyBtn =
     new JButton( new ImageIcon( "copy.gif" ) );
mToolBar.add( copyBtn );
copyBtn.setToolTipText( "Copy" );
copyBtn.setMargin( new Insets( 0, 0, 0, 0 ) );
copyBtn.addActionListener( this );
copyBtn.setActionCommand( "Copy" );

// Another button, just like the first.
pasteBtn =
     new JButton( new ImageIcon( "paste.gif" ) );
mToolBar.add( pasteBtn );
pasteBtn.setToolTipText( "Paste" );
pasteBtn.setMargin( new Insets( 0, 0, 0, 0 ) );
pasteBtn.addActionListener( this );
pasteBtn.setActionCommand( "Paste" );

// Set the frame's initial size.
setBounds( 0, 0, 100, 120 );
}


// This is called when one of the toolbar buttons is
// pressed.  It just prints out the button's command
// string.
public void actionPerformed( ActionEvent e )
{
   System.out.println( "Tool bar button pressed:  " +
                        e.getActionCommand() );
}

public void componentHidden( ComponentEvent e )
{
}
```

```
      public void componentMoved( ComponentEvent e )
      {
      }

      public void componentResized( ComponentEvent e )
      {
      }

      public void componentShown( ComponentEvent e )
      {
         System.out.println(
                 ((Component)(e.getSource())).getSize() );
         int extwidth = getSize().width -
                         getContentPane().getSize().width;
         int extheight = getSize().height -
                         getContentPane().getSize().height;

         System.out.println( extwidth+","+extheight );
      }
   }
}
```

JToolBar's Public Methods

`JButton add(Action a):`

Given an Action, create a JButton and add it to the JToolBar. This method returns the created JButton.

`void addSeparator():`

Adds space between the last item that was added to the JToolBar and the next one.

`AccessibleContext getAccessibleContext():`

Returns a subclass of AccessibleContext, which gives access to the JToolBar's accessibility information.

`Component getComponentAtIndex(int i):`

Returns the JToolBar's component with the given index.

`int getComponentIndex(Component c):`

Returns the index of the given JToolBar component.

`Insets getMargin():`

Returns the space, on each side of the JToolBar, between its border and its components.

`ToolBarUI getUI():`

Returns the JToolBar's current look-and-feel class.

`String getUIClassID():`

Returns the identifying string that the look-and-feel uses to assign a UI class to the JToolBar.

`boolean isBorderPainted():`

Returns true if the JToolBar allows its border to be painted.

`boolean isFloatable()`

Returns true if the JToolBar can be dragged around.

`void setBorderPainted(boolean b):`

Specifies whether the JToolBar allows its border to be painted.

`void setFloatable(boolean float)`

Specifies whether the JToolBar is allowed to be dragged around.

`void setMargin(Insets m):`

Specifies the distance, on each JToolBar side, between the JToolBar's border and its components.

`void setUI(ToolBarUI ui):`

Gives the JToolBar a new look-and-feel class.

`void updateUI():`

Tells the JToolBar that the look-and-feel class has been changed.

JTree

JTree is a component that helps you display data in a hierarchical way. It handles much of the functionality that you would otherwise have to program yourself (see Figure 8-125).

Ancestors

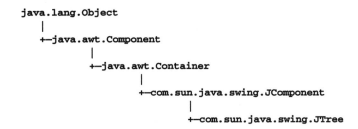

```
java.lang.Object
   |
   +—java.awt.Component
        |
        +—java.awt.Container
             |
             +—com.sun.java.swing.JComponent
                  |
                  +—com.sun.java.swing.JTree
```

NOTE: *For more information, see the "DefaultMutableTreeNode," "Default-TreeModel," "DefaultTreeSelectionModel," "DefaultCellEditor," "TreePath," and "JScrollPane" sections in this chapter. Also see the "Trees" section in Chapter 7, "JFC by Concept," as well as Chapters 10 and 11 that contain examples that use trees extensively.*

Steps in Creating and Using JTree

1. Create a tree node that will be your root node. All nodes in the tree will descend from this one. For this discussion, we will build a very incomplete inheritance tree from the Java libraries.

```
DefaultMutableTreeNode root = new DefaultMutableTreeNode(
                              "JComponent" );
```

There are several other useful constructors as well:

Create an empty JTree. If you use this constructor, you will need to separately create a TreeModel and use the JTree's setModel() method to apply it.

```
JTree()
```

Create a JTree with a root node but change the definition of what a leaf is. By default, a leaf is a node that has no child nodes, even if the node is allowed to have children. If you set 'asksAllowsChildren' to

Figure 8-125
A typical JTree.

true, the definition of a leaf becomes any node that is not allowed to have children. This is useful for things like file system browsers in which empty directories should still show up as directories. By default, empty directories would show up as files. This can also be set after construction by calling DefaultTreeModel's setAsksAllowsChildren(true).

```
JTree( TreeNode root, boolean asksAllowsChildren )
```

Create a JTree with a prebuilt TreeModel. This is like creating an empty JTree and then setting its model with the setModel() method. The TreeModel should normally be an instance of DefaultTreeModel.

```
JTree( TreeModel model )
```

2. Create more nodes and add them into the tree (not required, but a tree of one node is not of much use). Some nodes will be directly added to the root node, and others will be added to those nodes, and so on, building up a hierarchy:

```
// For this example we don't go very deep, so we just
// use a couple of levels.
DefaultMutableTreeNode sublevel1;
DefaultMutableTreeNode sublevel2;

// Add AbstractButton under JComponent.
sublevel1 = new DefaultMutableTreeNode( "AbstractButton" );
root.add( sublevel1 );

// Add JButton under AbstractButton
sublevel2 = new DefaultMutableTreeNode( "JButton" );
sublevel1.add( sublevel2 );

// Add BasicArrowButton under JButton.
sublevel2.add( new DefaultMutableTreeNode(
                "BasicArrowButton" ) );

// Add JMenuItem under AbstractButton.
sublevel2 = new DefaultMutableTreeNode( "JMenuItem" );
sublevel1.add( sublevel2 );

// Add two classes under JMenuItem.
sublevel2.add( new DefaultMutableTreeNode(
                "JCheckboxMenuItem" ) );
sublevel2.add( new DefaultMutableTreeNode( "JMenu" ) );

// Add JToggleButton under AbstractButton.
sublevel2 = new DefaultMutableTreeNode( "JToggleButton" );
sublevel1.add( sublevel2 );

// Add two classes under JToggleButton.
sublevel2.add( new DefaultMutableTreeNode( "JCheckbox" ) );
sublevel2.add( new DefaultMutableTreeNode( "JRadioButton" ) );
```

3. Create the JTree using the root node created previously:

```
JTree tree = new JTree( root );
```

4. Create a scroll pane to handle scrolling through the tree as its display needs change and add the scroll pane to the main panel (mPanel in this case, using a BorderLayout):

```
JScrollPane scrollpane = new JScrollPane(mTree);

mPanel.add( "Center", scrollpane );
```

5. Specify a class that will catch tree events. There are different types of events that may be caught:

To be notified when the tree selection changes, first tell the tree which class will be receiving the events. In this case, it is the class that contains the tree variable:

```
tree.addTreeSelectionListener( this );
```

Make the event-receiving class (MyFrame in this case) implement TreeSelectionListener:

```
public class MyFrame extends JFrame implements
        TreeSelectionListener
{
    .
    .
    .
    // When the selection changes, print the path whose
    // selection changed.
    public void valueChanged( TreeSelectionEvent e )
    {
        JTreePath paths[] = e.getPaths();

        for ( int i = 0; i < paths.length; i++ )
            System.out.println( i + ":  " + paths[i] );
    }
}
```

To be notified when a tree node is expanded or collapsed, first tell the tree which class should be notified when nodes are expanded/collapsed. In this class, it is the class that contains the JTree:

```
tree.addTreeExpansionListener( this );
```

Make the event-receiving class (MyFrame) implement the TreeExpansionListener interface:

```
public class MyFrame extends JFrame implements
        TreeExpansionListener
{
    .
    .
    .
```

```
public void treeExpanded( TreeExpansionEvent e )
{
   // Use the event's getPath() method to find out the path
   // that was expanded.
}

public void treeCollapsed( TreeExpansionEvent e )
{
   // Use the event's getPath() method to find out the path
   // that was collapsed.
}
}
```

6. To customize the appearance of the items in the tree by creating your own TreeCellRenderer, first tell the tree to use your renderer:

```
mTree.setCellRenderer( new MyCellRenderer() );
```

Create the TreeCellRenderer:

```
private class MyCellRenderer extends JLabel implements
   TreeCellRenderer
{
   private Icon mNodeIcon;
   private Icon mLeafIcon;

   public MyCellRenderer()
   {
      mNodeIcon = new ImageIcon( "dir.gif" );
      mLeafIcon = new ImageIcon( "leaf.gif" );
   }

   // This method is called when the tree is ready to have
   // a tree item drawn.  The method configures itself (as
   // the JLabel subclass that it is) so that when it is
   // drawn, it will represent the item being drawn.
   public Component getTreeCellRendererComponent( JTree tree,
                     Object value, boolean selected, boolean
                     expanded, boolean leaf, int row, boolean
                     hasFocus )
   {
      DefaultMutableTreeNode node =
                                 (DefaultMutableTreeNode)value;

      // Load the tree item's string into the JLabel.
      setText( ((MyNode)(node.getUserObject())).toString() );

      // Set the JLabel icon based on whether the node being
      // drawn is a leaf or a node.
      if ( leaf )
         setIcon( mLeafIcon );
      else
         setIcon( mNodeIcon );

      // Set the text fore-and background colors based on whether
      // the item being drawn is currently selected.
```

```
        if ( selected )
        {
            setForeground( SystemColor.textHighlightText );
            setBackground( SystemColor.textHighlight );
        }
        else
        {
            setForeground( SystemColor.textText );
            setBackground( SystemColor.window );
        }

        return this;
    }

    // This method draws the tree item as its state was set in the
    // call to getTreeCellRendererComponent().
    public void paint( Graphics g )
    {
        int textstart, textwidth;

        textstart = getIcon().getIconWidth() + getIconTextGap();
        textwidth = getSize().width - textstart;

        getIcon().paintIcon( this, g, 0, 0 );

        g.setColor( getBackground() );
        g.fillRect( textstart, 0, textwidth, getSize().height );
        g.setColor( getForeground() );
        g.drawString( getText(), textstart,
                        g.getFontMetrics().getAscent() );
    }
}
```

7. You will need to deal with TreePaths. A TreePath is basically just a list of the tree nodes required to get from one node to another one. If you get the selected path, the final node in the path will be the actual selected node.

Get the selected path or the first selected path if there are more than one:

```
TreePath path = tree.getSelectionPath();
```

Get all selected paths: This returns an array of TreePaths.

```
TreePath paths[] = tree.getSelectionPaths();
```

Get the last node in a TreePath:

```
TreeNode node = path.getLastPathComponent();
```

Get the path from the root node to a specific TreeNode. This uses the getPathToRoot() method from the JTree's DefaultTreeModel. Note that the method is not defined in the TreeModel interface, so you have to cast the return value of the getModel() method. The method

returns an array of TreeNodes which can be used to create a
TreePath.

```
DefaultTreeModel model = (DefaultTreeModel)tree.getModel();
TreeNode nodes[] = model.getPathToRoot( myNode );
TreePath path = new TreePath( nodes );
```

You can also do this by asking the node itself:

```
TreeNode nodes[] = myNode.getPath();
TreePath path = new TreePath( nodes );
```

Cause a node in the tree to be collapsed. This will make it so the
expandable node at the given path will still display, but its contents
won't. If the path is to a leaf node, nothing will happen.

```
tree.collapsePath( path );
```

Cause a node in the tree to be expanded. This will make it so the
expandable node at the given path will display its contents. It the
path is a leaf, its parent will be expanded so the leaf and all of its
sibling are displayed.

```
tree.expandPath( path );
```

Get the TreePath that corresponds to a pixel location. This is useful
when you are using a MouseListener on your JTree and you want to
know which node is at a MouseEvent's location, or when you are
dropping something onto the tree.

```
// Here, 'e' is a MouseEvent.
TreePath path = tree.getPathForLocation( e.getX(), e.getY() );
```

Get the TreePath that is closest to a pixel location. This is like the
getPathForLocation() method except that the click doesn't have to be
right on.

```
// Again, 'e' is a MouseEvent.
TreePath path = tree.getClosestPathForLocation( e.getX(),
                                                 e.getY() );
```

Get the TreePath of the node at a specific row:

```
TreePath path = tree.getPathForRow( 12 );
```

Find out if a TreePath is collapsed:

```
boolean pathCollapsed = tree.isCollapsed( path );
```

Find out if a TreePath is expanded:

```
boolean pathExpanded = tree.isExpanded( path );
```

Find out if a TreePath is currently selected:

```
boolean pathSelected = tree.isPathSelected( path );
```

Make sure the specified path is visible within the current JScrollPane (if any):

```
tree.scrollPathToVisible( path );
```

8. Dealing with rows. There are a number of methods that do the same as some of the above TreePath methods do.

Collapse the expandable node at the specified row:

This does nothing if the node at the given row is not expandable.

```
tree.collapseRow( 12 );
```

Expand the node at the specified row. If the node at the given row is a leaf, nothing happens.

```
tree.expandRow( 12 );
```

Find the row that is at the given pixel location:

```
// Here, 'e' is a MouseEvent.
int clickedRow = tree.getRowForLocation( e.getX(), e.getY() );
```

Find the row that is closest to the given pixel location:

```
// Here, 'e' is a MouseEvent.
int clickedRow = tree.getClosestRowForLocation( e.getX(),
                                                 e.getY() );
```

Get the path from the root node to the node at the given row:

```
TreePath path = tree.getPathForRow( 12 );
```

Get the row of the node specified by a given TreePath:

```
int row = tree.getRowForPath( path );
```

Find out if a specific row is selected:

```
boolean rowSelected = tree.isRowSelected( 12 );
```

Make sure the specified row is visible within the JScrollPane (if any):

```
tree.scrollRowToVisible( 12 );
```

Find out how many rows are currently visible. This applies whenever the JTree is too large for its container.

```
int numRows = tree.getVisibleRowCount();
```

Basic Code Examples

EXAMPLE 8-80 Basic Use of JTree

This example illustrates the ideas discussed previously plus a few more. It makes a simple tree that goes four levels deep and displays within a

JScrollPane so that you can get to the entire tree even though it is larger than the frame in which it displays. Figure 8-126 shows the example.

Important points to notice:

- The main class listens for events that are generated when a tree item is selected or when a node that has child nodes is expanded or compressed. When the selection changes, it prints out the selections. When a node is expanded or collapsed, the main class prints out a string describing what happened.

- In addition, it uses a custom TreeCellRenderer to make the leaf nodes draw differently than they do by default.

Here is the source code:

```
import com.sun.java.swing.*;
import com.sun.java.swing.tree.*;
import com.sun.java.swing.event.*;
import java.awt.*;
import java.util.*;

public class MyFrame extends JFrame implements
        TreeSelectionListener, TreeExpansionListener
{
    MyCellRenderer mRenderer;
    JTree mTree;
    boolean mCollapsing = false;

    public MyFrame()
    {
        setTitle( "JTree1" );

        // Store the content pane in a variable for easier
        // access.
        JPanel mPanel = (JPanel)getContentPane();

        // Set the layout manager so the tree's scroll pane
        // can completely overlay the content pane.
        mPanel.setLayout( new BorderLayout() );

        // We just create three tree nodes because a maximum
        // of three will be in use at a time — one for each
        // level of the tree.
        DefaultMutableTreeNode lev1, lev2, lev3;
```

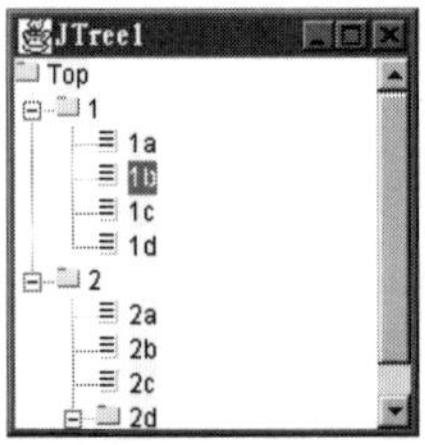

Figure 8-126
A simple JTree
example.

```
// Create the first node which is actually the root
// node.
DefaultMutableTreeNode top =
                    new DefaultMutableTreeNode(
                    new MyNode( "Top" ) );

// Create a new tree node and add it under the root
// node.
top.add( lev1 = new DefaultMutableTreeNode(
                            new MyNode( "1" ) ) );

// Create four nodes and add them to the one just
// created.
lev1.add( new DefaultMutableTreeNode(
                            new MyNode( "1a" ) ) );
lev1.add( new DefaultMutableTreeNode(
                            new MyNode( "1b" ) ) );
lev1.add( new DefaultMutableTreeNode(
                            new MyNode( "1c" ) ) );
lev1.add( new DefaultMutableTreeNode(
                            new MyNode( "1d" ) ) );

// Create a new node and add it under the root node.
top.add( lev1 = new DefaultMutableTreeNode(
                            new MyNode( "2" ) ) );

// Create three nodes and put them under the node we
// just created.
lev1.add( new DefaultMutableTreeNode(
                            new MyNode( "2a" ) ) );
lev1.add( new DefaultMutableTreeNode(
                            new MyNode( "2b" ) ) );
lev1.add( new DefaultMutableTreeNode(
                            new MyNode( "2c" ) ) );

// Create a fourth to add as we added the previous
// three, but it will also have children.
lev1.add( lev3 = new DefaultMutableTreeNode(
                            new MyNode( "2d" ) ) );

// Create a new node and add it below the one just
// created.
lev3.add( new DefaultMutableTreeNode(
                            new MyNode( "3a" ) ) );

// Create a new JTree with the root node.
mTree = new JTree( top );

// Specify that we have our own component for drawing
// the tree items.
mTree.setCellRenderer(
                    mRenderer = new MyCellRenderer() );

// We will have this class be notified when the
// selction state of the tree changes or when a node
```

```
      // is expanded.
      mTree.addTreeSelectionListener( this );
      mTree.addTreeExpansionListener( this );

      // Create a scroll pane that will control scrolling
      // of the tree if it gets too big for the frame.
      JScrollPane scrollpane = new JScrollPane();
      scrollpane.getViewport().add( mTree );

      // Add the scroll pane, having it take up all of the
      // frame's area.
      mPanel.add( "Center", scrollpane );
   }

   // This class holds the data for a tree node.
   private class MyNode
   {
      private String mText;

      public MyNode( String text )
      {
         mText = text;
      }

      public String toString()
      {
         return mText;
      }
   }

   // This class is used to draw the tree items.
   private class MyCellRenderer extends JLabel implements
            TreeCellRenderer
   {
      private Icon mNodeIcon;
      private Icon mLeafIcon;

      public MyCellRenderer()
      {
         mNodeIcon = new ImageIcon( "dir.gif" );
         mLeafIcon = new ImageIcon( "file.gif" );
      }

      // This method is called when the tree is ready to
      // have a tree item drawn.  The method configures
      // itself (as the JLabel subclass that it is) so that
      // when it is drawn, it will represent the item being
      // drawn.
      public Component getTreeCellRendererComponent(
                                    JTree tree,
                                    Object value,
                                    boolean selected,
                                    boolean expanded,
                                    boolean leaf,
                                    int row,
```

```
                                    boolean hasFocus )
{
    DefaultMutableTreeNode node =
                        (DefaultMutableTreeNode)value;

    // Load the tree item's string into the JLabel.
    setText( ((MyNode)(node.getUserObject())).
                                        toString() );

    // Set the JLabel icon based on whether the node
    // being drawn is a leaf or a node.
    if ( leaf )
        setIcon( mLeafIcon );
    else
        setIcon( mNodeIcon );

    // Set the text fore-and background colors based
    // on whether the item being drawn is currently
    // selected.
    if ( selected )
    {
        setForeground( SystemColor.textHighlightText );
        setBackground( SystemColor.textHighlight );
    }
    else
    {
        setForeground( SystemColor.textText );
        setBackground( SystemColor.window );
    }

    return this;
}


// This method draws the tree item as its state was
// set in the call to getTreeCellRendererComponent().
public void paint( Graphics g )
{
    int textstart, textwidth;

    textstart = getIcon().getIconWidth() +
                                    getIconTextGap();
    textwidth = getSize().width - textstart;

    getIcon().paintIcon( this, g, 0, 0 );

    g.setColor( getBackground() );
    g.fillRect( textstart, 0, textwidth,
                getSize().height );
    g.setColor( getForeground() );
    g.drawString( getText(), textstart,
                g.getFontMetrics().getAscent() );
}
}


// This is the method that is called when the selection
```

```
   // state of the tree changes.
   public void valueChanged( TreeSelectionEvent e )
   {
      TreePath paths[] = e.getPaths();

      for ( int i = 0; i < paths.length; i++ )
         System.out.println( i + ":  " + paths[i] );
   }

   // These methods are called when a tree node is expanded.
   public void treeExpanded( TreeExpansionEvent e )
   {
      System.out.println( "Expanded" );
   }

   public void treeCollapsed( TreeExpansionEvent e )
   {
      System.out.println( "Collapsed" );
   }
}
```

NOTE: *See Chapter 10, "Integrating JFC Example1: A File Browser" and Chapter 11, "Integrating JFC Example2: Adding Items to and Removing Items from JTrees" for examples of JTree's advanced capabilities.*

JTree's Public Methods

`void addSelectionInterval(int index0,int index1):`

Adds the paths between the given rows (inclusive) to the list of currently selected TreePaths.

`void addSelectionPath(TreePath path):`

Adds the given TreePath to the list of currently selected TreePaths.

`void addSelectionPaths(TreePath paths[]):`

Adds the TreePaths in the given array to the list of currently selected TreePaths.

`void addSelectionRow(int row):`

Adds the path at the given row to the list of currently selected TreePaths.

`void addSelectionRows(int rows[]):`

Adds the rows in the given array to the list of currently selected TreePaths.

```
void addTreeExpansionListener(TreeExpansionListener tel):
```

Tells the JTree to notify the given class whenever a tree node expands or collapses.

```
void addTreeSelectionListener(TreeSelectionListener tsl):
```

Tells the JTree to notify the given class whenever the JTree's selection state changes.

```
void clearSelection():
```

Makes it so no paths are selected.

```
void collapsePath(TreePath path):
```

Makes it so the child nodes of the given node are not visible.

```
void collapseRow(int row):
```

Makes it so the path at the given row is collapsed.

```
String convertValueToText(Object value,boolean selected,boolean
        expanded,boolean leaf,int row,boolean hasFocus):
```

TreeCellRenderers call this method to convert a node's value to a String. By default it just calls the Object's toString() method. Override to implement other behavior.

```
void expandPath(TreePath path):
```

Expands the given path and makes sure it is visible.

```
void expandRow(int row):
```

Expands the path at the given row.

```
void fireTreeCollapsed(TreePath path):
```

Causes TreeExpansionListeners to be notified that the given TreePath has been collapsed.

```
void fireTreeExpanded(TreePath path):
```

Causes TreeExpansionListeners to be notified that the given TreePath has been expanded.

```
AccessibleContext getAccessibleContext():
```

Returns a subclass of AccessibleContext which gives access to the JTree's accessibility information.

`TreeCellEditor getCellEditor():`

Returns the TreeCellEditor used to edit nodes in the JTree.

`TreeCellRenderer getCellRenderer():`

Returns the TreeCellRenderer used to draw the JTree's nodes.

`TreePath getClosestPathForLocation(int x,int y):`

Returns a TreePath for the node that is closest to the given point.

`int getClosestRowForLocation(int x,int y):`

Returns the row number for the node that is closest to the given point.

`TreePath getEditingPath():`

If a node is being edited, this returns the path to that node.

`boolean getInvokesStopCellEditing()`

Returns true if changes are not automatically discarded when editing is interrupted.

`Object getLastSelectedPathComponent():`

Returns the last node in the first currently selected path.

`TreePath getLeadSelectionPath():`

Returns the TreePath that was the last selection to be added to the list of selected paths.

`int getLeadSelectionRow():`

Returns the row representing the last selection added to the list of selected paths.

`int getMaxSelectionRow():`

Returns the row number that is the highest selected row number.

`int getMinSelectionRow():`

Returns the row number that is the lowest selected row number.

`TreeModel getModel():`

Returns the JTree's TreeModel.

`Rectangle getPathBounds(TreePath path):`

Returns the rectangle where the node at the end of the given TreePath will appear.

`TreePath getPathForLocation(int x,int y):`

Returns the path to the node at the given point.

`TreePath getPathForRow(int row):`

Gets the TreePath for the node at the given row.

`Dimension getPreferredScrollableViewportSize():`

Returns the size at which the JTree would like to be drawn, taking into account the current setting for visible row count and the preferred width.

`Rectangle getRowBounds(int row):`

Returns the rectangle in which the node in the given row appears.

`int getRowCount():`

Returns the number of rows in the JTree. This does not count nodes that are not expanded.

`int getRowForLocation(int x,int y):`

Returns the row where the given point falls.

`int getRowForPath(TreePath path):`

Returns the row where the given TreePath's last node is displayed.

`int getRowHeight():`

Returns the standard height for the JTree's rows.

`int getScrollableBlockIncrement(Rectangle visibleRect,int`
`                                orientation,int direction):`

Returns the amount the JTree would like to be scrolled when the user clicks between a scroll bar's thumbnail and end arrow.

`boolean getScrollableTracksViewportHeight():`

Overridden to return false.

```
boolean getScrollableTracksViewportWidth():
```

Overridden to return false.

```
int getScrollableUnitIncrement(Rectangle visibleRect,int
                                orientation,int direction):
```

Returns the distance the JTree wants to be scrolled when the user presses a scroll bar's end arrow.

```
int getSelectionCount():
```

Returns the number of currently selected nodes.

```
TreeSelectionModel getSelectionModel():
```

Returns the JTree's selection model.

```
TreePath getSelectionPath():
```

Returns the first selected TreePath.

```
TreePath[] getSelectionPaths():
```

Returns all of the currently selected TreePaths.

```
int[] getSelectionRows():
```

Returns all of the currently selected rows.

```
boolean getShowsRootHandles():
```

Returns true if the root node has the expand/collapse handle on it.

```
String getToolTipText(MouseEvent e)
```

Overridden to allow individual nodes to have different tool tips.

```
TreeUI getUI():
```

Returns the JTree's current look-and-feel class.

```
String getUIClassID():
```

Returns the identifying string that the look-and-feel uses to assign a UI class to the JTree.

```
int getVisibleRowCount():
```

Returns the number of rows that the JTree wants to have visible.

`boolean isCollapsed(int row):`

Returns true if the node at the given row is collapsed.

`boolean isCollapsed(TreePath path):`

Returns true if the given node is collapsed.

`boolean isEditable():`

Returns true if the JTree's nodes can be edited.

`boolean isEditing():`

Retruns true if a node in the JTree is currently being edited.

`boolean isExpanded(int row):`

Returns true if the node at the given row is expanded.

`boolean isExpanded(TreePath path):`

Returns true if the given node is expanded.

`boolean isFixedRowHeight():`

Returns true if all rows are a fixed height.

`boolean isLargeModel():`

Returns true if you are using the large model.

`boolean isOpaque():`

Returns true if the JTree paints its entire area.

`boolean isPathEditable(TreePath path)`

Returns true if the node at the given path can be edited.

`boolean isPathSelected(TreePath path):`

Returns true if the given TreePath is currently selected.

`boolean isRootVisible():`

Returns true if the root is displayed.

`boolean isRowSelected(int row):`

Returns true if the given row is currently selected.

`boolean isSelectionEmpty():`

Returns true if no nodes are currently selected.

`boolean isVisible(TreePath path):`

Returns true if the node described by the given TreePath is visible.

`void makeVisible(TreePath path):`

Makes it so the node represented by the given TreePath is visible.

`void removeSelectionInterval(int index0,int index1):`

Makes it so the nodes between the given rows (inclusive) are not selected.

`void removeSelectionPath(TreePath path):`

Makes it so that the given path is not selected.

`void removeSelectionPaths(TreePath paths[]):`

Makes it so that the paths in the given array are not selected.

`void removeSelectionRow(int row):`

Makes it so that the node at the given row is not selected.

`void removeSelectionRows(int rows[]):`

Makes it so that the nodes at the rows in the given array are not selected.

`void removeTreeExpansionListener(TreeExpansionListener tel):`

Tells the JTree to stop notifying the given class when nodes expand or collapse.

`void removeTreeSelectionListener(TreeSelectionListener tsl):`

Tells the JTree to stop notifying the given class when the selection state changes.

`void scrollPathToVisible(TreePath path):`

Makes it so the given TreePath is visible and expanded.

```
void scrollRowToVisible(int row):
```

Makes it so the node at the given row is visible.

```
void setCellEditor(TreeCellEditor cellEditor):
```

Specifies the TreeCellEditor to use when editing the JTree's nodes.

```
void setCellRenderer(TreeCellRenderer x):
```

Specifies the TreeCellRenderer to use when drawing the JTree's nodes.

```
void setEditable(boolean flag):
```

Specifies whether the JTree's nodes can be edited.

```
void setInvokesStopCellEditing(boolean flag)
```

Setting to true means changes are not automatically lost when editing is canceled.

```
void setLargeModel(boolean newValue):
```

Set to true if your tree will have many items visible at once, so the performance will be satisfactory.

```
void setModel(TreeModel newModel):
```

Replaces the JTree's TreeModel with another one.

```
void setRootVisible(boolean rootVisible):
```

Specifies whether the JTree's root node is visible.

```
void setRowHeight(int rowHeight):
```

Sets a row's height to the given pixel height.

```
void setSelectionInterval(int index0,int index1):
```

Makes it so the nodes between the given rows (inclusive) are the only selected nodes.

```
void setSelectionModel(TreeSelectionModel selectionModel):
```

Replaces the JTree's selection model.

```
void setSelectionPath(TreePath path):
```

Makes it so the given TreePath is the JTree's only selected path.

`void setSelectionPaths(TreePath paths[]):`

Makes it so the paths in the given array are the JTree's only selected paths.

`void setSelectionRow(int row):`

Makes it so the given row is the JTree's only selection.

`void setSelectionRows(int rows[]):`

Makes it so the nodes at the rows in the given array are the JTree's only selections.

`void setShowsRootHandles(boolean newValue):`

Specifies whether the nodes will display a collapse/expand handle.

`void setUI(TreeUI ui):`

Gives the JTree a new look-and-feel class.

`void setVisibleRowCount(int newCount):`

Specifies the number of rows the JTree wants visible at a time.

`void startEditingAtPath(TreePath path):`

Starts editing the node represented by the given TreePath.

`boolean stopEditing():`

Stops the current editing session, if there is one.

`void treeDidChange():`

Tells the JTree that it should resize itself, but not collapse any expanded nodes.

`void updateUI():`

Tells the JTree that the look-and-feel class has been changed.

JViewport

JViewport typically represents the visible area of a component that is being scrolled. It manages the relationship between the component being viewed and the visible area. JScrollPane uses a JViewport.

The default behavior of JViewport is to scroll a component in which one unit in the component being viewed is equal to one pixel on the screen. It is also possible to have a component that stores its coordinates in something other than pixels. For example, if you have a data set that represents a blueprint of a house, and the data points are in feet. Obviously, JViewport does not know how to convert between feet and pixels, so you have to provide a conversion. This is called logical scrolling. The visible area on the screen represents some number of feet, and the component being viewed is still storing its coordinates in feet. You have to subclass JViewport to support logical scrolling.

Terms

- View—The component being viewed. The view coordinates are screen areas and points defined in whatever coordinates the view component is using.
- Extent—The visible area of the view in view coordinates.
- View Size—The overall size of the view in view coordinates.
- View Position—The view coordinate represented by the upper lefthand corner of the visible area.
- Backing Store—An offscreen buffer used to improve performance when scrolling.

Ancestors

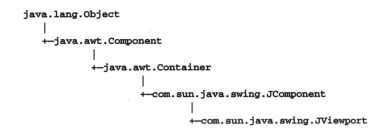

```
java.lang.Object
    |
    +—java.awt.Component
            |
            +—java.awt.Container
                    |
                    +—com.sun.java.swing.JComponent
                            |
                            +—com.sun.java.swing.JViewport
```

Steps in Creating and Using JViewport

1. If you are using a JViewport within a JScrollPane, you don't have to do anything—the JScrollPane creates the JViewport automatically and takes care of the scrolling interactions for you. If you want to create a JViewport for something different, you call the single constructor:

```
JViewport myViewport = new JViewport();
```

2. Specify the component that is being scrolled:

```
myViewport.setView( myComponent );
```

3. Tell the JViewport which part of the view component to display. You do this by specifying the view position:

```
myViewport.setViewPosition( new Point( 50, 50 ) );
```

4. Find out which part of the view component is being displayed:

```
Point viewPosition = myViewport.getViewPosition();
```

5. Listen for when anything about the JViewport changes. JViewport generates ChangeEvents.

Specify the class that should be notified of changes. In this case it is the current class:

```
myViewport.addChangeListener( this );
```

Make the event-receiving class (MyFrame) implement the ChangeListener interface:

```
public class MyFrame extends JFrame implements ChangeListener
{
    .
    .
    .
    public void stateChanged( ChangeEvent e )
    {
        // Now you know that something has changed.  You have to
        // ask the JViewport what it was.
    }
}
```

Basic Code Examples

EXAMPLE 8-81 Using JViewport Outside a JScrollPane

This example displays an image and, as you move the mouse over the image, a square part of the image, centered at the mouse position, displays in a smaller viewport. Figure 8-127 shows the example with the mouse positioned directly over one of the bird's faces.

Important points to notice:

■ The component that holds and draws the image and draws is called *RasterComponent* and is an inner class within the main frame class MyFrame.

Figure 8-127
An example of
JViewport.

- We offset the mouse position when setting the viewport's view position so that the viewport displays the mouse's location as centered.
- The component sets its preferred size to the size of the image. That is where the view size comes from.

Here is the source code:

```java
import com.sun.java.swing.*;
import java.awt.*;
import java.awt.event.*;

public class MyFrame extends JFrame implements
        MouseMotionListener
{
    JViewport vp;
    RasterComponent rc;
    RasterComponent rc2;

    public MyFrame()
    {
        setTitle( "JViewport1" );

        // Store the content pane in a variable for easy
        // access.
        JPanel mPanel = (JPanel)getContentPane();

        // Components will all be added to this panel.
        mPanel.setLayout( null );

        // Create a component containing the full-size image.
        rc =  new RasterComponent( "parrots.jpg" );

        // Place the component.
        rc.setBounds( 0, 0, rc.getPreferredSize().width,
```

```
                        rc.getPreferredSize().height );

        // Add the component.
        mPanel.add( rc );

        // Make it so this class is notified when the mouse
        // moves so we can update the viewport.
        rc.addMouseMotionListener( this );

        // Create a viewport.
        vp = new JViewport();

        // Create another component holding the image.
        rc2 = new RasterComponent( "parrots.jpg" );

        // Make the component into the viewport's view
        // component.
        vp.setView( rc2 );

        // Place the viewport.
        vp.setBounds( 0, 300, 100, 100 );

        // Add the viewport to the content pane.
        mPanel.add( vp );
    }

    // This is called when the mouse moves over the full
    // size image.
    public void mouseMoved( MouseEvent e )
    {
        // If we set the view position to the mouse position,
        // the spot where the mouse is will be in the
        // viewport's upper left corner.  We want it centered,
        // so we offset the view position.
        int viewX = e.getX() - vp.getExtentSize().width / 2;
        int viewY = e.getY() - vp.getExtentSize().height / 2;

        // Set the offset view position.
        vp.setViewPosition( new Point( viewX, viewY ) );
    }

    // For the MouseMotionListener interface.
    public void mouseDragged( MouseEvent e )
    {
    }

    // This is the class that displays an image and keeps
    // itself the image's size.
    private class RasterComponent extends JComponent
    {
        Image mImage;
        Dimension mSize;
        String mFilename;

        public RasterComponent( String filename )
        {
```

```
                mFilename = filename;

                // Load the image represented by the filename.
                loadImage();
            }

            // We set this to the size of the image.   The
            // viewport gets the view size here.
            public Dimension getPreferredSize()
            {
                return mSize;
            }

            // Paint the image on the component.
            public void paint( Graphics g )
            {
                g.drawImage( mImage, 0, 0, mSize.width,
                                 mSize.height, this );
            }

            // Load the full image and set the component's size
            // to match the image's.
            protected void loadImage()
            {
                MediaTracker tracker = new MediaTracker( this );

                mImage = Toolkit.getDefaultToolkit().getImage(
                                                      mFilename );

                tracker.addImage( mImage, 1 );

                try
                {
                    tracker.waitForAll();
                }
                catch( InterruptedException e ){}

                if ( mSize == null )
                    mSize = new Dimension( mImage.getWidth( this ),
                                        mImage.getHeight( this ) );

                setSize( mSize );
            }
        }
    }
```

JViewPort's Public Methods

```
void addChangeListener(ChangeListener l):
```

Tells the JViewport to notify the given class when view and visible area changes occur.

`AccessibleContext getAccessibleContext():`

Returns a subclass of AccessibleContext which gives access to the JViewport's accessibility information.

`Dimension getExtentSize():`

Returns the size of the visible area in view coordinates.

`final Insets getInsets():`

Overridden and final to prevent using insets.

`Component getView():`

Returns the view component.

`Point getViewPosition():`

Returns the position in the view component represented by the upper-lefthand corner of the visible area in view coordinates.

`Rectangle getViewRect():`

Returns a Rectangle made from the view position and the view size in view coordinates. Represents the visible area in view coordinates.

`Dimension getViewSize():`

Returns the size of the view component in view coordinates.

`boolean isBackingStoreEnabled():`

Returns true if the offscreen buffer is being used.

`boolean isOptimizedDrawingEnabled():`

Overridden for JViewport's special performance featues.

`void paint(Graphics g):`

Overridden for JViewport's custom painting.

`void remove(Component child):`

Removes the given component, presumably the view component.

`void removeChangeListener(ChangeListener l):`

Tells the JViewport to stop notifying the given class when view and visible area changes occur.

`void repaint(long tm,int x,int y, int w,int h):`

Overridden to maximize performance.

`void scrollRectToVisible(Rectangle contentRect):`

Overridden to make the given rectangle visible.

`void setBackingStoreEnabled(boolean x):`

Set true to enable the offscreen buffer.

`final void setBorder(Border border):`

Overridden to prevent using a border.

`void setBounds(int x,int y,int w,int h):`

Overridden to make additional view/extent calculations.

`void setExtentSize(Dimension newExtent):`

Sets the size of the visible area in view coordinates.

`void setView(Component view):`

Specifies the view component to use.

`void setViewPosition(Point p):`

Specifies the view coordinate position that should be displayed in the upper-lefthand corner of the visible area.

`void setViewSize(Dimension newSize):`

Specifies the view component's size in view coordinates.

`Dimension toViewCoordinates(Dimension size):`

Overridden by JViewport subclasses that support logical scrolling. Converts a size from pixels to view coordinates.

`Point toViewCoordinates(Point p):`

Overridden by JViewport subclasses that support logical scrolling. Converts a point from pixels to view coordinates.

JWindow

A JWindow is a container that, while associated with a particular JFrame, can float anywhere on the screen. A JWindow has no frame around it and in its default state is just a blank rectangle (see Figure 8-128).

As with JFrame, JDialog, JApplet, and JInternalFrame, access to the JWindow's display area should go through its JRootPane.

Ancestors

```
java.lang.Object
    |
    +—java.awt.Component
            |
            +—java.awt.Container
                    |
                    +—java.awt.Window
                            |
                            +—com.sun.java.swing.JWindow
```

NOTE: *For more information, see the "JRootPane," "JFrame," "JDialog," and "JInternalFrame" sections in this chapter. Also see the "Windows" section in Chapter 7, "JFC by Concept."*

Steps in Creating and Using JWindow

1. Create the window. JWindow's constructor requires a frame as its argument. In this case, the JWindow is being created within a subclass of JFrame, so its parent is the current class:

   ```
   JWindow win = new JWindow( this );
   ```

2. Specify the window's origin and size. Origin is in absolute screen coordinates, not relative to the parent frame:

   ```
   win.setBounds( 100, 100, 200, 300 );
   ```

Figure 8-133
A typical JWindow with a BevelBorder on its content pane.

This is a JWindow

3. Add a control to the window:

```
JButton btn = new JButton( "Ok" );
```

Set the content pane's layout manager (this is actually the content pane's default already):

```
win.getContentPane().setLayout( new BorderLayout() );
```

Add the button to the window.

```
win.getContentPane().add( "South", btn );
```

4. Show the window:

```
win.show();
```

You should not show the window until after any components are added.

5. Hide the window:

```
win.hide();
```

Basic Code Examples

EXAMPLE 8-82 A Basic JWindow

This simple example creates and displays a window after adding a button to it. Figure 8-129 shows the example as it first comes up.

Here is the source code:

```
import com.sun.java.swing.*;
import com.sun.java.swing.border.*;
import java.awt.*;

public class MyFrame extends JFrame
{
    public MyFrame()
    {
```

Figure 8-129

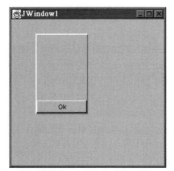

```
          setTitle( "JWindow1" );

          // Store the content pane in a variable for easier
          // access.
          JPanel contentPane = (JPanel)getContentPane();

          // Components will all be added to this panel.
          contentPane.setLayout( new BorderLayout() );

          //  Create the JWindow.
          JWindow win = new JWindow( this );

          // Set the window's size and origin (relative to the
          // upper-left corner of the display).
          win.setBounds( 50, 50, 100, 150 );

          // Create a button to add to the window.
          JButton btn = new JButton( "Ok" );

          // Store the window's content pane in a variable for
          // easier access.
          JPanel winPane = (JPanel)win.getContentPane();

          // Set the background color.
          winPane.setBackground( Color.lightGray );

          // Set the border so it is easier to see the window.
          winPane.setBorder( new BevelBorder(
                             BevelBorder.RAISED ) );

          // Set the window's content pane's layout.
          winPane.setLayout( new BorderLayout() );

          // Add the button to the window.
          winPane.add( "South", btn );

          // Display the window.
          win.setVisible( true );
     }
  }
```

Advanced Issues

EXAMPLE 8-83 Dragging a Component Around the Screen

This example creates a subclass of JWindow (FloatingComponent.java), which allows a component to be dragged around the screen. We use a JWindow because a JWindow can move outside the bounds of its parent container.

When the parent frame is initialized, the custom window is created. The parent frame specifies which component the custom window should contain. When the parent frame is first displayed (recognized by catching the windowOpened event), the window is moved to display directly over the frame's

center. When you drag the custom window around, it appears that you are dragging a component. Figure 8-130 shows the example as it first comes up.
Important points to notice:

- The custom window uses its glass pane to block events so the button does not appear to be pressed as we drag it.
- The custom window has to manage its own dragging and to make sure that while the drag is going on, the mouse pointer stays in the same spot within it.
- We use a WindowAdapter so we are notified when the main frame first appears.

The two main source files are the main frame (MyFrame.java) and the custom window (FloatingComponent.java).
Here is MyFrame's source code (FloatingComponent's follows it):

```java
import com.sun.java.swing.*;
import java.awt.*;
import java.awt.event.*;

public class MyFrame extends JFrame
{
    JButton b;
    FloatingComponent mFloatWindow;

    public MyFrame()
    {
        setTitle( "JWindow2" );

        // Store the content pane in a variable for easier access.
        JPanel mPanel = (JPanel)getContentPane();

        // The layout of the content pane doesn't really matter in this
        // example.
        mPanel.setLayout( new GridLayout( 7, 2 ) );

        // Create the button that will be placed into the floating
        // component window.
        b = new JButton( "Ok" );
        b.setBackground( Color.lightGray );

        // Create the floating component with the button as its
```

Figure 8-130

```
            component.
            mFloatWindow = new FloatingComponent( this, b );

            // Display the floating component.
            mFloatWindow.show();

            // We want to display the floating window in the frame's center
            // as soon as the frame is displayed.
            addWindowListener( new MyWindowAdapter() );
        }

        // This listens for the event that occurs when the frame is
            opened.
        private class MyWindowAdapter extends WindowAdapter
        {
            public void windowOpened( WindowEvent e )
            {
                // When the frame opens initially, place the floating window
                // in the frame's center.
                mFloatWindow.placeIt();
            }
        }
    }
```

Here is FloatingComponent's source code:

```
import com.sun.java.swing.*;
import java.awt.*;
import java.awt.event.*;

public class FloatingComponent extends JWindow implements
        MouseMotionListener
{
    private JComponent mComponent;
    private JFrame mParent;
    private int mRelX;
    private int mRelY;
    private boolean mDragging = false;

    public FloatingComponent( JFrame parent,
                              JComponent comp )
    {
        super( parent );

        // Save the parent so we can place the window at its
        // center.
        mParent = parent;

        // Store the component we will be displaying.
        mComponent = comp;

        // Size the window to its component's favorite size.
        // Can be a problem if the component has a very small
        // favorite size.
        setSize( comp.getPreferredSize() );
```

```java
        // Store the window's content pane in a variable for
        // easy access.
        JPanel pane = (JPanel)getContentPane();

        // Use a BorderLayout so we can make the component
        // fill the window.
        pane.setLayout( new BorderLayout() );

        // Add the component to the pane.
        pane.add( "Center", mComponent );

        // We use a transparent glass pane to catch mouse
        // events before the component does.
        setGlassPane( new TransPane() );

        // We have to call setVisible() or it won't get
        // events.
        getGlassPane().setVisible( true );
        getGlassPane().addMouseMotionListener( this );
    }

// Puts itself right in the center of its parent.
public void placeIt()
{
    setLocation( mParent.getLocation().x +
                  (mParent.getSize().width -
                  getSize().width) / 2,
                  mParent.getLocation().y +
                  (mParent.getSize().height -
                  getSize().height) / 2 );
}

// If the mouse is moving and we are not dragging, turn
// dragging off.
public void mouseMoved( MouseEvent e )
{
    if ( mDragging )
    {
        mDragging = false;
    }
}

// When dragging starts, save the relative location of
// the mouse within the component so we can make sure it
// stays there.  When we are dragging, find the absolute
// location of the source component and place the window
// at the mouse location relative to it.
public synchronized void mouseDragged( MouseEvent e )
{
    Component source = (Component)e.getSource();

    if ( !mDragging )
    {
        mRelX = e.getX();
```

```
                mRelY = e.getY();
                mDragging = true;
            }
            else
            {
                setLocation( source.getLocationOnScreen().x +
                             e.getX() - mRelX,
                             source.getLocationOnScreen().y +
                             e.getY() - mRelY );
            }
        }

        // A transparent panel.
        public class TransPane extends JPanel
        {
            // Override isOpaque() method so this can be
            // transparent.
            public boolean isOpaque()
            {
                return false;
            }

            // No painting required.
            public void paint( Graphics g )
            {
            }
        }
    }
```

JWindow's Public Methods

`AccessibleContext getAccessibleContext():`

Returns a subclass of AccessibleContext, which gives access to the JWindow's accessibility information.

`Container getContentPane():`

Returns the JWindow's root pane's content pane.

`Component getGlassPane():`

Returns the JWindow's root pane's glass pane.

`JLayeredPane getLayeredPane():`

Returns the JWindow's root pane's layered pane.

`JRootPane getRootPane():`

Returns the JWindow's root pane.

```
void setContentPane(Container content):
```

Replaces the JWindow's root pane's content pane with another container.

```
void setGlassPane(Component glass):
```

Replaces the JWindow's root pane's glass pane with another component.

```
void setLayeredPane(JLayeredPane layered):
```

Replaces the JWindow's root pane's layered pane with another one.

```
void setLayout(LayoutManager manager)
```

Overridden to remind you that you should be laying out the content pane instead.

Keymap

Keymap is an interface that defines the behavior of classes that contain a mapping of KeyStrokes to Actions. Text components typically have a Keymap that they use to keep track of what Action should occur when specific KeyStrokes happen. For example, a text field might have an entry in its Keymap that causes the cursor to move right when the right arrow key is pressed and the text field has the focus. The Keymap is usually created by a component's UI class.

You will usually use a Keymap to add KeyStroke/Action pairs to a component's existing Keymap.

Ancestors

Keymap is an interface that has no parent.

NOTE: *For more information, see the "KeyStroke," "AbstractAction," "JTextField," "JTextArea," "JTextPane," and "JTextComponent" sections in this chapter. Also see Chapter 5, "JFC Documents and Text Components."*

Steps in Creating and Using Keymap

1. Unless you create your own class to implement Keymap, you will want to modify a component's existing Keymap.

Get the component's Keymap:

```
Keymap map = myTextComp.getKeymap();
```

2. Get the KeyStroke that you want to use. The KeyStroke class can generate any combination of keys. In this case, we want to use Ctrl-C:

```
KeyStroke cut = KeyStroke.getKeyStroke( KeyEvent.VK_C,
                       ActionEvent.CTRL_MASK, false );
```

3. Create the Action that the Ctrl-C will trigger.

Define a subclass of AbstractAction:

```
private class CutAction extends AbstractAction
{
    public void actionPerformed(ActionEvent e)
    {
        JTextComponent tf = (JTextComponent)e.getSource();
        tf.cut();
    }
}
```

Create an instance of the Action:

```
CutAction cutAction = new CutAction();
```

4. Add the KeyStroke/Action pair to the Keymap:

```
map.addActionForKeyStroke( cut, cutAction );
```

5. Put the changed Keymap back:

```
myTextComp.setKeymap( map );
```

Basic Code Examples

EXAMPLE 8-84 Adding to a Keymap

This example shows how to make Ctrl-C cut a text field's selected text into the clipboard. It implements the steps described previously. Figure 8-131 shows the example just before the user presses Ctrl-C to cut the selected text.

Here is the source code:

```
import com.sun.java.swing.*;
import java.awt.*;
import java.awt.event.*;
import com.sun.java.swing.text.*;
```

Figure 8-131

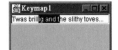

```java
public class MyFrame extends JFrame
{
    public MyFrame()
    {
        setTitle( "Keymap1" );

        // Store the content pane in a variable for easier
        // access.
        JPanel contentPane = (JPanel)getContentPane();

        // Components will all be added to this panel.
        contentPane.setLayout( new BorderLayout() );

        // Create a text field.
        JTextField myTextComp = new JTextField(
                    "Twas brillig and the slithy toves..." );

        // Put the text field at the top of the content pane.
        contentPane.add( "North", myTextComp );

        // Get the text field's Keymap.
        Keymap map = myTextComp.getKeymap();

        // Get the KeyStroke for 'Ctrl-C'
        KeyStroke cut = KeyStroke.getKeyStroke(
                    KeyEvent.VK_C,
                    ActionEvent.CTRL_MASK, false );

        // Create an Action.
        CutAction cutAction = new CutAction();

        // Add the KeyStroke/Action pair to the Keymap.
        map.addActionForKeyStroke( cut, cutAction );

        // Put the changed Keymap back.
        myTextComp.setKeymap( map );
    }

    // This is called when 'Ctrl-C' is pressed when the text
    // field has the focus.
    private class CutAction extends AbstractAction
    {
        public void actionPerformed(ActionEvent e)
        {
            // Get the text field.
            JTextComponent tf = (JTextComponent)e.getSource();

            // Cut any selected text into the clipboard.
            tf.cut();
        }
    }
}
```

Keymap's Public Methods

`void addActionForKeyStroke(KeyStroke key,Action a):`

Adds a KeyStroke/Action pair to the Keymap.

`Action getAction(KeyStroke key):`

Returns the Action associated with the given KeyStroke.

`Action[] getBoundActions():`

Returns all of the Actions in the Keymap.

`KeyStroke[] getBoundKeyStrokes():`

Returns all KeyStrokes in the Keymap.

`Action getDefaultAction()`

Returns the Action to trigger for KeyStrokes that are not mapped.

`void getDefaultAction(Action a)`

Specifies the Action to trigger for KeyStrokes that are not mapped.

`KeyStroke[] getKeyStrokesForAction(Action a):`

Returns a list of all KeyStrokes associated with the given Action.

`String getName():`

Returns the Keymap name.

`Keymap getResolveParent():`

Returns the inherited Keymap, if there is one.

`boolean isLocallyDefined(KeyStroke key):`

Returns true if the given KeyStroke is locally defined.

`void removeBindings():`

Clears the Keymap.

`void removeKeyStrokeBinding(KeyStroke keys):`

Removes the given KeyStroke and its associated Action from the Keymap.

```
void setResolveParent(Keymap parent):
```

Specifies a Keymap from which this Keymap can inherit KeyStroke/ Action pairs. KeyStroke/Action pairs are overridden by pairs in this Keymap that have the same KeyStroke.

KeyStroke

KeyStroke is a class that represents a key stroke occurrence, including all modifiers and whether the key is pressed or released. KeyStrokes are usually registered with a component and have an Action associated with them. For example, if you want a component to change state when the Alt-z combination is pressed, you create a KeyStroke to represent Alt-z, and you tell the component which Action to execute when that key stroke occurs.

Ancestors

```
java.lang.Object
    |
    +—com.sun.java.swing.KeyStroke
```

Steps in Creating and Using KeyStroke

1. KeyStroke has no constructors since the possible combinations of keys is finite. Instead it has a series of getKeyStroke() methods that create an instance of KeyStroke based on the properties you pass in.

    Get the KeyStroke representing the moment when Alt-z is released:

    ```
    KeyStroke stroke = KeyStroke.getKeyStroke( KeyEvent.VK_Z,
                        ActionEvent.ALT_MASK, true ),
    ```

    Notice that KeyEvent.VK_Z was used instead of 'z'.

    You can also get the KeyStroke that a KeyEvent contains using:

    ```
    KeyStroke.getKeyStrokeForEvent( keyEvent );
    ```

2. Get the parts of the KeyStroke:

    ```
    char ch = stroke.getKeyChar();
    ```

```
int code = stroke.getKeyCode();
int modifiers = stroke.getModifiers();
boolean onRelease = stroke.isOnKeyRelease();
```

Basic Code Examples

EXAMPLE 8-85 Registering KeyStrokes with JComponents

This example creates a custom component and registers a set of KeyStrokes that will change the component's state. When the component has the focus, pressing either the space bar or the enter key will change the component's state. When the component does not have the focus, pressing 'Alt-z' changes its state. The component displays a string that says whether it is selected and/or focused and changes color when its state changes. Figure 8-132 shows the example as it first comes up.

Important points to notice:

- In addition to the custom component, there is also a normal JButton. This lets you change the focus from the custom component so you can try out 'Alt-z'.

- The custom component class is MyComponent and is an inner class to the main frame class (MyFrame).

- There is also an inner class called ChangeAction that subclasses AbstractAction. It represents the action that is triggered when one of MyComponent's registered KeyStrokes happens.

- The registerKeyboardAction() method is how KeyStrokes and Actions are associated and is how JComponent subclasses know about them.

Here is the source code:

```
import com.sun.java.swing.*;
import java.awt.*;
import java.awt.event.*;

public class MyFrame extends JFrame
{
    public MyFrame()
    {
        setTitle( "KeyStroke1" );

        // Store the content pane in a variable for easier
        // access.
        JPanel contentPane = (JPanel)getContentPane();
```

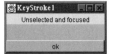

Figure 8-132

```
        // Components will all be added to this panel.
        contentPane.setLayout( new BorderLayout() );

        // Create an instance of the custom component.
        MyComponent m = new MyComponent();

        // Place the custom component at the top of the
        // content pane.
        contentPane.add( "North", m );

        // Create a standard button and put it at the bottom
        // of the content pane.
        JButton ok = new JButton( "ok" );
        contentPane.add( "South", ok );
    }

    // This class represents the Action that is triggered
    // when one of the custom component's registered
    // KeyStrokes happens.
    private class ChangeAction extends AbstractAction
    {
        public void actionPerformed( ActionEvent e )
        {
            // Cast the source so we can change its state.
            MyComponent comp = (MyComponent)e.getSource();

            // Change the custom component's state.
            comp.changeState();
        }
    }

    // This is the custom component class.
    private class MyComponent extends JComponent implements
            FocusListener
    {
        private boolean mIsSelected = false;

        public MyComponent()
        {
            // We listen for when the focus changes so we can
            // repaint the component, modifying its displayed
            // text string.
            addFocusListener( this );

            // Get rid of any pre-existing key stroke
            // registration.
            resetKeyboardActions();

            // Tell the component to execute a ChangeAction
            // when component has the focus and the space bar
            // is pressed with no modifier keys.
            registerKeyboardAction( new ChangeAction(),
                    KeyStroke.getKeyStroke( KeyEvent.VK_SPACE,
                    0 ), JComponent.WHEN_FOCUSED );
```

```
      // Tell the component to execute a ChangeAction
      // when component has the focus and the enter key
      // is pressed with no modifier keys.
      registerKeyboardAction( new ChangeAction(),
              KeyStroke.getKeyStroke( KeyEvent.VK_ENTER,
              0 ), JComponent.WHEN_FOCUSED );

      // Tell the component to execute a ChangeAction
      // when component has the focus or is in the
      // container of the component that has the focus,
      // and 'Alt-z' is pressed.
      registerKeyboardAction( new ChangeAction(),
              KeyStroke.getKeyStroke( KeyEvent.VK_Z,
              ActionEvent.ALT_MASK, true ),
              JComponent.WHEN_IN_FOCUSED_WINDOW );
   }

   // Toggles the component's selected state.  Calls
   // repaint() so the change is displayed.
   public void changeState()
   {
      mIsSelected = !mIsSelected;
      repaint();
   }

   // We override this so layout managers have an idea
   // of how big to make the component.
   public Dimension getPreferredSize()
   {
      return new Dimension( 100, 20 );
   }

   public void paint( Graphics g )
   {
      String text;

      // If the component is currently selected, draw
      // the background in red.  Otherwise draw it is
      // yellow.  Also start the 'text' string so it
      // reflects the state.
      if ( mIsSelected )
      {
         g.setColor( Color.red );
         text = "Selected and ";
      }
      else
      {
         g.setColor( Color.yellow );
         text = "Unselected and ";
      }

      // Draw the background rectangle.
```

```
        g.fillRect( 0, 0, getWidth(), getHeight() );

        // Set the text color.
        g.setColor( Color.black );

        // Add the focus state to the 'text' string.
        if ( hasFocus() )
            text = new String( text + "focused" );
        else
            text = new String( text + "unfocused" );

        // Get the current font metrics.
        FontMetrics metrics = g.getFontMetrics();

        // Figure out where to start drawing the 'text'
        // string so it is centered.
        int x = getWidth() / 2 -
                metrics.stringWidth( text ) / 2;
        int y = getHeight() / 2 +
                metrics.getAscent() / 2;

        // Draw the 'text' string.
        g.drawString( text, x, y );
    }

    // When the focus is lost, repaint so the change is
    // displayed.
    public void focusLost( FocusEvent e )
    {
        repaint();
    }

    // When the focus is gained, repaint so the change is
    // displayed.
    public void focusGained( FocusEvent e )
    {
        repaint();
    }
    }
}
```

KeyStroke's Public Methods

`boolean equals(Object anObject):`

Overridden to implement comparison.

`char getKeyChar():`

Returns the char part of the KeyStroke.

`int getKeyCode():`

Returns the key-code part of the KeyStroke.

`static KeyStroke getKeyStroke(char keyChar):`

Returns a KeyStroke that represents a press of the given char.

`static KeyStroke getKeyStroke(char c, boolean onKeyRelease)`

Returns a KeyStroke that represents a the char when it is pressed or released, depending on `'onKeyRelease'`.

`static KeyStroke getKeyStroke(int keyCode,int modifiers):`

Returns a KeyStroke that represents a press of the given key-code with the given modifiers.

`static KeyStroke getKeyStroke(int keyCode,int modifiers,boolean`
`onKeyRelease):`

Returns a KeyStroke that represents a press or release of the given keycode with the given modifiers.

`static KeyStroke getKeyStroke(String representation):`

Not implemented.

`static KeyStroke getKeyStrokeForEvent(KeyEvent anEvent):`

Makes a KeyStroke out of the key-code and modifiers in the given KeyEvent.

`int getModifiers():`

Returns the modifier part of the KeyStroke.

`int hashCode():`

Returns a hash code for the KeyStroke.

`boolean isOnKeyRelease():`

Returns true if the KeyStroke represents a key release rather than a key press.

`String toString()`

Overridden to provide custom formatting.

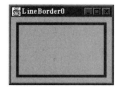

Figure 8-133
A typical LineBorder
inset from the frame
edge to distinguish it.

LineBorder

A line border is simply a line that follows the inside edge of a component (see Figure 8-133). Its width and color can be customized.

As with other borders, a LineBorder is painted when its paintBorder() method is called. If a component overrides its own paint() or paintBorder() method and does not call the border's paintBorder() method, the border will not draw.

Ancestors

```
java.lang.Object
    |
    +—com.sun.java.swing.border.AbstractBorder
         |
         +—com.sun.java.swing.border.LineBorder
```

NOTE: *For more information, see the "AbstractBorder" and "JPanel" sections in this chapter and the "Component Borders" section in Chapter 7, "JFC by Concept."*

Steps in Creating and Using LineBorder

1. Create a container that supports borders. This will typically be a JPanel:

   ```
   JPanel panel1 = new JPanel();
   ```

2. Create a line border. There are two constructors. The following one just sets the line color:

   ```
   LineBorder line1 = new LineBorder( Color.black );
   ```

   The next one sets both line color and line width in pixels:

   ```
   LineBorder line2 = new LineBorder( Color.red, 5 );
   ```

3. Apply the border to the container:

   ```
   panel1.setBorder( line1 );
   ```

Figure 8-134

Basic Code Examples

EXAMPLE 8-86 Basic LineBorder

This example creates a JPanel with a 1-pixel yellow border, a JPanel with a 5-pixel red border, and a JPanel with a titled border that incorporates an 8-pixel green line border. Figure 8-134 shows the example as it first comes up.

Here is the source code:

```
import com.sun.java.swing.*;
import com.sun.java.swing.border.*;
import java.awt.*;

public class MyFrame extends JFrame
{
    public MyFrame()
    {
        setTitle( "LineBorder1" );

        // Store the content pane for easy access.
        JPanel mPanel = (JPanel)getContentPane();

        // Components will all be added to this panel.
        mPanel.setLayout( new GridLayout( 3, 1 ) );

        // Create a panel that uses a 1-pixel wide black line
        // as a border.
        JPanel panel = new JPanel();

        // Create the line border in yellow.
        LineBorder line1 = new LineBorder( Color.yellow );

        // Apply the border.
        panel.setBorder( line1 );

        // Add the bordered pane to the buffered pane.
        mPanel.add( panel );

        // Create a panel with a 6-pixel wide red line as a
        // border.
        JPanel pane2 = new JPanel();

        // Create the line border in red with a width of 5
        // pixels.
```

```
        LineBorder line2 = new LineBorder( Color.red, 6 );

        // Apply the border.
        pane2.setBorder( line2 );

        // Add the panel to the content pane.
        mPanel.add( pane2 );

        // Create a panel that uses a titled border
        // incorporating a line border.
        JPanel pane3 = new JPanel();

        // Create the titled border.  Notice that it
        // incorporates a green line border with width 10.
        TitledBorder titled1 = new TitledBorder(
                        new LineBorder( Color.green, 10 ),
                        "Titled Using LineBorder" );

        // Apply the border.
        pane3.setBorder( titled1 );

        // Add the panel to the content pane.
        mPanel.add( pane3 );
    }
}
```

LineBorder's Public Methods

`Border createBlackLineBorder():`

This is a convenience method that generates a 1-pixel wide black LineBorder.

`Border createGrayLineBorder():`

This is a convenience method that generates a 1-pixel wide gray LineBorder.

`Insets getBorderInsets(Component c):`

Returns the distance that the border will take up of each of the target component's sides.

`Color getLineColor():`

Returns the color that the LineBorder will be drawn in.

`int getThickness():`

Returns the LineBorder's thickness.

`boolean isBorderOpaque():`

Returns true since the LineBorder paints its entire area.

```
void paintBorder(Component c,Graphics g,int x,int y,int width,int
                 height):
```

Actually paints the border onto the target component.

LookAndFeel

LookAndFeel is an abstract class that you can subclass to represent your own look-and-feel. Each LookAndFeel subclass has a name and a description as well as a list of UI classes and which component types they are associated with.

If you want to create your own special look-and-feel, you may want to consider subclassing an existing subclass of LookAndFeel like com.sun.java. swing.plaf.basic.BasicLookAndFeel.

Ancestors

```
java.lang.Object
   |
   +—com.sun.java.swing.LookAndFeel
```

NOTE: *For more information, see Chapter 4, "Pluggable Look-and-Feel," as well as the "UIManager" and "UIDefaults" sections in this chapter.*

NOTE: *For a complete discussion of look-and-feel options, see Chapter 4, "Pluggable Look-and-Feel."*

LookAndFeel's Public Methods

```
UIDefaults getDefaults():
```

Returns an instance of UIDefaults which contains a list of component UI identification strings and the UI classes that should be applied to them.

```
String getDescription():
```

Returns a brief description of the look-and-feel that this class represents.

`String getID()`

Returns a String that identifies the look-and-feel.

`String getName():`

Returns the official name for the look-and-feel that this class represents.

`void initialize():`

Called before getDefaults() is called the first time. Any start-up initialization should occur here.

`static void installBorder(JComponent c,String defaultBorderName):`

Makes the given component use the border resource associated with the given name if the component's border is null or is a UIResource.

`static void installColors(JComponent c,String defaultBgName,String defaultFgName):`

Makes the given component use the given foreground and background color resources associated with the names if its colors are null or are UIResources.

`static void installColorsAndFont(JComponent c, String defaultBgName, String defaultFgName,String defaultFontName):`

Makes the given component use the given foreground and background color resources and font resource associated with the names if its colors and font are null or are UIResources.

`boolean isNativeLookAndFeel():`

Returns true if this look-and-feel was designed to blend in with the look-and-feel of the platform the JVM is running on.

`boolean isSupportedLookAndFeel():`

Returns true if this look-and-feel is supported on the platform the JVM is running on. For example, the Windows look-and-feel is not supported on UNIX platforms.

`static Object makeIcon(Class baseClass, String gifFile)`

Creates an ImageIcon UIResource from the GIF file name.

```
String toString():
```

Overridden to custom format the string.

```
void uninitialize():
```

Undo any initialization that was done in the initialize() method. This is called right before a different look-and-feel replaces this one.

```
static void uninstallBorder(JComponent c):
```

Uninstalls the given component's border if the border is a UIResource.

MatteBorder

A MatteBorder is a border that fills the edge of its container with a solid color or an icon (see Figure 8-135). You can specify the border's width on all four sides.

If you use an icon to fill the border, you do not just get the icon repeated all the way around with the image always complete. Instead, you get the effect of filling the component with the icon in tiling fashion, and the pattern is just revealed where the border is.

Ancestors

```
java.lang.Object
    |
    +—com.sun.java.swing.border.AbstractBorder
        |
        +—com.sun.java.swing.border.EmptyBorder
            |
            +—com.sun.java.swing.border.MatteBorder
```

NOTE: *For more information, see the "AbstractBorder," "ImageIcon," and "JPanel" sections in this chapter. Also see the "Component Borders" section in Chapter 7, "JFC by Concept."*

Figure 8-135
A typical MatteBorder.

Steps in Creating and Using MatteBorder

1. Create a component to which the MatteBorder will be applied. This is typically a JPanel:

   ```
   JPanel panel = new JPanel();
   ```

2. Create a MatteBorder. There are three constructors. the following one creates a solid colored border that is the passed-in width on each side of its container:

   ```
   MatteBorder( int top, int left, int bottom, int right, Color
               borderColor )
   ```

   This constructor creates a patterned border that is the passed-in width on each side:

   ```
   MatteBorder( int top, int left, int bottom, int right, Icon
               borderIcon )
   ```

   To create a MatteBorder, use the following:

   ```
   MatteBorder border1 = new MatteBorder( 10, 10, 10, 10,
                                          Color.red );
   ```

3. Create a TitledBorder that includes a MatteBorder. This will put the MatteBorder all the way around the container, and the title string will appear as a solid-backgrounded text string in a break in the border:

   ```
   TitledBorder border = new TitledBorder( new MatteBorder( 16, 16,
                          16, 16, new ImageIcon( "delete.gif" ) ),
                          "Titled/Matted border" );
   ```

4. Make the panel use the border:

   ```
   pane3.setBorder( border );
   ```

Basic Code Examples

EXAMPLE 8-87 Basic MatteBorder

This example shows how to make a solid color MatteBorder, how to make an icon-patterned MatteBorder, and how to incorporate a MatteBorder into a TitledBorder. Figure 8-136 shows the example as it first comes up.

Here is the source code:

```
import com.sun.java.swing.*;
import com.sun.java.swing.border.*;
import java.awt.*;

public class MyFrame extends JFrame
{
```

```
public MyFrame()
{
    setTitle( "MatteBorder1" );

    // Store the content pane in a variable for easier
    // access.
    JPanel contentPane = (JPanel)getContentPane();

    // Components will all be added to this panel.
    contentPane.setLayout( new GridLayout( 3, 1 ) );

    // Create a panel that will have a 10-pixel wide red
    // border all the way around.
    JPanel panel1 = new JPanel();
    panel1.setBorder(
        new MatteBorder( 10, 10, 10, 10, Color.red ) );

    // Add the panel to the content pane.
    contentPane.add( panel1 );

    // Create a panel that uses an icon to fill a
    // 16-pixel wide border all the way around.
    JPanel pane2 = new JPanel();
    pane2.setBorder( new MatteBorder( 16, 16, 16, 16,
                        new ImageIcon( "print.gif" ) ) );

    // Add the panel to the content pane.
    contentPane.add( pane2 );

    // Create a panel that uses an icon to fill a
    // 16-pixel wide border all the way around.
    JPanel pane3 = new JPanel();
    TitledBorder border =
            new TitledBorder( new MatteBorder( 16, 16,
                16, 16, new ImageIcon( "delete.gif" ) ),
                "Titled/Matted border" );
    pane3.setBorder( border );

    // Add the panel to the content pane.
    contentPane.add( pane3 );
}
}
```

MatteBorder's Public Methods

```
Insets getBorderInsets(Component c)
```

Returns the distance the border will extend in from each side of the component.

```
boolean isBorderOpaque():
```

Returns true since MatteBorder paints its entire area.

```
void paintBorder(Component c,Graphics g,int x,int y,int width,int
     height):
```

Actually paints the border onto the target component.

OverlayLayout

OverlayLayout is a layout manager for putting things on top of each other. As you add components to a container that is using an OverlayLayout, the ones that are added later will go further down in the stacking order, so that the first one added will be topmost (see Figure 8-137). Of course, this doesn't extend to peer components from the AWT since they are *always* on top of lightweight components (which JFC components are). The OverlayLayout tries to expand each component out to fill its container's space if the container's space is fixed. If its container's preferred size is being queried, OverlayLayout will try to lay the components out at their preferred sizes with their alignment points on top of each other. It uses that information to calculate the container's preferred size.

Ancestors

```
java.lang.Object
   |
   +--com.sun.java.swing.OverlayLayout
```

NOTE: *For more information, see the "JFC Layout Managers" section in Chapter 7, "JFC by Concept."*

Steps in Creating and Using OverlayLayout

1. Create a container to use the overlay layout:

```
JPanel overlayPanel = new JPanel();
```

Figure 8-137
A transparent panel with white text overlaying another panel with radio buttons.

2. Create the OverlayLayout. Notice that you have to pass the container in as an argument to the constructor:

```
OverlayLayout layout = new OverlayLayout( overlayPanel );
```

3. Add components to the container. Remember that the first one added will be on top.

Create the component to be added:

```
JPanel paneOne = new JPanel();
```

Set its alignment value(s) if you want it offset from the other components added to the OverlayLayout:

```
paneOne.setAlignmentX( (float)0.5 );
```

Add the component to the container:

```
overlayPanel.add( paneOne );
```

Then do the same with whatever other components you want to add.

Basic Code Examples

EXAMPLE 8-88 Using OverlayLayout

In this example, we create three panels of different size and color and lay them out on top of each other using an OverlayLayout. Notice that the size is set using the setMaximumSize() method. This is because OverlayLayout will try to make each component added fill its container's space completely. If you specify that the component's maximum size is smaller than the container's, it will size the component to the component's maximum size. Also notice that the three panels are offset. By default, they would have been centered, but we used the setAlignmentX() method to accomplish this offset. Figure 8-138 shows the example as it looks when it first comes up.

Figure 8-138

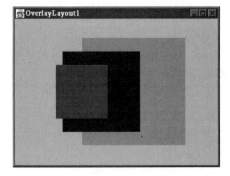

Here is the source code:

```java
import com.sun.java.swing.*;
import java.awt.*;

public class MyFrame extends JFrame
{
    public MyFrame()
    {
        setTitle( "OverlayLayout1" );

        // Store the content pane in a variable for easier
        // access.
        JPanel contentPane = (JPanel)getContentPane();

        // Give the content pane an OverlayLayout.
        contentPane.setLayout( new OverlayLayout( contentPane ) );

        // Create the topmost panel.  Make it 100x100 pixels
        // with a red color.  Its X alignment is 0.5 by
        // default.
        JPanel paneOne = new JPanel();
        paneOne.setBackground( Color.red );
        paneOne.setMaximumSize( new Dimension( 100, 100 ) );

        // Add the panel to the content pane.
        contentPane.add( paneOne );

        // Create the middle panel.  Make it 150x150 pixels
        // and give it a blue color.  Set the X alignment to
        // 0.25.
        JPanel paneTwo = new JPanel();
        paneTwo.setBackground( Color.blue );
        paneTwo.setMaximumSize( new Dimension( 150, 150 ) );
        paneTwo.setAlignmentX( (float)0.25 );

        // Add the panel to the content pane.
        contentPane.add( paneTwo );

        // Create the bottom-most panel.  Make it 200x200
        // pixels and give it a green color.  Set the X
        // alignment to 0.0.
        JPanel paneThree = new JPanel();
        paneThree.setBackground( Color.green );
        paneThree.setMaximumSize( new Dimension( 200, 200 ) );
        paneThree.setAlignmentX( (float)0.0 );

        // Add the panel to the content pane.
        contentPane.add( paneThree );
    }
}
```

OverlayLayout's Public Methods

`void addLayoutComponent(Component comp,Object constraints):`

Overridden to do nothing.

`void addLayoutComponent(String name,Component comp):`

Overridden to do nothing.

`float getLayoutAlignmentX(Container target):`

Returns the container's X alignment.

`float getLayoutAlignmentY(Container target):`

Returns the container's Y alignment.

`void invalidateLayout(Container target):`

Tells the OverlayLayout that one of its components has changed.

`void layoutContainer(Container target):`

Tells the OverlayLayout to layout its components.

`Dimension maximumLayoutSize(Container target):`

Returns the maximum size at which the OverlayLayout would like to layout its components.

`Dimension minimumLayoutSize(Container target):`

Returns the minimum size at which the OverlayLayout can satisfactorily layout its components.

`Dimension preferredLayoutSize(Container target):`

Returns the size at which the OverlayLayout wants to layout its components.

`void removeLayoutComponent(Component comp):`

Overridden to do nothing.

PlainDocument

PlainDocument is the default AbstractDocument subclass used to store the contents of JTextFields and JTextAreas.

Ancestors

```
java.lang.Object
    |
    +—com.sun.java.swing.text.AbstractDocument
              |
              +—com.sun.java.swing.text.PlainDocument
```

NOTE: *For more information, see the "AbstractDocument," "Element," "JTextField," and "JTextArea" sections in this chapter. Also see Chapter 5, "JFC Documents and Text Components."*

Steps in Creating and Using PlainDocument

1. You can either explicitly create a PlainDocument and tell a JTextField or JTextArea to use it or just create the JTextField or JTextArea and a PlainDocument will be created automatically.

   Create a PlainDocument and tell the text component to use it:

   ```
   PlainDocument doc = new PlainDocument();
   JTextField field = new JTextField();
   field.setDocument( doc );
   ```

   Or, create a text component that will automatically create a PlainDocument:

   ```
   JTextField field = new JTextField();
   PlainDocument doc = field.getDocument();
   ```

2. Get the number of characters in the PlainDocument.

   ```
   int length = doc.getLength();
   ```

3. Get a specific part of the PlainDocument's text. There are two getText() methods for this.

   Get a copy of the text in a range starting at character 3 and having a length of 4:

   ```
   String part = doc.getText( 3, 4 );
   ```

   Read the same range, but load it into a Segment that gives direct access to the PlainDocument's characters:

   ```
   Segment part = new Segment;
   String part = doc.getText( 3, 4, part );
   ```

   If you change the contents of the Segment, the text in the document is changed. You can access the characters directly through the Segment's 'array' variable.

4. Insert text into the PlainDocument at a specific index. This method takes an AttributeSet argument, but you can set it to null.

Insert the string "inserted string" into the PlainDocument at index 3.

```
doc.insertString( 3, "inserted string", null );
```

5. Listen for changes to the PlainDocument. You will be notified when text is inserted or deleted or when attributes change.

Specify a class that will be notified of PlainDocument changes. In this case it is the current class.

```
doc.addDocumentListener( this );
```

Make the event-receiving class (MyFrame) implement the DocumentListener interface:

```
public class MyFrame extends JFrame implements DocumentListener
{
    public void changedUpdate( DocumentEvent e )
    {
        // Atributes changed.
    }

    public void insertUpdate( DocumentEvent e )
    {
        // Text was inserted.
    }

    public void removeUpdate( DocumentEvent e )
    {
        // Text was deleted.
    }
}
```

6. Remove text from the PlainDocument.

This removes 4 characters starting at index 3:

```
doc.remove( 3, 4 );
```

NOTE: *For a simple PlainDocument example, see the "AbstractDocument" section in this chapter.*

PlainDocument's Public Methods

```
Element getDefaultRootElement():
```

Returns the main root element. Usually, there is only one root element.

SimpleAttributeSet

SimpleAttributeSet is the JFC's standard implementation of the Mutable-AttributeSet interface. It is used to store text attributes like font family name, font size, italic, color, etc. These attributes are applied to sets of characters within documents—mainly DefaultStyledDocuments—that are displayed and modified using JTextPanes.

A SimpleAttributeSet can also contain what is called a "resolve parent." This is another AttributeSet from which the SimpleAttributeSet can inherit attributes. The SimpleAttributeSet will use any of its resolve parent's attributes that it does not explicitly override.

Ancestors

```
java.lang.Object
    |
    +—com.sun.java.swing.text.SimpleAttributeSet
```

NOTE: *For more information, see the "DefaultStyledDocument," "JTextPane," "Element," "StyleContext," and "StyleConstants" sections in this chapter. Also see Chapter 5, "JFC Documents and Text Components," as well as Chapter 14, "JFC Integration Example5—A Simple Word Processor."*

Steps in Creating and Using SimpleAttributeSet

1. Create the SimpleAttributeSet. There are two ways to do this.

   Create an empty one (one that has no attributes and no resolve parent):

   ```
   SimpleAttributeSet set = new SimpleAttributeSet();
   ```

   Or, create one, initializing it with the attributes and resolve parent (if any) of another AttributeSet:

   ```
   SimpleAttributeSet set = new SimpleAttributeSet( otherSet );
   ```

   This is not the same as setting the resolve parent. In this case, you are essentially cloning 'otherSet'.

2. Add and modify attributes. You can do this by hand using methods like addAttribute(), but it is much easier to use the static methods defined in StyleConstants:

```
StyleConstants.setBold( set, true );
StyleConstants.setFontFamily( set, "TimesRoman" );
```

3. Specify a resolve parent. You can give a SimpleAttributeSet another AttributeSet from which it can inherit attributes. The resolve parent's attributes never override the SimpleAttributeSet's attributes, but any attributes in the resolve parent but not in the SimpleAttributeSet will be used by the SimpleAttributeSet.

```
SimpleAttributeSet set2 = new SompleAttributeSet();
set2.setResolveParent( set );
```

4. Apply the SimpleAttributeSet. There are a number of methods in DefaultStyledDocument and JTextPane that set various types of attributes. One of the most useful is JTextPane's setCharacterAttributes() method:

```
textPane.setCharacterAttributes( set, true );
```

Basic Code Examples

EXAMPLE 8-89 Using SimpleAttributeSet

This example shows how to create and use SimpleAttributeSets. It includes a JTextPane and two JRadioButtons. The JRadioButtons are used to specify which of two SimpleAttributeSets is in use in the JTextPane. There are a total of three SimpleAttributeSets defined in the example. 'mHeading1' is used when the "Heading 1" radio button is selected. 'mHeading2' is used when the "Heading 2" radio button is selected. 'mHeading0' serves as the resolve parent for 'mHeading1.' Figure 8-139 shows the example after some text has been typed in with alternating attributes.

Important points to notice:

■ 'mHeading1' is a 24-point bold Times Roman font.

■ 'mHeading2' is created by passing 'mHeading1' to its constructor and then overriding the font size.

■ After 'mHeading2' is created, we set mHeading1's resolve parent to 'mHeading0', which has its foreground color set to red. In this way, since its foreground color is not set, 'mHeading1' inherits 'mHeading0's red color. If we had set 'mHeading1's resolve parent before creating 'mHeading2', 'mHeading2' would have gotten 'mHeading0' as its resolve parent.

Here is the source code:

```
import com.sun.java.swing.*;
import com.sun.java.swing.text.*;
import java.awt.*;
import java.awt.event.*;
```

Figure 8-139

```
import java.util.*;

public class MyFrame extends JFrame implements ItemListener
{
    private JTextPane mPane;
    private SimpleAttributeSet mHeading0;
    private SimpleAttributeSet mHeading1;
    private SimpleAttributeSet mHeading2;
    private JRadioButton mButton1;
    private JRadioButton mButton2;

    public MyFrame()
    {
        setTitle( "SimpleAttributeSet1" );

        // Store the content pane in a variable for easier
        // access.
        JPanel contentPane = (JPanel)getContentPane();

        // Components will all be added to this panel.
        contentPane.setLayout( new BorderLayout() );

        // Create a text pane.
        mPane = new JTextPane();

        // Create a SimpleAttributeSet that will be used
        // solely as the resolve parent for mHeading1.
        mHeading0 = new SimpleAttributeSet();

        // Set the foreground color to red.
        StyleConstants.setForeground( mHeading0, Color.red );

        // Create a new SimpleAttributeSet.
        mHeading1 = new SimpleAttributeSet();

        // Specify attributes that give a large bold Times
        // Roman font.
        StyleConstants.setFontFamily( mHeading1,
                                      "TimesRoman" );
        StyleConstants.setFontSize( mHeading1, 24 );
        StyleConstants.setBold( mHeading1, true );
```

```
        StyleConstants.setLeftIndent( mHeading1, 72 );

        // Create a new SimpleAttributeSet, loading in
        // mHeading1's attributes.
        mHeading2 = new SimpleAttributeSet( mHeading1 );

        // Change the font size.
        StyleConstants.setFontSize( mHeading2, 14 );

        // Set mHeading1's resolve parent to mHeading0.  We
        // do this after creating mHeading2 so the resolve
        // parent is not also copied.
        mHeading1.setResolveParent( mHeading0 );

        // Place the text pane in the content pane's main
        // area.
        contentPane.add( "Center", mPane );

        // Create a box that will hold radio buttons for
        // switching between attribute sets.
        Box box = Box.createHorizontalBox();

        // Create the radio buttons.  We just listen to one
        // since it is all we need.
        mButton1 = new JRadioButton( "Heading 1" );
        mButton1.addItemListener( this );
        mButton2 = new JRadioButton( "Heading 2" );
        mButton2.addItemListener( this );

        // Create a ButtonGroup and add the radio buttons to
        // it.
        ButtonGroup group = new ButtonGroup();
        group.add( mButton1 );
        group.add( mButton2 );

        // Make heading 1 selected initially.  This will
        // trigger a call to itemStateChanged().
        mButton1.setSelected( true );

        // Add the radio buttons to the box.
        box.add( mButton1 );
        box.add( mButton2 );

        // Place the box at the bottom of the content pane.
        contentPane.add( "South", box );
    }

    // This is called when the Heading 1 radio button
    // changes state.
    public void itemStateChanged( ItemEvent e )
    {
        // If the button was selected, change to mHeading1,
        // otherwise, change to mHeading2.
        if ( e.getStateChange() == ItemEvent.SELECTED )
        {
            if ( e.getSource() == mButton1 )
```

```
            mPane.setCharacterAttributes( mHeading1, true );
        else
            mPane.setCharacterAttributes( mHeading2, true );

        mPane.requestFocus();
    }
  }
}
```

SimpleAttributeSet's Public Methods

`void addAttribute(Object name,Object value):`

Adds a new attribute name/value pair to the SimpleAttributeSet.

`void addAttributes(AttributeSet attributes):`

Adds all of the attributes from the given AttributeSet into the Simple-AttributeSet.

`Object clone():`

Makes a complete copy of the SimpleAttributeSet, including any resolve parent.

`boolean containsAttribute(Object name,Object value):`

Returns true if the SimpleAttributeSet contains an attribute matching 'name' whose value equals 'value'.

`boolean containsAttributes(AttributeSet attributes):`

Returns true if the SimpleAttributeSet contains all of the attributes (including values) in the given AttributeSet.

`AttributeSet copyAttributes():`

Copies the SimpleAttributeSet's attributes into a new AttributeSet. The copied attributes do not include those from a resolve parent.

`Object getAttribute(Object name):`

Returns the value associated with the given attribute name.

`int getAttributeCount():`

Returns the number of attributes stored in the SimpleAttributeSet. A resolve parent counts as one attribute, no matter how many it may contain.

`Enumeration getAttributeNames():`

Returns an enumeration of the SimpleAttributeSet's attribute names. A resolve parent shows up as a single name—the enumeration does not include the resolve parent's atrtributes.

`AttributeSet getResolveParent():`

Returns the AttributeSet (if any) from which the SimpleAttributeSet inherits values. This is set by calling the setResolveParent() method.

`boolean isDefined(Object attrName):`

Returns true if the given attribute name is stored in the SimpleAttributeSet.

`boolean isEmpty():`

Returns true if the SimpleAttributeSet has no attributes, including any inherited from a resolve parent.

`boolean isEqual(AttributeSet attr):`

Returns true if the SimpleAttributeSet matches the given AttributeSet. The two may have the same attributes but not be equal if one of them stores attributes in a resolve parent.

`void removeAttribute(Object name):`

Removes the attribute name/value pair matching the given name.

`void removeAttributes(AttributeSet attributes):`

Removes the set of name/value pairs matching the ones in the given AttributeSet.

`void removeAttributes(Enumeration names):`

Removes the attribute name/value pairs associated with the given enumeration's names.

`void setResolveParent(AttributeSet parent):`

Specifies an AttributeSet from which the SimpleAttributeSet can inherit attributes.

`String toString():`

Overridden to provide a special string.

Figure 8-140
A panel with both a
raised and a lowered
SoftBevelBorder.

SoftBevelBorder

A soft bevel border is a two-line border that makes it appear that the area
within is either raised or lowered relative to the surrounding area (see Figure
8-140). The SoftBevelBorder is identical to the BevelBorder except for the corners, which are slightly different.

Ancestors

```
java.lang.Object
    |
    +—com.sun.java.swing.border.AbstractBorder
           |
           +—com.sun.java.swing.border.BevelBorder
                  |
                  +—com.sun.java.swing.border.SoftBevelBorder
```

NOTE: *For more information, see the "AbstractBorder," "BevelBorder," and
"JPanel" sections in this chapter. Also see the "Component Borders" section in
Chapter 7, "JFC by Concept."*

Steps in Creating and Using SoftBevelBorder

1. Create a component that supports borders. Typically this will be a
   JPanel:

   ```
   Panel borderedPane = new JPanel();
   ```

2. Create a soft bevel border to apply to the component. In most cases
   the default colors will be used and all that needs to be set is whether
   the contents of the pane should appear raised or lowered:

   ```
   SoftBevelBorder bevel = new SoftBevelBorder(
                                       SoftBevelBorder.RAISED );
   SoftBevelBorder bevel = new SoftBevelBorder(
                                       SoftBevelBorder.LOWERED );
   ```

3. Apply the border to the pane:

```
borderedPane.setBorder( bevel );
```

When the bordered panel is displayed, the border will be automatically displayed.

4. Use a soft bevel border as part of a titled border. The border will appear as a normal soft bevel border except that it will be moved slightly in from the bordered pane's edge, and it will be interrupted by a string (title) at some point (left end of the top side by default):

```
JPanel pane3 = new JPanel();
pane3.setBorder( new TitledBorder(
                new SoftBevelBorder( SoftBevelBorder.RAISED ),
                "Raised" ) );
```

SoftBevelBorder's Public Methods

```
Insets getBorderInsets(Component c):
```

Returns the width of the border on all four sides.

```
boolean isBorderOpaque():
```

returns true since SoftBevelBorder paints its entire area.

```
void paintBorder(Component c,Graphics g,int x,int y,int width,int
     height):
```

Actually paints the SoftBevelBorder onto the target component.

StyleConstants

StyleConstants contains a set of static methods used in getting and setting attributes in classes that implement the AttributeSet interface, like SimpleAttributeSet. These attributes are used on characters in JTextPanes to change fonts, alignment, etc.

Ancestors

```
java.lang.Object
   |
   +-com.sun.java.swing.text.StyleConstants
```

NOTE: *For more information, see the "SimpleAttributeSet," "DefaultStyledDocument," and "JTextPane" sections in this chapter, as well as Chapter 5, "JFC Documents and Text Components."*

StyleConstants' Public Methods

```
int getAlignment(AttributeSet a):
```

Gets the alignment setting from the given AttributeSet.

```
Component getComponent(AttributeSet a):
```

Returns the Component attribute.

```
float getFirstLineIndent(AttributeSet a):
```

Returns the amount the first line of paragraphs should be indented in points.

```
String getFontFamily(AttributeSet a):
```

Returns a string like "TimesRoman" that defines the font family.

```
int getFontSize(AttributeSet a):
```

Returns an integer that defines the size of the font in points.

```
Color getForeground(AttributeSet a):
```

Returns the color used to draw text.

```
Icon getIcon(AttributeSet a):
```

Returns the icon attribute.

```
float getLeftIndent(AttributeSet a):
```

Returns the standard indent distance in points for the left side of the text.

```
float getLineSpacing(AttributeSet a):
```

Returns the spacing in points between lines.

```
float getRightIndent(AttributeSet a):
```

Returns the distance in points that the right margin is in from the right side.

`float getSpaceAbove(AttributeSet a):`

Returns the amount of space in points above a paragraph.

`float getSpaceBelow(AttributeSet a):`

Returns the amount of space in points below a paragraph.

`TabSet getTabSet()`

Returns the tab settings.

`boolean isBold(AttributeSet a):`

Returns true if bold is on.

`boolean isItalic(AttributeSet a):`

Returns true if italic is on.

`boolean isUnderline()`

Returns true if underlining is on.

`void setAlignment(MutableAttributeSet a,int align):`

Sets the alignment attribute to one of: ALIGN_CENTER, ALIGN_LEFT, ALIGN_RIGHT, or ALIGN_JUSTIFY.

`void setBold(MutableAttributeSet a,boolean b):`

Specifies whether bold is on or not.

`void setComponent(MutableAttributeSet a,Component c):`

Specifies the component attribute.

`void setFirstLineIndent(MutableAttributeSet a,float i):`

Specifies the distance in points that the first line should be indented.

`void setFontFamily(MutableAttributeSet a,String fam):`

Specifies the font family to use on text.

`void setFontSize(MutableAttributeSet a,int s):`

Specifies the font size in points to use.

`void setForeground(MutableAttributeSet a,Color fg):`

Specifies the text color to use.

```
void setIcon(MutableAttributeSet a,Icon c):
```

Specifies the icon attribute.

```
void setItalic(MutableAttributeSet a,boolean i):
```

Specifies whether italic is on or off.

```
void setLeftIndent(MutableAttributeSet a,float i):
```

Specifies the distance in points that the left side is indented.

```
void setLineSpacing(MutableAttributeSet a,float ls):
```

Specifies the spacing in points between lines.

```
void setRightIndent(MutableAttributeSet a,float ri):
```

Specifies the distance in points that the right margin is from the right side.

```
void setSpaceAbove(MutableAttributeSet a,float sa):
```

Specifies the space in points above a paragraph.

```
void setSpaceBelow(MutableAttributeSet a,float sb):
```

Specifies the space in points below a paragraph.

```
void setTabSet(MutableAttributeSet a, TabSet ts)
```

Specifies the tab settings.

```
void setUnderline(MutableAttributeSet a,boolean u):
```

Specifies whether underlining is on or off.

```
String toString()
```

Overridden for custom format.

StyleContext

StyleContext stores a set of Styles that may or may not have names associated with them. These Styles define commonly used attribute sets that can be applied to text in a JTextPane to alter its appearance and placement.

Style is an interface that extends the MutableAttributeSet interface, which in turn extends the AttributeSet interface. So, the Styles stored in a StyleContext can be modified using the StyleConstant's static methods.

Ancestors

```
java.lang.Object
    |
    +—com.sun.java.swing.text.StyleContext
```

NOTE: *For more information, see the "SimpleAttributeSet," "JTextPane," "Default-StyledDocument," "StyleConstants," and "Element" sections in this chapter. Also see Chapter 5, "JFC Documents and Text Components."*

Steps in Creating and Using StyleContext

1. You can either create a StyleContext and then use it to create a DefaultStyledDocument, or you can create a JTextPane or DefaultStyledDocument and let them create their own. If you do not create the StyleContext yourself, you must go through the JTextPane or DefaultStyledDocument's methods to access or modify the StyleContext.

   Create a StyleContext and use it to create a DefaultStyledDocument:

   ```
   StyleContext context = new StyleContext();
   DefaultStyledDocument doc = new DefaultStyledDocument( context );
   ```

2. Create a new empty style. The following creates a style named "Heading 1" with no parent Style and adds it to the StyleContext.

   ```
   Style heading1 = context.addStyle( "Heading 1", null );
   ```

   JTextPane and DefaultStyledDocument have identical addStyle() methods.

3. Create a new style based on an existing one. The following creates a style named "Heading 2" that inherits its initial attributes from 'heading1' and adds it to the StyleContext.

   ```
   Style heading2 = context.addStyle( "Heading 2", heading1 );
   ```

4. Add attributes to a style. The StyleConstants' static methods are the best way to do this.

   Set a Style's font family:

   ```
   StyleConstants.setFontFamily( heading2, "TimesRoman" );
   ```

   Set a Style's foreground color:

```
StyleConstants.setForeground( heading2, Color.red );
```

5. Get an enumeration of the style names within the StyleContext:

```
for ( Enumeration e = context.getStyleNames();
                                    e.hasMoreElements(); )
{
    String name = (String)e.nextElement();
}
```

6. Get the Style associated with a name:

```
Style s = context.getStyle( "Heading 1" );
```

7. Track when the contents of the StyleContext change. When Styles are added or deleted, a StyleContext generates a ChangeEvent.

Specify which class should be notified when Styles are added/deleted. In this case, it is the current class:

```
context.addChangeListener( this );
```

Make the event-receiving class (MyFrame) implement the ChangeListener interface:

```
public class MyFrame extends JFrame implements ChangeListener
{
    .
    .
    .
    public void stateChanged( ChangeEvent e )
    {
        // A Style was added or removed.
    }
}
```

Basic Code Examples

EXAMPLE 8-90 Working with StyleContexts

This example shows how to create a JTextPane using a custom StyleContext, how to add styles to the StyleContext, how to modify those styles, and how to switch among them. Figure 8-141 shows the example after three strings have been entered using three different styles.

Figure 8-141

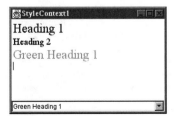

Important points to notice:

■ StyleContext is created with three custom styles. The StyleContext is used in creating a DefaultStyledDocument, which is in turn used in creating a JTextPane.

■ You can switch between styles in the context using the combo box at the bottom of the frame.

■ When a different style is selected, the name is retrieved from the combo box, and the JTextPane's getStyle() method() is used to get the corresponding style. We could have accessed the Style via the StyleContext, but this shows that styles can be accessed through the component itself.

Here is the source code:

```java
import com.sun.java.swing.*;
import com.sun.java.swing.text.*;
import java.awt.*;
import java.awt.event.*;
import java.util.*;

public class MyFrame extends JFrame implements ItemListener
{
    private JTextPane mPane;

    public MyFrame()
    {
        setTitle( "StyleContext1" );

        // Store the content pane in a variable for easier
        // access.
        JPanel contentPane = (JPanel)getContentPane();

        // Components will all be added to this panel.
        contentPane.setLayout( new BorderLayout() );

        // Create a StyleContext.
        StyleContext context = new StyleContext();

        // Create a Style and add it to the context.  It is
        // created with no initializing Style.  We set its
        // font family and font size.
        Style heading1 =
                    context.addStyle( "Heading 1", null );
        StyleConstants.setFontFamily( heading1,
                                        "TimesRoman" );
        StyleConstants.setFontSize( heading1, 24 );

        // Create a second Style, initializing it with the
        // attributes from the previously created Style.  We
        // override the font size to be smaller for this
        // Style.
        Style heading2 =
```

```
                           context.addStyle( "Heading 2", heading1 );
                StyleConstants.setFontSize( heading2, 18 );

                // Create a third style, initialized with the values
                // from the first Style.  We give it a green text
                // color.
                Style greenHeading1 =
                    context.addStyle( "Green Heading 1", heading1 );
                StyleConstants.setForeground( greenHeading1,
                                              Color.green );

                // Create a DefaultStyledDocument with the
                // StyleContext.
                DefaultStyledDocument doc =
                            new DefaultStyledDocument( context );

                // Create a JTextPane with the DefaultStyledDocument.
                mPane = new JTextPane( doc );

                // Make the text pane take up most of the content
                // pane.
                contentPane.add( "Center", mPane );

                // Create a combo box that will allow the user to
                // apply the different styles.
                JComboBox styles = new JComboBox();

                // We need to know when a new style is chosen so we
                // can apply it.
                styles.addItemListener( this );

                // Get an enumeration of the styles in the context,
                // and add each style name into the combo box.
                for ( Enumeration e = context.getStyleNames();
                      e.hasMoreElements(); )
                {
                    String name = (String)e.nextElement();
                    styles.addItem( name );
                }

                // Make heading 1 the initial style.
                styles.setSelectedItem( "Heading 1" );

                // Place the combo box at the bottom of the content
                // pane.
                contentPane.add( "South", styles );
    }

    // This is called when the selection in the styles combo
    // box changes.
    public void itemStateChanged( ItemEvent e )
    {
        // We ignore de-selects.
        if ( e.getStateChange() == ItemEvent.SELECTED )
        {
```

```
// Get the combo box from the event.
JComboBox box = (JComboBox)e.getSource();

// Get the currently selected style name.
String item = (String)box.getSelectedItem();

// Get the style associated with the name.
Style s = mPane.getStyle( item );

// Apply the style to the text pane.
mPane.setCharacterAttributes( s, true );
        }
    }

}
```

StyleContext's Public Methods

AttributeSet addAttribute(AttributeSet old,Object name,Object value):

Adds an attribute name/value pair to the given attribute set and returns the changed set.

AttributeSet addAttributes(AttributeSet old,AttributeSet attr):

Adds a set of attributes to the given 'old' attribute set and returns the result.

void addChangeListener(ChangeListener l):

Tells the StyleContext to notify the given class when styles are added or removed.

Style addStyle(String nm,Style parent):

This creates a style and adds it to the StyleContext. 'nm' is a string that may be used to retrieve the style, and 'parent' is an existing style with which the new style is initialized. Both arguments may be null. The method returns the created style.

static final StyleContext getDefaultStyleContext():

Returns the standard StyleContext. This is what is used if a StyleContext is not defined.

AttributeSet getEmptySet():

Returns an attribute set devoid of attributes.

`Font getFont(AttributeSet attr):`

Returns a Font instance from the given attribute set.

`Font getFont(String family,int style,int size):`

Generates a Font instance.

`FontMetrics getFontMetrics(Font f):`

Returns the metrics of the given font.

`Style getStyle(String nm):`

Returns the style associated with the given name.

`Enumeration getStyleNames():`

Returns an enumeration of all style names in the StyleContext.

`static void readAttributeSet(ObjectInputStream in,`
`    MutableAttributeSet a)`

Reads a MutableAttributeSet from the given ObjectInputStream.

`void reclaim(AttributeSet a):`

Tells the StyleContext that the given AttributeSet is no longer needed.

`static void registerStaticAttributeKey(Object key)`

Special method for serializing the key.

`AttributeSet removeAttribute(AttributeSet old,String name):`

Removes the attribute referred to by 'name' from the given attribute set and returns the changed set.

`AttributeSet removeAttributes(AttributeSet old,Enumeration names):`

Removes the attributes referred to by 'names' from the given attribute set and returns the changed set.

`AttributeSet removeAttributes(AttributeSet old,AttributeSet attrs):`

Removes the attributes in 'attrs' from the attribute set 'old,' and returns the changed set.

`void removeChangeListener(ChangeListener l):`

Tells the StyleContext to stop notifying the given class when styles are added or removed.

```
void removeStyle(String nm):
```

Removes the style associated with the given name from the StyleContext.

```
String toString():
```

Overridden to provide a special string format.

```
static void readAttributeSet(ObjectOutputStream out,
        MutableAttributeSet a)
```

Writes a MutableAttributeSet to the given ObjectOutputStream.

SwingUtilities

SwingUtilities is a set of static methods, some of which are designed for use by various Swing components, and some of which are general graphical utilities for programmers' use.

Ancestors

```
java.lang.Object
    |
    +—com.sun.java.swing.SwingUtilities
```

SwingUtilities Public Methods

```
static Rectangle[] computeDifference(Rectangle rectA,Rectangle
        rectB):
```

Given two rectangles 'rectA' and 'rectB,' returns an array of Rectangles that describe the part of 'rectA' that does not intersect with 'rectB.'

```
static Rectangle computeIntersection(int x,int y,int width,int
        height,Rectangle dest):
```

Returns the area where the rectangle described by 'x,' 'y,' 'width,' height' overlaps 'dest.'

```
static int computeStringWidth(FontMetrics fm,String str):
```

Returns the given string's width in pixels based on the FontMetrics. Same as calling the FontMetrics stringWidth() method.

```
static Rectangle computeUnion(int x,int y,int width,int
                             height,Rectangle dest):
```

Returns the smallest rectangle that contains `dest` and the Rectangle defined by `x`, `y`, `width`, `height`.

```
static MouseEvent convertMouseEvent(Component source,MouseEvent
                             sourceEvent,Component destination):
```

Given two components with a common ancestor and a MouseEvent, this creates a new MouseEvent whose X and Y coordinates have been converted from the 'source' coordinates to the 'destination' coordinates. One of the components may be an ancestor of the other.

```
static Point convertPoint(Component source,Point aPoint,Component
                             destination):
```

Given two components with a common ancestor, convert the given Point from the 'source' coordinates to the 'destination' coordinates. One component may be an ancestor of the other.

```
static Point convertPoint(Component source,int x,int y,Component
                             destination):
```

Given two components with a common ancestor, convert the given x,y coordinate from the 'source' coordinates to the 'destination' coordinates. One component may be an ancestor of the other.

```
static void convertPointFromScreen(Point p, Component c)
```

Converts `p` from screen to component coordinates.

```
static void convertPointToScreen(Point p, Component c)
```

Converts `p` from component to screen coordinates.

```
static Rectangle convertRectangle(Component source,Rectangle
                             aRectangle,Component destination):
```

Given two components with a common ancestor, convert the given Rectangle from the 'source' coordinates to the 'destination' coordinates. One component may be an ancestor of the other.

```
static Component findFocusOwner(Component c)
```

Returns the component's child that currently has the focus.

```
static Accessible getAccessibleAt(Component c,Point p):
```

Gets the accessible component contained in the given component, at the given point.

```
static Accessible getAccessibleChild(Component c,int i):
```

Returns the i-th accessible component contained in the given component.

```
static int getAccessibleChildrenCount(Component c):
```

Returns the number of accessible components in the given component.

```
static int getAccessibleIndexInParent(Component c)
```

Gets the given Component's accessible parent and returns the Component's accessible index within that parent.

```
static AccessibleStateSet getAccessibleStateSet(Component c):
```

Returns the accessible states that together describe the current state of the given component.

```
static Container getAncestorNamed(String name,Component comp):
```

Returns the first component with the given name above the given component in the display hierarchy.

```
static Container getAncestorOfClass(Class c,Component comp):
```

Returns the ancestor of 'comp' that is of type 'c', if any.

```
static Component getDeepestComponentAt(Component parent,int x,int y):
```

Returns the child of 'parent' that is nearest 'parent' and the given x,y coordinate.

```
static Rectangle getLocalBounds(Component aComponent):
```

Returns a Rectangle whose origin in 0,0 and whose width and height are set to the given component's width and height.

```
static JRootPane getRootPane(Component comp):
```

Returns the nearest root pane above the given component in the display hierarchy.

```
static void invokeAndWait(Runnable obj):
```

Causes the given Runnable object to be invoked after all outstanding events are processed. This method does not return until that has happened.

```
static void invokeLater(Runnable obj):
```

Causes the given Runnable object to be invoked after all outstanding events are processed.

```
static boolean isDescendingFrom(Component a,Component b):
```

Returns true of 'a' is a descendant of 'b'.

```
static boolean isLeftMouseButton(MouseEvent anEvent):
```

Returns true if the given MouseEvent represents a left mouse button click.

```
static boolean isMiddleMouseButton(MouseEvent anEvent):
```

Returns true if the given MouseEvent represents a middle mouse button click.

```
static final boolean isRectangleContainingRectangle(Rectangle
                                            a,Rectangle b):
```

Returns true if 'a' contains 'b'.

```
static boolean isRightMouseButton(MouseEvent anEvent):
```

Returns true if the given MouseEvent represents a right mouse button click.

```
static String layoutCompoundLabel(FontMetrics fm,String text,Icon
     icon,int verticalAlignment,int horizontalAlignment,int
     verticalTextPosition,int horizontalTextPosition,Rectangle
     viewR,Rectangle iconR,Rectangle textR,int textIconGap):
```

Used by JFC components like JButton to layout their text and icon based on alignment and position parameters.

```
static void paintComponent(Graphics g,Component c,Container
                           p,Rectangle r):
```

Causes the given component to be painted within the given rectangle.

```
static void paintComponent(Graphics g,Component c,Container p,int
                           x,int y,int w,int h):
```

Causes the given component to be painted within the given rectangle.

```
static void updateComponentTreeUI(Component c):
```

Given a component, this method goes through its tree and calls each component's updateUI() method.

```
static Window windowForComponent(Component aComponent):
```

Returns the window that the given component is displaying in.

TableColumn

TableColumn contains the graphical attributes for a single column of data in JTable's model. It is not a component itself, and it does not store the column's data. Instead, it stores information about the column header, the column height and width, and how cells in the column should be drawn and edited.

Ancestors

```
java.lang.Object
    |
    +—com.sun.java.swing.table.TableColumn
```

NOTE: *For more information, see the "DefaultTableColumnModel," "JTable," "DefaultTableModel," "AbstractTableModel," and "DefaultCellEditor" sections in this chapter. Also see the "JFC Tables" section in Chapter 7, "JFC by Concept."*

Steps in Creating and Using TableColumn

1. You will normally not want to create TableColumns of your own. instead, TableColumns will be created automatically when columns are added to the table model. A table's TableColumns are accessed through the table column model.

   Get the TableColumns associated with the currently selected columns:

   ```
   // Get the table column model from the 'mTable' table.
   DefaultTableColumnModel model =
           (DefaultTableColumnModel)mTable.getColumnModel();

   // Retrieve a list containing the column indices of all selected
   // columns.
   int columnIndices[] = model.getSelectedColumns();
   ```

```
// For each column index, get the associated TableColumn.
for ( int i = 0; i < columnIndices.length; i++ )
{
    TableColumn thisColumn = model.getColumn( columnIndices[i] );
}
```

Get all TableColumns

```
// Get the table column model from the 'mTable' table.
DefaultTableColumnModel model =
        (DefaultTableColumnModel)mTable.getColumnModel();

// Get an enumeration of all columns and iterate through.
for ( Enumeration enum = model.getColumns();
    enum.hasMoreElements(); )
{
    TableColumn col = (TableColumn)enum.nextElement();
}
```

2. Specify the TableCellEditor to use when editing the TableColumn's cells. DefaultCellEditor is usually sufficient, but you can create your own.

Create a cell editor that displays as a checkbox. The underlying data should be Boolean.

```
// Create a JCheckBox.
JCheckBox cbox = new JCheckBox();

// Make it so the check box displays centered.
cbox.setHorizontalAlignment( JCheckBox.CENTER );

// Create a cell editor using the checkbox.
DefaultCellEditor editor = new DefaultCellEditor( cbox );
```

Tell the TableColumn to use the editor:

```
tableColumn.setCellEditor( editor );
```

3. Change the column header:

```
tableColumn.setHeaderValue( "New Header" );
```

4. Change the column identifier. This is stored here, but is not used by the TableColumn. It can be any Object.

```
tableColumn.setIdentifier( "New Identifier" );
```

5. Get the index of the column that a TableColumn represents in the TableModel. This is different from the TableColumnModel index which represents the column order as displayed.

```
int modelIndex = tableColumn.getModelIndex();
```

Basic Code Examples

EXAMPLE 8-91 Using TableColumn

This example creates a simple GUI containing a JTable and some controls for monitoring and changing TableColumn information. The table is preloaded. The controls at the bottom display TableColumn attributes for the currently selected column. You can use the two text fields to change the currently selected column's identifier and header. Figure 8-142 shows the example after the first two columns have been swapped.

Important points to notice:

■ The first column (second in the figure) uses a custom cell renderer derived from JButton. The second column (first in the figure) uses a custom cell renderer derived from JCheckBox and the matching DefaultCellEditor. The third column uses the default renderer and editor.

■ The example's JTable uses a subclass of DefaultTableModel so the user can be kept from editing column0's values.

■ The controls are disabled if no column is currently selected.

■ The column header or identifier is applied to the current column when <Enter> is pressed in the text field.

■ Column selection events are caught by implementing the TableColumnModelListener interface and registering with the TableColumnModel as a listener.

Here is the source code:

```
import com.sun.java.swing.*;
import com.sun.java.swing.border.*;
import com.sun.java.swing.event.*;
import com.sun.java.swing.table.*;
import java.awt.*;
import java.awt.event.*;
import java.util.*;
```

Figure 8-142

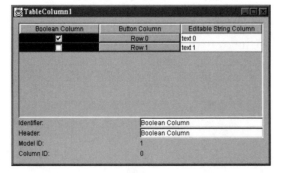

```
public class MyFrame extends JFrame implements
        TableColumnModelListener, ActionListener
{
    private JTable mTable;
    private JTextField mIdentifier;
    private JTextField mHeader;
    private JLabel mModelID;
    private JLabel mColumnID;

    public MyFrame()
    {
        setTitle( "TableColumn1" );

        // Store the content pane in a variable for easier
        // access.
        JPanel contentPane = (JPanel)getContentPane();

        // Components will all be added to this panel.
        contentPane.setLayout( new BorderLayout() );

        // Leave space around the edge.
        contentPane.setBorder(
                    new EmptyBorder( 10, 10, 10, 10 ) );

        // Create an array for the table's data and load it
        // up.
        Object data[][] = new Object[2][3];
        data[0][0] = "Row 0";
        data[0][1] = new Boolean( true );
        data[0][2] = "text 0";
        data[1][0] = "Row 1";
        data[1][1] = new Boolean( false );
        data[1][2] = "text 1";

        // Create an array for the table's column identifiers
        // and load it.
        Object headers[] = new Object[3];
        headers[0] = "Button Column";
        headers[1] = "Boolean Column";
        headers[2] = "Editable String Column";

        // Use a custom model that prohibits editing in
        // column 0.
        CustomTableModel model = new CustomTableModel( data,
                                    headers );

        // Use the arrays to create a JTable.
        mTable = new JTable( model );

        // Create a special scrollpane for the table.
        JScrollPane scroller =
                JTable.createScrollPaneForTable( mTable );

        // Make the scrollpane take up the content pane's
        // main area.
```

```
contentPane.add( "Center", scroller );

// Get the table column model from a JTable called
// 'myTable'.
TableColumnModel columnModel =
                                mTable.getColumnModel();

// Make it so this class is notified when table
// column events happen.
columnModel.addColumnModelListener( this );

// Make it so only one column may be selected at a
// time.
columnModel.getSelectionModel().setSelectionMode(
            ListSelectionModel.SINGLE_SELECTION );

// Get the TableColumn index associated with the
// given identifier.
int index = columnModel.getColumnIndex(
                                "Button Column" );

// Get the TableColumn at the index.
TableColumn col = columnModel.getColumn( index );

// Create a cell renderer that looks like a button.
ButtonRenderer brend = new ButtonRenderer();

// Apply the renderer to this TableColumn.
col.setCellRenderer( brend );

// Get the index for the second column.
index =
    columnModel.getColumnIndex( "Boolean Column" );

// Get the TableColumn at the index.
col = columnModel.getColumn( index );

// Create a cell renderer that looks like a check box.
CheckBoxRenderer cbrend = new CheckBoxRenderer();

// Create a cell editor that works like a check box.
JCheckBox cbox2 = new JCheckBox();
cbox2.setHorizontalAlignment( JCheckBox.CENTER );
DefaultCellEditor editor =
                        new DefaultCellEditor( cbox2 );

// Tell the TableColumn to use the renderer.
col.setCellRenderer( cbrend );

// Tell the TableColumn to use the editor.
col.setCellEditor( editor );

// Create a panel to hold the controls.
JPanel controlPane = new JPanel();
controlPane.setLayout( new GridLayout( 4, 3 ) );
```

```java
    // Create the identifier text field and accompanying
    // label and add them to the panel.
    JLabel lbl = new JLabel( "Identifier:  " );
    controlPane.add( lbl );
    mIdentifier = new JTextField();
    mIdentifier.addActionListener( this );
    controlPane.add( mIdentifier );

    // Create the header text field and accompanying
    // label and add them to the panel.
    lbl = new JLabel( "Header:  " );
    controlPane.add( lbl );
    mHeader = new JTextField();
    mHeader.addActionListener( this );
    controlPane.add( mHeader );

    // Create the model ID and accompanying label and
    // add them to the panel.
    lbl = new JLabel( "Model ID:  " );
    controlPane.add( lbl );
    mModelID = new JLabel();
    controlPane.add( mModelID );

    // Create the column ID and accompanying label and
    // add them to the panel.
    lbl = new JLabel( "Column ID:  " );
    controlPane.add( lbl );
    mColumnID = new JLabel();
    controlPane.add( mColumnID );

    // Place the control pane at the bottom of the
    // content pane.
    contentPane.add( "South", controlPane );

    // Make sure the controls are properly disabled.
    setControlEnableState();
}

// Call this to make sure the controls are enabled if a
// column is selected or disabled otherwise.
private void setControlEnableState()
{
    if ( mTable.getColumnModel().
         getSelectedColumnCount() == 0 )
    {
        mIdentifier.setEnabled( false );
        mHeader.setEnabled( false );
        mColumnID.setEnabled( false );
        mModelID.setEnabled( false );
    }
    else
    {
        mIdentifier.setEnabled( true );
        mHeader.setEnabled( true );
        mColumnID.setEnabled( true );
```

```
         mModelID.setEnabled( true );
      }


      repaint();
   }

   // Called when a column is added.
   public void columnAdded( TableColumnModelEvent e )
   {
   }

   // Called when the column margin changes.
   public void columnMarginChanged( ChangeEvent e )
   {
   }

   // Called when a column is moved.
   public void columnMoved( TableColumnModelEvent e )
   {
   }

   // Called when a column is deleted.
   public void columnRemoved( TableColumnModelEvent e )
   {
   }

   // Called when the column selection state changes.
   public void columnSelectionChanged(
                              ListSelectionEvent e )
   {
      // Get the table column model.
      DefaultTableColumnModel model =
         (DefaultTableColumnModel)mTable.getColumnModel();

      // Retrieve a list containing the column indices of
      // all selected columns.
      int columnIndices[] = model.getSelectedColumns();

      // For each column index, get the associated
      // TableColumn and display the TableColumn's
      // attributes.
      for ( int i = 0; i < columnIndices.length; i++ )
      {
         TableColumn thisColumn =
                     model.getColumn( columnIndices[i] );
         mIdentifier.setText(
                 thisColumn.getIdentifier().toString() );
         mHeader.setText(
                 thisColumn.getHeaderValue().toString() );
         mColumnID.setText(
                 String.valueOf( columnIndices[i] ) );
         mModelID.setText(
            String.valueOf( thisColumn.getModelIndex() ) );
      }
```

```
      // Update the controls' enable state.
      setControlEnableState();
   }

   // This is called when the user presses Enter in a text
   // field.
   public void actionPerformed( ActionEvent e )
   {
      // Get the table column model.
      DefaultTableColumnModel model =
          (DefaultTableColumnModel)mTable.getColumnModel();

      // Retrieve a list containing the column indices of
      // all selected columns.
      int columnIndices[] = model.getSelectedColumns();

      // For each column index, get the associated
      // TableColumn.
      TableColumn thisColumn =
                    model.getColumn( columnIndices[0] );

      if ( e.getSource() == mIdentifier )
      {
         // If Enter was pressed in the identifier text
         // field, update the selected TableColumn's
         // identifier.
         thisColumn.setIdentifier( mIdentifier.getText() );
      }
      else if ( e.getSource() == mHeader )
      {
         // If Enter was pressed in the header text field,
         // update the selected TableColumn's header.
         thisColumn.setHeaderValue( mHeader.getText() );
      }

      // Reflect the changes.
      repaint();
   }

   // This is a custom cell renderer that displays Boolean
   // values as center-aligned check boxes.
   private class CheckBoxRenderer extends JCheckBox
           implements TableCellRenderer
   {
      private Color mDefaultForeground;
      private Color mDefaultBackground;

      public CheckBoxRenderer()
      {
         super();
         setHorizontalAlignment( JCheckBox.CENTER );

         // Set initial colors so se can invert when
         // selected.
         mDefaultForeground = getForeground();
         mDefaultBackground = SystemColor.window;
```

```java
      setOpaque( true );
   }

   // This method is required, and returns the control
   // fully configured for this cell.
   public Component getTableCellRendererComponent(
                              JTable table,
                              Object value,
                              boolean isSelected,
                              boolean hasFocus,
                              int row,
                              int column )
   {
      Boolean b = (Boolean)value;

      if ( b != null )
         setSelected( b.booleanValue() );

      if ( isSelected )
      {
         setBackground( mDefaultForeground );
         setForeground( mDefaultBackground );
      }
      else
      {
         setBackground( mDefaultBackground );
         setForeground( mDefaultForeground );
      }

      return this;
   }
}

// This is a custom cell renderer that displays
// cells as buttons.
private class ButtonRenderer extends JButton
       implements TableCellRenderer
{
   public ButtonRenderer()
   {
      super();
      //setBackground( SystemColor.control );
      setOpaque( true );
   }

   // Required.  This configures the button for the
   // current cell, and returns it.
   public Component getTableCellRendererComponent(
                              JTable table,
                              Object value,
                              boolean isSelected,
                              boolean hasFocus,
                              int row,
                              int column )
   {
```

```
                    if ( value != null )
                        setText( value.toString() );

                    return this;
                }
            }

            // We create this to make it so the first column's
            // values cannot be edited.
            private class CustomTableModel extends DefaultTableModel
            {
                public CustomTableModel( Object data[][],
                                         Object headers[] )
                {
                    super( data, headers );
                }

                public boolean isCellEditable( int row, int col )
                {
                    if ( col == 0 )
                        return false;

                    return true;
                }
            }
        }
```

TableColumn's Public Methods

void addPropertyChangeListener(PropertyChangeListener listener):

Tells the TableColumn to notify the given class when properties change.

void disableResizedPosting():

Makes it so resize notifications are not sent until the resize is complete.

void enableResizedPosting():

Makes it so resize all resize notifications are sent.

TableCellEditor getCellEditor():

Returns the TableColumn's current cell editor.

TableCellRenderer getCellRenderer():

Returns the TableColumn's current cell renderer.

`TableCellRenderer getHeaderRenderer():`

Returns the cell renderer being used to draw the TableColumn's header.

`Object getHeaderValue():`

Returns the column header.

`Object getIdentifier():`

Returns the identifier object that other classes may use to track a column.

`int getMaxWidth():`

Returns the column's maximum width.

`int getMinWidth():`

Returns the column's minimum width;

`int getModelIndex():`

Returns the table model index that the TableColumn represents.

`boolean getResizable():`

Returns true if the column is resizable.

`int getWidth():`

Returns the column's width.

`void removePropertyChangeListener(PropertyChangeListener listener):`

Tells the TableColumn to stop notifying the given class when properties change.

`void setCellEditor(TableCellEditor anEditor):`

Replaces the TableColumn's current cell editor with the given one.

`void setCellRenderer(TableCellRenderer aRenderer):`

Replaces the TableColumn's current cell renderer with the given one.

`void setHeaderRenderer(TableCellRenderer aRenderer):`

Replaces the TableColumn's current header cell renderer with the given one.

```
void setHeaderValue(Object aValue):
```

Replaces the column header's value.

```
void setIdentifier(Object anIdentifier):
```

Replaces the column identifier.

```
void setMaxWidth(int newMaxWidth):
```

Changes the column's maximum width.

```
void setMinWidth(int newMinWidth):
```

Changes the column's minimum width.

```
void setModelIndex(int anIndex):
```

Specifies with which TableModel column the TableColumn is associated.

```
void setResizable(boolean flag):
```

Specifies whether the column may be resized.

```
void setWidth(int newWidth):
```

Specifies the column's width.

```
void sizeWidthToFit():
```

Tells the column to change its width to match its header width.

Timer

A Timer is a nongraphical class used to cause something to happen at a specific interval or to cause something to happen at some set amount of time in the future. Timers do not keep perfect time, but are useful for making something like animation frames happen at approximately regular intervals.

Ancestors

```
java.lang.Object
   |
   +—com.sun.java.swing.Timer
```

Steps in Creating and Using Timer

1. Create a Timer. The constructor takes an interval in milliseconds and an ActionListener to which it can send events. The interval is the amount of time between generating events. For this example, the event-receiving class is the same one that contains the Timer.

```
Timer timer1 = new Timer( 1000, this );
```

2. Make the listening class implement the ActionListener interface. Here, the listening class is a private class called TimerDisplay:

```
private class TimerDisplay extends JLabel implements
    ActionListener
{
    .
    .
    .
    public void actionPerformed( ActionEvent e )
    {
        // Execute whatever action the timer is supposed to
        // trigger.
    }
}
```

3. Set the timer's initial delay. This is useful if you don't want the timer to begin generating events for awhile. The initial delay is in milliseconds:

```
timer1.setInitialDelay( 5000 );
```

4. Specify whether you want the timer to keep generating events or just generate the first one. By default, the timer keeps repeating until it is stopped.

```
timer1.setRepeats( false );
```

This makes it generate just one event when the initial delay is up.

5. Start the timer running. The timer won't start counting time until you run start().

```
timer1.start();
```

Basic Code Examples

EXAMPLE 8-92 Using Multiple Timers

This example includes a class called TimerDisplay that contains a Timer and, as the Timer runs, displays its progress. TimerDisplay extends JLabel to make displaying simpler. Each of the five instances of TimerDisplay is different. One has a longer initial delay. The others have varying intervals between events.

Figure 8-143

Each TimerDisplay keeps track of how much time it thinks has elapsed based on its initial delay, its interval between events, and how many events have been received. Figure 8-143 shows the example after it has been running for about 10 seconds.

Here is the source code:

```java
import com.sun.java.swing.*;
import java.awt.*;
import java.awt.event.*;

public class MyFrame extends JFrame
{
    public MyFrame()
    {
        setTitle( "Timer1" );

        // Store the content pane in a variable for easier
        // access.
        JPanel mPanel = (JPanel)getContentPane();

        mPanel.setLayout( new GridLayout( 5, 1 ) );

        // Create five instances of the class defined later
        // in this file, specifying initial delay and
        // interval.  Add them to the buffered pane.
        mPanel.add( new TimerDisplay( 0, 500 ) );
        mPanel.add( new TimerDisplay( 0, 1000 ) );
        mPanel.add( new TimerDisplay( 0, 3000 ) );
        mPanel.add( new TimerDisplay( 3000, 5000 ) );
        mPanel.add( new TimerDisplay( 0, 10000 ) );
    }

    // This class contains a timer.  It extends JLabel so it
    // can display the timer's progress.
    private class TimerDisplay extends JLabel implements
            ActionListener
    {
        // Use this variable to track how long this class
        // thinks it has been running.  This is calculated by
        // taking the initial delay, then adding the interval
        // each time the timer generates an ActionEvent
        // (after the first one).
        private int mApparentElapsed = -1;
        private Timer mTimer;
```

```
public TimerDisplay( int initialDelay, int interval )
{
    // Create a Timer with interval between
    // ActionEvents and which class will be receiving
    // the events.
    mTimer = new Timer( interval, this );

    // Set how long the timer will wait before
    // starting to generate events.
    mTimer.setInitialDelay( initialDelay );

    // Start the timer.
    mTimer.start();

    // Build the text string that gets displayed in
    // the label.
    loadText();
}

private void loadText()
{
    setText( "Start:  " + mTimer.getInitialDelay() +
             ", " + "Interval:  " +
             mTimer.getDelay() + ", " +
             "Elapsed:  " + mApparentElapsed );
}

public void actionPerformed( ActionEvent e )
{
    // If this is the first event, set the apparent
    // elapsed time to the initial delay.  Otherwise,
    // add the interval.
    if ( mApparentElapsed == -1 )
        mApparentElapsed = mTimer.getInitialDelay();
    else
        mApparentElapsed += mTimer.getDelay();

    // Rebuild the label string updated to the new
    // apparent elapsed time.
    loadText();

    // Cause the label to redisplay.
    repaint();
    }
  }
}
```

Timer's Public Methods

```
void addActionListener(ActionListener listener):
```

Tells the Timer to notify the given class whenever it completes an interval.

`int getDelay():`

Returns the time in milliseconds between generating ActionEvents.

`int getInitialDelay():`

Returns the amount of time in milliseconds before the Timer starts generating ActionEvents.

`boolean getLogTimers():`

Returns true if the Timer will print out messages when events are triggered.

`boolean isCoalesce():`

Returns true if the Timer combines multiple messages that haven't been delivered yet into one.

`boolean isRepeats():`

Returns true if the Timer will keep counting after its first interval.

`boolean isRunning():`

Returns true if the Timers is currently running.

`void removeActionListener(ActionListener listener):`

Tells the Timer to stop notifying the given class when intervals are up.

`void restart():`

Tells the Timer to stop where it is and then start generating ActionEvents back with its initial delay.

`void setCoalesce(boolean flag):`

Specifies whether multiple messages that haven't been delivered yet will be combined.

`void setDelay(int delay):`

Specifies the interval in milliseconds between generating ActionEvents.

`void setInitialDelay(int initialDelay):`

Specifies how long in milliseconds the Timer will wait before generating its first ActionEvent.

`void setLogTimers(boolean flag):`

Specifies whether the Timer will print out messages when events happen.

`void setRepeats(boolean flag):`

Specifies whether the Timer keeps going after its first interval or not.

`void start():`

Starts up the Timer.

`void stop():`

Stops the Timer.

TitledBorder

A TitledBorder is a component border that allows you to place a string in a break of another border. This is particularly useful not only for grouping related components in a user interface, but also for identifying how the grouped components are related (see Figure 8-144).

Ancestors

```
java.lang.Object
   |
   +—com.sun.java.swing.border.AbstractBorder
          |
          +—com.sun.java.swing.border.TitledBorder
```

NOTE: *For more information, see the "AbstractBorder," "EtchedBorder," and "JPanel" sections in this chapter. Also see the "Component Borders" section in Chapter 7, "JFC by Concept."*

Figure 8-144
A typical TitledBorder that incorporates an EtchedBorder.

Steps in Creating and Using TitledBorder

1. Create a TitledBorder. There are six constructors. Five accept a separate border into which the title string will be placed:

```
TitledBorder( Border border )
TitledBorder( Border border, String title )
TitledBorder( Border border, String title,
            int titleJustification, int titlePosition )
TitledBorder( Border border, String title,
            int titleJustification, int titlePosition,
            Font titleFont )
TitledBorder( Border border, String title,
            int titleJustification, int titlePosition,
            Font titleFont, Color titleColor )
```

where 'border' is the other border (EtchedBorder, BevelBorder, etc.) to which the title string should be applied; 'title' is the title string; 'titleJustification' tells whether the title string will appear to the left, center, or right side of the border; 'titlePosition' tells whether the title string will be on the top or bottom edge of the border, and whether it will appear above, on, or below the border; 'titleFont' is the font to use for the title string; and 'titleColor' is the color that will be used for the title string.

The sixth constructor just takes the title string:

```
TitledBorder( String title )
```

It uses an EtchedBorder and the default title justification and position.

The following produces a border that has a dark gray title string in Times Roman. It uses an EtchedBorder. The title will appear as a break in the top line of the border, at its right end:

```
TitledBorder complexBorder = new TitledBorder( mPanel, new
            EtchedBorder(),
            "Title String", TitledBorder.RIGHT,
            TitledBorder.TOP, new Font( "TimesRoman",
            Font.PLAIN, 14 ), Color.darkGray );
```

Or, you can create a simple TitledBorder:

```
TitledBorder simpleBorder = new TitledBorder( "Title String" );
```

This will have use an EtchedBorder. The title string will appear in a break in the left end of the top edge of the EtchedBorder.

2. Add the border to a container. This container will normally be a JPanel:

```
JPanel complexPane = new JPanel();
complexPane.setBorder( complexBorder );
```

Or, you could use the border as the edge of a component like JInternalFrame:

```
JInternalFrame inFrame = new JInternalFrame( "Bordered Frame" );
inFrame.setBorder( complexBorder );
```

Many Swing components (all JComponent subclasses) have a setBorder() method like JInternalFrame's used here. Whether calling setBorder() with a new border will actually change the component's appearance depends on the component's UI for the current look-and-feel. And just because you *can* change the border, it doesn't mean the change will be attractive. TitledBorder is generally most useful with a JPanel.

3. Customize the TitledBorder. Everything that can be set using the constructors can be set using methods. If you want to use the simplest constructor, then change its title justification:

```
TitledBorder border1 = new TitledBorder(
                                    "Change  Justification" );
border1.setTitleJustification( TitledBorder.RIGHT );
```

You can also set the border, title, position, font, and color:

```
border1.setBorder( new BevelBorder( BevelBorder.RAISED ) );
border1.setTitle( "Changed Title" );
border1.setTitlePosition( TitledBorder.BELOW_BOTTOM );
border1.setTitleFont( new Font( "TimesRoman", Font.ITALIC,
                                16 ) );
border1.setTitleColor( Color.white );
```

Basic Code Examples

EXAMPLE 8-93 Basic TitledBorder

This example puts the concepts discussed previously to work. It includes:

- A simple TitledBorder
- A TitledBorder with a changed font, text color, and text location
- A TitledBorder in which the text, font, text color, and text location were all set separate from the constructor. The background color for the pane has been changed
- A TitledBorder with the text centered above
- A TitledBorder that uses a LineBorder
- A TitledBorder with the text on the inside-right
- A TitledBorder using an EmptyBorder

Figure 8-145 shows the example as it looks when it first starts up. Here is the source:

Figure 8-145

```java
import com.sun.java.swing.*;
import com.sun.java.swing.border.*;
import java.awt.*;

public class MyFrame extends JFrame
{
    public MyFrame()
    {
        setTitle( "TitledBorder1" );

        // Store the content pane for easier access.
        JPanel contentPane = (JPanel)getContentPane();

        // Components will all be added to this panel.
        contentPane.setLayout( new GridLayout( 7, 1 ) );

        // Create a panel that will take a border.
        JPanel pane1 = new JPanel();

        // Set the pane's border to a TitledBorder whose
        // title will appear in a break in an EtchedBorder
        // with default justification and position.
        pane1.setBorder( new TitledBorder(
                        new EtchedBorder(),
                        "First Pane" ) );

        // Add the bordered pane to the main panel.
        contentPane.add( pane1 );

        // Create a TitledBorder that uses the most complex
        // constructor, explicitly setting everything.
        TitledBorder complexBorder =
                    new TitledBorder( new EtchedBorder(),
                    "Title String", TitledBorder.RIGHT,
                    TitledBorder.TOP, new Font( "TimesRoman",
                    Font.PLAIN, 14 ), Color.darkGray );

        // Create a panel that uses the just-created border.
        JPanel pane2 = new JPanel();
        pane2.setBorder( complexBorder );
```

```
// Add the panel to the main panel.
contentPane.add( pane2 );

// Create a panel that will take a border and set its
// background color.
JPanel pane3 = new JPanel();
pane3.setBackground( Color.green );

// Create a TitledBorder using the simplest
// constructor, then use TitledBorder's attribute-
// setting methods to customize.
TitledBorder border1 =
        new TitledBorder( "Change Justification" );
border1.setTitleJustification( TitledBorder.RIGHT );
border1.setBorder( new BevelBorder(
                    BevelBorder.RAISED ) );
border1.setTitle( "Changed Title" );
border1.setTitlePosition( TitledBorder.BELOW_BOTTOM );
border1.setTitleFont( new Font( "TimesRoman",
                                Font.ITALIC, 16 ) );
border1.setTitleColor( Color.white );

// Set the panel's border to the one we just created.
pane3.setBorder( border1 );

// Add the panel to the main panel.
contentPane.add( pane3 );

TitledBorder border2 =
                new TitledBorder( new EtchedBorder(),
                "Centered above the Top",
                TitledBorder.CENTER,
                TitledBorder.ABOVE_TOP );
JPanel pane4 = new JPanel();
pane4.setBorder( border2 );
contentPane.add( pane4 );

// Create a TitledBorder that uses a 3-pixel thick
// LineBorder and places the title in a break in the
// center of the border's top line.
TitledBorder border3 = new TitledBorder(
                new LineBorder( Color.black, 3 ),
                "Centered on the Top Line",
                TitledBorder.CENTER,
                TitledBorder.TOP );

// Create a panel that uses the just-created border.
JPanel pane5 = new JPanel();
pane5.setBorder( border3 );

// Add the panel to the main panel.
contentPane.add( pane5 );

// Create a TitledBorder that uses the default
// EtchedBorder, then customize it so the title
```

```
                    // string appears inside the lower-right corner of
                    // the border.
                    TitledBorder border4 =
                            new TitledBorder( "Inside Lower-Right" );
                    border4.setTitleJustification( TitledBorder.RIGHT );
                    border4.setTitlePosition( TitledBorder.ABOVE_BOTTOM );

                    // Create a panel that uses the just-created border.
                    JPanel pane6 = new JPanel();
                    pane6.setBorder( border4 );

                    // Add the panel to the main panel.
                    contentPane.add( pane6 );

                    // Create a TitledBorder that uses an EmptyBorder.
                    TitledBorder border5 = new TitledBorder(
                            new EmptyBorder( 10, 10, 10, 10 ),
                            "Empty Border" );

                    // Create a panel that uses the just-created border.
                    JPanel pane7 = new JPanel();
                    pane7.setBorder( border5 );

                    // Add the panel to the main panel.
                    contentPane.add( pane7 );
            }
    }
```

TitledBorder's Public Methods

Border getBorder():

Returns the border that the TitledBorder is using.

Insets getBorderInsets(Component c):

Returns the width of the border on each side.

Dimension getMinimumSize(Component c)

Returns the minimum size the given component can be in order for the border to draw properly.

String getTitle():

Returns the border's title text string.

Color getTitleColor():

Returns the color used to draw the title text.

`Font getTitleFont():`

Returns the font being used to draw the title text.

`int getTitleJustification():`

Returns where, horizontally, the title text will appear. May be: LEFT, CENTER, or RIGHT.

`int getTitlePosition():`

Returns where the title will appear vertically relative to the border; may be: ABOVE_BOTTOM, ABOVE_TOP, BELOW_BOTTOM, or BELOW_TOP.

`boolean isBorderOpaque():`

Returns true if the TitledBorder paints its entire area.

`void paintBorder(Component c,Graphics g,int x,int y,int width,int`
`                 height):`

Actually paints the TitledBorder onto the target component.

`void setBorder(Border border):`

Specifies which border the TitledBorder should incorporate.

`void setTitle(String title):`

Sets the title text string.

`void setTitleColor(Color titleColor):`

Specifies the title text string's color.

`void setTitleFont(Font titleFont):`

Specifies which font to use to draw the title text string.

`void setTitleJustification(int titleJustification):`

Specifies where, horizontally, the title text string is placed.

`void setTitlePosition(int titlePosition):`

Specifies where, vertically, the title text string should be relative to the border.

TreePath

A TreePath represents the path through a tree from one tree node to another. It contains the starting node, the ending node, and all nodes in between.

Ancestors

```
java.lang.Object
    |
    +—com.sun.java.swing.tree.TreePath
```

NOTE: *For more information, see the "JTree," "DefaultTreeModel," "DefaultTree-SelectionModel," and "DefaultMutableTreeNode" sections in this chapter. Also see the "Trees" section in Chapter 7, "JFC by Concept."*

Steps in Creating and Using TreePath

1. Although you can create TreePaths from scratch, you will normally be using TreePaths returned from various Swing tree methods.

   For example, when you want to get the path to the last node selected by the user, you can call JTree's getLeadSelectionPath() method which returns a TreePath:

   ```
   TreePath leadSelection = tree.getLeadSelectionPath();
   ```

   One time when you will create a new TreePath is when you have a method like DefaultTreeModel's protected getPathToRoot() method. This method returns an array of TreeNodes instead of a TreePath, so if you want to make the array of TreeNodes into a TreePath, you just call the TreePath constructor:

   ```
   TreePath newPath = new TreePath( model.getPathToRoot( node ) );
   ```

2. Get the node that the TreePath represents. When you select a node in a tree, just that node gets highlighted, but if you ask for the selection, you get a TreePath ending with the node you selected. You can get the actual node from the TreePath using:

   ```
   TreeNode selectedNode = leadSelection.getLastPathComponent();
   ```

3. Get the nodes that make up the TreePath:

   ```
   TreeNode nodes[] = leadSelection.getPath();
   ```

NOTE: *For examples of the use of TreePaths, see the "DefaultTreeSelectionModel"
section in this chapter, as well as Chapter 10, "Integrating JFC Example 1: A File
Browser."*

TreePath's Public Methods

```
boolean equals(Object o):
```

Compares each node in 'o' with each node in this TreePath and returns
true if all are equal.

```
Object getLastPathComponent():
```

Gets the node that the path represents.

```
Object[] getPath():
```

Returns the array of TreeNodes that make up the path.

```
Object getPathComponent(int n)
```

Returns the nth node in the TreePath.

```
int getPathCount()
```

Returns the number of nodes in the TreePath.

```
in hashCode()
```

Returns the TreePath's hash code.

```
boolean isDescendant(TreePath aTreePath):
```

Returns true if the given TreePath is a descendant of this TreePath.

```
String toString():
```

Overridden to return TreePath's own special string.

TypedFile

TypedFile is used to associate a file type with a file. It is typically used with
DirectoryModel, JFileChooser, or JDirectoryPane because those classes are
involved in using a file's type to decide how to display a file or directory.

TypedFile is a subclass of java.io.File plus it has information about the type of file it is.

NOTE: *For JFC 1.1, TypedFile has been moved to the com.sun.java.swing.preview package. This means that its API is likely to change in the near future.*

Ancestors

```
java.lang.Object
   |
   +—java.io.File
         |
         +—com.sun.java.swing.preview.TypedFile
```

NOTE: *For more information, see the "FileType," "DirectoryModel," "JDirectoryPane," and "JFileChooser" sections in this chapter. Also see the File Browsing section in Chapter 7, "JFC by Concept," as well as Chapter 10, "Integrating JFC Example 1: A File Browser."*

Steps in Creating and Using TypedFile

1. There are two constructors, both of which take a file and a file type. The first takes the complete path to a file or directory and a file type:

   ```
   TypedFile myFile = new TypedFile( "c:\\autoexec.bat",
           FileType.SharedGenericFolder );
   ```

   The other takes a path to a directory, a file or directory within that, directory and a file type:

   ```
   TypedFile myFile = new TypedFile( "c:\\", "autoexec.bat",
           FileType.SharedGenericFolder );
   ```

   The FileType interface includes a number of basic types that refer to generic files, folders, floppy drives, hard drives, etc. You can create your own FileTypes as well.

2. When you use a JFileChooser or JDirectoryPane, you retrieve the selected files using the getSelectedFile() or getSelectedFiles() method. These methods return TypedFiles, either directly with getSelectedFile() or in a Vector with getSelectedFiles().

3. When you use a DirectoryModel, you get the contents of a directory using one of the following methods: getTypedFile(), getTypedFiles(), or getTypedFilesForDirectory(). Each of these methods returns either a single TypedFile or a Vector full of TypedFiles.

4. You can get a TypedFile's type using the getType() method. This returns a class that implements FileType.

```
FileType thisType = myFile.getType();
```

5. You can also get the icon associated with the TypedFile. This is actually stored as part of the FileType.

```
Icon fileIcon = myFile.getIcon();
```

This is the same as:

```
Icon fileIcon = myFile.getType().getIcon();
```

6. As a subclass of File, TypedFile has access to all of File's methods and can be used as a File.

NOTE: *See the "DirectoryModel," "JDirectoryPane," and "JFileChooser" sections for examples.*

TypedFile's Public Methods

```
Icon getIcon():
```

Returns the icon associated with this file's type.

```
FileType getType():
```

Returns the file's associated FileType class.

```
void setType(FileType type):
```

Changes the FileType associated with this file.

```
String toString():
```

Overridden for TypedFile's own special string format.

UIDefaults

UIDefaults holds a look-and-feel's list of UI classes and the look-and-feel ID's for the components that they should be applied to. This list is critical because otherwise a look-and-feel doesn't know which of its classes to use on which components. The look-and-feel ID string for a component is the same string returned by that component's getUIClassID() method and will be something like "CheckBoxUI".

As you can see in "Ancestors" below, UIDefaults is a descendant of java.util.Hashtable. Its keys are UI class ID strings like "CheckBoxUI," and its values are UI class names like "com.sun.java.swing.plaf.motif.Mo-tifCheckBoxUI." You can also store resources like colors, fonts, and strings as values in a UIDefaults instance. These are stored as UI resource classes like FontUIResource and ColorUIResource which can be found in the com.sun.java.swing.plaf package.

Ancestors

```
java.lang.Object
    |
    +—java.util.Dictionary
            |
            +—java.util.Hashtable
                    |
                    +—com.sun.java.swing.UIDefaults
```

NOTE: *For more information, see Chapter 4, "Pluggable Look-and-Feel," and also the "LookAndFeel" and "UIManager" sections in this chapter.*

Steps in Creating and Using UIDefaults

1. Create a UIDefaults instance. You only have to do this if you are creating a custom look-and-feel by directly subclassing LookAndFeel. You will probably want to do it in the LookAndFeel subclass' initialize() method.

   You can create an empty list:

   ```
   UIDefaults myDefaults = new UIDefaults();
   ```

   Or, you can create a list from an array of Objects representing keys and values:

   ```
   Object[] deflist =
   {
       "CheckBoxUI", "MyLookAndFeel.MyCheckBoxUI",
       "RadioButtonUI", "MyLookAndFeel.MyRadioButtonUI",
       "CheckBox.Foreground", new ColorUIResource( 200, 200, 200 )
   }
   UIDefaults myUIDefaults = new UIDefaults( deflist );
   ```

   If you are creating a custom look-and-feel by subclassing an existing look-and-feel like BasicLookAndFeel, that class has already created an UIDefaults instance, so you can just change its values.

2. Get the name of the UI class associated with a component's look-and-feel ID string:

   ```
   String uiClassName = myUIDefaults.getUIClass( "CheckBoxUI" );
   ```

3. Put a new key/value pair into the UIDefaults list. If an item with the given key already exists in the list, it is replaced with the new one.

```
put( "CheckBoxUI", "com.sun.java.swing.plaf.motif.MotifCheckBoxUI" );
```

4. Put a list of key/value pairs into the UIDefaults list. The list is an array of Objects representing key/value pairs.

```
Object[] deflist =
{
    "CheckBoxUI", "MyLookAndFeel.MyCheckBoxUI",
    "RadioButtonUI", "MyLookAndFeel.MyRadioButtonUI",
    "CheckBox.Foreground", new ColorUIResource( 200, 200, 200 ),
    "InternalFrameBorder",
        new BorderUIResource( new BevelBorder(
                                BevelBorder.LOWERED ) ),
}
myUIDefaults.putDefaults( deflist );
```

5. Get the UIResource associated with a string key. Each of these methods checks to make sure that the value associated with the given string is a class of the correct type. Since the key strings are only used by the look-and-feel that the UIDefaults is associated with, there is no standard set.

```
ColorUIResource checkboxForeground =
                            myUIDefaults.getColor(
                            "CheckBox.Foreground" );

BorderUIResource internalFrameBorder =
                            myUIDefaults.getBorder(
                            "InternalFrameBorder" );
```

There are also methods for getting font, icon, and string resources. The UIResource classes are just the equivalent AWT classes implementing the empty UIResource interface so they can be identified as having come from the look-and-feel.

6. Create an instance of the UI class associated with a component:

```
JCheckBox checkBox = new JCheckBox( "A Check Box" );
ComponentUI checkBoxUIClass = myUIDefaults.getUI( checkBox );
```

NOTE: *See Chapter 4, "Pluggable Look-and-Feel" to see UIDefaults in use.*

UIDefaults's Public Methods

```
void addPropertyChangeListener(PropertyChangeListener listener):
```

Tells the UIDefaults to notify the given class when the defaults list changes in any way.

`Object get(Object key):`

Returns the value associated with the given key which is normally a String.

`Border getBorder(Object key):`

Returns the Border or BorderUIResource associated with the given key, if there is one.

`Color getColor(Object key):`

Returns the Color or ColorUIResource associated with the given key, if there is one.

`Font getFont(Object key):`

Returns the Font or FontUIResource associated with the given key, if there is one.

`Icon getIcon(Object key):`

Returns the Icon or IconUIResource associated with the given key, if there is one.

`String getString(Object key):`

Returns the String associated with the given key, if there is one.

`ComponentUI getUI(JComponent target):`

Creates an instance of the given component's current UI class.

`Class getUIClass(String uiClassID):`

Returns the name of the UI class that is associated with the given look-and-feel ID string.

`Object put(Object key,Object value):`

Puts the given key/value pair into the UIDefaults list. If an entry already exists with the given key, the new one replaces it.

`void putDefaults(Object keyValueList[]):`

Adds the list of key/values into the UIDefaults list.

`void removePropertyChangeListener(PropertyChangeListener listener):`

Tells the UIDefaults to stop notifying the given class about changes to the defaults list.

UIManager

UIManager is the class that keeps track of what the current look-and-feel is and allows you to change to a new look-and-feel and access or modify that its properties. You do not create the UIManager yourself—the JVM creates it. Since there is always only one look-and-feel installed, all of UIManager's methods are static.

Ancestors

```
java.lang.Object
    |
    +—com.sun.java.swing.UIManager
```

NOTE: *For more information, see Chapter 4, "Pluggable Look-and-Feel," and the "LookAndFeel" and "UIDefaults" sections in this chapter.*

Steps in Using UIManager

1. Change the look-and-feel.

Create a look-and-feel class and tell the UIManager to install it as the look-and-feel (notice the exception that must be caught):

```
JLFLookAndFeel newLook = new JLFLookAndFeel();
try
{
    UIManager.setLookAndFeel( newLook );
}
catch ( UnsupportedLookAndFeelException ex )
{
    System.out.println( "JLF is not supported" );
}
```

Or, you can let the UIManager create the instance of the look-and-feel class by giving it the class name (notice the multiple exceptions that must be caught):

```
try
{
    UIManager.setLookAndFeel(
            "com.sun.java.swing.plaf.motif.MotifLookAndFeel");
```

```
    }
catch ( ClassNotFoundException ex )
{
System.err.println( "Motif:  Could not find the look-and-feel" );
}
catch ( InstantiationException ex )
{
System.err.println( "Motif:  Could not create the look-and-feel" );
}
catch ( IllegalAccessException ex )
{
System.err.println( "Motif:  Could not access the look-and-feel" );
}
```

JFC components created after the look-and-feel is changed will use it, as will any existing components that are explicitly told to do so.

2. Read the look-and-feel's properties. These are convenience methods for access to the current look-and-feel's UIDefaults instance.

```
ColorUIResource checkBoxForeground = UIManager.getColor(
                                    "CheckBox.Foreground" );
```

There are also methods for getting font, border, icon, and string resources. These property methods will check to make sure that the resource returned is the correct type.

3. Add a property key/value pair to the UIDefaults' list of defaults. This can include resources or UI class names.

```
UIManager.put( "CheckBoxUI",
                "com.sun.java.swing.plaf.motif.motifCheckBoxUI" );
```

4. Get the currently installed look-and-feel (a subclass of LookAndFeel):

```
LookAndFeel currentLF = UIManager.getLookAndFeel();
```

NOTE: *See Chapter 4, "Pluggable Look-and-Feel" for examples of how to use UIManager.*

UIManager's Public Methods

```
static synchronized void addPropertyChangeListener(
    PropertyChangeListener listener):
```

Tells the UIManager to notify the given class when the look-and-feel or other properties change.

```
static Object get(Object key):
```

Returns the value Object associated with the given key in the current look-and-feel's UIDefaults list. The key is usually a String.

```
static AbstractLookAndFeel[] getAuxiliaryLookAndFeels():
```

Returns a list of all of the look-and-feels that the UIManager knows.

```
static Border getBorder(Object key):
```

Returns the Border or BorderUIResource associated with the given key in the current look-and-feel's UIDefaults list.

```
static Color getColor(Object key) :
```

Returns the Color or ColorUIResource associated with the given key in the current look-and-feel's UIDefaults list.

```
static String getCrossPlatformLookAndFeelClassName()
```

Returns the name of the look-and-feel that is the default platform-independent look-and-feel. This should be "com.sun.java.swing.plaf.metal.MetalLookAndFeel."

```
static UIDefaults getDefaults():
```

Returns the current look-and-feel's UIDefaults list.

```
static Font getFont(Object key):
```

Returns the Font or FontUIResource associated with the given key in the current look-and-feel's UIDefaults list.

```
static Icon getIcon(Object key):
```

Returns the Icon or IconUIResource associated with the given key in the current look-and-feel's UIDefaults list.

```
static UIManager.LookAndFeelInfo[] getInstalledLookAndFeels()
```

This returns information about the JVM's currently installed look-and-feel classes. Use the LookAndFeelInfo class getName() or getClassName() methods.

```
static LookAndFeel getLookAndFeel():
```

Returns the currently installed look-and-feel.

```
static UIDefaults getLookAndFeelDefaults()
```

Returns the UIDefaults from the current look-and-feel.

```
static String getString(Object key) :
```

Returns the String associated with the given key in the current look-and-feel's UIDefaults list.

```
static String getSystemLookAndFeelClassName()
```

Returns the name of the look-and-feel class that mimics the current platform's native look-and-feel.

```
static ComponentUI getUI(JComponent target):
```

Creates and returns an instance of the current look-and-feel's UI class associated with the given component.

```
static Object put(Object key,Object value):
```

Adds the given key/value pair to the current look-and-feel's UIDefaults list. Any existing item with the same key in the list will be replaced.

```
static synchronized void removePropertyChangeListener(
        PropertyChangeListener listener):
```

Tells the UIManager to stop notifying the given class when the look-and-feel or its properties change.

```
static void setLookAndFeel(LookAndFeel lnf):
```

Sets the look-and-feel to the given one.

```
static void setLookAndFeel(String className):
```

Creates an instance of the given look-and-feel class and makes it the new look-and-feel.

SUMMARY

This chapter is the heart of the book. It discusses the most important classes in the JFC, giving instructions for their use as well as examples putting them to work. The intent of this chapter is to get you started with a class quickly and then give you an example so you can see it interact with related classes.

Future JFC Technologies

Parts of the JFC require changes to the JDK, so these parts are on a different schedule than the Swing and Accessibility parts, which are 100 percent Java. This chapter briefly discusses the parts that will come out with JDK 1.2, including the following:

- Drag-and-Drop
- Custom Cursors
- Java 2D

NOTE: *Because the discussions and examples in this chapter are based on an early beta release of JDK 1.2, these topics could not be covered as fully as topics in other chapters. There are also likely to be major API changes by the time the final release comes out.*

Drag-and-Drop

One of the things Java has always been missing has been built-in drag-and-drop capabilities. In the past, you have had to use a package that supports drag-and-drop, such as Netscape's IFC, or implement it yourself. Either way, you were restricted to dragging within a single window. The drag-and-drop classes in JDK 1.2 will allow you to have drag-and-drop not only between windows, but also between Java applications and non-Java applications.

Java drag-and-drop isn't incredibly straightforward, but it's quite flexible. It's made up of a set of classes that work together in interesting ways. Here's a list of the most important classes and interfaces and what they do:

■ **DragSource:** This class generates a drag operation. It's not a component, but it will generally be associated with a component. The DragSource does not respond to drag or other mouse events—a component must recognize that a drag is starting, and then tells the DragSource to start a drag session.

■ **DragSourceListener:** This interface defines the methods a class has to implement to be kept up-to-date on the status of the drag operation from the DragSource's point of view. A DragSourceListener is notified when the drag cursor enters a potential drop target, exits a potential drop target, moves while over a potential drop target, and when the drop has occurred. DragSourceListener methods get either DragSourceDragEvents or DragSourceDropEvents, depending on what happened. These events are where a listener can get access to the drag operation's DragSourceContext.

■ **DragSourceContext:** This class is created when the DragSource starts a drag session, and keeps track of what's going on with the drag operation for registered DragSourceListeners. The DragSourceContext stores the data that's being dragged.

■ **DropTarget:** This class isn't a component, but is always associated with a component. When a component wants to be able to have things dropped on it, it creates a DropTarget for itself and the DropTarget waits for things to happen.

■ **DropTargetListener:** This interface defines the methods a class has to implement to be kept up-to-date on the status of a drag operation from the point of view of the DropTarget. A DropTargetListener is notified when a drag cursor enters or exits its associated component, when a drag cursor is over its associated component, or when a drop occurs on its associated component. DropTargetListener methods get either DropTargetDragEvents or DropTargetDropEvents, depending on what happened. These events are where listeners can get access to the drag operation's DropTargetContext.

- **DropTargetContext:** This is the class that actually tracks a drag operation from the DropTarget's point of view. It's the one that notifies registered DropTargetListeners when interesting things happen. The DropTargetContext contains the data being dragged.

- **DnDConstants:** This class contains the constants that define the type of actions that can be done in a drag operation, like moving, copying, and so forth.

- **DataFlavor:** When data is being dragged, the destination isn't known, so the data must be stored in a general format. A DataFlavor represents a way of presenting data. Normally, an object being transferred stores its data in one way, but can make it available to drop targets in multiple ways.

- **Transferable:** This interface represents an object being dragged. A class that implements it contains the data being dragged and includes DataFlavors specifying the forms in which the data can be presented.

Steps in a Typical Drag-and-Drop Operation

1. Create a component that things will be dragged from. When the user clicks an item in this component and drags the cursor, the drag-and-drop operation begins. For this example, we will subclass java.awt.List:

```
import java.awt.*;

public class SourceList extends List
{
    public SourceList()
    {
        super();
    }
}
```

2. Create an instance of the DragSource class for the component we just created. We need a DragSource as the doorway to starting a drag-and-drop operation.

   Here's the code for the component we just created with changes in italic:

```
import java.awt.*;
import java.awt.dnd.*;

public class SourceList extends List
{
    private DragSource mSource;

    public SourceList()
    {
        super();

        mSource = new DragSource();
    }
}
```

3. The DragSource doesn't automatically start a drag-and-drop operation when the user clicks and drags the mouse. Our component is responsible for recognizing the mouse events and telling the DragSource to start the operation. What we will do is catch the event when the mouse is pressed. Then, while the mouse is down, we will catch events when the mouse is dragged. Once the mouse is dragged a certain distance away from the point where it was initially pressed, we will decide that a drag-and-drop operation has been started.

Modify the preceding source code so that an inner class listens for both mouse events and mouse-drag events. When the mouse is pressed, the inner class saves the MouseEvent for comparison to later mouse-drag events. If the mouse is released, the saved MouseEvent is discarded. When a mouse-drag event is received, if the position has moved more than 5 pixels away from the starting point in X or Y, we consider this a real drag.

Here's the previous source code, modified to recognize the start of a drag-and-drop.

```
import java.awt.*;
import java.awt.event.*;
import java.awt.dnd.*;

public class SourceList extends List
{
    private DragSource mSource;

    public SourceList()
    {
        super();

        // Create our mouse listener and make it listen to
        // this component's mouse and mouse motion events.
        SourceMouseListener sma = new SourceMouseListener();
        addMouseListener( sma );
        addMouseMotionListener( sma );
```

```
                mSource = new DragSource();
        }

        // This inner class contains everything we need to
        // recognize when a drag starts.
        private class SourceMouseListener extends MouseAdapter
                implements MouseMotionListener
        {
            // Save where the drag started.
            private MouseEvent mPressedEvent;

            // When the mouse is pressed, save the mouse event.
            public void mousePressed( MouseEvent e )
            {
                mPressedEvent = e;
            }

            // When the mouse is released, discard the mouse
            // event so there won't be any confusion.
            public void mouseReleased( MouseEvent e )
            {
                mPressedEvent = null;
            }

            // When the mouse drags more than 5 pixels away from
            // where it was pressed, if there is a selected item
            // and a saved mouse event, we consider it the start
            // of a drag.
            public void mouseDragged( MouseEvent e )
            {
                // Get the selected list item.
                String selectedItem = getSelectedItem();

                if ( mPressedEvent != null &&
                     selectedItem != null &&
                     (Math.abs( mPressedEvent.getX() - e.getX() )
                     > 5 ||
                     Math.abs( mPressedEvent.getY() - e.getY() )
                     > 5 ) )
                {
                    System.out.println( "Drag started" );

                    mPressedEvent = null;
                }
            }

            // Completes the MouseMotionListener interface.
            public void mouseMoved( MouseEvent e )
            {
            }
        }
    }
```

4. To tell a DragSource to start a drag-and-drop operation, you have to call its startDrag() method, whose definition is as follows:

```
public void startDrag( Component c,
                       AWTEvent trigger,
                       int actions,
                       Cursor dragCursor,
                       Image dragImage,
                       Point imageOffset,
                       Transferable transferable,
                       DragSourceListener dsl )
```

Here's what the arguments mean:

- **Component c:** This is the component in which the drag started. For this example, it would be our SourceList component.

- **AWTEvent trigger:** This is the event that triggered the operation. It's used to figure out what event will trigger the drop. Our trigger is the MouseEvent we saved when the mouse was initially pressed.

- **int actions:** The DnDConstants class defines the following actions: ACTION_COPY, ACTION_COPY_OR_MOVE, ACTION_LINK, ACTION_MOVE, ACTION_NONE, and ACTION_REFERENCE. Choose one to define the kind of drag interaction you expect to have. We will use ACTION_COPY so a DropTarget can get a copy of the dragged list item.

- **Cursor dragCursor:** This is the cursor used while dragging over places where a drop can't take place. You can use any Cursor, but the DragSource class defines the following ones: DefaultCopyDrop, , DefaultCopyNoDrop, DefaultLinkDrop, DefaultLinkNoDrop, DefaultMoveDrop, DefaultMoveNoDrop. We will use DragSource.DefaultCopyNoDrop.

- **Image dragImage:** This image moves around with the drag cursor and further defines what is happening. We will use null, expecting the drag cursor to be enough.

- **Point imageOffset:** This position is where the the dragImage's hotspot should be. We use (0,0).

- **Transferable transferable:** Transferable is an interface in the java.awt.datatransfer package. It contains the object being dragged—in our case a list item, which is a String. It also contains the data flavors that the object being dragged can be delivered in. We use an implementation of Transferable called StringSelection, also found in java.awt.datatransfer. It allows the DropTraget to access the object being dragged via a java.io.StringReader.

- **DragSourceListener dsl:** We need to be notified of events that happen during the drag-and-drop operation, so we implement the

DragSourceListener interface in our SourceList class and pass it into the startDrag() method.

Here's the modified source code. The changes are in italic and include the implementation of the DragSourceListener and the call to startDrag():

```java
import java.awt.*;
import java.awt.event.*;
import java.awt.dnd.*;
import java.awt.datatransfer.*;

public class SourceList extends List implements
        DragSourceListener
{
    private DragSource mSource;

    public SourceList()
    {
        super();

        // Create our mouse listener and make it listen to
        // this component's mouse and mouse motion events.
        SourceMouseListener sma = new SourceMouseListener();
        addMouseListener( sma );
        addMouseMotionListener( sma );

        mSource = new DragSource();
    }

    // This is called when the item has been dropped on a
    // DropTarget and the target has called the
    // TargetContext's dropComplete() method.
    public void dragDropEnd( DragSourceDropEvent e )
    {
    }

    // This is called when the drag cursor enters a
    // DropTarget where the item can be dropped.
    public void dragEnter( DragSourceDragEvent e )
    {
    }

    // This is called when the drag cursor exits a
    // DropTarget where the item can be dropped.
    public void dragExit( DragSourceEvent e )
    {
    }

    // This is called when the drag events change.
    public void dragGestureChanged( DragSourceDragEvent e )
    {
    }
```

```java
// This is called when the drag cursor is being dragged
// over a DropTarget where the item can be dropped.
public void dragOver( DragSourceDragEvent e )
{
}

// This inner class contains everything we need to
// recognize when a drag starts.
private class SourceMouseListener extends MouseAdapter
        implements MouseMotionListener
{
    // Save where the drag started.
    private MouseEvent mPressedEvent;

    // When the mouse is pressed, save the mouse event.
    public void mousePressed( MouseEvent e )
    {
        mPressedEvent = e;
    }

    // When the mouse is released, discard the mouse
    // event so there won't be any confusion.
    public void mouseReleased( MouseEvent e )
    {
        mPressedEvent = null;
    }

    // When the mouse drags more than 5 pixels away from
    // where it was pressed, if there is a selected item
    // and a saved mouse event, we consider it the start
    // of a drag.
    public void mouseDragged( MouseEvent e )
    {
        // Get the selected list item.
        String selectedItem = getSelectedItem();

        if ( mPressedEvent != null &&
             selectedItem != null &&
             (Math.abs( mPressedEvent.getX() - e.getX() )
             > 5 ||
             Math.abs( mPressedEvent.getY() - e.getY() )
             > 5 ) )
        {
            // Tell the DragSource to start the drag.
            mSource.startDrag( SourceList.this,
                    mPressedEvent,
                    DnDConstants.ACTION_COPY,
                    DragSource.DefaultCopyNoDrop,
                    null,
                    new Point( 0, 0 ),
                    new StringSelection( selectedItem ),
                    SourceList.this );

            mPressedEvent = null;
        }
```

```
        }

        // Completes the MouseMotionListener interface.
        public void mouseMoved( MouseEvent e )
        {
        }
    }
}
```

5. Create a component that accepts dropped information. We will create another subclass of java.awt.List. If the user is dragging something from our SourceList class and releases the mouse within our new class, the dropped item will be added to the end of the list. Here is the skeleton:

```
import java.awt.*;

public class TargetList extends List
{
    public TargetList()
    {
        super();
    }
}
```

6. To accept drops, the component needs to have a DropTarget associated with it. The DropTarget creates a DropTargetContext that notifies any listeners about drag-and-drop events that happen on the component, so we will implement the DropTargetListener interface. The dragEnter() method is called when a drag cursor touches the component's edge on entering. We call the DropTargetDragEvent's acceptDrag() method to let the DropTargetContext know what types of drops this component accepts. If the drag isn't of that type, the drag cursor is a no-drop cursor while over the component. Otherwise, it becomes a drop cursor over the component.

Here's the source code after it has been modified to create a DropTarget and implement the DropTargetListener interface.

```
import java.awt.*;
import java.awt.dnd.*;

public class TargetList extends List implements
        DropTargetListener
{
    private DropTarget mTarget;

    public TargetList()
    {
        super();

        // Create the DropTarget, passing in the component it
        // is associated with, and the class that implements
```

```
        // the DropTargetListener interface.
        mTarget = new DropTarget( this , this );
    }

    // This is called when the drag cursor enters the
    // component.  We call the DropTargetDragEvent's
    // acceptDrag() method to tell the DropTargetContext
    // that this component will accept ACTION_COPY type
    // drops only.
    public void dragEnter( DropTargetDragEvent e )
    {
        e.acceptDrag( DnDConstants.ACTION_COPY );
    }

    // This is called when the drag cursor exits the
    // component.
    public void dragExit( DropTargetEvent e )
    {
    }

    // This is called when the drag cursor drags over the
    // component.
    public void dragOver( DropTargetDragEvent e )
    {
    }

    // This is called when the drag cursor causes the
    // component to scroll.
    public void dragScroll( DropTargetDragEvent e )
    {
    }

    // This is called when the drop occurs.
    public void drop( DropTargetDropEvent e )
    {
    }
}
```

At this point, the drag cursor will change when it passes over the component, but nothing happens to the dropped data.

7. Now we need to fill in the drop() method to get the dragged data and put it into the target list.

Get the dragged data from the DropTargetDropEvent "e." It's stored in a Transferable, just as it was when we called startDrag() in the SourceList.

```
Transferable tr = e.getTransferable();
```

Find out if the dragged data can be delivered in a format we can understand. Transferables can deliver their data in one or more formats. When you receive a drop, you should try your most sophisticated formats first so you get the best possible information.

```
if ( tr.isDataFlavorSupported( DataFlavor.stringFlavor ) )
{
    // The Transferable can give us what we want.
}
```

If we can get the Transferable's data, tell the DropTargetDropEvent that we accept the drop:

```
e.acceptDrop();
```

Get the data. In this example, we get the data as a StringReader:

```
StringReader reader = (StringReader)tr.getTransferData(
                          DataFlavor.plainTextFlavor );
```

Notify the DragSource that the drop has been successful. The notification goes through the DropTargetContext, which notifies the DragSourceContext, which notifies the DragSource by calling its dragDropEnd() method. If you don't call this method, the operation won't end:

```
e.getDropTargetContext().dropComplete( true );
```

EXAMPLE 9-1 Dragging Items from One List to Another

This example puts together the steps discussed previously to create a simple application with a list on the left and a list on the right. You can drag copies of items from the left-hand list into the right-hand list. The example has a main frame class called "MyFrame," a class called "SourceList" for the list that can be dragged from, and a class called "TargetList" for the list where items can be dropped. Figure 9-1 shows the example after two items have been dragged and dropped.

Here is the source for MyFrame.java (SourceList.java and TargetList.java follow):

```
import java.awt.*;

public class MyFrame extends Frame
{
    public MyFrame()
```

Figure 9-1
Dragging items from
one list to another.

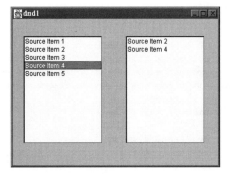

```
{
    setTitle( "dnd1" );

    setBackground( Color.lightGray );

    setLayout( null );

    // Create the source list.
    SourceList list1 = new SourceList();

    // Load the source list.
    list1.add( "Source Item 1" );
    list1.add( "Source Item 2" );
    list1.add( "Source Item 3" );
    list1.add( "Source Item 4" );
    list1.add( "Source Item 5" );

    // Place the source list.
    list1.setBounds( 25, 55, 150, 200 );
    add( list1 );

    // Create the target list.
    TargetList list2 = new TargetList();

    // Place the target list.
    list2.setBounds( 220, 55, 150, 200 );
    add( list2 );
    }
}
```

Here is the source for SourceList.java:

```
import java.awt.*;
import java.awt.event.*;
import java.awt.dnd.*;
import java.awt.datatransfer.*;

public class SourceList extends List implements
        DragSourceListener
{
    private DragSource mSource;

    public SourceList()
    {
        super();

        // Create our mouse listener and make it listen to
        // this component's mouse and mouse motion events.
        SourceMouseListener sma = new SourceMouseListener();
        addMouseListener( sma );
        addMouseMotionListener( sma );

        mSource = new DragSource();
    }
```

```java
// This is called when the item has been dropped on a
// DropTarget and the target has called the
// TargetContext's dropComplete() method.
public void dragDropEnd( DragSourceDropEvent e )
{
}

// This is called when the drag cursor enters a
// DropTarget where the item can be dropped.
public void dragEnter( DragSourceDragEvent e )
{
}

// This is called when the drag cursor exits a
// DropTarget where the item can be dropped.
public void dragExit( DragSourceEvent e )
{
}

// This is called when the drag events change.
public void dragGestureChanged( DragSourceDragEvent e )
{
}

// This is called when the drag cursor is being dragged
// over a DropTarget where the item can be dropped.
public void dragOver( DragSourceDragEvent e )
{
}

// This inner class contains everything we need to
// recognize when a drag starts.
private class SourceMouseListener extends MouseAdapter
        implements MouseMotionListener
{
    // Save where the drag started.
    private MouseEvent mPressedEvent;

    // When the mouse is pressed, save the mouse event.
    public void mousePressed( MouseEvent e )
    {
        mPressedEvent = e;
    }

    // When the mouse is released, discard the mouse
    // event so there won't be any confusion.
    public void mouseReleased( MouseEvent e )
    {
        mPressedEvent = null;
    }

    // When the mouse drags more than 5 pixels away from
    // where it was pressed, if there is a selected item
```

```
        // and a saved mouse event, we consider it the start
        // of a drag.
        public void mouseDragged( MouseEvent e )
        {
            // Get the selected list item.
            String selectedItem = getSelectedItem();

            if ( mPressedEvent != null &&
                 selectedItem != null &&
                 (Math.abs( mPressedEvent.getX() - e.getX() )
                 > 5 ||
                 Math.abs( mPressedEvent.getY() - e.getY() )
                 > 5 ) )
            {
                // Tell the DragSource to start the drag.
                mSource.startDrag( SourceList.this,
                        mPressedEvent,
                        DnDConstants.ACTION_COPY,
                        DragSource.DefaultCopyNoDrop,
                        null,
                        new Point( 0, 0 ),
                        new StringSelection( selectedItem ),
                        SourceList.this );

                mPressedEvent = null;
            }
        }

        // Completes the MouseMotionListener interface.
        public void mouseMoved( MouseEvent e )
        {
        }
    }
}
```

Here is the source for TargetList.java:

```
import java.awt.*;
import java.awt.dnd.*;
import java.awt.datatransfer.*;
import java.io.*;

public class TargetList extends List implements
        DropTargetListener
{
    private DropTarget mTarget;

    public TargetList()
    {
        super();

        // Create the DropTarget, passing in the component it
        // is associated with, and the class that implements
        // the DropTargetListener interface.
```

```
        mTarget = new DropTarget( this , this );
    }

    // This is called when the drag cursor enters the
    // component.  We call the DropTargetDragEvent's
    // acceptDrag() method to tell the DropTargetContext
    // that this component will accept ACTION_COPY type
    // drops only.
    public void dragEnter( DropTargetDragEvent e )
    {
        e.acceptDrag( DnDConstants.ACTION_COPY );
    }

    // This is called when the drag cursor exits the
    // component.
    public void dragExit( DropTargetEvent e )
    {
    }

    // This is called when the drag cursor drags over the
    // component.
    public void dragOver( DropTargetDragEvent e )
    {
    }

    // This is called when the drag cursor causes the
    // component to scroll.
    public void dragScroll( DropTargetDragEvent e )
    {
    }

    // This is called when the drop occurs.
    public void drop( DropTargetDropEvent e )
    {
        // Get the Transferable.
        Transferable tr = e.getTransferable();

        // If the Transferable's data can be delivered in the
        // format we understand, we can continue.
        if ( tr.isDataFlavorSupported(
                            DataFlavor.stringFlavor ) )
        {
            // Accept the drop.
            e.acceptDrop( DnDConstants.ACTION_MOVE );

            try
            {
                // Get the dragged data from the Transferable.
                StringReader reader =
                        (StringReader)tr.getTransferData(
                        DataFlavor.plainTextFlavor );

                // Read the item into a character array and add
                // it as a list item.
                char ch[] = new char[100];
```

```
        int len;

        len = reader.read( ch );

        add( new String( ch, 0, len ) );
    }
    catch ( UnsupportedFlavorException ex )
    {
        ex.printStackTrace();
    }
    catch ( IOException ex )
    {
        ex.printStackTrace();
    }

    // Notify the DropTargetContext that the drop is
    // successfully complete.
    e.getDropTargetContext().dropComplete( true );
    }
    else
    {
    // We couldn't get the data, so we reject the drop.
    e.rejectDrop();
    }
    }
    }
}
```

Custom Cursors

In the old AWT, the only cursors you had access to were a handful of predefined ones. Part of the new JFC functionality in JDK 1.2 is the ability to create and use custom cursors. The key to custom cursors is the Toolkit createCustomCursor() method:

```
public Cursor createCustomCursor( Image cursorImage, Point hotspot,
    String name )
```

Here's what the arguments mean:

- **cursorImage:** This is the image that's displayed.
- **hotspot:** This is the coordinate within the image that indicates where a click occurs.
- **name:** This argument is used for accessibility information.

Different environments might have limitations on cursor size and number of colors. For this reason, Toolkit also supplies a method called getBestCursorSize(xsize, ysize), which returns the available cursor size closest to the given size, and a method called getMaximumCursorColors(), which returns the maximum number of colors a cursor can have in its palette.

EXAMPLE 9-2 Creating a Custom Cursor

This example reads an image from a GIF file and uses it to create a custom cursor. Here is the source code:

```
import com.sun.java.swing.*;
import java.awt.*;

public class MyFrame extends JFrame
{
    public MyFrame()
    {
        setTitle( "CustomCursor" );

        // Store the content pane in a variable for easier
        // access.
        JPanel contentPane = (JPanel)getContentPane();

        // Components will all be added to this panel.
        contentPane.setLayout( new BorderLayout() );

        // Read the GIF file into an ImageIcon.
        ImageIcon icon = new ImageIcon( "delete.gif" );

        // Create the custom cursor using the image from the
        // icon.
        Cursor custom = Toolkit.getDefaultToolkit().
                        createCustomCursor( icon.getImage(),
                        new Point( 0, 0 ), "delete" );

        // Apply the custom cursor.
        setCursor( custom );

        // Print out cursor size and palette information.
        System.out.println(
            Toolkit.getDefaultToolkit().getBestCursorSize(
            16, 16 ) );
        System.out.println(
            Toolkit.getDefaultToolkit().getBestCursorSize(
            32, 32 ) );
        System.out.println(
            Toolkit.getDefaultToolkit().getBestCursorSize(
            64, 64 ) );
        System.out.println(
            Toolkit.getDefaultToolkit().
            getMaximumCursorColors() );
    }
}
```

Java 2D

Java2D is a set of classes and packages that have been added into the java.awt.* hierarchy and are used to implement sophisticated graphical capabilities that weren't previously available. These capabilities include the following:

- **Wide lines:** The AWT could only draw 1-pixel wide lines. Java2D lets you specify line width.
- **Dashed lines:** The AWT did not support dashing. Java2D lets you define your own line styles.
- **Line caps:** You can select from butt, round, and square ends.
- **Line joins:** You can select from bevel, miter, and round joins.
- **Gradient fill:** The AWT supported only solid fill. Java2D supports both cyclic and acyclic gradient fills.
- **Texture fill:** You can specify a raster image to use to fill a shape.
- **Different fill rules:** Non-zero and even-odd winding rules are supported.
- **Arcs:** You can define a three-point arc as open, closed with a chord, or a pie shape.
- **Ellipses:** You can define a rectangle in which an ellipse will be fit.
- **Curves:** You can define quadratic parametric curves and cubic parametric curves.
- **Transformations:** Java2D supports translation, rotation, and shearing transformations.
- **Image-processing filters:** Java2D includes classes for advanced image filtering.
- **Full access to local fonts:** The AWT was restricted to just a few fonts. Java2D gives you access to all your fonts.
- **Color merging:** Java2D supports an alpha channel that allows degrees of transparency.
- **Multiple color spaces:** Java2D supports several color spaces.
- **Improved access to printers and other local graphical devices:** Java2D gives you more direct control over the printing process, as well as better information about local graphical devices.
- **Lines, polygons, and text all treated as paths:** This means that transformations all work the same, and you can fill text as though it were polygons.

Graphics2D

It used to be that when you wanted to draw inside an AWT component, you would override the component's paint() method. The paint() method would look something like this:

```
public void paint( Graphics g )
{
    g. setColor( Color.red );
    g. drawLine( 0, 0, 100, 100 );
}
```

With Java2D, you can still override the paint() method, but you cast the passed-in Graphics instance to a Graphics2D instance. Graphics2D is a subclass of Graphics. Your revised paint() method would look something like this:

```
public void paint( Graphics g )
{
    Graphics2D g2D = (Graphics2D)g;
    g2D.setColor( Color.red );
    GeneralPath path = new GeneralPath();
    path.moveTo( 0, 0 ):
    path.lineTo( 100, 100 );
    g2D.draw( path );
}
```

All Java2D drawing is done through Graphics2D.

Paths and the Shape Interface

The Shape interface has existed within the AWT for a while, but didn't get much use. In Java2D, however, Shape and its implementors play a large part. These *implementors* include lines, arcs, curves, rectangles, and even text. This is very useful because all these Shape implementors can be treated the same —they can be stroked using the same methods, filled using the same methods, and transformed using the same methods. So once you have a Shape, you can draw its outline, fill it, rotate it, shear it, or whatever.

Java2D also includes the idea of a *path*, which essentially contains one or more Shapes. So you can make a simple line, and then add a three-point arc to the end of it, or you can include the Shapes that make up a text string into a single path. The best thing about paths is that they are also Shapes, so you can do anything to a path that you could to any other Shape.

The following sections cover each Shape implementor. After those explanations, an example shows them in use.

RECTANGLE Rectangle replaces the old java.awt.Rectangle class. It even has different ancestors.

ANCESTORS
```
java.lang.Object
     |
     +—java.awt.geom.RectangularShape
            |
            +—java.awt.geom.Rectangle2D
                   |
                   +—java.awt.Rectangle
```

STEPS IN CREATING AND USING RECTANGLE
1. You can still use Rectangle as you did in the old AWT. For use with Graphics2D, you might create it as usual:

   ```
   Rectangle r = new Rectangle( 10, 10, 100, 100 );
   ```

   This statement creates a rectangular shape whose upper-left corner is at 10,10; it's 100 pixels wide and 100 pixels high.

2. Draw the rectangle's outline, assuming "g2D" is a Graphics2D instance:

   ```
   g2D.draw( r );
   ```

3. Fill the rectangle, assuming "g2D" is a Graphics2D instance:
   ```
   g2D.fill( r );
   ```

ARC2D.FLOAT Arc2D.Float is an inner class of the abstract Arc2D class and extends it. It allows you to create a three-point arc Shape and to leave it open, close it with a chord, or resolve it into a pie area.

ANCESTORS
```
java.lang.Object
     |
     +—java.awt.geom.RectangularShape
            |
            +—java.awt.geom.Arc2D
                   |
                   +—java.awt.geom.Arc2D.Float
```

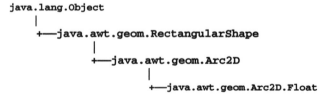

NOTE: *For more information on how to set a Shape's line attributes, fill its interior, and transform its coordinates, see the "Stroking Paths," "Applying Color," and "Transformations" sections in this chapter.*

STEPS IN CREATING AND USING ARC2D.FLOAT
1. Create the Arc2D.Float. There are several constructors, but this one

takes a rectangle that defines the ellipse the arc is part of, plus the start and extent angles in degrees, and a constant that specifies whether (and how) to close the arc:

```
Arc2D.Float arc = new Arc2D.Float( 200, 120, 200, 90,
                                   30, 60, Arc2D.PIE );
```

The ellipse the arc is part of has its bounding rectangle's origin at 200,120, and is 200 pixels wide and 90 pixels tall. The arc starts at 30 degrees along the ellipse and continues for 60 degrees. The ends of the arc attach to the center of the ellipse, forming a pie shape. You can also leave the arc open or close it with a chord.

2. Draw the outline of the arc, assuming "g2D" is an instance of Graphics2D:

```
g2D.draw( arc );
```

3. Fill the the arc (if it was closed), assuming "g2D" is an instance of Graphics2D:

```
g2D.fill( arc );
```

CUBICCURVE2D.FLOAT CubicCurve2D is an inner class of the abstract CubicCurve2D class and extends it. It takes a start and an end point plus two other points used to define what the curve does between the start and end points.

ANCESTORS

```
java.lang.Object
   |
   +—java.awt.geom.CubicCurve2D
        |
        +—java.awt.geom.CubicCurve2D.Float
```

NOTE: *For more information on how to set a Shape's line attributes, fill its interior, and transform its coordinates, see the "Stroking Paths," "Applying Color," and "Transformations" sections in this chapter.*

STEPS IN CREATING AND USING CUBICCURVE2D.FLOAT

1. Create the CubicCurve2D.Float. There are two constructors. The following one takes the start point, followed by the two intermediate points, followed by the end point:

```
CubicCurve2D.Float cc = new CubicCurve2D.Float( 50, 120, 10, 130,
                                                100, 180, 20,
                                                200 );
```

The start point is 50,120, and the end point is 20,200. The intermediate points are 10,130 and 100,180.

2. Draw the outline of the curve, assuming "g2D" is an instance of Graphics2D:

```
g2D.draw( cc );
```

ELLIPSE2D.FLOAT   Ellipse2D.Float is an inner class of the abstract Ellipse2D class and extends it. The ellipse is defined by giving it a rectangle bounding area.

ANCESTORS
```
java.lang.Object
    |
    +——java.awt.geom.RectangularShape
            |
            +——java.awt.geom.Ellipse2D
                    |
                    +——java.awt.geom.Ellipse2D.Float
```

NOTE: *For more information on how to set a Shape's line attributes, fill its interior, and transform its coordinates, see the "Stroking Paths," "Applying Color," and "Transformations" sections in this chapter.*

STEPS IN CREATING AND USING ELLIPSE2D.FLOAT

1. Create the Ellipse2D.Float. There are two constructors. This one specifies a rectangle for the ellipse to place itself inside:

```
Ellipse2D.Float e = new Ellipse2D.Float( 10, 260, 80, 120 );
```

The rectangle has it upper-left corner at 10,260; it's 80 pixels wide and 120 pixels tall.

2. Draw the outline of the ellipse, assuming "g2D" is an instance of Graphics2D:

```
g2D.draw( e );
```

3. Fill the the ellipse, assuming "g2D" is an instance of Graphics2D:

```
g2D.fill( e );
```

GENERALPATH   GeneralPath is the Java2D class that implements the path idea. It's initially a path with no points. It has a set of methods for adding straight line segments, cubic curves, quad curves, and other shapes to itself. Because it implements the Shape interface, it can be drawn, filled, and transformed like any other shape.

ANCESTORS
```
java.lang.Object
    |
    +——java.awt.geom.GeneralPath
```

NOTE: *For more information on how to set a Shape's line attributes, fill its interior, and transform its coordinates, see the "Stroking Paths," "Applying Color," and "Transformations" sections in this chapter.*

STEPS IN CREATING AND USING GENERALPATH

1. Create the GeneralPath. There are three constructors. This one allows you to set the winding rule that determines how parts of a path that overlap are drawn:

   ```
   GeneralPath gp = new GeneralPath( PathIterator.EVEN_ODD );
   ```

   This statement sets the winding rule to even-odd. It's non-zero by default.

2. Add an unattached point to the path. This point won't draw as a point. It's more likely to be used as the beginning of a line segment:

   ```
   gp.moveTo( 120, 10 );
   ```

3. Add a line segment to the path. This command represents a straight line from the path's last point to the given point:

   ```
   gp.lineTo( 200, 10 );
   ```

4. Add a quad curve to the path. This represents a curve from the path's last point to the given ending point, using the intermediate point to determine what the curve does between the points:

   ```
   gp.quadTo( 300, 100, 150, 100 );
   ```

5. Add a cubic curve to the path. This represents a curve from the path's last point to the given end point, with two intermediate points determining how the added curve will be shaped:

   ```
   gp.curveTo( 120, 120, 180, 230, 120, 250 );
   ```

6. Add an existing Shape to the path. This statement adds the Shape after the path's last point. A line will be drawn from the path's last point to the Shape's first if the last argument is true:

   ```
   Rectangle r = new Rectangle( 10, 10, 100, 100 );
   gp.append( r, true );
   ```

7. Close the path. If you want to fill a path, you must close it. You can either do so yourself or have GeneralPath do it for you:

   ```
   gp.closePath();
   ```

   This statement adds a line segment back to where the last Shape in the path started.

8. Draw the outline of the path, assuming "g2D" is an instance of Graphics2D:

   ```
   g2D.draw( gp );
   ```

9. Fill the path (if it was closed), assuming "g2D" is an instance of Graphics2D:

```
g2D.fill( gp );
```

LINE2D.FLOAT   Line2D is an inner class of the abstract Line2D class and extends it. It contains two points and represents a straight line segment.

ANCESTORS
```
java.lang.Object
    |
    +—java.awt.geom.Line2D
        |
        +—java.awt.geom.Line2D.Float
```

NOTE: *For more information on how to set a Shape's line attributes, fill its interior, and transform its coordinates, see the "Stroking Paths," "Applying Color," and "Transformations" sections in this chapter.*

STEPS IN CREATING AND USING LINE2D.FLOAT

1. Create the Line2D.Float. You can assign the points using either X and Y coordinates or actual Points. This constructor uses X and Y coordinates:

```
Line2D.Float line = new Line2D.Float( 10, 10, 100, 100 );
```

This statement creates a line from 10,10 to 100,100.

2. Draw the line, assuming "g2D" is an instance of Graphics2D:

```
g2D.draw( line );
```

QUADCURVE2D.FLOAT   QuadCurve2D.Float is an inner class of the abstract QuadCurve2D class and extends it. It takes a start point and an end point, plus an intermediate point that determines what the curve looks like.

ANCESTORS
```
java.lang.Object
    |
    +—java.awt.geom.QuadCurve2D
        |
        +—java.awt.geom.QuadCurve2D.Float
```

NOTE: *For more information on how to set a Shape's line attributes, fill its interior, and transform its coordinates, see the "Stroking Paths," "Applying Color," and "Transformations" sections in this chapter.*

STEPS IN CREATING AND USING QUADCURVE2D.FLOAT

1. Create the QuadCurve2D.Float. The most useful constructor is the one that takes the start, end, and intermediate points:

```
QuadCurve2D.Float qcurve = new QuadCurve2D.Float( 0, 100, 120,
                           300, 200, 100 );
```

The start point is 0,100, the end point is 200,100, and the intermediate point is 120,300.

2. Draw the outline of the curve, assuming "g2D" is an instance of Graphics2D:

```
g2D.draw( qcurve );
```

RECTANGLE2D.FLOAT   Rectangle2D.Float is an inner class of the abstract Rectangle2D class and extends it. It represents a rectangle. There's a similar class called Rectangle2D.Double.

ANCESTORS

```
java.lang.Object
    |
    +——java.awt.geom.RectangularShape
           |
           +——java.awt.geom.Rectangle2D
                  |
                  +——java.awt.geom.Rectangle2D.Float
```

NOTE: *For more information on how to set a Shape's line attributes, fill its interior, and transform its coordinates, see the "Stroking Paths," "Applying Color," and "Transformations" sections in this chapter.*

STEPS IN CREATING AND USING RECTANGLE2D.FLOAT

1. Create the Rectangle2D.Float. The most useful constructor is the one that takes the upper-left corner plus the width and height:

```
Rectangle2D.Float rf = new Rectangle2D.Float( 10, 20, 100, 200 );
```

The rectangle's upper-left corner is 10,20; it's 100 pixels wide and 200 pixels tall.

2. Draw the outline of the rectangle, assuming "g2D" is an instance of Graphics2D:

```
g2D.draw( rf );
```

3. Fill the the rectangle, assuming "g2D" is an instance of Graphics2D:

```
g2D.fill( rf );
```

ROUNDRECTANGLE2D.FLOAT   RoundRectangle2D.Float is an inner class of the abstract RoundRectangle2D class and extends it. It represents a rectangle with rounded corners.

ANCESTORS
```
java.lang.Object
     |
     +——java.awt.geom.RectangularShape
              |
              +——java.awt.geom.RoundRectangle2D
                        |
                        +——java.awt.geom.RoundRectangle2D.Float
```

■■ ■■

NOTE: *For more information on how to set a Shape's line attributes, fill its interior, and transform its coordinates, see the "Stroking Paths," "Applying Color," and "Transformations" sections in this chapter.*

STEPS IN CREATING AND USING ROUNDRECTANGLE2D.FLOAT

1. Create the RoundRectangle2D.Float. The most useful constructor is the one that takes the upper-left corner, the width and height, and the arc width and height that will be used on the corners:

```
RoundRectangle2D.Float rr = new RoundRectangle2D.Float( 250, 10,
                                                          70, 100,
                                                          10, 20 );
```

The round rectangle's upper-left corner is 250,10; it's 70 pixels wide and 100 pixels tall. The arc width is 10, and the arc height is 20.

2. Draw the outline of the round rectangle, assuming "g2D" is an instance of Graphics2D:

```
g2D.draw( rr );
```

Fill the the round rectangle, assuming "g2D" is an instance of Graphics2D:

```
g2D.fill( rr );
```

EXAMPLE 9-3 USING THE SHAPE IMPLEMENTORS

This example illustrates how to use the Shape-implementing Java2D classes. It doesn't include the Rectangle2D classes because they are just like the Rectangle class for this example. Each Shape has a letter within or next to it. These letters aren't in the example—they were added so we could identify each shape (see Figure 9-2):

■ A: This is a Rectangle with a Line2D.Float drawn through it.

■ B: This is a GeneralPath made up of line segments and curves.

■ C: This is a RoundRectangle2D.Float.

■ D: This is a CubicCurve2D.Float.

■ E: This is a three-point arc closed in a pie shape.

Figure 9-2
The Shapes used in
this example.

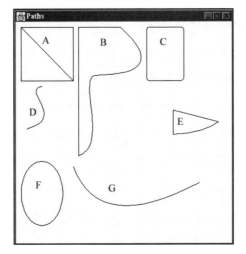

■ F: This is an Ellipse2D.Float.

■ G: This is a QuadCurve2D.Float.

Here's the source code for the canvas on which the paths are drawn. The simple supporting classes are included on the CD-ROM:

```java
import java.awt.*;
import java.awt.image.*;
import java.awt.geom.*;

public class MyCanvas extends Canvas
{
    public void paint( Graphics g )
    {
        // Cast the Graphics to Graphics2D.
        Graphics2D g2D = (Graphics2D)g;

        // Set the drawing color to black.
        g2D.setColor( Color.black );

        // Create a rectangle and draw its outline.
        Rectangle r = new Rectangle( 10, 10, 100, 100 );
        g2D.draw( r );

        // Create a line segment and draw it.
        Line2D.Float l = new Line2D.Float( 10, 10, 110, 110 );
        g2D.draw( l );

        // Create a path that contains line segments and
        // curves, and draw it.
        GeneralPath gp = new GeneralPath();
        gp.moveTo( 120, 10 );
        gp.lineTo( 200, 10 );
        gp.quadTo( 300, 100, 150, 100 );
```

```
gp.curveTo( 120, 120, 180, 230, 120, 250 );
gp.closePath();
g2D.draw( gp );

// Create a round rectangle and draw its outline.
RoundRectangle2D.Float rr =
                new RoundRectangle2D.Float( 250, 10,
                70, 100, 10, 10 );
g2D.draw( rr );

// Create a cubic curve and draw it.
CubicCurve2D.Float cc =
            new CubicCurve2D.Float( 50, 120, 10, 130,
                                    100, 180, 20, 200 );
g2D.draw( cc );

// Create a 3-point arc, closed as a pie segment, and
// draw its outline.
Arc2D.Float arc = new Arc2D.Float( 200, 120, 200, 90,
                    30, 60, Arc2D.PIE );
g2D.draw( arc );

// Create an ellipse and draw its outline.
Ellipse2D.Float e =
            new Ellipse2D.Float( 10, 260, 80, 120 );
g2D.draw( e );

// Create a quad curve and draw its outline.
QuadCurve2D.Float q =
            new QuadCurve2D.Float( 110, 270, 160, 400,
                                    350, 300 );
g2D.draw( q );
    }
}
```

Applying Color

Java2D has an interface called Paint that defines the behavior for classes
that can be used to color Shapes. There are three classes that implement this
interface:

■ **Color:** This class has been modifed to implement Paint and is used to
apply solid colors.

■ **GradientPaint:** This class allows you to specify two points and
assign a color to each point. GradientPaint takes care of making the
color gradually change from one color at one point to the other color at
the other point.

■ **TexturePaint:** This class lets you fill a shape with a raster image,
repeated over and over.

When you specify a Paint class, that Paint is applied to all Shapes until a new Paint class is specified. This way, you can use any of these Paint styles not just for filling the interiors of Shapes, but for drawing their outlines. The current Paint class is also applied to text.

Each Paint class's role as a Paint implementor is covered in the following sections, and then an example uses all three classes.

COLOR Use Color to apply a solid color to Shapes:

1. In the sample code, assume "g2D" is a Graphics2D object. Tell the Graphics2D object to use a Color. You can do this by using the method that has always been used with Graphics objects:

```
g2D.setColor( Color.red );
```

Or, you can use the new method for specifying gradient or texture fills:

```
g2D.setPaint( Color.red );
```

GRADIENTPAINT Use GradientPaint to apply a color range to Shapes:

1. Create a GradientPaint object. GradientPaint needs two points and two colors—one for each point. You can also pass it a Boolean specifying what should happen in the area that isn't between the points. That value tells whether the gradation from one point's color to the other's will repeat or not:

```
GradientPaint gp = new GradientPaint( 50, 200, Color.red,
                    350, 200, Color.blue, true );
```

This statement places the color red at 50,200 and the color blue at 350,200 and generates a gradation of color between them. The "true" tells the GradientPaint to repeat the pattern to the left of the red point and to the right of the blue point, if there's room.

2. Tell the Graphics2D object to use our GradientPaint on all Shapes that are added to it until a new Paint class is specified, assuming "g2D" is a Graphics2D object:

```
g2D.setPaint( gp );
```

TEXTUREPAINT Use TexturePaint to fill a shape with a repeated raster image:

1. TexturePaint's constructor takes three arguments: a BufferedImage containing the image to repeat, a Rectangle2D that specifies an anchor point for repeating the image and a size at which the image should display, and an interpolation constant that will be either BILINEAR or NEAREST_NEIGHBOR. Here's the constructor:

```
TexturePane tp = new TexturePaint( bufferedImage,
                 new Rectangle2D.Float( 0, 0, 30, 30 ),
                 TexturePaint.BILINEAR );
```

2. Tell the Graphics2D object to use the TexturePaint on all Shapes that are added to it until a new Paint class is specified, assuming "g2D" is a Graphics2D object:

```
g2D.setPaint( tp );
```

EXAMPLE 9-4 **Using the Paint Implementors**

This example shows the three types of Paint interface implementors: Color, GradientPaint, and TexturePaint. It includes four rectangles. The upper-left rectangle uses a cyclic GradientPaint. The upper-right rectangle uses an acyclic GradientPaint. The lower-left rectangle uses a solid fill. The lower-right rectangle is filled with a repeating raster image of a star. Figure 9-3 shows the four rectangles.

Important points to notice:

- The two points for the GradientPaint rectangles are in the rectangle's upper-left and lower-right corners.
- The BufferedImage for the TexturePaint is loaded from a GIF file. We create a special inner class called RasterThingy that takes care of the image's normal loading. We then create a BufferedImage the same size as the GIF image and paint the image into a Graphics2D associated with the BufferedImage.

Here's the source code for the canvas on which the painting is done; the simple supporting classes are included on the CD-ROM:

```
import java.awt.*;
import java.awt.image.*;
import java.awt.geom.*;
```

Figure 9-3
Using the Paint implementors.

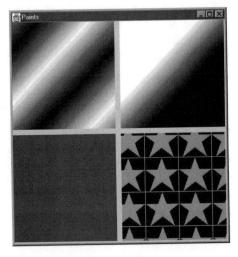

```java
public class MyCanvas extends Canvas
{
    RasterThingy mRC;

    public MyCanvas()
    {
        super();

        mRC = new RasterThingy( "brnzstar.gif" );
    }

    public void paint( Graphics g )
    {
        Graphics2D g2D = (Graphics2D)g;

        // Cyclic gradient paint.
        Rectangle rect = new Rectangle( 0, 0, 200, 200 );
        Point2D.Float p1 = new Point2D.Float( 75f, 75f );
        Point2D.Float p2 = new Point2D.Float( 125f, 125f );
        GradientPaint gp = new GradientPaint( p1, Color.white,
                              p2, Color.black, true );
        g2D.setPaint( gp );
        g2D.fill( rect );

        // Acyclic gradient paint
        rect = new Rectangle( 210, 0, 200, 200 );
        p1 = new Point2D.Float( 285f, 75f );
        p2 = new Point2D.Float( 335f, 125f );
        gp = new GradientPaint( p1, Color.white, p2,
                                  Color.black, false );
        g2D.setPaint( gp );
        g2D.fill( rect );

        // Color paint.
        rect = new Rectangle( 0, 210, 200, 200 );
        g2D.setPaint( Color.red );
        g2D.fill( rect );

        // Texture paint.
        rect = new Rectangle( 210, 210, 200, 200 );
        BufferedImage bi = new BufferedImage(
                        mRC.getSize().width,
                        mRC.getSize().height,
                        BufferedImage.TYPE_INT_ARGB );
        Graphics2D galso = (Graphics2D)bi.getGraphics();
        AffineTransform at = new AffineTransform();
        galso.drawImage( mRC.getImage(), at, this );
        TexturePaint tp = new TexturePaint( bi,
                        new Rectangle2D.Float( 0, 0,
                        mRC.getSize().width,
                        mRC.getSize().height ),
                        TexturePaint.BILINEAR );
        g2D.setPaint( tp );
        g2D.fill( rect );
    }
```

```java
// This is the class that displays an image and keeps
// itself the image's size.
private class RasterThingy extends Component
{
    Image mImage;
    Dimension mSize;
    String mFilename;

    public RasterThingy( String filename )
    {
        mFilename = filename;

        // Load the image represented by the filename.
        loadImage();
    }

    public Image getImage()
    {
        return mImage;
    }

    // Paint the image on the component.
    public void paint( Graphics g )
    {
        g.drawImage( mImage, 0, 0, mSize.width,
                    mSize.height, this );
    }

    // Load the full image and set the component's size
    // to match the image's.
    protected void loadImage()
    {
        MediaTracker tracker = new MediaTracker( this );

        mImage = Toolkit.getDefaultToolkit().getImage(
                                        mFilename );

        tracker.addImage( mImage, 1 );

        try
        {
            tracker.waitForAll();
        }
        catch( InterruptedException e ){}

        if ( mSize == null )
            mSize = new Dimension( mImage.getWidth( this ),
                            mImage.getHeight( this ) );

        setSize( mSize );
    }
}
```

Stroking Paths

Java2D provides the ability to set line attributes when you draw a path. You can set the line end type, line join type, and line width, and you can define and use line styles (dashing). The Java2D class that holds line attributes is called BasicStroke. Once you create a BasicStroke and tell a Graphics2D object to use it, all subsequent path draw commands will use it until a new one is specified.

BASICSTROKE   Use BasicStroke to define line attributes. You can also use it to create a Shape that holds the outline of a stroked line, which is useful when you want to draw a wide line and make its edge different from its fill:

1. Create the BasicStroke. There are several constructors, but they are all variations on this one:

```
BasicStroke( float width, int endstyle, int joinstyle,
             float miterlimit, float dash[],
             float dash_phase )
```

In this statement, here's what the arguments mean:

- "width" is the line width.
- "endstyle" is the line end style and should be CAP_BUTT, CAP_ROUND, or CAP_SQUARE.
- "joinstyle" is the line join style and should be JOIN_MITER, JOIN_ROUND, or JOIN_BEVEL.
- "miterlimit" is the miter limit to use with miter joins. Using a miter join with a wide line that has acute angles can cause the join to stick out too far. If it's longer than the line width multiplied by the miter limit, it's cut back to a bevel join so it won't stick out.
- "dash[]" is an array that defines a line style. The even items in the array are dash lengths, and the odd ones are gap lengths.
- "dash_phase" is the distance from the start of the line to offset the start of the line style. It's usually 0.

A dash array could look like the following if you wanted a line style where the dashes and gaps between dashes are the same length:

```
float dashes[] = new float[2];
dashes[0] = 20;
dashes[1] = 20;
```

The following line creates a BasicStroke that contains a line width of 10, an end style of round, a join style of beveled, no miter limit (using beveled joins), a dash array, and a dash phase of 0:

```
BasicStroke bs = new BasicStroke( 10, BasicStroke.CAP_ROUND,
              BasicStroke.JOIN_BEVEL, 0, dash, 0 );
```

2. Tell the Graphics2D object to use our BasicStroke, assuming "g2D" is a Graphics2D object:

```
g2D.setStroke( bs );
```

3. Create a path to stroke:

```
Rectangle rect = new Rectangle( 20, 20, 100, 100 );
```

4. Draw the dashed path's outline:

```
g2D.draw( rect );
```

5. Create a new Shape that holds the outline of the given path as it would be stroked:

```
Shape dashedRectOutline = bs.createStrokedShape( rect );
```

EXAMPLE 9-5 **Using Line Attributes**

This example illustrates how to apply line weight, line end types, line join types, and line styles to a path. The top row in Figure 9-4 shows examples of changing the line width, end style, and join style. Below that are four lines that display four different line styles. At the bottom is a wide line drawn with a GradientPaint, but its edge is drawn in solid black by using the createStrokedShape() method.

Here is the source code for the canvas on which the lines are drawn; the simple supporting classes are included on the CD-ROM:

```
import java.awt.*;
import java.awt.image.*;
import java.awt.geom.*;

public class MyCanvas extends Canvas
{
    public void paint( Graphics g )
    {
        // Cast the Graphics to Graphics2D.
        Graphics2D g2D = (Graphics2D)g;

        // Create a rectangle.
        Rectangle r = new Rectangle( 20, 20, 100, 100 );

        // Create a stroke description with width 10, butt
        // ends, and round joins.
        BasicStroke bs =
                new BasicStroke( 10, BasicStroke.CAP_BUTT,
                                 BasicStroke.JOIN_ROUND );

        // Apply the stroke description for use in subsequent
        // drawing.
        g2D.setStroke( bs );

        // Draw the rectangle using the stroke description.
```

Figure 9-4
Applying Line attributes to a path.

```
g2D.draw( r );

// Create a U-shpaed path.
GeneralPath gp = new GeneralPath();
gp.moveTo( 150, 20 );
gp.lineTo( 150, 120 );
gp.lineTo( 250, 120 );
gp.lineTo( 250, 20 );

// Create a stroke description with width 25, round
// ends and bevel joins.
bs = new BasicStroke( 25, BasicStroke.CAP_ROUND,
                          BasicStroke.JOIN_BEVEL );

// Apply the stroke description for use in subsequent
// drawing.
g2D.setStroke( bs );

// Draw the path using the stroke description.
g2D.draw( gp );

// Create a V-shaped path.
gp = new GeneralPath();
gp.moveTo( 280, 20 );
gp.lineTo( 330, 120 );
gp.lineTo( 380, 20 );

// Create a new stroke description with width 15,
// square ends, miter joins, and a miter limit of 3.
bs = new BasicStroke( 15, BasicStroke.CAP_SQUARE,
                          BasicStroke.JOIN_MITER, 3 );

// Apply the stroke description for use in subsequent
// drawing.
g2D.setStroke( bs );
```

```
// Draw the path using the stroke description.
g2D.draw( gp );

// Create an array defining a linestyle whose dashes
// and gaps are both 16 points.
float dashes[] = new float[2];
dashes[0] = 15;
dashes[1] = 15;

// Creata a new stroke description with width 1, butt
// ends, round joins, a miter limit of 0, the just-
// created dash/gap array, and no initial offset.
bs = new BasicStroke( 1, BasicStroke.CAP_BUTT,
            BasicStroke.JOIN_ROUND, 0, dashes, 0 );

// Create a horizontal line segment.
Line2D.Float l =
            new Line2D.Float( 20, 170, 390, 170 );

// Apply the stroke description for use in subsequent
// drawing.
g2D.setStroke( bs );

// Draw the line segment using the stroke description.
g2D.draw( l );

// Create an array describing a linestyle whose
// dashes are 20 points and whose gaps are 5 points.
dashes = new float[2];
dashes[0] = 20;
dashes[1] = 5;

// Create a stroke description using the linestyle
// array.
bs = new BasicStroke( 1, BasicStroke.CAP_BUTT,
            BasicStroke.JOIN_ROUND, 0, dashes, 0 );

// Create a horizontal line.
l = new Line2D.Float( 20, 190, 390, 190 );

// Apply the stroke description.
g2D.setStroke( bs );

// Draw the line using the stroke description.
g2D.draw( l );

// Create a linestyle that will generate a dash-dot
// pattern.
dashes = new float[4];
dashes[0] = 20;
dashes[1] = 5;
dashes[2] = 1;
dashes[3] = 5;

// Create a stroke description using the linestyle
```

```
// array.
bs = new BasicStroke( 1, BasicStroke.CAP_BUTT,
                BasicStroke.JOIN_ROUND, 0, dashes, 0 );

// Create a horizontal line.
l = new Line2D.Float( 20, 210, 390, 210 );

// Apply the stroke description.
g2D.setStroke( bs );

// Draw the line using the stroke description.
g2D.draw( l );

// Create an array that will generate a linestyle on
// long and short dashes separated by dots.
dashes = new float[8];
dashes[0] = 20;
dashes[1] = 5;
dashes[2] = 1;
dashes[3] = 5;
dashes[4] = 8;
dashes[5] = 5;
dashes[6] = 1;
dashes[7] = 5;

// Create a stroke description using the linestyle
// array.
bs = new BasicStroke( 1, BasicStroke.CAP_BUTT,
                BasicStroke.JOIN_ROUND, 0, dashes, 0 );

// Create a horizontal line.
l = new Line2D.Float( 20, 230, 390, 230 );

// Apply the stroke description.
g2D.setStroke( bs );

// Draw the line using the stroke description.
g2D.draw( l );

// Create a rectangle.
r = new Rectangle( 20, 280, 100, 100 );

// Create an array that will generate long and short
// dashes.
dashes = new float[4];
dashes[0] = 80;
dashes[1] = 10;
dashes[2] = 40;
dashes[3] = 10;

// Create a stroke description that will generate
// wide lines using the above array for linestyles.
bs = new BasicStroke( 20, BasicStroke.CAP_BUTT,
                BasicStroke.JOIN_ROUND, 0, dashes, 0 );
```

```
    // Create a new Shape composed of the outlines of the
    // rectangle's dashes.
    Shape s = bs.createStrokedShape( r );

    // Reset the stroke description to the default.
    g2D.setStroke( new BasicStroke() );

    // Set up a GradientPaint.
    GradientPaint gpaint =
            new GradientPaint( 20, 280, Color.lightGray,
                               120, 380, Color.black );

    // Apply the GradientPaint.
    g2D.setPaint( gpaint );

    // Fill the new shape using the GradientPaint.
    g2D.fill( s );

    // Set the color to solid black.
    g2D.setColor( Color.black );

    // Draw the outline of the new shape.
    g2D.draw( s );
    }
}
```

Transformations

If you have dealt much with the old AWT, you're familiar with specifying coordinates within a component. When you draw a line from 0,0 to 100,100, you
expect the line to start at the upper-left corner of the component and end at
a point 100 pixels right and 100 pixels down from the start. In this case, the
coordinates you specify are component coordinates. Most advanced graphics
libraries include the concept of *transformations*; they represent a relationship between the coordinates you use and the component coordinates that's
not necessarily one-to-one. Although they can be confusing, transformations
can also make some operations much easier.

Java2D includes four types of transformations:

■ **Translation:** Moves the origin by some amount.

■ **Rotation:** Rotates the X and Y axes.

■ **Shear:** Makes the X and Y axes non-perpendicular.

■ **Scale:** Makes the coordinates along the axes not equal to one pixel.

TRANSLATION   You can use a translation transformation to move the coordinate space origin around. Normally, if you specify the point 0,0, it maps
to the component's 0,0. If you use a translation of 100,0 and then specify the
point 0,0, it maps to the component's 100,0.

ROTATION You can use a rotation transformation to rotate the coordinate space around a point. Normally, if you draw a line from 0,0 to 100,0, it maps onto the same points on the component, and you get a 100-pixel-long horizontal line. If you use a rotation of PI/2, the same line is rotated 90 degrees clockwise around the origin, so the line maps onto the component starting at 0,0 and ending at 0,100. It has become a vertical line. You can also make the rotation take place around a point other than the origin.

SHEAR You can use a shear transformation to make lines that would usually be perpendicular become non-perpendicular. A shear value is specified for each axis. The value for the X axis is a factor by which X coordinates should be moved to the right, depending on their Y coordinate. For example, if you draw a line from 0,0 to 0,100, you get a vertical line from the point 0,0 to 0,100. If you specify an X shear value of 1.0, each coordinate is shifted right one pixel for its Y value. So, although the first point wouldn't be changed because its Y value is 0, the second point's X value would move right by the amount of Y $\times$ 1.0, which is 100. The line will map onto the component from 0,0 to 100,100.

SCALE You can use a scaling transformation to make coordinates map closer to or farther away from the origin than they normally would. You can also specify a scale for each axis. If you draw a line from 0,0 to 100,100 and then apply a scaling transformation of 2.0,0.5, each coordinate's X value would be multiplied by 2.0 and each coordinate's Y value would be multiplied by 0.5. Therefore, the line you specified from 0,0 to 100,100 would map onto the component from 0,0 to 200,50.

Using Transformations in Java2D

Java2D has a single class called "AffineTransform" that you use when you want to apply a transformation. It allows you to specify translations, rotations, shearing, and scaling. AffineTransform allows access to the transformation matrix, but we'll discuss just the methods that manipulate the matrix for you.

AFFINETRANSFORMATION This class contains 10 main methods for changing the transformation:

- **setToRotation(double rotation):** Rotates the coordinate system around the origin.
- **setToRotation(double rotation, double x, double y):** Rotates the coordinate system around the given point.
- **rotate(double rotation):** Adds a rotation around the origin onto the current transformation.
- **rotate(double rotation, double x, double y):** Adds a rotation around the given point onto the current transformation.

- **setToScale(double xscale, double yscale):** Scales the X and Y axes.
- **scale(double xscale, double yscale):** Adds a scaling of the X and Y axes onto the current transformation.
- **setToShear(double xshear, double yshear):** Shears the X and Y axes.
- **shear(double xshear, double yshear):** Adds a shearing onto the current transform.
- **setToTranslation(double xshift, double yshift):** Shifts the origin.
- **translate(double xshift, double yshift):** Adds an origin shift onto the current translation.

As you can see, each "set" method has a corresponding method that applies the change to the transformation, instead of replacing it. This can be clarified with a simple example:

```
public void paint( Graphics g )
{
    Graphics2D g2D = (Graphics2D)g;
    g2D.setColor( Color.black );
    AffineTransformation at = new AffineTransformation();
    at.setToTranslation( 100, 100 );
    g2D.setTransform( at );
    at.setToTranslation( 100,0 );
    g2D.setTransform( at );
    Rectangle rect = new Rectangle( 0, 0, 100, 100 );
    g2D.draw( rect );
}
```

The preceding code would move the origin to 100,100, then move it to 100,0, and then draw a rectangle. The rectangle would map its origin from 0,0 to 100,0 on the component.

```
public void paint( Graphics g )
{
    Graphics2D g2D = (Graphics2D)g;
    g2D.setColor( Color.black );
    AffineTransformation at = new AffineTransformation();
    at.setToTranslation( 100, 100 );
    g2D.setTransform( at );
    at.translate( 100,0 );
    g2D.setTransform( at );
    Rectangle rect = new Rectangle( 0, 0, 100, 100 );
    g2D.draw( rect );
}
```

This preceding code is different because the translate() method is used instead of setToTranslation(). Instead of moving the origin to 100,0, translate(100,0) adds the translation of 100,0 onto the translation of 100,100. The net effect is to move the origin to 200,100 and draw the rectangle there.

The Graphics2D class has two ways of applying a transformation. It can either replace its current transformation with the new one or add the new one on. The setTransform() method used previously replaces the current transformation; the transform() method adds the new one on.

EXAMPLE 9-6 Using Transformations

This example illustrates the use of all four types of transformations, as well as how to combine transformations. The example has a method for drawing four colored squares with the words *Up* and *Down* printed on top. Its drawing always starts at 0,0. The point of the example is to apply transformations, and then call this method and see what effect it has.

First, we draw the picture without any transformations. That copy is the one that appears in the upper-left corner. Second, we translate the origin to 100,0 and draw the picture again. It appears to the right of the first. Third, we translate the origin to 250,50. At that point, we create a rotation transformation that rotates the coordinate system by PI/16 around the point 50,50 (in relation to the translated origin). We apply that transformation 32 times, telling the Graphics2D object to add the rotation transformation instead of using it to replace its current one, which causes the rotations to be cumulative. We draw the picture after every rotation. Fourth, we translate the origin to 0,100 and apply a shear of 1,0. Then we draw the picture again. Fifth, we translate the origin by 0,100, adding it to the Graphics2D's current transformation. This causes the translation to be sheared. Then we reverse the shear by applying a shear of −1,0, and draw the picture. Sixth, we translate the origin to 300,200 and apply a scaling transformation of 0.5,2.1 and draw the picture. Figure 9-5 shows the end result.

Here is the source code for the canvas we drew on; the simple supporting classes are included in the example on the CD-ROM:

```
import java.awt.*;
import java.awt.font.*;
import java.awt.image.*;
import java.awt.geom.*;

public class MyCanvas extends Canvas
{
    public void paint( Graphics g )
    {
        // Cast the Graphics to Graphics2D.
        Graphics2D g2D = (Graphics2D)g;

        // Draw the picture untransformed.
        drawIt( g2D );

        // Create the transform.
        AffineTransform at = new AffineTransform();
```

Figure 9-5
Using
transformations.

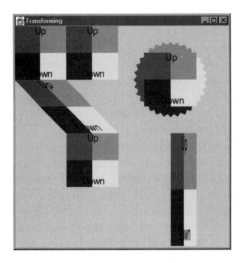

```
// Translate the origin to 100,0.
at.translate( 100, 0 );

// Replace the Graphics2D's current transformation.
// This applies the translation.
g2D.setTransform( at );

// Draw the picture.
drawIt( g2D );

// Translate the origin to 250,50.
at.setToTranslation( 250, 50 );

// Apply the new transformation as the Graphics2D's
// transformation.
g2D.setTransform( at );

// Create a rotation transformation of PI/16 which
// will rotate the coordinate system around the point
// 50,50 (relative to the translated origin).
at.setToRotation( Math.PI / 16, 50, 50 );

// 2*PI makes a full circle, so we rotate enough
// times to get all the way around.
for ( int i = 0; i < 32; i++ )
{
    // Tell the Graphics2D to add the rotation
    // transformation to its current transformation.
    g2D.transform( at );

    // Draw the picture.
    drawIt( g2D );
}

// Translate the origin to 0,100.
```

```
                  at.setToTranslation( 0, 100 );

                  // Replace the Graphics2D transformation.
                  g2D.setTransform( at );

                  // Create a shear transformation.
                  at.setToShear( 1, 0 );

                  // Add the transformation to the Graphics2D's do we
                  // don't lose the origin translation.
                  g2D.transform( at );

                  // Draw the picture.
                  drawIt( g2D );

                  // Create a translation of the origin to 0,100.
                  at.setToTranslation( 0, 100 );

                  // Add the translation to the Graphics2D's
                  // transformation.
                  g2D.transform( at );

                  // Reverse the shear.
                  at.setToShear( -1, 0 );

                  // Add the shear reversal to the Graphics2D's
                  // transformation.  This lets us keep the same
                  // origin.
                  g2D.transform( at );

                  // Draw the picture.
                  drawIt( g2D );

                  // Translate the origin to 300,200.
                  at.setToTranslation( 300, 200 );

                  // Replace the Graphics2D's transformation with our
                  // translation transformation.
                  g2D.setTransform( at );

                  // Create a scaling transformation.
                  at.setToScale( 0.5f, 2.1f );

                  // Add the scaling to the Graphics2D's transformation
                  // so we keep the same origin.
                  g2D.transform( at );

                  // Draw the picture.
                  drawIt( g2D );
      }

      // This draws four colored squares with the words "Up":
      // and "Down" on top.
      private void drawIt( Graphics2D g )
      {
```

```
Rectangle r1 = new Rectangle( 0, 0, 50, 50 );
g.setColor( Color.red );
g.fill( r1 );

Rectangle r2 = new Rectangle( 50, 0, 50, 50 );
g.setColor( Color.green );
g.fill( r2 );

Rectangle r3 = new Rectangle( 0, 50, 50, 50 );
g.setColor( Color.blue );
g.fill( r3 );

Rectangle r4 = new Rectangle( 50, 50, 50, 50 );
g.setColor( Color.yellow );
g.fill( r4 );

Font f = new Font( "Helvetica", Font.BOLD, 18 );
StyledString ss = new StyledString( "Up", f );
g.setColor( Color.black );
g.drawString( ss, 40f, 15f );

ss = new StyledString( "Down", f );
g.drawString( ss, 30f, 95f );
    }
}
```

Colors

COLOR MODELS Java2D supports several color models in the java.awt.color package.

COLOR BLENDING Java2D supplies a class called "AlphaComposite" that lets you specify how a Shape's color blends in with the underlying Shapes. Normally, a Shape is opaque, so it obscures everything beneath it. By using AlphaComposite, however, you can let the underlying shapes show through.

ALPHACOMPOSITE AlphaComposite has eight switches you can use to do color blending:

- CLEAR
- DST_IN
- DST_OUT
- DST_OVER
- SRC
- SRC_IN
- SRC_OUT
- SRC_OVER

To apply an AlphaComposite, use its static getInstance() method. The float argument is the alpha value:

```
AlphaComposite ac = AlphaComposite.getInstance(
                    AlphaComposite.DST_IN, 0.5f );
```

Then apply it to the Graphics2d object:

```
g2D.setComposite( ac );
```

Everything after this statement will be affected.

EXAMPLE 9-7 Using AlphaComposite to Blend Colors

This example uses all eight compositing rules and varies their alpha value from 0.0 to 1.0. It creates two rectangles for each rule/alpha combination—a yellow one, then a red one. The two rectangles overlap to show the effect of the color blend on the combined rectangles. In the example, each column represents a compositing rule in this order from left to right: CLEAR, DST_IN, DST_OUT, DST_OVER, SRC, SRC_IN, SRC_OUT, and SRC_OVER. Each row represents the overlaying rectangle's alpha value, starting at 0.0 at the top and increasing by 0.1 as you go down. Figure 9-6 shows the example as it first comes up.

Here is the source code for the canvas on which the example is drawn; the simple supporting classes are included on the CD-ROM:

```
import java.awt.*;
import java.awt.image.*;
import java.awt.geom.*;

public class MyCanvas extends Canvas
{
    // Possible compositing modes.
    int modes[] = {
           AlphaComposite.CLEAR, AlphaComposite.DST_IN,
           AlphaComposite.DST_OUT, AlphaComposite.DST_OVER,
           AlphaComposite.SRC, AlphaComposite.SRC_IN,
           AlphaComposite.SRC_OUT, AlphaComposite.SRC_OVER };

    public void paint( Graphics g )
    {
        int x = 0;
        Graphics2D g2D = (Graphics2D)g;

        // Save the initial composite.
        Composite initialComposite = g2D.getComposite();

        // Use a translation to move the boxes while we
        // iterate through different compositing options.
        AffineTransform at = new AffineTransform();
```

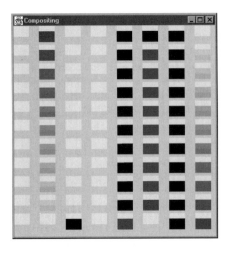

```
// For each composite mode, draw a column of boxes
// using it.
for ( int i = 0; i < 8; i++ )
{
    at.setToTranslation( x, 0 );
    g2D.setTransform( at );
    doColumn( g2D, modes[i], initialComposite );
    x += 50;
}
}

// Given a compositing mode, draw a column of boxes
// showing what the mode looks like when used on the
// overlying box.
private void doColumn( Graphics2D g2D, int mode,
                       Composite initialComposite )
{
    float value = 0f;
    AffineTransform at = new AffineTransform();

    for ( int i = 0; i <= 100; i += 10 )
    {
        // Draw two overlapping rectangles with the lower
        // one using the default composite mode and the
        // upper one using the given mode.
        doItem( g2D, mode, value, initialComposite );

        // Move the origin down for the next iteration.
        at.setToTranslation( 0, 35 );
        g2D.transform( at );

        // Increment the composite value.
        value += 0.1f;
    }
}
```

```
// Draw a box using the default composite.  Then draw
// another, partially overlapping box using the
// composite mode being tested.
private void doItem( Graphics2D g2D, int mode,
                            float value,
                            Composite initialComposite )
{
    if ( value > 1f )
       value = 1f;
    g2D.setComposite( initialComposite );
    g2D.setColor( Color.yellow );
    Rectangle r1 = new Rectangle( 0, 0, 30, 20 );
    g2D.fill( r1 );
    AlphaComposite ac =
               AlphaComposite.getInstance( mode, value );
    g2D.setComposite( ac );
    g2D.setColor( Color.red );
    Rectangle r2 = new Rectangle( 0, 10, 30, 20 );
    g2D.fill( r2 );
}
}
```

Fonts and Text

Java2D offers improved text capabilities, especially the number of fonts that are available.

ACCESSING ALL AVAILABLE FONTS   To give you access to fonts that vary from machine to machine and are stored in different ways under different operating systems, Java2D has to supply a generic interface into the local machine. It does this by using a class called "GraphicsEnvironment." GraphicsEnvironment is an abstract class that contains a static method called getLocalGraphicsEnvironment() to return a subclass of itself that has been loaded with information about the local system. Using this subclass, you can call its getAllFonts() method to retrieve a list of Font objects representing all available fonts.

EXAMPLE 9-8   Accessing All Local Fonts

This example finds out all the fonts available on the local system and puts their names into a combo box. Figure 9-7 shows the combo box.

Here is the source code (there's a simple supporting class that isn't listed here but is included on the CD-ROM):

```
import java.awt.*;
import com.sun.java.swing.*;
```

Figure 9-7
Accessing a system's
local fonts.

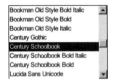

```java
public class MyFrame extends Frame
{
    public MyFrame()
    {
        setTitle( "AllFonts" );

        setLayout( new BorderLayout() );

        // Get the list of available fonts.
        Font fontList[] = GraphicsEnvironment.
                getLocalGraphicsEnvironment().getAllFonts();

        // Create the combo box.
        JComboBox fontBox = new JComboBox();

        // Load the font names into the combo box.
        for ( int i = 0; i < fontList.length; i++ )
        {
            fontBox.addItem( fontList[i].getFontName() );
        }

        // Place the combo box at the top of the frame.
        add( "North", fontBox );
    }
}
```

Images

Java2D provides additions to the java.awt.image package that help you manipulate images more easily. These manipulations typically require a BufferedImage and a BufferedImageOp. This section will show variations on one of these BufferedImageOps at work on a BufferedImage.

EXAMPLE 9-9   Using Sharpening on an Image

This example takes a picture of two parrots and applies three versions of a convolve operation on it (see Figure 9-8). A ConvolveOp uses what is called a "Kernel." Kernel defines a matrix that holds information about how a pixel's surrounding pixels will affect it. Kernel contains three constant matrices called SHARPEN3×3_1, SHARPEN3×3_2, and SHARPEN3×3_3. The example applies each of these matrices to the raster image by using a ConvolveOp.

Figure 9-8
Using sharpening on
an image.

Important points to notice:

- The canvas has an inner class called RasterThingy that takes care of loading the image and making it available.
- The four images are in this order: SHARPEN3×3_3 to the upper-left, SHARPEN3×3_2 to the lower-left, SHARPEN3×3_1 to the upper-right, and the unfiltered image to the lower-right.

Here is the source to the canvas where all the interesting things happen; the simple supporting classes are included on the CD-ROM:

```java
import java.awt.*;
import java.awt.image.*;
import java.awt.geom.*;

public class MyCanvas extends Canvas
{
    private RasterThingy mRC;

    public MyCanvas()
    {
        super();

        // This class loads the image and makes it available.
        mRC = new RasterThingy( "parrots.jpg" );
    }

    public void paint( Graphics g )
    {
        // Prepare a transform.
        AffineTransform at = new AffineTransform();
```

```
    // Get the local graphics environment.
    GraphicsEnvironment ge =
       GraphicsEnvironment.getLocalGraphicsEnvironment();

    // Cast the graphics.
    Graphics2D g2D = (Graphics2D)g;

    // Create a BufferedImage the same size as the image.
    BufferedImage bi = new BufferedImage(
                       mRC.getSize().width,
                       mRC.getSize().height,
                       BufferedImage.TYPE_INT_RGB );

    // Use the graphics environment to create a
    // Graphics2D for the image.
    Graphics2D galso = ge.createGraphics( bi );

    // Draw the image into the BufferedImage.
    galso.drawImage( mRC.getImage(), at, this );

    // Create the first Kernel.
    Kernel k = new Kernel( 3, 3, Kernel.SHARPEN3x3_3 );

    // Draw the SHARPEN3x3_3 image at the origin.
    g2D.drawImage( bi, new ConvolveOp( k ), 0, 0 );

    // Create the second kernel.
    k = new Kernel( 3, 3, Kernel.SHARPEN3x3_2 );

    // Draw the SHARPEN3x3_2 image below the previous
    // one.
    g2D.drawImage( bi, new ConvolveOp( k ), 0, 250 );

    // Create the third kernel.
    k = new Kernel( 3, 3, Kernel.SHARPEN3x3_1 );

    // Draw the SHARPEN3x3_1 image to the right of the
    // first one.
    g2D.drawImage( bi, new ConvolveOp( k ), 370, 0 );

    // Set a translation to draw the image unfiltered in
    // the lower right corner.
    at.setToTranslation( 370, 250 );

    // Draw the unfiltered image using the translation.
    g2D.drawImage( bi, at, this );
}

// This is the class that loads and holds an image and
// keeps itself the image's size.
private class RasterThingy extends Component
{
    Image mImage;
    Dimension mSize;
```

```
                    String mFilename;

                    public RasterThingy( String filename )
                    {
                       mFilename = filename;

                       // Load the image represented by the filename.
                       loadImage();
                    }

                    public Image getImage()
                    {
                       return mImage;
                    }

                    // Paint the image on the component.
                    public void paint( Graphics g )
                    {
                       g.drawImage( mImage, 0, 0, mSize.width,
                                    mSize.height, this );
                    }

                    // Load the full image and set the component's size
                    // to match the image's.
                    protected void loadImage()
                    {
                       MediaTracker tracker = new MediaTracker( this );

                       mImage = Toolkit.getDefaultToolkit().getImage(
                                                      mFilename );

                       tracker.addImage( mImage, 1 );

                       try
                       {
                          tracker.waitForAll();
                       }
                       catch( InterruptedException e ){}

                       if ( mSize == null )
                          mSize = new Dimension( mImage.getWidth( this ),
                                                 mImage.getHeight( this ) );

                       setSize( mSize );
                    }
                 }
              }
```

Printing

Printing from Java has changed since previous releases of the JDK. When
the user chooses to print, your application will now generate a book with one

or more pages, and that will be printed. Here are the main printing classes plus one interface:

- **Paper:** This describes the area in which drawing can take place. In the future, it might also include information about the media.
- **PageFormat:** This includes an instance of Paper and also contains orientation information about a page.
- **Printable:** This interface specifies a single method called print(). There should be a Printable implementor associated with each page to be printed. When the print job runs, the Printables' print() methods are called to actually draw the pages. If you have a single page, you can just cause the print() method to call your paint() method. If there are multiple pages, you might have to create special Printable classes that contain enough information about the page they're associated with to cause it to be printed when the print() method is called.
- **Book:** This is where all the information about pages to be printed is stored. Each page has a PageFormat/Printable pair. The PageFormat defines the page's printable area, and the Printable will draw there.
- **PrintJob2D:** This is used to interact with the print system and to print Books.

The steps to printing in Java2D go something like this:

1. The user chooses to print.
2. Create an empty Book.
3. For each page to be printed, provide a PageFormat and a class that implements the Printable interface.
4. Append the PageFormat/Printable pairs onto the Book.
5. Create a PrintJob2D.
6. Set up the print job via the PrintJob2D.
7. Print the Book.

SUMMARY

This chapter has given you a quick introduction to many of the parts of the JFC that are still in the works. Some of the classes and methods will change before these parts are ultimately released, but I hope the discussions and examples here will help you understand the basic relationships more quickly.

Integrating JFC
Example1: A File
Browser

DirectoryModel and JTree are two of the important new classes in the JFC. DirectoryModel lets you navigate the file system under any operating system without having to write any native code, and JTree allows you to visually organize items in a hierarchy. In this chapter, we use DirectoryModel and JTree to create a file browser that should work on any operating system.

We won't just go through the example step-by-step; we'll discuss the JFC classes that were used, how they were used, and why.

The File Browser

This file browser is a single pane that allows the user to navigate throughout the file system. For Windows systems, it displays one drive at a time, but supplies a combo box that can be used to change to another drive. If you double-click on a directory, its contents become visible. You can single-click to select a single file, use Shift+click to select a range of adjacent files, or use Ctrl+click to select multiple separate files. Figure 10-1 shows what the file browser looks like.

This example consists of five separate classes:

- **Test.java:** This simple class contains the main() method, creates an instance of the main frame class, and places the frame onscreen.
- **MyFrame.java:** This main frame class is also quite simple. A subclass of JFrame, it creates an instance of the file browser, places it in a JScrollPane, and then makes the JScrollPane take up the frame's main area. It also places the JComboBox (if available), which allows the user to change the actively displayed drive.
- **WorkingDirectoryModel.java:** This subclass of DirectoryModel gives access to the file system and includes workarounds for some annoying JDK 1.x problems.
- **FileBrowser.java:** The class that controls the file browser. A subclass of JPanel, it controls interaction between the user and the tree and between the tree and the file system.
- **FileTreeCellRenderer.java:** This class defines what tree items look like in all their different states.

Test.java and MyFrame.java are just an example of how to use the file browser. The browser itself is made up of the other three classes.

Figure 10-1
The file browser.

The following sections cover each class and the JFC classes and concepts they use.

Test.java

This class is extremely simple. It contains the main() method, which creates an instance of Test. Test's constructor creates an instance of the main frame class MyFrame and places the frame onscreen.

Test.java uses the UIManager class to force the current platform's native look-and-feel to be used. This includes a call to the getSystemLookAndFeelClassName() method to get the native look-and-feel, and a call to the setLookAndFeel() method to apply it.

Here's the source code:

```java
import com.sun.java.swing.*;

public class Test
{
    public Test()
    {
        // Use the current platform's native look-and-feel
        // if there is one.  Otherwise, just use the default
        // Metal look-and-feel.
        String lf = UIManager.getSystemLookAndFeelClassName();

        if ( lf != null )
        {
            try
            {
                UIManager.setLookAndFeel( lf );
            }
            catch ( Exception ex )
            {
                ex.printStackTrace();
            }
        }

        // Create the main frame and place it.
        MyFrame mf = new MyFrame();
        mf.setSize( 300, 400 );
        mf.show();
    }

    // The main() method just creates an instance of this
    // class.
    public static void main( String args[] )
    {
        new Test();
    }
}
```

MyFrame.java

This is the main frame for the application and shows an example of how the file browser can be used. It does the following:

- Creates an instance of the FileBrowser class.
- Puts the FileBrowser panel into a JScrollPane so the user can scroll around it.
- Adds the JScrollPane to its content pane so it covers the frame's main area.
- Gets the drives combo box from the FileBrowser (null on non-Windows systems).
- Places the drives combo box (if non-null) at the bottom of the content pane.

JFC CLASSES USED IN MYFRAME.JAVA   Following is a list of the JFC classes that were used in MyFrame.java, along with explanations of how and why they were used:

- **JFrame:** MyFrame is a subclass of JFrame. The only interesting thing about this is that we have to add components to the frame through the content pane (which is part of the root pane).
- **JPanel:** We use a JPanel to hold the content pane so we don't have to keep calling the frame's getContentPane() method. This JPanel is where the JScrollPane (with the FileBrowser inside) and the drives combo box are added.
- **JComboBox:** The FileBrowser's drives list is a JComboBox. You would normally want to catch the combo box's events, but the FileBrowser does so automatically. The combo box is separate from the FileBrowser so you can place them where you want them.
- **JScrollPane:** This is used so that the user can scroll around the FileBrowser when its display area becomes too big for the frame to show in its entirety. You place the FileBrowser in the JScrollPane with the JScrollPane's constructor. The JScrollPane takes care of everything after that.

RELATIONSHIPS TO OTHER FILE BROWSER CLASSES   Following is a explanation of MyFrame's interactions with the other classes in this example:

- **Test:** MyFrame is displayed by Test.
- **FileBrowser:** MyFrame creates a FileBrowser and places it in a JScrollPane. It also asks the FileBrowser for its drives combo box, which is null on non-Windows platforms. If the combo box is not null,

MyFrame places it at the bottom of the content pane.

Here's the source code:

```java
import com.sun.java.swing.*;
import java.awt.*;

public class MyFrame extends JFrame
{
    public MyFrame()
    {
        setTitle( "FileBrowser" );

        // Store the content pane in a variable for easier
        // access.
        JPanel contentPane = (JPanel)getContentPane();

        // Components will all be added to this panel.
        contentPane.setLayout( new BorderLayout() );

        // Create the file browser pane with its initial
        // directory set to the current one.
        FileBrowser fb = new FileBrowser( "." );

        // Get the file browser's combo bo that can be used
        // to show and change the active drive on Windows
        // systems.
        JComboBox driveBox = fb.getDriveBox();

        // Create a scroll pane so we can scroll around the
        // file browser pane.
        JScrollPane scroller = new JScrollPane( fb );

        // Fill the content pane with the scroller.
        contentPane.add( "Center", scroller );

        // If the drives combo box is not null (it is null on
        // non-Windows systems), display the combo box at the
        // bottom of the content pane.
        if ( driveBox != null )
        {
            contentPane.add( "South", driveBox );
        }
    }
}
```

WorkingDirectoryModel.java

This class is a subclass of DirectoryModel. It adds some intelligence for working around bugs in the pre-JDK 1.2 File class, as well as a method for getting all available drives on a Windows system.

NOTE: *For Swing 1.0, the classes and interfaces relating to file browsing have been moved to the com.sun.java.swing.preview package. Their APIs are likely to change in the near future.*

Following is a list of the JFC classes used in this class:

■ **DirectoryModel:** This is WorkingDirectoryModel's super class, used to navigate through the local file system, get the contents of directories, and get the available drives on Windows systems. We overrode the getTypedFilesForDirectory() method to get around problems with how DirectoryModel deals with certain situations. DirectoryModel uses the File class behind the scenes, and File has a couple of problems. First, if you create a File in Windows using the path "c:\," File doesn't access that directory's contents properly. Second, if you create the DirectoryModel with a File made from the path ".," you get an extra level of directory that's just the current directory with a "." on the end. We also overrode the canGoUp() method because DirectoryModel says you can still go up from a Windows root directory, but the goUp() method doesn't take you anywhere new. We added a getDrives() method that returns a Vector with a list of available drives under Windows. Notice, too, that DirectoryModel's isWindowsFileSystem() and getCurrentDirectory() methods are used.

RELATIONSHIPS TO OTHER FILE BROWSER CLASSES The only other file browser class that WorkingDirectoryModel interacts with is FileBrowser itself. When FileBrowser needs the list of Windows drives or the contents of a directory, it asks this class. It also calls canGoUp() and goUp() when it's building the tree.

Here's the source code:

```
import com.sun.java.swing.*;
import com.sun.java.swing.preview.*;
import java.io.*;
import java.util.*;

public class WorkingDirectoryModel extends DirectoryModel
{
    // Special variable that tells us if we have to work
    // around pre JDK 1.2 bugs in the File class.
    private boolean mIsOldJDK;

    // Creates a directory model with its current directory
    // set to the user's home directory.
    public WorkingDirectoryModel()
    {
        super();
```

```
        mIsOldJDK = isOldJDK();
}

// Creates a directory model with its current directory
// set to the specified one.
public WorkingDirectoryModel( File dir )
{
    super( dir );
    mIsOldJDK = isOldJDK();
}

// For Windows systems, this returns a Vector filled
// with the available drive letters.  On other systems
// it returns null.
public Vector getDrives()
{
    if ( isWindowsFileSystem() )
    {
        TypedFile driveFile;
        String driveName;

        // Until there is a valid way to get the
        // Windows drive letters, we have to fake it.
        // Create a TypedFile for the "A" drive (even
        // if it is empty).  Ignore the possibility
        // that there might be a "B" drive.  Then step
        // through drive letters "C" through "Z", and
        // if they exist create TypedFiles for them
        // as well.
        Vector drives = new Vector();
        driveFile = new TypedFile( "A:\\",
                    FileType.SharedFolder );
        drives.addElement( driveFile );

        for ( char ch = 'C'; ch <= 'Z'; ch++ )
        {
            driveName = new String( ch + ":\\" );
            driveFile = new TypedFile( driveName,
                        FileType.SharedFolder );
            if ( driveFile != null && driveFile.exists() )
            {
                drives.addElement( driveFile );
            }
        }

        return drives;
    }
    else
    {
        return null;
    }
}

// Override so we can work around some JDK strangeness.
public Vector getTypedFilesForDirectory( File dir )
```

```
{
   File newDir = dir;
   String name = dir.getAbsolutePath();

   if ( mIsOldJDK && name.endsWith( ":\\" ) )
   {
      // In Windows, the File class will not find
      // children of root directories like "c:\".
      // Getting rid of the path separator does the
      // trick.
      name = name.substring( 0, 2 );
      newDir = new File( name );
   }
   else if ( name.endsWith( File.separator + "." ) )
   {
      // If a path ends with "/." on UNIX or "\." on
      // Windows, if you use the directory model goUp()
      // method, it doesn't actually go up.  So we strip
      // the "/." or "\.".
      name = new String( name.substring( 0,
                         name.length() - 2 ) );
      newDir = new File( name );
   }

   return super.getTypedFilesForDirectory( newDir );
}

public boolean canGoUp()
{
   // This may ultimately be fixed in JFC, but for now,
   // the directory model thinks it can go up from a
   // Windows root directory, but won't actually do so.
   if ( isWindowsFileSystem() &&
        getCurrentDirectory().getAbsolutePath().endsWith(
        ":" ) )
   {
      return false;
   }

   return super.canGoUp();
}

// Returns true is the JDK version is less than 1.2.
private boolean isOldJDK()
{
   String version = System.getProperty( "java.version" );

   System.out.println( "Version:  " + version );
   if ( version.charAt( 0 ) <= '1' &&
        version.charAt( 2 ) <= '1' )
   {
      System.out.println( "Old JDK" );
      return true;
   }
```

```
        return false;
    }

    // Allows public access to the protected
    // isWindowsFileSystem() method.
    public boolean isWindows()
    {
        return isWindowsFileSystem();
    }
}
```

FileBrowser.java

FileBrowser is a subclass of JPanel. It always has its area covered by a directory tree that lets the user navigate the contents of a file system. On Windows systems, which have multiple file systems (one per drive), FileBrowser can swap one file system's tree for another one, restoring the new tree to its previous state if it was swapped. It does this by maintaining a hash table containing one JTree for each drive that has been accessed since the file browser started up.

Each JTree has its own tree model where the actual file system data is stored. In the interest of efficiency, a directory's contents are loaded from disk only when needed. If a directory is never expanded, its contents are never loaded, although that fact isn't visually evident to the user. Each item in the JTree is of type DefaultMutableTreeNode and contains a TypedFile that represents a directory or file.

FileBrowser also stores a JComboBox that can be used on Windows systems to allow the user to select a different drive to display. This is null on non-Windows systems. This combo box's events are caught by FileBrowser so that changes in the combo box can be automatically reflected in the main FileBrowser.

JFC CLASSES USED IN FILEBROWSER.JAVA Following is a list of which JFC classes are used in this class and what they are used for:

- **JPanel:** FileBrowser is a subclass of JPanel. It could have been a subclass of JTree except for the need to be able to swap different JTrees on Windows systems. This class uses a BorderLayout so that the active JTree can be layed out to completely cover it.

- **JTree:** Each file system is held in its own JTree, and only one is active at a time. Each JTree has its own tree model of type DefaultTreeModel. JTree's setLargeModel() method is called to make the browser perform well with many nodes displayed. The different JTrees are stored in a hash table and can be accessed there by using their drive letters as a key. When the FileBrowser initially accesses a file system, it loads only the contents of directories being displayed. As the user navigates the file system, expanding new directories, the contents of these directories are loaded. FileBrowser knows when a directory becomes expanded because it catches the JTree's TreeExpansionEvents. When it receives one of these events, it checks whether the directory being expanded has any children in the JTree. If it doesn't, FileBrowser gets the directory's contents from the WorkingDirectoryModel and loads them into the JTree with its tree model. Each file is added as a non-expandable tree node, and each directory is added as an expandable tree node. After the new nodes are added to the tree model, FileBrowser tells the tree model that its structure has changed; then the tree model tells the JTree.

- **DefaultTreeModel:** This class, where the actual tree nodes are stored, implements the TreeModel interface. When we first create a JTree, we give its constructor a DefaultTreeModel that already has at least a root node. JTree is the graphical representation of this tree model. If you want to explicitly tell the tree to display a directory and its contents, you use the tree model to create a TreePath, which is just a list of tree nodes. You then pass that tree path to JTree's expandPath() method. When you add nodes into the tree model, they aren't automatically reflected in the associated JTree. Instead, you have to call the DefaultTreeModel's nodeStructureChanged() method to tell the tree model its structure has changed. Then the tree model tells the JTree, and the JTree updates.

- **DefaultMutableTreeNode:** This class implements the MutableTreeNode interface. These tree nodes are what makes up the tree model. Each tree node stores a single TypedFile that represents a file or folder on the file system. A new tree node is created by giving its constructor the TypedFile it will be associated with. This TypedFile can later be accessed with the tree node's getUserObject() method. When you create a tree model, you give it a tree node it uses as its root node. At one point, we need to find out which tree node holds a particular TypedFile. To do this, we get the parent folder's children by using its children() method, and then go through each child, comparing the TypedFile to the child's contents. A node in our example represents either a file or a directory. A file can't contain other files, so it shouldn't appear to be expandable; however, a directory can contain other files, so it *should* appear expandable. You tell a node it's expandable with the setAllowsChildren() method. A file node doesn't allow children, but a directory node does. When you have a directory node and you want to add a child node to it, use the add() method.

- **TreeExpansionEvent:** When an expandable node in a JTree is expanded (by double-clicking or by calling JTree's expandPath() method), a TreeExpansionEvent is generated, and any registered TreeExpansionListeners are notified through their treeExpanded() method. These events are *very* important to this example because we load a directory's contents only when the directory is first expanded and the events tell us when a directory is about to be expanded. When treeExpanded() is called, we find out the path being expanded by using the event's getPath() method. Then we see if the last directory on that path (the directory being expanded) has any tree node children. If so, its contents have already been loaded; if not, we load the directory's children.

- **TreeExpansionListener:** As discussed previously, TreeExpansionEvents are very important to this example. To listen for these events, your listening class must implement the TreeExpansionListener interface that consists of two methods: treeExpanded() and treeCollapsed(). We don't use treeCollapsed().

- **TreePath:** A TreePath is just a list of tree nodes that embodies the path in the tree model from one node to another. For this example, the tree path is always from the tree model's root node to another node. The path for c:\windows\system32\myfile.dll would be a series of tree nodes that represent each directory (C:\, windows, system32) and the file itself (myfile.dll). We use a TreePath to make sure the path is completely expanded by passing it to JTree's expandPath() method. We had to build up the path one node at a time.

- **TypedFile:** This subclass of File is used to associate a file type with a file. Each TypedFile has a variable of type FileType that stores the file's type. When you interact with a DirectoryModel, it's usually through TypedFiles rather than Files.

- **FileType:** This interface can be used to create classes that define file types. Each file type knows if it can contain other files (as directories contain other files), what the file type's icon is, what the description of the type is, and how to tell if a file is of that type. The FileType interface defines a group of types, such as SharedFolder and SharedGenericFile.

- **JComboBox:** On a Windows system, the available drives are stored in a JComboBox, which you can get from FileBrowser and place on the screen as you please. FileBrowser catches the combo box's ItemEvents so it can make the active file system change.

RELATIONSHIP TO OTHER FILE BROWSER CLASSES FileBrowser has interactions with three of the other four classes in the example:

- **MyFrame:** This class creates the FileBrowser. It places the FileBrowser in a JScrollPane because file browsers generally need to scroll. It also asks for the Windows drives combo box and displays it.

- **WorkingDirectoryModel:** FileBrowser uses this class when it needs information about the file system, whether it's the list of available drives on Windows, information about the current directory's parent, or a list of a directory's contents.

■ **FileTreeCellRenderer:** FileBrowser interacts with this class only indirectly. It just tells the JTrees to use this class to display their tree nodes.

Here's the source code:

```
import com.sun.java.swing.*;
import com.sun.java.swing.preview.*;
import com.sun.java.swing.tree.*;
import com.sun.java.swing.event.*;
import java.util.*;
import java.io.*;
import java.awt.*;
import java.awt.event.*;

public class FileBrowser extends JPanel implements
        TreeExpansionListener, ItemListener
{
   // This stores the JTree instances for all drives.  On
   // non-Windows, there will just be one.
   private Hashtable mDriveTrees;

   // This is the combo box that can be used to display and
   // change drives on Windows systems.
   private JComboBox mDriveBox;

   // The directory model.
   private WorkingDirectoryModel mDirModel;

   // The currently displayed JTree.
   private JTree mCurrentTree;

   // Create a file browser panel starting at the given
   // directory.
   public FileBrowser( String startDir )
   {
      // This layout allows the currently active JTree to
      // take up all of the FileBrowser's area.
      setLayout( new BorderLayout() );

      // Using the explicit current working directory
      // instead of "."  makes dealing with File paths
      // simpler (no trailing ".").
      if ( startDir.equals( "." ) )
         startDir = System.getProperty( "user.dir" );

      // Create a TypedFile from the given path.
      TypedFile thisDir = new TypedFile( startDir,
                           FileType.SharedFolder );

      // Initialize the table that stores each drive's
      // JTree.
      mDriveTrees = new Hashtable();
```

```
      // Create the combo box that can hold the drive
      // letters.
      createDrivesBox();

      // If the drives combo box was created (Windows
      // only), we want to listen so the active JTree can
      // be changed.
      if ( mDriveBox != null )
      {
         mDriveBox.addItemListener( this );
      }

      // Cause the directory and its parents to be loaded
      // into the tree if they aren't already.
      loadDirectory( thisDir );
   }

   // For Windows systems, we provide a combo box that
   // contains all available drives so the user can change
   // from one to another.  The combo box is null on non-
   // Windows systems.
   private void createDrivesBox()
   {
      // Create a directory model from which we will get
      // the list of available drives.
      WorkingDirectoryModel tmpModel =
                        new WorkingDirectoryModel();

      // Get the list of drives (null on non-Windows
      // systems).
      Vector files = tmpModel.getDrives();

      // If the list of drives was returned, create the
      // combo box and load the drive letters into it.
      if ( files != null )
      {
         mDriveBox = new JComboBox();

         // For each drive letter...
         for ( int i = 0; i < files.size(); i++ )
         {
            // Put it in a TypedFile variable for easier
            // understanding.
            TypedFile thisDrive =
                        (TypedFile)files.elementAt(i);

            // Get the drive's absolute path and store just
            // its drive letter followed by ':'.
            mDriveBox.addItem(
                  thisDrive.getAbsolutePath().substring(
                  0, 2 ) );
         }
      }
   }
```

```
// Return the combo box that holds the drive letters.
public JComboBox getDriveBox()
{
   return mDriveBox;
}

// Cause the specified directory and its parents to be
// loaded if they haven't.
private void loadDirectory( TypedFile dir )
{
   DefaultTreeModel treeModel;

   // Create the directory model if it hasn't been.
   // Otherwise set its current directory to the one
   // passed in.
   if ( mDirModel == null )
   {
      mDirModel = new WorkingDirectoryModel( dir );
   }
   else
   {
      mDirModel.setCurrentDirectory( dir );
   }

   // Make a vector that stores the current directory's
   // TypedFile and each of its parents'.
   Vector dirPathItems = new Vector();

   // Starting at the specified directory, put the
   // directory and its parents into the vector.  Each
   // higher level is inserted at the vector's start.
   while ( mDirModel.canGoUp() )
   {
      // DirectoryModel bug - still thinks it can go up
      // from '/' on UNIX.
      if ( mDirModel.getCurrentDirectory().
                        getAbsolutePath().equals( "/" ) )
      {
         break;
      }

      dirPathItems.insertElementAt( getTypedFolder(
                mDirModel.getCurrentDirectory() ), 0 );
      mDirModel.goUp();
   }

   dirPathItems.insertElementAt( getTypedFolder(
             mDirModel.getCurrentDirectory() ), 0 );

   // Store the root TypedFile in this variable to make
   // the code easier to read.
   TypedFile rootDir =
                  (TypedFile)dirPathItems.elementAt(0);

   // See which tree from the tree hash table this path
```

```
// uses.
JTree tree = getTree( rootDir );

// If its tree has not been created, create it and
// add it to the hash table.
if ( tree == null )
{
   // Create a root tree node from the file system's
   // root directory.
   DefaultMutableTreeNode root =
              new DefaultMutableTreeNode( rootDir );

   // Create a new tree model with the just-created
   // node as its root.  'true' is so that tree nodes
   // will appear expandable even if they currently
   // have no children.  This is required since we
   // only load a directory's contents when it
   // becomes expanded and we want a directory node
   // to look the same whether it has been loaded yet
   // or not.
   treeModel = new DefaultTreeModel( root, true );

   // Create a new JTree for this file system using
   // the just-created tree model.
   tree = new JTree( treeModel );

   // Use the large model since the total of
   // displayed nodes can be large.
   tree.setLargeModel( true );

   // Add the JTree into the hash table that stores
   // each drive's JTree.
   mDriveTrees.put( getDriveHash( rootDir ), tree );

   // Make it so this class is notified when a node
   // on this JTree is expanded so we can get its
   // children if they haven't been loaded yet.
   tree.addTreeExpansionListener( this );

   // Tell the JTree to use our custom renderer to
   // display its items.
   tree.setCellRenderer( new FileTreeCellRenderer() );

   // Make sure the drives combo box (if it exists)
   // reflects the drive of the new JTree.
   if ( mDriveBox != null )
   {
      mDriveBox.setSelectedItem(
         rootDir.getAbsolutePath().substring( 0, 2 ) );
   }
}

// If the tree is the current one, don't bother
// reloading it.  Otherwise, replace the currently
// active JTree with the new one.
```

```
if ( tree != mCurrentTree )
{
   replaceTree( tree );
}

// This array accumulates nodes as they are put on
// the tree.  Since we are going through the path
// from root down, we add another level each time
// through the loop.
DefaultMutableTreeNode allInPath[] =
     new DefaultMutableTreeNode[dirPathItems.size()];

TreePath thisPath = null;

// For the new directory and each of its parents...
for ( int i = 0; i < dirPathItems.size(); i++ )
{
   // This makes it easier to read.  'thisFile' is
   // the TypedFile representation  of the directory
   // we are working on.
   TypedFile thisFile =
               (TypedFile)dirPathItems.elementAt(i);

   // Append the directory's node to the array.
   if ( i == 0 )
   {
      allInPath[i] =
         (DefaultMutableTreeNode)mCurrentTree.
                                getModel().getRoot();
   }
   else
      allInPath[i] = findChild( thisFile,
                               allInPath[i-1] );

   // We want the directory and its contents to be
   // visible in the JTree.  To do that we have to
   // build a TreePath.
   DefaultMutableTreeNode pathSoFar[] =
               new DefaultMutableTreeNode[i+1];

   for ( int j = 0; j <= i; j++ )
   {
      pathSoFar[j] = allInPath[j];
   }

   thisPath = new TreePath( pathSoFar );

   // Tell the tree to expand the path (show it and
   // its children).
   mCurrentTree.expandPath( thisPath );

   // In some cases calling the JTree's expand()
   // method does not cause the JTree to generate a
   // TreeExpansionEvent.  This forces it.
   treeExpanded( new TreeExpansionEvent(
```

```
                                    mCurrentTree, thisPath ) );
      }

      // Make the full path visible.
      mCurrentTree.scrollPathToVisible( thisPath );
   }


   // Replace the currently active JTree with the passed in
   // one.
   private void replaceTree( JTree tree )
   {
      // If this is not the first JTree to be displayed,
      // remove the active one from the JPanel.
      if ( mCurrentTree != null )
         remove( mCurrentTree );

      // Store the new JTree as the active one.
      mCurrentTree = tree;

      // Add the JTree so it fills the file browser's area.
      add( "Center", mCurrentTree );

      // Make sure the JTree displays properly.
      validate();
   }


   // Retrieve the TypedFile's JTree if it is in the hash
   // table.  If the JTree has not been created yet, this
   // returns null.
   private JTree getTree( TypedFile rootDirectory )
   {
      return (JTree)mDriveTrees.get(
                         getDriveHash( rootDirectory ) );
   }


   // Get the one-character drive letter or '/' on UNIX.
   private String getDriveHash( TypedFile dir )
   {
      return dir.getAbsolutePath().substring( 0, 1 );
   }


   // Find the parent's child that matches the TypedFile.
   // On Windows, we have to do this by comparing the
   // file names in a case-insensitive way.
   private DefaultMutableTreeNode findChild(
                         TypedFile thisFile,
                         DefaultMutableTreeNode parent )
   {
      DefaultMutableTreeNode thisNode;

      if ( mDirModel.isWindows() )
      {
         File newFile;
         String newPath;
         String thisPath =
```

```
                thisFile.getAbsolutePath().toLowerCase();

     for ( Enumeration e = parent.children();
           e.hasMoreElements(); )
     {
        thisNode =
              (DefaultMutableTreeNode)e.nextElement();
        newFile = (File)thisNode.getUserObject();
        newPath =
              newFile.getAbsolutePath().toLowerCase();
        if ( newPath.equals( thisPath ) )
           return thisNode;
     }
  }
  else
  {
     for ( Enumeration e = parent.children();
           e.hasMoreElements(); )
     {
        thisNode =
              (DefaultMutableTreeNode)e.nextElement();
        if ( ((TypedFile)thisNode.getUserObject()).
                                equals( thisFile ) )
        {
           return thisNode;
        }
     }
  }

  return null;
}

// Converts a File to a TypedFile of type
// FileType.SharedFolder.
private TypedFile getTypedFolder( File dir )
{
   return new TypedFile( dir.getAbsolutePath(),
                      FileType.SharedFolder );
}

// This is called when the drive combo box's value
// changes.  We check the hash table to see if the newly
// selected file system has already been loaded.  If so,
// make it the currently active JTree.  Otherwise,
// cause it's root directory to be loaded.
public void itemStateChanged( ItemEvent e )
{
   if ( e.getStateChange() == ItemEvent.SELECTED )
   {
      // If the tree model for the new drive is already
      // built, reload it into the tree.  Otherwise,
      // create a path representing the drive's root
      // directory and call loadDirectory().
      String path = (String)mDriveBox.getSelectedItem()
                   + "\\";
```

```java
      // Get the JTree from the hash table that
      // corresponds to the drive letter.
      JTree tree = (JTree)mDriveTrees.get(
                                  path.substring( 0, 1 ) );

      if ( tree == null )
      {
         // Cause the file system's root directory to be
         // loaded.
         loadDirectory( new TypedFile( path,
                        FileType.SharedFolder ) );
      }
      else
      {
         // Make this JTree the active one.
         replaceTree( tree );
      }

      // Make sure the scrollpane adjusts for the
      // different length trees.
      revalidate();
   }
}

// This is called when the active JTree has one of its
// directories expanded.  If the directory's contents
// have not been loaded yet, load them.
public void treeExpanded( TreeExpansionEvent e )
{
   DefaultMutableTreeNode endOfPath =
               (DefaultMutableTreeNode)e.getPath().
                                  getLastPathComponent();

   if ( endOfPath.getChildCount() == 0 )
   {
      loadEmptyNode( endOfPath );
   }
}

// Load a directory's contents.
private void loadEmptyNode(
                     DefaultMutableTreeNode emptyNode )
{
   // Get the TypedFile object from the tree node.
   TypedFile thisFolder =
                  (TypedFile)emptyNode.getUserObject();

   // Get the directory's contents.
   Vector contents =
      mDirModel.getTypedFilesForDirectory( thisFolder );

   // If there are no contents, return.
   if ( contents.size() == 0 )
      return;
```

```
TypedFile thisFile;
DefaultMutableTreeNode thisNode;

// Get the tree model.
DefaultTreeModel model =
            (DefaultTreeModel)mCurrentTree.getModel();

// For each item within the directory, create a new
// tree node.  If the item is a file, make it so the
// tree node doesn't allow children.  Otherwise, the
// tree node does.
for ( int i = 0; i < contents.size(); i++ )
{
    // This makes it easier to read.
    thisFile = (TypedFile)contents.elementAt(i);

    // Create the new tree node, storing the TypedFile
    // within it.
    thisNode = new DefaultMutableTreeNode( thisFile );

    // If the TypedFile's type is a container type (it
    // can hold other files), make it so the tree will
    // display it as expandable.
    if ( thisFile.getType().isContainer() )
        thisNode.setAllowsChildren( true );
    else
        thisNode.setAllowsChildren( false );

    // Add the tree node to the previously empty node.
    model.insertNodeInto( thisNode, emptyNode, i );
}

// Tell the JTree's model that things have been added
// to it.  The tree model will inturn tell the JTree
// to refresh itself.
((DefaultTreeModel)mCurrentTree.getModel()).
                    nodeStructureChanged( emptyNode );
}

// For the TreeExpansionListener interface.
public void treeCollapsed( TreeExpansionEvent e )
{
}
}
```

FileTreeCellRenderer.java

This class is used by the JTrees to draw their tree nodes. It subclasses
JLabel because JLabel can display text and an icon, and that's the kind of
functionality we want for displaying tree nodes. The most crucial method is

getTreeCellRendererComponent(). This is our chance to look at the tree node's current state, set the text and icon and colors to match that state, and return an instance of the class. Then, when the node is painting, this class' paint() method is called. We use this instead of JLabel's default paint() method because we have to support the ability to highlight a tree node.

Here's the source code:

```
import com.sun.java.swing.*;
import com.sun.java.swing.preview.*;
import com.sun.java.swing.tree.*;
import java.awt.*;


//————————————————————————————
// public class FileTreeCellRenderer
//————————————————————————————
/* This is an example of making your own TreeCellRenderer
 * so you can get more control of how tree items look. */
public class FileTreeCellRenderer extends JLabel implements
        TreeCellRenderer
{
   private Icon mExpandedIcon;
   private Icon mCollapsedIcon;
   private Icon mLeafIcon;

   //————————————————————————————
   // FileTreeCellRenderer()
   //————————————————————————————
   /* Load up the icons that reflect a tree item's state. */
   public FileTreeCellRenderer()
   {
      mExpandedIcon = new ImageIcon( "TreeOpen.gif" );
      mCollapsedIcon = new ImageIcon( "TreeClosed.gif" );
      mLeafIcon = new ImageIcon( "file.gif" );
   }


   //————————————————————————————
   // getIconHeight()
   //————————————————————————————
   /* If you have big icons, you could use this information
    * to change the row height. */
   public int getIconHeight()
   {
      return mExpandedIcon.getIconHeight();
   }


   //————————————————————————————
   // getTreeCellRendererComponent()
   //————————————————————————————
   public Component getTreeCellRendererComponent(
                        JTree tree,
                        Object value,
                        boolean selected,
                        boolean expanded,
```

```
                              boolean leaf,
                              int row,
                              boolean hasFocus )
    {
       DefaultMutableTreeNode node =
                              (DefaultMutableTreeNode)value;
       TypedFile file = (TypedFile)node.getUserObject();

       if ( file.getName().length() == 0 )
          setText( file.getAbsolutePath() );
       else
          setText( file.getName() );

       if ( leaf )
          setIcon( mLeafIcon );
       else if ( expanded )
          setIcon( mExpandedIcon );
       else
          setIcon( mCollapsedIcon );

       if ( selected )
       {
          // Hack for X where the system colors are not all
          // defined properly.
          if ( SystemColor.textHighlightText.getRGB() ==
               SystemColor.textHighlight.getRGB() )
          {
             setForeground( Color.white );
             setBackground( Color.blue );
          }
          else
          {
             setForeground( SystemColor.textHighlightText );
             setBackground( SystemColor.textHighlight );
          }
       }
       else
       {
          // Hack for X where the system colors are not all
          // defined properly.
          if ( SystemColor.textText.getRGB() ==
               tree.getBackground().getRGB() )
          {
             setForeground( Color.black );
          }
          else
          {
             setForeground( SystemColor.textText );
          }

          setBackground( tree.getBackground() );
       }

       return this;
    }
```

```
//————————————————
// paint()
//————————————————
/* Paint the tree item. */
public void paint( Graphics g )
{
    int textstart, textwidth;

    textstart = getIcon().getIconWidth() +
                getIconTextGap();
    textwidth = getSize().width - textstart;

    getIcon().paintIcon( this, g, 0, 0 );

    g.setColor( getBackground() );
    g.fillRect( textstart, 0, textwidth,
                getSize().height );
    g.setColor( getForeground() );
    g.drawString( getText(), textstart,
            (getSize().height +
            g.getFontMetrics().getAscent()) / 2 );
}
}
```

SUMMARY

This chapter has illustrated creating a file browser as an excuse to show how a variety of JFC classes can be used together to create something useful. It's particularly nice for seeing how some of the tree-related classes interact.

The emphasis is not only on the end product, but also on explaining what JFC classes went into the example and why.

11

Integrating JFC Example 2: Adding Items to and Removing Items from JTrees

Working with the JTree class requires an understanding of how all its supporting classes work, including DefaultTreeModel, DefaultTreeSelectionModel, DefaultMutableTreeNode, and TreePath. This example illustrates the relationships between these classes. Although by itself this application isn't of much practical use, it's useful for showing how to handle the types of situations that *do* arise in practical applications.

The Application

This example creates two internal frames, each with a JTree displayed in it. Each frame also contains a JToolBar with three buttons. You use these buttons to delete an item from the current tree, copy an item from one tree to the other, or move an item from one tree to the other. Figure 11-1 shows the example just after a directory has been copied from Frame 2 to Frame 1.

The example consists of three separate classes:

■ **Test.java:** This simple class contains the main() method that just serves to create an instance of the Test class. The Test constructor creates and places our main frame.

■ **MyFrame.java:** Our main frame, this class creates and displays the two internal frames, each containing a tree. It listens for events from the internal frames. When MyFrame receives notification of these events, it triggers the action of deleting, copying, or moving tree items.

■ **TreeFrame.java:** Each of MyFrame's internal frames is a TreeFrame. Each TreeFrame contains a JTree and a JToolBar with three buttons. This class controls loading and interacting with the JTree.

Following is a discussion of each class, which JFC classes it uses and why, and how it interacts with the other classes in the example.

Test.java

This is a very simple class. It contains the main() method, which just creates an instance of the Test class. Test's constructor creates an instance of the MyFrame class and places it on the display. Test.java uses two methods from the

Figure 11-1
The JTree example.

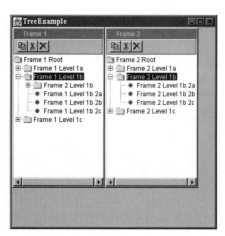

UIManager class. It uses the getSystemLookAndFeelClassName() method to get the native look-nad-feel. It uses the setLookAndFeel() method to apply the native look-and-feel.

Here's the source code:

```
import com.sun.java.swing.*;

public class Test
{
    // Create an instance of MyFrame and place it.
    public Test()
    {
        // Use the native look-and-feel if there is one.
        String lf = UIManager.getSystemLookAndFeelClassName();

        if ( lf != null )
        {
            try
            {
                UIManager.setLookAndFeel( lf );
            }
            catch ( Exception ex )
            {
                ex.printStackTrace();
            }
        }

        MyFrame mf = new MyFrame();
        mf.setSize( 400, 400 );
        mf.show();
    }

    // When the application starts, create an instance of
    // this class.
    public static void main( String args[] )
    {
        new Test();
    }
}
```

MyFrame.java

This class, a subclass of JFrame, serves as the main workspace for the example. It does the following:

- Creates the two TreeFrames.
- Creates a JDesktop pane.
- Adds the TreeFrames as windows in the desktop pane.

- Makes the desktop pane fill its content pane.
- Is notified when one of the toolbar buttons in one of the TreeFrames is clicked.
- Based on the TreeFrame action events, controls deleting, copying, and moving tree nodes.

JFC CLASSES USED IN MYFRAME.JAVA   Following is a list of the JFC classes used in MyFrame.java, including how and why they were used:

- **JFrame:** MyFrame is a subclass of JFrame. This is noteworthy only because the JDesktopPane that the TreeFrames are added to is placed in the frame's content pane.
- **JPanel:** We use a JPanel as a reference to the frame's content pane so we don't have to keep calling the frame's getContentPane() method. The JDesktopPane is placed in this JPanel.
- **JDesktopPane:** Because the TreeFrames are subclasses of JInternalFrame, we use a JDesktopPane to manage them. This JDesktopPane is added to MyFrame's content pane so that it covers it completely.
- **JInternalFrame:** The TreeFrame class is an extension of JInternalFrame, and we use some of JInternalFrame's methods. We use setBounds() to place the TreeFrame within the JDesktopPane and setResizable() so the user can resize the TreeFrame.
- **DefaultMutableTreeNode:** When the user wants to copy or move a tree node from one TreeFrame to the other, MyFrame has the node while it's in transit.

RELATIONSHIPS TO OTHER CLASSES IN THE EXAMPLE   Here's how MyFrame interacts with the other two classes in the example:

- **Test.java:** The Test class creates MyFrame and causes it to be displayed onscreen.
- **TreeFrame.java:** MyFrame creates two TreeFrames and places them within a JDesktopPane. It calls TreeFrame's addActionListener() method so it's notified when either of the TreeFrames' toolbar buttons is clicked. When one of those buttons is clicked and MyFrame's actionPerformed() method is called, MyFrame gets the TreeFrame that generated the event from the ActionEvent's getSource() method. MyFrame knows whether the action is meant to trigger a tree node deletion, copy, or move based on the ActionEvent's command string. If the button click is meant to trigger a tree node copy or move between the TreeFrames, MyFrame calls the event-generating TreeFrame's getSelectedNode() method to get the tree

node that's being moved or copied, and then calls the other TreeFrame's insertNode() method. If the button is meant to trigger a deletion, MyFrame calls the event-generating TreeFrame's deleteSelectedNode() method. MyFrame also calls this method as the last step in a move operation—after the tree node has been copied across.

Here's the source code for MyFrame.java:

```java
import com.sun.java.swing.*;
import com.sun.java.swing.tree.*;
import java.awt.*;
import java.awt.event.*;

public class MyFrame extends JFrame implements
        ActionListener
{
    // The two internal frames are instance variables so
    // actionPerformed() can see them.
    TreeFrame mFrame1;
    TreeFrame mFrame2;

    public MyFrame()
    {
        setTitle( "TreeExample" );

        // Store the content pane in a variable for easier
        // access.
        JPanel contentPane = (JPanel)getContentPane();

        // Components will all be added to this panel.
        contentPane.setLayout( new BorderLayout() );

        // Create a desktop pane into which the internal
        // frames will be added.
        JDesktopPane desktop = new JDesktopPane();

        // Create the first frame.
        mFrame1 = new TreeFrame( "Frame 1" );

        // Place it relative to the desktop pane.
        mFrame1.setBounds( 0, 0, 180, 300 );

        // Make it resizable.
        mFrame1.setResizable( true );

        // This class will get action events from the
        // internal frames when their toolbar buttons are
        // pressed.
        mFrame1.addActionListener( this );

        // Add the internal frame to the desktop.
```

```
      desktop.add( mFrame1 );

      // Same steps for the other internal frame, except it
      // is placed to the right of the first.
      mFrame2 = new TreeFrame( "Frame 2" );
      mFrame2.setBounds( 180, 0, 180, 300 );
      mFrame2.setResizable( true );
      mFrame2.addActionListener( this );
      desktop.add( mFrame2 );

      // Make it so the desktop pane completely covers the
      // content pane.
      contentPane.add( "Center", desktop );
   }

   // This is called when one of the internal frames'
   // toolbar buttons is pushed.  Each button has a command
   // string that tells us which button was pushed, and we
   // can find out which internal frame generated the event
   // using the event's getSource() method.
   public void actionPerformed( ActionEvent e )
   {
      // Store the event's command string.
      String actionCommand = e.getActionCommand();

      // Get the internal frame that generated the event.
      TreeFrame thisFrame = (TreeFrame)e.getSource();

      // Store the frame that did not generate the event.
      TreeFrame otherFrame;

      if ( thisFrame == mFrame1 )
         otherFrame = mFrame2;
      else
         otherFrame = mFrame1;

      if ( actionCommand.equals( "Copy" ) )
      {
         // If the "Copy" button was pressed, get the
         // selected node from the internal frame where the
         // event was generated, and insert that node into
         // the other internal frame.
         DefaultMutableTreeNode node =
                     (DefaultMutableTreeNode)thisFrame.
                                       getSelectedNode();
         otherFrame.insertNode( node );
      }
      else if ( actionCommand.equals( "Delete" ) )
      {
         // If the "Delete" button was pressed, tell the
         // internal frame that generated the event to
         // delete the selected node.
         thisFrame.deleteSelectedNode();
      }
      else if ( actionCommand.equals( "Move" ) )
```

```
            {
                    // If the "Move" button was pressed, get the
                    // selected node from the internal frame that
                    // generated the event, insert it into the other
                    // internal frame, and delete it from the
                    // originating frame.  We delete after moving
                    // because the node isn't copied until it is
                    // inserted.
                    DefaultMutableTreeNode node =
                                (DefaultMutableTreeNode)thisFrame.
                                                getSelectedNode();
                    otherFrame.insertNode( node );
                    thisFrame.deleteSelectedNode();
            }
        }
    }
```

TreeFrame.java

TreeFrame is a subclass of JInternalFrame that contains a scrolling JTree and a JToolBar. The JTree is initially filled with a set of strings, which is the same across all TreeFrames except that each string gets the TreeFrame's title added to it so we can identify where it originated.

The JTree is configured to allow only one node to be selected at a time. The JToolBar, placed at the top of the TreeFrame, contains three icon buttons. Each button is used to trigger one of three operations on the currently selected node: copy the node and its children to the other TreeFrame, move the node and its children to the other TreeFrame, or delete the node and its children. When one of these buttons is clicked, it generates an action event that TreeFrame catches and passes on (slightly modified) to its listener (MyFrame).

JFC CLASSES USED IN TREEFRAME.JAVA   The following are the JFC classes used in this class, with an explanation of how and why they were used:

- ■ **JInternalFrame:** TreeFrame is a subclass of JInternalFrame because we wanted to be able to have two TreeFrames onscreen at once and make them resizable in case they needed more space. The getTitle() method is called so we can add a string to each tree node, making its source readily identifiable.

- ■ **EventListenerList:** Because TreeFrame needs to generate ActionEvents and send them to listeners, EventListenerList was used to handle the list of listeners. TreeFrame calls EventListenerList's add(), remove(), and getListenerList() methods. We could have coded the same functionality, but the whole point of using EventListenerList is so you don't have to.

- **JTree:** TreeFrame contains a single JTree that covers most of its area. This tree is initially loaded with a group of strings—three levels deep, including the root. We limited the number of tree nodes that can be selected at once to one by using the tree's TreeSelectionModel, which has a method called setSelectionModel(). We set the initially selected node to be the root node (always in the tree's first row) using the setSelectionRow() method. We got the path of the currently selected node from the tree with the getSelectionPath() method, which returns a TreePath. We got the tree's TreeModel by using the getModel() method, and we used the setSelectionPath() method to specify which tree node should be the selected one.

- **JScrollPane:** We placed the JTree within one of these JScrollPanes so the user can scroll around the tree as it gets larger.

- **JToolBar:** This class holds the Copy, Move, and Delete buttons. It's placed at the top of the TreeFrame. The toolbar can be moved around and docked in other locations on the TreeFrame.

- **JButton:** The three toolbar buttons are JButtons that have an icon but no text. The buttons' margins are set to zero with the setMargin() method, which gets rid of the default padding around the button's text/icon. Each button has a tool tip added by using the setToolTipText() method so the user can find out what the button is for. The setActionCommand() method is used to designate a string that's delivered with any ActionEvents the button might generate. The addActionListener() method specifies which class should be notified when the button is clicked.

- **DefaultTreeModel:** By creating the JTree by directly specifying a root node in its constructor, the JTree's model is automatically created and is a DefaultTreeModel. This model holds all of the JTree's nodes and allows access to them. We could have created a DefaultTreeModel with the root node, and then passed the model to the JTree's constructor. This method might have been preferable because in that constructor you can specify that expandable nodes should look expandable, even if they have no children. By default, a node that's expandable but has no children looks just like a node that isn't expandable. You can get the same effect by calling the model's setAsksAllowsChildren() method.

  We use the model's removeNodeFromParent() method to remove a node. We could have removed the node with the tree node's remove() method, but this way we don't have to notify the model that it has been changed. Given a tree node, we use the model's getPathToRoot() method to return the path from the root node to the node in question. Oddly, getPathToRoot() returns an array of tree nodes instead of a TreePath. We use the insertNodeInto() method to insert a node under a parent. We could have used the tree node's insert() method, but then we would have had to notify the model that we had done so. The getRoot() method is used to access the tree's root node.

■ **DefaultTreeSelectionModel:** This is the selection model that's automatically associated with a JTree. It manages which nodes are selected and controls how selections can be made. The only method we call from this class is the setSelectionMode() method, which we use to specify that only one item can be selected at a time. However, the selection model is called indirectly through JTree convenience methods, such as setSelectionRow(), getSelectionPath(), and setSelectionPath().

■ **DefaultMutableTreeNode:** All the tree model's nodes are of this type. It's the standard tree node class that comes with the JFC. Each of the example's nodes is constructed with a string, which is what will be displayed by the default TreeCellRenderer. The add() method is used to add child nodes to a parent node. The setAllowsChildren() method specifies whether the node can have child nodes added or whether it's a leaf node. Initially, a root node is created and the rest of the nodes are added under it (to it or to its child nodes). Then the root node is passed to the JTree's constructor. This causes the root node to be loaded into a DefaultTreeModel that's subsequently used to add, remove, and access nodes. The getParent() method is used to find the tree node that contains the current node. The getIndex() method can be used on a node that allows children. It returns the index of the specified child. A node that allows children can also use the getChildCount() method to find out how many children it has, and it can use the getChildAt() method to return its child at the specified index.

■ **TreePath:** This is a list of the tree nodes required to get from one point in the tree to another. For our purposes, it's typically the path from the root node to the current node. A TreePath is returned from JTree's getSelectionPath() method. The tree model's getPathToRoot() method actually returns an array of tree nodes instead of a TreePath, but we can create a TreePath using a constructor that accepts an array of tree nodes. This is necessary because if we want to use JTree's setSelectionPath() method, we must have a TreePath. The only TreePath method we actually call is the getLastPathComponent(), which gets the final node in the path. In this example, that node generally represents the currently selected node on the tree.

RELATIONSHIPS TO OTHER CLASSES IN THE EXAMPLE
TreeFrame doesn't interact with Test.java at all. It does, however, use MyFrame to help it do its main job.

Initially, MyFrame creates the TreeFrames and places them in a JDesktopPane. After that, MyFrame responds to the TreeFrames' action events and controls deleting tree nodes, copying nodes from one TreeFrame to the other, and moving nodes from one TreeFrame to the other.

Here's the source code for TreeFrame.java:

```java
import com.sun.java.swing.*;
import com.sun.java.swing.event.*;
import com.sun.java.swing.tree.*;
import java.awt.event.*;
import java.awt.*;

public class TreeFrame extends JInternalFrame implements
        ActionListener
{
    // List of action listeners to which we should send
    // notification when one of the toolbar buttons is
    // pressed.
    private EventListenerList mActionListenerList;

    // The tree.
    private JTree mTree;

    public TreeFrame( String title )
    {
        // Call JInternalFrame's constructor.
        super( title );

        // Set the content pane's layout so we can add the
        // tree and toolbar.
        getContentPane().setLayout( new BorderLayout() );

        // Create the action listener list.
        mActionListenerList = new EventListenerList();

        // Create the tool bar.
        JToolBar toolBar = new JToolBar();

        // Put the toolbar at the top of the frame.
        getContentPane().add( "North", toolBar );

        // Create the toolbar buttons.  Give each a tool tip
        // and a unique action command string.  Tell it that
        // this class should be notified when it is pressed
        // and add it to the toolbar.
        JButton copy =
                new JButton( new ImageIcon( "copy.gif" ) );
        copy.setMargin( new Insets( 0, 0, 0, 0 ) );
        copy.setToolTipText(
                "Copy selected item(s) to other tree" );
        copy.setActionCommand( "Copy" );
        copy.addActionListener( this );
        toolBar.add( copy );

        JButton move =
```

```
                           new JButton( new ImageIcon( "cut.gif" ) );
       move.setMargin( new Insets( 0, 0, 0, 0 ) );
       move.setToolTipText(
                  "Move selected item(s) to other tree" );
       move.setActionCommand( "Move" );
       move.addActionListener( this );
       toolBar.add( move );

       JButton delete =
              new JButton( new ImageIcon( "delete.gif" ) );
       delete.setMargin( new Insets( 0, 0, 0, 0 ) );
       delete.setToolTipText( "Delete selected item(s)" );
       delete.setActionCommand( "Delete" );
       delete.addActionListener( this );
       toolBar.add( delete );

       // Call the method that loads the tree.
       MutableTreeNode root = generateTree();

       // Create the tree and load it up.
       mTree = new JTree( root );

       // Specify that only one item in the tree may be
       // selected at a time.
       mTree.getSelectionModel().setSelectionMode(
              TreeSelectionModel.SINGLE_TREE_SELECTION );

       // Make it so the root item in the tree is initially
       // selected.
       mTree.setSelectionRow( 0 );

       // Put the tree in a scroll pane since it may get
       // larger than the frame.
       JScrollPane scroller = new JScrollPane( mTree );

       // Place the scroll pane so it takes all of the
       // internal frame's area left after the toolbar was
       // placed.
       getContentPane().add( "Center", scroller );
   }

   // Load the tree's data.
   private MutableTreeNode generateTree()
   {
      DefaultMutableTreeNode root =
         new DefaultMutableTreeNode( getTitle() +
                                        " Root" );

      DefaultMutableTreeNode lev1a =
         new DefaultMutableTreeNode( getTitle() +
                                        " Level 1a" );
      DefaultMutableTreeNode lev1a2a =
         new DefaultMutableTreeNode( getTitle() +
                                        " Level 1a 2a" );
```

```
DefaultMutableTreeNode lev1a2b =
   new DefaultMutableTreeNode( getTitle() +
                                 " Level 1a 2b" );
DefaultMutableTreeNode lev1a2c =
   new DefaultMutableTreeNode( getTitle() +
                                 " Level 1a 2c" );
lev1a.add( lev1a2a );
lev1a.add( lev1a2b );
lev1a.add( lev1a2c );
lev1a2a.setAllowsChildren( false );
lev1a2b.setAllowsChildren( false );
lev1a2c.setAllowsChildren( false );

DefaultMutableTreeNode lev1b =
        new DefaultMutableTreeNode( getTitle() +
                                     " Level 1b" );
DefaultMutableTreeNode lev1b2a =
        new DefaultMutableTreeNode( getTitle() +
                                     " Level 1b 2a" );
DefaultMutableTreeNode lev1b2b =
        new DefaultMutableTreeNode( getTitle() +
                                     " Level 1b 2b" );
DefaultMutableTreeNode lev1b2c =
        new DefaultMutableTreeNode( getTitle() +
                                     " Level 1b 2c" );
lev1b.add( lev1b2a );
lev1b.add( lev1b2b );
lev1b.add( lev1b2c );
lev1b2a.setAllowsChildren( false );
lev1b2b.setAllowsChildren( false );
lev1b2c.setAllowsChildren( false );

DefaultMutableTreeNode lev1c =
        new DefaultMutableTreeNode( getTitle() +
                                     " Level 1c" );
DefaultMutableTreeNode lev1c2a =
        new DefaultMutableTreeNode( getTitle() +
                                     " Level 1c 2a" );
DefaultMutableTreeNode lev1c2b =
        new DefaultMutableTreeNode( getTitle() +
                                     " Level 1c 2b" );
DefaultMutableTreeNode lev1c2c =
        new DefaultMutableTreeNode( getTitle() +
                                     " Level 1c 2c" );
lev1c.add( lev1c2a );
lev1c.add( lev1c2b );
lev1c.add( lev1c2c );
lev1c2a.setAllowsChildren( false );
lev1c2b.setAllowsChildren( false );
lev1c2c.setAllowsChildren( false );

root.add( lev1a );
root.add( lev1b );
root.add( lev1c );
```

```
            return root;
        }

        // Return the currently selected node.
        public MutableTreeNode getSelectedNode()
        {
            return (MutableTreeNode)mTree.getSelectionPath().
                                        getLastPathComponent();
        }

        // Delete the selected node.
        public void deleteSelectedNode()
        {
            // Get the tree model.
            DefaultTreeModel model =
                        (DefaultTreeModel)mTree.getModel();

            // Find the selected node.
            MutableTreeNode node =
                (MutableTreeNode)mTree.getSelectionPath().
                                getLastPathComponent();

            // We don't allow deleting the root node.
            if ( node != model.getRoot() )
            {
                // Get the parent of the node to be deleted.
                MutableTreeNode parent =
                                (MutableTreeNode)node.getParent();

                // Get the node's index so we can decide which
                // node to set as selected after this one is
                // deleted.
                int index = parent.getIndex( node );

                // Remove the node from its parent.
                model.removeNodeFromParent( node );

                // 'newSelection' will be the node that is
                // selected.
                MutableTreeNode newSelection;

                if ( parent.getChildCount() == 0 )
                {
                    // If the parent now has no children, make it
                    // the selected item.
                    newSelection = parent;
                }
                else if ( index >= parent.getChildCount() )
                {
                    // If the deleted node was the bottom child,
                    // set the one that was before it to be
                    // selected.
                    newSelection =
                                (MutableTreeNode)parent.getChildAt(
                                                    index - 1 );
```

```
            }
            else
            {
                // Set the node that used to be after the
                // deleted one to be the selected one.
                newSelection =
                    (MutableTreeNode)parent.getChildAt( index );
            }

            // Find the path from the root node to the one
            // that will be selected.  Notice that
            // getPathToRoot() actually returns an array of
            // tree nodes instead of a tree path, so we have
            // to use that array to create a tree path which
            // is what the setSelectionPath() method needs.
            TreePath rootToIndexNode =
                    new TreePath( model.getPathToRoot(
                                    newSelection ) );

            // Make the path selected.
            mTree.setSelectionPath( rootToIndexNode );
        }
    }

// Given a tree node, insert it after the currently
// selected item.
public void insertNode(
                    DefaultMutableTreeNode nodeToCopy )
{
    // Make a copy of the node and its children.
    DefaultMutableTreeNode newNode =
                    cloneNodeAndContents( nodeToCopy );

    // Get the tree model.
    DefaultTreeModel model =
                    (DefaultTreeModel)mTree.getModel();

    // Get the currently selected node.
    DefaultMutableTreeNode node =
        (DefaultMutableTreeNode)mTree.getSelectionPath().
                                getLastPathComponent();

    if ( node.getAllowsChildren() )
    {
        // If the selected node is expandable, add the
        // copy node as its first child.
        model.insertNodeInto( newNode, node, 0 );
    }
    else
    {
        // If the selected node is a leaf, add the copy
        // node directly after it.

        // Get the index where the copy node should be
        // inserted.
```

```
            int index = node.getParent().getIndex( node ) + 1;

            // Get the parent node.
            DefaultMutableTreeNode parent =
                    (DefaultMutableTreeNode)node.getParent();

            // Insert the node.
            model.insertNodeInto( newNode, parent, index );
        }
    }

    // Recursive method that, given a tree node, makes a
    // copy of it and its tree.
    private DefaultMutableTreeNode cloneNodeAndContents(
                            DefaultMutableTreeNode node )
    {
        // Clone this node.
        DefaultMutableTreeNode theClone =
                    (DefaultMutableTreeNode)node.clone();

        if ( node.getAllowsChildren() )
        {
            // For each of the node's children, call this
            // method again.
            int count = node.getChildCount();

            for ( int i = 0; i < count; i++ )
            {
                theClone.add( cloneNodeAndContents(
                    (DefaultMutableTreeNode)node.getChildAt(i)));
            }
        }

        // Return the cloned node.
        return theClone;
    }

    // Add classes that want to be notified when toolbar
    // buttons are pressed.
    public void addActionListener( ActionListener listener )
    {
        mActionListenerList.add( ActionListener.class,
                                listener );
    }

    // Remove listeners.
    public void removeActionListener(
                                ActionListener listener )
    {
        mActionListenerList.remove( ActionListener.class,
                                listener );
    }

    // Notify action listeners that one of the toolbar
    // buttons was pressed.
```

```
protected void fireActionEvent( ActionEvent e )
{
    // Get the list of listeners.
    Object[] listeners =
                    mActionListenerList.getListenerList();

    // Create a new event just like the one that came
    // from the toolbar button, except with this class as
    // its source.
    ActionEvent newEvent = new ActionEvent( this,
                                e.getID(),
                                e.getActionCommand() );

    // Call each listener's actionPerformed() method.
    for ( int i = listeners.length-2; i >= 0; i -=2 )
    {
        if ( listeners[i] == ActionListener.class )
        {
            ((ActionListener)listeners[i+1]).
                            actionPerformed( newEvent );
        }
    }
}

// When one of the toolbar buttons is pressed, fire an
// action event to the listening classes.
public void actionPerformed( ActionEvent e )
{
    fireActionEvent( e );
}
}
```

SUMMARY ▬ ▬ ▬ ▬ ▬ ▬ ▬ ▬

I have explained how the tree-related classes interact in Chapter 7, "JFC by Concept," gone into the details of those classes in Chapter 8, "JFC by Class", and used some of them in Chapter 10, "Integrating JFC Example 1: A File Browser." However, it's difficult to understand how the classes work together without seeing an example dedicated to showing exactly that. This chapter has, I hope, filled any gaps left from previous ones.

12

Integrating JFC Example 3: A Simple Paint Program

One of the standard GUI applications is the paint application. It usually has a toolbar that lets the user choose from several drawing tools and a color palette that can be applied to the drawing's elements. This example shows how to make a simple paint application by using the JFC. It does not have all the features a commercial paint application would have, but it shows that the JFC can be used to create the kinds of user interface applications people expect these days. Figure 12-1 shows a typical paint session.

Figure 12-1
A typical GUI paint
application.

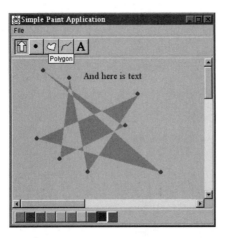

The Application

This example has three main parts:

■ A toolbar that displays drawing tools, including a selection tool, dot tool, polygon tool, polyline tool, and text tool.

■ A toolbar that displays the current color palette, which is generated randomly.

■ The main drawing area encased in a scroll pane. All drawing takes place in this area.

The way this application works is that you select a tool and draw a dot, polyline, polygon, or text string. The element currently being drawn is highlighted either by small squares around the element's points or, for text elements, a JTextField that's actually displayed where the text should go. The current element's color can be changed by selecting a different button from the color palette.

You can make an already drawn element the current element by choosing the select tool and clicking on the element. The algorithm that decides which element you just clicked is fairly simple.

In the color palette, you can change a button's color by right-clicking on the button. This action brings up a JColorChooser dialog where you can choose a new color. After you click the dialog's OK button, the new color is applied to the palette button. If the palette button is the currently selected button, the new color is also applied to the current element being drawn.

Both the drawing toolbar and color toolbar contain JToggleButtons, which are grouped within ButtonGroups so that only one button can be selected at a time within a toolbar.

The following sections cover each class in the example, explain which JFC classes it uses and why, and discuss how it interacts with the other classes in the example.

Test.java

This simple class contains the main() method, which just creates an instance of the Test class. Test's constructor creates an instance of the main frame class and makes sure the application ends when the frame's close button is clicked. This class uses a Window/Adapter to make sure the application closes when the main window closes. It also uses two methods from the UIManager class. These are the getSystemLookAndFeelClassName() and setLookAndFeel() methods.

Here's the source code:

```java
import com.sun.java.swing.*;
import java.awt.event.*;

public class Test
{
    public Test()
    {
        // Use the system's native look-and-feel.
        String lf = UIManager.getSystemLookAndFeelClassName();

        if ( lf != null )
        {
            try
            {
                UIManager.setLookAndFeel( lf );
            }
            catch ( Exception ex )
            {
                ex.printStackTrace();
            }
        }

        // Create the main frame.
        MyFrame mf = new MyFrame();

        // Make it so this class catches the main frame's
        // window events.
        mf.addWindowListener( new MyWindowAdapter() );

        // Size the main frame.
        mf.setSize( 400, 400 );

        // Display the main frame.
        mf.show();
    }

    // This class is used to catch the main frame's window
    // closing event which is generated when the frame's
    // close button is pressed.  It causes the application
    // to end when that event is received.
    private class MyWindowAdapter extends WindowAdapter
```

```
    {
        public void windowClosing( WindowEvent e )
        {
            System.exit( 0 );
        }
    }

    // The main method — just creates an instance of this
    // class.
    public static void main( String args[] )
    {
        new Test();
    }
}
```

MyFrame.java

This class is a subclass of JFrame and serves as the main workspace for the example. It does the following:

■ Creates a menu bar with a File menu that contains an Exit item.

■ Creates the toolbar that contains the color palette, and places it at the bottom of the frame.

■ Creates the toolbar that contains the drawing tools, and places it at the top of the frame.

■ Creates the main drawing area, passing in the color toolbar and the drawing toolbar.

■ Creates a JScrollPane, so the user can scroll around the main drawing area, and places it in the center of the frame.

JFC CLASSES USED IN MYFRAME.JAVA   Following is a list of the JFC classes used in MyFrame.java, including how and why they were used:

■ **JFrame:** MyFrame is a subclass of JFrame. The only interesting thing is how the menu bar, the two toolbars, and the JScrollPane containing the main drawing area are added to the frame through its root pane.

■ **JPanel:** We use a JPanel as a reference to the frame's content pane so we aren't constantly calling the frame's getContentPane() method. The toolbars and scroll pane are added to it.

■ **JMenuBar:** We create a JMenuBar and tell the frame's root pane to use it as the main menu bar.

■ **JMenu:** The menu bar contains a single JMenu labeled "File." This JMenu contains a single JMenuItem that's used as a way for the user to end the application.

- **JMenuItem:** The JMenu's single JMenuItem is labeled "Exit." MyFrame listens for when this item generates an ActionEvent, signaling that it has been pressed. When that happens, the application exits.

- **JRootPane:** This class is used indirectly to get the frame's content pane and to set its menu bar. The root pane is accessed by using the JFrame's getRootPane() method. The content pane is accessed through the JFrame's getContentPane() method, which is a convenience method that's the same as calling getRootPane().getContentPane(). The frame's menu bar is set by calling getRootPane().setMenuBar(mbar).

- **JScrollPane:** The main drawing area is too big to be shown all at once, so it's necessary to use a JScrollPane that the user can scroll around to see the entire drawing area. We do this by passing the main drawing area to the JScrollPane's constructor. Then we add the JScrollPane so it fills the center of the frame.

RELATIONSHIPS TO OTHER CLASSES IN THE EXAMPLE Here's how MyFrame interacts with other classes in the example:

- **Test.java:** The Test class creates MyFrame and causes it to be displayed.

- **ColorToolBar.java:** MyFrame creates the ColorToolBar, which is the toolbar that holds the color palette. It places the ColorToolBar on the bottom edge of the frame and passes it as an argument to DrawArea —the main drawing class.

- **PaintToolBar.java:** MyFrame creates the PaintToolBar, which is the toolbar that contains the drawing tools. It places the PaintToolBar along the top edge of the frame, just under the menu bar. Then it passes the PaintToolBar to DrawArea through its constructor.

- **DrawArea.java:** MyFrame creates DrawArea, which is where all the drawing takes place. It passes the ColorToolBar and PaintToolBar to DrawArea's constructor. MyFrame then adds DrawArea to a JScrollPane so the user can see and work in the whole thing.

Here's the source for MyFrame.java:

```
import com.sun.java.swing.*;
import java.awt.*;
import java.awt.event.*;

public class MyFrame extends JFrame implements
        ActionListener
{
    public MyFrame()
    {
        setTitle( "Simple Paint Application" );
```

```java
// Store the content pane in a variable for easier
// access.
JPanel contentPane = (JPanel)getContentPane();

// Create the menu bar.
JMenuBar mbar = new JMenuBar();

// Create the "File" menu.
JMenu fileMenu = new JMenu( "File" );

// Add the menu to the menu bar.
mbar.add( fileMenu );

// Create an "Exit" item.
JMenuItem exitItem = new JMenuItem( "Exit" );

// Add the menu item to the menu.
fileMenu.add( exitItem );

// Associate a command string with the menu item.
exitItem.setActionCommand( "exit" );

// Designate a class to listen for when the menu item
// is pressed.
exitItem.addActionListener( this );

// Tell the frame that this menu bar will be its main
// menu bar.
getRootPane().setMenuBar( mbar );

// We use a border layout so we can place the tool
// bars around the edges and the main scrolling pane
// in the middle.
contentPane.setLayout( new BorderLayout() );

// Create the color palette tool bar.
ColorToolBar ctb = new ColorToolBar( 10 );

// Place the color palette tool bar along the frames
// bottom edge.
contentPane.add( "South", ctb );

// Create the drawing tool bar.
PaintToolBar ptb = new PaintToolBar();

// Place the drawing tool bar along the frame's top
// edge.
contentPane.add( "North", ptb );

// Create the main painting area.
DrawArea da = new DrawArea( ptb, ctb );

// Create a scroll pane that will allow the user to
// scroll around the drawing area.
JScrollPane scroller = new JScrollPane( da );
```

```
                    // Make the scroll pane take up the remaining part of
                    // the frame.
                    contentPane.add( "Center", scroller );
                }

                // This method is called when the "Exit" menu item is
                // pressed.  It will cause the application to close.
                public void actionPerformed( ActionEvent e )
                {
                    if ( e.getActionCommand().equals( "exit" ) )
                    {
                        System.exit( 0 );
                    }
                }
            }
        }
```

ColorToolBar.java

ColorToolBar is a subclass of JToolBar that's used to maintain the application's color palette. Its constructor takes an integer that specifies how many colors the palette should show. These colors are then generated randomly. Each color is held in a ColorButton that's a subclass of JToggleButton. These buttons are added to a ButtonGroup so that only one is selected at a time. ColorToolBar has a getColor() method other classes use to find out what color is currently selected.

Each time one of the ColorButtons is clicked, ColorToolBar captures the resulting ItemEvent. Also, ColorButtons can change their color, which generates a ChangeEvent when the changed button is also the currently selected button. ColorToolBar also captures these events. Clicking a ColorButton or changing the color of the selected ColorButton represents a change in the ColorToolBar's current color. In response to these events, ColorToolBar generates ChangeEvents. So that these ChangeEvents can be heard by other classes, ColorToolBar implements an EventListenerList that manages the list of registered ChangeListeners.

JFC CLASSES USED IN COLORTOOLBAR.JAVA The following are JFC classes used in this class, including how and why they were used:

■ **JToolBar:** ColorToolBar is a subclass of JToolBar. Presumably, we could have used a JPanel with a BoxLayout, but this way we get JToolBar's docking capabilities. ColorToolBar uses the add() method to add ColorButtons to the toolbar.

■ **ChangeListener:** A ColorButton generates a ChangeEvent when its color value is changed and it's the selected button. ColorToolBar implements the ChangeListener interface to capture those events. In response, it generates its own ChangeEvents to tell its listeners that its current color has changed.

- **ChangeEvent:** As just discussed, ColorToolBar implements the ChangeListener interface so it can capture the ColorButtons' ChangeEvents. When the color changes this way, or by the user clicking on a new ColorButton, ColorToolBar generates its own ChangeEvent and multicasts it to its registered ChangeListeners.

- **EventListenerList:** Because ColorToolBar needs to multicast ChangeEvents, it needs a way for other classes to register as ChangeListeners. It uses an EventListenerList to help with this task. It implements three methods: addChangeListener() registers a class that wants to be notified when the current color changes, removeChangeListener() tells ColorToolBar that a class no longer wants to be notified, and fireChangeEvent() actually goes through the list of registered ChangeListeners and calls their stateChanged() methods. When the listeners hear that the ColorToolBar's current color has changed, they have to call its getColor() method to find out the new color.

- **ButtonGroup:** The color palette is displayed as a set of colored toggle buttons called "ColorButtons." Because only one color can be chosen at a time, only one ColorButton should be able to be selected at a time. We do this by adding the ColorButtons to a ButtonGroup, much as we do with JRadioButtons. The ButtonGroup makes sure only one ColorButton is selected. ColorToolBar calls ButtonGroup's add() method to add ColorButtons to the group.

- **JToggleButton:** ColorToolBar interacts with JToggleButton only indirectly—as the superclass of ColorButtons. It calls the JToggleButton setSelected() method to set the first ColorButton as the initially selected one.

- **BoxLayout:** JToolBar's default layout manager is BoxLayout. ColorToolBar inherits this property.

RELATIONSHIPS TO OTHER CLASSES IN THE EXAMPLE   Here's how ColorToolBar interacts with other classes in the example:

- **MyFrame.java:** MyFrame creates a ColorToolBar, places it on the frame, and passes it to DrawArea.

- **ColorButton.java:** ColorToolBar contains multiple ColorButtons, each of which represents a color in the color palette. When a new ColorButton is clicked, or the selected button's color changes, the button generates a ChangeEvent that ColorToolBar catches and passes on to any interested parties.

- **DrawArea.java:** DrawArea's constructor takes a ColorToolBar as one of its arguments. DrawArea registers itself as a ChangeListener so that it knows when ColorToolBar's current color changes.

Here's the source for ColorToolBar.java:

```java
import com.sun.java.swing.*;
import com.sun.java.swing.event.*;
import java.util.*;
import java.awt.*;
import java.awt.event.*;

public class ColorToolBar extends JToolBar implements
        ItemListener, ChangeListener
{
    // Store the current color so we can give it out when
    // asked.
    private Color mCurrentColor;

    // This helps manage the list of change listsners.
    private EventListenerList mChangeListeners;

    public ColorToolBar( int numColors )
    {
        super();

        float red, green, blue;

        // Initialize the class that will help us manage our
        // change listeners.
        mChangeListeners = new EventListenerList();

        // We will use random numbers to generate the color
        // palette.
        Random rand = new Random();

        // This will hold each of the tool bar's buttons as
        // they are created.
        ColorButton button;

        // We only want one of the color buttons pressed, so
        // we put them all into a ButtonGroup so only one can
        // be pressed at a time.
        ButtonGroup group = new ButtonGroup();

        for ( int i = 0; i < numColors; i++ )
        {
            // Generate random RGB values.
            red = rand.nextFloat();
            green = rand.nextFloat();
            blue = rand.nextFloat();

            // Create a color button with the new color.
            button = new ColorButton(
                            new Color( red, green, blue ) );

            // Listen for the buttons changes of state.
            button.addItemListener( this );

            // Listen for when the color of the pressed button
            // is changed.
```

```
      button.addChangeListener( this );

      // Make the first button the selected one.
      if ( i == 0 )
         button.setSelected( true );

      // Add the button to the tool bar.
      add( button );

      // Add the button to the button group.
      group.add( button );
   }
}

// Return the tool bar's currently selected color.
public Color getColor()
{
   return mCurrentColor;
}

// Other classes can register to listen for changes in
// the tool bar's current color.  This method is used to
// register a class to be notified when the current
// color changes.
public void addChangeListener( ChangeListener listener )
{
   mChangeListeners.add( ChangeListener.class,
                         listener );
}

// If a class no longer wants to know when the tool bar's
// current color changes, it can un-register itself
// using this method.
public void removeChangeListener(
                         ChangeListener listener )
{
   mChangeListeners.remove( ChangeListener.class,
                            listener );
}

// This causes a change event to be multicast to all
// registered change listeners.
protected void fireChangeEvent( ChangeEvent newEvent )
{
   // Get the listener class type / listener class
   // instance pairs.
   Object[] listeners =
               mChangeListeners.getListenerList();

   // We step through the pairs from last to first.  The
   // first is the pair is the class type, then is the
   // class instance.  This is why we step through the
   // list two at a time.
   for ( int i = listeners.length-2; i >= 0; i -= 2 )
   {
```

```
                    // Make sure this listener is the right type.
                    if ( listeners[i] == ChangeListener.class )
                    {
                        ((ChangeListener)listeners[i+1]).stateChanged(
                                                        newEvent );
                    }
                }
            }
        }

        // This method is called when a new color button is
        // pressed.
        public void itemStateChanged( ItemEvent e )
        {
            if ( e.getStateChange() == ItemEvent.SELECTED )
            {
                // Change the tool bar's current color.
                mCurrentColor =
                        ((ColorButton)e.getSource()).getColor();

                // Create a new change event to be sent to all
                // registered ChangeListeners.
                ChangeEvent evt = new ChangeEvent( this );

                // Cause the event to be sent out.
                fireChangeEvent( evt );
            }
        }

        // This is called when a color button's color is changed
        // by bringing up and using the color chooser.
        public void stateChanged( ChangeEvent e )
        {
            // Change the tool bar's current color.
            mCurrentColor =
                        ((ColorButton)e.getSource()).getColor();

            // Create a new event to be sent to all registered
            // listeners.
            ChangeEvent evt = new ChangeEvent( this );

            // Send the event out.
            fireChangeEvent( evt );
        }
    }
```

ColorButton.java

ColorButton is a subclass of JToggleButton and paints its main area with the color it represents. A set of ColorButtons represents the application's color palette. The ColorButton's color is initially set through its constructor, and can later be changed with a JColorChooser that can be brought up by right-clicking the ColorButton. The JColorChooser comes up in a dialog; when the user chooses a new color and clicks the dialog's OK button, the new color is applied to the ColorButton. When a ColorButton is clicked, it generates an ItemEvent as part of its JToggleButton ancestry. When the color is changed with the JColorChooser, the button generates a ChangeEvent if it's currently selected. We don't need special management of ChangeListeners as ColorToolBar did because JToggleButton takes care of it for us.

JFC CLASSES USED IN COLORBUTTON.JAVA   Following is a list of the JFC classes used in ColorButton.java, including how and why they were used:

▓ **JToggleButton:** ColorButton is a subclass of JToggleButton because we needed a control that could show a color and show clearly that it was selected. We could also use the controls' ability to be added to a ButtonGroup, making sure only one was selected at a time. We called the setBackground() method to give the ColorButton the SystemColor used for buttons and the setMargin() method to remove the default padding around the main button area. We called setToolTipText() to specify that the ColorButton could show its RGB value to the user. We overrode getMinimumSize(), getPreferredSize(), and getMaximumSize() so that the ColorButtons would be layed out as we wanted. We overrode the paintComponent() method so we could draw on the button's main area without messing up the border because the border is so important in showing the selection state. We overrode the processMouseEvent() method so we could use the right-click to trigger the display of the color chooser dialog without causing the button to become selected. We used the getInsets() method to find out the extent of the border so we didn't paint over it in paintComponent().

▓ **JColorChooser:** ColorButton uses a JColorChooser to set a new color. It calls the showDialog() method to display a JColorChooser in a dialog. It could have used the createDialog() method instead, which, although it takes a little more work, gives more flexibility in relocating the dialog. The showDialog() method returns the new color if its OK button is clicked or null if its Cancel button is clicked. You should notice that the JColorChooser is part of the com.sun.java. swing.preview package. This means that its API is likely to change in the next JFC release. It also means that the class has a few bugs.

▓ **ChangeEvent:** ColorButton generates a ChangeEvent when its color is changed with the color chooser, but only if it's the currently selected ColorButton. There seems little point in notifying others that a button's color has changed when the button isn't in use. ColorButton uses its ancestor's fireStateChange() method to tell registered ChangeListeners that the color has changed. Listeners have to call the ColorButton's getColor() method to find out what the change was.

RELATIONSHIPS TO OTHER CLASSES IN THE EXAMPLE Here's how ColorButton interacts with other classes in the example:

■ **ColorToolBar:** This class creates and contains multiple ColorButtons. It catches the ItemEvents generated when one is selected, as well as the ChangeEvents generated when the selected ColorButton's color is changed. ColorToolBar acts as a layer between the ColorButtons and the rest of the example, so ColorButton doesn't interact with any other classes.

Here's the source for ColorButton.java:

```java
import java.awt.*;
import java.awt.event.*;
import com.sun.java.swing.*;
import com.sun.java.swing.preview.*;
import com.sun.java.swing.event.*;

public class ColorButton extends JToggleButton
{
    // The size of the button, not counting the border.
    private final int WIDTH = 16;
    private final int HEIGHT = 16;

    // The button's current color.
    private Color mColor;

    public ColorButton( Color initialColor )
    {
        super();

        // Make the button's background into the system color
        // of buttons.
        setBackground( SystemColor.control );

        // Set the current color to the passed-in color.
        mColor = initialColor;

        // Remove the default padding around the button's
        // icon.
        setMargin( new Insets( 0, 0, 0, 0 ) );

        // Make it so the button's too tip shows the button's
        // RGB value.
        setToolTipText( mColor.getRed() + "," +
                        mColor.getGreen() + "," +
                        mColor.getBlue() );
    }

    // Return the button's current color.
    public Color getColor()
    {
        return mColor;
```

```
}

// Calculate the button's preferred size based on the
// inner size and the border size.
public Dimension getPreferredSize()
{
   // getInsets() gets the size of the border.  Add it
   // to the inner size of the button and you get the
   // size at which the button should be displayed.
   int width = getInsets().left + WIDTH +
              getInsets().right;
   int height = getInsets().top + HEIGHT +
              getInsets().bottom;

   return new Dimension( width, height );
}

// The button should not display smaller than the
// preferred size, or the icon will not show up
// properly.
public Dimension getMinimumSize()
{
   return getPreferredSize();
}

// The button does not look as good if it is expanded so
// it has extra space around the icon.
public Dimension getMaximumSize()
{
   return getPreferredSize();
}

// This method is called by JToggleButton's paint()
// method to paint the part of the button within the
// border.  We just fill it with the button's current
// color.
public void paintComponent( Graphics g )
{
   // Make sure we don't draw on the border.
   int x = getInsets().left;
   int y = getInsets().top;

   // Fill a rectangle covering the button's inner area.
   g.setColor( mColor );
   g.fillRect( x, y, WIDTH, HEIGHT );
}

// We override this method so we can catch a right-click
// before it causes the button to be selected.  The
// right-click will cause a color chooser to come up
// allowing the user to change the button's color.
protected void processMouseEvent( MouseEvent e )
{
   // Check to see if the click is a right-click and the
   // event is a mouse pressed event.  We don't want to
```

```
                    // catch the other mouse events (released, clicked,
                    // entered, exited).
                    if ( (e.getModifiers() &
                         InputEvent.BUTTON3_MASK) != 0 &&
                         e.getID() == MouseEvent.MOUSE_PRESSED )
                    {
                        // Display the color chooser and get the color it
                        // returns.
                        Color newColor = JColorChooser.showDialog( this,
                                        "Choose a color", mColor );

                        // If the color chooser's Ok button was pressed,
                        // the return has the new color.  Otherwise it is
                        // null.
                        if ( newColor != null )
                        {
                            // Store the changed color.
                            mColor = newColor;

                            // Update the tool tip to show the changed
                            // color.
                            setToolTipText( mColor.getRed() + "," +
                                            mColor.getGreen() + "," +
                                            mColor.getBlue() );

                            // Cause the button to reflect the change.
                            repaint();

                            // If the changed button is the currently
                            // selected one, cause any change listeners to
                            // be notified so the element being drawn can
                            // be updated.
                            if ( isSelected() )
                            {
                                // Cause the event to be sent to all
                                // registered ChangeListeners.
                                fireStateChanged();
                            }
                        }
                    }
                    else
                    {
                        // Pass the event through for default processing.
                        super.processMouseEvent( e );
                    }
                }
            }
```

PaintToolBar.java

PaintToolBar is a subclass of JToolBar. It contains a set of JToggleButtons that
represent the tools that can be used for drawing. These tools are for selecting

already drawn elements, drawing polygons, drawing polylines, drawing dots, and drawing text. PaintToolBar defines a set of constants—one for each tool. Other classes can call its getTool() method to find out which tool is currently selected. The JToggleButtons are added to a ButtonGroup so that only one tool can be selected at a time. When a new tool is selected, PaintToolBar generates an ActionEvent. Because JToolBar doesn't already handle ActionListeners, PaintToolBar had to use an EventListenerList to take care of them.

JFC CLASSES USED IN PAINTTOOLBAR   Following is a list of the JFC classes used in PaintToolBar.java, including how and why they were used:

■ **JToolBar:** PaintToolBar is a subclass of this class. JToolBar was selected because it already has the functionality to contain a set of buttons in a row, and it can be docked. The add() method is used to add JToggleButtons to the toolbar.

■ **EventListenerList:** PaintToolBar uses this class to help manage its ActionListeners. It implements addActionListener() to register new ActionListeners, removeActionListener() to stop sending events to a class, and fireActionEvent() to cause an ActionEvent to be multicast to all registered listeners.

■ **ButtonGroup:** All the JToggleButtons are added to a Button group so that only one can be selected at a time. They are added with ButtonGroup's add() method. When PaintToolBar's getTool() method is called, it calls ButtonGroup's getSelection() method to help find out which of the JToggleButtons is currently selected.

■ **JToggleButton:** As discussed, each of the tools in PaintToolBar is represented as a JToggleButton. Each JToggleButton is created with only an icon—no text. The default padding around the icon is removed by using the setMargin() method. Each JToggleButton sets its own action command string with setActionCommand(), which helps differentiate between them. Because the buttons have no text, we gave them tool tips by using setToolTipText().

RELATIONSHIPS TO OTHER CLASSES IN THE EXAMPLE   Here's how PaintToolBar interacts with other classes in the example:

■ **MyFrame.java:** MyFrame creates the PaintToolBar, places it along the frame's top edge just under the menu bar, and passes it to the DrawArea's constructor.

■ **DrawArea.java:** When DrawArea is ready to draw a new element, it asks the PaintToolBar which tool is active by calling its getTool() method. DrawArea also captures the ActionEvents that PaintToolBar generates when the user selects a new tool. In response, it closes out whatever drawing it's currently doing and prepares to start something new.

Here's the source for PaintToolBar.java:

```java
import java.awt.*;
import java.awt.event.*;
import com.sun.java.swing.*;
import com.sun.java.swing.event.*;

public class PaintToolBar extends JToolBar implements
        ActionListener
{
    // Use this class to help manage action listeners.
    private EventListenerList mActionListenerList;

    // We use this group to make sure that only one of the
    // tool bar's buttons is pressed at a time.  We also use
    // it to find out which button is the currently selected
    // one.
    private ButtonGroup mGroup;

    // Constants referring to the tool bar's buttons.
    public static final int SELECT   = 0;
    public static final int POLYGON  = 1;
    public static final int POLYLINE = 2;
    public static final int DOT      = 3;
    public static final int TEXT     = 4;

    public PaintToolBar()
    {
        // Initialize the class that will help us manage
        // action listeners.
        mActionListenerList = new EventListenerList();

        // Create the first button.
        JToggleButton select = new JToggleButton(
                            new ImageIcon( "select.gif" ) );

        // Get rid of the default padding around the icon.
        select.setMargin( new Insets( 0, 0, 0, 0 ) );

        // Specify a string that will differentiate this
        // button from the others.
        select.setActionCommand( "PaintToolBar - select" );

        // Cause this class to be notified when the button is
        // pressed.
        select.addActionListener( this );

        // Set its tool tip.
        select.setToolTipText( "Select" );

        // Add the button to the tool bar.
        add( select );

        // Do the same for the second button as we did for
```

```
    // the first.
    JToggleButton dot = new JToggleButton(
                     new ImageIcon( "dot.gif" ) );
    dot.setMargin( new Insets( 0, 0, 0, 0 ) );
    dot.setActionCommand( "PaintToolBar - dot" );
    dot.addActionListener( this );
    dot.setToolTipText( "Dot" );
    add( dot );

    // Do the same for the third button as we did for the
    // first.
    JToggleButton polygon = new JToggleButton(
                     new ImageIcon( "polygon.gif" ) );
    polygon.setMargin( new Insets( 0, 0, 0, 0 ) );
    polygon.setActionCommand( "PaintToolBar - polygon" );
    polygon.addActionListener( this );
    polygon.setToolTipText( "Polygon" );
    add( polygon );

    // Do the same for the fourth button as we did for
    // the first.
    JToggleButton polyline = new JToggleButton(
                    new ImageIcon( "polyline.gif" ) );
    polyline.setMargin( new Insets( 0, 0, 0, 0 ) );
    polyline.setActionCommand( "PaintToolBar - polyline" );
    polyline.addActionListener( this );
    polyline.setToolTipText( "Polyline" );
    add( polyline );

    // Do the same for the fifth button as we did for the
    // first.
    JToggleButton text = new JToggleButton(
                     new ImageIcon( "text.gif" ) );
    text.setMargin( new Insets( 0, 0, 0, 0 ) );
    text.setActionCommand( "PaintToolBar - text" );
    text.addActionListener( this );
    text.setToolTipText( "Text" );
    add( text );

    // Create a button group and add the buttons into it
    // so only one can be selected at a time.
    mGroup = new ButtonGroup();
    mGroup.add( select );
    mGroup.add( dot );
    mGroup.add( polygon );
    mGroup.add( polyline );
    mGroup.add( text );

    // Make the select button initially set.
    select.setSelected( true );
}

// This returns the currently selected tool.
public int getTool()
{
```

```
            // Get the currently selected button's command string.
            String selected =
                        mGroup.getSelection().getActionCommand();

            // Use the selected button's command string to figure
            // out which button is selected.
            if ( selected.equals( "PaintToolBar - select" ) )
            {
               return SELECT;
            }
            else if ( selected.equals( "PaintToolBar - polygon" ) )
            {
               return POLYGON;
            }
            else if ( selected.equals(
                                  "PaintToolBar - polyline" ) )
            {
               return POLYLINE;
            }
            else if ( selected.equals( "PaintToolBar - dot" ) )
            {
               return DOT;
            }
            else
            {
               return TEXT;
            }
         }

         // This is called when one of the buttons is pressed.
         public void actionPerformed( ActionEvent e )
         {
            // Create a new action event like the one sent to
            // this method except that the source is changed to
            // this class.
            ActionEvent newEvent = new ActionEvent( this,
                                     e.getID(),
                                     e.getActionCommand() );

            // Cause all registered ActionListeners to be
            // notified that a tool change has taken place.
            fireActionEvent( newEvent );
         }

         // This method is called to register a class that will
         // be notified when the current tool changes.
         public void addActionListener( ActionListener listener )
         {
            mActionListenerList.add( ActionListener.class,
                                     listener );
         }

         // If an action listener no longer wants to know about
         // tool changes, it can be un-registered.
         public void removeActionListener(
```

```
                                        ActionListener listener )
{
    mActionListenerList.remove( ActionListener.class,
                                listener );
}

// Cause the event to be sent to each registered
// ActionListener.
protected void fireActionEvent( ActionEvent newEvent )
{
    // Get the listener class type / listener class
    // instance pairs.
    Object[] listeners =
                mActionListenerList.getListenerList();

    // We step through the pairs from last to first.  The
    // first is the pair is the class type, then is the
    // class instance.  This is why we step through the
    // list two at a time.
    for ( int i = listeners.length-2; i >= 0; i -= 2 )
    {
        // Make sure this listener is the right type.
        if ( listeners[i] == ActionListener.class )
        {
            // Call the ActionListener method.
            ((ActionListener)listeners[i+1]).
                            actionPerformed( newEvent );
        }
    }
}
}
}
```

DrawArea.java

DrawArea, a subclass of JPanel, is where all the drawing happens. It keeps a list of all the elements that have already been created and controls their painting. DrawArea contains references to both the ColorToolBar and the PaintToolBar and listens to their events so that it knows when the current color changes or when a new tool has been selected.

Element drawing is in response to mouse clicks. When the mouse is clicked within the DrawArea, it first asks the PaintToolBar which tool is active. If the Select tool is active, DrawArea tries to figure out which (if any) existing element was clicked on. If the Dot tool is active, DrawArea creates a new DotElement with its center at the mouse click and adds it to its list of elements to draw.

If the Polygon tool is active, one of two things happens. If we're already drawing a polygon, the mouse click is just added as another point in the polygon. If not, DrawArea creates a new PolygonElement, adds the mouse click as its first point, and adds the PolygonElement to its list of things to draw. If the Polyline tool is active, it acts much like the Polygon tool. If we're already drawing a polyline, the mouse click is added as a new point. If not, a new PolylineElement is created, the mouse click is added as its first point, and the PolylineElement is added to DrawArea's list of things to draw.

If the Text tool is active, a new TextElement is created and added to the DrawArea's list of things to draw. A JTextField is created and placed at the mouse click so that the user can enter a text string.

The currently selected element (either just created or clicked on with the Select tool) looks different from other, not selected, elements. For DotElements, PolylineElements, and PolygonElements, each point of the selected element has a small square drawn around it. TextElements that are selected appear as JTextFields. If they're not selected, they are drawn as JLabels with a transparent background.

When the user chooses a new tool from the PaintToolBar, it ends any current editing going on and deselects the current element. When the user changes the ColorToolBar's current color, the change is applied to the current element, if there is one.

JFC CLASSES USED IN DRAWAREA.JAVA Following is a list of the JFC classes used in DrawArea.java, including how and why they were used:

- ■ **JPanel:** DrawArea is a subclass of JPanel as a good choice for a drawing canvas. It uses a null layout so that the TextElement's JTextField can be placed at the correct position when it's in use. DrawArea overrides the getMinimumSize(), getPreferredSize(), and getMaximumSize() methods to stay at the hard-coded size of 1000 × 1000 pixels. It also overrides the paint() method so it can draw the elements in its list. We could have overridden paintComponent() instead; then we wouldn't have had to call the paintChildren() method because the default paint() method does so for you. DrawArea uses the add() method to add the text field to its area and the validate() method to make sure the layout is valid.

- ■ **ChangeListener:** ColorToolBar generates ChangeEvents when its current color is changed by the user. DrawArea captures those events. When one is received, DrawArea calls the ColorToolBar's getColor() method to get the new color, then applies it to the current element, if any.

- ■ **JTextField:** A TextElement, when it's the current element, is displayed using a JTextField so that the user has full editing capabilities. This JTextField is gotten from the TextElement being edited. The JTextField goes away when the user selects another tool from the PaintToolBar or clicks the mouse outside the JTextField, but within the DrawArea.

RELATIONSHIPS TO OTHER CLASSES IN THE EXAMPLE Here's how DrawArea interacts with other classes in the example:

- **MyFrame.java:** MyFrame creates the DrawArea and puts it into a JScrollPane so the user can scroll around in it. MyFrame also creates the ColorToolBar and PaintToolBar that it passes to DrawArea's constructor.

- **ColorToolBar.java:** DrawArea listens for ColorToolBar's ChangeEvents, which signify that its current color has been changed. When DrawArea gets one of these events, it calls ColorToolBar's getColor() method to see what the new color is, and then applies it to the current element, if any.

- **PaintToolBar.java:** DrawArea listens for PaintToolBar's ActionEvents, which indicate that the user has selected a new tool. When DrawArea gets one of these events, it calls PaintToolBar's getTool() method, ends any editing, and deselects the current element, if any. DrawArea bases much of its activities on which tool is PaintToolBar's current one.

- **DotElement.java:** This class represents a dot to be drawn on DrawArea. While the Dot tool is selected in PaintToolBar, each mouse click within the DrawArea causes a new dot to be added to DrawArea's list of elements. DrawArea's paint() method calls this class's draw() method.

- **PolygonElement.java:** This class represents a polygon to be drawn on DrawArea. If the Polygon tool is selected in PaintToolBar, one of two things happens when the mouse is clicked. First, if there's no polygon currently being drawn, a new PolygonElement is created, added to DrawArea's list of elements, and given a single starting point. Second, if there's a polygon already in progress, the left click is added to the PolygonElement being drawn as its next point. DrawArea's paint() method calls this class's draw() method.

- **PolylineElement.java:** This class represents a polyline to be drawn on DrawArea. It works much like the PolygonElement—in fact, they are both descendants of the abstract class PolyElement. DrawArea's paint() method calls this class's draw() method.

- **TextElement.java:** This class represents a text string to be drawn on DrawArea. If the Text tool is selected in PaintToolBar, each time you click the mouse in the DrawArea, a new TextElement is created and added to DrawArea's list of elements. When the TextElement is the current element, it appears as a JTextField that the user can use to modify the text string. Other times, the text is drawn as a JLabel. DrawArea's paint() method calls this class's draw() method.

Here's the source for DrawArea.java:

```java
import com.sun.java.swing.*;
import com.sun.java.swing.event.*;
import java.awt.*;
import java.awt.event.*;
import java.util.*;

public class DrawArea extends JPanel implements
        ActionListener, ChangeListener, MouseListener
{
    // Stores the canvas' size.
    private Dimension mSize;

    // Stores the drawing tool bar.
    private PaintToolBar mPaintToolBar;

    // Stores the tool bar that controls the color.
    private ColorToolBar mColorToolBar;

    // Stores all elements to be drawn.
    private Vector mElements;

    // Stores the element that is currently active.
    private DrawingElement mCurrentElement;

    // Stores the text field that is used to edit a text
    // element when it is the active element.
    private JTextField mField;

    public DrawArea( PaintToolBar painttoolbar,
                     ColorToolBar colortoolbar )
    {
        // Hard code the size.
        mSize = new Dimension( 1000, 1000 );

        // Store the drawing tool bar.
        mPaintToolBar = painttoolbar;

        // Specify that this class wants to be notified when
        // a new tool is selected.
        mPaintToolBar.addActionListener( this );

        // Store the color tool bar.
        mColorToolBar = colortoolbar;

        // Specify that this class wants to be notified when
        // the color changes.
        mColorToolBar.addChangeListener( this );

        // Specify that this class wants to know when the
        // mouse is clicked in its area.
        addMouseListener( this );

        // Initialize the vector that will hold all of the
        // drawing elements.
        mElements = new Vector();
```

```
      // Set the layout to null so we can place the text
      // field where it needs to be.
      setLayout( null );
}


// This component always wants to be its hard-coded size.
public Dimension getMinimumSize()
{
   return mSize;
}


// This component always wants to be its hard-coded size.
public Dimension getPreferredSize()
{
   return mSize;
}


// This component always wants to be its hard-coded size.
public Dimension getMaximumSize()
{
   return mSize;
}


// Paint the drawing elements.
public void paint( Graphics g )
{
   // Draw the background rectangle.
   g.setColor( getBackground() );
   g.fillRect( 0, 0, getSize().width, getSize().height );

   // For each element to be drawn, draw.
   for ( Enumeration e = mElements.elements();
         e.hasMoreElements(); )
   {
      // Get the next element to be drawn.
      DrawingElement element =
                     (DrawingElement)e.nextElement();

      // If the element being drawn is the active one,
      // pass 'true' to its draw() method.
      if ( element == mCurrentElement )
         element.draw( g, true );
      else
         element.draw( g, false );
   }

   // This is required so the text field gets drawn.
   // This would happen automatically but we have to do
   // it since we overrode the paint method.
   paintChildren( g );
}


// This method locates the drawing element at the given
// point.
private DrawingElement findElementAt( int x, int y )
```

```
{
   DrawingElement closest = null;
   int lowDistance = 1000000;
   int thisDist;

   // For each drawing element...
   for ( Enumeration e = mElements.elements();
           e.hasMoreElements(); )
   {
       DrawingElement elem =
                    (DrawingElement)e.nextElement();

       // Ask the element how close to the given point it
       // gets.  This method returns -1 if the point is
       // not within the element's bounding box or a
       // greater number that is the distance in pixels
       // from the point to the element's closest point.
       thisDist = elem.getClosestPoint( x, y );

       // If the point is within the element's bounding
       // box...
       if ( thisDist >= 0 )
       {
           // If this is the closest element yet, keep
           // track of which element it is.
           if ( lowDistance > thisDist )
           {
               lowDistance = Math.min( lowDistance,
                                          thisDist );
               closest = elem;
           }
       }
   }

   // Return the element that was closest.  It may be
   // null.
   return closest;
}

// This method is called when the drawing tool bar's
// current tool is changed.
public void actionPerformed( ActionEvent e )
{
   // If the text field is active, make it go away.
   getRidOfTextField();

   // Set the current element to null since it is no
   // longer active when the tool changes.
   mCurrentElement = null;

   // Repaint.  This makes it so the squares that mark
   // the active element are removed.
   repaint();
}
```

```java
// Complete the text element edit.
private void getRidOfTextField()
{
    // If the text field is active, there should be an
    // active element and it should be a text element.
    if ( mField != null && mCurrentElement != null )
    {
        if ( mCurrentElement instanceof TextElement )
        {
            // Copy the text field's value into the text
            // element.
            ((TextElement)mCurrentElement).setText(
                                    mField.getText() );

            // Make it so the text field is no longer
            // contained in this panel.
            remove( mField );

            // Tell the text element to delete the text
            // field.
            ((TextElement)mCurrentElement).fieldDone();

            // Set the field null here since we are done
            // with it.
            mField = null;
        }
        else
        {
            System.out.println(
                    "Field not null, but not text element" );
        }
    }
}

// This is called when the color tool bar's current
// color changes.
public void stateChanged( ChangeEvent e )
{
    // If there is a currently active element, change
    // it's color to reflect the change in the color tool
    // bar.  Then repaint so the change is updated to the
    // screen.
    if ( mCurrentElement != null )
    {
        mCurrentElement.setColor(
                            mColorToolBar.getColor() );
        repaint();
    }
}

// Pressing the mouse has a different effect depending
// on the tool that is currently selected.
public void mousePressed( MouseEvent e )
{
    // If the text field is active, copy its contents to
```

```
            // the current element and remove it.
            getRidOfTextField();

            // Switch depending on the currently selected tool.
            switch( mPaintToolBar.getTool() )
            {
                case PaintToolBar.SELECT:

                    // Find which element (if any) we have just
                    // selected to become the active element.
                    mCurrentElement =
                            findElementAt( e.getX(), e.getY() );

                    // If the newly active element is a text
                    // element, make it so a text field shows up on
                    // the screen so the user can change the value.
                    if ( mCurrentElement instanceof TextElement )
                        activateTextField();

                    // Update the display.
                    repaint();

                    break;

                case PaintToolBar.POLYGON:

                    // If the active element is null, create a new
                    // polygon element.  Otherwise, the click
                    // represents the next point in the polygon.
                    if ( mCurrentElement == null )
                    {
                        // Create the polygon element.
                        mCurrentElement = new PolygonElement();

                        // Set its color.
                        mCurrentElement.setColor(
                                mColorToolBar.getColor() );

                        // Add the polygon element to the list of
                        // elements on the canvas.
                        mElements.addElement( mCurrentElement );
                    }

                    // Add the mouse-click point to the polygon
                    // element.
                    mCurrentElement.addPoint(
                            new Point( e.getX(), e.getY() ) );

                    // Update the display to show the addition.
                    repaint();

                    break;

                case PaintToolBar.POLYLINE:
```

```
                // If the current element is null, we need to
                // create a new polyline element.
                if ( mCurrentElement == null )
                {
                    // Create the polyline element.
                    mCurrentElement = new PolylineElement();

                    // Set the element's color.
                    mCurrentElement.setColor(
                                mColorToolBar.getColor() );

                    // Add the element to the list of elements
                    // to be drawn.
                    mElements.addElement( mCurrentElement );
                }

                // Add the mouse-click point to the polyline.
                mCurrentElement.addPoint(
                            new Point( e.getX(), e.getY() ) );

                // Update the display to show the added point.
                repaint();

                break;

            case PaintToolBar.DOT:

                // Create a new dot element.
                mCurrentElement = new DotElement();

                // Set the dot's center point.
                mCurrentElement.addPoint(
                            new Point( e.getX(), e.getY() ) );

                // Set the dot's color.
                mCurrentElement.setColor(
                                mColorToolBar.getColor() );

                // Add the dot to the elements to be drawn.
                mElements.addElement( mCurrentElement );

                // Update the display to show the added dot.
                repaint();

                break;

            case PaintToolBar.TEXT:

                // Create a new text element.
                mCurrentElement =
                            new TextElement( "Text Field" );

                // Set the point at which the element will draw.
                mCurrentElement.addPoint(
                            new Point( e.getX(), e.getY() ) );
```

```
                      // Set the element's color.
                      mCurrentElement.setColor(
                                            mColorToolBar.getColor() );

                      // Add the text element to the list of elements
                      // to be drawn.
                      mElements.addElement( mCurrentElement );

                      // Cause a text field to be drawn so the user
                      // can edit the text.
                      activateTextField();

                      // Update the display to show the addition.
                      repaint();

                      break;
            }
    }

    // Get a text field from the current text element and
    // place it on the screen.
    private void activateTextField()
    {
        // Get the pre-loaded, pre-placed text field.
        mField =
                ((TextElement)mCurrentElement).getTextField();

        // Add the text field to the panel.
        add( mField );

        // Cause the display to update.
        validate();
    }

    // Part of the MouseListener interface.
    public void mouseReleased( MouseEvent e )
    {
    }

    // Part of the MouseListener interface.
    public void mouseClicked( MouseEvent e )
    {
    }

    // Part of the MouseListener interface.
    public void mouseEntered( MouseEvent e )
    {
    }

    // Part of the MouseListener interface.
    public void mouseExited( MouseEvent e )
    {
    }
}
```

DrawingElement.java

DrawingElement is an interface that must be implemented by each type of element that DrawArea can draw. In this way, DrawArea can, as much as possible, treat the different types of elements the same. No JFC classes are used in this interface.

RELATIONSHIPS TO OTHER CLASSES IN THE EXAMPLE Here's how DrawingElement interacts with other classes in the example:

- **DrawArea.java:** All four of the methods specified in DrawingElement are called from DrawArea. DrawArea calls the draw() method to allow the DrawingElement to draw itself. It calls addPoint() to add the only point (in the case of Dot and Text elements) or to add another point (in the case of Polygon and Polyline elements). It calls setColor() when the ColorToolBar's current color changes, and it calls getClosestPoint() when it gets a mouse click and the Select tool is the PaintToolBar's active tool.
- **DotElement.java:** This class implements DrawingElement.
- **PolyElement.java:** This abstract class implements DrawingElement and is extended to create the PolygonElement and PolylineElement classes.
- **TextElement.java:** Implements DrawingElement. It's different from the other implementors in that its active state is represented by placing a JTextField on the DrawArea, instead of just slightly changing the way the element is painted.

Here's the source for DrawingElement.java:

```java
import java.awt.*;

// This interface defines the methods common to all of the
// drawing elements.
public interface DrawingElement
{
    // Draw the element.  Drawing is different if the
    // element is the active element.
    public void draw( Graphics g, boolean isActive );

    // Add a point to the element.  For dots and text, this
    // is the only point.
    public void addPoint( Point p );

    // Set the element's color.

    public void setColor( Color c );

    // Figure out how close the given point is to the
    // element.  This will return -1 if the point is not
    // within the element's bounding box.
```

```
        public int getClosestPoint( int x, int y );
    }
```

DotElement.java

DotElement implements the DrawingElement interface and represents a Dot
to be drawn in the DrawArea. A Dot is just a circle with a hard-coded radius
of four pixels drawn around a given center point. No JFC classes are used in
this class.

RELATIONSHIPS TO OTHER CLASSES IN THE EXAMPLE   Here's
how DotElement interacts with other classes in the example:

■ **DrawArea.java:** If the mouse is clicked within the DrawArea and
the PaintToolBar's current tool is the Dot tool, a new DotElement is
created and added to the DrawArea's list of elements to draw. At the
same time, the mouse-clicked point is passed to the DotElement to
serve as its center point. When the DotElement is created, or when a
DotElement is the current element and the ColorToolBar changes its
current color, DrawArea calls the DotElement's setColor() method to
change its color. When DrawArea paints, it calls each DotElement's
draw() method. When the Select tool is the current tool and the mouse
is clicked in the DrawArea, DrawArea goes through its list of elements, calling their getClosestPoint() methods in an attempt to find
out which element is the one the user wants.

Here's the source for DotElement.java:

```
import java.awt.*;

public class DotElement implements DrawingElement
{
    // Stores the dot's center point.
    private Point mPoint;

    // Stores the dot's color.
    private Color mColor;

    private static final int RADIUS = 4;

    public DotElement()
    {
    }

    // Allows the user to change the dot's color.
    public void setColor( Color c )
    {
        mColor = c;
```

```
    }

    // Draw the dot.  If it is the active element, draw a
    // square around it so the user knows it is the active
    // element.
    public void draw( Graphics g, boolean isActive )
    {
        int x = mPoint.x - RADIUS;
        int y = mPoint.y - RADIUS;
        int width = RADIUS * 2;
        int height = RADIUS * 2;

        g.setColor( mColor );
        g.fillOval( x, y, width, height );

        if ( isActive )
            g.drawRect( x, y, width, height );
    }

    // Set the dot's center point.
    public void addPoint( Point p )
    {
        mPoint = p;
    }

    // This method is intended to return the pixel distance
    // between this element and the given point, or -1 if it
    // is not in the element's bounding box.  This returns 0
    // if the point is in the element's bounding box or -1
    // if not.
    public int getClosestPoint( int x, int y )
    {
        int loX = mPoint.x - RADIUS;
        int loY = mPoint.y - RADIUS;
        int hiX = loX + RADIUS * 2;
        int hiY = loY + RADIUS * 2;

        if ( x >= loX && x <= hiX && y >= loY && y <= hiY )
        {
            return 0;
        }

        return -1;
    }
}
```

TextElement.java

This is perhaps the most complicated of the implementors of the
DrawingElement interface because it requires DrawArea to call methods
beyond the DrawingElement methods. The problem is that when a TextElement

is the current element, it doesn't draw itself on DrawArea as the other elements do. Instead, it causes a JTextField to be displayed within DrawArea so the user can edit its contents. When a TextElement is *not* the current element, it draws by using its draw() method as the other elements do.

When the Text tool is the PaintToolBar's active tool and the mouse is clicked in the DrawArea, a TextElement is created and added to the DrawArea's list of elements to draw. At that point, the TextElement is the DrawArea's current element. It can also become the current element when the Select tool is PaintToolBar's active tool and a TextElement is clicked on. When a TextElement becomes the current element, DrawArea asks the TextElement for a preloaded, preplaced JTextField so that the user can edit its text. DrawArea then adds the JTextField to itself. If the user selects another tool from the PaintToolBar or clicks outside the JTextField, the edited text is sent back to the TextElement, the TextElement is told that editing is complete, and the JTextField is removed from the DrawArea and set to null.

DrawArea calls a TextElement's setColor() method if the TextElement has just been created or if it's the current element and the ColorToolBar's current color changes. It calls a TextElement's getTextField() method to get a preloaded, preplaced JTextField when the TextElement becomes the current element. It calls the setText() method when editing is complete. It calls the draw() method when it's time to draw a TextElement; this method is called even when the TextElement is the current element, but returns immediately. DrawArea calls the addPoint() method to set the TextElement's upper-left corner, and calls getClosestPoint() when the Select tool is active and it's trying to figure out which element was clicked.

JFC CLASSES USED IN TEXTELEMENT.JAVA Following is a list of the JFC classes used in TextElement.java, including how and why they were used:

- **JTextField:** This class is used to allow the user to edit a TextElement's text string. It's created in a call to getTextField(), in which its color, font, and text are set so that it matches the current state of the TextElement. The setBounds() method is then called to size it to its preferred size and place it at its point. When editing is complete, DrawArea calls the JTextField's getText() method to get the edited string and pass it back to the TextElement.

- **JLabel:** TextElement uses a JLabel to draw its text string when the TextElement isn't the current element. It calls the setText() method to set the JLabel's text, the setForeground() method to set its text color, the setFont() method to set its font, the setSize() method to set its size, and the getPreferredSize() method to find out how big to size it.

RELATIONSHIPS TO OTHER CLASSES IN THE EXAMPLE Here's how TextElement interacts with other classes in the example:

■ **DrawArea.java:** DrawArea is responsible for creating TextElements and stores them in its list of elements to draw. It creates a TextElement when the Text tool is the PaintToolBar's active tool and the user clicks the mouse within the DrawArea. The other interactions are described at the start of the section discussing TextElement.java

Here's the source for TextElement.java:

```java
import java.awt.*;
import com.sun.java.swing.*;

public class TextElement implements DrawingElement
{
    // Stores the text's upper-left corner.
    private Point mPoint;

    // Stores the element's color.
    private Color mColor;

    // Stores the element's text string.
    private String mText;

    // Stores the element's text field which only exists
    // while the element is the active element.
    private JTextField mTextField;

    // Stores the label that is used to draw the element.
    private JLabel mTextLabel;

    // Stores the element's font.
    private Font mFont;

    public TextElement( String text )
    {
        // Store the element's initial value.
        mText = text;

        // Make the label used to draw the text.
        mTextLabel = new JLabel( text );

        // Initialize the font.
        mFont = new Font( "TimesRoman", Font.PLAIN, 18 );
    }

    // This creates a text field that can be displayed so
    // the user can edit this element's value.
    public JTextField getTextField()
    {
        // Create the field.
        mTextField = new JTextField( mText );

        // Set the field's font and color.
        mTextField.setFont( mFont );
        mTextField.setForeground( mColor );
```

```
            // Specify where the field should display and how
            // large it should be.
            mTextField.setBounds( mPoint.x, mPoint.y,
                            mTextField.getPreferredSize().width,
                            mTextField.getPreferredSize().height );

        return mTextField;
    }

    // This is typically called to set the element's text
    // after it has been edited.
    public void setText( String text )
    {
        mText = text;
        mTextLabel.setText( text );
    }

    // Change the element's color.  Make sure to also change
    // it in the text field if it is in use.
    public void setColor( Color c )
    {
        mColor = c;
        if ( mTextField != null )
            mTextField.setForeground( mColor );
    }

    // This informs us that the text field needs to be done
    // away with.
    public void fieldDone()
    {
        mTextField = null;
    }

    // Draw the text field as a JLabel.
    public void draw( Graphics g, boolean isActive )
    {
        // If the element is being edited, the text field is
        // already up, so there is no point drawing the label.
        if ( mTextField != null )
        {
            return;
        }

        int x = mPoint.x;
        int y = mPoint.y;

        // Translate the coordinates so the label draws in
        // the right place.
        g.translate( x, y );

        // Set the text field's font to match the element's.
        mTextLabel.setFont( mFont );

        // Size the text field properly.
```

```
        mTextLabel.setSize( mTextLabel.getPreferredSize() );

        // Set the text field's color to match the element's.
        mTextLabel.setForeground( mColor );

        // Tell the label to paint itself.
        mTextLabel.paint( g );

        // Un-translate.
        g.translate( -x, -y );
    }

    // Set the text field's upper-left corner.
    public void addPoint( Point p )
    {
        mPoint = p;
    }

    // If the given point is within the bounds of the text,
    // return 0 to say that this element should be made
    // active.  Otherwise return -1 to say it should not.
    public int getClosestPoint( int x, int y )
    {
        FontMetrics metrics =
          Toolkit.getDefaultToolkit().getFontMetrics( mFont );

        int width = metrics.stringWidth( mText );
        int height = metrics.getHeight();

        // Check to see if the point is within the text's
        // rectangle.
        if ( x >= mPoint.x && x <= mPoint.x + width &&
             y >= mPoint.y && y <= mPoint.y + height )
        {
            return 0;
        }

        return -1;
    }
}
```

PolyElement.java

PolyElement is an abstract class that implements the DrawingElement interface and contains the common functionality shared by the PolygonElement and PolylineElement classes that extend it. It implements the setColor(), addPoint(), and getClosestPoint() methods that PolygonElement and PolylineElement use. It also includes an empty draw() method that they override. No JFC classes are used in this class.

RELATIONSHIPS TO OTHER CLASSES IN THE EXAMPLE   Here's how PolyElement interacts with other classes in the example:

■ **PolygonElement.java:** PolyElement is PolygonElement's superclass. PolygonElement overrides the draw() method.

■ **PolylineElement.java:** PolyElement is PolylineElement's superclass. PolylineElement overrides the draw() method.

Here's the source for PolyElement.java:

```java
import java.awt.*;
import java.util.*;

// This is the superclass for PolygonElement and
// PolylineElement.  They provide their own constructors
// and override draw().
public abstract class PolyElement implements DrawingElement
{
    // Stores the element's points.
    protected Vector mPoints;

    // Stores the element's color.
    protected Color mColor;

    // Change the element's color.
    public void setColor( Color c )
    {
        mColor = c;
    }

    // Draw the element.
    public void draw( Graphics g, boolean isActive )
    {
    }

    // Add a point to the element's list of points.
    public void addPoint( Point p )
    {
        mPoints.addElement( p );
    }

    // Get the distance between two points.  This is used in
    // figuring out how close the element is to a given
    // point.
    private int getDistance( int x1, int y1, int x2, int y2 )
    {
        // Use the standard a squared plus b squared equals c
        // squared.
        double a = Math.pow( (double)(x2 - x1), 2.0 );
        double b = Math.pow( (double)(y2 - y1), 2.0 );
        double c = Math.sqrt( a + b );
```

```
        // Return a pixel distance.
        return (int)Math.rint( c );
}


// Given a point, this method attempts to figure out how
// close the point is to the element.  It actually
// checks each point in the element and returns the
// distance to the one that is closest to the given
// point.  It returns -1 if the given point is not
// within the element's bounding box.  This algorithm
// is not the best, but is good for this example.
public int getClosestPoint( int x, int y )
{
    int loX = 100000;
    int loY = 100000;
    int hiX = -100000;
    int hiY = -100000;
    int thisDist;
    int lowDist = 100000;

    // Figure out the element's bounding box which is
    // just its highest and lowest x and y values.  Also
    // use the getDistance() method to find out how close
    // the point is to the given point.  If it is closer
    // than the previously closest, it becomes the
    // closest.
    for ( Enumeration e = mPoints.elements();
            e.hasMoreElements(); )
    {
        Point p = (Point)e.nextElement();

        loX = Math.min( loX, p.x );
        loY = Math.min( loY, p.y );
        hiX = Math.max( hiX, p.x );
        hiY = Math.max( hiY, p.y );

        thisDist = getDistance( p.x, p.y, x, y );
        lowDist = Math.min( thisDist, lowDist );
    }

    // If the given point is not within the element's
    // bounding box, return -1.
    if ( x < loX || x > hiX || y < loY || y > hiY )
    {
        return -1;
    }

    // Return the distance from the given point to the
    // element's closest point.
    return lowDist;
}
}
```

PolygonElement.java

PolygonElement, a subclass of PolyElement, implements the DrawingElement interface. It represents a polygon that DrawArea will draw. When the Paint-ToolBar's active tool is the Polygon tool, and the user clicks in the DrawArea, one of two things happens. If we aren't currently making a polygon, a new PolygonElement is created and added to DrawArea's list of elements. Or, if we *are* currently making a polygon, the mouse click is added as the polygon's next point. No JFC classes are used in this class.

RELATIONSHIPS TO OTHER CLASSES IN THE EXAMPLE   Here's how PolygonElement interacts with other classes in the example:

■ **PolyElement.java:** This is PolygonElement's superclass that takes care of implementing the DrawingElement interface except for the draw() method, which PolygonElement takes care of.

■ **DrawArea.java:** DrawArea creates PolygonElements and stores them in its list of things to draw. DrawArea also calls each PolygonElement's draw() method so it can draw itself.

Here's the source for PolygonElement.java:

```
import java.awt.*;
import java.util.*;

// This class' superclass implements the parts of the
// DrawingElement interface that are not implemented here.
public class PolygonElement extends PolyElement
{
    public PolygonElement()
    {
        // mPoints comes from PolyElement.
        mPoints = new Vector();
    }

    // Draw the element.  If it is the active element, draw
    // a little square around each point.
    public void draw( Graphics g, boolean isActive )
    {
        g.setColor( mColor );

        // Create arrays to hold the element's x and y
        // values.
        int size = mPoints.size();
        int x[] = new int[size];
        int y[] = new int[size];
        int count = 0;

        // For each element...
        for ( Enumeration e = mPoints.elements();
              e.hasMoreElements(); )
```

```
{
    Point pt = (Point)e.nextElement();

    // Store the point's x and y values.
    x[count] = pt.x;
    y[count] = pt.y;

    count++;
}

// Fill the polygon.
g.fillPolygon( x, y, size );

// If the element is the active element draw squares
// around its points.
if ( isActive )
{
    for ( int i = 0; i < size; i++ )
    {
        g.drawRect( x[i] - 2, y[i] - 2, 4, 4 );
    }
}
}
}
```

PolylineElement.java

PolylineElement, a subclass of PolyElement, implements the DrawingElement interface. It represents a polyline that DrawArea will draw. When the PaintToolBar's active tool is the Polyline tool, and the user clicks in the DrawArea, one of two things happens. If we aren't currently making a polyline, a new PolylineElement is created and added to DrawArea's list of elements. Or, if we *are* currently making a polyline, the mouse click is added as the polyline's next point. No JFC classes are used in this class.

RELATIONSHIPS TO OTHER CLASSES IN THE EXAMPLE   Here's how PolylineElement interacts with other classes in the example:

- **PolyElement.java:** This is PolylineElement's superclass that takes care of implementing the DrawingElement interface except for the draw() method, which PolylineElement takes care of.

- **DrawArea.java:** DrawArea creates PolylineElements and stores them in its list of things to draw. DrawArea also calls each PolylineElement's draw() method so it can draw itself.

Here's the source for PolylineElement.java:

```java
import java.awt.*;
import java.util.*;

// This class' superclass implements the parts of the
// DrawingElement interface not implemented here.
public class PolylineElement extends PolyElement
{
    public PolylineElement()
    {
        // mPoints is from PolyElement.
        mPoints = new Vector();
    }

    // Draw the polyline.  If it is the active element, draw
    // little squares around its points.
    public void draw( Graphics g, boolean isActive )
    {
        int prevX = -100000, prevY = -100000;
        int thisX, thisY;

        g.setColor( mColor );

        // For each point.
        for ( Enumeration e = mPoints.elements();
                e.hasMoreElements(); )
        {
            Point pt = (Point)e.nextElement();

            // Store the current point.
            thisX = pt.x;
            thisY = pt.y;

            // If prevX is way negative, it means this is the
            // first time through the loop, so we don't have
            // two points to draw between.
            if ( prevX > -100000 )
            {
                g.drawLine( prevX, prevY, thisX, thisY );
            }

            // Draw a square around each point if this is the
            // active element.
            if ( isActive )
            {
                g.drawRect( thisX - 2, thisY - 2, 4, 4 );
            }

            // Store this point so we can use it to draw the
            // next line segment.
            prevX = thisX;
            prevY = thisY;
        }
    }
}
```

SUMMARY

In this chapter, we've created a simple application that uses many of the classes in the JFC. The end product is only marginally interesting, however; the real goal has been to make these JFC classes work together in a real application and to see what they could do and how they could be used.

13

JFC Integration Example 4: A Simple Word Processor

The JFC offers much richer tools for text display and editing than the AWT did. It makes it relatively easy to implement word processing functions, such as the following:

- Using multiple fonts in a document
- Changing text and background colors
- Copying, cutting, and pasting content by using the Clipboard
- Adjusting text alignment
- Setting other attributes, such as paragraph indentation

This example exercises many of these capabilities and shows how they can be integrated with other JFC features to create a complete application.

The Application

The application has a large editing area where you can manipulate text, plus a menu and a toolbar. The toolbar lets you change text attributes and copy, cut, and paste text. The menu gives you access to the copy, cut, and paste functions, and also lets you save your work and read in previously saved files. The files are stored in an ASCII-readable format that places attribute changes in angle brackets (< and >). It you want to modify the example to read and write HTML or rich text format (RTF), it shouldn't be too difficult. Figure 14-1 shows the word processor in action.

The example consists of six separate classes:

- **Test.java:** This simple class contains the main() method, which causes an instance of Test to be created. Test's constructor creates and places the main frame.

- **MyFrame.java:** This is the main frame class. It loads up the menu items and the toolbar, and places the text pane. It also keeps the toolbar in sync with the current text attributes, tracks whether the document needs saving, and handles the copy, cut, and paste operations.

- **FontBox.java:** This is the font family combo box that appears in the toolbar. It takes care of getting the available fonts and loading them into the combo box.

- **SizeBox.java:** This is the font size combo box that appears in the toolbar. It loads a series of hard-coded sizes into the combo box.

- **MyStyledDocument.java:** This subclass of DefaultStyledDocument enables the user to read documents from file and write them to file.

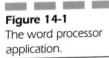

Figure 14-1
The word processor application.

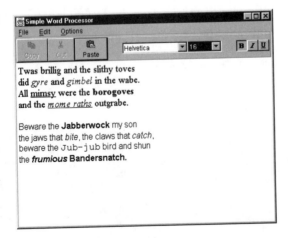

■ **FilterFileType.java:** This takes one or more file extensions, a file type name, and an icon and creates a new FileType that you can use in a JFileChooser's file type filter.

Following is a discussion of each class, which JFC classes it uses and why, and how it interacts with the other classes in the example.

Test.java

This is a very simple class. It contains the main() method, which just creates an instance of the Test class. Test's constructor creates an instance of the MyFrame class and places it on the display. Test.java includes calls to two UIManager methods: getSystemLookAndFeelClassName() and setLookAndFeel(). These are used to find out the system's native look-and-feel and to apply it.

Here's the source code:

```java
import com.sun.java.swing.*;

public class Test
{
    public Test()
    {
        // Use the system's native look-and-feel.
        String lf = UIManager.getSystemLookAndFeelClassName();

        if ( lf != null )
        {
            try
            {
                UIManager.setLookAndFeel( lf );
            }
            catch ( Exception ex )
            {
                ex.printStackTrace();
            }
        }

        MyFrame mf = new MyFrame();
        mf.setSize( 500, 400 );
        mf.show();
    }

    public static void main( String args[] )
    {
        new Test();
    }
}
```

MyFrame.java

This is the most complex class in the example. It's a subclass of JFrame and serves as the main workspace for the application. It does the following:

- Creates the menu bar, menus, and menu items and puts them all together.
- Creates the toolbar and adds the toolbar buttons, the font combo box, and the font size combo box.
- Creates a text pane.
- Tracks Caret motion within the text pane.
- Keeps toolbar settings consistent with the text attributes at the caret position.
- Handles events from the menu items and the toolbar components.
- Keeps track of whether the document has changed since it was loaded or last saved.
- Executes copy, cut, and paste commands.
- Displays the file chooser to get the names of files to open and save.

JFC CLASSES USED IN MYFRAME.JAVA   Following is a list of the JFC classes used in MyFrame.java, including how and why they were used:

- **JFrame:** MyFrame is a subclass of JFrame. The menu bar, toolbar, and text pane are all added into its root pane.
- **JTextPane:** The main text editing area is a JTextPane. JTextPane, used with our custom subclass of DefaultStyledModel, lets the user change text attributes basic to this application. The getCaret() method is used to track the current position as it moves, and the getCaretPosition() method is used to find where the caret position is currently. The getSelectedText() method is used to find out if text is currently selected because that affects whether the cut and copy buttons are enabled, and is also useful for supplying different behavior when applying attributes to the caret position and to a selected string. The setCharacterAttributes() method is used to apply newly changed attributes to either the caret position or a text selection. The getStyledDocument() method is used to get the text pane's copy of our MyStyledDocument. The getSelectionStart() and getSelectionEnd() methods are used to find the actual selected area. The setStyledDocument() method is used when we open a file and have to replace the text pane's contents. The copy(), cut(), and paste() methods are used to execute Clipboard actions.
- **JPanel:** The content pane is stored in a JPanel so we don't have to call getContentPane() constantly.

▤ **JToolBar:** This class contains the Copy, Cut, and Paste buttons, the font and font size combo boxes, and the Bold, Italic, and Underline buttons. By taking advantage of being able to add Actions to a JToolBar, we can use them to create JButtons. We create a CutAction, a CopyAction, and a PasteAction button and add them to both the toolbar and the Edit menu. By doing that, we can treat actions from menu items and toolbar buttons in the same way. We left space between the toolbar items by using Box's createHorizontalGlue() method, taking advantage of JToolBar's BoxLayout.

▤ **Caret:** Text panes have a Caret class that keeps track of the current position in the displayed document. We track Caret movements so we can update the toolbar settings as the caret moves through the text. We do this by making MyFrame a ChangeListener for the Caret.

▤ **AbstractAction:** MyFrame includes three inner subclasses of AbstractAction: CopyAction, CutAction, and PasteAction. Each contains a name string and an icon. We create an instance of each, and then add them to the Edit menu and the toolbar. Because the Cut and Copy menu items and buttons shouldn't be active if no text is currently selected, we find out when there's no text selection and use the CopyAction and CutAction to disable the menu items and toolbar buttons. These Actions have actionPerformed() methods that actually cause the copy, cut, and paste actions to happen.

▤ **JMenuBar:** The main menu in MyFrame is a JMenuBar. We add three menus to it.

▤ **JMenu:** There are three JMenus: File, Edit, and Options. They are added to the JMenuBar, and menu items are added into them. We create the items in the Edit menu by passing Actions into JMenu's add() method. JMenu creates a JMenuItem with the Action's text string, adds the JMenuItem to itself, and returns the created JMenuItem. Each menu has an accelerator key assigned so the menu can be used through the keyboard, too.

▤ **JMenuItem:** The menu items in the File and Options menus are created explicitly as JMenuItems. The ones in the Edit menu are created by JMenus from passed-in Actions. MyFrame listens for the menu items' ActionEvents, and then acts on them. Each menu item has an accelerator key, too.

▤ **JButton:** The Copy, Cut, and Paste buttons in the toolbar are JButtons created by passing an Action into the JToolBar's add() method. The JToolBar automatically creates a JButton using the Action's icon and text and adds the JButton into itself. The add() method then returns the created JButton. When clicked, the JButtons' ActionEvents are sent to the Actions used to create them.

▤ **JToggleButton:** The attribute buttons in the toolbar are all JToggleButtons because it's important to see what attributes are currently set. The Bold, Italic, and Underline buttons are not in a ButtonGroup because it's possible to have more than one selected simultaneously. The isSelected() method is used to create an attribute set that matches the current toolbar attribute settings. MyFrame listens for these JToggleButtons' ItemEvents so it can update the character attributes in the text pane. The setAlignmentY() method is used to make the buttons align with the combo boxes in the toolbar. The setMargin() method is used to remove the normal padding around the icon.

- **SimpleAttributeSet:** We use this to build up a set of attributes that are applied to the text pane.

- **StyleConstants:** This class's static methods are used to modify SimpleAttributeSets.

- **JOptionPane:** If the current document has been modified since it was loaded or last saved, we put up a JOptionPane to prompt the user to save the changes.

- **JRootPane**: We use MyFrame's JRootPane to access the content pane and add the menu bar.

- **Element:** To keep the toolbar's attributes current with the Caret position in the document, we have to retrieve the Element at the Caret position. We call its getAttributes() method to get the attribute set to reflect in the toolbar.

- **DefaultStyledDocument:** MyStyledDocument is a subclass of DefaultStyledDocument, and MyFrame calls several DefaultStyledDocument methods. It calls addDocumentListener() so MyFrame can be notified when the document changes in any way. In this way, it keeps track of whether the document has changed and needs to be saved. It calls the setCharacterAttributes() method to change the attributes in a specific range of characters. It calls the dump() method to get a listing of the document's elements sent to standard out. It calls getEndPosition() to get the character position at the end of the document, and it calls the getCharacterElement() method to get the Element associated with a particular character position.

- **JComboBox:** The font family and font size controls are subclasses of JComboBox. MyFrame listens for their ItemEvents so it can update the attributes in the text pane.

- **JFileChooser:** MyFrame displays a JFileChooser when the user wants to open a file or save the current document to file. Since JFileChooser is incomplete in Swing 1.0, it looks the same whether you are opening or saving a file. It also will not allow you to save to a file that does not exist.

RELATIONSHIPS TO OTHER CLASSES IN THE EXAMPLE   Here's how MyFrame interacts with the other classes in the example:

- **Test.java:** The Test class creates and places MyFrame.
- **MyStyledDocument.java:** MyFrame creates it when it needs to load a new document into the text pane. It also tells it to load new files or save the current document. MyFrame listens for when the document changes so it can keep track of whether the document needs saving.
- **FontBox.java:** MyFrame creates this and puts it into the toolbar. It listens for FontBox's ItemEvents.
- **SizeBox.java:** MyFrame creates this and puts it into the toolbar. It listens for SizeBox's ItemEvents.

Here's the source code:

```java
import com.sun.java.swing.*;
import com.sun.java.swing.preview.*;
import com.sun.java.swing.text.*;
import com.sun.java.swing.event.*;
import java.awt.*;
import java.awt.event.*;
import java.util.*;
import java.io.*;

public class MyFrame extends JFrame implements
        DocumentListener, ItemListener, ActionListener
{
    private JTextPane mTextPane;
    private CopyAction mCopyAction;
    private CutAction mCutAction;
    private PasteAction mPasteAction;
    private JToggleButton mBold;
    private JToggleButton mItalic;
    private JToggleButton mUnderline;
    private FontBox mFonts;
    private SizeBox mSizes;
    private SimpleAttributeSet mInitialAttributes;
    private boolean mHasChanged = false;
    private String mFileName = null;
    private JFileChooser mChooser;
    private String mCurrentFile = "";
    private Position mNextPosition = null;

    public MyFrame()
    {
        setTitle( "Simple Word Processor" );

        // Create the copy, cut, and paste actions.
        createActions();

        // Create the menu bar, menus, and menu items.
        createMenu();

        // Store the content pane in a variable for easier
        // access.
        JPanel contentPane = (JPanel)getContentPane();
```

```
// Components will all be added to this panel.
contentPane.setLayout( new BorderLayout() );

// Create a toolbar for attribute tools.
JToolBar fontTools = new JToolBar();

// Create the copy, cut, and paste buttons and put
// them in the toolbar.
addEditButtons( fontTools );

// Leave some space.
fontTools.add( Box.createHorizontalGlue() );

// Create the font family and font size combo boxes
// and put them in the toolbar.
addFontControls( fontTools );

// Leave some space after the sizes combo box.
fontTools.add( Box.createHorizontalGlue() );

// Create the bold, italic, and underline buttons and
// put them in the toolbar.
addAttributeButtons( fontTools );

// Place the tool bar at the top of the content pane.
contentPane.add( "North", fontTools );

// Create an instance of the custom document.
MyStyledDocument doc = new MyStyledDocument();

// Create the text pane, giving it the custom
// document.
mTextPane = new JTextPane( doc );

// Listen for when the caret changes position.
mTextPane.getCaret().addChangeListener(
                              new CaretListener() );

// Add the text pane to cover the content pane's main
// area.
contentPane.add( "Center", mTextPane );

// Listen for when characters are added or erased or
// attributes change.
doc.addDocumentListener( this );

// Set the current attributes to those represented by
// the tool bar buttons.
updateStyle();

// Store the initial attributes so they can be
// restored before loading a new file.
mInitialAttributes = getSetAttributes();
```

```
        // Make sure the cut and copy items are in the proper
        // state.
        checkSelection();

        // Give the focus to the text pane.
        mTextPane.requestFocus();
    }

    // Create the actions that control the cut, copy, and
    // paste menu items and toolbar buttons.
    private void createActions()
    {
        mCopyAction = new CopyAction();
        mCutAction = new CutAction();
        mPasteAction = new PasteAction();
    }

    // Create the menu bar, menus, and menu items.
    private void createMenu()
    {
        // Create the menu bar and apply it to the frame's
        // root pane.
        JMenuBar mbar = new JMenuBar();
        getRootPane().setMenuBar( mbar );

        // Create a file menu and add it to the menu bar.
        JMenu fileMenu = new JMenu( "File" );
        fileMenu.setMnemonic( 'f' );
        mbar.add( fileMenu );

        // Create a New item and make it so this class is
        // notified when the item is pressed.
        JMenuItem newItem = new JMenuItem( "New" );
        newItem.setMnemonic( 'n' );
        newItem.setActionCommand( "New" );
        newItem.addActionListener( this );

        // Add the item to the file menu.
        fileMenu.add( newItem );

        // Create an Open item and make it so this class is
        // notified when the item is pressed.
        JMenuItem openItem = new JMenuItem( "Open" );
        openItem.setMnemonic( 'o' );
        openItem.setActionCommand( "Open" );
        openItem.addActionListener( this );

        // Add the item to the file menu.
        fileMenu.add( openItem );

        // Create a Save item and make it so this class is
        // notified when the item is pressed.
        JMenuItem saveItem = new JMenuItem( "Save" );
        saveItem.setMnemonic( 's' );
        saveItem.setActionCommand( "Save" );
```

```
        saveItem.addActionListener( this );

        // Add the item to the file menu.
        fileMenu.add( saveItem );

        // Create an Exit item and make it so this class is
        // notified when the item is pressed.
        JMenuItem exitItem = new JMenuItem( "Exit" );
        exitItem.setMnemonic( 'x' );
        exitItem.setActionCommand( "Exit" );
        exitItem.addActionListener( this );

        // Add the item to the menu.
        fileMenu.add( exitItem );

        // Create the Edit menu and add it to the menu bar.
        JMenu editMenu = new JMenu( "Edit" );
        editMenu.setMnemonic( 'e' );
        mbar.add( editMenu );

        // Using the actions created by createActions(), let
        // the menu generate new menu items.
        JMenuItem item;

        item = editMenu.add( mCopyAction );
        item.setMnemonic( 'c' );
        item = editMenu.add( mCutAction );
        item.setMnemonic( 'u' );
        item = editMenu.add( mPasteAction );
        item.setMnemonic( 'p' );

        // Create the Options menu and add it to the menu bar.
        JMenu optionMenu = new JMenu( "Options" );
        optionMenu.setMnemonic( 'o' );
        mbar.add( optionMenu );

        // Create a Dump menu item and make it so this class
        // is notified when the item is pressed.
        JMenuItem dump = new JMenuItem( "Dump" );
        item.setMnemonic( 'd' );
        dump.addActionListener( this );
        dump.setActionCommand( "Dump" );

        // Add the item to the options menu.
        optionMenu.add( dump );
    }

// Create the cut, copy, and paste buttons and put them
// in the toolbar.
private void addEditButtons( JToolBar toolbar )
{
    JButton button;

    // Using the actions generated by createActions(),
    // let the toolbar create the edit buttons.
```

```java
    button = toolbar.add( mCopyAction );
    button.setToolTipText(
                "Copy selected text to the clipboard" );
    button.setAlignmentY( 0.5f );

    button = toolbar.add( mCutAction );
    button.setToolTipText(
                "Move selected text to the clipboard" );
    button.setAlignmentY( 0.5f );

    button = toolbar.add( mPasteAction );
    button.setToolTipText(
                    "Insert text from the clipboard" );
    button.setAlignmentY( 0.5f );
}

// Create the font family and font size combo boxes and
// put them into the toolbar.
private void addFontControls( JToolBar toolbar )
{
    // Create and load a combo box holding font names.
    mFonts = new FontBox();

    // Listen for when a new font is selected.
    mFonts.addItemListener( this );

    // Add the combo box to the toolbar.
    toolbar.add( mFonts );

    // Create and load a combo box holding font sizes.
    mSizes = new SizeBox();

    // Listen for when a new font size is selected.
    mSizes.addItemListener( this );

    // Add the sizes combo box to the toolbar.
    toolbar.add( mSizes );
}

// Create the bold, italic, and underline buttons and
// add them to the toolbar.
private void addAttributeButtons( JToolBar toolbar )
{
    // Make the Bold toggle button.
    mBold = new JToggleButton(
                        new ImageIcon( "bold.gif" ) );
    mBold.setMargin( new Insets( 0, 0, 0, 0 ) );
    mBold.setAlignmentY( 0.5f );

    // Listen for when the button changes state.
    mBold.addItemListener( this );

    // Add the button to the tool bar.
    toolbar.add( mBold );
```

```
    // Make the Italic toggle button.
    mItalic = new JToggleButton(
                        new ImageIcon( "italic.gif" ) );
    mItalic.setMargin( new Insets( 0, 0, 0, 0 ) );
    mItalic.setAlignmentY( 0.5f );

    // Listen for when the button changes state.
    mItalic.addItemListener( this );

    // Add the button to the tool bar.
    toolbar.add( mItalic );

    // Make the Underline toggle button.
    mUnderline = new JToggleButton(
                    new ImageIcon( "underline.gif" ) );
    mUnderline.setMargin( new Insets( 0, 0, 0, 0 ) );
    mUnderline.setAlignmentY( 0.5f );

    // Listen for when the button changes state.
    mUnderline.addItemListener( this );

    // Add the button to the tool bar.
    toolbar.add( mUnderline );
}

// This is called when attributes change in the text
// pane's document.
public void changedUpdate( DocumentEvent e )
{
    mHasChanged = true;
}

// Called when text is inserted into the text pane's
// document.
public void insertUpdate( DocumentEvent e )
{
    mHasChanged = true;
}

// Called when text is removed from the text pane's
// document.
public void removeUpdate( DocumentEvent e )
{
    mHasChanged = true;
}

// This is called when any of the toggle buttons change
// state or the font name or size is changed.
public void itemStateChanged( ItemEvent e )
{
    // Update the current character attributes to reflect
    // the new settings.
    updateStyle();

    // Try to get the focus back to the text pane so the
```

```
        // user can get right back to work in the same place
        // with the new attributes.
        mTextPane.requestFocus();
    }


    // Create a new attribute set and make it match the
    // toolbar settings.
    private SimpleAttributeSet getSetAttributes()
    {
        // Create a new, empty set.
        SimpleAttributeSet set = new SimpleAttributeSet();

        // Set attributes based on the bold, italic, and
        // underline toggle buttons.
        StyleConstants.setItalic( set, mItalic.isSelected() );
        StyleConstants.setBold( set, mBold.isSelected() );
        StyleConstants.setUnderline( set,
                                    mUnderline.isSelected() );

        // Set attributes based on the currently selected
        // font family and size.
        StyleConstants.setFontFamily( set,
                        (String)mFonts.getSelectedItem() );
        StyleConstants.setFontSize( set, Integer.parseInt(
                        (String)mSizes.getSelectedItem() ) );

        // Return the attribute set.
        return set;
    }


    // This updates the current character attributes to
    // reflect the toolbar settings.
    private void updateStyle()
    {
        // Create a new attribute set that reflects the
        // toolbar settings, and use it.  If the attribute
        // set will be applied to a text selection, merge
        // the attributes.  Otherwise, replace them.
        if ( mTextPane.getSelectedText() == null )
            mTextPane.setCharacterAttributes(
                                    getSetAttributes(), true );
        else
        {
            StyledDocument doc = mTextPane.getStyledDocument();
            int start = mTextPane.getSelectionStart();
            int length = mTextPane.getSelectionEnd() - start;
            doc.setCharacterAttributes( start, length,
                                    getSetAttributes(),
                                    false );
        }
    }


    // This is called when one of the menu items is pressed.
    public void actionPerformed( ActionEvent e )
    {
```

```
String command = e.getActionCommand();
if ( command == null )
    command = "";

if ( command.equals( "Save" ) )
{
    // Save the current document to file.
    saveContents();
}
else if ( command.equals( "New" ) )
{
    if ( promptToSaveIfChanged() )
    {
        // No existing file is being edited.
        mCurrentFile = "";

        // Clear the contents.
        MyStyledDocument doc = new MyStyledDocument();
        mTextPane.setStyledDocument( doc );

        // Restore the attributes we had initially.
        mTextPane.setCharacterAttributes(
                            mInitialAttributes, true );

        // Update the tool bar to match.
        updateToolBar();

        // Since we have a new document, we have to
        // reattach.
        doc.addDocumentListener( this );

        mHasChanged = false;
    }
}
else if ( command.equals( "Open" ) )
{
    if ( promptToSaveIfChanged() )
    {
        // Open a new file and load its contents.
        loadFile();

        mHasChanged = false;
    }
}
else if ( command.equals( "Exit" ) )
{
    if ( promptToSaveIfChanged() )
    {
        // Exit the application.
        System.exit( 0 );
    }
}
else if ( command.equals( "Dump" ) )
{
    // Dump the document's contents.
```

```
        AbstractDocument doc =
            (AbstractDocument)mTextPane.getStyledDocument();

        // Call the document's dump().
        doc.dump( System.out );
    }
}


// This checks the current document to see if it has
// changed since it was loaded or last saved.  If so,
// it prompts the user to save, not save, or cancel.
// If the user cancels (presses the cancel button or
// the dialog's close button), this returns false.
// Otherwise it returns true.
private boolean promptToSaveIfChanged()
{
    if ( mHasChanged )
    {
        // Display the dialog.
        int retval = JOptionPane.showConfirmDialog(
                getJMenuBar(),
                "The document has changed.  Save it?" );

        switch ( retval )
        {
            case JOptionPane.YES_OPTION:

                // If the user chose to save the current
                // document, then save it.
                saveContents();
                return true;

            case JOptionPane.NO_OPTION:

                // If the user chose not to save the
                // current document, just continue.
                return true;

            case JOptionPane.CANCEL_OPTION:
            case JOptionPane.CLOSED_OPTION:

                // If the user cancelled the dialog, they do
                // not want to do whatever operation was
                // going to replace the current document in
                // the text pane, so return false.
                return false;
        }
    }

    // The current document hasn't changed, so just
    // continue.
    return true;
}

// This opens an existing file and loads it into the
```

```
// text pane.
private void loadFile()
{
    // If the file chooser has not been created, create
    // it and specify a custom filter file type.
    if ( mChooser == null )
    {
        mChooser = new JFileChooser( "." );

        FilterFileType filetype =
                new FilterFileType( "txt",
                            "Custom files (*.txt)",
                            new ImageIcon( "txt.gif" ) );

        mChooser.addChoosableFileType( filetype );
    }

    // Display the file chooser in a dialog.
    int retval = mChooser.showDialog( this );

    // If the file chooser exited sucessfully, and a file
    // was selected, continue.
    if ( retval == 0 &&
         mChooser.getSelectedFile() != null )
    {
        // Save the file name.
        String mCurrentFile =
                mChooser.getSelectedFile().getAbsolutePath();

        // Create a new document containing the given
        // file's contents.
        MyStyledDocument doc =
                    new MyStyledDocument( mCurrentFile,
                                    mInitialAttributes );

        // Replace the text pane's document with the new
        // one.
        mTextPane.setStyledDocument( doc );

        // Since we have a new document, we have to
        // reattach.
        doc.addDocumentListener( this );

        // Update the toolbar to match the attributes at
        // the start of the new document.
        updateToolBar();
    }
}

// Save the text pane's contents to file.
private void saveContents()
{
    // If the file chooser has not been created, create
    // it and add a special filter type.
    if ( mChooser == null )
```

```
    {
        mChooser = new JFileChooser( "." );

        FilterFileType filetype =
                new FilterFileType( "txt",
                            "Custom files (*.txt)",
                            new ImageIcon( "txt.gif" ) );

        mChooser.addChoosableFileType( filetype );
    }

    // Display the file chaooser in a dialog.
    int retval = mChooser.showDialog( this );

    // If the user selected a file name, continue.
    if ( retval == 0 &&
        mChooser.getSelectedFile() != null )
    {
        // Save the file name.
        String mCurrentFile =
            mChooser.getSelectedFile().getAbsolutePath();

        // Get the text pane's document.
        MyStyledDocument doc =
            (MyStyledDocument)mTextPane.getStyledDocument();

        // Make the document write itself out to the given
        // file.
        doc.saveToFile( mCurrentFile, mInitialAttributes );

        // We just saved, so the document has not changed
        // since its last save.
        mHasChanged = false;
    }
}

// Get the attributes at the current position, and make
// the toolbar buttons reflect those attributes.
private void updateToolBar()
{
    // Get the text pane's document.
    StyledDocument doc = mTextPane.getStyledDocument();

    // Get the new position from which we want to get the
    // attributes.
    int pos = mTextPane.getCaretPosition();

    // If the caret is at the end of the text, use the
    // attributes from the place before.
    if ( pos > 0 &&
        pos == doc.getEndPosition().getOffset() - 1 )
    {
        pos--;
    }
```

```
// Retrieve the element at the given position.
Element el = doc.getCharacterElement( pos );

// Get the element's attributes.
AttributeSet set = el.getAttributes();

// If the caret was moved as part of selecting text,
// don't change the toolbar.
if ( mTextPane.getSelectedText() == null )
{
    mBold.setSelected( StyleConstants.isBold( set ) );
    mItalic.setSelected(
                    StyleConstants.isItalic( set ) );
    mUnderline.setSelected(
                StyleConstants.isUnderline( set ) );
    mFonts.setSelectedItem(
                StyleConstants.getFontFamily( set ) );
    mSizes.setSelectedItem( String.valueOf(
                StyleConstants.getFontSize( set ) ) );
}

// Make sure the cut and copy buttons and menu items
// are properly enabled/disabled.
checkSelection();
}

// When the caret position changes, we want to make sure
// the toolbar reflects the attributes at the new
// position.
public class CaretListener implements ChangeListener
{
    public void stateChanged( ChangeEvent e )
    {
        // If the caret changed because a character was
        // typed, we don't want to update the toolbar
        // since it will already be up-to-date.  So, we
        // save a position 'mNextPosition' which is the
        // position after the current one.  When the caret
        // moves, the caret position will be one character
        // before the saved one if the caret move came
        // from a character being entered.  Otherwise,
        // we save a new position and update the toolbar.
        try
        {
            // Get a Position at the caret.
            Position caretpos =
                    mTextPane.getDocument().createPosition(
                            mTextPane.getCaretPosition() );

            // If there is no saved position or it is not
            // at the next character, update the toolbar
            // and save a new position.
            if ( mNextPosition == null ||
                caretpos.getOffset() !=
                mNextPosition.getOffset() - 1 )
```

```
                    {
                      updateToolBar();

                      // Make sure we don't try to save a position
                      // beyond the end of the document.
                      if ( caretpos ==
                        mTextPane.getDocument().getEndPosition() )
                      {
                        mNextPosition = caretpos;
                      }
                      else
                      {
                        mNextPosition =
                          mTextPane.getDocument().createPosition(
                                        caretpos.getOffset() + 1 );
                      }
                    }
                  }
                  catch ( BadLocationException ex )
                  {
                    ex.printStackTrace();
                  }
                }
              }


    // If there is a current text selection, the cut and
    // copy buttons and menu items should be enabled.
    // Otherwise they should be disabled.  They are
    // enabled/disabled using the Actions that were used to
    // create them.
    private void checkSelection()
    {
      if ( mTextPane.getSelectedText() == null )
      {
        mCopyAction.setEnabled( false );
        mCutAction.setEnabled( false );
      }
      else
      {
        mCopyAction.setEnabled( true );
        mCutAction.setEnabled( true );
      }
    }


    // This action is used to create the Edit-Copy menu
    // item, and is also associated with the toolbar button.
    private class CopyAction extends AbstractAction
    {
      public CopyAction()
      {
        // Create the action with a string for the menu
        // item this will be used to create and an icon
        // for the toolbar buuton.
        super( "Copy", new ImageIcon( "copy.gif" ) );
      }
```

```
      public void actionPerformed( ActionEvent e )
      {
          // Copy the selected text to the clipboard.
          mTextPane.copy();

          // Send focus back to the text pane.
          mTextPane.requestFocus();
      }
  }

  // This action is used to create the Edit-Cut menu item,
  // and is also associated with the toolbar button.
  private class CutAction extends AbstractAction
  {
      public CutAction()
      {
          // Create the action with a string for the menu
          // item this will be used to create and an icon
          // for the toolbar button.
          super( "Cut", new ImageIcon( "cut.gif" ) );
      }

      public void actionPerformed( ActionEvent e )
      {
          // Remove the selected text from the text pane and
          // put it into the clipboard.
          mTextPane.cut();

          // Send focus back to the text pane.
          mTextPane.requestFocus();
      }
  }

  // This action is used to create the Edit-Paste menu
  // item and is also associated with the toolbar button.
  private class PasteAction extends AbstractAction
  {
      public PasteAction()
      {
          // Create the action with a string for the menu
          // item this will be used to create and an icon
          // for the toolbar button.
          super( "Paste", new ImageIcon( "paste.gif" ) );
      }

      public void actionPerformed( ActionEvent e )
      {
          // Paste the clipboard text into the text pane.
          mTextPane.paste();

          // Send focus back to the text pane.
          mTextPane.requestFocus();
      }
  }
}
```

MyStyledDocument.java

This subclass of DefaultStyledDocument extends that class to enable the user to read the document in from file and save it to file. It does the following:

- Stores the current document, including text and attributes.
- Notifies listeners when text is added or removed or when attributes change.
- Loads itself from file.
- Saves itself to file.

JFC CLASSES USED IN MYSTYLEDDOCUMENT.JAVA Following is a list of the JFC classes used in MyStyledDocument, including how and why they were used:

- **DefaultStyledDocument:** MyStyledDocument's superclass, it takes care of storing the text and attributes and giving access to them. The getDefaultRootElement() method is called to get the start of the Element tree so it can write the document contents to file. The insertString() method is called while reading from file to insert a chunk of text with the same attributes.
- **SimpleAttributeSet:** This is used to build up attributes as a file is being read in, or is read from the document so attributes can be written to file.
- **Element:** Starting with the root Element, MyStyledDocument reads through the Element tree and writes it to file. The isLeaf() method is called because only leaf nodes are actually written out. The getStartOffset() and getEndOffset() methods are called to get the text associated with the Element. The getAttributes() method gets the Element's attributes so they can be written to file. The getDocument() method is used to read the Element's text. The getElement() method is called for non-leaf Elements so we can walk through child Elements while writing to file.
- **StyleConstants:** This class's static methods are useful for getting and setting attributes in SimpleAttributeSets.

RELATIONSHIPS TO OTHER CLASSES IN THE EXAMPLE Here's how MyStyledDocument interacts with other classes in the example:

- **MyFrame.java:** This is the only class in the example that MyStyled-Document interacts with. MyFrame creates a MyStyledDocument and uses it to set the contents of its text pane. MyFrame.java also makes MyStyledDocument read in documents from file and save them out.

Here's the source code:

```java
import com.sun.java.swing.*;
import com.sun.java.swing.text.*;
import java.io.*;

public class MyStyledDocument extends DefaultStyledDocument
{
    public MyStyledDocument()
    {
        super();
    }

    public MyStyledDocument( String filename,
                    SimpleAttributeSet initialAttributes )
    {
        super();

        loadFile( filename, initialAttributes );
    }

    public void saveToFile( String filename,
                    SimpleAttributeSet initialAttributes )
    {
        // Make a copy of the attributes that are in effect
        // when a document is first started up.
        SimpleAttributeSet attribs =
                (SimpleAttributeSet)initialAttributes.clone();

        // Get the document's root element.
        Element els = getDefaultRootElement();

        try
        {
            // Open the output file.
            FileWriter writer = new FileWriter( filename );

            // Call the routine that recursively saves the
            // elements.
            saveElement( els, attribs, writer );

            // Close the file.
            writer.close();
        }
        catch ( IOException e )
        {
            System.out.println( "Can't open:  " + filename );
        }
    }

    // Recursively saves the given element and its child
    // elements (if any).
    private AttributeSet saveElement( Element el,
                                      AttributeSet attribs,
                                      FileWriter writer )
            throws IOException
    {
```

```
        AttributeSet current;

        // If the element is a leaf element, write it out.
        if ( el.isLeaf() )
        {
            // Write the element's attributes, taking care of
            // differences between the current attributes and
            // the element's.
            writer.write( reconcileAttributes( attribs,
                                    el.getAttributes() ) );

            // Get the start and end of the element's text.
            int start = el.getStartOffset();
            int end = el.getEndOffset();

            try
            {
                // Get the text from the document and write it
                // out.
                writer.write( el.getDocument().getText( start,
                                        end - start ) );
            }
            catch ( BadLocationException e )
            {
                System.out.println( "Bad location:  " + start +
                                "|" + end );
            }

            // Set the attributes that will be returned.
            current = el.getAttributes();
        }
        else
        {
            current = attribs;

            // Call this method again for each child element.
            // 'current' stores the attributes after each
            // element is written.
            for ( int i = 0; i < el.getElementCount(); i++ )
            {
                current = saveElement( el.getElement( i ),
                                    current, writer );
            }
        }

        // Return the attributes in effect after the element
        // is written.
        return current;
    }

    // Given a starting set of attributes and an element's
    // attributes, create an output string that contains
    // the attribute tags required to get from one to the
    // other.
    private String reconcileAttributes(
```

```
                                    AttributeSet startSet,
                                    AttributeSet thisSet )
{
   String bold = getToggleString(
                    StyleConstants.isBold( startSet ),
                    StyleConstants.isBold( thisSet ),
                    "<Start Bold>", "<End Bold>" );
      String italic = getToggleString(
                    StyleConstants.isItalic( startSet ),
                    StyleConstants.isItalic( thisSet ),
                    "<Start Italic>", "<End Italic>" );
      String underline = getToggleString(
                    StyleConstants.isUnderline( startSet ),
                    StyleConstants.isUnderline( thisSet ),
                    "<Start Underline>",
                    "<End Underline>" );
      String fontName = "";
      if ( StyleConstants.getFontFamily( startSet ) !=
           StyleConstants.getFontFamily( thisSet ) )
      {
         fontName = "<Font Name=" +
                    StyleConstants.getFontFamily( thisSet ) +
                    ">";
      }

      String fontSize = "";
      if ( StyleConstants.getFontSize( startSet ) !=
           StyleConstants.getFontSize( thisSet ) )
      {
         fontSize = "<Font Size=" +
                    StyleConstants.getFontSize( thisSet ) +
                    ">";
      }

      return bold + italic + underline + fontName +
             fontSize;
}

// Given two states and two strings, return the string
// that should be added to the output stream.
private String getToggleString( boolean state1,
                                boolean state2,
                                String on, String off )
{
   if ( state1 != state2 )
   {
      if ( state1 )
         return off;
      return on;
   }

   return "";
}

private void loadFile( String filename,
```

```
                            SimpleAttributeSet initialAttributes )
{
    // Make a copy of the attributes that the application
    // starts up with.
    SimpleAttributeSet attribs =
            (SimpleAttributeSet)initialAttributes.clone();

    try
    {
        int intch;
        char ch;

        // Open the new file.
        FileReader reader = new FileReader( filename );

        // Initialize buffers and status flags.

        // True if we are reading an attribute tag.
        boolean readingTag = false;

        // True if we are reading an attribute value.
        boolean readingValue = false;

        // Holds the attribute tag we are reading (if any).
        StringBuffer tag = new StringBuffer();;

        // Holds the text element we are reading (if any).
        StringBuffer element = new StringBuffer();

        // Holds the attribute value we are reading (if
        // any).
        StringBuffer value = new StringBuffer();

        // While we still have characters.
        while ( (intch = reader.read()) != -1 )
        {
            ch = (char)intch;

            // '<' starts an attribute tag.
            if ( ch == '<' )
            {
                if ( element.length() > 0 )
                {
                    // If we are currently reading a text
                    // string, store the string.
                    insertString( getLength(),
                                  element.toString(),
                                  attribs );

                    // Clear the element for next time.
                    element = new StringBuffer();
                }

                // Set the flag that says we are now reading
                // a tag instead of a text element.
```

```
      readingTag = true;

      // Clear the attribute tag.
      tag = new StringBuffer();

      // Clear the attribute value.
      value = new StringBuffer();
}
else if ( readingTag && ch == '>' )
{
      // '>' ends an attribute.
      String tagString = tag.toString();
      String valueString = value.toString();

      // Modify the current attributes to reflect
      // the attribute we just read.
      if ( tagString.equals( "Start Bold" ) )
      {
            StyleConstants.setBold( attribs, true );
      }
      else if ( tagString.equals( "End Bold" ) )
      {
            StyleConstants.setBold( attribs, false );
      }
      else if ( tagString.equals(
                                "Start Italic" ) )
      {
            StyleConstants.setItalic( attribs, true );
      }
      else if ( tagString.equals( "End Italic" ) )
      {
            StyleConstants.setItalic( attribs,
                                        false );
      }
      else if ( tagString.equals(
                                "Start Underline" ) )
      {
            StyleConstants.setUnderline( attribs,
                                          true );
      }
      else if ( tagString.equals(
                                "End Underline" ) )
      {
            StyleConstants.setUnderline( attribs,
                                          false );
      }
      else if ( tagString.equals( "Font Name" ) )
      {
            StyleConstants.setFontFamily( attribs,
                                          valueString );
      }
      else if ( tagString.equals( "Font Size" ) )
      {
            StyleConstants.setFontSize( attribs,
                    Integer.parseInt( valueString ) );
```

```
                    }

                    // The tag is over, so we are not reading an
                    // attribute or an attribute value.
                    readingTag = false;
                    readingValue = false;
                }
                else if ( readingTag && ch == '=' )
                {
                    // We are in an attribute and we got '=', so
                    // we now start reading an attribute value.
                    readingValue = true;
                }
                else if ( readingTag )
                {
                    // We are reading an tag, so this character
                    // is either part of an attribute or of an
                    // attribute value, depending on whether we
                    // encountered a '='.
                    if ( readingValue )
                        value = value.append( ch );
                    else
                        tag = tag.append( ch );
                }
                else
                {
                    // This character must be part of a text
                    // element.
                    element = element.append( ch );
                }
            }

            // If we reached the end of the file and were in
            // the midst of a text element, read it in.
            if ( element.length() > 0 )
            {
                insertString( getLength(), element.toString(),
                              attribs );
            }
        }
        catch ( FileNotFoundException e )
        {
            System.out.println( "Can't find:  " + filename );
        }
        catch ( IOException e )
        {
            System.out.println( "IOException with Reader" );
        }
        catch ( BadLocationException e )
        {
            System.out.println( "Bad Location on open" );
        }
    }
}
```

FontBox.java

FontBox is a subclass of JComboBox and does the following:

- Loads the available font family names into itself.
- Sets the initial font family to use.

JFC CLASSES USED IN FONTBOX.JAVA   Following is a list of the JFC classes used in FontBox.java, including how and why they were used:

- **JComboBox:** FontBox, a subclass of JComboBox, calls the addItem() method to add a font family name to its list. It calls the setSelectedItem() to specify which font family name is initially selected.

RELATIONSHIPS TO OTHER CLASSES IN THE EXAMPLE   Here's how FontBox interacts with other classes in the example:

- **MyFrame.java:** This is the only other class in the example that FontBox interacts with. MyFrame creates a FontBox and puts it into the toolbar. It listens for when a new font family name is selected by the user so it can update the text pane's attributes. It also changes the current selection when the Caret is moved to a character position drawn in a different font.

Here's the source code:

```java
import com.sun.java.swing.*;
import java.awt.*;

public class FontBox extends JComboBox
{
    public FontBox()
    {
        super();

        // Get the list of available fonts.
        String fontList[] =
                Toolkit.getDefaultToolkit().getFontList();

        // Load the font names into the combo box.
        for ( int i = 0; i < fontList.length; i++ )
        {
            addItem( fontList[i] );
        }

        // Make times roman the current font.
        setSelectedItem( "TimesRoman" );
    }
}
```

SizeBox.java

SizeBox is a subclass of JComboBox and does the following:

■ Loads a hard-coded set of font point sizes into itself.
■ Sets the initial font size.

JFC CLASSES USED IN SIZEBOX.JAVA   Following is a list of the JFC classes used in SizeBox.java, including how and why they were used:

■ **JComboBox:** SizeBox, a subclass of JComboBox, calls the addItem() method to add a font size to its list. It calls the setSelectedItem() to specify which font size is initially selected.

RELATIONSHIPS TO OTHER CLASSES IN THE EXAMPLE   Here's how SizeBox interacts with other classes in the example:

■ **MyFrame.java:** This is the only other class in the example that SizeBox interacts with. MyFrame creates a SizeBox and puts it into the toolbar. It listens for when a new font size is selected by the user so it can update the text pane's attributes. It also changes the current selection when the Caret is moved to a character position drawn in a different font size.

Here's the source code:

```java
import com.sun.java.swing.*;
import java.awt.*;

public class SizeBox extends JComboBox
{
    public SizeBox()
    {
        super();

        // Hard-code a set of font size values.
        int sizeList[] = { 6, 7, 8, 9, 10, 11, 12, 14,
                          16, 18, 20, 22, 24, 28, 32,
                          36, 44, 52, 60, 66, 72 };

        // Load the values into the combo box.
        for ( int i = 0; i < sizeList.length; i++ )
        {
            addItem( String.valueOf( sizeList[i] ) );
        }

        // Make the initial font size 14 point.
        setSelectedItem( "14" );
    }
}
```

FilterFileType.java

FilterFileType implements the FileType interface and is used to create a FileType that can be used in a JFileChooser filter combo box. FilterFileType accepts one or more extensions, a FileType description, and an icon. The description is used as the FileType's presentation name. The extensions are used to decide whether a file is of this FileType. The icon is displayed next to files with one of the given extensions in the JFileChooser.

JFC CLASSES USED IN FILTERFILETYPE.JAVA   FilterFileType doesn't actually use any JFC classes, but it does accept Icons and implements the FileType interface.

RELATIONSHIPS TO OTHER CLASSES IN THE EXAMPLE   Here's how FilterFileType interacts with other classes in the example:

■ **MyFrame.java:** This is the only other class in the example that this class interacts with. When MyFrame creates the JFileChooser, it also creates a FilterFileType that recognizes the "txt" extension and adds the new type to the JFileChooser with the addChoosableFileType() method.

Here's the source code:

```
import com.sun.java.swing.*;
import com.sun.java.swing.preview.*;
import java.io.*;

// This implementation of FileType accepts a file extension
// or an array of extensions and corresponding string
// description through the constructor.
public class FilterFileType implements FileType
{
    // Storage for the file extension and description.
    private String mExts[];
    private String mName;
    private Icon mIcon;

    public FilterFileType( String ext, String name,
                           Icon icon )
    {
        mExts = new String[1];
        mExts[0] = "." + ext;

        mName = name;
        mIcon = icon;
    }

    public FilterFileType( String exts[], String name,
                           Icon icon )
```

```
    {
        int num = exts.length;
        mExts = new String[num];

        for ( int i = 0; i < num; i++ )
        {
            mExts[i] = "." + exts[i];
        }

        mName = name;
        mIcon = icon;
    }

    // Return this file type's description.
    public String getPresentationName()
    {
        return mName;
    }

    // Return an icon that can be placed next to files of
    // this type in a file browser.
    public Icon getIcon()
    {
        return mIcon;
    }

    // Return false because this file type is not able to
    // contain others.
    public boolean isContainer()
    {
        return false;
    }

    // If the file's name ends with one of the extensions,
    // the file is of this type.
    public boolean testFile( File file )
    {
        String name = file.getAbsolutePath();

        int num = mExts.length;

        for ( int i = 0; i < num; i++ )
        {
            if ( name.endsWith( mExts[i] ) )
                return true;
        }

        return false;
    }

    public String toString()
    {
        return mName;
    }
}
```

SUMMARY

Although this chapter focuses mainly on illustrating how to use Styled-Documents and many of the associated classes, it also makes use of other JFC features, including JFileChooser, Actions, menu accelerators, and JToolBar, among others.

Index